From Code to Cloud

From Code to Cloud
Developing Web Applications

Maura A. Deek   0009-0008-2023-971X
Fadi P. Deek   0009-0001-1022-4118
Wei Yao   0000-0001-5019-3216

CRC Press

Boca Raton and London

AN AUERBACH BOOK

Designed cover image: Concept and idea: Fadi P. Deek; Code: Maura A. Deek; and Image: shutterstock.com

First edition published
by CRC Press 2027
2385 NW Executive Center Drive, Suite 320, Boca Raton FL 33431

and by CRC Press
4 Park Square, Milton Park, Abingdon, Oxon, OX14 4RN

CRC Press is an imprint of Taylor & Francis Group, LLC

Library of Congress Cataloging-in-Publication Data
A catalog record for this title has been requested.

ISBN: 978-1-041-20735-1 (hbk)
ISBN: 978-1-041-21520-2 (pbk)
ISBN: 978-1-003-72765-1 (ebk)

DOI: 10.1201/9781003727651

Typeset in Times Roman
by Maura A. Deek, Fadi P. Deek, and Wei Yao

About the Front Cover

The design of the front cover is inspired by symbolic elements found in Roman temple design. These elements can be interpreted as broadcasting messages deliberately, especially during key moments of the year, to different audiences regarding authority, symbolism, and cosmology. Many Roman temples were oriented with precise alignment to celestial events, with the sun's position in mind, during solstices or equinoxes. One such ancient archaeological site is in Baalbek, Lebanon, referred to as Heliopolis, translated as "City of the Sun."

Architecturally, the main structure is the Temple of Jupiter, the largest and most famous, renowned for its colossal stone blocks that are among the largest ever quarried. The site also includes the Temple of Bacchus and the Temple of Venus. While not necessarily a "code" in the modern sense, this complex of temples retains symbolic significance linking the earthly realm to the cosmic order. Such linkages of semiotic meaning drive the book you are about to read.

Dedication

This book is dedicated to the memory of Professor James A. McHugh (1944–2022), whose life continues to inspire.

Dr. McHugh left us too soon, but left so much behind. His insight, voice, and heart are woven into every chapter. This book would not exist without him. It began as a shared vision between Jim and Fadi, whose scholarly collaborations, and friendship, spanned multiple decades. Subsequently, when Fadi's administrative assignments took him away from this project, Jim teamed up with Maura, who shared a deep interest in the topic, taught it side-by-side with him for many years, and worked closely on developing content for the course. Jim brought not only brilliance to the project, but also perspective and passion. Jim passed in the middle of this journey but his influence remains everywhere in these pages. Completing this book has been an act of appreciation of, and a tribute to, Jim. Thank you, Jim, for everything.

Contents

Preface

About this book

The web is one of the most transformative technologies of our time. It has reshaped nearly every aspect of modern life. Yet, for all its ubiquity, the inner workings of web technologies often remain obscure to those outside the field. We have chosen to write this book out of a desire to present a clear, structured, and comprehensive overview of how modern web systems are built, and function, from foundational protocols to full-stack development.

Our motivation stems from both observation and experience. Over the years, as educators, researchers, and developers, we have encountered a range of learner, from students and professionals transitioning into tech to experienced developers and technical managers, who struggled with existing resources and materials that focus narrowly on certain technologies or delve directly into frameworks without establishing a strong understanding of the underlying principles. Often, the result, is trained developers who can build applications, but may lack the broader perspective necessary to diagnose, optimize, or secure them.

This book is an attempt to respond to such a gap by covering a range of core topics both from a breadth and depth point of views. This includes fundamental topics such as Internet protocols, HTML and CSS standards, client side programming with JavaScript, server-side programming with PHP and MySQL, and crucial topics like web application security and modern development practices. The structure of the book is intentional: it begins with foundational knowledge, gradually builds technical complexity, and ends with contemporary challenges and trends in web development.

It is our hope that this text serves multiple audiences: students in academic programs, self-taught developers seeking structure and focus, and professionals looking to reinforce or revisit key concepts. Emphasis is placed not only on the how, but also on the why: why standards matter, why security must be integral, and why a deep understanding of the web stack leads to better, more robust applications.

In a field that evolves rapidly, there is enduring value in mastering the fundamentals. This book is both a guide and a resource to support our stated aims.

Understanding the complexities of building robust, dynamic, and secure web applications has become an invaluable skill. Whether you are an aspiring software developer, a tech enthusiast, or a professional looking to expand your knowledge, *From Code to Cloud: Developing Web Applications* provides a roadmap to mastering the fundamental technologies for building successful websites and applications.

This book takes a practical approach to learning, equipping you with the knowledge and skills needed to navigate the complexities of web development from the ground up. From the foundational building blocks of internet protocols and HTML to the intricacies of modern web development frameworks and security practices, this book is an essential guide for anyone looking to understand how internet applications are created and maintained.

From Code to Cloud: Developing Web Applications not only covers the technical skills required to build websites and web applications but also teaches you the principles behind creating applications that are efficient and user-friendly. By the end of this book, you will have a complete understanding of the technologies and tools that form the foundation of the modern internet, empowering you to build, deploy, and maintain robust and secure web applications.

This book is not just for developers; it is for anyone looking to deepen their understanding of how the internet works and how dynamic applications come to life. Whether you are a beginner looking to enter into the field of web development or an experienced developer aiming to polish your skills, you will find valuable insights and practical suggestions that will take your web development knowledge to the next level. Mastering these skills will open up for you a world of opportunities in the fast-paced, ever-evolving realm of internet applications. With *From Code to Cloud: Developing Web Applications*, you will have all the tools you need to bring your ideas to life on the web.

Organization and Learning Path

Foundation First: Understanding the Web's Infrastructure

This book follows a deliberate progression designed to build comprehensive understanding. We begin with Internet protocols in Chapter 2, establishing how data moves across networks. This foundation proves essential for debugging connection issues, optimizing performance, and understanding security implications. Without grasping protocols, developers remain dependent on memorized patterns rather than principled understanding.

Chapters 3 and 4 explore HTML in depth, progressing from basic document structure to forms and modern HTML5 features. While seemingly elementary, thorough HTML knowledge distinguishes professional developers. Semantic markup improves accessibility and SEO. Proper form structure enhances usability. Understanding standards ensures cross-browser compatibility. These chapters establish patterns that echo throughout web development.

Building Interactive Experiences

Chapter 5 introduces CSS, transforming bare HTML into polished interfaces. Beyond basic styling, you will master layout systems, responsive design principles, and performance optimization. Modern CSS capabilities like Grid and Flexbox solve layout challenges that once required JavaScript. Animations and transitions create engaging experiences. Understanding the cascade and specificity rules prevents frustrating debugging sessions.

Chapter 6 brings interactivity through JavaScript, covering everything from basic DOM manipulation to asynchronous programming. You will learn event handling, form validation, AJAX communication, and modern ES6+ features. The chapter emphasizes practical patterns while explaining underlying concepts. By chapter's end, you will create dynamic interfaces that respond instantly to user actions.

Server-Side Development and Data Management

Chapter 7 addresses security before diving into server-side programming, establishing a security-first mindset. You will learn about common vulnerabilities, authentication patterns, and defensive programming techniques. This knowledge proves invaluable when building the dynamic features covered in subsequent chapters.

Chapter 8 introduces PHP, focusing on its web-specific features and integration with HTML. You will process forms, manage sessions, handle file uploads, and generate dynamic content. The chapter emphasizes practical examples while explaining important concepts like variable scope and security considerations.

Chapter 9 covers SQL and MySQL, teaching database design principles alongside practical query skills. You will learn normalization, indexing strategies, and query optimization. Understanding these concepts enables efficient data management regardless of the specific database system used.

Chapter 10 integrates PHP and MySQL, demonstrating how server-side code interacts with databases. You will build complete features like user authentication, content management, and search functionality. This integration chapter consolidates previous learning into practical applications.

Professional Development Practices

Chapter 11 explores deployment and operations, covering web server configuration, cloud platforms, and DevOps practices. You will learn to move applications from development to production, implement monitoring, and handle scaling challenges. These skills distinguish hobbyists from professionals.

Chapter 12 examines modern web development trends and practices. You will explore contemporary frameworks, development workflows, and architectural patterns. This forward-looking chapter prepares you for continued learning as the field evolves.

Customized Learning Paths

While sequential reading provides the most comprehensive understanding, different readers benefit from customized approaches based on their backgrounds and goals.

For Complete Beginners: Follow the book sequentially, completing all problems in the chapter review section. Begin with Chapters 1–2 to understand web fundamentals. Spend extra time on Chapters 3–4 (HTML) and 5 (CSS) to build a solid foundation. Take breaks between chapters to practice and consolidate learning. Take your time working through the material with consistent daily practice.

For Front-End Developers Expanding to Full-Stack: Start with a quick review of Chapters 3–6 to ensure no gaps in fundamental knowledge. Focus intensively on Chapters 7–10, which cover server-side development and database integration. Pay special attention to security concepts in Chapter 7, as server-side code introduces new vulnerabilities. Chapter 11's deployment content will prove particularly valuable for understanding production environments.

For Back-End Developers Learning Front-End: Begin with Chapter 2 to understand client-server communication from the client perspective. Study Chapters 3–6 carefully, as front-end development requires different thinking than server-side programming. Focus particularly on CSS (Chapter 5) and JavaScript (Chapter 6), as these represent the biggest departures from server-side work. Chapter 12's coverage of modern front-end frameworks will accelerate your transition.

For Experienced Developers Refreshing Knowledge: Use the table of contents to identify areas needing reinforcement. Read Chapter 1 for perspective on web evolution. Review Chapter 7 for current security best practices. Examine Chapters 11–12 for modern deployment and development approaches. Focus on problems that explore unfamiliar concepts rather than those reinforcing existing knowledge.

Hands-On Learning Strategy

Each chapter includes carefully designed problems that reinforce concepts through implementation. These progress from isolated concept demonstration to integrated feature development. Completing them provides practical experience essential for skill development.

Resist the temptation to merely read code examples. The physical act of typing, debugging, and modifying code commits knowledge to memory and promotes understanding. Errors you encounter and resolve become valuable learning experiences. Keep a development journal documenting challenges faced and solutions discovered. This reflection accelerates learning and provides a personal reference.

Create a portfolio of completed problems and personal projects. This demonstrates competence to potential employers while providing code examples for future reference. Consider sharing your learning journey, as teaching others reinforces your own understanding.

Prerequisites and Preparation

This book assumes basic computer literacy and some programming exposure, though not necessarily with web technologies. Familiarity with any programming language helps, as concepts like variables, functions, and control structures appear throughout. Basic networking understanding proves helpful but not essential. However, necessary concepts are explained as introduced.

More important than specific knowledge is mindset. Web development involves numerous interconnected technologies. Initial confusion is normal and expected. Persistence through early challenges leads to moments of clarity where connections become apparent. Cultivate patience with yourself and curiosity about how things work.

Prepare your learning environment before beginning. Install required software, configure your editor, and establish a consistent workspace. Create a dedicated folder structure for problems and projects. Establish regular study times when you can focus without interruption.

Beyond This Book: Continuing Your Journey

Web development is a vast and evolving field. This book provides solid foundations, but continued learning remains essential. Key areas for further study include:

Front-End Frameworks: React, Vue, and Angular dominate modern front-end development. Each offers different approaches to building complex user interfaces. Choose one based on job market demands or personal preference, but understand that framework knowledge builds upon JavaScript fundamentals.

Back-End Frameworks: Laravel and Symfony for PHP, Django for Python, or Express for Node.js provide structure for large applications. These frameworks implement patterns introduced in this book while adding conventions and utilities that accelerate development.

Cloud Platforms: AWS, Google Cloud, and Azure offer services beyond basic hosting. Understanding cloud services enables building scalable, globally distributed applications. Start with basic compute and storage services before exploring specialized offerings.

DevOps and Automation: Infrastructure as Code, continuous integration/deployment, and container orchestration represent essential modern skills. These practices reduce deployment friction and improve reliability.

Join developer communities to accelerate learning through shared knowledge. Local meetups provide networking opportunities and exposure to diverse perspectives. Online forums offer quick answers to specific questions. Open source contribution develops skills while giving back to the community. Conference attendance, whether virtual or in-person, exposes you to new ideas and best practices.

Remember that becoming a proficient web developer is a journey, not a destination. Technologies evolve, new patterns emerge, and best practices shift. The fundamental understanding gained from this book—how the web works, how to structure applications, how to think about security and performance—remains valuable regardless of specific technology changes. Embrace continuous learning as both a professional necessity and an intellectual adventure.

Making the Most of Your Learning

Success in mastering web development depends not just on reading but on active engagement with the material. Set specific learning goals for each study session. Write code as often as you can. Build projects that interest you personally, as passion sustains effort through challenging periods.

Connect concepts across chapters rather than treating them in isolation. Notice how HTML forms (Chapter 4) connect to PHP processing (Chapter 8) and database storage (Chapter 10). Observe how security principles (Chapter 7) apply throughout all development activities. These connections transform individual techniques into comprehensive understanding.

Most importantly, maintain perspective on the learning process. Every expert began as a beginner. Every complex application started with a single line of code. Your journey from novice to professional follows a path traveled by many before you. With dedication, curiosity, and the structured approach provided by this book, you will master the art and science of web development.

We hope that this book serves as a clear and useful guide as you engage with the material and learn important skills for developing web applications. Whether you are studying such topics for the first time or expanding on your knowledge, we wish you a productive and intellectually rewarding learning experience.

Maura A. Deek is a seasoned educator and technologist with extensive experience in academia and industry. She currently serves as a Senior University Lecturer in the Department of Informatics at New Jersey Institute of Technology (NJIT). With four decades of professional affiliation at NJIT, Professor Deek has taught undergraduate and graduate courses, engaged in curriculum development, and participated in interdisciplinary educational initiatives. She holds an M.S. in Computer Science from NJIT, a B.S. in Environmental Science from Rutgers University, and an A.S. in Liberal Arts from Middlesex College.

Maura's interdisciplinary academic background reflects a commitment to bridging science, computing, and education. In addition to college teaching, Maura has contributed to K–12 STEM education through her work with NJIT's Center for Pre-College Programs, where she served as a Research Associate and Investigator on state- and federally-funded projects. In this role, she developed curricula, trained educators, and participated in educational assessment efforts aimed at enhancing STEM learning in elementary and secondary schools. Maura's scholarly work explores the intersection of technology, pedagogy, and interdisciplinary learning, with notable contributions including studies on virtual classrooms, the role of problem-solving in computer science education, and technology integration in pre-college and special education curricula. She has co-authored journal and conference papers reporting on the results of her scholarship activities.

Prior to her academic career, Maura worked in the energy sector where she held several technical roles, ultimately serving as a Lead Knowledge Engineer and Systems Analyst. In this context, she led software engineering teams developing intelligent systems for energy applications and played a key role in business software design and development. With a rare blend of academic dedication, industry experience, and a passion for education at all levels, Maura brings a unique profile for teaching and mentoring future generations of computing professionals.

Fadi P. Deek is a Distinguished Professor at New Jersey Institute of Technology (NJIT) where he began his academic career as a student in the early 1980s. He received his B.S. and M.S. in Computer Science, and PhD in Computer and Information Science; all from NJIT. Dr. Deek's faculty appointments are in two departments: Informatics (in the College of Computing) and Mathematical Sciences (in the College of Science and Liberal Arts). Dr. Deek also serves as a member of the Graduate Faculty at Rutgers University-Newark. He has similarly progressed through administrative ranks at NJIT, culminating with Provost and Senior Executive Vice President for a decade, and Dean of the College of Science and Liberal Arts the prior decade.

Over the four decades of his professional affiliation with NJIT, Dr. Deek has taught students of differing abilities, from special needs to honors, and courses at all university levels in a variety of modalities, including face-to-face and online, from first-year to advanced graduate courses. Dr. Deek has received numerous teaching awards including the NJIT Student Senate Faculty of the Year Award, given to him in 1992 and 1993; the NJIT Honors Program Outstanding Teacher Award in 1992; the NJIT Excellence in Teaching Award in 1990 and 1999; the NJIT Master Teacher Designation in 2001 and the NJIT Robert W. Van Houten Award for Teaching Excellence in 2002. Also, in 2015, Dr. Deek was given the NJIT National Society of Black Engineers Chapter's Martin Luther King Jr. University Award and, in 2022, the Exemplar Model Award by NJIT's Society of

Hispanic Professional Engineers.

Dr. Deek maintains an active research program with interests primarily focusing in the areas of software engineering and open source software development, and most recently a keen interest in the intersection of philosophical, ethical, and technological aspects of artificial intelligence. Dr. Deek has mentored 16 PhD students. He has published over 200 articles in journals and conference proceedings, 14 book chapters, five edited collections, and six books. Dr. Deek has also given over 50 invited/professional presentations and keynotes.

Wei Yao is a researcher and educator with extensive expertise in blockchain technology, web applications, decentralized systems, privacy, and computer security. He earned his Ph.D. in Computer Science at New Jersey Institute of Technology (NJIT), where he also served as a Research Assistant in the Fintech Lab. Additionally, he received his M.S. in Computer Science from Central Connecticut State University and M.S. in Electrical Engineering from the University of Hartford, as well as a B.S. in Computer Science from Huazhong University of Science and Technology. Dr. Yao is an Assistant Professor of Mathematics, Statistics and Computer Science at the Polytechnic Campus of the University of Wisconsin-Stout, with a commitment to teaching, research, and mentoring in web applications and blockchain technologies. He previously served as a Postdoctoral Researcher at NJIT.

Dr. Yao's research explores the integration of blockchain technology with web-based systems, emphasizing the creation of secure and trustworthy distributed applications. His scholarly contributions include numerous peer-reviewed journal articles and conference presentations focused on blockchain-enabled web applications, decentralized key management, identity systems, and secure frameworks for web and mobile platforms. He is an active mentor, guiding undergraduate and graduate students as well as open-source developers, particularly within the web development and blockchain communities.

1. Introduction

The web has evolved from a simple document-sharing system to become one of the most transformative technologies of our time. It has reshaped human interaction, commerce, education, government, entertainment, and virtually every aspect of modern life. Yet for all its ubiquity, the inner workings of web technologies often remain opaque to those seeking to master them. This book aims to demystify web development by presenting a clear, structured, and comprehensive journey from foundational protocols to full-stack development.

This book addresses that gap by building knowledge systematically. We begin with the protocols that enable web communication, progress through the technologies that structure and style content, explore dynamic programming on both client and server sides, and culminate with modern deployment and development practices. Each chapter builds upon previous foundations while introducing concepts that will prove essential in subsequent sections. By the end of this journey, you will possess not just practical skills but the theoretical understanding that distinguishes professional developers from casual practitioners.

Learning Objectives

By the end of this chapter, you should be able to:

- Trace the evolution of web applications from static document repositories to dynamic, interactive platforms, understanding the key technological advances that enabled each transformation.
- Identify and explain the components of modern web architecture, including the roles of clients, servers, databases, and the protocols that enable their communication.
- Understand the purpose and relationship of each technology in the LAMP stack (Linux, Apache, MySQL, PHP) and how these components work together to create dynamic web applications.
- Establish a functional development environment suitable for web development, with appropriate tools and software configurations for effective learning.
- Recognize and differentiate between common application architecture patterns, understanding when to apply monolithic, service-oriented, or microservices approaches.
- Navigate this book's organization effectively, creating a personalized learning path based on your background, goals, and time constraints.

1.1 Evolution of Internet Applications

1.1.1 The Foundation: From ARPANET to HTTP

The Internet's genesis in 1969 as Advanced Research Projects Agency Network (ARPANET) established principles that remain fundamental today. This experimental network, connecting four university computers, demonstrated that decentralized, packet-switched communication could create resilient information systems. Throughout the following decades, networking protocols evolved and standardized, culminating in Transmission Control Protocol/Internet Protocol (TCP/IP)'s adoption in 1983. This created the technical foundation for global internetworking, but the Internet remained primarily a tool for researchers and technologists.

DOI: 10.1201/9781003727651-1

The transformation from Internet to World Wide Web occurred through Tim Berners-Lee's 1989 proposal at the European Organization for Nuclear Research (CERN). His vision elegantly combined three innovations: HTML for document structure, HyperText Transfer Protocol (HTTP) for transmission, and Uniform Resource Locators (URLs) for addressing. This trinity of technologies transformed the Internet from a file transfer and communication medium into an interconnected information space. The first web server went online in 1991, hosting simple HTML documents that demonstrated the power of hypertext linking.

1.1.2   The Static Era: Information Architecture (1991–1995)

Early websites functioned as digital publications. Developers hand-crafted HTML files, uploaded them via File Transfer Protocol (FTP), and organized them in directory hierarchies. A typical website might contain dozens or hundreds of static pages, interconnected through hyperlinks. The 1993 release of Mosaic, the first graphical web browser, catalyzed adoption beyond academic circles. Suddenly, the web became accessible to anyone with a computer and Internet connection.

This period established fundamental patterns that persist today. The request–response cycle, URL structure, and basic HTML elements from this era remain cornerstones of web development. However, limitations quickly became apparent. Static sites required manual updates, could not respond to user input beyond simple navigation, and offered identical content to every visitor. These constraints drove demand for dynamic capabilities.

1.1.3   The Dynamic Revolution: Server-Side Processing (1995–2005)

The introduction of the Common Gateway Interface (CGI) in 1993 had planted seeds that bloomed fully by 1995. Server-side scripting transformed websites from static documents into interactive applications. PHP's 1995 release democratized dynamic web development by embedding scripting directly within HTML. Simultaneously, JavaScript brought client-side interactivity, enabling immediate responses without server round-trips.

This era witnessed explosive growth in web capabilities. E-commerce sites processed transactions, forums enabled user discussions, and content management systems automated publishing. The Linux, Apache, MySQL, and PHP (LAMP) stack emerged as a dominant architecture, combining Linux's stability, Apache's flexibility, MySQL's data management, and PHP's accessibility. By 2005, platforms like WordPress and Drupal allowed non-programmers to create sophisticated websites, while frameworks provided structure for custom application development.

Figure 1.1 illustrates this evolution across four distinct eras of web development. The progression from static HTML pages with manual updates and one-way communication through to today's mobile-first, cloud-native applications demonstrates how each era built upon previous foundations while introducing revolutionary capabilities. The dynamic web era (1995–2005) marked the critical transition from static documents to interactive applications through the introduction of server-side scripting and database integration. As the diagram shows, the progression of web technologies from the static HTML era through to modern cloud-native applications has been eventful. Each era introduced transformative capabilities that built upon previous foundations while addressing emerging user needs and technological possibilities.

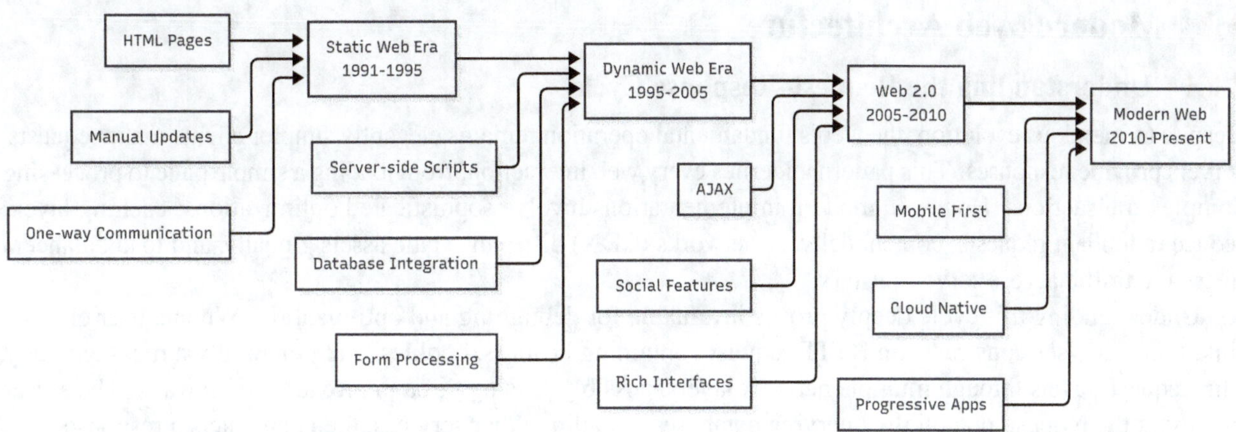

Figure 1.1: Evolution of web development eras.

1.1.4 Web 2.0: The Participatory Web (2005–2010)

The term "Web 2.0" captured a fundamental shift in web philosophy. Users transformed from passive consumers to active participants. Social networks redefined online interaction, while platforms like YouTube and Wikipedia demonstrated the power of user-generated content. Technically, AJAX (Asynchronous JavaScript and Extensible Markup Language (XML)) enabled fluid interfaces that updated without page reloads, creating experiences comparable to desktop applications.

Behind the scenes, architectural patterns evolved to support these richer interactions. Representational State Transfer Application Programming Interfaces (RESTful APIs) emerged as a standard for service communication. Cloud computing began abstracting infrastructure concerns. The traditional model of monolithic applications on dedicated servers gave way to distributed systems and service-oriented architectures. These changes laid the groundwork for the modern web's scalability and flexibility.

1.1.5 The Modern Era: Mobile, Cloud, and Beyond (2010–Present)

Smartphones and tablets forced a fundamental reconsideration of web design. Responsive design emerged to handle diverse screen sizes and interaction models. Mobile-first development acknowledged that many users primarily accessed the web through touch devices. Progressive Web Apps (PWA) began delivering app-like experiences through browsers, blurring distinctions between web and native applications.

Simultaneously, cloud computing matured from experimental technology to standard practice. Infrastructure as Code, containerization with Docker, and orchestration with Kubernetes revolutionized deployment. Front-end frameworks like React, Angular, and Vue.js enabled sophisticated single-page applications. The back-end evolved with microservices, serverless functions, and API-first development. Modern web development demands expertise across this expanded technology landscape.

1.2   Modern Web Architecture

1.2.1   Understanding the Request–Response Cycle

Despite tremendous evolution, the web's fundamental operation remains elegantly simple: clients make requests; servers provide responses. This pattern underlies every web interaction, from loading a simple page to processing complex transactions. However, modern implementations involve sophisticated optimizations: caching layers reduce redundant requests, content delivery networks (CDN) distribute static assets globally, and load balancers distribute traffic across server clusters.

Understanding this cycle deeply proves invaluable for debugging and optimization. When a user clicks a link, their browser constructs an HTTP request containing headers, cookies, and potentially a message body. This request travels through multiple network layers, possibly passing through proxies and firewalls. The server processes the request, potentially querying databases or calling other services, then constructs a response. The response journey reverses the request path, with each layer potentially modifying or caching the content.

Figure 1.2 depicts a complete request–response cycle in modern web architecture. The sequence diagram shows how a simple user action triggers a complex choreography of interactions across multiple infrastructure components. From initial DNS resolution through CDN caching, load balancing, application processing, and database queries, each component plays a crucial role in delivering the final response. Understanding this flow enables developers to optimize performance at each stage and diagnose issues when requests fail or perform poorly. This sequence depicts the complete flow of a typical web request in a modern multi-tier architecture. The interaction begins with user action and flows through various infrastructure components including Domain Name System (DNS) resolution, Content Delivery Networks (CDN), load balancing, and database queries before returning the rendered page to the user. Each component plays a crucial role in delivering fast, reliable web experiences at scale.

1.2.2   Multi-Tier Architecture

Enterprise web applications typically employ multi-tier architecture, separating concerns across presentation, application, and data layers. This separation enables independent scaling, specialized optimization, and clear boundaries between components. The presentation tier handles user interface rendering and client-side logic. The application tier implements business rules and orchestrates data flow. The data tier manages persistence and ensures consistency.

Each tier presents unique challenges and opportunities. Presentation tier optimization focuses on perceived performance through techniques like lazy loading and progressive rendering. Application tier concerns include session management, authentication, and API design. Data tier considerations encompass query optimization, replication strategies, and backup procedures. Success requires understanding each tier's role while maintaining a holistic system view.

1.2.3   Front-End Technologies and Evolution

Modern front-end development has evolved into a specialized discipline requiring deep expertise. While HTML, CSS, and JavaScript remain fundamental, their application has grown increasingly sophisticated. HTML5 introduced semantic elements that improve accessibility and Search Engine Optimization (SEO). CSS3 brought animations, transitions, and layout systems like Flexbox and CSS Grid. JavaScript evolved from simple scripting

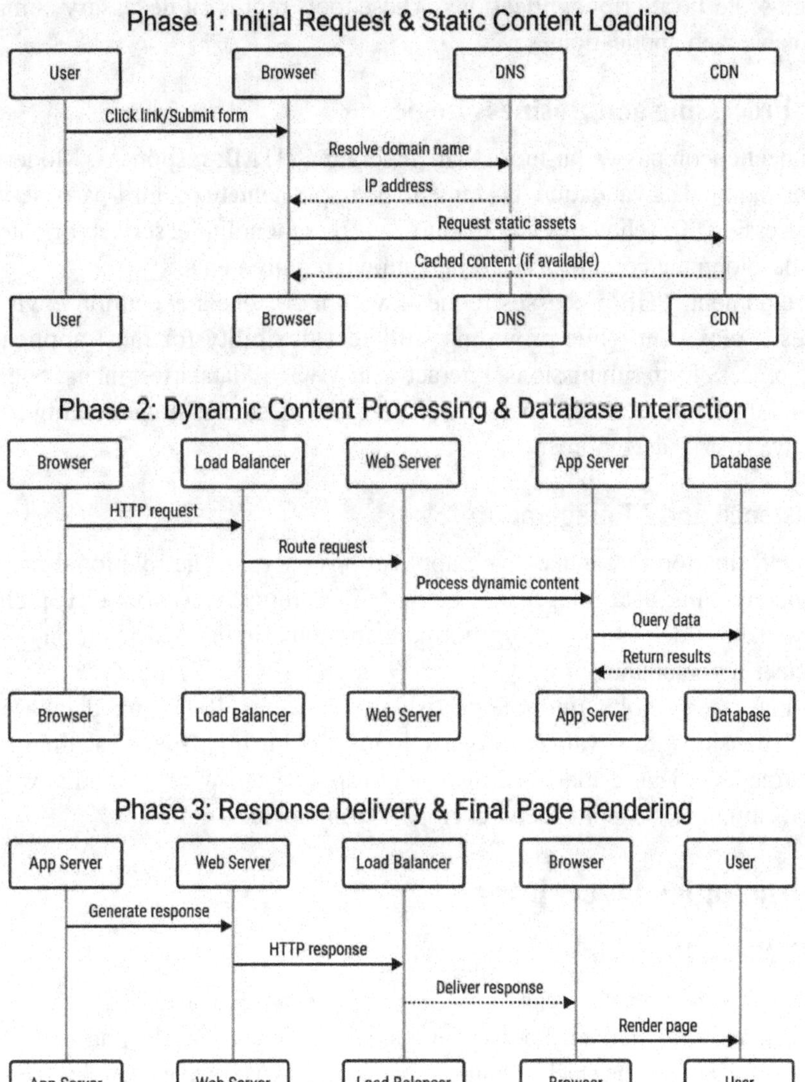

Figure 1.2: Modern web application request-response cycle.

to a full-featured programming language supporting complex application development.

Contemporary front-end development involves build pipelines that transform and optimize code. Transpilers like Babel enable modern JavaScript features while maintaining browser compatibility. Bundlers like Webpack optimize asset delivery. CSS preprocessors add programming constructs to stylesheets. TypeScript provides static typing for large-scale JavaScript applications. These tools represent necessary complexity for building performant, maintainable web applications.

1.2.4　Back-End Processing and Business Logic

Server-side development encompasses far more than generating HTML responses. Modern back-ends handle authentication, authorization, data validation, business logic implementation, third-party service integration, and asynchronous job processing. The choice of architecture, whether monolithic, service-oriented, or microservices, profoundly impacts development complexity and operational requirements.

In LAMP stack development, PHP processes requests within Apache's execution environment. This tight integration simplifies deployment while providing sufficient flexibility for most applications. PHP scripts handle URL routing, process form submissions, interact with MySQL databases, manage sessions, and generate responses. Understanding this flow, from Apache receiving a request to PHP generating a response, forms the foundation for effective LAMP development.

1.2.5　Data Persistence and Management

Databases store the information that makes web applications useful. The relational model, exemplified by MySQL, excels at maintaining data integrity through ACID properties (Atomicity, Consistency, Isolation, Durability). Proper database design, including normalization and index optimization, significantly impacts application performance and maintainability.

Modern applications often employ multiple persistence strategies. Relational databases handle structured data with complex relationships. Key–value stores like Redis provide high-speed caching. Document databases accommodate semi-structured data. Understanding when to apply each approach, and how to integrate multiple systems effectively, distinguishes experienced developers from novices.

1.3　Core Technologies Overview

1.3.1　The LAMP Stack Philosophy

The LAMP stack represents more than a technology choice. It embodies a development philosophy emphasizing openness, accessibility, and pragmatism. Each component is open source, eliminating licensing barriers and enabling complete customization. The stack's maturity means edge cases have been discovered and documented. Its ubiquity ensures abundant learning resources and hosting options.

LAMP's enduring relevance stems from its balance of simplicity and capability. Unlike some modern stacks requiring extensive configuration and tooling, LAMP applications can run on modest hardware with minimal setup. This accessibility makes it ideal for learning web development fundamentals. The principles mastered through LAMP development such as request handling, database interaction, session management, security considerations transfer directly to other technology stacks.

1.3.2 Linux: The Foundation

Linux provides the operating system foundation, offering stability, security, and flexibility essential for web servers. Its open-source nature eliminates licensing costs while providing complete control over system configuration. Linux's permission system enables fine-grained security controls. Its process management efficiently handles concurrent requests. Its networking stack, refined over decades, provides robust communication capabilities.

For web developers, Linux knowledge pays dividends beyond basic operation. Understanding file permissions prevents security vulnerabilities. Familiarity with command-line tools enables efficient debugging and deployment. Knowledge of process management helps diagnose performance issues. While graphical tools exist, command-line proficiency remains invaluable for server administration and automation.

1.3.3 Apache: The Web Server

Apache HTTP Server has powered the web for over two decades, consistently ranking among the most deployed web servers globally. Its modular architecture enables administrators to include only necessary functionality, improving security and performance. Modules handle diverse requirements from URL rewriting to authentication to compression.

Apache's configuration flexibility accommodates virtually any deployment scenario. Virtual hosts enable one server to host multiple websites with distinct configurations. Directory-level `.htaccess` files allow granular control without server-wide changes. `mod_rewrite` enables SEO-friendly URLs and complex routing rules. Understanding Apache configuration empowers developers to optimize application delivery and diagnose deployment issues.

1.3.4 MySQL: Data Management

MySQL brings enterprise-grade data management to the LAMP stack. As a relational database management system, it organizes information into structured tables with defined relationships. SQL provides a standardized interface for data manipulation, while MySQL's storage engines offer different performance and feature trade-offs for various use cases.

Effective MySQL usage requires understanding both theoretical concepts and practical considerations. Database normalization eliminates redundancy and prevents anomalies. Indexes accelerate queries but require storage and maintenance overhead. Transaction isolation levels balance consistency with concurrency. Query optimization can improve performance by orders of magnitude. These skills prove invaluable regardless of the specific database system used.

1.3.5 PHP: Dynamic Processing

PHP transforms static web servers into dynamic application platforms. Designed specifically for web development, PHP integrates seamlessly with HTML while providing full programming language capabilities. Its extensive standard library includes functions for common web tasks: form processing, session management, database interaction, file manipulation, and email sending.

Modern PHP bears little resemblance to its early versions. Object-oriented programming support enables well-structured applications. Namespaces prevent naming conflicts in large codebases. Type declarations catch errors during development. Composer manages dependencies professionally. Frameworks like Laravel and

Symfony provide structure for complex applications. Understanding both PHP's fundamentals and modern practices enables building maintainable, secure applications.

1.4 Development Environment

1.4.1 Establishing Your Workspace

Professional web development requires a properly configured environment that balances production fidelity with development convenience. For LAMP development, this means installing and configuring Linux (or suitable alternatives), Apache, MySQL, and PHP on your development machine. While production servers typically run Linux, developers can work effectively on Windows using WSL (Windows Subsystem for Linux) or macOS using its Unix foundation.

Package managers streamline installation and maintenance. On Ubuntu or Debian, `apt-get` installs the entire stack with a few commands. Red Hat-based systems use `yum` or `dnf`. macOS developers often prefer `Homebrew`. These tools manage dependencies, handle updates, and ensure compatible versions. Understanding package management proves essential for maintaining both development and production environments.

1.4.2 Integrated Development Environments and Tools

Effective development requires more than just the LAMP stack. A capable code editor or IDE dramatically improves productivity through syntax highlighting, auto-completion, debugging integration, and refactoring support. Popular choices include Visual Studio Code for its extensive extension ecosystem, PhpStorm for comprehensive PHP support, and Sublime Text for speed and flexibility.

Version control, particularly Git, has become non-negotiable for professional development. Git tracks code changes, enables collaboration, facilitates code review, and provides recovery from mistakes. Platforms like GitHub, GitLab, and Bitbucket add issue tracking, continuous integration, and deployment automation. Mastering Git workflows including branching, merging, rebasing is essential for team development.

1.4.3 Development Workflow and Best Practices

Professional web development follows established workflows that ensure code quality and team productivity. Development begins with requirement analysis and planning, progresses through implementation and testing, and culminates in deployment and maintenance. Each phase demands specific skills and tools.

Modern workflows emphasize automation and continuous improvement. Automated testing catches regressions before they reach production. Code linters enforce consistent style. Continuous integration validates changes across environments. Deployment pipelines eliminate manual errors. These practices, while requiring initial investment, pay dividends through reduced bugs and faster delivery.

1.5 Application Architecture Patterns

1.5.1 Monolithic Architecture: Simplicity and Trade-offs

Traditional web applications follow monolithic architecture, packaging all functionality within a single deployable unit. This approach offers genuine advantages: simplified development, straightforward debugging, easy transaction management, and minimal operational complexity. For many applications, especially those with modest scale requirements, monolithic architecture remains the most pragmatic choice.

However, monoliths present challenges as applications grow. Large codebases become difficult to comprehend and modify. Scaling requires replicating the entire application even when only specific components need additional resources. Technology choices made early constrain future options. Team coordination becomes complex when many developers work on a single codebase. Understanding these trade-offs helps architects choose appropriate patterns for specific contexts.

1.5.2 Service-Oriented and Microservices Architectures

Service-oriented architecture (SOA) addresses monolithic limitations by decomposing applications into discrete services communicating through well-defined interfaces. Each service encapsulates specific business capabilities and maintains its own data. This separation enables independent development, deployment, and scaling of services.

Microservices architecture extends SOA principles to create many small, focused services. Each microservice typically handles a single business function, maintains its own database, and communicates via lightweight protocols. This approach maximizes flexibility and scalability but introduces complexity in service coordination, data consistency, and operational management. Success requires sophisticated tooling, monitoring, and organizational maturity.

1.5.3 Model-View-Controller and Its Variations

The Model-View-Controller (MVC) pattern provides internal structure regardless of overall architecture. Models encapsulate data and business logic. Views present information to users. Controllers coordinate between models and views, handling user input and selecting appropriate responses. This separation of concerns improves code organization and enables parallel development.

Many frameworks implement MVC variations adapted to web development realities. Model-View-Presenter (MVP) clarifies responsibilities by making views passive. Model-View-ViewModel (MVVM) introduces view models that prepare data for display. Understanding these patterns helps developers work effectively with frameworks and organize code logically even without framework support.

1.5.4 RESTful Architecture and API Design

Representational State Transfer (REST) has become the dominant architectural style for web APIs. RESTful services treat URLs as resource identifiers and HTTP methods as operations. GET retrieves resources, POST creates them, PUT updates them, and DELETE removes them. This alignment with HTTP semantics creates intuitive, cacheable APIs.

Effective REST API design requires careful consideration of resource modeling, URL structure, response formats, and error handling. Resources should represent business concepts, not database tables. URLs should be predictable and hierarchical. Responses should include appropriate status codes and headers. Versioning strategies must balance stability with evolution. These design decisions profoundly impact API usability and longevity.

1.6   Concluding Remarks

This introductory chapter has established the context for your web development journey. We have traced the web's evolution from simple document sharing to today's sophisticated application platforms. We have examined modern web architecture, understanding how multiple technologies collaborate to create seamless user experiences. We have introduced the LAMP stack that forms this book's foundation while acknowledging the broader technology ecosystem.

As you progress through subsequent chapters, remember that web development combines technical precision with creative problem-solving. Each technology you master becomes a tool in your professional toolkit. Understanding when and how to apply these tools, not just memorizing their syntax, distinguishes competent developers from exceptional ones.

The web continues evolving, presenting endless opportunities for those who understand its foundations. Whether building personal projects, contributing to open source, or developing commercial applications, the knowledge gained here enables meaningful participation in the digital future. Welcome to the rewarding challenge of web development. Let us begin building tomorrow's web together.

2. Internet Protocols

The Internet is built on a suite of protocols that enable computers and networks to communicate. Understanding these protocols, from how data is packaged and addressed to how connections are established is crucial for developers and network engineers. This chapter explores core Internet protocols, illustrates their operations with diagrams, and provides real-world examples of both successes and failures. We also include hands-on problems to reinforce key concepts, and discuss security considerations, such as vulnerabilities and defenses, for each protocol.

Learning Objectives

By the end of this chapter, you should be able to:
- Explain the key functions of each layer in the TCP/IP protocol stack and how this model compares to the OSI model.
- Describe the client-server architecture and how clients and servers communicate over the Internet.
- Explain the role of the Internet Protocol (IP) in addressing and routing data across networks, and distinguish between IPv4 and IPv6 addresses.
- Differentiate between TCP and User Datagram Protocol (UDP) in terms of connection setup, reliability, and appropriate use cases for each.
- Describe how the Domain Name System (DNS) translates domain names into IP addresses to route requests to the correct server.
- Interpret and construct HTTP request and response messages, understanding common HTTP methods (e.g., GET, POST) and status codes.
- Explain how HTTPS (HTTP Secure) uses Transport Layer Security (TLS) encryption to protect data in transit and why this is important for web security.
- Outline the fundamentals of web server operation, including how a web server handles incoming requests and delivers responses to clients.
- Identify common security vulnerabilities associated with core Internet protocols (such as HTTP, DNS, or TCP) and describe basic defenses against these threats.
- Use common networking tools (like `ping`, `traceroute`, or `nslookup`) to test connectivity and troubleshoot network issues.

2.1   Network Architecture

Modern networks follow a layered architecture. Each layer in the network stack is responsible for specific functions, and protocols at each layer cooperate to deliver data from source to destination. The predominant model in use is the TCP/IP protocol stack, which abstracts networking into four layers:
- Application Layer: Protocols for specific network services and data exchange at the application level (e.g., HTTP for the web, DNS for domain name resolution, SMTP for email).

DOI: 10.1201/9781003727651-2

- Transport Layer: End-to-end communication between hosts, managing how data is reliably or unreliably delivered (e.g., TCP for reliable byte streams, UDP for connectionless datagrams).
- Network Layer: Packet routing and addressing across networks (e.g., IP, the Internet Protocol, for logical addressing and routing of packets).
- Link Layer: Physical and data link connectivity on local network segments (e.g., Ethernet and Wi-Fi, the protocols that operate over a particular medium or local link).

Open Systems Interconnection (OSI) vs. TCP/IP Models: In networking theory, the OSI model divides communication into 7 layers, whereas the Internet's TCP/IP model uses a more streamlined 4-layer approach. However, the concepts are similar, in that higher layers build on services of lower layers, but the TCP/IP model merges some of the OSI layers. For example, OSI's Physical and Data Link layers are often collectively referred to as the "Link layer" in TCP/IP, and OSI's Session and Presentation layers are typically considered part of the Application layer in TCP/IP. In practice, discussions of Internet protocols usually refer to the TCP/IP model, as it reflects the actual protocols in use. Figure 2.1 illustrates how the seven OSI layers correspond to the four layers of the TCP/IP model.

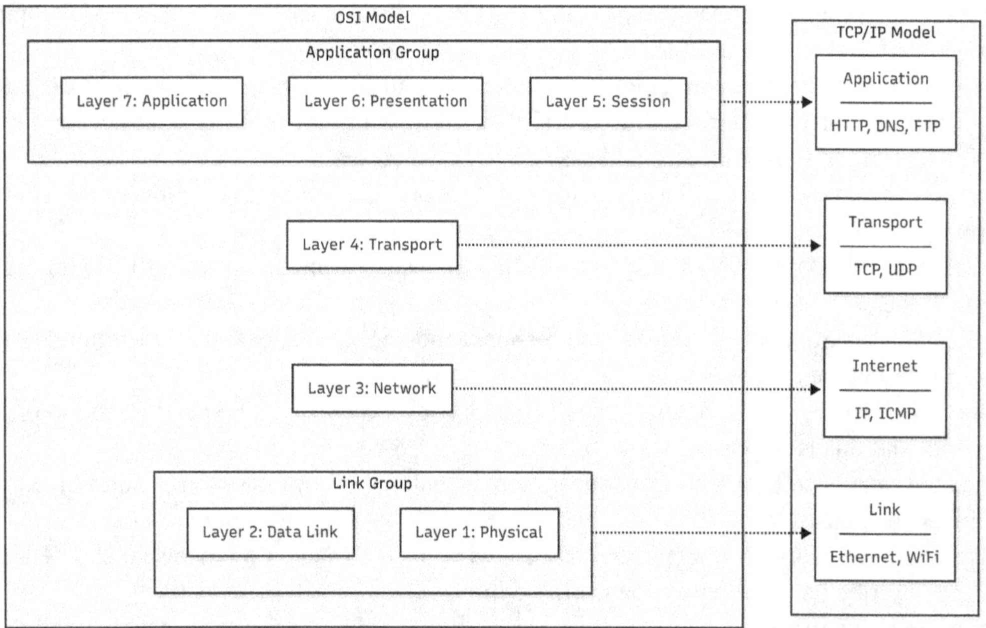

Figure 2.1: The OSI and TCP/IP layers.

Understanding both models helps developers conceptualize where different protocols and technologies fit within the networking landscape. In the TCP/IP model (which we will use throughout this book), the Application layer corresponds to all high-level protocols (HTTP, DNS, etc.), the Transport layer handles host-to-host communication (TCP, UDP), the Internet layer handles routing (IP), and the Link layer covers the network interface (Ethernet, Wi-Fi, and other link technologies).

2.1.1 Client-Server Architecture

Most Internet applications use a client-server architecture. A client (for example, your web browser) initiates a connection to a server (for example, a web server) to request some resource or service. Servers generally listen for incoming requests on well-known ports that designate specific services. Clients connect from arbitrary, typically high-numbered source ports on their end. For instance, a web server typically listens on TCP port 80 for HTTP or 443 for HTTPS, while the browser may use a random port like 50234 as its source. This client-server pattern underpins the Web (browser-to-webserver communication), email (mail client to mail server), domain name resolution, and many other services. It allows for a clear separation of roles: servers provide resources or services, and clients consume them on demand.

2.1.2 Routing in the Internet (BGP and Beyond)

While a client-server model describes who initiates communication, routing describes how the data actually travels across networks to reach the correct destination. At the Network layer, routers forward packets toward their destinations based on IP addresses. In the Internet , a "network of networks", your packet may hop through many intermediate networks (and routers) before arriving at the target server.

Within a single organization or autonomous system (a network under one administrative entity), interior routing protocols like Open Shortest Path First (OSPF) or Intermediate System to Intermediate System (IS-IS) determine the best paths for data. Between different networks on the global Internet, the protocol that "glues" everything together is BGP (Border Gateway Protocol). BGP allows the many independent networks ((Internet Service Providers (ISPs), large companies, etc.) to exchange information about which IP address blocks (prefixes) they can deliver traffic to. In essence, each network advertises to its neighbors which destinations it can reach, and BGP propagates this information so that routers across the world know how to get to any given block of IP addresses.

A dramatic real-world example of routing's importance occurred in October 2021, when a misconfiguration in BGP made Facebook and its services (WhatsApp, Instagram) unreachable worldwide for several hours. In that incident, Facebook's routers accidentally stopped advertising the routes to Facebook's own IP addresses. As a result, other networks had no way to route packets to Facebook's servers, effectively making Facebook "disappear" from the Internet. Even Facebook's DNS servers became inaccessible (since DNS queries could not reach them), compounding the problem. This outage highlighted how critical and yet fragile BGP is: a single incorrect routing update can cause large portions of the Internet to become unreachable. Since then, there have been renewed calls for improving routing security (for example, using route filtering and cryptographic route validation) to prevent such incidents or malicious route hijacks.

Routing protocols generally operate on trust. For example, BGP assumes that networks truthfully advertise only the routes they are authorized to. Misconfigurations or attacks (such as BGP route hijacking) can exploit this trust. Networking professionals use tools like route filters and monitoring systems to mitigate these risks, but the fundamental openness that makes the Internet flexible can also introduce vulnerabilities if not managed carefully.

2.2 Core Internet Protocols

Now we turn our attention to the core protocols of the Internet. These include the Internet Protocol (IP) itself at the Network layer, the major Transport-layer protocols (TCP and UDP), and important supporting systems like DNS for naming. Each of these protocols plays a specific role in enabling Internet communication.

2.2.1 Internet Protocol

The Internet Protocol (IP) is the workhorse of the Internet's Network layer. IP is responsible for addressing and routing packets across interconnected networks. It provides a connectionless, best-effort packet delivery service. "Connectionless" means that IP does not establish a dedicated end-to-end connection before sending data; instead, it simply forwards individual packets independently. "Best-effort" means that IP does not guarantee delivery. Packets may be lost, arrive out of order, or be duplicated but it will do its best to move packets towards their destination. Reliability (ensuring all data arrives and in order) is left to higher-level protocols if needed (for example, TCP builds reliability on top of IP).

IPv4 and IPv6 Addressing

IP addresses provide the addressing scheme that identifies senders and recipients in the network. There are currently two versions of IP in use on the Internet: IPv4 and IPv6.

- IPv4 addresses are 32-bit numbers, typically written in the familiar "dotted decimal" notation (e.g., `203.0.113.5`). There are around 4.3 billion possible IPv4 addresses. This finite pool was exhausted in the 2010s due to the explosive growth of the Internet. As a short-term workaround, techniques like NAT (Network Address Translation) allow multiple devices to share a single IPv4 address (for example, your home router uses one public IPv4 address for all your devices by translating their addresses). However, NAT is a stop-gap; it breaks the end-to-end addressing model of the Internet and adds complexity.

- IPv6 addresses are 128-bit numbers, usually written in hexadecimal and separated by colons (e.g., `2001:0db8:85a3::8a2e:0370:7334`, often abbreviated by omitting consecutive zeros). The IPv6 address space is astronomical (approximately 3.4×10^{38} possible addresses), enough to give virtually every device a unique address many times over. Besides a vastly larger address space, IPv6 also simplified some aspects of IP (like more efficient routing and built-in autoconfiguration through Neighbor Discovery). Despite these advantages, IPv6 adoption has been gradual. Both protocols coexist today in a "dual stack" Internet: many systems support both IPv4 and IPv6. Over time, IPv6 is expected to become dominant as legacy IPv4 networks are upgraded.

Domain Names and DNS

While IP addresses are the numbers that identify machines on the network, they are not convenient for humans to remember. This is where the Domain Name System (DNS) comes in. DNS is often called the "phonebook of the Internet" because it translates human-friendly domain names (like `www.example.com`) into IP addresses (like `93.184.216.34`) that computers use to route traffic. Whenever you type a URL in your browser or send an email, your system will use DNS to resolve the domain name to the corresponding IP address before making a connection.

A DNS lookup involves multiple steps in a hierarchical, distributed database of name servers. The process is usually as follows:

1. Recursive Resolver: Your computer sends the domain name query to a recursive resolver (often operated by your ISP or a public DNS service like Cloudflare's `1.1.1.1` or Google's `8.8.8.8`). The recursive resolver's job is to find the answer (the IP address for the domain) on your behalf. It will query other DNS servers as needed and return the final answer to you. From your perspective, you ask one server (the resolver) and get an answer. The resolver performs this recursive process through the DNS hierarchy for you.

2. Root Name Server: The recursive resolver first contacts a DNS root server. There are 13 logical root servers (named `A` through `M`) distributed globally. The root servers know which servers are responsible for top-level domains (TLDs). For example, if you are looking up `example.com`, the resolver asks a root server, "Who can tell me about the `.com` domain?" The root server responds with a referral to the TLD name servers for `.com`.

3. TLD Name Server: Next, the resolver contacts the appropriate TLD name server (for `.com` in our example) and asks, "Who is the DNS authority for `example.com`?" The TLD server replies with the address of the authoritative name server for the `example.com` domain.

4. Authoritative Name Server: Finally, the resolver contacts the authoritative DNS server for `example.com` and asks for the specific record: "What is the IP address for `www.example.com`?" The authoritative server looks up that host name in its DNS records and responds with the IP address (for instance, `93.184.216.34`).

5. Response to Client: The recursive resolver now has the answer. It returns the IP address to your computer (the client) that originally made the request. Your browser can then use that IP address to connect to the web server for `www.example.com`. Additionally, the resolver will typically cache the result for a period of time (specified by the DNS record's TTL, or time-to-live) to speed up future queries for the same name. Your own computer may also cache the result for a short time.

(The above process is called iterative resolution from the perspective of the resolver. The client makes a single recursive query to the resolver, and the resolver then makes a series of iterative queries to find the answer. The client does not see all those intermediate steps; it just waits for the final answer.)

DNS is a distributed, hierarchical database. No single server contains all domain information; instead, responsibility is delegated downward: from the root zone to top-level domains (like `.com`), and then to each domain's authoritative servers. This design is what makes DNS scalable and resilient. If one DNS server does not know the answer, it knows someone else to ask (or at least where to direct the query next).

DNS resolution example:

To tie this together, consider what happens when you visit `https://www.example.com/` in a browser. Your system will use DNS to resolve `www.example.com` to an IP address via the steps above. Once the IP is obtained (possibly via cached results if available), the browser will initiate a TCP connection to that IP on port 443 (for HTTPS). Only after the DNS step succeeds can the web request proceed. In practice, DNS caching (by your operating system or browser, and by resolvers) often makes this process quicker, as many lookups can be answered immediately from cache if they were recently performed.

Figure 3.1 illustrates the DNS lookup process step-by-step showing how a recursive resolver sequentially queries a root server, a TLD server, and the authoritative name server to resolve a domain name to its IP address after the section on DNS resolution steps.

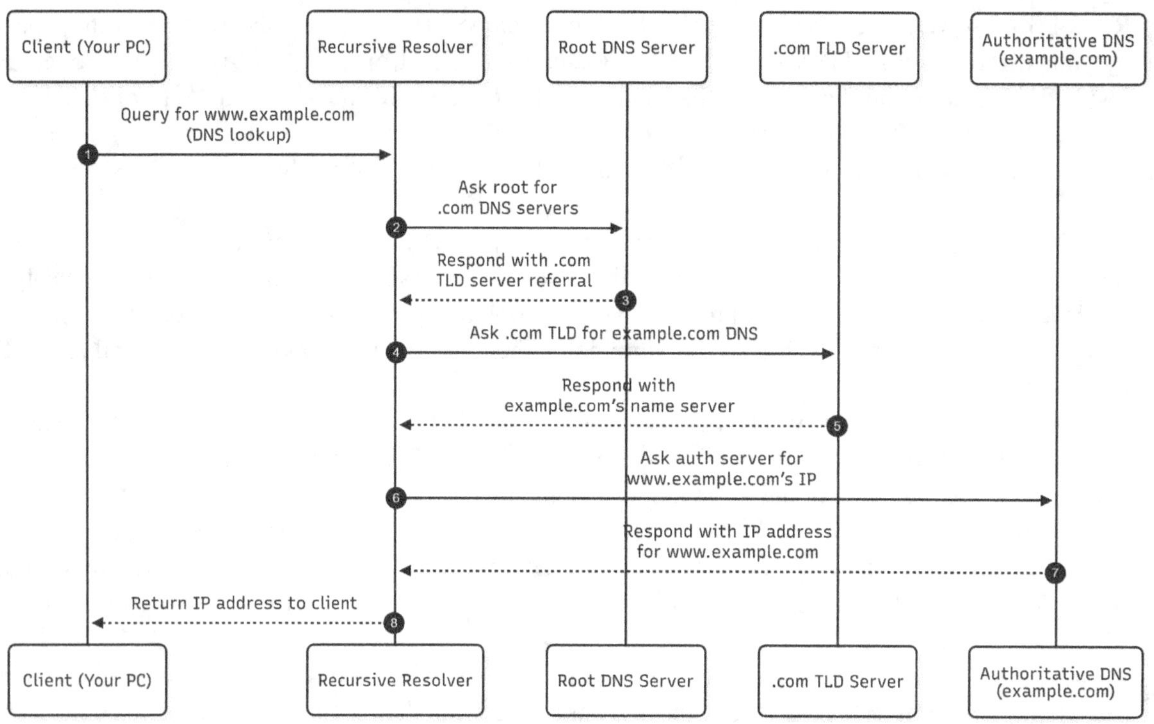

Figure 2.2: The DNS lookup process.

DNS makes the use of human-readable addresses possible, but it was designed in an earlier, more trusting era of the Internet. As we will see in the security section, standard DNS queries and responses are neither encrypted nor authenticated, which opens the door to certain attacks.

DNS Security Considerations:

Because vanilla DNS has no built-in authentication, attackers can attempt to provide false DNS information. One well-known attack is DNS cache poisoning, where a malicious actor tricks a DNS resolver into caching an incorrect mapping for a domain name. For example, an attacker might succeed in making a resolver cache an answer that says `bank.example.com` map to an attacker-controlled IP address. Subsequent users querying that resolver for `bank.example.com` would get the fake IP and could be directed to a phishing site. Cache poisoning typically involves the attacker sending forged DNS response packets to the resolver, hoping to race the real response and have the fake one accepted. Because DNS predominantly uses UDP (which is connectionless and has no handshake), it is easier for an attacker to spoof replies as there is no easy built-in verification.

Several measures exist to counter DNS attacks. DNSSEC (Domain Name System Security Extensions) adds digital signatures to DNS data so that resolvers can verify a response's authenticity (i.e., confirm it truly came from the authoritative server for the domain and was not tampered with). When DNSSEC is properly implemented, a DNS resolver will reject forged answers that are not signed with the correct key. However,

DNSSEC requires support by both the domain owner and the resolver, and adoption has been slow since not all domains have DNSSEC enabled, and not all clients request DNSSEC validation. Another set of protections involves encrypting DNS queries to protect privacy and integrity: protocols like DoT (DNS over TLS) and DoH (DNS over HTTPS) ensure that DNS queries and answers are encrypted on the wire, preventing eavesdropping or tampering by intermediaries. Major public resolvers and modern operating systems increasingly support these encrypted DNS methods.

In summary, DNS is fundamental to Internet usability, but it must be secured and managed carefully. Misconfigurations (like forgetting to update a DNS record or letting a domain expire) can break connectivity, while deliberate attacks on DNS can hijack or disrupt traffic. Whether you are a developer or administrator, using trusted DNS services, enabling DNSSEC for your domains, and being aware of DNS's role in your application's availability are all important.

2.2.2 TCP (Transmission Control Protocol)

The Transmission Control Protocol (TCP) operates at the Transport layer and provides a reliable, connection-oriented data stream between applications. Most core Internet services including web (HTTP/HTTPS), email (Simple Mail Transfer Protocol (SMTP) / Internet Message Access Protocol (IMAP)), file transfer (FTP), and many others rely on TCP for transporting data. TCP's job is to ensure that data sent by one end of a connection is received at the other end completely and in order. If data is lost or corrupted in transit, TCP detects it and retransmits as needed. If packets arrive out of order, TCP reorders them before delivering to the application. It also manages flow control (so a fast sender does not overwhelm a slow receiver) and congestion control (to avoid swamping the network).

TCP Handshake (Connection Establishment)

Before two devices can exchange data using TCP, they must establish a connection. This is done via the famous three-way handshake. The handshake synchronizes sequence numbers and sets up initial connection parameters:

1. SYN: The client (e.g., a browser) initiates by sending a TCP segment with the "SYN" (synchronize) flag set. This segment includes an initial sequence number (a random 32-bit value, say X). The SYN signifies "I'd like to start a connection, and my starting sequence number is X."
2. SYN-ACK: The server, upon receiving the SYN, responds with a segment that has both the SYN and ACK (acknowledge) flags set. In this single response, the server is doing two things: acknowledging the client's SYN and sequence number, and sending its own SYN to the client. The ACK portion contains X+1 (to acknowledge receipt of the client's sequence X and indicate the next expected number), and the SYN portion of this packet carries the server's own initial sequence number (say Y).
3. ACK: Finally, the client sends an ACK back to the server, acknowledging the server's sequence number by sending Y+1. After this step, the connection is established; both sides have agreed on the initial sequence numbers and are ready to transmit data.

After the three-way handshake, both the client and server have "synchronized" sequence numbers and the TCP connection is considered open. Now, data can flow in both directions. Every byte of data is numbered (as part of the sequence), and each acknowledgment (ACK) indicates the next byte expected, providing reliable delivery.

It is worth noting that TCP connection teardown involves a separate handshake with Finish (FIN) and ACK flags, often a "four-way" exchange because each side closes independently. But for now, the key concept is that establishing a TCP connection requires this preliminary exchange to set up the connection state.

TCP Data Transfer and Reliability

Once a TCP connection is established, data can be sent using TCP segments. Each segment carries a chunk of the byte stream along with sequence numbers and acknowledgments. TCP uses the sequence numbers and ACKs to provide reliability:

- Acknowledgments: When a receiver (client or server) gets TCP data, it sends back an ACK with the sequence number of the next byte it expects. For example, if a server has received bytes 0–1023 from the client, it might send ACK 1024, meaning "I have everything up to byte 1023, send me byte 1024 next." This ACK mechanism lets the sender know which data has arrived successfully.
- Retransmission: If the sender does not receive an ACK for certain data within a timeout period, it assumes those packets were lost and retransmits them. This ensures that eventually all data is received (assuming the network is not completely down).
- Ordering: If packets arrive out of order, the receiver can buffer them until missing pieces arrive, then reassemble the data in the correct order before delivering it to the Application layer. The sequence numbers enable this reordering.
- Flow Control: TCP uses a sliding window mechanism to implement flow control. The receiver advertises a "window size", essentially indicating "I can receive X more bytes; please don't send more than that before waiting for an ACK." This prevents a fast sender from overflowing a slow receiver's buffer.
- Congestion Control: Perhaps one of TCP's most significant contributions is its congestion control algorithms. TCP detects network congestion (often via missing ACKs or delay increases) and will throttle back its sending rate to alleviate congestion. Classic algorithms like TCP Tahoe/Reno (and many variants since) dynamically adjust how much data can be "in flight" based on perceived network conditions. This prevents routers and links from being overwhelmed by too much traffic and was crucial in preventing Internet meltdown due to congestion. A famous example: in the late 1980s, early TCP implementations did not handle congestion well, leading to severe network collapses. Van Jacobson's congestion control algorithms (additive increase/multiplicative decrease, slow start, etc.) introduced around 1988 saved the Internet from repeated congestion collapse. These algorithms (with refinements) are still in use today and allow the Internet to handle massive amounts of traffic in a stable way.

TCP in Practice: Socket Example in PHP

To see TCP's reliability and connection-oriented service in action, let us walk through a simple example using PHP. We will connect to a web server and fetch a page using raw socket calls, essentially doing manually what a browser does automatically under the hood:

```php
<?php
// Create a TCP socket connection to example.com on port 80 (HTTP)
$socket = fsockopen("www.example.com", 80);
if (!$socket) {
```

```php
5      die("Unable to connect to server");
6  }
7
8  // Send an HTTP GET request over the TCP connection
9  $request = "GET / HTTP/1.1\r\nHost: www.example.com\r\nConnection: Close\r\n\r\n";
10 fwrite($socket, $request);
11
12 // Receive the first 1024 bytes of the response
13 $response = fread($socket, 1024);
14 echo "Response from server:\n";
15 echo $response;
16
17 // Close the socket
18 fclose($socket);
19 ?>
```

Output (excerpt): Running this PHP script should print an HTTP response starting with a status line and headers, for example:

Output (excerpt)

```
Response from server:
HTTP/1.1 200 OK
Content-Type: text/html; charset=UTF-8
Content-Length: 1256
... (other headers) ...
<html>
  <head><title>Example Domain</title> ... </head>
  <body> ... </body>
</html>
```

In this code, we manually opened a TCP connection to www.example.com and sent a simple HTTP GET request. The `fsockopen` function handled the low-level detail of the TCP three-way handshake for us when establishing the connection. We then sent text down the socket (which under the hood was packaged into TCP segments), and we read back the response. This illustrates how TCP provides the pipe for application protocols like HTTP: once the connection is established, the application can send requests and receive responses as a stream of bytes, without worrying about packet loss or ordering, allowing TCP to take care of those.

TCP Vulnerabilities and Security

While TCP's design ensures reliable delivery, it is not without security concerns. Two common issues to be aware of:

- SYN Flood (Denial-of-Service): Because establishing a TCP connection requires a three-way handshake, a malicious actor can exploit this by initiating a large number of connections and never completing the handshake. In a TCP SYN flood attack, an attacker sends a barrage of SYN packets to a server, but never sends back the final ACK to complete the handshakes. This leaves the server with many half-open connections (in the SYN-RECEIVED state) consuming resources (each half-open connection ties up a bit of memory for control structures). If enough are opened, the server may run out of resources to accept new legitimate connections, causing a Denial of Service for real users. Mitigations for SYN floods include techniques like SYN cookies (where the server does not allocate resources until the handshake is completed; it encodes necessary connection info in the SYN-ACK it sends back, and if the final ACK is received, the info can be recovered to create the connection). Rate-limiting incoming SYNs or using firewalls/load balancers to screen out attack traffic are other defenses.
- TCP RST Injection / Session Hijacking: TCP assumes that the IP addresses in packets are not spoofed (at least for the purpose of establishing a connection) and that sequence numbers are hard to guess. However, if an attacker can guess the sequence numbers in an ongoing connection (which can be feasible if sequence numbers are not random enough or via observing the traffic path), they could send a forged packet with the RST (reset) flag to tear down the connection. Then the receiver of a RST will immediately close the connection, thinking the other side sent it. Similarly, an attacker might inject fake data into a connection if they can predict sequence numbers and source/dest addresses/ports. Modern TCP implementations use random initial sequence numbers to mitigate trivial prediction, and the widespread use of encryption (TLS) on top of TCP now means that even if an attacker injects raw TCP packets, they will not be able to craft valid encrypted payloads. Still, on unencrypted connections, these risks exist.
- Resource Exhaustion / Slowloris: Another class of attack is to hold a TCP connection open and not send data, or send data extremely slowly, to tie up server resources (for example, the Slowloris attack on web servers). Servers can mitigate this by setting timeouts for connections and using strategies to handle many connections efficiently (threads or async handling).

In general, pairing TCP with additional security protocols (like TLS for encryption and authenticity) is important for protecting the data transmitted. Also, network-level defenses (like firewalls, intrusion prevention systems) can help detect anomalies like floods or strange packet patterns and protect TCP services.

2.2.3   UDP (User Datagram Protocol)

The User Datagram Protocol (UDP) is the other major Transport layer protocol in the Internet suite, offering a contrast to TCP. UDP provides a much simpler service: it is connectionless and unreliable (in the sense that it does not guarantee delivery, ordering, or integrity, although it has an optional checksum to detect corruption). UDP is often described as sending "datagrams" like sending letters or postcards: you just send them off with a destination address, but you do not get a built-in acknowledgment that they arrived.

Key characteristics of UDP include:

- No Connection Handshake: UDP does not establish a connection before sending data. One host can just start sending packets to another at any time. This means there is no handshake or setup delay, and therefore communication can be very fast to start. It also means there is no built-in mechanism to manage session state or sequence numbers.
- Message-Oriented: UDP preserves message boundaries. If you send a UDP datagram of 500 bytes, the

receiver will either receive that 500-byte message in one piece or not at all (unless it is fragmented at the IP layer due to size, but that is handled transparently). In contrast, TCP is a byte stream that has no concept of message boundaries, you just get a continuous stream of bytes. UDP messages (datagrams) are sent as distinct packets.

- Unreliable Delivery: UDP does not guarantee that packets arrive. Packets may be lost, duplicated, or arrive out of order. There are no acknowledgments or retransmissions at the UDP layer. If reliability is needed, it has to be handled by the Application layer (or by using a protocol built on top of UDP that adds reliability).
- Minimal Overhead: The UDP header is very short (only 8 bytes versus 20 bytes minimum for TCP, not counting IP headers). The UDP header contains source port, destination port, length, and a checksum. There is no sequence number, no ACK field, etc., which makes UDP packets lightweight. The checksum covers the data and parts of the IP headers to detect corruption; it is optional in IPv4 (but mandatory in IPv6).

Because UDP is lightweight and has no flow control or congestion control, it is ideal for use cases where speed is critical and occasional loss is acceptable. Common examples include: DNS (each lookup is a single short query/response, and if a packet is lost, the application can retry), multimedia streaming or VoIP (where it is better to drop a lost packet than to wait for it to be retransmitted, which would cause delay/jitter), and certain online games (which can tolerate some packet loss but need low latency).

However, if an application does need reliability or ordering on top of UDP, it must implement those itself. Some protocols built on UDP, such as TFTP (Trivial File Transfer Protocol), add simple acknowledgments and retransmissions at the Application layer. More modern examples include Quick UDP Internet Connections (QUIC), a protocol used for HTTP/3, which runs over UDP but implements its own equivalent of TCP's reliability and congestion control in user space (with improvements like faster handshakes).

UDP Example: Socket Communication in PHP

To demonstrate UDP in action, let us do a simple exercise: we will create a UDP "server" socket that listens on a certain port, and a UDP "client" that sends a message to that port. We will use PHP's socket functions for this example. Both server and client can be in the same script for demonstration, since UDP does not require a persistent connection.

```php
<?php
// Create a UDP server socket and bind it to localhost:5005
$serverSock = socket_create(AF_INET, SOCK_DGRAM, SOL_UDP);
socket_bind($serverSock, "127.0.0.1", 5005);
echo "UDP server listening on 127.0.0.1:5005\n";

// Prepare a UDP client socket (no need to bind for client, we will just send)
$clientSock = socket_create(AF_INET, SOCK_DGRAM, SOL_UDP);

// Client sends a message to the server
$message = "Hello, UDP!";
```

```php
12 socket_sendto($clientSock, $message, strlen($message), 0, "127.0.0.1", 5005);
13 echo "UDP client sent: $message\n";
14
15 // Server receives the message
16 $buf = '';
17 $from = ''; $port = 0;
18 socket_recvfrom($serverSock, $buf, 1024, 0, $from, $port);
19 echo "UDP server received: $buf from $from:$port\n";
20
21 // Close sockets
22 socket_close($clientSock);
23 socket_close($serverSock);
24 ?>
```

Expected Output:

Expected Output

```
UDP server listening on 127.0.0.1:5005
UDP client sent: Hello, UDP!
UDP server received: Hello, UDP! from 127.0.0.1:xxxxx
```

(Here xxxxx would be the ephemeral source port that the OS chose for the client socket.)

This example shows that the server, after binding to a port, can receive a message from the client with no prior handshake. The client simply sent a datagram to the server's IP and port, and the server (which was waiting on that port) received it. If the server was not running or listening on that port, the UDP packet would have been sent into the void (and possibly an "ICMP Port Unreachable" message would be returned to the sender by the OS). There was no connection establishment: the first packet from the client contained the actual data ("Hello, UDP!").

Characteristics of UDP: In this example, if the UDP packet were lost in transit (not likely in a local host scenario, but possible on a real network), the client would not know and the server would never receive anything. UDP does not automatically retry. It is up to the application to detect lost data (maybe by expecting a response and using a timeout) or to simply tolerate loss. Many UDP-based applications are designed to tolerate some loss. For instance, losing a few voice or video packets might only cause a minor glitch that is preferable to the delay of retransmission. In contrast, TCP's reliable delivery would pause the stream to recover lost data, which in a live call could be worse than a momentary blip.

Because UDP has no congestion control, a misbehaving UDP application can flood the network (sending packets as fast as it wants). Well-behaved applications implement their own rate control if needed, or rely on the fact that their data rates are inherently limited (e.g., by media encoding bitrates).

UDP Security Considerations: Attackers often exploit UDP's lack of handshake in various ways. One is UDP flooding that simply overwhelms a target with a high volume of UDP packets, which can consume bandwidth and processing power (the target might try to process or respond with ICMP errors). Another major issue is UDP amplification in DDoS attacks: an attacker sends small UDP queries to certain services that respond with much larger replies, and the attacker spoofs the source IP of the packets to be the victim's IP. The result is the unwitting service sends large responses to the victim, amplifying the attack traffic. DNS, NTP, SSDP, and other protocols have been abused this way when their servers are left open to the public. Mitigations include disabling or securing UDP services that can be abused and implementing network egress filters (so that spoofed outgoing packets are blocked). Additionally, because UDP does not verify source IPs, it is trivial to forge the source of a UDP packet, explaining why many reflective attacks are possible. From an application developer perspective, if you build a UDP service, you should implement logic to detect and ignore abnormal or excessive requests (rate limiting, not responding to obvious spoofed traffic, etc.).

To summarize: UDP is simple and fast, making it useful for certain applications, but it shifts the responsibility for reliability and congestion management to the application and can be a vector for abuse if not handled carefully.

2.3 Application Layer Protocols

Moving up to the Application layer, we examine how the foundational transport and network layers support real-world network applications. We will focus primarily on HTTP, the protocol of the World Wide Web, along with its secure variant HTTPS. HTTP is especially relevant to LAMP stack development, as it is the protocol through which web servers (like Apache with PHP) communicate with clients (browsers). We will break down the basics of HTTP, and also demonstrate a simple HTTP interaction.

2.3.1 HTTP and HTTPS: The Hypertext Transfer Protocol

The Hypertext Transfer Protocol (HTTP) is the foundation of data communication for the Web. It is an Application-layer protocol that defines how web clients (browsers, for example) request resources from web servers, and how servers respond with those resources. HTTP is a text-based, stateless, request-response protocol:

- Text-based: HTTP messages (requests and responses) are human-readable text (at least the headers are; the body can be binary for things like images). This makes them easy to construct and debug with simple tools.
- Stateless: Each HTTP request from a client to server is independent as the protocol itself does not retain memory of previous requests. If state is needed (like remembering a logged-in user), it has to be managed via other means (cookies, sessions on the server, etc.). Being stateless makes the protocol simpler and scalable (the server does not have to remember context between requests).
- Request-response: The client always initiates an HTTP transaction by sending a request, and the server replies with a response. The server does not spontaneously send data without a request.

Request-Response Model

An HTTP request message from client to server typically consists of:

- Start Line: This has the HTTP method, the path (URL) of the resource, and the HTTP version. For example: `GET /index.html HTTP/1.1`. This means "GET the resource `/index.html` using HTTP version 1.1".

- Headers: These are key-value pairs (one per line following the start line) that provide additional information about the request. For instance, `Host: www.example.com` (required in HTTP/1.1 to indicate which host the request is for, since one server might host multiple domains), `User-Agent: ...` (to identify the client software), `Accept: ...` (what content types the client can accept), etc. There are many standard headers.
- Blank Line: A blank line indicates the end of headers.
- Body: (Optional) For some requests, like POST or PUT, the request may include a body after the headers, which could contain data being sent to the server (such as form field values, JSON payload, file upload, etc.). For GET requests, typically there is no body (the request is just asking for a resource).

An HTTP response message from server to client consists of:

- Status Line: This has the HTTP version, a numeric status code, and a textual reason phrase. For example: `HTTP/1.1 200 OK`. This indicates the result of the request (200 is a success code, and "OK" is a human-readable reason).
- Headers: Similar to requests, responses have headers too, providing metadata about the response. Common response headers include `Content-Type` (telling the client the media type of the response, e.g., HTML or JSON), `Content-Length` (size of the response body in bytes), `Server` (software the server is running, e.g., Apache), `Set-Cookie` (instructing the client to store a cookie), etc.
- Blank Line
- Body: The content of the response (optional, depending on the status code and nature of the request). For example, for a 200 OK response to a GET request, the body would contain the requested resource (e.g., the HTML of the webpage). In a 204 No Content response, there would be no body. For a 301 Redirect, the body might be empty or just contain a short message, because the main info is in the headers (Location header telling the client where to go next).

For example, a very simple exchange might look like this (as text):

Request:

```
GET /hello.txt HTTP/1.1
Host: www.example.com
```

Note: the blank line after the Host header terminates the headers.

Response:

```
HTTP/1.1 200 OK
Content-Type: text/plain
Content-Length: 14

Hello, world!
```

Here the client requested `/hello.txt`. The server replied with a 200 OK, indicating success, and included headers saying it is plain text of length 14 bytes. After the blank line, the body "Hello, world!" is the content of the file.

HTTP Methods

HTTP defines a set of methods (also called verbs) that specify the desired action for a given request. The most common methods you will encounter are:

- GET: Retrieve a resource. (Requests data from the server; should not cause any side-effects on the server. Used for most navigation, like clicking a link or loading an image.)
- POST: Submit data to the server (often resulting in a change in state or side-effects on the server, e.g., submitting a form, creating a new record).
- PUT: Upload or replace a resource at a specific URL. (Often used in APIs to update a resource entirely.)
- DELETE: Remove the resource at a given URL.
- HEAD: Same as GET but ask only for headers (no body). This is useful if you want to check if something exists or get metadata (like content length or modified date) without downloading the whole resource.
- PATCH: Apply a partial update to a resource (a more fine-grained update than PUT).
- OPTIONS: Ask the server what methods are allowed or what capabilities are available for a resource (often used in CORS preflight requests in browsers).

In practice, for web browsing and basic forms:

- GET and POST are by far the most common. Browsers use GET for navigating to pages and fetching most resources. POST is typically used when submitting a form (especially if it changes data on the server or is sending user input that should not be on the URL).
- PUT, DELETE, PATCH, etc., are more commonly used in RESTful APIs or web services rather than in standard browser-website interactions (browsers do not generate PUT or DELETE requests from a normal form without help from JavaScript or specific client code).

The server will handle each method according to its semantics. For example, a web server might map GET requests to reading files or generating content, POST requests to handling form submissions or API calls that modify data, etc.

Status Codes

HTTP responses use status codes to indicate the outcome of the request. These are three-digit numbers grouped into categories by their first digit:

- 1xx: Informational: These are rare in practice. An example is 100 Continue, which is part of a protocol handshake for large payloads. 1xx codes are mostly used internally by client-server communications and not often seen by end users.
- 2xx: Success: The request was successfully received, understood, and accepted.
    - 200 OK: The standard success code for GET, POST, or really any successful request where there is a response body.
    - 201 Created: Often used for POST requests that result in the creation of a new resource. The response may include a Location header pointing to the new resource.
    - 204 No Content: Success but no content to return (often used for successful requests that have nothing to display, for example a DELETE request might return 204 on success).
- 3xx: Redirection: The client must take additional action to complete the request (usually by making a new request to a different URL).

- 301 Moved Permanently: The resource has moved to a new URL (given in the Location header). The client (and search engines) should update their references to use the new URL henceforth.
- 302 Found: A temporary redirect. The client is told to go to another URL for this request, but future requests may still use the original URL.
- 303 See Other / 307 Temporary Redirect / 308 Permanent Redirect: Other variants of redirection used in different scenarios (HTTP/1.1 refined the definition of 302 with 303 and 307; 308 is a permanent redirect similar to 301 but for cases that preserve method).
- 304 Not Modified: Not a redirect to a different URL, but an instruction that the client's cached version of the resource is still valid (so the client can use its cache and does not need a new copy). This is used in response to conditional GET requests.

- **4xx: Client Errors:** The request was not successful due to an error from the client side (bad input, unauthorized, etc.).
  - 400 Bad Request: The request was malformed or invalid (the server could not understand it).
  - 401 Unauthorized: The request requires authentication (or the authentication provided is invalid). Typically, the server includes a `WWW-Authenticate` header prompting for credentials. (Despite the name "Unauthorized," it really means "unauthenticated," 403 is used for unauthorized in the sense of not allowed.)
  - 403 Forbidden: The server understood the request but refuses to authorize it (the client is not allowed to access this resource).
  - 404 Not Found: The requested resource does not exist on the server.
  - 405 Method Not Allowed: The requested HTTP method is not supported for this resource.
  - 418 I'm a teapot: An Easter-egg status code from a joke RFC (RFC 2324) but not actually used in real HTTP, but often cited humorously.

- **5xx: Server Errors:** The server failed to fulfill a valid request due to an internal error on the server side.
  - 500 Internal Server Error: A generic catch-all for unexpected server-side errors.
  - 502 Bad Gateway: The server was acting as a gateway or proxy and received an invalid response from the upstream server.
  - 503 Service Unavailable: The server is currently unable to handle the request (due to maintenance or overload). Often used to indicate temporary downtime.
  - 504 Gateway Timeout: Used by a gateway or proxy when the upstream server failed to send a request in time.

Status codes let the client automate certain behaviors (like following redirects, prompting for authentication, etc.) and inform the user or client application about what happened. As a developer, you will encounter these frequently when debugging your web applications (e.g., figuring out why you got a 404 or 500 error).

These methods and status codes together define the protocol of HTTP and make it extensible (new methods or headers can be added over time) and flexible (it is used not just for human-facing websites but also for API communication, web services, and more).

HTTP/1.1 vs. HTTP/2 (and HTTP/3)

The HTTP protocol has evolved to improve performance and address some limitations of earlier versions:

- HTTP/1.1: This is the classic version that introduced persistent connections (the ability to reuse a single

TCP connection for multiple requests/responses, rather than opening a new connection for every single request). HTTP/1.1 also introduced chunked transfer encoding (to send responses of unknown length in pieces), additional caching controls, and more. However, HTTP/1.1 still has a limitation: by default, requests are served one after another over a connection (strict pipelining was introduced but not widely used because of head-of-line blocking issues). If a page requires 100 resources (images, scripts, etc.), the browser has to make many requests, and it typically opens multiple connections in parallel (browsers would open 4–8 connections per host) to fetch resources concurrently. This can cause overhead due to multiple TCP handshakes and contention.

- HTTP/2: Published in 2015, HTTP/2 is a major revision designed to improve performance. It is binary (not text like HTTP/1.1, though as developers we still see essentially the same semantics). The key improvements are:
  - Multiplexing: Multiple requests and responses can be in flight simultaneously over a single TCP connection. This means a browser does not need to open many connections to load a page with many assets; one connection can handle many parallel streams. This eliminates head-of-line blocking at the Application layer (although if the single TCP connection experiences packet loss, it can block all streams, a downside of multiplexing over TCP).
  - Header Compression: HTTP/2 compresses headers (which in HTTP/1.1 can be quite repetitive, e.g., sending the same cookies and long user-agent string with every request). This reduces overhead, especially for pages with many small requests.
  - Server Push: HTTP/2 allows the server to push responses the client has not yet requested (e.g., when the client asks for an HTML page, the server can proactively send some associated CSS or JS files it knows the page will need, without waiting for the browser to request them).
  - These changes are mostly transparent to developers writing applications, but they greatly improve page load times and efficiency.
- HTTP/3: In progress (as of the 2020s) and already used in some places (notably, it is the basis of the latest QUIC transport and used for HTTPS by some major services). HTTP/3 departs from using TCP as the transport; instead, it runs over QUIC, which is a transport protocol built on UDP. QUIC (and thus HTTP/3) brings benefits like:
  - Reduced latency for handshakes: QUIC can establish a secure connection with fewer round trips than TCP+TLS requires.
  - No head-of-line blocking at the Transport layer: Because QUIC streams are independent within a connection, a lost packet only affects the particular stream it was part of, not all streams. In TCP, loss causes a stall for the entire connection until the packet is retransmitted.
  - Essentially, HTTP/3 aims to further reduce latency and improve reliability in real-world networks (especially on cellular/mobile where packet loss or reordering is common).

(R) For developers building web applications, you typically do not need to worry about the differences between HTTP/1.1, 2, or 3 in your server-side code or client-side code; your web server and browser handle the details. But it is useful to know why, for example, modern sites can load many assets quickly (HTTP/2 multiplexing) or why moving to HTTPS no longer has the performance penalty it once did (HTTP/2 and HTTP/3 mitigate that). When tuning a web server, you might enable HTTP/2 or HTTP/3 support. And understanding these versions can explain behaviors (like why in HTTP/1.1 we used to concatenate files or use image sprites to reduce requests, optimizations that HTTP/2 makes less necessary).

For typical web development using the LAMP stack, ensure your server is configured to use the latest HTTP versions (if possible) for efficiency, but you will primarily interact with HTTP at the level of requests and responses, which remain conceptually the same across versions.

HTTP over TCP and TLS: It is worth noting that HTTP/1.1 and HTTP/2 are usually used over a TCP connection (HTTP/3 over QUIC/UDP). When we add encryption (TLS) to HTTP, it becomes HTTPS. We will say more on that shortly. For now, remember that each HTTP request/response in HTTP/1.1 might involve a separate TCP handshake unless persistent connections are used (which they are, by default in HTTP/1.1). HTTP/2 by design uses one TCP connection per origin to handle many requests. A consequence: under HTTP/1.1, having many small files could incur overhead; under HTTP/2, that overhead is reduced. This has influenced web performance best practices over time.

Direct HTTP Request to Web Server (Manual Exercise)

In the early days of learning web protocols, a common exercise is to interact with a web server manually using low-level tools (like Telnet or Netcat) to really see the raw HTTP communication. Let us briefly describe how you could do this, because it demystifies what your browser does in milliseconds every time you navigate the web:

1. Establish a TCP Connection: You can open a raw TCP connection to a web server on the HTTP port. For example, in a terminal, you might type `telnet www.example.com 80`. This attempts to open a connection to `www.example.com` on port 80. If successful, your terminal will go blank (or show a connection message) meaning it is connected and waiting. (Telnet is a tool that creates a raw TCP connection and lets you type characters which will be sent as bytes to the server. Netcat (typically `nc` command on Unix) can do similarly.)

2. Send an HTTP Request: Once connected, you can manually type an HTTP request. For instance:

```
GET / HTTP/1.1
Host: www.example.com
```

   It is important to include the `Host` header (required for HTTP/1.1). After typing the headers, you must send a blank line (press Enter on an empty line) to indicate the end of the request. At that point, the server will start processing the request. (Typing this by hand can be tricky because if you make a typo, especially in Telnet, backspace might not work as expected, so one has to type carefully.)

3. View the Response: The server will respond with an HTTP status line and headers, followed by the HTML content of the page (if you requested / and it is an HTML page). For example, if you connected to `example.com` and sent the above request, you should see something like:

```
HTTP/1.1 200 OK
Content-Type: text/html; charset=UTF-8
Content-Length: 1256
... (other headers) ...

<html>
    <head><title>Example Domain</title> ... </head>
    <body> ... </body>
</html>
```

If you had connected to google.com on port 80 and sent a similar HTTP/1.1 request, Google likely would respond with a redirect (since Google prefers HTTPS). You might see HTTP/1.1 301 Moved Permanently and a Location: https://www.google.com/ header, indicating that you need to use HTTPS.

4. Close the Connection: Depending on the server and the HTTP version/protocol, the server might close the connection after sending the response (HTTP/1.0 behavior or if Connection: close is sent). With HTTP/1.1 persistent connections, the server might leave it open waiting for another request for a short time. You can close it from your side by just closing Telnet or pressing the escape sequence. In any case, once the exchange is done, the connection will eventually be torn down (with FIN packets at the TCP level).

This manual process shows exactly what a browser does under the hood: open connection, send request text, get response text, and then interpret it (render HTML, etc.). Doing this once or twice can help you understand HTTP headers and responses. We essentially did the same thing in our earlier PHP socket example where we manually constructed and sent the request and printed the response.

If you prefer not to use Telnet, you could also simulate this with a simple PHP or Python script (as we demonstrated with sockets). In fact, let us see an example of using a high-level HTTP client in PHP to perform the same task more easily.

Hands-On: Fetching a Web Page with PHP

Instead of manually handling sockets and constructing HTTP requests, you can use high-level libraries or functions in most languages that handle HTTP for you. In PHP, one convenient way is to use the built-in file_get_contents() for simple requests, or the cURL library for more control. Here is a quick example using PHP's file functions to fetch a web page and inspect the response:

```php
<?php
$url = "http://httpbin.org/get";
// Fetch the URL and capture the response body
$responseBody = file_get_contents($url);

// Get the response headers (available in $http_response_header after file_get_contents)
$responseHeaders = $http_response_header ?? [];

// Extract the status code from the first header
$statusCode = "Unknown";
if (!empty($responseHeaders)) {
    // The first header is a status line like "HTTP/1.1 200 OK"
    if (preg_match('#HTTP/\d+\.\d+\s+(\d+)#', $responseHeaders[0], $matches)) {
        $statusCode = $matches[1];
    }
}

```

```php
18  // Find the Content-Type header (if any)
19  $contentType = "Unknown";
20  foreach ($responseHeaders as $hdr) {
21      if (stripos($hdr, "Content-Type:") === 0) {
22          $contentType = trim(substr($hdr, strlen("Content-Type:")));
23          break;
24      }
25  }
26
27  // Print out some information
28  echo "Status code: $statusCode\n";
29  echo "Content-Type header: $contentType\n";
30  echo "Body text (first 100 chars): " . substr($responseBody, 0, 100) . "...\n";
31  ?>
```

In this code, we use `file_get_contents` to perform an HTTP GET request to a sample URL (httpbin.org is a public service that returns information about your request). The `$http_response_header` variable is a special PHP variable that gets populated with the response headers after using `file_get_contents` on a URL. We parse it to get the status code and Content-Type, then show a snippet of the body. If you run this script, you might see output like:

Example Output

```
Status code: 200
Content-Type header: application/json
Body text (first 100 chars): {
  "args": {},
  "headers": {
    "Accept": "*/*",
    "Host": "httpbin.org",
    "User-Agent": "PHP...
```

This indicates a successful 200 response, the server reported the content type as JSON, and the body (which we truncated) is a JSON object containing details of our request (httpbin conveniently returns the request data in the response). The `file_get_contents` (or cURL, or any HTTP library) handled all the low-level work for us: it opened a socket, sent the HTTP request, followed any redirects (PHP's `file_get_contents` will not automatically follow redirects unless configured, but cURL can if set), and gathered the response.

Using such high-level tools is how you will usually work with HTTP in applications (for example, PHP scripts might use cURL to call an API). But it is valuable to understand the raw protocol as we have covered, so you know what those tools are doing behind the scenes and can troubleshoot issues like missing headers or incorrect status codes.

HTTPS: HTTP Secure (TLS)

On the modern web, HTTP is almost always used in its secure form, HTTPS. HTTPS means that the HTTP communication is encrypted and authenticated using TLS (Transport Layer Security). From a user's perspective, HTTPS is seen as the `https://` in URLs and the padlock icon in browsers indicating the connection between the browser (client) and the server is secure.

What does "secure" entail? Essentially, TLS (formerly known as SSL(Secure Sockets Layer)) provides two main benefits:

- Encryption: The data exchanged between client and server is encrypted, so eavesdroppers on the network cannot read sensitive information (like passwords or credit card numbers). Even for non-sensitive content, encryption prevents malicious intermediaries from injecting or altering content unnoticed.
- Authentication: The server (and optionally the client) is authenticated. Typically, the server presents a digital certificate (issued by a trusted Certificate Authority) that proves its identity. The browser/OS verifies this certificate (checking that it is valid, not expired, issued by a trusted CA, and matches the domain you are visiting). This prevents an attacker from impersonating, say, your bank's website without detection, because they would not have the bank's valid certificate.

When a client initiates an HTTPS connection (usually to port 443), the process is:

1. TLS Handshake: Immediately after the TCP three-way handshake, the client and server perform a TLS handshake. This involves the exchange of messages to agree on cryptographic algorithms (cipher suite), exchange keys, and perform mutual authentication (the server presents its certificate, the client verifies it; if client certificates are used, the client also presents one, but that is rare for public websites).
   - During this handshake, the client and server establish a shared secret key that will be used to encrypt the rest of the session. Modern TLS (TLS 1.3) has a very streamlined handshake requiring just 1–1.5 round trips. Older TLS (1.2) usually required a couple of round trips.
   - The server's certificate is verified against a store of trusted Certificate Authorities (CAs) that your browser/OS maintains. If the certificate is self-signed or from an untrusted CA, the browser will show a security warning. If it is valid, the handshake proceeds.
   - The result of the handshake is that both client and server have a session key for symmetric encryption, and the client is sure it is talking to the genuine server (and not an impostor). The integrity of the handshake is also protected, meaning no one can tamper with it without detection.
2. Encrypted HTTP: After the TLS handshake, the HTTP request and response are sent over the now-secure channel. They are encrypted (along with being integrity-checked). Anyone sniffing the traffic on the network only sees gibberish (ciphertext), not the actual headers or content of the HTTP messages.
3. Connection Reuse and Resumption: The TLS session can be reused for multiple HTTP requests (just like a TCP connection can be persistent for multiple HTTP/1.1 requests, the TLS layer on top can remain in place). If you visit multiple pages on the same site, your browser typically reuses the existing HTTPS connection rather than doing a full handshake each time, to avoid the overhead. Even between distinct visits, there are mechanisms like TLS session resumption that avoid the full handshake if you recently connected to the same server.

From a developer's point of view: always use HTTPS for any website or application in production, even if the content does not seem sensitive. Modern best practices and user expectations demand encryption everywhere. Browsers flag non-HTTPS sites as "not secure," and features like HTTP/2 and HTTP/3 often require TLS in browsers. Tools like Let's Encrypt make obtaining and renewing certificates free and automated. And frameworks or server configurations typically allow enabling HTTPS with relative ease. In a LAMP stack, that often means setting up Apache with `mod_ssl` and a certificate, so that your PHP application is served over HTTPS.

Security of HTTPS

Properly implemented HTTPS (TLS) is very secure. It prevents attackers from eavesdropping on data or tampering with it in transit. For example, if you are on a public Wi-Fi, an attacker could potentially intercept or modify traffic on that network if it is not encrypted. However, if you are using HTTPS, they cannot decipher the content or alter it without breaking cryptographic protections. There are a few caveats to understand:

- HTTPS does not magically make your website internally secure; it secures the transport. You still need to worry about things like SQL injection or XSS in your application. But HTTPS will stop an attacker on the same network from stealing session cookies or injecting malicious scripts into an HTTP page (which were real threats on unencrypted connections).
- The trust in HTTPS is only as strong as the trust in Certificate Authorities (CAs). Users must also be trained not to ignore certificate warnings. If an attacker somehow gets a fraudulent certificate issued for your domain (through a compromised or coerced CA), they could impersonate your site. This is rare and mitigated by improvements like Certificate Transparency logs and browsers being very strict about certificates.
- TLS itself has had vulnerabilities (old versions like SSL 3.0 or TLS 1.0 are broken and should not be used; even TLS 1.2 had some problematic cipher suites). Always use up-to-date TLS libraries and configurations. As of now, TLS 1.2 and TLS 1.3 are the standards, with 1.3 being preferred when available.

In summary, HTTPS is now the norm for web traffic. As a LAMP developer, you will want to ensure your Apache server is configured for HTTPS (which likely means obtaining a certificate and updating Apache's config). This will be covered in practical setup chapters, but at the protocol level, just remember HTTPS = HTTP + encryption/authentication via TLS.

Figure 2.3 illustrates the TCP three-way handshake between a client and a server, depicting the exchange of SYN, SYN-ACK, and ACK packets to establish a TCP connection. It also summarizes an HTTP request over a secure connection, including the TCP and TLS handshakes.

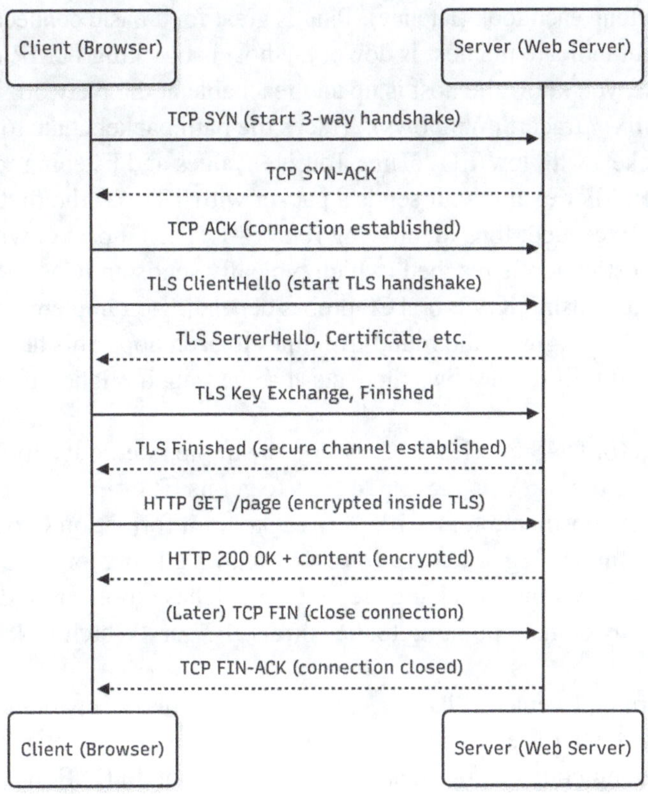

Figure 2.3: TCP three-way handshake.

In the above diagram, the HTTP GET and response are shown in bold to highlight them, and they occur after the TCP and TLS handshakes. All HTTP data is encrypted during transit in HTTPS. This whole process (TCP + TLS + HTTP) typically happens in fractions of a second. Modern TLS (1.3) has optimized the handshake to be very fast, often adding as little as a few tens of milliseconds in typical cases. This is a small price for significant security gains.

2.3.2   Network Tools and Diagnostics

Understanding and working with network protocols is much easier if you are familiar with some common network tools. These tools let you observe the behavior of network protocols and diagnose issues. Here are several useful ones:

Command Line Tools

- ping: Uses ICMP (Internet Control Message Protocol) Echo Request and Echo Reply messages to check if a host is reachable and measure round-trip time. When you run `ping example.com`, your computer sends ICMP Echo Request packets to the target and waits for Echo Replies. The output tells you if replies are received and how long each took (latency). Ping is great for a basic connectivity test. When ping fails (no replies), this might indicate the host is down, the host is blocking ICMP, or there is no route to that host. If ping succeeds, you know the host is up and reachable at the Network layer.

- traceroute (Linux/Unix) / tracert (Windows): Traces the path packets take to a destination. Traceroute works by sending packets with low TTL (Time To Live) values and listening for ICMP "Time Exceeded" messages from routers. For example, it sends a packet with TTL=1; the first router drops it and sends back an ICMP Time Exceeded, thus identifying router #1. Then a packet with TTL=2 finds router #2, and so on, until the destination is reached (which typically sends an ICMP Port Unreachable for UDP probes, or just responds if using ICMP or TCP probes depending on implementation). The output is a list of router hostnames/IPs along with the round-trip times to each hop. This helps identify where delays or failures are occurring. If traceroute shows timeouts at some step, it might indicate a firewall or an issue at that hop.
- nslookup / dig: Tools for DNS queries. `nslookup` is a simple interactive tool to find DNS records; for example, you can do `nslookup www.example.com` to get its IP, or `nslookup 93.184.216.34` to do a reverse lookup (find the hostname for an IP). `dig` (Domain Information Groper) is more powerful and script-friendly. For example, `dig example.com ANY` shows all sorts of DNS records for example.com, `dig google.com MX` shows mail exchange records, etc. These tools are indispensable for debugging DNS issues (e.g., "Is my domain pointing to the correct IP?" or "Which DNS server is authoritative for this domain?").
- netstat (and its modern replacements like `ss on Linux)`: Displays network connections, routing tables, and a variety of network interface statistics. For example, `netstat -an` might show all active TCP/UDP connections and listening ports on your machine (with `-n` to not do DNS lookups for speed). `netstat -anp` on Linux will also show which process is associated with each socket. This is useful for confirming if your server program is listening on the expected port or if a client connection is established. On Linux, `ss -tulpn` is a similar command that shows listening ports and processes.
- cURL / HTTPie: These are command-line tools for making HTTP (and other protocol) requests. `curl` is extremely versatile: you can use it to fetch a webpage (`curl http://example.com`), download a file, send data via POST, add custom headers, and so on. The `-v` (verbose) flag is helpful because it will show the raw request being sent and the raw response (headers and body) received, which is great for debugging web servers or APIs. For example, `curl -v https://www.example.com` will print the HTTP request and response headers along with the content. HTTPie is a friendlier alternative to curl for interactive use, with syntax like `http GET httpbin.org/get X-Header:Value`. Both are useful for testing your web applications (e.g., to simulate API calls, check responses, etc.) without needing a browser.

Protocol Analysis

- tcpdump: A command-line packet capture tool. It allows you to sniff network traffic on an interface and apply filters to see only what you are interested in. For example, `tcpdump -i eth0 port 80` might show all packets going to or from port 80 on interface eth0 (which would capture HTTP traffic). tcpdump outputs in a decoded text form by default, which can be verbose, but it is extremely powerful for debugging at the packet level. It is commonly used by network engineers and can be run on servers to capture traffic for analysis, often capturing to a file in pcap format for later analysis in Wireshark.

- Wireshark: A graphical packet analysis tool. Wireshark can capture packets (or you can open a capture file made by tcpdump). It then parses the protocols and provides a nice GUI to inspect them. For example, you can capture the packets while loading a webpage and then use Wireshark to follow the TCP stream, which will reassemble all the packets into a coherent view of the HTTP conversation. Wireshark will show you, for instance, the DNS request and response, the TCP handshake, the HTTP GET request your browser sent, and the HTTP response from the server, all nicely parsed. It is an excellent way to see the concepts from this chapter literally in action. Note that capturing your own machine's traffic on modern OSes may require running Wireshark with elevated privileges, and capturing other people's traffic on a network may be illegal or against policy. Always ensure you have permission for whatever traffic you sniff.

Using Wireshark or tcpdump, you could, for example, verify that when your browser makes a request to your LAMP web server, the TCP handshake occurs, then the TLS handshake (if using HTTPS), then the HTTP request/response, etc., exactly as described. You can also debug problems: e.g., if a browser is not connecting to your server, does the TCP SYN packet arrive at the server? Does anything come back? This can help distinguish firewall issues from application issues.

 Running packet sniffers might require root/administrator privileges. Also, if you are not on a network you control (say, a public Wi-Fi), capturing traffic could violate privacy or laws. Typically, you use these tools on your own machine or network for testing or troubleshooting.

Overall, these diagnostic tools are extremely useful when developing and deploying network applications. As a LAMP developer, you will primarily use tools like cURL to test your web APIs and maybe ping or traceroute to ensure connectivity. If you run into low-level network issues or need to optimize network performance, tools like tcpdump/Wireshark can provide insight into what is happening on the wire.

2.4   Security Considerations

Throughout this chapter we have touched on various security issues relevant to each protocol. Let us summarize some key points and best practices to keep in mind:

- IP Layer Security: IP itself does not have built-in authentication or encryption. This means attackers can send packets with spoofed source IP addresses (pretending to be someone else). One mitigation at the network level is for ISPs to perform ingress filtering (BCP 38), refusing to forward packets with source addresses that should not come from that direction. This helps reduce IP spoofing on the Internet. Also, because IP has no encryption, sensitive data could theoretically be intercepted at this layer (though higher layers like TLS usually take care of encryption). Tools like Virtual Private Networks (VPNs) use IPsec (a suite of protocols for IP security) to add confidentiality and authenticity at the IP layer when needed (e.g., corporate VPNs encrypt all IP traffic between your laptop and the company network). From a developer standpoint, be aware that scanning and spoofing can happen: e.g., an attacker can send ping sweeps to map out your network or spoof their IP in a DDoS attack so the traffic is hard to trace. Network administrators employ firewalls to block unwanted traffic and intrusion detection systems to monitor for suspicious patterns at this layer.
- TCP Security: As discussed, TCP is vulnerable to certain denial-of-service and connection-hijacking attacks. SYN floods abuse the handshake to exhaust server resources, but the use of SYN cookies and connection limits can mitigate this. RST injection and sequence prediction attacks aim to terminate or

hijack sessions. Using TLS on top (so that an injected RST would not carry the right cryptographic signature and would be ignored) is a strong mitigation. Additionally, modern TCP implementations randomize initial sequence numbers and have mechanisms like TCP timestamps and window scaling that somewhat complicate naive hijacking. Another consideration is telnet vs. SSH: historically, protocols like Telnet used plain TCP for remote logins, meaning everything (including passwords) was sent in cleartext. Nowadays Telnet is obsolete for this reason, replaced by SSH (Secure Shell) which runs over TCP but encrypts the traffic. The lesson: wherever TCP is used for potentially sensitive interactions (remote logins, transmitting credentials, etc.), it should be combined with encryption (TLS, SSH, etc.) to prevent eavesdropping or tampering.

- UDP Security: UDP's simplicity makes it a common vector for abuse. Because it is easy to spoof UDP packets, attacks like amplification exploits (DNS, NTP, etc. as described) are prevalent. As a developer, if you run a UDP service (say, a game server or a custom protocol), you should implement measures like rate limiting responses to any one source, and not responding at all if a request does not make sense or is malformed (to avoid your server being used as an amplifier). Many servers for UDP-based protocols also implement authentication or puzzles to ensure the client is legitimate. Also, be mindful of the lack of encryption. If you were to design a new protocol on UDP and it carries sensitive data, you would want to add encryption at the Application layer or run it through a VPN or DTLS (Datagram TLS). A noteworthy incident underscoring DNS (which is UDP-based) security was the Dyn DNS DDoS attack in 2016. Attackers used a botnet (Mirai) to send a huge volume of DNS queries to Dyn's servers, taking down major websites (Twitter, Netflix, etc.) that relied on Dyn for DNS. This was a reflection attack combined with sheer volume. In its aftermath, many DNS providers bolstered their infrastructure (using anycast networks of distributed servers, etc.) and rate-limiting to handle such floods.

- DNS Security: We elaborated on cache poisoning and DNSSEC in the DNS section. To reiterate: use DNSSEC where possible to protect against forgery. On the client side (or in web applications), be cautious about assuming DNS is 100% trustworthy or fast; sometimes apps double-check important addresses or have fallbacks. Also, consider privacy since traditional DNS queries reveal every site you are looking up to anyone who can monitor your traffic (like your ISP or someone on the same Wi-Fi). Technologies like DNS over HTTPS (DoH) or DNS over TLS (DoT) encrypt queries to the resolver, which improves privacy (though the resolver itself will know, so trusting a reputable resolver is important). If you run your own server, ensure your DNS records (like MX for mail) are correct and monitor them. DNS hijacking (either by compromising a registrar or nameserver) can lead to users being redirected to malicious sites.

- HTTP/HTTPS Security: The most important thing is use HTTPS for any web service that handles sensitive data (in fact, use HTTPS for everything by default). On plain HTTP, any data can be intercepted or modified. There have been cases where ISPs or hotspot providers inject ads or malware into HTTP pages, or where attackers on public networks steal session cookies from HTTP sites (a classic example was Firesheep, a tool that let people snoop logins on open Wi-Fi back in 2010, which accelerated the adoption of HTTPS by sites like Facebook). Beyond using HTTPS, web developers need to be aware of application-level security: HTTP itself will not prevent attacks like XSS (cross-site scripting) or CSRF; those are issues with how the application handles user input and state. Set cookies with the Secure flag (so they are not sent over HTTP by mistake) and HttpOnly flag (so they are not accessible to JavaScript if not needed, as a defense against XSS stealing them). Consider using HTTP security headers like Content Security Policy (CSP) to restrict what external scripts or resources can be loaded,

X-Frame-Options/Frame-Ancestors to prevent clickjacking in iframes, HSTS (HTTP Strict Transport Security) to tell browsers to always use HTTPS for your site, etc. While those topics go beyond basic protocol mechanics, they are part of making the most of HTTP's features to secure an application. Also, manage your TLS certificates properly: if you are using Apache with `mod_ssl`, you will have a certificate (perhaps from Let's Encrypt). Keep it renewed and correctly configured. An expired certificate or a misconfigured trust chain can break access for users. Monitoring tools can alert you if your site's certificate is about to expire.

- Email/Other Protocols: Though not the focus of this chapter, similar principles apply to other application protocols. For instance, use SSH instead of Telnet (as noted), use Secure File Transfer Protocol (SFTP) or File Transfer Protocol Secure (FTPS) instead of FTP for file transfers to encrypt credentials and data, etc.

In conclusion, understanding the protocols gives you a lens to understand their security implications. Each layer has its potential weaknesses: IP can be spoofed, TCP can be flooded or hijacked, UDP can be abused for amplification, DNS can be poisoned, HTTP can be eavesdropped or manipulated if not encrypted. As a developer or engineer, you should use the protective technologies available (TLS, DNSSEC, firewalls, etc.) and follow best practices (like input validation to prevent injection attacks on your web app) to mitigate these threats. Security is an ongoing process, but building on a strong foundation of protocol knowledge will help you make informed decisions in designing and deploying applications.

2.5 Web Server Fundamentals

To connect this knowledge of Internet protocols to the LAMP stack, let us discuss how a web server operates in the context of these protocols and how it serves dynamic applications.

In a LAMP stack, the web server is typically Apache HTTP Server (the "A" in LAMP), running on a Linux OS. Apache's job is to listen for HTTP requests (usually on port 80 for HTTP and port 443 for HTTPS) and respond to them, either by serving static content (files from the filesystem) or by passing the request to server-side scripts (like PHP, the "P" in LAMP) for dynamic content.

Basic Web Server Operation:

1. Listening on a Port: When Apache starts, it opens a network socket on the designated port(s). For example, it will bind to `0.0.0.0:80` (all network interfaces on port 80) for HTTP. This means it is ready to accept TCP connections on that port.
2. Accepting Connections (TCP/TLS): When a client (browser) initiates a TCP connection (and completes a TLS handshake if using HTTPS) to the server, Apache accepts the connection. It then waits for the client to send an HTTP request over that connection.
3. Handling an HTTP Request: Apache reads the request line and headers. It determines which resource is being requested by looking at the path (and Host header to know which virtual host, if Apache is serving multiple sites on one server). Based on its configuration, Apache decides how to handle the request:
    - If the request is for a static file (like an image, CSS file, or a static HTML page) that resides in the website's document root, Apache will retrieve that file from the filesystem and send it back in the HTTP response (with appropriate headers like Content-Type).
    - If the request is for a dynamic resource (for example, a PHP script like `index.php`), Apache will forward the request to the PHP interpreter. Historically, this was done via a module like `mod_php` (which runs PHP in-process with Apache) or now commonly via PHP-FPM (FastCGI Process

Manager), where Apache communicates with a separate PHP process over a socket. In either case, the PHP code is executed server-side.

4. The Role of PHP and MySQL: For dynamic pages, PHP will often need to fetch or store data, which involves communicating with the MySQL database (the "M" in LAMP). For instance, if the page is a blog article, the PHP script might query the MySQL database to get the article content. This query happens over a separate connection (usually TCP to the MySQL server, which might be localhost or another host, using the MySQL protocol). MySQL will return the results, PHP will use those to build an HTML page (mixing the data with templates, etc.). All of this happens within the server, and the client at this point is just waiting while the server is working.

5. Sending the Response: Once the content is ready (be it read directly from a file or generated by a PHP script), Apache sends the HTTP response back to the client over the established connection. This includes sending the status line (`200 OK` if all is well, or an error code if something went wrong), response headers (Content-Type, Content-Length, etc.), and the body (the file content or HTML output of the PHP script). If the response is large, it might be sent in chunks or streamed.

6. Persistent vs. Closed Connection: After sending the response, Apache may keep the connection open for a short time (if using HTTP/1.1 with Keep-Alive or if the client supports HTTP/2 multiplexing) to see if the client will request another resource (which is common: a single webpage might lead to many requests for images, scripts, etc.). If the connection is kept alive, subsequent requests can reuse it. Otherwise, Apache closes the TCP connection. In HTTPS, closing the connection also tears down the TLS session (although TLS sessions could be resumed later to avoid full handshake).

7. Concurrency: A web server like Apache is handling potentially many requests from many clients at once. Apache can spawn multiple processes or threads to handle multiple connections concurrently (or use newer asynchronous modes, depending on configuration like Worker vs. Event MPM in Apache). The details are not relevant here, but know that a production web server is highly parallel; each browser might open several connections, and there could be hundreds or thousands of users simultaneously. Apache (and other servers) have configurations for maximum connections, timeouts, etc., to manage this load.

8. Virtual Hosting: Apache often serves multiple websites on one machine (virtual hosts). It uses the Host header in HTTP requests to decide which site's content to serve. This way, one server process can handle `www.siteA.com` and `www.siteB.com` on the same IP, differentiating by Host header. As a LAMP developer, if you are setting up a dev environment, you might configure Apache virtual hosts for each of your projects.

Figure 2.4 illustrates the flow of a dynamic page request in a LAMP stack. In this sequence:
- The browser makes a request to Apache.
- Apache sees the URL corresponds to a PHP script, so it calls out to PHP to handle it (either via an internal module or an external FCGI (Fast Common Gateway Interface) call).
- The PHP code executes; if it needs data, it queries MySQL.
- MySQL returns data; PHP generates the HTML (or other output) for the page.
- PHP returns the generated content to Apache.
- Apache sends that content back to the browser in an HTTP response.

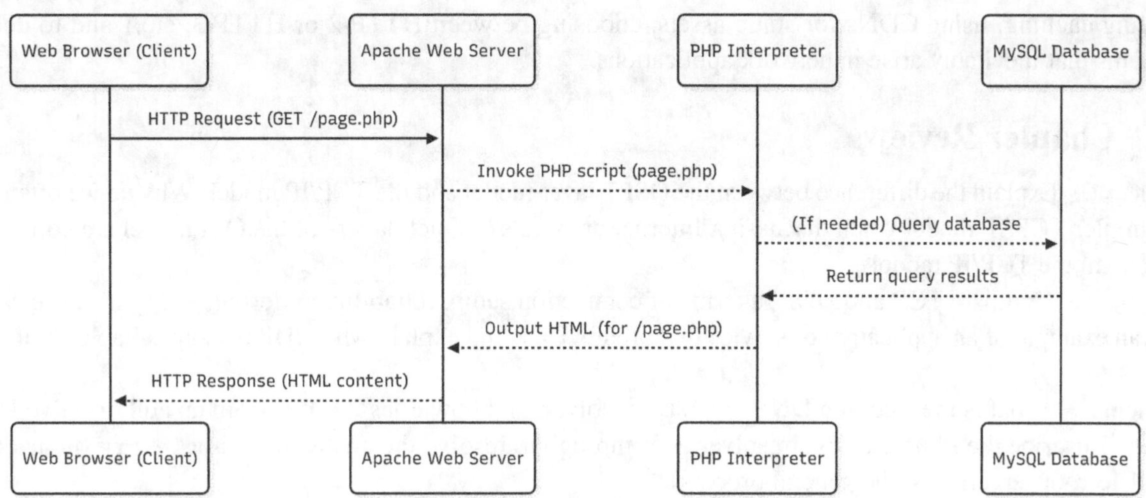

Figure 2.4: The flow of a dynamic page request in a LAMP stack.

This is a simplified view, but it shows how the layers we discussed earlier come into play:

- The HTTP request/response is the Application layer protocol carrying the content.
- Apache and the browser are doing the TCP handshake, possibly TLS if HTTPS (Transport and Security layers).
- Underneath, IP is routing the packets, etc.
- Within the server, the application stack (PHP, MySQL) is doing its own data handling.

Static vs. Dynamic content: Not all pages hit the database or even involve PHP. For example, static images (PNG, JPEG files) are just read by Apache from disk and sent directly. Those might be handled extremely quickly (often optimized through caching, so they may not even hit the disk if cached in memory, and with HTTP headers that allow the browser to cache them on the client side). Dynamic requests are typically slower (because code executes, databases are read, etc.) but offer functionality (e.g., user-specific content, forms, etc.).

Connecting to Other Chapters: In the next chapters, we will delve into creating the content that the web server will serve. Chapter 3 covers HTML, the structure and content of web pages, which is what our HTTP responses will largely contain. You will learn how to write HTML that the browser will render. Later chapters cover how to style those pages (CSS), how to make them interactive in the browser (JavaScript), and how to program the server-side logic (PHP) to generate responses and interact with databases (MySQL). All of that operates on top of the protocols we have discussed in this chapter. Whenever you deploy a PHP web application on a LAMP server, remember that underneath your code, TCP connections are being opened, HTTP requests are flowing in, and responses (with HTML/JSON/etc.) are flowing out, DNS is resolving your domain name to an IP, and so on. A solid grasp of these fundamentals will help you troubleshoot issues (like "Why is my site slow?"—maybe DNS lookup is slow or too many TCP handshakes; or "Why can't users reach my server?"—maybe a firewall is blocking the port or BGP is not routing correctly to your IP).

In practice, much of this complexity is handled by system administrators or cloud platforms, but as a developer, knowing what is happening at the protocol level empowers you to make better decisions (like enabling caching, using CDNs for static assets, choosing between HTTP/2 or HTTP/3, etc.) and to debug problems that inevitably arise in network applications.

2.6   Chapter Review

Problem 2.1 Explain the difference between the OSI 7-layer model and the TCP/IP model. Why do we often use the simpler TCP/IP model when discussing Internet protocols? Which layers of the OSI model are combined into one in the TCP/IP model?

Problem 2.2 Compare TCP and UDP in terms of connection setup, reliability, ordering, and typical use cases. Give an example of an application or service that prefers UDP and explain why UDP is more suitable for it than TCP.

Problem 2.3 What is the role of a DNS recursive resolver, and how does it differ from an authoritative DNS server? Describe the steps the DNS resolver goes through to resolve the hostname `example.org` (no need to list all 13 root servers, just the general process).

Problem 2.4 What are the three steps of TCP's three-way handshake and what is accomplished by each step? Why is a handshake necessary before data transmission, and how does it contribute to TCP's reliability?

Problem 2.5 When a browser makes an HTTP request for a web page, what are the key parts of that request? Similarly, what are the key parts of an HTTP response? Describe the purpose of at least two HTTP request headers and two HTTP response headers.

Problem 2.6 A client receives a response with status code 404. What does this mean, and what are some possible reasons for a 404 error? The client then tries a different URL and gets a 301 status code. What should the client do when it sees a 301, and how is that different from a 404 in terms of action?

Problem 2.7 Why is using HTTPS important even for websites that do not handle sensitive information? Describe at least two security threats that are mitigated by HTTPS. Additionally, what is DNS cache poisoning and how does DNSSEC help prevent it?

Problem 2.8 In the context of a LAMP stack, explain the roles of Apache and PHP. How does a web server like Apache delegate work to the PHP interpreter when a dynamic page is requested? What role does MySQL play in this process?

Problem 2.9 If a user reports that they cannot reach your website, list a series of troubleshooting steps you would take using the tools discussed (e.g., ping, traceroute, etc.) to isolate the problem. What might it mean if ping works but a browser cannot load the site? What if ping does not work at all?

Problem 2.10 Imagine you deployed a new PHP web application, but it is running very slowly when serving pages to users. Based on this chapter's topics, list three possible areas you would investigate (for example: DNS lookup time, TCP connection issues, server-side processing, etc.) and briefly describe how each could cause slowdowns and how you might detect or resolve it.

Problem 2.11 Using your command line, perform DNS lookups for three different websites (you can use `nslookup` or `dig`). For each site, note the IP addresses returned. Do you notice any patterns or interesting findings (for example, multiple IPs for one site indicating load balancing or global servers)? Explain what you observe about how DNS is resolving those names.

Problem 2.12 Pick three popular websites and use a tool like `curl -I` (which fetches just the headers) or an online service to retrieve the HTTP response headers from their homepage. Compare the headers and look especially at the `Server` header (what software and version the site is running, if disclosed), caching headers like

`Cache-Control` or `ETag`, and security headers (such as `Content-Security-Policy`, `Strict-Transport-Security`, `X-Frame-Options`, etc.). What differences do you see in how these sites configure their responses? What might those differences indicate about each site's infrastructure or priorities (e.g., one might have a very long cache duration for static content, another might not)?

Problem 2.13 Attempt a manual HTTP request to a server using Telnet or Netcat (as described in the chapter). For example, connect to `port 80` of a website (you can use a small site like `example.com`). Send an HTTP/1.0 request (remember to include the Host header and end with a blank line). Record the response you get. Then, try an HTTP/1.1 request with a Host header. What differences do you notice in the responses, especially regarding connection closure or additional headers like `Connection:`? (If direct telnet is not possible from your environment, you can simulate this with a script or even use an online TCP client.)

Problem 2.14 Use `ping` to measure the latency to servers in different regions of the world. For instance, try pinging a server in North America, one in Europe, one in Asia (you can use known hosts like `nytimes.com`, `bbc.co.uk`, `nic.ad.jp` for example, or any others you know). Note the round-trip times. Then run `traceroute` to those same servers. How many hops does it take to reach each, and what are some of the intermediate network locations (looking at DNS names of routers can give clues)? Explain the differences in latency in terms of geographic distance and number of hops.

Problem 2.15 Write a short PHP script that uses sockets to send a message over TCP to a service and one that sends a message over UDP. (For example, you could test TCP by connecting to `telehack.com` on port 23, an open Telnet service, and UDP by sending a dummy packet to a public NTP server or echo server.) If you can, capture the traffic with Wireshark while running your scripts. Observe the TCP handshake in the TCP case and the lack thereof in the UDP case. What happens in each when you try to communicate? (Be mindful of what data you send; for UPD, it might just go and you get no reply unless the server is expecting it; for TCP, you might actually establish a connection to a telnet service.)

Problem 2.16 Draw a diagram or flowchart (you can use Mermaid as we did, or draw on paper) illustrating the complete sequence of events when a user types

`http://www.example.com/index.html` into their web browser and presses Enter. Include: DNS resolution, TCP handshake, HTTP request/response, and the closing of the connection. Assume HTTP (not HTTPS) for simplicity in this diagram. Label each step with what protocol and which layer it is at (e.g., "DNS query (Application layer over UDP)", "TCP SYN (Transport layer)", etc.). This exercise will test your understanding of how all the pieces fit together in context.

3. HTML I: Core Elements and Markup

HTML (HyperText Markup Language) is the standard markup language used to create documents for the World Wide Web. It provides a textual syntax (using tags) to structure content (text, images, media) and describe how that content should be organized and presented in a browser. In this chapter, we introduce the core elements of HTML and how they are used to build the content layer of web applications. We focus on fundamental HTML structures such as text paragraphs and headings, links for navigation, images for graphics, and tables for tabular data. Rather than covering web page graphic design, our emphasis is on the basic ideas, tools, and techniques underlying web page implementation. Mastering these HTML foundations will not only enable you to create simple web pages, but also help you understand broader web development concepts (like how browsers and servers interact) in the context of modern Internet applications.

Modern web applications typically follow a three-tier architecture consisting of: (1) web servers that store and deliver content, (2) web browsers (clients) that render HTML content and provide an interface for users, and (3) back-end databases or services that web pages can interact with through server-side code. HTML is central to this model, as it defines the structure of the content that web servers send to browsers for presentation. An HTML file (commonly with a `.html` or `.htm` extension) contains text intermingled with HTML tags, special strings in angle brackets (e.g., `<p>...</p>`), that indicate how pieces of content should be interpreted by the browser. A basic HTML page begins with an `<html>` tag and ends with a closing `</html>` tag, encompassing two main sections: a head and a body. The `<head>...</head>` section contains metadata about the page (such as its `<title>` that appears in the browser's title bar or tab, as well as links to Cascading Style Sheets (CSS), scripts, etc.), while the `<body>...</body>` section contains the actual content that will display in the browser window. By learning how to mark up content using HTML tags, you gain the ability to turn plain text into a structured web page.

Learning Objectives

By the end of this chapter, you should be able to:

- Explain the role of HTML in web applications and describe how an HTML document is structured (with head, body, and tags) to organize content.
- Create well-structured HTML pages using fundamental elements such as paragraphs, line breaks, headings, lists, links, images, and tables.
- Distinguish between block-level and inline elements in HTML, and know how each type of element affects the layout of content on the page.
- Use text formatting and grouping tags (for example, emphasis, bold, blockquotes, etc.) to mark up textual content appropriately for semantic meaning and appearance.
- Add hyperlinks to connect pages and resources, including external links, internal navigation links, and in-page anchors, and utilize attributes like `target` and `title` for enhanced link behavior.
- Embed images into a webpage using the `<img>` tag with proper `src` paths, and provide alternate text using the `alt` attribute for accessibility and good practice.

DOI: 10.1201/9781003727651-3

- Explain the use of attributes such as `alt`, `title`, `width`, `height`, etc., for providing additional information and control over how content (images, links, etc.) is presented.
- Understand relative vs. absolute paths and URLs for referencing resources, and appreciate the importance of relative paths in making webpages portable (relocatable across directory structures or servers).
- Construct HTML tables to represent tabular data, using table tags (`<table>`, `<tr>`, `<td>`, `<th>`) and attributes like `border`, `cellspacing`, `cellpadding`, as well as merging cells with `rowspan` and `colspan`.
- Recognize deprecated HTML features such as certain presentational attributes and understand the push toward using CSS for styling, as well as the concept of validation and "tidying" tools to clean up HTML.
- Utilize basic development tools for HTML, such as graphical HTML editors or browser developer consoles, to write, inspect, and debug HTML code more efficiently.
- Understand the role of content management tools (e.g., content management systems) in organizing and deploying websites, especially when handling large amounts of content without manually editing HTML for every page.

3.1 Basic Text Markup

One of the first steps in learning HTML is to mark up plain text into structured paragraphs, headings, lists, and other textual groupings. HTML provides a set of elements to denote different logical parts of text and to distinguish between block-level containers (which typically start on a new line) and inline elements (which flow within a line of text). By correctly using these elements, you ensure that your content is not only displayed appropriately in browsers but is also meaningful to search engines and assistive technologies.

3.1.1 Paragraphs and Text Flow

A paragraph is the fundamental block-level container for text in an HTML document. Paragraphs are marked up with the `<p>` tag (with a corresponding `</p>` closing tag). In modern HTML (HTML5), it is permitted to have text directly in the body without wrapping it in a paragraph tag, but it is good practice (and required in older XHTML/HTML4 strict standards) to enclose standalone text in paragraphs or other container elements for clarity. Browsers render paragraph text with a blank line (margin) before and after, visually separating it from other content.

When a browser displays a paragraph of text, it will treat consecutive whitespace characters (spaces, newlines, tabs) as a single space when rendering. For example, extra spaces or line breaks inside the HTML source of a paragraph will not appear as extra gaps in the output. Instead, the text will re-flow to fit the browser window. If you need multiple spaces or precise spacing in the content, special characters like ` ` (non-breaking space) must be used, or the text should be placed in a preformatted context (discussed below).

HTML elements are often categorized as block-level or inline. Block-level elements (such as paragraphs, headings, lists, and divisions) typically start on a new line in the browser and may contain other blocks or inline elements. They inherently create a vertical separation from the content before and after. By contrast, inline elements (such as links, emphasized text, or images) do not start on a new line; they appear in the flow of surrounding text and generally should only contain text or other inline elements (not block elements). For example, you can have an inline `<span>` or an `<img>` inside a paragraph, but you cannot put a block like a second `<p>` or a `<h1>` directly inside a paragraph.

To illustrate this, consider the following HTML snippet:

```
1  <p> This is a paragraph with an inline image
2      <img src="dog.jpg" alt="A small dog" />
3      and some <b>bold text</b>.
4  </p>
```

In the rendered page, the image and the bold text will appear within the same line-flow as the rest of the paragraph. The paragraph as a whole will be separated from content before and after it by default margins. Block elements cannot be nested inside a paragraph. For instance, you should not start a new `<h2>` or another `<p>` before the `</p>` closing the current paragraph.

Another useful text container is the preformatted text element, `<pre>...</pre>`. The `<pre>` element is a block element that instructs the browser to preserve whitespace and line breaks within it. Text wrapped in `<pre>` is displayed in a fixed-width (monospaced) font and exactly as it is typed in the HTML source (multiple spaces and line breaks are not collapsed or merged). Use `<pre>` when you want to show text exactly as formatted (for example, code listings or poem stanzas where spacing is significant).

Line Breaks and Comments

Within a paragraph or any block of text, if you want to force a line break (move subsequent text to a new line) without starting a new paragraph, you can use the line break tag `<br>`. The `<br>` tag is a void element) that does not have a separate closing tag (you write `<br>` and do not use `</br>`). In XHTML syntax you would close it with `/>` (for instance, `<br />`), but in HTML5 it is fine to just end with `>` as above.

A `<br>` simply breaks the current line at that point, continuing the content on a new line in the rendered output. Use `<br>` sparingly. For instance, in an address or poem where line breaks are part of the content rather than to create vertical spacing (use CSS margin/padding or paragraphs for controlling spacing in general).

HTML also allows comments that will not be displayed in the browser. A comment begins with `<!--` and ends with `-->`. For example:

```
1  <!-- This is a comment and will not appear in the output -->
```

Comments can span multiple lines and are often used to leave notes or temporarily remove code from being rendered. They can appear in the HTML body or head (essentially anywhere in the HTML document outside other tags), but they should not be nested inside actual tags or disturb the HTML structure. One common use of comments during development is to "comment out" sections of HTML code to test or debug by preventing certain parts from rendering without deleting the code.

3.1.2 Headings and Document Structure

HTML provides six levels of headings for section titles or subtitles, `<h1>` through `<h6>`. `<h1>` represents the highest-level (usually largest) heading, and `<h6>` the lowest-level (smallest) heading. Headings are block-level elements, typically rendered in bold and with some space above and below. They also have inherent semantic meaning (browsers and search engines assume an `<h1>` is a top-level heading, etc.), which is important for accessibility and Search Engine Optimization (SEO). Use heading levels in a logical, hierarchical way (like an outline). For example, use `<h1>` for the page's main title, `<h2>` for major section headings, `<h3>` for subsections, and so on.

Another block element for textual content is blockquote (`<blockquote>...</blockquote>`), used to indicate extended quotations. Browsers usually render blockquotes with indentation (margins on the left and right), to set off the quoted material from the main text. Inside a `<blockquote>`, you can put text and other block elements like paragraphs. In effect, a blockquote is like a specialized container for a section of text, typically italicized or indented to show it is a quote from another source.

To insert a thematic break or division between sections of text, you can use the horizontal rule tag `<hr>`. This is a void (empty) element that generates a horizontal line across the page. It is commonly used to visually separate content (for instance, between different topics or between the main content and footnotes). In HTML5, `<hr>` is more semantically defined as a paragraph-level thematic break (rather than just a visual ruler). By default, browsers draw it as a shaded line that takes up 100% of the width of its container, but like other elements it can be styled via CSS.

3.1.3 Text Formatting Elements

For basic text formatting within a line, HTML includes inline tags such as `<b>` (or `<strong>`) for bold text and `<i>` (or `<em>`) for italicized text. There are also `<sub>` and `<sup>` for subscripted and superscripted text (e.g., for chemical formulas or footnote markers), and `<small>` or `<big>` (deprecated in HTML5) for slightly smaller or larger text than the surrounding text. These tags affect the appearance of text but ideally should be used in a way that also conveys meaning (for example, `<strong>` implies importance, and browsers typically render it as bold). Modern HTML encourages using CSS for purely presentational effects and using these tags when the semantic meaning is appropriate (e.g., `<em>` for emphasis, which by default italicizes).

In practice, headings are very common (almost every page has at least an `<h1>`), whereas elements like `<blockquote>` and `<hr>` might be used less frequently depending on the content. Surveys of web pages have shown that elements like `<p>`, `<a>` (links), and `<img>` (images) are among the most frequently used, while `<blockquote>` or `<h5>` and `<h6>` headings are relatively rare. Nonetheless, it is important to know these elements so you can use them when appropriate.

3.1.4 Lists and Navigation

HTML supports several types of lists for organizing content into structured, hierarchical lists of items. The three basic list types are:

- Unordered list (`<ul>`): Displays a bulleted list of items (by default, each list item is preceded by a bullet or disc).
- Ordered list (`<ol>`): Displays a numbered list of items (each item is numbered in sequence, e.g., 1, 2, 3, ... by default).
- Description list (`<dl>`): Formerly known as definition lists, this displays a list of terms and their descriptions. Inside a `<dl>`, use `<dt>` for each term (definition term) and `<dd>` for its description (definition description).

Each individual item in an unordered or ordered list is wrapped in an `<li>` (list item) tag. For example:

```
<ul>
  <li>Dogs</li>
  <li>Cats</li>
</ul>
```

This would be rendered as a bulleted list with "Dogs" and "Cats" as two separate items. Similarly, an ordered list using `<ol>` with `<li>` items would by default number the items (1, 2, 3, ...). The numbering style (decimal, roman numerals, etc.) can be changed with CSS or deprecated attributes, but the default is decimal numerals.

Description lists are structured slightly differently since they pair terms with descriptions. A simple example:

```
<dl>
  <dt>HTML</dt>
  <dd>HyperText Markup Language, the standard language for creating web pages.</dd>
  <dt>CSS</dt>
  <dd>Cascading Style Sheets, used for styling HTML content.</dd>
</dl>
```

This would typically render with "HTML" and "CSS" as terms, possibly in a distinct typographic style (like bold), and their corresponding descriptions indented on the next line.

Nested lists (sub-lists): Lists can be nested inside list items to represent sub-categories or hierarchical structures. For example, you might have an unordered list of categories, and within the "Dogs" item, embed an ordered list of dog breeds:

```
<ul>
  <li>Dogs
    <ol>
      <li>Boxers</li>
      <li>Hounds</li>
    </ol>
  </li>
  <li>Cats</li>
</ul>
```

This code creates an unordered list with two top-level items ("Dogs" and "Cats"). Under "Dogs", there is a nested ordered list with two items ("Boxers" and "Hounds"). Browsers will indent the nested list further and, in this case, number the dog breeds as 1 and 2. When nesting lists, the rule is that the nested `<ul>` or `<ol>` must be placed inside an `<li>` of the parent list because you cannot directly put one `<ul>` inside another without it being within a list item.

Lists (especially unordered lists) are not only used for content in sentences; they are also often used for navigation menus or other grouping of links, because they provide a nice semantic way to group items. You can then use CSS to style the list (for instance, turning a `<ul>` into a horizontal menu by removing bullets and styling the `<li>` elements).

Using Lists for Navigation

One of the most common uses of lists in modern web development is creating navigation menus. By combining unordered lists with hyperlinks, we can create both vertical and horizontal navigation bars.

Vertical Navigation Bar

```html
<ul>
   <li><a href = "index.html">Home</a></li>
   <li><a href = "about.html">About Me</a></li>
   <li><a href = "contact.html">Contact Me</a></li>
</ul>
```

By default, this creates a vertical list of links. Each list item appears on its own line, creating a sidebar-style navigation.

Horizontal Navigation Bar

To create a horizontal navigation bar, we use CSS to change the display of list items:

```html
<!DOCTYPE html>
<html>
<head>
  <style>
    li
    {
       display:inline;
    }
  </style>
</head>
<body>
  <ul>
     <li><a href = "index.html">Home</a></li>
```

```
14     <li><a href = "about.html">About Me</a></li>
15     <li><a href = "contact.html">Contact Me</a></li>
16   </ul>
17 </body>
18 </html>
```

The CSS rule `display: inline` makes the list items appear side by side instead of stacked vertically. This is a common pattern for top navigation bars on websites.

3.1.5 Special Characters and Entities

HTML provides special codes called character entities to display characters that have special meaning in HTML or are not easily typed on a keyboard. These begin with `&` and end with `;` and are shown in along with their descriptions in Table 3.1.

Table 3.1: Common special characters and their descriptions.

Entity	Character	Description
`&`	&	Ampersand
`<`	<	Less than sign
`>`	>	Greater than sign
`©`	©	Copyright symbol
`®`	®	Registered trademark sign
`™`	™	Trademark sign
`°`	°	Degree sign
`±`	±	Plus/minus sign
`¢`	¢	Cent sign
`£`	£	Pound sign
`€`	€	Euro sign
`¥`	¥	Yen sign
`"`	"	Double quote
`‘`	'	Opening single quote
`’`	'	Closing single quote/apostrophe
` `		Non-breaking space

Use character entities when:

- You need to display characters that have special meaning in HTML (like < or &)
- You want to include symbols not on your keyboard
- You need a non-breaking space to keep words together on the same line

For example, to display "AT&T" correctly, you should write `AT&T` in your HTML. To show a temperature like "98.6Â°F", write `98.6°F`.

3.1.6 Generic Containers (div and span)

HTML offers two generic container elements that have no semantic meaning on their own but are useful for grouping other content: <div> (division) and <span>. The <div> is a block-level container, and <span> is an inline container. They do not inherently do anything to the content (no visual change) unless styled, but they allow you to apply identification or styling to grouped content.

A <div> can wrap other blocks of content. For example, you might wrap a section of your page in a <div id="intro"> ... </div> to target it with specific styles or scripts. A <span> is for wrapping inline content, such as a word or phrase within a paragraph, often to change its style or to mark it for scripting.

Both <div> and <span> are commonly used in conjunction with the class or id attributes (or other attributes like data-* attributes) to hook them to CSS rules or JavaScript. For instance:

```
1  <div class = "notice">
2    <p><span class = "urgent">Important:</span> Your session will expire in 1 minute.</p>
3  </div>
```

Here, the <div> with class "notice" might be styled with a special background color in CSS, and the <span> with class "urgent" might be styled to be bold or red.

Although the <div> and <span> elements themselves are just neutral containers, their power comes from applying styles to them. This brings us to the concept of using CSS (Cascading Style Sheets) for presentation. We will cover CSS in detail in a later chapter, but a brief introduction is useful here, since presentational attributes in HTML (like the now-deprecated align or font color attributes) have largely been replaced by CSS.

A style rule in CSS sets a presentation property (like text color, font size, margins, etc.) for HTML elements. Styles can be applied in several ways. One straightforward way is in an HTML page is via a <style> element in the head. For example:

```
1  <head>
2    <style>
3      .highlight
4      {
5        color: blue;
6      }
7    </style>
8  </head>
```

This defines a CSS class selector named "highlight" that makes text blue. We could then apply this style to a <div> or <span> by using the class="highlight" attribute on that element. For instance:

```
1  <p>This is a <span class = "highlight">highlighted</span> word.</p>
```

The word "highlighted" would appear blue (assuming the above style rule is in effect), because the `<span>` wraps it and has class "highlight", which the style rule targets. Similarly, you could give an element a unique id and target it with CSS (though using classes is more common for multiple elements).

In summary, `<div>` and `<span>` are structural tools to group content when no other semantic element is appropriate. They become extremely useful when combined with CSS or JavaScript. In modern web development, you will often see many `<div>`s used to layout sections of a page (though HTML5 introduced more semantic containers like `<header>`, `<nav>`, `<section>`, etc., which we will discuss later), and `<span>` to apply styles to parts of text without breaking the flow.

3.1.7 HTML Validation and Clean Code

As you start writing HTML code, it is easy to introduce minor errors such as forgetting a closing tag, nesting elements incorrectly, or using deprecated markup. Browsers are generally forgiving and will attempt to fix or ignore many errors, but sloppy HTML can lead to unpredictable display or difficulties in maintenance. It is therefore important to keep HTML code tidy and valid.

HTML Tidy is a tool originally developed by Dave Raggett (and available in open-source form) that can automatically clean up HTML. There are online interfaces (for example, the W3C's HTML Validator can also offer tidying suggestions, and there are standalone versions as well). Feeding your HTML into such a tool can help by: (1) indenting and formatting the code consistently (making it more readable), and (2) identifying certain errors or suggest fixes for common mistakes. For instance, if you omitted a required DOCTYPE or a closing tag, a tidying tool might insert it or alert you.

It is important to note that tidying is not the same as validation. A validator (such as the official W3C Markup Validation Service) checks your HTML against the formal specification (for HTML5, or for HTML 4.01 Transitional/Strict, etc.) to ensure the code is valid. A tidy tool may correct some issues and make the HTML more uniform, but it does not guarantee the code is fully standards-compliant. For example, Tidy might clean up nested tags and add missing quotes, but your code might still contain deprecated elements that are allowed under Transitional HTML but not under Strict HTML.

Best Practices: Clean HTML

Consider the following suggestions for clean HTML code:
- Use a good code editor with syntax highlighting
- Format your code clearly (indent nested elements)
- Validate early and often, especially after major edits
- Close all tags properly and nest them correctly
- Use lowercase for all tags and attributes
- Quote all attribute values
- Include proper DOCTYPE and character encoding declarations

3.2 Hyperlinks

One of the defining features of HTML (and the "Web" in general) is hyperlinking, which is the ability to link from one document or resource to another. In fact, the "HT" in HTML stands for "HyperText," reflecting that web pages can contain links (hypertext) that users click to retrieve other pages or resources. Hyperlinks turn static documents into a navigable web of information.

In HTML, hyperlinks are created using the anchor tag `<a>`. An anchor can serve as a source (the clickable link in your page) that points to a destination (another resource, which could be another HTML page, a specific part of the current page, an image, a file to download, etc.). The basic syntax is:

```
<a href = "URL">Link text or content</a>
```

Here, the `href` attribute (short for hypertext reference) specifies the target location, typically a URL or a path to another file, and the content between the `<a>` and `</a>` is what the user clicks on. This clickable content (often just text, but it could also be an image or any HTML content) is usually styled by browsers to indicate that it is a link (by default, most browsers underline it and color it blue, and perhaps purple if it is a link the user has visited before).

For example:

```
<a href = "https://www.wikipedia.org/">Visit Wikipedia</a>
```

This creates a link that says "Visit Wikipedia," and when clicked, the browser will navigate to the URL `https://www.wikipedia.org/`. If the `href` value is a relative path (e.g., `href="about.html"` with no `http://`), the browser will look for that file on the same server and directory as the current page. If it is an absolute URL starting with `http://` or `https://` (or other protocols like `ftp://`), the browser will go to that address on the Internet.

Hyperlinks are not limited to linking HTML pages. The `href` can point to any resource, including an image, a PDF, an audio file, a video, or even trigger an email (`href="mailto:someone@example.com"` opens an email client). If the resource is something the browser can display or handle, it will do so; otherwise it might prompt the user to download it.

A link can also include query parameters to pass data to server programs. For instance:

```
<a href="https://www.google.com/search?q=hyperlink">Search for "hyperlink"</a>
```

This link goes to Google's search page with a query parameter q=hyperlink. Clicking it would effectively search Google for the term "hyperlink." The part after the ? in the URL (q=hyperlink) is data being sent to the server's search program. This illustrates that hyperlinks can not only retrieve static pages but also invoke server-side scripts or programs (like search engines), making the web interactive even without forms (forms provide a more structured way to send data, which we will cover in the next chapter).

By default, when a user clicks a link, the new page/resource replaces the current page in the browser window. The user can navigate back using the browser's back button. We can modify this behavior with attributes, as we will see soon (for example, opening in a new tab or window).

From a user interface perspective, browsers typically render hyperlinks in a distinct way. Using CSS, these defaults can be changed, but historically a blue underline indicated a link, and a purple underline indicated a visited link. Additionally, many browsers change the cursor to a pointing hand when hovering over a link, giving a visual cue that something is clickable. It is important when designing pages to make links obvious to users (through consistent styling or cues), so they know where they can click.

In terms of conceptualizing a website, you can think of each page as a node in a graph, and each hyperlink as a directed edge connecting one node to another. This is why we call it the "web"; everything can be connected via links, forming a giant network of information.

In Figure 3.1 we show a simple visualization of a hyperlink as a directed connection from a source anchor to a destination resource. The hyperlink is depicted as an arrow from the source anchor (the link in the page you click) to the destination (the page or resource it leads to). Hyperlinks enable non-linear navigation through information, which was a revolutionary aspect of the web's development.

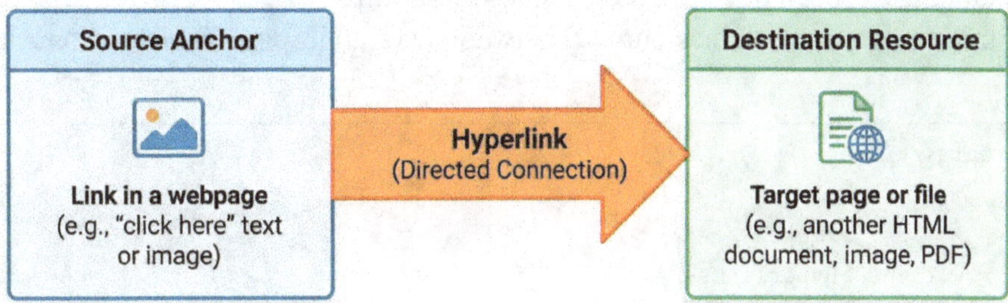

Figure 3.1: A simple visualization of hyperlink as a directed connection.

A hyperlink can be placed around any inline content. Often it is text ("click here" or a descriptive phrase), but it could just as well be an image:

```
<a href = "cat.jpg"><img src = "thumb_cat.jpg" alt = "Small cat picture"></a>
```

In this case, clicking the thumbnail image (`thumb_cat.jpg`) might lead the user to the full-size image `cat.jpg` as the image itself is the clickable anchor content.

3.2.1 Name, Target, and Title Attributes

The anchor tag `<a>` supports several attributes that add functionality to hyperlinks:
- `name (or id) attribute`: In older HTML, `name` could turn an `<a>` tag into a destination anchor within the page (an anchor point). For example, `<a name="section2"></a>` placed before a section acts as a bookmark. You could then link to this section from the same page (or another page) with `href="#section2"`, which tells the browser to scroll to the element with that name/id. In modern HTML, any element can have an `id` attribute to mark a spot, and you link to it with `href="#thatID"`. This is useful for creating a table of contents or "back to top" links that jump to certain parts of the page.
- `target attribute`: This attribute specifies where to open the linked document. Common values are _self (the default, opens in the same frame or window), _blank (opens the link in a new browser tab or

window), _parent, or a specific frame name if using frames (frames are now largely obsolete). For example, `<a href="page2.html" target="_blank">Open Page 2 in new tab</a>` will cause the link to launch a new tab. Use this carefully because opening many new tabs/windows can be considered bad user experience unless there is a good reason (like an external site or a PDF that you want to keep separate).

- `title` attribute: This attribute provides additional advisory information about the link. The `title` text typically appears as a tooltip when the user hovers over the link. For instance:

```
1  <a href = "archive.html" title = "View the archive of previous articles">Archive</a>
```

Here, hovering over "Archive" might show a tooltip that says "View the archive of previous articles." The `title` attribute can be used on many elements (not just links) to provide supplementary information. It is good for usability but not crucial; it should not be relied on for essential info because not all users will see it (for example, on touch devices there is no hover tooltip).

Using these attributes, we can enhance our earlier example of an in-page Table of Contents:

```
1  <h2>Table of Contents</h2>
2  <ul>
3    <li><a href = "#section1">Images</a></li>
4    <li><a href = "#section2">Hyperlinks</a></li>
5    <li><a href = "#section3">Tables</a></li>
6  </ul>
7
8  <!-- Later in the page, the sections might be: -->
9  <h3 id = "section1">Images</h3>
10 <p> ...content... </p>
11
12 <h3 id = "section2">Hyperlinks</h3>
13 <p> ...content... </p>
14
15 <h3 id = "section3">Tables</h3>
16 <p> ...content... </p>
```

In the code above, clicking "Images" in the TOC will jump to the element with `id="section1"`. Note that in modern HTML5, `id` is used instead of `name` for in-page anchors, and we did that with `<h3 id="section1">` etc.

Finally, an anchor's `href` can be any valid URL or path. It could even reference a specific part of another page by combining both: `href="otherpage.html#chapter2"` would go to `otherpage.html` and, once loaded, scroll to the element with `id="chapter2"` on that page.

In summary, hyperlinks (`<a href="...">`) are the glue of the web, connecting documents and resources. Attributes like `name`/`id` allow linking to fragments within a page, `target` can change where the link opens, and `title` can provide helpful hover text. These make links more powerful and user-friendly.

Best Practices: Hyperlinks

Consider the following suggestions for creating your HTML code:

- Use descriptive link text (avoid "click here")
- Include title attributes for additional context when helpful
- Use `target="_blank"` sparingly and only when appropriate
- Ensure links are visually distinct from regular text
- Test all links to ensure they work correctly

3.3 Images

A web page without images can feel feel dry; images provide visual interest, illustrations, logos, and so on. In HTML, the `<img>` tag is used to embed images into a page. Like the `<br>` tag, `<img>` is a void element (empty tag), it does not wrap content, and is self-contained (in HTML5 you can just write `<img...>` without a closing tag).

The simplest form of an image tag is:

```
<img src = "photo.png" alt="Description of the image">
```

Here, the required attribute `src` (source) specifies the path or URL to the image file. The browser will retrieve that image and display it at the location of the `<img>` tag. The `alt` attribute is also required (per HTML5) for accessibility. It provides alternative text that describes the image's content or purpose (more on `alt` below). In the example above, if `photo.png` is in the same directory as the HTML page, just the file name is given. If it were in an `images` subfolder, we would write `src="images/photo.png"`, or a full URL could be used like `src="https://example.com/images/photo.png"` to load from a remote server.

By default, the image will display at its native size, the pixel dimensions of the actual image file. If the image is 800 pixels wide and 600 pixels tall, that is how it will appear (unless the browser or CSS resizes it). However, you can specify width and height attributes on the `<img>` tag to control the displayed size:

```
<img src = "photo.png" alt = "Description" width="400" height = "300">
```

This would attempt to display the image at 400Ã—300 pixels, regardless of its original size. It is important to maintain the aspect ratio (the proportional relationship between width and height) when resizing images to avoid distortion. The browser does not automatically preserve aspect ratio if you set both width and height, and will stretch/squash the image to exactly those values. If you provide only one dimension (say, `width="400"` and omit height), the browser will scale the image preserving aspect ratio (so height auto-adjusts). In CSS, you can also constrain one dimension and set the other to `auto`.

Providing the width and height attributes that match the image's actual size can also help the browser lay out the page faster (because it can allocate the correct space even before the image loads). Many developers use these attributes for that reason. If unknown, you can omit them, but the page might reflow when the image loads.

Alt and Title Attributes

The `alt attribute` (alternative text) is meant to provide a textual alternative to the image, primarily for users who cannot see the image. This could be because the image failed to load, or because the user is visually impaired and using a screen reader, or because they have images turned off in their browser. The content of `alt` should succinctly describe the image or its function. For instance, if the image is a company logo, `alt="Acme Corp Logo"` would be appropriate. If the image is purely decorative and has no informational value, it is acceptable to use `alt=""` (an empty alt), which signals to screen readers to skip it.

If an `<img>` tag is missing an alt attribute, HTML5 will consider it a validation error (because of the importance of alt text for accessibility). Always include an alt, even if it is empty.

The `title attribute` on images (and on links or other elements) can provide additional information, often shown as a tooltip on hover. For an image, `title` might give more detail than alt, or a different kind of info (alt is supposed to stand in for the image if it is not shown, whereas title might be supplementary). For example:

```
1  <img src = "chart.png" alt = "Bar chart of quarterly sales" title = "Sales increased 15% in Q4">
```

If a user's browser displays tooltips on hover (most do for the title attribute), they would see "Sales increased 15% in Q4" when they hover over the image, whereas if the image fails to load, they would see the alt text "Bar chart of quarterly sales" (often displayed in place of the image or read by a screen reader).

It is worth noting that not all browsers handle these attributes in exactly the same way. Historically, Internet Explorer would show the `alt` text as a tooltip on hover instead of the title if no title was present (which was actually incorrect behavior, as only title is meant for that). Modern versions in standards mode have corrected this. Firefox and others correctly use `title` for hover tooltips and only use `alt` for actual alternate text when the image cannot be shown.

In summary, always use meaningful alt text for images. It is crucial for accessibility and for scenarios where images cannot be seen. Use `title` if you want to provide a bit more detail on hover, but remember that not everyone will see it (touchscreen users, for example, have no hover).

3.3.1   Relative Paths, Absolute Paths, and URLs

When specifying the `src` for images (and similarly `href` for links), you can use relative paths or absolute paths/URLs. A relative path describes how to get to the resource starting from the current page's location, whereas an absolute path (in context of file system) or a URL describes the full location irrespective of the current page.

Consider you have an HTML file located in a directory, and an image in a subdirectory or parent directory. You might have a directory structure like the sample showing in Figure 3.2, showing HTML files, an images folder with subfolders, and a docs folder.

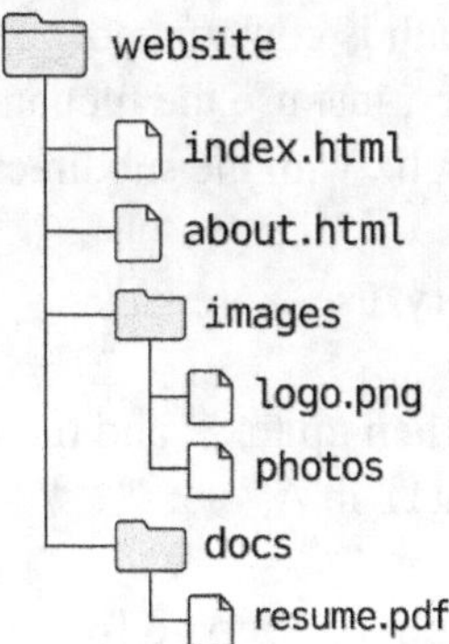

Figure 3.2: A website directory structure.

If `index.html` wants to include `logo.png`, since `logo.png` is in an `images` subfolder of the current directory, the `src` could be `"images/logo.png"`. That is a relative path (relative to where `index.html` is). If `about.html` (in the same directory as index) wants to include `team.jpg`, which is in a deeper subfolder (`images/photos/`), the path would be `"images/photos/team.jpg"`.

To reference a file in a parent directory, use `..` which stands for "up one directory." For example, if you had another HTML file inside `docs/` that wants to show the `logo.png` from above, the path would be `../images/logo.png` (go up from `docs` to `website/`, then into `images/` and find `logo.png`).

Now consider Figure 3.3, which shows an example directory tree illustrating relative path notation. In this hypothetical structure, an HTML file in directory C references image files in various locations: F1.gif in the same folder, F2.gif in a subfolder E, F3.gif in the parent folder B, F4.gif in a sibling folder D, and F5.gif in the grandparent folder A.

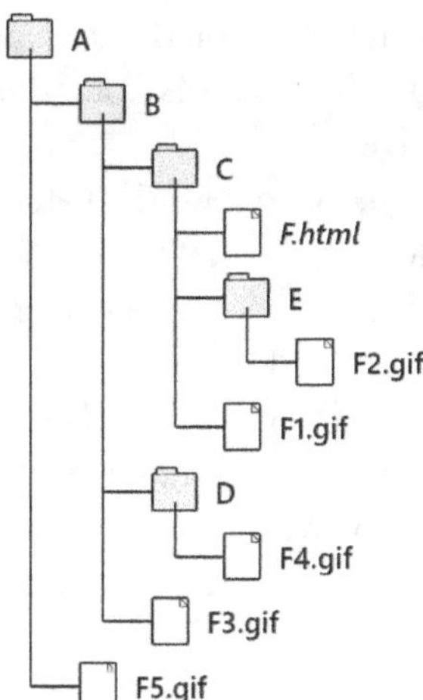

Figure 3.3: Directory tree illustrating relative path notation.

In this figure, notice how each relative path is constructed:

- To reference a file in the same directory, just use the filename (e.g., `src="F1.gif"`).
- To reference a file in a subdirectory, prefix with the subdirectory name (e.g., `src="E/F2.gif"` to go into subfolder E).
- To reference a file in the parent directory, use `..` (e.g., `src="../F3.gif"` from C goes up to B and finds `F3.gif`).
- To go up two levels (from C up to B, then up to A, and then into another branch), you can chain `../...` For example, from C to reference `F5.gif` in A, `src="../../F5.gif"` goes up to B (`../`), then up to A (`../` again), then looks for `F5.gif` there.
- A sibling directory reference is a combination: to go from C to D (which share the same parent B), you go up to B (`..`), then down into D: `src="../D/F4.gif"`.

Using relative paths keeps links portable. If you move the whole website folder to a new domain or another location, the internal links still work, because they are relative to each other. If you had used absolute file paths (like `C:\Users\Name\website\images\logo.png` on your computer), that would only work on your computer and break elsewhere. On a web server, absolute URLs (like `http://mywebsite.com/images/logo.png`) will work, but if you copy the site to another domain or test it locally, those would need changing. Hence, relative paths are generally preferred for linking resources within your own site.

Sometimes, however, you will use full URLs in `src` or `href`. For instance, linking to an external site's image or an external webpage obviously requires a full URL. Example:

```
1  <img src = "https://www.w3schools.com/images/w3schools_logo.png" alt = "W3Schools logo">
```

This `<img>` pulls an image directly from `w3schools.com`. When the browser sees an `http` or `https` URL in the `src`, it will make a separate request to that server to fetch the image. Keep in mind that linking images from other sites (hotlinking) can be problematic if you do not have permission or if the site changes the image. It is often better to host the image yourself unless it is something like a third-party content delivery (like a library or a known resource). To summarize:

- Relative paths (no protocol or domain, just directories) are resolved relative to the current page's location.
- Absolute paths in the context of a local file system (like starting with / on a server) are resolved from the root of the website or drive. For example, `src="/images/logo.png"` (starting with a slash) would look for an `images` directory at the root of the domain.
- Full URLs include the protocol (`http://` or `https://` etc.) and domain, and they are needed to reference anything on a different server or outside the current site.

Using relative paths enhances portability. You could move your entire site directory to a different domain or folder and internal links would still work. On the other hand, if your links are absolute and your domain changes, you would have to edit them all.

3.3.2   Flowing Text Around Images

By default, an `<img>` is an inline element. This means if you place an `<img>` in the middle of a paragraph, the browser treats it like a giant character and continues the text on the same line (if space permits) or wraps text around to the next lines as needed. The bottom of an image aligns roughly with the baseline of text by default (so small text might appear vertically centered around the image's height, if the image is taller than one line of text).

Sometimes you want text to wrap around an image, especially for a layout like an article with a thumbnail floated to one side. Historically, HTML provided an `align` attribute on images for this: `align="left"` or `align="right"` on an `<img>` would cause the image to "float" to that side and text would wrap around the other side of it. For example:

```
<img src = "portrait.jpg" alt = "Portrait of Jane" align = "left">
<p>Jane Doe is a software engineer with 10 years of experience... (text continues)</p>
```

With `align="left"`, the image will sit at the left margin, and the paragraph text will flow to the right of the image, wrapping under it once the text extends beyond the image's height. This can create a nice effect where the image is embedded to one side of a block of text.

However, the `align` attribute for images (as well as similar presentational attributes) is deprecated in modern HTML. The recommended approach now is to use CSS to achieve the same effect, typically using the `float` property:

```
<img src = "portrait.jpg" alt = "Portrait of Jane" style = "float: left; margin: 0 1em 1em 0;">
```

In the example above, `style="float: left; margin: 0 1em 1em 0;"` will float the image to the left and also add some margin to the right and bottom of the image so that the text does not butt right up against it. This accomplishes the same as the old align attribute but with more control. `float:right` would analogously push it to the right side with text wrapping on the left.

Whether using the deprecated `align` or modern CSS `float`, the behavior is similar: the floated image is taken out of the normal document flow (block flow) and positioned to the side, and subsequent text flows around it.

One thing to be careful about: if you have multiple images or floats, you might need to "clear" the float (using the CSS clear property on a block element that follows) to avoid layout issues. But a deep dive into floats and clears is a CSS topic. For now, understand that you can wrap text around images and that modern practice is to use CSS to do so.

Centering an image: Often people want to center an image. There is no `align="center"` for inline elements (that was only for block elements like `<p align="center">` which is also deprecated). The easiest way to center an image is to wrap it in a block-level container (like a `<div>` or `<p>`) and apply `text-align: center;` to that container, or use CSS margin auto on the image if it is turned into a block (`display: block; margin: auto;`). Again, this veers into CSS, but keep in mind that plain HTML attributes have limitations which CSS overcomes.

3.3.3   Deprecated Features in HTML (Presentational Markup)

Earlier versions of HTML included many presentational elements and attributes – things like `<font>` tags to change text color or face, attributes like `bgcolor` on `<table>` or `align` on various tags to achieve visual layout, etc. The standards body for the web, the W3C, in HTML 4 and beyond, began phasing these out in favor of CSS, a process known as deprecation. A feature being deprecated means it is marked as outdated and slated for removal in future standards, though browsers may continue to support it for a while for backward compatibility.

For example, the `align` attribute on `<img>` (and on `<table>`, `<p>`, etc.) is deprecated in HTML4 Strict and not part of HTML5 at all, because CSS should be used (`float` or `text-align` or other techniques). Another example: the `<font>` tag and its `color` attribute were deprecated. Instead of `<font color="red">Hello</font>` you would write `<span style="color: red;">Hello</span>` or define a CSS class.

Deprecation does not mean immediate disappearance. In fact, browsers still support many deprecated tags and attributes (like `<center>`, `<font>`, etc.) to ensure old websites do not break. However, if you are writing new code (and especially if you aim to meet modern standards like HTML5), you should avoid deprecated features. Not only do they separate content from design poorly (mixing style into your HTML), they also might not be supported forever. Writing modern HTML means using semantic markup for structure and CSS for styling.

For learning purposes, you might encounter deprecated usage (especially when maintaining older code or looking at examples from the early 2000s). It is useful to recognize them: e.g., `<b>` and `<i>` are actually not deprecated (they are still valid but with semantic considerations), while `<u>` (underline) was deprecated in HTML4 (but is reintroduced with semantic meaning in HTML5), and attributes like `bgcolor`, `border` on tables, `align` on most elements, etc., are deprecated/obsolete. In this chapter, when we used `align` in an example, we noted it was for illustration and that it is deprecated, showing a CSS alternative.

Always try to follow the principle: use HTML for structure and meaning, use CSS for layout and appearance. This approach will future-proof your pages and make them easier to maintain.

3.3.4   The Browser Cache and Image Loading

When discussing images, it is important to consider performance aspects. Images are often the bulk of a webpage's download size. Browsers use a mechanism called caching to store copies of resources (HTML pages, images, scripts, etc.) on the user's computer so that if they are needed again, they can be loaded from the local cache (much faster) instead of downloaded again. By default, browsers will cache images after downloading them the first time, which is why if you visit a page and then revisit it, it loads faster (images and other resources might come from cache).

Users can control some browser settings regarding images. For instance, one can choose not to display images to speed up browsing on a slow connection or for accessibility reasons. In most browsers, this is an advanced setting (for example, in Chrome, it is under Site Settings → Images; in older IE, it was an option "Show Pictures"). If images are turned off, the browser will not even download them. Instead, it will just show the alt text (and maybe a placeholder icon).

Let us walk through what happens when a browser loads a page with images:

1. The browser requests the HTML page from the server (say `index.html`).
2. The server sends the HTML file to the browser.
3. The browser starts parsing the HTML. As it encounters an `<img src="...">` tag, it notes that it needs

that image. It does not stop everything; it continues parsing, but it also issues a new HTTP request to fetch the image file.

4. The page can finish loading its HTML and even display text while the images might still be on their way. The images will fill in once downloaded.

5. If an image is in cache (perhaps the same image was used on a previous page you visited on the same site), the browser may load it from cache instantly rather than downloading again (depending on cache settings and server headers).

If the user has turned off images, step 3 (downloading the image) will not happen at all. The browser will just display the alt text (or nothing, if alt is empty) in place of the image. This saves bandwidth and time. We can do a simple experiment (hypothetically) to illustrate browser cache behavior:

- Clear the browser cache completely.
- Disable images in the browser settings.
- Visit a webpage that has images (e.g., a news article with photos). The browser will load the HTML and any non-image resources, but not the images, so the page will show placeholders or alt text.
- If you check the local cache (browser's temporary files), you would see that those images were not downloaded at all.
- Now enable images and refresh the page. The browser will download the images and show them.
- If you refresh again, the browser will likely load the images from cache (if the cache policy allows) rather than re-downloading, since it already has them stored.

Latency and image size: Every image adds to the total load time of the page. The delay experienced by the user depends on:

- Network bandwidth (how many bytes per second can be transferred).
- Network latency and traffic (time to establish connections, plus any slowdowns due to congestion).
- Server speed (how fast the server responds with the data).
- File size of the content (a larger image file takes more bytes, obviously).

To improve performance, developers optimize images (more on formats and compression below), and browsers might download multiple images in parallel (web servers and browsers often allow 4–6 parallel connections per domain).

If a user has a slow connection, disabling images can dramatically speed up loading, since the text of a page is usually much smaller than the images. This is one reason the `alt` text is important: it ensures some information is available even if the image itself is not.

The browser cache is also crucial for performance. If your site uses the same logo on every page, the user's browser should ideally download it once, cache it, and then instantly reuse it from cache on subsequent pages. Web developers can control caching behavior by sending certain HTTP headers (e.g., `Cache-Control`) with images, indicating how long they can be stored.

3.3.5 Transmission Delay and Data Compression

Large images can be slow to transmit. As mentioned, the file size of an image is a big factor in how quickly it loads. Two images with the same pixel dimensions can have vastly different file sizes depending on their format and content.

For example, consider a simple graphic like an icon with solid colors and maybe 100×100 pixels. If saved as an uncompressed bitmap, it might be 10 KB. If saved as a compressed PNG or GIF, it might be 2 KB. A photograph at 1920×1080 might be 2 MB as an uncompressed BMP, but as a JPEG compressed, maybe only 200 KB at quality 80%. These differences are due to compression algorithms.

Compression can be lossless or lossy:

- Lossless compression means the image data is compressed in a way that you can recover 100% of the original data. PNG and GIF are generally lossless (though GIF is limited in color depth to 256 colors). Lossless methods exploit patterns and redundancy in the data. One simple form is run-length encoding: if a row of pixels has 50 white pixels in a row, instead of storing "white, white, white..." 50 times, you store "50×white". The GIF format uses a more complex algorithm called LZW (Lempel-Ziv-Welch), which builds a dictionary of repeated patterns in the data to compress it. LZW was at one time patented, which caused some issues in the past (more on that soon).

- Lossy compression means some information is discarded to achieve higher compression. JPEG is a lossy format commonly used for photographs. It uses techniques from signal processing to throw away details that the human eye might not notice much (like very subtle color changes), achieving great compression ratios. A high-quality JPEG may look identical to the original photo but be one tenth the file size, because it has thrown away some data in a clever way. If you compress too much (too low quality setting), you start seeing artifacts (blurriness or blocky patterns).

Example: A simple image of the U.S. flag (which has large areas of solid color and repeated patterns) might compress extremely well in GIF/PNG. Suppose it is 412×217 pixels (which raw would be about 89,000 pixels; at 1 byte per pixel for a 256-color GIF, raw ~89 KB). Using LZW compression, because of the repetition (stripes), the GIF might end up only ~2 KB! The repeated red and white stripes are ideal for compression. That is over 40× smaller than raw. That is lossless compression, and the decompressed image is pixel-for-pixel the same as the original.

Now, if that were a detailed photograph with many colors and little repetition, a GIF would not compress well (and is limited to 256 colors). A JPEG would do better for a photograph by being lossy, perhaps taking a 500 KB raw photo down to 50 KB with minimal quality loss.

The key takeaway for web development: optimize your images. Choose the right format (more about formats in a moment), and compress images to the smallest size that still looks good. This reduces transmission delay (latency). Users on slow connections or mobile devices appreciate sites that load fast.

3.3.6   Image Formats, Patents, and the History of GIF/PNG

It is interesting that even image formats have had their drama in terms of intellectual property. As a web developer or content creator, you normally just use formats like PNG, JPEG, GIF without worrying about their internal algorithms. But historically, the GIF format (which was very popular for small images and animations in the early web) used the LZW compression algorithm, which was patented by Unisys. In the late 1990s, Unisys started to enforce licensing fees for software that created GIFs, which caused a stir in the developer community. This spurred the development of the PNG format as a patent-free alternative to GIF.

A brief overview:

- GIF (Graphics Interchange Format): Supports up to 256 colors (8-bit color) and simple animations (by combining multiple frames). Uses LZW compression (which was patented until 2003). Ideal for simple graphics, logos, icons, and animations with limited colors. Not great for photographs due to color limitation.

- PNG (Portable Network Graphics): Created as an improved, patent-free replacement for GIF. Supports lossless compression, can handle 24-bit truecolor (millions of colors) as well as transparency. PNGs come in two flavors typically, PNG-8 (like GIF's 256-color) and PNG-24 (truecolor). PNG also supports an alpha channel for partial transparency (GIF only has binary transparency, thus making a pixel either opaque or fully transparent). PNG compression is also quite effective and generally produces smaller files than GIF for similar images (especially for images with more than 256 colors).
- JPEG (Joint Photographic Experts Group format, usually with extension .jpg or .jpeg): Designed for photographs and complex imagery. Supports 24-bit color, no transparency, and uses lossy compression (typically). Great for photos, not suitable for sharp-edged graphics or images with text (because compression artifacts can blur edges). You can choose the quality level to trade off size vs fidelity.
- TIFF (Tagged Image File Format): Not commonly used on the web (browsers do not display TIFF by default). It is more of a print/scanner image format, supports multiple color depths, can be lossless or use compression like LZW or others. TIFF files can be very large and are not optimized for web delivery.

The free software movement (open source movement) rallied around the PNG format in the late 90s and early 2000s as a stand against the patented GIF. Advocates like Richard Stallman, the founder of the Free Software Foundation (FSF), argued that software patents (like the one covering LZW) were harmful because they restrict the ability of developers to implement standard features without legal barriers. PNG was deliberately created to avoid any patented algorithms. By the time the LZW patent expired (around 2003 globally), the web had largely moved on and PNG became a widely supported standard for images. Today, PNG, GIF, and JPEG all coexist: use GIF for simple animations (PNG does not support animation in its basic form, though there is APNG extensions and others), use PNG (or SVG) for crisp graphics/line art, and use JPEG for photographs.

The licensing issue for GIFs is now history, but it was a crucial lesson in how an intellectual property constraint could influence technology adoption on the web. Now, virtually all common web standards for images, audio, video have to consider patent encumbrances. For example, modern video codecs have similar patent pools issues, leading to patent-free ones like AV1 being developed by consortiums.

The open source angle: developers value formats that anyone can implement and use freely. That is why HTML, CSS, and JavaScript are open standards. In the case of images, PNG's development was a community-driven effort to ensure the web's basic media formats remain open.

3.3.7 The PNG, GIF, JPG, and TIFF Formats – When to Use Each

To recap and add context on the image formats:

- PNG ("Ping"): Great for images that need lossless quality or transparency. Web designers use PNG for logos, icons, UI elements, or any image that has text or sharp lines (since PNG will not blur them as JPEG might). PNG supports up to 48-bit color (far beyond typical monitors) and can handle gradations well, though for very high-detail photographic images, PNG files can be larger than JPEG. PNG also supports progressive rendering (interlacing) – an interlaced PNG loads in passes (blurry to sharp), similar to interlaced GIF.
- GIF: Limited to 256 colors, which is a big constraint for photographs or smooth gradients. But GIF supports animation (multiple frames in one file) and is still used for simple animations or memes on the web. GIF also supports a single transparent color. If you have a simple graphic with just a few colors (like

a black-and-white diagram or a small icon), a GIF might be as efficient as a PNG. But typically PNG has largely replaced GIF for static images because of better compression and color support. For animations, new formats like APNG (animated PNG) or even video snippets (MP4/WebM) are more efficient, but GIF remains popular due to universal support.

- JPEG (JPG): The go-to format for photographs on the web. A typical use case: a 4MB high-res photo can be compressed to, say, 200KB as a JPEG with negligible visible quality loss on screen. JPEG's lossy nature makes it unsuitable for images with text or diagrams because it introduces noise around sharp edges. Also, every time you re-save a JPEG, it can lose quality (so keep originals in a lossless format if you need to edit repeatedly). There is also a progressive JPEG option, which loads the image as a low-res full image then gradually sharpens it, which is useful for user experience to see something quickly.
- TIFF: Rarely (if ever) used in web pages because browser support is not universal and file sizes are typically large. TIFF is more for archival images, printing, or use in software like Photoshop. It can use lossless compression (like LZW or Zip) and can store high bit-depth images (like 16-bit per channel from cameras or scanners).

In practice, for web development:

- Use JPEG for photographs or images with many gradients/colors.
- Use PNG for graphics, logos, icons, especially if transparency is needed or if it has few colors (the PNG will compress well).
- Use GIF if you need an animated image or for very small icons with a limited palette (though PNG can often do those too).
- Avoid using BMP or TIFF or other raw formats on web pages.

Newer image formats like WebP and SVG:

- WebP is a newer image format from Google that can be lossy or lossless, often producing smaller files than JPEG or PNG. It supports animation and alpha transparency. Browser support is now widespread (except some older versions or specific browsers). You may encounter it, but since this is an intro, we stick to the classics.
- SVG (Scalable Vector Graphics) is an XML-based vector image format. Great for logos and icons as it is resolution-independent (it scales without losing quality) and often very small in file size for simple graphics. Modern websites use SVGs a lot for logos, icons, illustrations that are vector art. Being text-based, it can be directly embedded or styled with CSS.

Finally, always remember to balance image quality with file size. Overly heavy pages (with huge images) can harm user experience, especially on mobile devices. Tools exist to optimize images (compressing them as much as possible without visible loss). As a developer, it is part of your job to ensure images are web-optimized.

Best Practices: Images

Consider the following suggestions when working with images:

- Always include meaningful alt text for accessibility
- Optimize image file sizes before uploading
- Choose appropriate formats: JPEG for photos, PNG for graphics
- Use relative paths for portability
- Consider responsive images for different screen sizes

- Specify width and height attributes when known
- Test your site with images disabled to ensure it remains usable

3.3.8 Concepts and Terminology

Let us summarize some key concepts and terms introduced in this chapter:

- Elements, Tags, and Attributes: HTML uses tags (like `<p>`, `<img>`) to create elements. Many tags come in pairs with content between (opening `<p>` and closing `</p>`), while some are self-closing (like `<br>` or `<img>`). Attributes (like `src`, `href`, `alt`, `width`, `class`, etc.) are additional pieces of information included in the opening tag to modify or provide data about the element.
- Block-level vs Inline: Block-level elements (paragraphs `<p>`, headings `<h1>`–`<h6>`, lists `<ul>`/`<ol>`, `<div>`, etc.) typically start on a new line and can contain other blocks or inline elements. Inline elements (`<a>`, `<span>`, `<img>`, `<em>`, etc.) flow within a line of text and generally only contain text or other inline elements.
- Basic Text Elements: Paragraphs (`<p>`), line breaks (`<br>`), headings (`<h1>`...`<h6>`), bold (`<b>` or `<strong>`), italic (`<i>` or `<em>`), blockquote (`<blockquote>`), horizontal rule (`<hr>`), subscript (`<sub>`), superscript (`<sup>`), etc.
- Lists: Unordered lists (`<ul>`) with `<li>` items (bulleted), ordered lists (`<ol>`) with `<li>` items (numbered), and description/definition lists (`<dl>` with `<dt>` terms and `<dd>` descriptions). Lists can be nested inside list items to create sub-lists.
- Div and Span: Generic containers for grouping content (block-level `<div>`, inline `<span>`). Often used with `class` or `id` attributes to apply CSS styles or for scripting.
- Hyperlinks: Created with `<a href="...">...</a>` (anchor tag). The `href` attribute holds the URL or path to the target resource. Anchors can also link to an internal page fragment (`href="#section2"` for example). Attributes: `target` (like `_blank` for new tab), `title` (tooltip text), and in older usage `name` (for anchor name, replaced by using `id` nowadays).
- Images: Embedded with `<img src="..." alt="...">`. Key attributes: `src` (source URL/path), `alt` (alternative text for accessibility), `title` (optional tooltip), `width`/`height` (to specify displayed dimensions, optional but useful). Understand the concept of aspect ratio and that altering width/height can distort if not proportional. Images are inline elements by default.
- Paths and URLs: Relative path (relative to current page's location, e.g. `images/pic.png`, `../docs/file.pdf`), Absolute path (starting from root `/`, e.g. `/images/pic.png` might refer to root of current domain), URL (including protocol and domain, e.g. `https://example.com/images/pic.png`). Relative paths help with portability of the site `..` The `..` notation moves up directories.
- Floats and Alignment (Images/Text): Using deprecated `align` attribute or modern CSS `float` to wrap text around images (float left or right). Also know that these presentational attributes are deprecated and replaced by CSS (we briefly introduced `style="float:left"` as an example).
- Deprecated vs Standard practices: Awareness that some HTML features (like `<font>` tag, `align` attribute, etc.) are deprecated, meaning they are outdated and replaced by CSS or other mechanisms. Modern HTML5 focuses on using semantic elements and CSS for styling. Deprecated features may still work but should not be used in new code.
- Browser Cache: The browser's local storage of pages and images to speed up subsequent loads. If images

are cached, the browser may not re-download them every time. Users can toggle image loading; if images are off, `alt` text is displayed and no request is made for the image file, reducing load time (useful on slow connections or for accessibility). Cache can be observed by checking the browser's temporary files; images not loaded will not appear there.

- Factors in Page Load Time: Bandwidth, latency, server response, file sizes. Particularly, images and other media often dominate file size, so optimizing them (compressing, choosing appropriate formats) greatly affects user experience. High latency or low bandwidth makes large files very slow to load.
- Compression (Lossless vs Lossy): Lossless compression (as in PNG, GIF's LZW) reduces file size without losing any data (the original can be exactly reconstructed). Lossy compression (as in JPEG) sacrifices some fidelity for much greater size reduction. Lossy is acceptable for photographs where a slight loss of detail is not noticeable, but not for text or precise graphics.
- Image Formats:
    - GIF: 8-bit color (256 colors), supports animation and transparency (1 color fully transparent). Uses LZW compression (lossless for images with ≤ 256 colors). Good for simple graphics/animations, not for high-color images.
    - PNG: Supports 24-bit (or more) color, full alpha transparency, lossless compression (generally produces smaller files than GIF for similar content). Great for graphics, screenshots, images requiring transparency or sharp details.
    - JPEG: 24-bit color, lossy compression (degree adjustable). Best for photographs or complex imagery where slight loss is acceptable for huge reduction in size. Not good for text or simple graphics (causes blur).
    - TIFF: Mentioned for completeness, and is a versatile format often lossless, used outside web (scanning/print). Not a web format (browsers typically do not display TIFF).

  (Also noted modern developments like patent issues with GIF leading to PNG, and open source movement's role.)
- Accessibility considerations: Using `alt` text for images, using proper heading hierarchy (`<h1>`...`<h6>` in order), using lists for listable content, etc., all contribute to making content understandable by screen readers and assistive tech.
- Character Entities: Special codes for displaying reserved or special characters in HTML, always starting with & and ending with ;.

3.4   HTML Tables

For displaying information in a structured grid (rows and columns), HTML provides the table elements. Tables are useful for showing tabular data (like spreadsheets on a web page). It is important to note that in modern web design, tables should not be used for page layout (as was common in the 1990s) but purely for actual data tables. CSS has taken over layout duties. However, understanding HTML tables is crucial for cases where you have data that naturally fits into a matrix form (e.g., comparison charts, schedules, etc.).

An HTML table is defined with the `<table>` tag, containing one or more `<tr>` (table row) elements. Inside each `<tr>`, you put table cells – either `<td>` (table data cell) for normal cells or `<th>` (table header cell) for header cells (which are typically displayed in bold and centered by default). Conceptually, each `<tr>` creates a new row, and cells within it (`<td>` or `<th>`) form the columns of that row.

3.4.1 Table Element Structure

The basic structure of a table in HTML:

```html
<table>
  <tr>
    <th>Header 1</th>
    <th>Header 2</th>
    <th>Header 3</th>
  </tr>
  <tr>
    <td>Row1, Col1</td>
    <td>Row1, Col2</td>
    <td>Row1, Col3</td>
  </tr>
  <tr>
    <td>Row2, Col1</td>
    <td>Row2, Col2</td>
    <td>Row2, Col3</td>
  </tr>
</table>
```

This would produce a table with 3 columns and 3 rows (if you count the header row). The first row uses `<th>` for cells, which by default renders as bold and centered text (and some browsers may slightly shade header cells). The subsequent rows use `<td>` for standard cells. By default, most browsers draw a borderless table (no gridlines). In older HTML, one would often use `border="1"` attribute on the table to quickly add a border, but that is another presentational attribute which is better done with CSS now. For example, you could do `<table style="border: 1px solid black; border-collapse: collapse;">` and also style the `td`, `th` with borders to get a grid.

Each table cell can contain virtually any content: text, images, links, even other tables. However, be cautious with nesting tables as it can get complicated. Typically, cells contain text or form elements or images. All cells in a row will by default be the same height (matching the tallest cell in that row), and all cells in a column will align under each other.

By default, a table will be only as wide as needed to fit its content. If content is narrow, the table is narrow. If a cell has a long word or large image, it can stretch the column width. You can set a table's width (and other properties) with attributes or CSS.

Example of a simple table with some styling and how it looks in HTML:

```html
<table border = "1">
  <tr>
    <th>Name</th>
```

```html
 4    <th>Age</th>
 5    <th>Gender</th>
 6   </tr>
 7   <tr>
 8    <td>Bert</td>
 9    <td>22</td>
10    <td>Male</td>
11   </tr>
12   <tr>
13    <td>Mary</td>
14    <td>33</td>
15    <td>Female</td>
16   </tr>
17 </table>
```

If using the deprecated `border` attribute with value "1", the browser draws a simple 1-pixel border around each cell. The above would render as a 2-row, 3-column table with headers "Name, Age, Gender" and two data rows. The header cells are bold and centered by default.

Using modern style, we might instead do:

```html
 1 <table style = "border: 2px solid blue; border-collapse: collapse;">
 2   <tr>
 3     <th>Name</th><th>Age</th><th>Gender</th>
 4   </tr>
 5   <tr>
 6     <td>Bert</td><td>22</td><td>Male</td>
 7   </tr>
 8   <tr>
 9     <td>Mary</td><td>33</td><td>Female</td>
10   </tr>
11 </table>
```

And in CSS define `th, td { border: 1px solid blue; padding: 4px; }`.
The `border-collapse: collapse;` on the table makes adjacent cell borders collapse into a single border (so you do not get double lines between cells).

By default, text in `<td>` is left-aligned and vertically centered within the cell (some browsers might baseline-align it, but generally middle vertically). In `<th>`, text is centered both horizontally and vertically by default.

3.4.2 Table Attributes: Width, Cellspacing, Cellpadding, Alignment

There are a number of legacy attributes for tables that control layout. While these can be done with CSS now, you will encounter them or might use them for quick prototypes:

- `width` attribute on `<table>`: Specifies the width of the table. Can be in pixels or percentage. For example, `<table width="100%">` makes the table span the full width of its container (often the browser viewport or parent element). `<table width="500">` fixes it at 500 pixels wide. If the content does not naturally fill that width, the extra space will either create padding or be distributed somehow (in practice, the browser will make columns wider to meet the width).
- `cellspacing` attribute: This sets the space between table cells (the gap between each cell's border, essentially). In older HTML, `cellspacing="10"` would put 10 pixels of space between cells. If you have seen a table with big gaps, that is cellspacing. Setting `cellspacing="0"` (or using CSS `border-collapse: collapse;`) removes that gap so cells are flush with each other (shared borders).
- `cellpadding` attribute: This sets the space between the cell border and the cell content, and is essentially the padding inside each cell. E.g., `cellpadding="5"` gives a 5-pixel cushion inside each cell so text is not jammed right against the cell border. In CSS terms, this corresponds to padding. If you omit it, some browsers default to 1px or 2px padding, others to 0.

Think of a cell like a little box: cellpadding is inside it (between text and the edge), cellspacing is outside (between this cell and the neighboring cell).

- `align` and `valign` on `<td>` or `<tr>`: `align` can be "left", "center", "right" to horizontally align the cell's content. `valign` can be "top", "middle", "bottom" to vertically align the content within the cell. For example: `<td align="right" valign="top">` would put that cell's content at the top-right corner of the cell. By default, `<td>` align is left and valign is middle. `<th>` defaults to center/middle (for most browsers).

These attributes can be handy. For instance, if you want a column of numbers to align to the right (common in tables of figures to line up the decimal places, etc.), you could put `align="right"` on those `<td>` cells or on the `<col>` or via CSS.

Let us modify our earlier table example to use some of these attributes:

```html
<table width = "50%" cellspacing = "10" cellpadding = "20" border = "2">
  <tr>
    <th valign = "top">Name<br><br><br></th>
    <th valign = "middle">Age</th>
    <th valign = "bottom" align = "right">Gender</th>
  </tr>
  <tr>
    <td>Bert</td>
    <td align = "center">22</td>
    <td align = "right">Male</td>
  </tr>
  <tr>
    <td>Mary</td>
```

```html
14    <td align = "center">33</td>
15    <td align = "right">Female</td>
16   </tr>
17 </table>
```

We set width to 50%, so the table will take half the available width of the page (centered by default? Actually, not centered, just 50% of width, aligned to the left unless specified otherwise). We put `cellspacing=10` so there is a noticeable gap between cells, and `cellpadding=20` to make cells quite roomy inside. We gave the table a border of 2 (so outer border and inner cell borders are thicker).

In the header row:

- The "Name" header cell has `valign="top"` and we inserted a few `<br>` (line breaks) after the word to demonstrate top alignment. Adding breaks makes that cell taller, and with valign top, the word "Name" sticks to the top of the cell, whereas "Age" (middle) stays in the middle of its cell, and "Gender" (bottom) goes to bottom. We also gave "Gender" `align="right"` so the text "Gender" is pushed to the right side of that header cell.
- In data rows, we aligned the Age column center (so numbers appear centered in their cells) and the Gender column right (so "Male" and "Female" text align to the right side of that cell). This is just to illustrate alignment.

With the breaks in the Name header, that cell becomes taller than the others in that row; because of how table row height works, the entire row gets that height, and "Age" and "Gender" cells also become that tall, but since their content is middle or bottom aligned, you see them positioned differently (Age in middle, Gender at bottom of those cells).

This is a bit contrived, but it shows the effect of `valign`. Usually, you would not put `<br>` like that just for alignment; instead, you would use CSS to set cell height or padding to achieve visible spacing.

Different attribute combinations can conflict or interact. For example, if you set a table `width` too small to fit its content plus cellpadding, the browser will still make it big enough to fit everything (it will not cut off content; instead the specified width might be ignored or the content will overflow). If you set a very large cellpadding and a fixed width, that leaves less room for text.

A note: the `border` attribute, when combined with cellspacing, can produce double-line borders if cellspacing > 0 (since each cell's border is separate). That is why in CSS using `border-collapse: collapse` is often better (it merges the border between two adjacent cells into one border).

3.4.3   Spanning Rows and Columns (Colspan and Rowspan)

Sometimes, you need a cell that spans multiple columns or rows. For instance, you might have a table header that spans two columns, or a cell that acts as a category label spanning several rows.

- `colspan` attribute on a `<th>` or `<td>`: indicates that the cell extends across multiple columns. For example, `<td colspan="3">` in a row means that cell takes up the space of 3 cells horizontally in that row. You would use this and then not include the individual cells that it covers. So if a row has a cell with `colspan=3`, that row might have fewer `<td>` elements because one is spanning over what would have been others.

- `rowspan` attribute: similar idea, but vertically. A cell with `rowspan="2"` will occupy two rows vertically. It will merge with the cell position directly below (assuming it is in a row below). When you use a rowspan, in the subsequent row that it spans into, you have one less cell to specify because the spanning cell is covering a slot in that row.

Example scenario: A table where the first cell spans two rows (like a side header), and maybe the second cell spans two columns in the second row, etc. It can get confusing to visualize, but let us do a simple example:

Suppose we want a table like:

1	2		4
	3	3a	

Where cell "1" spans two rows (a tall cell on the left), cell "2" spans two columns (a wide cell on the top row), and then on the second row we have "3" and "3a" under that "2", and "4" is a cell that spans two rows on the right. This is tricky, but let us simplify: we will make a table demonstrating one cell spanning rows and one spanning columns:

```
<table border = "1">
  <tr>
    <th rowspan = "2">Countries</th>
    <th colspan = "2">Cities</th>
  </tr>
  <tr>
    <td>New York</td>
    <td>Los Angeles</td>
  </tr>
</table>
```

In this example:
- The first `<th>` has `rowspan="2"` and contains "Countries". It appears as a tall cell covering both the first and second rows in the first column.
- The second `<th>` in the first row has `colspan="2"` with content "Cities". It stretches across two columns in that first row.
- On the second row, we only put two `<td>` cells ("New York" and "Los Angeles"). Why only two? Because the first column is already occupied by the `rowspan=2` cell "Countries" from the first row.

Using row/col spans can create complex layouts. Sometimes it is easier to sketch the table grid and label each cell with how many spans it should cover.

Key points when spanning:

- If you span into a space, you omit what would have been cells in that space in the HTML, otherwise you will have too many cells in a row or column.
- Browsers will calculate the layout such that spanned cells expand appropriately. If row heights differ, the spanned cell's height is sum of the spanned rows, similarly for column widths.

3.4.4   Additional Table Elements

Beyond the basic table structure, HTML provides several elements for better organization and semantics:

Caption Element

The `<caption>` element provides a title or description for the table. It should be the first child of the `<table>` element:

```html
<table>
  <caption>Table 1: Quarterly Sales Data</caption>
  <tr>
    <th>Quarter</th>
    <th>Sales</th>
  </tr>
  ...
</table>
```

By default, captions appear centered above the table. You can use CSS to position them below or style them differently. Captions are important for accessibility and documentation.

Table Sections: thead, tbody, and tfoot

These elements group rows by function, which helps with:
- Styling different sections separately
- Printing (headers/footers can repeat on each page)
- Scrolling (body can scroll while header stays fixed)
- Screen reader navigation

```html
<table>
  <caption>Table of Authors and Their Books</caption>

  <colgroup>
    <col style = "background-color:lightblue">
    <col style = "background-color:lightyellow">
    <col style = "background-color:lightgreen">
  </colgroup>

```

```
10    <thead>
11      <tr>
12        <th>Author Name</th>
13        <th>Title of Book</th>
14        <th>Year Published</th>
15      </tr>
16    </thead>
17
18    <tfoot>
19      <tr>
20        <td>Number of Authors</td>
21        <td colspan = "2">4</td>
22      </tr>
23    </tfoot>
24
25    <tbody>
26      <tr>
27        <td>Beatrix Potter</td>
28        <td>The Tale of Peter Rabbit</td>
29        <td>1902</td>
30      </tr>
31      <tr>
32        <td>A.A. Milne</td>
33        <td>Winnie the Pooh</td>
34        <td>1926</td>
35      </tr>
36      <tr>
37        <td>Eric Carle</td>
38        <td>The Very Hungry Caterpillar</td>
39        <td>1969</td>
40      </tr>
41      <tr>
42        <td>Marcus Pfister</td>
43        <td>The Rainbow Fish</td>
44        <td>1999</td>
45      </tr>
46    </tbody>
47 </table>
```

Note that `<tfoot>` appears before `<tbody>` in the HTML but browsers render it at the bottom. This allows the footer to load before potentially long body content.

Column Grouping: col and colgroup

The `<colgroup>` and `<col>` elements allow you to apply styles to entire columns:

```html
<table>
  <colgroup>
    <col span = "1" style = "background-color: #f0f0f0">
    <col span = "2" style = "background-color: #e0e0e0">
  </colgroup>
  <tr>
    <th>Product</th>
    <th>Price</th>
    <th>Quantity</th>
  </tr>
  <tr>
    <td>Widget</td>
    <td>$10.00</td>
    <td>5</td>
  </tr>
</table>
```

The first `<col>` styles the first column, the second `<col>` with `span="2"` styles the next two columns. This is more efficient than styling individual cells.

Important notes about col and colgroup:

- They must appear after `<caption>` (if present) but before any `<thead>`, `<tbody>`, `<tfoot>`, or `<tr>` elements
- They only affect certain style properties (like background, border, width, visibility)
- Individual cell styles override column styles

Table Summary (Accessibility)

For accessibility, the `summary` attribute was used in HTML4/XHTML to provide a description of the table's structure for screen reader users:

```html
<table summary="This table lists student names and their scores on midterm and final exams.">
```

However, `summary` is obsolete in HTML5. Instead, use:

- `<caption>` for visible titles
- Proper `<th>` elements with appropriate scope
- Clear, descriptive text around the table
- ARIA attributes if needed for complex tables

Aligning a Table on the Page

By default, a table (being a block element) will be left-aligned. If you want to center a table in the page, older HTML allowed `align="center"` on the `<table>` tag. That is deprecated in Strict HTML, but still works in many cases or in Transitional doctype.

For example: `<table align="center">...</table>` would center the table in the window. `align="right"` would float it to the right (with text wrapping on the left side of it potentially).

However, the `align` attribute on tables is deprecated, so instead you can use CSS. The common CSS trick to center a block (like a table) is `margin-left: auto; margin-right: auto;` provided you have given it a set width or it can shrink-wrap its content. Setting both margins to auto causes equal distribution of leftover space, centering the element.

For instance, if we had:

```
1  <table style = "width:50%; margin-left:auto; margin-right:auto;">
2    ... rows ...
3  </table>
```

This would center the table horizontally in its container. The table is 50% wide, and the auto margins center it.

In summary: to center a table, do not use `<table align="center">` in modern HTML, use CSS margin auto or a container with `text-align: center` (and then reset text-align inside).

Best Practices: Tables

Consider the following suggestions when using tables in your HTML documents:
- Use tables only for tabular data, not for layout
- Always include header cells (`<th>`) for better accessibility
- Use caption to provide context
- Consider using thead, tbody, tfoot for complex tables
- Keep tables simple when possible as complex spanning can confuse screen readers
- Style with CSS rather than deprecated attributes
- Test tables at different screen sizes

Common Pitfalls: Tables

Similarly, consider the following suggestions to avoid certain pitfalls:
- Do not use tables for page layout (use CSS instead)
- Remember that colspan reduces the number of `<td>` elements needed in that row
- Always validate when using rowspan/colspan to ensure correct structure
- Consider accessibility: use `<th>` for headers and scope attributes for complex tables

3.5   Development Tools for HTML

Writing HTML by hand in a text editor (like Notepad or VS Code) is fine for learning and for small pages, but as projects grow, using HTML development tools can greatly improve productivity and reduce errors. These tools range from feature-rich code editors to WYSIWYG (What You See Is What You Get) editors that let you design pages visually.

Some categories of development tools for HTML include:

- Text Editors / IDEs with HTML support: Modern code editors such as Visual Studio Code, Atom, Sublime Text, or IDEs like WebStorm or Adobe Dreamweaver provide syntax highlighting, auto-completion, and error checking for HTML (as well as CSS and JavaScript). As you type <, they might show a list of tag suggestions. When you type an opening tag, many will auto-insert the closing tag. They often also have snippets (e.g., you type ! in VS Code in an HTML file and press tab, it can expand to a full HTML5 boilerplate template). These features speed up writing code.
- WYSIWYG HTML Editors: These allow users to design a page visually, similar to using a word processor or desktop publishing software, and the tool generates the HTML code for you. Examples historically include Adobe Dreamweaver (which has both code and design view), Microsoft FrontPage (older), KompoZer (open source), etc. Even word processors like Microsoft Word can export to HTML (though usually not very clean code). Modern replacements might be more along the lines of website builders (which are online tools) or content management systems with rich text editors (like editing in WordPress's GUI). These tools often let you drag-and-drop images, draw tables by clicking, etc., and they produce the underlying markup.
- Browser Developer Tools: Every modern browser has developer tools (press F12 in Chrome/Firefox, or right-click "Inspect"). These are not for writing pages from scratch, but they are invaluable for debugging and tweaking HTML/CSS/JS on the fly. In the context of HTML, you can use them to inspect the DOM (Document Object Model) which is the browser's internal representation of the HTML. You can live-edit HTML elements or attributes in the dev tools to see how changes would look, without reloading. This is more for testing changes or debugging layout issues.
- Other Utilities: There are tools for validating HTML (we mentioned W3C's validator). Some editors have built-in validators or linters that will underline mistakes in your HTML code (like forgetting to close a tag). There are also tools for formatting or tidying code (some editors auto-format on save, or you can use specific HTML tidy tools as discussed).

Specifically mentioned in the original text:

- MS Expression Web: This was a Microsoft web development tool, part of the Expression Studio, intended to replace FrontPage. It had a design view and code view, support for modern standards (at the time), etc. It is discontinued now (last version around 2012). But it exemplified a high-level editor where you could visually design or get help with code.
- Adobe Dreamweaver: Still around as part of Adobe Creative Cloud. It provides a visual design interface as well as coding environment, and integrates with site management (FTP upload, etc.). It is a commercial product popular with designers who want some visual editing capability.
- Aptana Studio: An open-source web development IDE (built on Eclipse). It supports HTML, CSS, JS, and server languages. Provides code completion, project management, etc. It might be a bit dated now (most have moved to lighter editors like VS Code), but it was notable especially around the 2000s.

- These tools often have features like drag-and-drop for creating tables or forms, color pickers for styles, and site management features (like keeping track of all files, doing search/replace across the site, etc.).

Using an HTML editor can dramatically increase productivity because:

- You do not have to remember every tag or attribute by heart; the editor can suggest them and auto-complete them.
- They can catch errors (e.g., some editors will give a warning that you started a `<table>` but forgot to close it).
- Many have built-in templates or generators for common structures.
- Split view or live preview: some editors show you a live rendering as you code.
- They handle mundane tasks like properly indenting code, closing tags, etc., letting you focus on content and structure.

Additionally, these tools often integrate with CSS editing and JavaScript debugging. For beginners, a graphical editor can be appealing because you can design something without deep knowledge of code, but as you learn HTML, you might prefer writing code directly to have cleaner and more controlled output.

High level editors also help with things like:

- Link management: If you rename a file, they can update all links that pointed to it.
- Path auto-calculation: If you insert an image from somewhere, they can automatically figure out the relative path and insert it for you, reducing mistakes in references.
- Snippet libraries: Quick insertion of common patterns (like a standard table or form snippet).
- Project preview: Some can run a local server or show the page in multiple browsers to preview.

One should be cautious: WYSIWYG editors in the past had a reputation for generating bloated or non-semantic code (e.g., lots of nested tables or inline styles). Modern ones have improved, but it is still valuable to know HTML to go in and clean up or tweak the code that the editor produces.

In summary, as you move from learning HTML to building real projects, leveraging development tools is wise. They reduce errors and speed up your workflow. At the same time, try not to rely blindly on them â€" understanding the code is crucial, because you might need to fix or optimize what the tool generates.

3.6   Content Management Tools

Hand-coding individual HTML files is feasible for small websites, but as a site grows (dozens or hundreds of pages) or when non-technical users need to contribute content, a more scalable approach is needed. This is where Content Management Systems (CMS) and related tools come into play. Content management tools are software platforms that allow creating, organizing, and publishing web content without manually editing HTML for every change.

A Content Management System typically provides:

- A web-based interface (or application) where users can create and edit content in a rich text editor (similar to a word processor interface) instead of writing HTML. The CMS will handle converting that into proper HTML behind the scenes.
- Organization of content into categories, with features like menus, navigation, search, etc., generated automatically.
- Templates or themes that separate design from content. The site's look and feel is defined in templates, and the content is plugged into those templates. This way, if you want to redesign the site, you modify

the template rather than every page.
- User management, so multiple people can contribute with different roles (authors, editors, admins).
- Often, dynamic features like commenting, workflow (draft $\to$ review $\to$ publish processes), and media management (uploading images/documents and reusing them).

Examples of popular CMS:
- WordPress: By far one of the most widely used CMS platforms (powers a significant portion of websites). It started as a blogging platform but now is used for everything from simple blogs to complex websites. It is PHP-based and open source. Users can pick themes, install plugins for extra features, and add posts/pages through an admin interface. WordPress generates the HTML pages dynamically from a database.
- Drupal: Another open source CMS, more technical/flexible in some ways (often used for larger, complex sites with custom content types).
- Joomla: Somewhere between WordPress and Drupal in complexity.
- Wix, Squarespace, Weebly: These are proprietary website builder platforms (Software as a Service (SaaS)) where users build sites via drag-and-drop in a browser. They handle hosting and everything, often for small business/personal sites.
- Enterprise CMS: For large organizations, systems like Adobe Experience Manager, Sitecore, or SharePoint might be used, which integrate with other enterprise systems.

The advantage of using a CMS:
- Non-developers can manage content. For example, a marketing team can post news articles or update text on the site through a friendly interface. They do not need to know HTML (though a little knowledge still helps to fix minor formatting issues).
- Consistency: Since pages use templates, the header, footer, navigation, etc., are consistent across all pages and centrally managed. You change the template once to affect all pages.
- Maintenance: Need to update a sidebar across all pages? In a CMS, that sidebar might be a single include or widget, updated in one place. In static HTML, you would have to edit every page or use a server-side include mechanism.
- Features: Many CMS come with built-in features like search, SEO-friendly URLs, caching for performance, etc., which you would otherwise have to implement yourself.
- Scalability: They often use a database to store content, which is better for large amounts of content than having hundreds of .html files to manage.

That said, CMS have a learning curve and overhead. For a small site, it might be overkill to set up a whole WordPress installation if a few static pages would do. But as soon as you want a blog or frequently updated content, a CMS shines.

Another aspect of content management is version control and deployment:
- If you still code pages manually or have a team of developers, using a version control system (like Git) helps manage changes to the HTML/CSS/JS files. It is not a CMS per se, but a tool to manage content code.
- There are static site generators (like Jekyll, Hugo) which are a kind of middle ground: you write content in a simpler format (Markdown, etc.) and the generator builds static HTML files. This is great for blogs or documentation sites where you want the performance of static files but the convenience of templates and not writing raw HTML each time.

Content management in a broader sense could also refer to managing digital assets (images, PDFs), ensuring broken links are avoided, and making content updates in a structured way. Tools like link checkers or site-wide search/replace scripts can assist in content maintenance for static sites.

In professional environments, content might go through a staging process (make changes in a test environment, review, then publish to live). CMS often support such workflows; without a CMS, teams use manual processes or automated deployment pipelines.

In summary, content management tools and systems enable you to handle web content at scale. They abstract much of the low-level HTML editing away, which reduces human error and allows people to focus on content quality. As a developer or power user, knowing how to work with a CMS (and occasionally drop into the code if needed) is a valuable skill. While this textbook focuses on the fundamentals of building pages, be aware that in many real-world scenarios, you will be adding content through a CMS interface rather than typing `<div>`s from scratch, but understanding HTML deeply will help you make better use of those systems (for example, when something in the What You See Is What You Get (WYSIWYG) editor does not look right, you can switch to the HTML view and fix a nested tag).

3.7 Chapter Review

Problem 3.1 What is the purpose of HTML in the context of web development?

Explain how HTML is used in a three-tier web application (client-server-database) and why it is often called the structure or skeleton of a webpage.

Problem 3.2 Describe the basic structure of an HTML document.

What are the roles of the `<head>` and `<body>` sections in an HTML page? Name a few elements that belong in the head, and a few that belong in the body.

Problem 3.3 What is the difference between a block-level element and an inline element in HTML?

Give two examples of each and describe how each type of element affects the layout of content on the page.

Problem 3.4 How do you create a paragraph break and a line break in HTML?

Which tag would you use for a new paragraph versus just moving to a new line within the same paragraph?

Problem 3.5 List three HTML tags that are used for text formatting and explain their effect.

For example, what do `<strong>`, `<em>`, `<sub>` tags do when applied to text?

Problem 3.6 What tag would you use to create a hyperlink and what are the minimum attributes required?

Write a sample anchor (`<a>`) tag that links to `https://www.example.com` with the link text "Visit Example". Also mention what `target="_blank"` does.

Problem 3.7 Explain the use of the `alt` attribute in an `<img>` tag. Why is it important?

What happens if an image fails to load or a user is using a screen reader? Provide an example of a good alt text for an image of a chart.

Problem 3.8 How do relative file paths differ from absolute URLs in the context of linking or embedding content?

If your page is at `http://mywebsite.com/about/team.html`, what would `src="images/photo.jpg"` refer to versus `src="http://mywebsite.com/images/photo.jpg"`? Why might you use one over the other?

Problem 3.9 What is the effect of using `float: left` on an image in CSS (or `align="left"` in old HTML)?

Describe how text will flow around an image that is floated to the left side of a paragraph. How would this differ if the image were not floated?

Problem 3.10 Define "deprecated" in terms of HTML features and provide an example.

What does it mean if an element or attribute is deprecated? Name one deprecated element or attribute (like `<font>` or `align`) and the modern alternative to achieve the same effect.

Problem 3.11 How can you create a bulleted list and a numbered list in HTML?

Which tags are used for lists and list items? Write a short example of an unordered list with three items and an ordered list with three items.

Problem 3.12 In an HTML table, what do the `<tr>`, `<td>`, and `<th>` tags represent?

Explain the structure of an HTML table row and how header cells differ from data cells. How would a browser typically render a `<th>` differently from a `<td>`?

Problem 3.13 How would you make a single table cell span across two columns in a table?

Which attribute is used and how does it affect the HTML you write for that row? Similarly, what attribute would make a cell span multiple rows?

Problem 3.14 What are `cellpadding` and `cellspacing` in tables, and how do they affect the appearance of a table?

If a table has `cellpadding="10"`, what will you notice compared to one with `cellpadding="2"`? What does `cellspacing="0"` achieve? (If these attributes are deprecated, mention the CSS equivalent.)

Problem 3.15 What is a content management system (CMS) and why might a company use one instead of static HTML files?

Discuss how a CMS like WordPress or Drupal changes the way content is created and maintained. What are some advantages of using a CMS for a website with a lot of content or multiple editors?

Problem 3.16 Identify two features of advanced HTML editors or development tools that make coding HTML easier or less error-prone.

For instance, how do code autocompletion or syntax highlighting help a developer? Name a specific tool (like VS Code, Dreamweaver, etc.) and a feature you find useful.

Problem 3.17 Explain the concept of browser caching in relation to images on a webpage.

If you visit a webpage twice, why do images often load faster the second time? What role does the `alt` attribute play if images are turned off or fail to load?

Problem 3.18 Why is it important to include alternative text (`alt`) and use proper headings (`<h1>`, `<h2>`, etc.) beyond just visual considerations?

Relate your answer to accessibility and search engines: how do these practices benefit users with disabilities and search engine optimization (SEO)?

Problem 3.19 What are HTML character entities and when would you use them?

Give three examples of common character entities (like `&`, `<`, `©`) and explain why you cannot just type the literal character in some cases.

Problem 3.20 Describe the purpose and structure of the `<thead>`, `<tbody>`, and `<tfoot>` elements in HTML tables.

How do these elements help organize table content? What benefits do they provide for styling, printing, or accessibility?

4. HTML II: Forms, Standards, and Advanced Features

In the previous chapter, we introduced the basics of HTML, suitable for creating static web pages. In this chapter, we delve into more advanced HTML topics that enable interactive and modern web applications. In particular, we focus on HTML forms, that allow users to input data and send requests to web servers, the cornerstone of dynamic, data-driven websites. We also explore the standards that govern HTML, including the differences between standard HTML and XHTML (a stricter XML-based formulation of HTML), and how to ensure our HTML conforms to standards through validation. Additionally, we discuss character encodings (such as Unicode) and MIME types, which are essential for proper interpretation of content on the web. Finally, we examine the improvements and new capabilities introduced with HTML5, which modernized web development with semantic elements, native multimedia support, and enhanced form controls. By mastering these topics, you will be able to create forms that interact with server-side programs, write standards-compliant code, and leverage modern HTML5 features to build robust web applications.

Learning Objectives

By the end of this chapter, you should be able to:

- Create and structure HTML forms with various input elements (text fields, menus, radio buttons, checkboxes, file uploads, etc.) and understand how form data is sent to a server via GET or POST.
- Distinguish between HTML and XHTML, understand the goals of XHTML and key syntax differences (such as case-sensitivity and required closures), and include proper document declarations (DOCTYPE, character encoding, namespaces) in your pages.
- Validate HTML/XHTML documents using W3C standards, identify and fix common markup errors, and understand the importance of writing standard-compliant code (and the consequences of quirks mode if you do not).
- Explain character encodings and how Unicode enables multi-language text. Also, specify a page's encoding (like UTF-8) and use HTML character entities for special characters.
- Understand MIME types and their role in web communications, from how servers label content types (HTML, CSS, images, etc.) to how browsers choose plugins or handlers for content, and why certain form submissions and email attachments require special encoding (like `multipart/form-data` or Base64).
- Use HTML5 enhancements, including new input types (e.g. email, date, color) and attributes (e.g. required, placeholder), as well as incorporate semantic structural elements, media playback, and basic graphics (canvas/SVG) into web pages.

4.1 HTML Forms

A basic HTML page becomes far more powerful when it includes a form. Forms enable user interactivity by collecting input in the browser and sending it to a web server for processing. In a typical web application, a form submission will trigger a server-side program (for example, a PHP script) to run and generate a response

DOI: 10.1201/9781003727651-4

(such as a results page). In this section, we cover how to construct forms and their elements, how the browser sends form data to the server, and simple examples illustrating form behavior. We will also briefly touch on how client-side and server-side scripts interact with forms (though the server-side programming (PHP, etc.) will be explored in later chapters.)

4.1.1 What a Form Needs to Do

At a high level, an HTML form's job is to collect user input and send it to the right place for processing. To perform this job, a form requires three essential components. First, it needs input controls for user data through form elements like text fields, checkboxes, radio buttons, and drop-down menus where users enter or select information. Second, it must identify a target program on the server, typically specified via an action URL that points to a server-side script (for example, a `.php` program) which will handle the input. Third, it needs a submission mechanism, usually one or more submit buttons that the user can click to send the form data. When triggered, the browser packages up the data and sends an HTTP request to the server.

In HTML, several elements work together to accomplish these tasks. The main container is the `<form>` element, and inside it we include various form widgets (the input controls and other interactive elements). Each input control that should be sent to the server is given a name and a current value (for example, a text field might have `name="username"` and whatever the user types as its value). When the user submits the form, the browser collects the name/value pairs from all the form's inputs and sends them to the server as part of the request.

4.1.2 The `<form>` Element

The `<form>` element is a container for all the input elements and labels that make up the user input interface. A simple form tag looks like:

```
1  <form action = "server-script.php" method = "GET">
2      ...form fields...
3      <input type = "submit" value = "Submit Form">
4  </form>
```

The form tag in this example includes two essential attributes that control how the form operates. The action attribute specifies the URL of the server-side program that will process the form data. This can be an absolute URL (including `http://` or `https://` and a domain) or a relative URL pointing to a script on the same server. Without an action specified, the form cannot be properly processed, since the browser would not know where to send the data. If the `action` attribute is left empty or is omitted entirely, the form will by default submit to the current page URL, which is rarely useful unless that page is specifically designed to handle the incoming data. The method attribute specifies the HTTP method the browser will use when sending the form data. The two common methods are `"GET"` and `"POST"`, which we will discuss in detail shortly. If you omit the method attribute, the browser defaults to `"GET"`.

The `<form>` element typically contains other elements like `<input>`, `<select>`, `<textarea>`, and so on, which define the actual input controls. It can also contain non-interactive elements (text, images, etc.) and layout elements to arrange the form. A form can include multiple submit buttons or other specialized inputs to enhance functionality (like reset buttons or image-based submission, discussed later).

 A single HTML page can contain multiple `<form>` sections, but forms cannot be nested inside one another.

4.1.3 GET versus POST Methods

When a user submits a form, the browser sends an HTTP request to the server URL specified by the form's action. The method attribute of the form determines how the form data is included in that request. Understanding the distinction between GET and POST is fundamental to web development, as each method has specific characteristics that make it appropriate for different situations.

The GET Method

With the GET method, form data is appended to the URL as a query string. The browser takes each named form field and its value, URL-encodes them (converting spaces, special characters, and other unsafe characters to a safe format), and appends them to the target URL after a `?` character. For example, if the form action is `search.php` and has fields `q=Arctic` and `hl=en`, the browser might request `search.php?hl=en&q=Arctic`. Multiple name/value pairs are joined with `&` characters.

Using GET has several important implications. First, the submitted data is visible in the URL, which is useful for debugging and allows users to bookmark or share specific queries, but may expose sensitive information if used inappropriately. Second, URLs (including the query string) have length limits, typically a few thousand characters at most, and so GET is not suitable for very large form submissions. Third, GET requests are intended to be idempotent and safe, meaning they should not change server state. The W3C recommends using GET for forms that do not cause side effects such as database modifications. If a user refreshes a page that resulted from a GET request, the browser simply re-fetches the same URL, which is usually harmless for read-only operations. However, if a GET request had caused a database insert, refreshing could accidentally repeat the insertion. Finally, because of how browsers handle caching and the browser history, a form submitted with GET may be resubmitted inadvertently if the user refreshes the result page or shares the URL with others.

The POST Method

With the POST method, form data is sent in the HTTP request body rather than in the URL. The URL of the request contains only the form action without any query parameters. This method is suitable for larger amounts of data and for operations that change server-side state, such as updating a database or processing a purchase.

POST offers several advantages over GET for appropriate use cases. POST requests can send much more data than GET, since they are not constrained by URL length limits. While the HTTP specification does not set a hard limit on POST body size, servers may impose their own limits, often allowing many kilobytes or even megabytes of data. Because the data is not embedded in the URL, POST submissions are not cached by browsers and cannot be bookmarked with their parameters, which is desirable for actions that should not be repeated by simply revisiting a URL. Browsers typically warn users or ask for confirmation when attempting to refresh or resend a POST request, helping prevent accidental duplicate submissions. This makes POST more appropriate for form actions that have side effects, such as placing an order or creating a user account.

As a general guideline, use POST whenever a form performs an action that creates or updates data on the server, submits passwords or other sensitive information, or transmits data too large or sensitive to include in a

URL.

In summary, use GET for simple data retrieval queries (especially if you want the convenience of book-markable or shareable URLs), and use POST for anything that changes server state or submits large or sensitive data. Many search forms use GET so that search results pages have unique URLs, whereas forms for logging in, uploading files, or posting messages use POST.

4.1.4　Query Strings

When form data is sent (especially via GET), it is packaged into a query string, which is a series of `name=value` pairs separated by ampersands (`\&`). Understanding query string format is essential for debugging forms and understanding how data is transmitted.

Query String Format:

```
?name1=value1&name2=value2&name3=value3...
```

URL Encoding Rules: Query strings must follow certain rules defined by the HTTP protocol. Certain characters cannot appear in their raw form within a query string. Spaces are converted to plus signs (+) or the encoded sequence `%20`. Special characters are encoded as `%HH`, where HH represents two hexadecimal digits corresponding to the character's ASCII or Unicode code point. Punctuation symbols and characters from non-ASCII alphabets must also be encoded.

To illustrate, the string `"John Doe"` becomes `John+Doe` or `John%20Doe`. The hash symbol `"#"` becomes `%23`. Square brackets are encoded as `%5B` for `"["` and `%5D` for `"]"`.

The browser automatically performs this URL encoding when submitting forms. Understanding this helps when debugging. For example if you see odd sequences like `%5B%5D` or + in an address bar after submitting a form, that is just the encoded representation of special characters.

4.1.5　Protocol Interaction Diagrams

To better understand how forms work in the context of web applications, let us visualize the request-response cycle as shown in Figure 4.1. The process begins when a user requests the page containing the form, and the server responds by sending the HTML page with the form markup. When the user fills out the form and clicks submit, the browser packages the form data and sends it to the server as a new HTTP request. The server then processes this data that may include storing it in a database, performing a calculation, or validating user credentials, and then sends back a result page. This stateless request-response pattern is fundamental to web applications: each request-response is a discrete transaction, and the server does not retain the form data except as needed to produce the response.

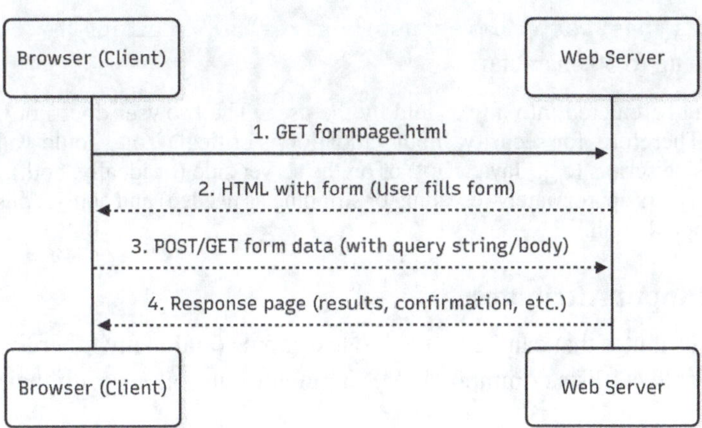

Figure 4.1: The fundamental request-response cycle.

4.1.6 Text Input Fields

One of the most common form controls is a single-line text field. In HTML, a simple text field is created with an <input> element of type `"text"`. For example:

```
<input type = "text" name = "lastname" value = "Enter last name here">
```

This produces a one-line text input box. The <input> tag is an empty element. It does not have a separate closing tag (you write <input ... /> and do not use </input>). In XHTML syntax you would close it with /> (for instance, <input type="text" ... />), but in HTML5 it is fine to just end with > as above.

Several attributes control the behavior and appearance of a text input. The type attribute specifies the kind of input control; here it is `"text"` for a regular text box, though other type values create different controls as we will see later. The name attribute provides the identifier used as the key when the browser transmits the field's value to the server. If an input lacks a name attribute, it will not contribute any data when the form is submitted, so this attribute is essential for any field whose data you want to collect.

The value attribute specifies an initial value for the field. This is optional, if provided, it populates the text box with a default string that the user can see and edit; if omitted, the text box starts empty. In the example above, the field would initially display "Enter last name here," which the user can then replace with their own input.

Two additional attributes control the field's dimensions and input limits. The size attribute specifies the visible width of the text field in characters, though this only affects the display width and does not prevent users from typing more characters (the field will scroll horizontally). Most browsers default to a size of approximately 20 characters. The maxlength attribute specifies the maximum number of characters the user is allowed to type; if set to 100, the browser will prevent entry beyond 100 characters. Note that `maxlength` applies only to single-line <input type="text"> fields, not to <textarea> elements.

For example, `<input type="text" name="user" size="30" maxlength="50">` would create a wider text box that only accepts up to 50 characters.

 Any characters can be entered into a text field by the user. The browser does not filter out potentially dangerous input. Therefore, for security, input validation is critical. You should validate text field data either with client-side scripts (e.g., JavaScript) or on the server side (or ideally, both). Always ensure you handle special characters appropriately (escaping or stripping as needed) and consider using the `maxlength` attribute to limit input length.

4.1.7   Common Text Input Attributes

HTML provides several attributes that can be applied to text inputs (and many other form elements) to improve behavior and usability. Table 4.1 lists common HTML input attributes along with their descriptions.

Table 4.1: Common HTML input attributes.

Attribute	Description
`id`	An id that can be utilized by client-side scripts and CSS
`name`	A name that is used as the key when submitting form data
`value`	Specifies an initial default value for an input field
`disabled`	A Boolean attribute that disables the control, preventing it from receiving focus, being tabbed to, or having its value submitted
`readonly`	A Boolean attribute that prohibits a user from changing the element's value, but it can still receive focus, be tabbed to, and its value is submitted
`required`	Indicates that the field must be filled out before submitting (HTML5)
`placeholder`	Provides a hint to the user about what to enter (HTML5)
`autofocus`	Automatically focuses this field when the page loads (HTML5)
`autocomplete`	Allows the browser to display predictive values based on previous input
`pattern`	Specifies a regular expression that the input must match (HTML5)
`title`	Displays text when the user hovers over the field

4.1.8   Text Input Variations

HTML provides several specialized text input types for specific purposes:

Password fields: `<input type="password" name="pass">` works just like a text input, except the characters typed are obscured (shown as asterisks or dots) so that sensitive information is not visible on-screen. The value submitted (the actual text) is still in plain form to the server, only the display is masked.

```
1  <label>Enter your password:</label>
2  <input type = "password" id = "myPassword" name = "myPassword">
```

Hidden fields: `<input type="hidden" name="token" value="abc123">` creates an input that is not shown in the page at all, but its value is included when the form is submitted. Hidden fields are useful for including data that the user does not directly enter (for example, a session ID, or a fixed value like the "hl=en" language parameter). They can be used to store state between requests or to subtly pass additional info to the server.

```
1 Enter your Name: <input type = "text">
2 <br>
3 SSN: <input type = "hidden" value = "123-45-6789">
```

Email fields (HTML5): `<input type="email" name="user_email">` for email addresses. Browsers that support it may validate that the entered text looks like an email address (contains "@", etc.) before allowing form submission, and on mobile devices, the keyboard may be optimized for typing emails (for example, showing an "@" key prominently).

```
1 <label>Enter an email address:</label>
2 <input type = "email" id = "myEmail" name = "myEmail">
```

URL fields (HTML5): `<input type="url" name="homepage">` for web URLs. Browsers can validate the text looks like a URL (e.g., starts with http:// or https://).

```
1 <label>Enter a URL:</label>
2 <input type = "url" id = "myURL" name = "myURL">
```

Tel fields (HTML5): `<input type="tel" name="phone">` for telephone numbers. No specific format enforcement by default (since phone formats vary), but mobile browsers might show a numeric keypad.

```
1 <label>Enter a telephone number:</label>
2 <input type = "tel" id = "myPhone" name = "myPhone">
```

Search fields (HTML5): `<input type="search" name="query">`, not drastically different from a normal text input, but some browsers style it slightly differently (e.g., Safari puts a rounded search field with a clear "×" button to clear the text).

```
1 <label>Enter a string for the word to search for:</label>
2 <input type="search" id="searchString" name="searchString">
```

4.1.9   Textareas (Multi-line Text Input)

For multi-line text input (such as a large comment or address box), HTML provides the `<textarea>` element. A `<textarea>` is not an `<input>` tag; it has a distinct syntax with an opening and closing tag. For example:

```html
<textarea name = "comments" rows = "5" cols = "30">Enter your comments here.</textarea>
```

This would produce a text area 5 lines tall and 30 columns wide (approximately 30 characters per line, using a fixed default character width). The content between the opening `<textarea>` and closing `</textarea>` tags ("Enter your comments here." in this case) is the initial text content of the textarea, which the user can then edit. If you want the textarea to start empty, you would leave that content blank (e.g., `<textarea name="comments" rows="5" cols="30"></textarea>` with no text between the tags).

The `<textarea>` element has several characteristics that distinguish it from single-line text inputs. The `rows` attribute sets how many text lines are visible in the display area, while `cols` sets the width in characters. Unlike `<input type="text">` where the `value` attribute defines the initial content, a textarea's initial text is placed between the opening and closing tags. This content can include line breaks and spaces and, importantly, such whitespace is preserved as part of the textarea's value rather than being collapsed as it would be in regular HTML text.

Users can type or paste multiple lines of text into a textarea. If the content exceeds the visible area defined by the rows and columns attributes, scrollbars will typically appear to allow navigation within the text area. As with other form controls, the `<textarea>` element requires a `name` attribute for its contents to be transmitted on form submission. The entire text, including any line breaks entered by the user, will be sent as the value associated with that name. Extended example:

```html
<label>Enter a brief statement about yourself:</label>
<textarea rows = "6" cols = "50" id = "statement" name = "statement"></textarea>
```

4.1.10   Drop-down Menus

Another common form control for user input is a drop-down menu, created with the `<select>` element in HTML. A drop-down allows users to choose one option from a list (or multiple options, if configured to allow multiple selections). The basic structure of a drop-down menu is:

```html
<select name="category">
    <option value = "1">Option 1</option>
    <option value = "2">Option 2</option>
    <option value = "3">Option 3</option>
</select>
```

In this example, the `<select>` element defines a menu control named `"category"`. Inside it, each `<option>` element defines one choice in the menu. The `value` attribute of an option is the actual value that will be sent if that option is selected, whereas the content of the `<option>` tag (the text between `<option>` and `</option>`) is what the user sees in the dropdown list. Here, if the user selects "Option 2" from the menu, the form will send `category=2` as the data.

By default, a `<select>` allows only one selection at a time (it acts like a typical drop-down). The first `<option>` is usually selected by default unless you specify otherwise. You can set an option as initially selected by adding the `selected` attribute to one of the `<option>` tags, for example:

```html
<option value = "2" selected>Option 2</option>
```

This would make "Option 2" the initially shown choice.

Size attribute: The `size` attribute specifies the number of visible options in a drop-down list. If its value is greater than 1, but lower than the total number of options in the list, the browser will add a scroll bar to indicate more options to view:

```html
<label>Choose a Country to Visit</label>
<select id = "country" name = "country" size = "2">
    <option>Ireland</option>
    <option>Italy</option>
    <option>Spain</option>
</select>
```

Multiple selections: If you want to allow multiple selections (where the user can choose more than one item from the list), you can add the attribute `multiple` to the `<select>` element. A multi-select is typically rendered as a list box rather than a drop-down (showing multiple lines at once, often with Ctrl+Click or Shift+Click to select multiple items). When multiple items are selected, the form will send multiple values for the same field name. This requires special handling on the server side (similar to handling checkbox groups, which we discuss below).

```html
<select id = "country" name = "country" multiple>
    <option>Choose countries to visit</option>
    <option value = "Ireland">Ireland</option>
    <option value = "Italy">Italy</option>
    <option value = "Spain">Spain</option>
</select>
<p>Please PRESS the Ctrl (Windows) or Command (Mac) key to allow for selection of multiple
options</p>
```

Drop-down menus are ideal when you have a predefined set of options and want to conserve space on the form (since a collapsed drop-down only shows one value at a time). They are functionally similar to a group of radio buttons (only one selection allowed), especially when the list is long. A long list of radio buttons would take up a lot of space, so a `<select>` is preferable.

Linking to a Live Site Example:

To illustrate a practical drop-down, consider we want a form that lets a user choose a department from a list and then go to that department's page on an external site. For instance, the U.S. National Science Foundation (NSF) might have a page where selecting a division leads you to that division's section of the site. We could mimic a portion of their menu with:

```html
<form action = "https://www.nsf.gov/dir/index.jsp" method="GET">
    <select name="org">
        <option value = "BIO">Biology</option>
        <option value = "CISE">Computer & Information Science & Engineering</option>
        <option value = "OCI">Cyberinfrastructure</option>
    </select>
    <input type = "submit" value = "Go">
</form>
```

Here, the form's action is set to an NSF URL (`index.jsp`), which expects a query parameter `org` to indicate the organization code. We have three options with values corresponding to actual NSF organization codes (BIO, CISE, OCI). If the user picks "Cyberinfrastructure" and clicks Go, the browser will request:

```
https://www.nsf.gov/dir/index.jsp?org=OCI
```

This will navigate to the NSF site's Cyberinfrastructure page.

4.1.11   Grouping Options and Submenus

Sometimes, it is helpful to visually group related options within a drop-down menu. HTML provides the `<optgroup>` element for this purpose. An `<optgroup>` lets you define a labeled group of options, which most browsers render as a non-selectable heading within the drop-down list.

For example:

```html
<select name = "product">
    <option value = "" selected>-- Select an item --</option>
    <optgroup label = "Phones">
        <option value = "iph">iPhone</option>
        <option value = "and">Android Phone</option>
    </optgroup>
    <optgroup label="Laptops">
```

```
8          <option value = "mac">MacBook</option>
9          <option value = "win">Windows Laptop</option>
10     </optgroup>
11 </select>
```

In this menu, the first option is a placeholder ("– Select an item –"). Then we have two groups: "Phones" and "Laptops". Under "Phones", two phone options; under "Laptops", two laptop options. The `label` attribute of `<optgroup>` provides the heading text for each group. The user cannot select the label itself (it is just a label, not an option with a value), but it creates a submenu-like visual grouping in the list.

Extended example with city groupings:

```
1  <select id = "country" name = "country">
2      <option>Choose a city in a country</option>
3      <optgroup label = "Treland">
4          <option>Dublin</option>
5          <option>Donegal</option>
6          <option>Dingle</option>
7      </optgroup>
8      <optgroup label = "Italy">
9          <option>Florence</option>
10         <option>Rome</option>
11         <option>Venice</option>
12     </optgroup>
13     <optgroup label = "Spain">
14         <option>Barcelona</option>
15         <option>Madrid</option>
16         <option>Valencia</option>
17     </optgroup>
18 </select>
```

This grouping creates a submenu effect with related choices are clustered together under a heading, which can make long lists easier to navigate. In terms of data, the grouping does not change how the form is submitted; it is purely for the user interface clarity.

4.1.12   Client-side Scripts and Dynamic Menus

Thus far, our forms are static, with the options and inputs being fixed in the HTML. However, forms can be enhanced with client-side scripts (JavaScript) to provide dynamic behavior without requiring a server round-trip. For instance, one common scenario is having one form field's choices depend on another (like a "state" dropdown that populates a "city" dropdown). Achieving that requires JavaScript to update the form on the fly when a selection changes.

While a full discussion of the capabilities of JavaScript comes later in the book, we will give a brief example of client-side scripting with forms, to show how it can work. Consider a drop-down menu where we want to show a popup alert with details whenever the user selects a different option. We can use the `onchange` event on the `<select>` to trigger a JavaScript function when the selection changes. For example:

```html
<form>
    <select name = "color" onchange = "alert('Selected index: ' + this.selectedIndex + '\nText: ' +
    this.options[this.selectedIndex].text)">
        <option value = "cyan">Cyan</option>
        <option value = "red">Red</option>
        <option value = "tan">Tan</option>
    </select>
</form>
```

This code demonstrates how JavaScript can respond to user selections in a dropdown menu. The `onchange` attribute contains an inline script that executes whenever the user picks a different option. Within this script, `this.selectedIndex` refers to the zero-based index of the currently selected option, while `this.options[this.selectedIndex].text` retrieves the display text of that option. The `alert()` function then displays a popup message showing both the index and text of the selection.

If the user chooses "Red" (which is index 1 in the list, assuming "Cyan" is index 0), the script would alert something like:

```
Selected index: 1
Text: Red
```

This example illustrates two important concepts for form development. First, it shows how JavaScript can be embedded directly in form element event attributes to add interactivity without writing separate script blocks. Second, it demonstrates that the `<select>` element exposes useful properties, such as `.selectedIndex` and the `.options` collection, that scripts can inspect or manipulate. Client-side scripting enables form validation (checking that required fields are filled or values are properly formatted before submission) and dynamic interfaces (showing or hiding fields, adding new options, etc.). We will cover JavaScript in detail in a later chapter, but it is important to understand that forms and JavaScript often work together to improve user experience.

4.1.13   Radio Buttons

A radio button group is a set of related options of which only one may be selected at a time. Radio buttons are those small round selectors; when one in the group is clicked "on", any other previously selected one in the same group is automatically turned off (like presets on an old car radio).

In HTML, radio buttons are created with `<input type="radio">` elements. To make them function as a group, all radio inputs in the group share the same `name`. Each radio button in the group should have a distinct `value` so the server can tell which option was chosen.

For example, suppose we have a survey question with three options (Not Useful, Useful, Very Useful) and we only want one choice:

```html
<form action = "rate.php" method="GET">
    <p>Rate this example:</p>
    <input type = "radio" name = "rating" value = "1"> Not useful<br>
    <input type = "radio" name = "rating" value = "2"> Useful<br>
    <input type = "radio" name = "rating" value = "3" checked> Very useful<br>
    <input type = "submit" value = "Submit Rating">
</form>
```

This example demonstrates several key aspects of radio button implementation. All three `<input>` elements share the same `type="radio"` and `name="rating"`, which makes them a linked group where the browser enforces that only one can be checked at a time. Each radio button has a different `value` attribute (1, 2, and 3 in this case). These could be numeric codes or descriptive strings, whatever makes sense for your application. The value of the selected radio button is what will be sent under the field name "rating" when the form is submitted.

The third option includes the `checked` attribute, meaning "Very useful" is pre-selected when the page loads. If you want no selection initially, you can omit `checked` from all options, though some browsers will automatically select the first one. Radio groups are typically designed to have one option selected by default, so it is common practice to specify an initial selection. Users can click a different radio button at any time to change their selection, which will automatically deselect the previously chosen option.

Extended example with country selection:

```html
<form>
    <label>Choose a Country to Visit</label>
    <br>
    <input type = "radio" id = "country" name = "country" value = "Ireland" checked>Ireland
    <br>
    <input type = "radio" id = "country" name = "country" value = "Italy"> Italy
    <br>
    <input type = "radio" id = "country" name = "country" value = "Spain"> Spain
</form>
```

Radio buttons are appropriate when you have a small, fixed number of choices and the user is to pick exactly one. If you have a lot of choices (dozens), a drop-down might be more space-efficient. But radio buttons have the advantage of showing all options at once without needing to open a menu, which can be quicker for user input in many cases.

On the server side, a radio group behaves like a single field: the server will receive at most one value for the given name. If no radio button was selected (which can happen if none were marked checked and the user did not click any, or if the group was optional), then that field name might not appear at all in the submitted data.

Note about multiple selection override: As stated previously, HTML allows you to override the default single radio button selection by giving each radio button a unique name attribute value. However, this defeats the purpose of radio buttons and should generally be avoided:

```
1  <!-- NOT RECOMMENDED - defeats radio button purpose -->
2  <input type = "radio" id = "country" name = "country1" value = "Ireland">Ireland
3  <input type = "radio" id = "country" name = "country2" value = "Italy"> Italy
4  <input type = "radio" id = "country" name = "country3" value = "Spain"> Spain
```

4.1.14   Checkbox Groups

A checkbox is similar to a radio button in appearance, but with an important difference: checkboxes are not mutually exclusive. Each checkbox is essentially a toggle that can be either checked (on/true) or unchecked (off/false). Checkboxes typically come in groups as well, but in a group of checkboxes the user can select multiple items simultaneously. Think of checkboxes as on/off switches for a set of independent options, whereas radio buttons are like a multiple-choice question where only one answer can be chosen.

In HTML, checkboxes are created with `<input type="checkbox">`. Like radio buttons, you give each checkbox a `name` and a `value`. When the form is submitted, each checked checkbox contributes a name-value pair to the submitted data, while unchecked checkboxes do not send anything at all.

If you have multiple checkboxes with the same name (which effectively makes them a group), and more than one of them is checked, the form submission will include that field name multiple times (once for each checked box). How to handle that depends on the server-side processing language.

For example, consider a form that lets a user select multiple interests:

```
1  <form action = "interests.php" method = "GET">
2     <p>Select your interests:</p>
3     <input type = "checkbox" name = "interest" value = "sports">Sports<br>
4     <input type = "checkbox" name = "interest" value = "music">Music<br>
5     <input type = "checkbox" name = "interest" value = "tech">Technology<br>
6     <input type = "submit" value = "Submit">
7  </form>
```

If the user checks "Sports" and "Technology" and submits, the browser will send `interest=sports& interest=tech` as part of the query string (assuming GET). Note that the parameter name "interest" appears twice. Many server frameworks will interpret that as an array or list of values for "interest".

Several details about checkbox behavior are worth noting. Each checkbox should have a `value` attribute specifying what data to send when that checkbox is checked. If you omit the value attribute and the checkbox is checked, some browsers send the default value "on" for that field, which may not be meaningful to your server-side code.

When a checkbox is unchecked, it behaves as if it does not exist in the form and the server receives no indication that the checkbox was present but unchecked. If your application logic requires distinguishing between "not checked" and "not present," you may need to handle this on the server by detecting when an expected field name is absent from the submitted data.

You can pre-check a checkbox by including the `checked` attribute in the HTML, such as `<input type="checkbox" name="subscribe" value="yes" checked>`. This is useful for default selections where you expect most users to want the option enabled. Unlike radio buttons, users can toggle each checkbox independently as there is no automatic exclusive behavior between checkboxes, even those sharing the same name.

Extended example with country selection:

```html
<form>
    <label>Choose Countries to Visit</label>
    <br>
    <input type = "checkbox" id = "country" name = "country" value = "Ireland" checked>Ireland
    <br>
    <input type = "checkbox" id = "country" name = "country" value = "Italy">Italy
    <br>
    <input type = "checkbox" id = "country" name = "country" value = "Spain">Spain
</form>
```

> (R) The `checked` attribute is a Boolean attribute meaning it can have two values: on or off. When turned on as in the examples above, the related checkbox/radio button is checked when the page is rendered.

Checkbox groups and server-side processing: When multiple checkboxes share the same name (like the "interest" example above), the server may receive multiple values for that single field name. For instance, if a user selected two interests, the query string might look like `...?interest=sports&interest=tech`. How servers handle this varies by programming language and framework.

In PHP, if you simply use `$_GET["interest"]`, you would by default receive only one of the values (typically the last one). To properly handle multiple values, you can name the field with square brackets, such as `name="interest[]"`, which tells PHP to collect them into an array. With this approach, `$_GET["interest"]` becomes an array containing all selected values. Other frameworks have analogous techniques or automatically treat repeated fields as arrays.

Using a shared name for related checkboxes is the common approach when they represent multiple values for one logical field (like "interests"). Alternatively, you could give each checkbox a unique name, in which case each acts as its own boolean field (sending `sports=yes` or nothing at all). However, this approach makes server-side handling more cumbersome, so the shared-name pattern is generally preferred.

To illustrate, consider a more explicit example with array notation (as one would in PHP):

```html
<form action = "checkbox.php" method = "GET">
    <input type = "checkbox" name = "item[]" value = "1">Item 1<br>
```

```
3      <input type = "checkbox" name = "item[]" value = "2">Item 2<br>
4      <input type = "checkbox" name = "item[]" value = "3">Item 3<br>
5      <input type = "submit" value = "Choose">
6  </form>
```

If the user checks Item 1 and Item 3, the resulting request URL might contain `item%5B%5D=1&item%5B %5D=3`. Here `%5B%5D` is the URL-encoded form of `[]` (the square brackets in the field name). This is how the browser encodes the array-style name. It effectively means `item[]=1` and `item[]=3`. On the server, `$_GET["item"]` would then be an array `["1","3"]`. The order of values in the array corresponds to the order of the checkboxes in the HTML form (browsers list fields in document order when constructing the query string).

We will not dig further into PHP here, but in a simple PHP script (`checkbox.php`), one might retrieve and use these values like:

```
1  $a = $_GET["item"];
2  $n = count($a);
3  echo "$n item(s) selected:<br>";
4  for ($i = 0; $i < $n; $i++) {
5      echo "Value " . $a[$i] . "<br>";
6  }
```

If the user had selected Item 1 and 3, `$n` would be 2 and the script might output:

```
2 item(s) selected:
Value 1
Value 3
```

This matches the values of the checked boxes.

The main takeaway: radio buttons vs. checkboxes – use radio when only one choice can be made, use checkboxes when multiple choices are allowed. And remember that with checkboxes, the server may get multiple values for the same field name, requiring careful handling.

4.1.15   Using Labels with Radio Buttons and Checkboxes

The `<label>` element can be used with both radio buttons and checkboxes to improve usability. Instead of having to click on a small button or box, this option allows a user to click on the text in the `<label>` element when choosing an option.

This is accomplished by setting the `for` attribute of the `<label>` element to the `id` attribute of the radio button or checkbox:

```
1  <form>
2      <h1>Dessert Menu</h1>
3      <input type = "radio" name = "dessert" id = "dessert1" value = "cheesecake">
4      <label for = "dessert1">Cheese Cake</label>
5      <br>
6      <input type = "radio" name = "dessert" id = "dessert2" value = "applepie">
7      <label for = "dessert2">Apple Pie</label>
8      <br>
9      <input type = "radio" name = "dessert" id = "dessert3" value = "brownie">
10     <label for = "dessert3">Chocolate Brownie</label>
11     <br>
12
13     <h1>Toppings</h1>
14     <input type = "checkbox" name = "topping" id = "topping1" value = "whipcream">
15     <label for = "topping1">Whip Cream</label>
16     <br>
17     <input type = "checkbox" name = "topping" id = "topping2" value = "icecream">
18     <label for = "topping2">Ice Cream</label>
19     <br>
20     <input type = "checkbox" name = "topping" id = "topping3" value = "hotfudge">
21     <label for = "topping3">Hot Fudge</label>
22 </form>
```

This creates a more user-friendly interface where clicking anywhere on the label text will toggle the associated checkbox or select the radio button.

4.1.16 Submit and Reset Buttons

No form is complete without a way to submit it. The primary way to do this is using a Submit button, created by `<input type="submit">` or the `<button>` element with type submit. When the user clicks a submit button (or presses Enter in certain contexts, like a single text field form), the browser will gather all the form data and send it to the form's action URL using the specified method.

A basic submit button we have seen looks like:

```
1  <input type = "submit" value = "Search">
```

The `value` attribute on a submit input defines the text that appears on the button (in this case "Search"). If no value is provided, browsers will typically display a default label like "Submit".

HTML also provides a Reset button, `<input type="reset">`, which when clicked will reset all form controls in that form to their initial values (the values they had when the form was first loaded, or the default values specified in the HTML). For example:

```
1  <input type = "reset" value = "Clear Form">
```

This would create a button labeled "Clear Form" that, if clicked, undoes any changes the user made, and the text fields revert to their original text, selections go back to the initial option, checkboxes and radios return to their initial checked/unchecked state, etc.

Reset buttons can be useful, but be cautious: users sometimes click "Reset" by accident when they meant to click "Submit", losing what they have typed. For that reason, reset buttons are less common in modern web forms unless there is a clear need to quickly clear a form (for example, a complex search filter form). If used, ensure they are labeled clearly and placed where accidental clicks are unlikely.

It is also possible to have multiple submit buttons in one form. This is typically done if the form can be submitted to do different things depending on which button is pressed. For instance:

```
1  <input type = "submit" name = "action" value = "Preview">
2  <input type = "submit" name = "action" value = "Post">
```

If both are in the same form, clicking "Preview" will submit the form with the additional data `action=Preview`, which the server could detect and respond by showing a preview, whereas clicking "Post" would send `action=Post` and the server would actually post the data. Both submit buttons still send the whole form data; they just include an extra piece of data (their own name/value) to distinguish the intention. Using the `name` attribute on submit inputs is optional and mainly useful in such scenarios.

4.1.17   Other Button Types

HTML defines several different types of buttons beyond submit and reset:

Custom button: `<input type="button">` creates a button that does not have any default behavior. It requires JavaScript to perform any function. The default text is usually "Button" but can be customized with the `value` attribute:

```
1  <input type = "button" value = "Click Me" onclick = "alert('Hello!')">
```

Image button: `<input type="image">` creates a submit button that displays an image instead of text:

```
1  <input type = "image" src = "send.png" alt = "SEND">
```

This works just like a submit button but displays an image. Additionally, when clicked, it reports the coordinates of the click as `name.x` and `name.y` parameters (useful for image maps).

Button element: The `<button>` element is more flexible than input buttons because it can contain HTML content:

```
1 <button type = "submit"><img src = "send.png" alt = "SEND">SEND</button>
```

This allows you to combine images and text in a button, or even include other HTML elements.

4.1.18 Form Organization with Fieldset and Legend

HTML provides the `<fieldset>` and `<legend>` elements to group related form controls together visually and semantically:

```
1  <form>
2      <fieldset>
3          <legend>Personal Information</legend>
4          <label>First Name: <input type = "text" name = "fname"></label><br>
5          <label>Last Name: <input type = "text" name = "lname"></label><br>
6          <label>Email: <input type = "email" name = "email"></label>
7      </fieldset>
8
9      <fieldset>
10         <legend>Preferences</legend>
11         <input type = "checkbox" name = "newsletter" id = "news">
12         <label for = "news">Subscribe to newsletter</label><br>
13         <input type = "checkbox" name = "updates" id = "upd">
14         <label for = "upd">Receive updates</label>
15     </fieldset>
16 </form>
```

The `<fieldset>` creates a visual box around the grouped elements (usually with a border), and the `<legend>` provides a title for that group. This improves form organization and accessibility.

4.1.19 Advanced Input Types and Controls

Number inputs: HTML5 introduces `<input type="number">` for numeric input:

```
1 <label>Employee Name: <input type = "text"></label><br>
2 <label>Number of Hours Worked: <input type = "number" min = "0" max = "168" step = "0.5"></label>
```

This creates a field that only accepts numbers, often with spinner controls. The `min`, `max`, and `step` attributes control the allowed range and increments.

Range inputs: `<input type="range">` creates a slider control:

```
1 <label>Pain Level</label><br>
2 Minimal
3 <input type = "range" min = "1" max = "10" step = "1" value = "5">
4 Severe
```

This renders as a slider that the user can drag to select a value between the min and max.

Date and time inputs: HTML5 provides several specialized input types for date and time selection, each with native browser controls that provide consistent user interfaces and built-in validation.

The `date` type creates a date picker for selecting a calendar date in yyyy-mm-dd format:

```
1 <input type = "date" name = "birthday">
```

The `time` type provides a time selector in HH:MM:SS format:

```
1 <input type = "time" name = "appointment">
```

For situations requiring both date and time, the `datetime-local` type combines both selectors:

```
1 <input type = "datetime-local" name = "meeting">
```

The `month` type allows selection of a month and year in yyyy-mm format, useful for credit card expiration dates:

```
1 <input type = "month" name = "expiry">
```

The `week` type enables selection of a specific week within a year:

```
1 <input type = "week" name = "vacation">
```

Color picker: `<input type="color">` provides a color selection interface:

```
1 <label>Favorite Color: <input type = "color" name = "favcolor" value = "#ff0000"></label>
```

4.1.20 Datalist Element

The `<datalist>` element provides autocomplete suggestions for text inputs:

```html
<label>Choose a browser:</label>
<input list = "browsers" name = "browser">
<datalist id = "browsers">
    <option value = "Chrome">
    <option value = "Firefox">
    <option value = "Safari">
    <option value = "Edge">
    <option value = "Opera">
</datalist>
```

This creates a text input with a dropdown of suggestions that filters as the user types.

4.1.21 Output Element

The `<output>` element represents the result of a calculation or user action:

```html
<form oninput="result.value=parseInt(a.value)+parseInt(b.value)">
    <input type = "number" id = "a" value = "0"> +
    <input type = "number" id = "b" value = "0"> =
    <output name = "result" for = "a b">0</output>
</form>
```

4.1.22 Simple Form Example

Let us construct a very simple form to solidify these concepts. Suppose we want a form that asks for a person's last name and has a submit button. We are not actually processing it with a server script yet; we just want to see what happens on submission. We could write:

```html
<form action = "" method = "GET">
    <input type = "text" name = "lastname" value = "Doe">
    <input type = "submit" value = "Submit">
</form>
```

Here we left the `action` attribute empty. By doing so, we are indicating (in HTML5) that the form will submit to the current page (itself). If this file is just opened locally (not through a server), clicking submit will simply reload the page with the form parameters appended to the URL (since method GET is used by default if not specified). This is a partial example because we have no server script; but it lets us observe the browser's behavior.

If this form is saved as `Form01.html` and opened from a server (say at `http://example.com/Form01.html`), and the user types "Smith" in place of "Doe" and presses Submit, the browser will attempt to request:

```
http://example.com/Form01.html?lastname=Smith
```

When this form is submitted, a sequence of events occurs. Since the `action` attribute was empty, the browser assumes the current page (`Form01.html`) is the target. The query string `?lastname=Smith` gets appended to that page's URL. The server receives the request for `Form01.html?lastname=Smith`, but in this case there is no server program to handle the data. The server simply treats it like a request for the same HTML file and will likely ignore the query string, returning the `Form01.html` file again. The browser loads the page, and if nothing processes the query parameters, it might appear that nothing happened, though you will see the query string in the address bar.

Even without a server script, the browser still generated a query string and sent the data. If you were watching the browser's address bar, you would see `?lastname=Smith` appear after the page URL when you hit Submit. This is a clear demonstration of how GET works. The form data was encoded into the URL.

4.1.23   Google Search Form Example

To illustrate a form that actually does something useful without us writing a server script, we can imitate a well-known service. Consider the Google search homepage: it features a text input and a submit button (and some hidden fields). When you type a query and hit search, Google's servers receive the query and return results. We can make our own HTML page that piggybacks on Google's search by sending a request to Google's search URL with the right parameters.

Through either examining Google's HTML or observing the URL of a search result, one can determine the key parameters of Google's search interface. The action URL is `https://www.google.com/search`. The main query parameter is `q`, which contains the search term. Additional parameters control various aspects of the search, such as `hl` (host language) which specifies the language for the interface.

For simplicity, let us use `hl=en` (English) as a fixed hidden parameter. We can create a mini Google search form as follows:

```
1  <form action = "https://www.google.com/search" method =" GET">
2      <input type = "hidden" name = "hl" value = "en">
3      <input type = "text" name = "q" placeholder = "Search Google">
4      <input type = "submit" value = "Google Search">
5  </form>
```

This form demonstrates how to create a custom search interface that submits to Google. The form is configured to submit via GET to Google's search endpoint. A hidden field sets `hl=en` to ensure results are displayed in English (the "hl" parameter stands for host language). The text field named `q` captures the user's search query, which is the main parameter Google expects.

If the user enters "Arctic" and clicks the button, the browser will navigate to:

```
https://www.google.com/search?hl=en&q=Arctic
```

Google's servers interpret q=Arctic and return the search results page for "Arctic".

This example demonstrates that HTML forms can point to any server, not just the one from which the form came. As long as you know the correct action URL and parameter names expected, your form can send a request there. This also shows how hidden fields can supply preset values (like the hl parameter) without user intervention.

4.1.24 Simple PHP Processing Example (Text and Radio Inputs)

While server-side programming is beyond just HTML, it is useful to understand what the server receives and how it might handle it. We have touched on it a bit with mention of PHP's $_GET. Let us outline a very basic example:

Imagine we have a form with a text field for name and a radio button group for gender, and we wrote a simple PHP script to handle it. First, here is the HTML form:

```
1 <form action = "hello.php" method = "GET">
2     Name: <input type = "text" name = "username"><br>
3     Gender:
4     <input type = "radio" name = "gender" value = "M">Male
5     <input type = "radio" name = "gender" value = "F">Female<br>
6     <input type = "submit" value = "Go">
7 </form>
```

Now, the PHP script hello.php could look like this:

```
1  <?php
2  $name = $_GET["username"];
3  $gen  = $_GET["gender"];
4  if ($name == "") {
5      echo "Hello, anonymous!";
6  } else {
7      $salutation = ($gen == "F") ? "Ms." : "Mr.";
8      echo "Hello, $salutation $name!";
9  }
10 ?>
```

If the user enters "Alice" and selects Female, the request to server would be hello.php?username=Alice&gender=F. The PHP script would output: Hello, Ms. Alice!. If the name field was left blank and Male was selected, it might output: Hello, Mr. ! (or Hello, anonymous! in our logic above if we chose to handle blank differently).

The details of PHP are not important right now; the key concept is that each form field's name becomes a variable the server can access. Text fields provide strings, radio groups provide one of the predefined values, etc.

4.1.25 `<input type="file">` (File Uploads)

One very powerful form element is the file upload control, which allows the user to select a file from their local computer to send to the server. This is how, for example, you attach a file in an email or upload a profile picture on a website.

A file chooser is created with:

```
<input type = "file" name = "uploaded_file">
```

When rendered, this typically appears as a text input field and a "Browse..." button (the exact label depends on the browser and OS; it might say "Choose File" or something similar). The user can either type the path to a file or (more commonly) click the Browse button to open a file picker dialog and choose a file. Once chosen, the file's name (and path) appear in the input field (though for security, browsers often only show the base name, not the full path, to the webpage).

File uploads require specific form configuration to work correctly. Most importantly, the form must use `method="POST"` because files can contain substantial amounts of data (potentially megabytes) that must be sent in the request body. Attempting to send a file via GET would be impractical since file content cannot be meaningfully encoded into a URL query string.

In addition to using POST, the form tag must specify `enctype="multipart/form-data"`. The `enctype` (encoding type) attribute tells the browser how to encode the form data for transmission. The default encoding, `application/x-www-form-urlencoded`, works well for regular text fields but cannot properly handle binary file data. The `multipart/form-data` encoding instructs the browser to send each form field as a separate part of the request, with boundary markers separating the parts. Each part includes its own headers, and the file part will specify the file's MIME type and contain the raw binary data. We will discuss MIME types in detail later in this chapter, but the essential rule is straightforward: for file uploads, always include `enctype="multipart/form-data" on your form tag`.

When a file is uploaded, the browser sends only the file's name and binary content, not the full path from the user's system. This is a security measure as the server does not learn about the user's local filesystem structure. If a user uploads "photo.jpg," the server receives the filename and the file's binary contents, but has no knowledge that it originated from a path like `C:\Users\Alice\Pictures\`.

HTML5 introduced the ability to select multiple files in a single input by adding the `multiple` attribute to `<input type="file">`. When this attribute is present, users can select multiple files from the file dialog, and the form will transmit all of them. For the server to properly receive multiple files, the input's `name` attribute should use array notation, such as `name="photos[]"`, and each file will be sent as a separate part in the multipart form data.

File uploads also raise important security considerations on the server side. The server must be configured to accept uploaded files, typically through a server-side script that moves files from a temporary location to a permanent directory. File permissions must be set correctly to allow the script to save files while preventing unauthorized access. Servers often impose limits on file size and type to prevent abuse because without such limits, malicious users could consume storage with huge files or attempt to upload executable files. These server-side concerns go beyond HTML and are handled through server configuration and programming. When we cover server-side programming with PHP in a later chapter, we will examine how to handle file uploads securely, including checking the $_FILES array, validating file types, and moving uploaded files to their final destinations.

For now, from an HTML perspective, here is a minimal example:

```
1  <form action = "upload.php" method = "POST" enctype = "multipart/form-data">
2      <p>Select a file to upload:</p>
3      <input type = "file" name = "myfile"><br>
4      <input type = "submit" value = "Upload">
5  </form>
```

This form will let the user pick a file. When submitted, the browser will POST to upload.php with a multipart/form-data body that includes the file. Without a server script at upload.php, nothing useful happens (the server might just return an error or do nothing). To make it functional, upload.php would need to be a script that reads the uploaded file and saves it somewhere or processes it. But writing that script requires PHP or another language, which is beyond our HTML scope here.

The crucial parts again are method="POST" and enctype="multipart/form-data". If you forget one of these, the file upload will not work properly. Using GET instead of POST will cause the form to submit, but the file will not actually be sent. You might end up with just myfile=filename in the URL query string, which contains only the filename, not the file contents. If you use POST but omit the correct enctype, the file also will not transmit properly; the browser would attempt to URL-encode the binary data, which is both inefficient and often exceeds server limits.

4.1.26 Putting it All Together: Comprehensive Form Example

To recap, here is a comprehensive form incorporating many of the elements we have discussed:

```
1  <!DOCTYPE html>
2  <html>
3  <head>
4      <meta charset = "UTF-8">
5      <title>Registration Form</title>
6  </head>
7  <body>
8      <h1>User Registration</h1>
9
10     <form action = "submit.php" method = "POST" enctype = "multipart/form-data">
11         <fieldset>
```

```html
12            <legend>Personal Information</legend>
13            Name: <input type = "text" name = "name" maxlength = "100" required><br>
14            Email: <input type = "email" name = "email" required><br>
15            Phone: <input type = "tel" name = "phone"><br>
16            Birthday: <input type = "date" name = "birthday"><br>
17            Gender:
18                <input type = "radio" name = "gender" value = "M" id = "male">
19                <label for = "male">Male</label>
20                <input type = "radio" name = "gender" value = "F" id = "female">
21                <label for = "female">Female</label><br>
22        </fieldset>
23
24        <fieldset>
25            <legend>Preferences</legend>
26            Interests:<br>
27                <input type = "checkbox" name = "interest[]" value = "music" id = "music">
28                <label for= "music">Music</label><br>
29                <input type = "checkbox" name = "interest[]" value = "sports" id = "sports">
30                <label for = "sports">Sports</label><br>
31                <input type = "checkbox" name = "interest[]" value = "reading" id = "reading">
32                <label for = "reading">Reading</label><br>
33
34            Preferred Contact Time:
35            <input type = "time" name = "contact_time"><br>
36
37            Experience Level:
38            <input type = "range" name = "experience" min = "1" max = "10" value = "5"><br>
39        </fieldset>
40
41        <fieldset>
42            <legend>Account Setup</legend>
43            Username: <input type = "text" name = "username" required
44                       pattern = "[A-Za-z0-9]{3,}"
45                       title = "At least 3 alphanumeric characters"><br>
46            Password: <input type = "password" name = "password" required minlength = "8"><br>
47            Profile Picture: <input type = "file" name = "photo" accept = "image/*"><br>
48            Bio: <textarea name = "bio" rows = "4" cols = "50"
49                       placeholder = "Tell us about yourself..."></textarea><br>
50        </fieldset>
51
52        <input type = "submit" value = "Register">
53        <input type = "reset" value = "Clear Form">
54    </form>
```

```
55  </body>
56  </html>
```

This comprehensive form example demonstrates several HTML5 form features working together. It includes text inputs with validation attributes that enforce required fields, minimum and maximum lengths, and pattern matching. Email and telephone inputs use specialized types that provide appropriate keyboard layouts on mobile devices and built-in format validation. Date and time inputs offer native picker interfaces. The range input creates a slider control for numeric selection. Dropdown menus, radio buttons, and checkboxes provide various selection mechanisms. A textarea allows multi-line text entry, and file inputs enable document uploads. Together, these elements showcase the breadth of HTML5's form capabilities.

4.2   HTML and XHTML Standards and Validation

HTML has evolved over time with various versions and standards. XHTML was an effort to reformulate HTML as an XML-based language with stricter rules. In this section, we discuss what XHTML is, how it differs from traditional HTML, why standards (like DOCTYPE declarations and validation) are important, and how to ensure your HTML or XHTML is properly structured and valid. We will also cover common syntax errors developers make and how to avoid them.

4.2.1   HTML versus XHTML

HTML (HyperText Markup Language) was originally a relatively loose language in terms of syntax, where browsers could handle tags in various cases, tolerate missing closing tags, etc. HTML 4.01 (1999) was a widely used specification that defined much of what we consider "classic HTML".

XHTML (eXtensible HyperText Markup Language), introduced in 2000, is essentially HTML 4 reformulated as an XML application. The idea was to impose XML's stricter rules and extensibility on HTML. The W3C expected XHTML to gradually replace HTML, because XML-based web documents could be parsed with standard XML parsers, could be extended with other XML vocabularies (MathML, SVG, etc.) through namespaces, and in theory lead to a more disciplined web.

However, the transition to XHTML did not happen as quickly or as smoothly as hoped. Many web developers stuck with HTML 4 or used "XHTML" but served it as `text/html`, meaning browsers still treated it like HTML rather than applying strict XML parsing. Older browsers, especially Internet Explorer through version 8, had poor or no support for true XHTML served with the `application/xhtml+xml` content type. Browsers did not enforce strict XML rules when processing documents served as `text/html`, so authors often did not notice when their markup was not well-formed. Essentially, the large installed base of existing content and browsers kept HTML with its forgiving error handling as the common denominator for web development.

As Tim Berners-Lee (a computer scientist credited with the inventor of the web and then-director of the W3C) noted in 2006, the attempt to get everyone to "switch to XML... all at once did not work. The large HTML-generating public did not move, largely because the browsers did not complain." Instead, it became clear that HTML needed to evolve incrementally. This realization was part of what led to HTML5, which took a more pragmatic approach (maintaining compatibility while adding new features, rather than forcing an XML-only world).

That said, understanding XHTML is still useful, because it emphasizes writing cleaner code and some folks still use XHTML syntax. Also, XHTML 1.0/1.1 are still W3C recommendations; XHTML 2 was abandoned, but the concept lives on in the XHTML5 (basically the XML serialization of HTML5).

Next, we will outline the differences and requirements of XHTML compared to HTML.

4.2.2   The Goals of XHTML

XHTML was designed with several goals in mind. Strictness and consistency were paramount: XHTML forces well-formed markup where every tag must be closed, properly nested, and all attributes must be quoted. The idea was to catch errors early and avoid the kind of "tag soup" that browsers would forgivingly try to fix.

XML integration was another key goal. Since XHTML is XML, it can be mixed with other XML-based languages using XML namespaces. For example, you could embed MathML or SVG markup directly in an XHTML document. Modern HTML5 also allows inline SVG and MathML, but XHTML made this concept explicit through its namespace mechanism.

Future extensibility was envisioned as a step toward the "Semantic Web", a vision where documents could contain rich, meaningful markup (possibly custom XML tags for specific purposes) that machines could understand. Using XML namespaces, new tags could be introduced without waiting for HTML standards to catch up.

Finally, XHTML promised better parsing. An XHTML document, being valid XML, can be parsed by any standard XML parser. This could theoretically simplify browser implementations and enable other XML tools to process web content. HTML, in contrast, required custom parsing with extensive error-handling for malformed code.

In principle, an XHTML document served with the correct content type (`application/xhtml+xml`) will be handled by browsers in XML mode. This has significant implications for error handling and document processing. If the document is not well-formed XML, the browser will stop rendering and display an error message rather than attempting to recover from mistakes as HTML parsers do. The document can use XML tools like XSLT for transformations, and the DOM is an XML DOM (which in practice is similar to the HTML DOM but with some differences in case-sensitivity and element handling).

In practice, because IE (until v9) did not support `application/xhtml+xml`, many sites that claimed to be XHTML just served it as `text/html`, which meant browsers treated it as tag-soup HTML anyway. Thus the benefits were not realized unless you truly served as XML (which only advanced or niche sites did, since IE users would get a download prompt or broken page).

Fast forward to today: HTML5 specification is written to encompass both an HTML serialization (`text/html`, with all the forgiving parsing rules specified in detail) and an XML serialization (XHTML5, which basically is HTML5 but you send it as XML and follow XML rules). So you can still use XHTML-style syntax in HTML5 if you want (self-closing tags, lowercase, etc.), and you can serve pages as XML for browsers that support it. But it is optional.

Nevertheless, understanding XHTML rules is essentially understanding how to write really clean, well-structured HTML. Next, we will go over the key syntactical differences (most of which you can apply to writing better HTML too):

4.2.3   Syntax Differences between HTML and XHTML

1. Case Sensitivity (Capitalization):

HTML (prior to HTML5) is case-insensitive for element and attribute names. `<DIV>` is the same as `<div>`. Authors often wrote tags in lowercase anyway (as a convention), but it was not required. XHTML, being XML, is case-sensitive and requires all tags and attributes to be in lowercase (since the XHTML Document Type Definition (DTD) defines them in lowercase). So `<Html>` or `<BODY>` would not be recognized in XHTML; you must use `<html>` and `<body>`, etc.

In practice: Always use lowercase for tags and attributes in modern HTML. HTML5 even recommends lowercase for consistency (and if you ever switch to XML mode, you will be fine).

2. Attribute Values Quoting:

In HTML, attribute values should be quoted, especially if they contain spaces, but there were cases you could omit quotes (like `<input type=text value=hello>` would technically work in HTML). Some older HTML attributes (like boolean attributes, e.g., `checked` on a checkbox) could be written without a value (`<input type="checkbox" checked>`). XHTML is strict: all attribute values must be enclosed in quotes (single or double). Even values that are numeric or could be boolean must have a value and quotes. For example, in XHTML you would write `<input type="text" name="user" value="John">` (quotes around "John"), and a boolean attribute like checked must be written as `checked="checked"` (or `checked="true"` depending on DTD, but generally the value is the same name or something).

So, `<option selected>` is fine in HTML, but XHTML would require `<option selected="selected">`. HTML5 (even in HTML serialization) allows the minimized boolean attribute (selected without value) and considers it equivalent to `selected="selected"`. But if you write XHTML, you cannot minimize and you must provide the full attribute with a value.

3. Closing Tags:

HTML has a number of elements where the closing tag can be omitted if context makes it clear (called optional end tags). For example, `<p>Paragraph 1<p>Paragraph 2` where the first `</p>` is implicitly closed when the second `<p>` begins. Or `<li>` tags do not strictly need closing `</li>` in some cases, etc. HTML also forbids a few closing tags entirely: e.g., you should not put a `</br>` or `</img>` because those tags are self-closing in effect (or simply empty).

XHTML, by XML rules, requires every tag to have a closing tag unless it is declared as an empty element. In XHTML, empty elements (like `<br>`, `<img>`, `<input>`, etc.) must be self-closed by adding `/>` at the end (with a space before the slash as a typical convention). For example: `<br />`, `<img src="photo.png" alt="Photo" />`, `<input type="text" name="x" />`. Non-void elements must have explicit closing tags: you cannot omit `</p>` or `</li>` as they all must be present.

The requirement to close all elements means that in XHTML you must write `<p>Para 1</p><p>Para 2</p>` with explicit closing tags, rather than relying on implicit closure. Empty elements must use self-closing syntax: `<br />` instead of `<br>`, and `<hr />` instead of `<hr>`. Similarly, image tags must be written as `<img src="..." alt="..." />` with the trailing slash.

It is worth noting that HTML5 defines these as void elements (no closing tag allowed, and not needing the slash), but it allows the slash and just ignores it in HTML mode. So writing `<br />` in HTML5 is acceptable (it is just treated as `<br>`). But writing `<br>` in XHTML would not be well-formed (you would need the slash).

Also, in XHTML you cannot have stray unclosed tags. For instance, in HTML a `<p>` can wrap text until maybe a closing `</div>` is encountered, at which point browsers infer the `<p>` was closed before the `</div>`. In XHTML, that scenario would be an error as all tags must nest properly (more on nesting below).

4. Element Nesting Rules:

XHTML demands well-formedness, which includes proper nesting. That means if element A contains element B, B must be closed before A is closed. You cannot overlap. Example of incorrect nesting in HTML (which some browsers might fix):

```
<b><i>Bold-italic text</b></i>
```

This is not well-formed (the tags overlap improperly). Browsers might render it as `<b><i>Bold-italic text</i></b>` or something. In XHTML (or any XML), overlapping tags would cause a fatal parse error. The correct nesting must be:

```
<b><i>Bold-italic text</i></b>
```

Close the inner `<i>` before closing the outer `<b>`.

Furthermore, HTML (especially older versions) allowed some tags to be left open or not nested strictly, and browsers would auto-correct the structure. XHTML and modern HTML5 require logical nesting of elements. You cannot directly place block elements inside inline elements without properly closing the outer element first. While HTML5 is more flexible about content models than XHTML was, certain combinations remain invalid in both. For example, `<p><div>...</div></p>` is not permitted because a paragraph cannot contain a division. Forms cannot be nested inside other forms in any version of HTML or XHTML. Table structure must be correct, with `<tr>` elements inside `<table>` and `<td>` or `<th>` inside `<tr>`. While browsers often fix missing or misplaced tags automatically, XHTML expects them to be present and correctly nested from the start.

In short, XHTML enforces that your document must be a well-formed XML tree. Each start tag has a matching end tag in the correct place, elements are properly nested without overlap, and all attribute quotes are in place.

Summary of Common XHTML Syntax Requirements

Compared to HTML, XHTML imposes several stricter syntax requirements. All tag and attribute names must be lowercase. All attribute values must be quoted. Every non-void element must have a closing tag, and void (empty) elements must use self-closing syntax with `/>`. Elements must be nested properly with no overlapping or missing closures.

4.2.4 Identifying the W3C Standard of a Document

One of the first lines in any HTML or XHTML document is typically a `<!DOCTYPE ...>` declaration. This declaration is not an HTML tag; it is an instruction to the browser (and validators) about which version of HTML/XHTML the page is written in.

For example, an HTML 4.01 Strict document might start with:

```
<!DOCTYPE HTML PUBLIC "-//W3C//DTD HTML 4.01//EN" "http://www.w3.org/TR/html4/strict.dtd">
```

An XHTML 1.0 Transitional might have:

```
<!DOCTYPE html PUBLIC "-//W3C//DTD XHTML 1.0 Transitional//EN"
 "http://www.w3.org/TR/xhtml1/DTD/xhtml1-transitional.dtd">
```

And HTML5 simplified this drastically to:

```
<!DOCTYPE html>
```

HTML5's doctype is short and case-insensitive. It is basically just a trigger to tell the browser "use standard mode and HTML5 rules".

Why is the DOCTYPE important:

Browsers use the DOCTYPE declaration to determine their rendering mode. In older times, if you omitted the DOCTYPE or used an outdated one, browsers (especially Internet Explorer) might enter "quirks mode," which emulates old browser behaviors intended for legacy pages. This could cause significant layout problems, particularly with CSS. A correct DOCTYPE ensures the page is rendered in standards mode, where the browser follows W3C standards consistently. For HTML5, the simple `<!DOCTYPE html>` declaration is sufficient to trigger standards mode in all modern browsers.

In the early 2000s, web developers commonly used several DOCTYPE declarations depending on their needs. HTML 4.01 Transitional allowed some older presentational elements like `<font>`, making it suitable for pages migrating from older practices. HTML 4.01 Strict prohibited deprecated elements, requiring purely structural markup with CSS for presentation. XHTML 1.0 offered both Transitional and Strict variants with similar distinctions but requiring XHTML syntax rules.

For example, transitional DOCTYPE:

```
<!DOCTYPE HTML PUBLIC "-//W3C//DTD HTML 4.01 Transitional//EN"
 "http://www.w3.org/TR/html4/loose.dtd">
```

The presence of "Transitional" or "Strict" in that identifier was key.

Quirks mode note: If no recognizable DOCTYPE is present at the top, many browsers (especially older IE) will go into quirks mode where they handle CSS box models and other things the old way (making modern CSS layout very difficult). So always include a DOCTYPE. HTML5 made it easy with `<!DOCTYPE html>` because it triggers standards mode in all browsers and implies HTML5. You do not need to memorize the long ones anymore unless working with legacy pages.

One edge case: If an XHTML page is served as `application/xhtml+xml`, Internet Explorer (pre-Edge) would not render it at all (it would prompt to download or show an XML tree or error). Modern browsers (Firefox, Chrome, Safari, Edge) will render it in standards mode and treat it as XML. They look at the DOCTYPE and the `xmlns` to know it is XHTML 1.0 or 1.1 for instance. But typically, if you are using HTML5, you would either just do HTML serialization (text/html with `<!DOCTYPE html>`) or if you really need XML (rarely necessary), you might use `<!DOCTYPE html>` and serve as XML which is actually still fine. HTML5 spec defines how to parse HTML5 as XML too.

In summary, always include a DOCTYPE declaration at the top of your documents. Use the simplest correct DOCTYPE for your needs. Therefore, in most cases, `<!DOCTYPE html>` is recommended. Remember that the DOCTYPE influences both browser rendering mode and validation behavior.

4.2.5   Identifying the Character Encoding of a Document

Besides telling the browser what HTML standard to use, you should also tell it what character encoding the document is in. Characters (letters, symbols) are stored as numeric codes; the encoding is the mapping of those codes to actual bytes. For instance, the character "A" in ASCII or UTF-8 is 65 (0x41), while in UTF-16 it might be 0x0041 (because UTF-16 uses 2 bytes for that).

Modern web pages typically use UTF-8, a Unicode encoding that can represent virtually all characters in all languages and is backward-compatible with ASCII for the first 128 characters.

Character encoding can be declared in two ways. The server can send an HTTP header like `Content-Type: text/html; charset=UTF-8`, which is highly reliable since browsers give precedence to encoding information from headers. Alternatively, the encoding can be specified within the HTML document itself via a meta tag in the head section. In HTML5, the recommended syntax is simply `<meta charset="UTF-8">`, which should appear as early as possible in the document, ideally within the first 1024 bytes.

In HTML4/XHTML, you might see:

```
<meta http-equiv="Content-Type" content="text/html; charset=UTF-8">
```

That was the older syntax. HTML5 simplified it to the shorter `<meta charset="...">`.

For XHTML served as XML, you can also declare encoding in the XML prolog:

```
<?xml version = "1.0" encoding = "UTF-8"?>
```

If you serve XHTML as `application/xhtml+xml`, you should have that XML declaration at the very top (before the DOCTYPE).

If you drop an HTML file from your local system into a browser (file:// URL), and there is no header, the browser will rely on the meta tag or otherwise guess (often defaulting to some locale-specific encoding like

Windows-1252 for Western systems, which can lead to garbled characters if the file was actually UTF-8 without a declaration).

So always specify your encoding. UTF-8 is strongly recommended for all new web content for several compelling reasons. It can represent any character you might need, enabling mixed languages, special symbols, and emojis in a single document. While UTF-8 is the default for HTML5 if no encoding is specified, that default can be overridden by server headers or other factors, so explicit declaration is still advisable. Most validators and modern development tools expect UTF-8 encoding, making it the path of least resistance for standards compliance.

If you do not specify and the server does not either, browsers might heuristically sniff the content, but that is not reliable.

When a meta charset is present, as long as it is very early, the browser can re-interpret the stream from that point on correctly. If, however, you had some accented characters before the meta tag, and the browser was guessing a wrong encoding for those, they might appear wrong. That is why meta charset should be at the top. (Ideally within first 512 bytes, definitely within first 1024 bytes as recommended by W3C).

A meta character set example:

```html
<!DOCTYPE html>
<html lang = "en">
<head>
  <meta charset = "UTF-8">
  <title>Sample Page</title>
</head>
<body>
  <p>This page is in UTF-8. Characters like @ and [Chinese: zhong] should display correctly.</p>
</body>
</html>
```

The `lang="en"` attribute in html (or xml:lang in XHTML) is distinct. It declares the natural language of the content (useful for accessibility, search, etc.), whereas charset deals with character encoding.

One more note: if you serve XHTML as `application/xhtml+xml`, the content-type header must have a charset parameter or an XML declaration in the file must have encoding. If there is a mismatch or none given, the default per XML rules is UTF-8 or UTF-16 (if it sees a Byte Order Mark (BOM)). But it is best to be explicit.

Character encodings and Unicode are fundamental concepts for understanding how text is represented in web documents. Unicode is a character set. A mapping of code points to characters (like U+00E9 for 'é'). UTF-8 is an encoding that specifies how those code points are represented as bytes. An HTML or XHTML document is essentially a sequence of bytes that the browser must interpret as characters. If the browser assumes the wrong encoding, you get mojibake (garbled text where characters display incorrectly). Common legacy encodings like ISO-8859-1 (nearly identical to Windows-1252 for practical HTML purposes) or Shift_JIS (for Japanese) can only represent certain languages properly. Unicode, particularly in its UTF-8 encoding, covers all writing systems and has become the universal standard.

When you validate an HTML page, the validator also needs to know encoding. If you use the W3C validator and it complains "No character encoding declared at document level", it is urging you to include that `<meta charset>` or send a proper header.

For standards compliance and to avoid encoding-related errors, follow these practices. Include `<meta charset="UTF-8">` in your document's head section when using HTML5. Verify that your server is not overriding this declaration with a different charset in the HTTP header. Use UTF-8 consistently throughout your development workflow, especially if your content includes any non-ASCII characters or if scripts and stylesheets might contain special symbols.

4.2.6 Identifying XML Namespace (XHTML only)

In an XML document like XHTML, the root element can (and should) declare an XML namespace to disambiguate elements by the vocabulary they belong to.

For XHTML 1.x, the namespace is `http://www.w3.org /1999/xhtml`. Thus, an XHTML document's root `<html>` tag usually looks like:

```
<html xmlns="http://www.w3.org/1999/xhtml" xml:lang="en" lang="en">
```

The `xmlns="..."` attribute declares the default namespace for the document, indicating that any un-prefixed element (like `<p>` or `<div>`) in this document belongs to the XHTML namespace. The `xml:lang="en"` attribute is the XML way to specify language, while `lang="en"` is included for backwards compatibility with HTML processors. XHTML requires the `xml:lang` attribute and suggests also including `lang` for HTML compatibility.

The namespace declaration serves several important purposes in XHTML. When embedding other XML vocabularies, you use prefixes and different xmlns declarations to distinguish them. For example, including an SVG snippet in an XHTML file requires declaring the SVG namespace: `<svg xmlns="http://www.w3.org /2000/svg" ...>`. Because the SVG elements are in their own namespace, the XHTML parser treats them differently, and the browser knows to handle those elements with its SVG renderer.

Namespaces also prevent naming collisions between different XML vocabularies. Without proper namespace declarations, an `<svg>` tag might be mistaken for an XHTML element named "svg." This namespace mechanism is fundamental to the XML nature of XHTML: all elements belong to some namespace, even if it is the default namespace inherited from the root element.

If you do not include `xmlns` in an XHTML document served as XML, the parser might not know what kind of elements these are and could generate an error or treat them as belonging to no namespace (which might break CSS or scripts expecting them to be in XHTML Namespace (NS)).

For HTML5, if you serve as XML, you should still use `xmlns="http://www.w3.org/1999/xhtml"` on the html element. The `xml:lang` vs. `lang` difference becomes moot in HTML5 (it says just use `lang` even in XML serialization, IIRC, but having both is fine).

In plain HTML (text/html), you do not need to and should not include XML namespace declarations (browsers will just ignore `xmlns` attributes in HTML mode, but it is unnecessary clutter unless you are writing polyglot markup that can be both parsed as HTML or XML).

To summarize namespace requirements in XHTML: ensure the root element carries the correct XML namespace for XHTML, which identifies the document's elements as XHTML elements. Also use appropriate language attributes (`xml:lang` for XML processors and `lang` for HTML compatibility) and include any other required XML prolog elements such as the XML declaration (`<?xml version="1.0" encoding="UTF-8"?>`) if you want the document to be well-formed XML.

4.2.7 Validation of HTML Pages

Validation is the process of checking your HTML (or XHTML) against the rules of a specific standard (like HTML5, or XHTML 1.0 Strict, etc.). The W3C provides a validator service where you can upload a page or give a URL and it will report any deviations from the specification.

Why validate your HTML? Validation helps catch mistakes that could lead to inconsistent display across different browsers. It ensures you are using markup correctly rather than relying on browser quirks or error-correction behavior. A valid page is more likely to work properly with assistive technologies like screen readers, search engine parsers, and future browsers that may handle errors differently than current ones.

When you run a validator, it will parse the page and list errors or warnings. For example, if you forgot a `</head>` or you nested something improperly, or used an attribute that is not allowed, etc.

If you have a page with `<head><title>Test</head>` (missing closing `</title>` or mis-nested), a validator might report an error like:

```
Line 10, Column 6: end tag for "HEAD" which is not finished.
</head>
```

And often a hint:

```
Most likely, you nested tags and closed them in the wrong order...
<p><em>...</p> is not acceptable, as <em> must be closed before <p>.
```

This clue is telling you an example of improper nesting and the correct way (`<p><em>...</em></p>`). It might specifically be hinting maybe you forgot to close a title or a paragraph, etc.

If you forget the meta charset and the validator cannot determine encoding, it might warn:

```
No Character Encoding Found! Falling back to UTF-8.
... Without encoding information it is impossible to reliably validate ...
```

So it would prefer you include one.

Or if you omit the required `<title>` in the head, the validator will throw an error (as `<title>` is required in HTML/XHTML). If you had an empty or missing title, it might show a message about head not finished or missing required element.

Validation messages can sometimes be verbose or confusing. The key is to scan for the first error, because one error (like a missing closing tag) can cascade into many subsequent error messages. Fixing the first error often causes a lot of the following errors to disappear on the next validation attempt.

Doctypes and validation: The validator uses the DOCTYPE to know what set of rules to apply. If you use an HTML5 doctype, the validator knows you might use modern elements (`<article>`, `<nav>`, etc.). If you used an XHTML 1.0 Strict doctype, it will complain if you use, say, a deprecated attribute like `bgcolor` on a table (since Strict disallowed that).

Common validation issues fall into several categories. Missing closing tags or improper nesting is very common and can cause unpredictable layout behavior. Using attributes that are not allowed in the declared HTML version will trigger errors. For example, using `border="1"` on a `<table>` when your DOCTYPE specifies HTML5 or XHTML Strict, which require CSS for visual styling. Forgetting required attributes such as the `alt` attribute on every `<img>` element will cause validation failures. Using uppercase tag names or unquoted attribute values in XHTML mode violates XML requirements. A stray ampersand in text that is not part of a known entity reference (or written as `&`) will be flagged. Duplicate ID values on elements violate the HTML requirement that IDs be unique within a document. Placing elements in disallowed contexts, such as putting a block element inside an inline element, will cause errors in older HTML and XHTML versions, though HTML5 has relaxed many of these rules.

Note that the HTML5 validator is more forgiving in some areas because HTML5 defines content models more flexibly. It often issues warnings rather than errors for certain practices, such as using obsolete elements that are still technically supported.

Using the validator effectively: If you have a lot of errors, concentrate on the first few unique ones. Often one error (like an unclosed quote or tag) can throw off the rest of the parse. Fix that and re-run.

Keep in mind validation does not guarantee a site looks or functions as intended; it only ensures the code is syntactically correct according to spec. You could have a perfectly valid page that still has logical issues or CSS bugs, etc. But it eliminates one category of problem.

Also, you might occasionally have to use non-standard markup (e.g., a custom data- attribute or an SVG embed). HTML5 is extensible with data-* attributes and allows SVG, so usually that is fine. But if you include something truly non-standard, you can still validate by creating a custom DTD or by using HTML5 which is designed to accommodate unknown elements (it allows any tag, treating unknown ones as inline by default).

The bottom line: Validate your pages during development. It is much easier to catch an unclosed tag via a validator than by manually scanning or wondering why the layout is broken in one browser. Most modern editors and Integrated Development Environments (IDEs) also have linting that catches these, but the W3C validator is the authority.

4.2.8   Common Errors in HTML

Even experienced developers sometimes make simple HTML mistakes. Here are some of the most common errors to watch out for (some we have already touched on):

- Omitting a closing quote on an attribute value: For example `<input type="text" name="user value="John">`, here the `name` attribute's quote was opened but not closed properly before value. This can wreak havoc on the parser (suddenly lots of subsequent text might be seen as part of the attribute value). Many editors highlight attribute values in a color; if you forget a quote, you might see the rest of the page highlighted as a string. Always double-check quotes. A validator would flag an error at the point of the next quote or tag.
- Omitting the closing bracket `>` of a tag: e.g., `<div<p>Text</p>`, the `<div` tag never closed `>`, so the browser might ignore it or assume something. This often results in the browser treating the `<div <p>` as literal text or ignoring the div start. The rest of your page might appear as plain text or elements not recognized until the next `>` is found. This error can make almost the entire remainder of the HTML invalid. It is easy to accidentally do when manually editing. Always ensure every `<` has a matching `>` for

the tag (and each attribute's quotes are closed, as mentioned).

- Mis-nested tags: e.g., `<em><strong>Important</em></strong>`, closing in the wrong order. Browsers might fix it internally (most would assume you meant `<em><strong>Important</strong></em>`). But it is invalid HTML. Use a structured approach to writing HTML and indent your code logically to spot overlap.
- Missing required elements: For instance, forgetting to include a `<title>` in the head. The page might still render, but it is technically invalid and you will have no title in bookmarks or browser tabs (which is a usability issue). The validator will remind you if you left it out.
- Using deprecated elements or attributes in Strict modes: For example, using `<font>` or the `align` attribute on a `<p>` when using XHTML Strict or HTML5. They still "work" in browsers (for now) but they are not part of modern specs. The validator will warn or error out on those if using a doctype that disallows them.
- Duplicate `id values:` Each id in a document should be unique. If you accidentally copy-paste elements and leave them with the same id, it is invalid (and can cause script or style issues since id selectors or getElementById might find the first one only). Some validators or linters catch this.
- Non-HTML content in HTML: e.g., putting a `<script>` or `<style>` in the body with an unescaped < that looks like a tag. For example, writing a JavaScript snippet that includes HTML in a string but forgetting to escape or quote it properly, leading to broken HTML structure.
- Forgetting to self-close an empty tag in XHTML: If you are writing XHTML, `<img>` must be `<img ... />`. If you forget the slash, the validator will complain since in XML, `<img>` would require a separate `</img>` which is not allowed by DTD.
- Typos in tag names or attribute names: e.g., writing `<dib>` instead of `<div>`. Browsers typically ignore unknown tags (they treat them as inline elements) but it is not what you intended. Or `clsas` instead of `class`. Those will not apply style and are hard to spot by eye.
- Using & or `< in text without escaping:` If you need to literally output "AT&T" in HTML, you should write `AT&T` (or include it in a context like `<pre>` where it might be taken literally, but generally use `&`). Same with the < if you want it to appear (like writing `x < y` should be `x < y`). If you do not, the parser might think you started a tag or entity. `&something;` will try to parse an entity; if it is not a valid one, some browsers leave it as is, others might drop it. The validator will catch an & that is not followed by a valid entity name or #.
- Leaving off closing `</table> or \CVerb{</tr>} etc.:` Browsers often handle it, but it can lead to weird layouts. Better to explicitly close all table tags. The validator will definitely flag those.
- Inline in block mis-nesting or vice versa: Historically, HTML had a concept of block-level and inline elements and rules like `<p>` cannot contain another `<p>` directly, etc. HTML5 relaxed some rules, but e.g., you should not put a `<div>` inside a `<span>` (block inside inline) because it is generally not allowed (browser will probably close the span before the div automatically). The validator might warn about element not allowed in that context.

To avoid these errors, use a code editor with syntax highlighting that shows mismatched quotes or tags. Format your code clearly with proper indentation for nested elements. Validate early and often, especially after major edits. Consider integrating HTML linters or validators into your development workflow to catch errors automatically.

Remember that browsers try their best to recover from errors, which is good for users but can hide problems from developers. Different browsers may recover differently from the same malformed markup, so a page that looks fine in one browser might break in another. A validated page is more likely to behave consistently across all browsers.

4.3   Character Encodings

As discussed in Chapter 3, the web is a global medium, and content can be written in any of the world's languages and scripts. To handle this, modern HTML relies on Unicode, a universal character set that assigns a code point (a number) to every character in nearly every writing system, including Latin, Cyrillic, Chinese, Arabic, emojis, etc. However, these code points need to be stored as bytes, and that is where encodings come in.

Let us now expand on this topic for forms and advanced HTML features.

4.3.1   Unicode

Unicode is a standard that defines a unique number, called a code point, for every character across all writing systems. The letter A is assigned code point U+0041 (hexadecimal 41). The accented letter é has code point U+00E9. The Chinese character meaning "middle" or "center" is U+4E2D. Even emojis are included. For example, the grinning face is U+1F600. This universal character set allows any text from any language to be represented and processed by computers.

Unicode does not tell how these numbers are stored in memory or files; it is just the numbering scheme (the character set). It currently has over 143,000 characters defined, covering historical scripts as well.

Web pages internally use Unicode for representing characters (the DOM deals in code points). But when it comes to files and network transmission, we have to choose a specific encoding that turns those code points into bytes.

4.3.2   Encodings of Unicode Characters

There are several Unicode encodings, each with different characteristics:
- UTF-8: The most popular encoding on the web. It uses 1 byte for common ASCII characters (U+0000 to U+007F), and more bytes for other characters (up to 4 bytes for characters in the range U+10000 and beyond). It is a variable-length encoding but very efficient for texts that are primarily in English/ASCII range (as those remain one byte each). UTF-8 is backward compatible with ASCII as any valid ASCII text is also valid UTF-8 (the bytes mean the same characters).
- UTF-16: Uses 2 bytes (16 bits) for most common characters, and 4 bytes for those outside the Basic Multilingual Plane (characters above U+FFFF). There are two flavors (little-endian and big-endian) depending on byte order. In UTF-16, ASCII characters actually become 2 bytes each (for example "A" is 0x0041).
- UTF-32: Uses 4 bytes for every character (enough to encode every code point directly as one number). It is not commonly used for file or network because it is space-inefficient (lots of 0x00 bytes for ASCII).
- Legacy encodings: Before Unicode took over, many regions had their own encodings: ISO-8859-1 (Latin-1) for Western Europe (which covers A-Z, a-z, and common accented letters for Western European languages), ISO-8859-5 for Cyrillic, Shift_JIS or EUC-JP for Japanese, GB2312 for Chinese, etc., and Windows code pages like Windows-1252 (an extension of Latin-1). These encodings typically only handle a subset of characters (often 256 characters possible, one byte per char). They cannot represent

characters outside their range (for example, you cannot show Chinese characters in ISO-8859-1, or Russian in ISO-8859-1).

When we say "the page is encoded in UTF-8", it means the bytes that make up the .html file are interpreted via UTF-8 rules to recover the Unicode code points.

How Characters Are Represented in Different Encodings

The following examples demonstrate how the same characters are encoded differently depending on which character encoding scheme is used. Understanding these differences helps explain why encoding mismatches cause display problems.

Consider the character 'A' (Unicode code point U+0041). In ASCII, this character is represented as the single byte 0x41. UTF-8 uses the same representation for ASCII characters, so 'A' is also 0x41 in UTF-8. However, UTF-16 uses two bytes for every character, so 'A' becomes 0x41 0x00 in little-endian UTF-16 (the bytes are stored with the least significant byte first).

The accented character 'é' (U+00E9) shows more variation. In Latin-1 (ISO-8859-1), this character maps directly to the byte 0xE9. UTF-8 encodes it as the two-byte sequence 0xC3 0xA9, since UTF-8 uses multiple bytes for characters outside the ASCII range. UTF-16 represents it as 0xE9 0x00 in little-endian format.

The Chinese character [Chinese: zhong/middle] (U+4E2D) illustrates the limitations of legacy encodings. UTF-8 encodes this character as three bytes: 0xE4 0xB8 0xAD. UTF-16 uses two bytes: 0x2D 0x4E in little-endian format. However, this character simply cannot be represented in ISO-8859-1 or other Western legacy encodings. Attempting to display it in such an encoding would produce a fallback character or question mark.

These examples demonstrate that the same text produces different byte sequences depending on the encoding. This is precisely why web pages must correctly declare their encoding: if a browser interprets bytes using the wrong encoding, characters will display incorrectly or not at all.

Why Unicode and UTF-8 Are Favored

Unicode and UTF-8 have become the standard for web content because they solve the fundamental problems of legacy encodings. With UTF-8, developers do not need to guess which encoding a document uses. If everything is UTF-8, any language can be displayed on any page seamlessly. There is no longer a need for separate pages or encoding declarations for different languages, as was common in the era of regional encodings.

Modern web platforms have standardized on UTF-8: JSON requires it, XML defaults to it, and HTML5 strongly recommends it. This standardization eliminates the frustrating situation where characters appear incorrectly because a file was saved in one encoding but interpreted as another. In the past, a file saved in Windows-1252 but read as ISO-8859-1 would display some characters incorrectly, and reading a Shift_JIS Japanese file as Latin-1 would produce complete gibberish. UTF-8 adoption has largely eliminated these problems from modern web development.

4.3.3 Identifying Encodings in HTML

Always declare the encoding of your HTML pages, even if you believe the server will do it for you, including a meta tag provides a safety net. The standard approach in HTML5 is to include `<meta charset="UTF-`

8"> in the head section. For XHTML served as XML, use the XML declaration `<?xml version="1.0"`
`encoding="UTF-8"?>` at the very beginning of the file, before the DOCTYPE.

The HTTP header is the most authoritative way to declare encoding if you can configure your server:
`Content-Type: text/html; charset=UTF-8`. When both an HTTP header and a meta tag are present, the
HTTP header takes precedence as the browser trusts the server's declaration over the document's. However,
when opening a file directly from disk, there is no HTTP header, so the meta tag becomes the browser's only
source of encoding information.

If an encoding is not specified, browsers must guess which encoding to use. They often assume a default
based on the user's locale or browser settings, frequently choosing Latin-1 or Windows-1252 for Western
language versions. Browsers may also attempt to detect the encoding by examining the content for certain
patterns, such as the byte sequences characteristic of UTF-8 or the presence of a UTF-8 BOM (byte order mark).
However, this detection is unreliable and may guess incorrectly, resulting in garbled characters.

Even when you do specify an encoding, you must ensure your file is actually saved in that encoding. A
common problem occurs when a developer includes `<meta charset="UTF-8">` in their HTML, but the text
editor actually saved the file in Windows-1252. If that file contains characters that differ between the two
encodings, such as em dashes or curly quotation marks, the browser will misinterpret those bytes when trying to
decode them as UTF-8, resulting in strange replacement characters or gibberish at those points. Always verify
your editor's encoding setting and, ideally, configure it to use UTF-8 without BOM by default.

So always double-check your file encoding in your editor (most allow you to choose or will show it). Ideally,
set your editor to use UTF-8 without BOM by default.

4.3.4   Unicode and HTML Entities

As we covered in Chapter 3, sometimes you need to include characters that have special meaning in HTML
syntax (like <, >, or &), but you cannot easily type on your keyboard, or that you want to ensure display correctly
regardless of potential encoding issues. HTML provides character entities and numeric character references for
these situations.

For these cases, HTML and XML provide character references as a way to include characters that cannot be
typed directly or that have special meaning in markup. Named entities (also called character entity references)
use mnemonic names beginning with & and ending with ;. For example, `<` represents the less-than sign (<).
Named entities exist for many symbols, particularly punctuation and common special characters.

Numeric character references specify characters by their Unicode code point. These come in two forms:
decimal notation like `<` and hexadecimal notation like `<`. Both examples represent the less-than
sign(<), since 60 decimal (or 3C hexadecimal) is the code point for that character. Numeric references can
represent any Unicode character, making them useful when no named entity exists.

The most commonly used character entities handle characters with special meaning in HTML. The entity
`<` produces the less-than sign (<), which must be escaped in text content to avoid being interpreted as
the start of a tag. The entity `>` produces the greater-than sign (>), and while it is generally safe in text
content, escaping it maintains consistency. The entity `&` produces the ampersand (&), which must always
be escaped since it introduces entity references. The entity `"` produces a double quotation mark, useful
within attribute values. The entity `'` produces a single quotation mark. This was not available in HTML4
but is supported in XHTML and HTML5. The entity ` ` produces a non-breaking space, which prevents

line breaks between words and is also used when multiple consecutive spaces are needed.

For instance, if you wanted to write 5 > 4 in an HTML file but not have it be confused, you should write 5 > 4 so that the > is not seen as a tag delimiter (in text content it is fine to just put > though, as that is not ambiguous, < is the main one that must be escaped in text to avoid starting an element).

The ampersand always introduces an entity. If you actually want to output an ampersand, you must write &. If you forget and write something like AT&T, the parser will see AT& and think an entity is coming. AT&T might result in "AT" and then an error or it might ignore &T as unknown entity. So do AT&T.

Numeric references usage

In addition to named entities, HTML supports numeric character references that specify characters by their Unicode code point. Decimal references use the format &#NNN; where NNN is the decimal code point. For example, © produces the copyright symbol (©) because 169 decimal equals 0xA9 hexadecimal, the code point for that character. Hexadecimal references use &#xHHH; where HHH is the hexadecimal code point, so © also produces the copyright symbol. These numeric references can represent any Unicode character. For example, the smiley face at code point U+263A can be written as ☺ (decimal) or ☺ (hexadecimal).

However, if you are using UTF-8 and your file is saved in UTF-8, you can often just put the actual character directly in your HTML and it will work (as long as your editor can input it). Entities are a fallback or for clarity.

One area where entities remain commonly used is for spaces and typographic characters. The non-breaking space   prevents line breaks between words, useful for keeping an honorific with a name (such as "Dr. Smith") on the same line. Typographic dashes have their own entities: – for the en dash and — for the em dash. Symbols like copyright (©) and trademark (™) can be written as entities, though in UTF-8 you can also type © and ™ directly. The less-than sign and ampersand must always be escaped in contexts where they could be misinterpreted as markup.

Entities in XHTML Context

In XML-based XHTML, the requirements for escaping special characters are stricter than in HTML. You cannot have an unescaped < anywhere in the document content. In HTML served as text/html, a parser might treat an unexpected < as literal text if it does not look like the start of a valid tag. But in XHTML served as XML, an unescaped < outside of a tag causes a well-formedness error that stops parsing entirely. You must use < for any literal less-than sign and & for any ampersand that is not introducing a valid entity reference.

Entities vs. encoding

Using a numeric character reference ensures that character shows up as intended even if the encoding might not normally support it. For example, if you were stuck using ISO-8859-1 encoding but wanted to display a character outside its range (like U+0411, Cyrillic capital letter Be), you could include it as Б. The browser will interpret that code point and render the appropriate Cyrillic character even though Latin1 has no direct byte representation for it. The rest of page might still be Latin1.

But rather than doing that for multiple characters, it is far better to just use Unicode encoding (UTF-8) so you can directly include any character.

One caution: The HTML5 parser (in text/html mode) has some pre-defined named entities. Some obscure ones from XHTML MathML or older sets might not be recognized in an HTML5 page unless a doctype or DTD is known. However, HTML5 covers essentially all commonly used named entities. If an entity is not recognized, you will see it rendered as the literal text (&something; stays on page). The validator would catch an unknown entity reference.

When to Use Character References

Use character references for special characters like < and & in any context where they might be misinterpreted, particularly in text content and attribute values. Use them for non-breaking spaces and other specific whitespace characters when you need precise control over spacing and line breaks. Character references are also useful when you cannot easily input a character on your keyboard or when you want to make a character's presence explicit in the source code for clarity. Some developers prefer `é` over the literal é to avoid potential encoding confusion. However, when using UTF-8 encoding (which you should be), prefer typing characters directly when possible. This keeps the HTML source more readable, especially for documents containing text in non-Latin scripts.

4.3.5   Summary of Encodings and Entities in Practice

Character encodings and HTML entities work together to ensure that web content displays correctly across different systems, browsers, and languages. Understanding how to use them properly is essential for creating robust, internationalized web applications.

The most important practical decision is choosing UTF-8 as your page encoding. UTF-8 has become the de facto standard for the web because it can represent any Unicode character while remaining backward-compatible with ASCII. When you declare UTF-8 encoding, you can include characters from any language directly in your HTML source, from Western European accented letters to Chinese characters to emojis. This declaration should appear early in your document, either through a `<meta charset="UTF-8">` tag in the head section or through an HTTP `Content-Type` header from the server.

Equally important is ensuring that your entire toolchain is aligned to UTF-8. Your text editor must save files in UTF-8 encoding (not Latin-1 or another legacy encoding). Your web server must be configured to send the correct `Content-Type` header with the UTF-8 charset parameter. If any part of this chain uses a different encoding, characters may become corrupted or display as garbled text. Many frustrating encoding problems stem from a mismatch between the declared encoding and the actual encoding used to save the file.

Even when using UTF-8, certain characters require escaping with HTML entities. The less-than sign (<) must be written as `<` when it appears in text content, because browsers would otherwise interpret it as the start of an HTML tag. The ampersand (&) must be written as `&` because it introduces entity references. In attribute values, quotation marks may need escaping as `"` if you are using double quotes as the attribute delimiter. The greater-than sign (>) is technically safe in most contexts but is often escaped as `>` for consistency and to avoid any edge cases.

The non-breaking space entity (` `) serves a specific purpose: it prevents line breaks between words that should stay together, such as "Dr. Smith" or "100 km". Regular spaces allow the browser to break lines for text wrapping, but non-breaking spaces keep adjacent words on the same line. This entity is also sometimes used (though not ideally) to create multiple consecutive spaces, since HTML collapses sequences of regular spaces into a single space.

Finally, validating your pages helps catch encoding-related errors that might otherwise go unnoticed. The W3C validator will flag unescaped ampersands, unknown entity references, and other character-related issues. Running validation regularly during development prevents these small errors from accumulating into larger problems that are harder to diagnose later.

4.4 MIME Types

When a browser requests a resource from a web server – whether an HTML page, an image, a CSS file, or any other content – the server responds with not just the content itself, but also metadata in the form of HTTP headers. Among the most important of these headers is the MIME type (also known as the content type), which tells the browser what kind of content it is receiving. MIME stands for Multipurpose Internet Mail Extensions; the standard originated from email protocols where it was used to describe the type of email attachments, but it has become equally essential in HTTP for describing the type of any file sent over the web. Understanding MIME types is fundamental for web developers because they determine how browsers interpret and display content, and incorrect MIME types can lead to rendering failures or security vulnerabilities.

A MIME type follows the format `type/subtype`, where the type indicates the general category of content and the subtype specifies the exact format. For example, `text/html` indicates an HTML page, `text/css` identifies a CSS stylesheet, `image/png` represents a PNG image, `application/javascript` (or the older `text/javascript`) denotes JavaScript files, and `application/pdf` indicates PDF documents. The browser uses the MIME type to decide how to handle the content: if it receives `text/html`, it renders the content as a web page; if it receives `image/jpeg`, it displays it as an image; and if it receives something like `application/octet-stream` (generic binary) or an unrecognized type, the browser might prompt the user to download the file or ask what action to take.

Servers typically determine the MIME type by examining the file extension or consulting their configuration. For instance, Apache might be configured so that `.html` files are served as `text/html`, `.jpg` files as `image/jpeg`, and so on. This configuration is crucial because browsers rely on the MIME type header rather than the file extension to determine how to process content.

4.4.1 MIME Types and Subtypes

The structure `type/subtype` provides a hierarchical classification system for content. The type represents a general category such as `text`, `image`, `audio`, `video`, `application`, or `multipart`. The subtype provides the specific format within that category. Some subtypes are further subdivided by standards bodies or vendors. For example, `application/vnd.ms-excel` specifically identifies Microsoft Excel files, where `vnd` indicates a vendor-specific type.

The `text` type encompasses human-readable content where newlines might be standardized to CRLF (carriage return plus line feed) in the protocol. Common examples include `text/plain` for plain text, `text/html` for HTML documents, and `text/css` for stylesheets. The `image` type covers visual content such as `image/png`, `image/jpeg`, `image/gif`, and `image/svg+xml`. Note that SVG is actually XML text but is typically served with an image type to indicate its visual purpose.

The `audio` type includes formats like `audio/mpeg` for MP3 files and `audio/ogg` for Ogg Vorbis audio. Similarly, the `video` type covers formats like `video/mp4` and `video/webm`. The `application` type is used for content that is binary or not naturally viewed as text, including `application/pdf` for PDF documents, `application/zip` for compressed archives, `application/json` for JSON data, and `application/xhtml+xml` for XHTML documents. Notice that XML-based types often use the `application` type when they are not directly intended as human-readable text.

The `multipart` type is mainly used in emails and form submissions. The `multipart/form-data` type, which we discussed in the context of file uploads, packages form data with file content separated by boundary markers. HTTP responses can also be multipart in some server-push technologies, though this is less common in standard web browsing.

Wildcard types like `image/*` can be used in certain contexts to indicate "any image type." This becomes particularly relevant in content negotiation, where browsers indicate what types they can accept.

Understanding why MIME types matter requires recognizing their role in browser behavior. Browsers use MIME types to decide how to render or handle a resource. If a server mistakenly sends an HTML file with MIME type `text/plain`, the browser will display the raw HTML code as plain text instead of rendering it as a web page. Conversely, if a server sends a CSS file with type `text/html`, the browser might try to parse it as HTML, which will fail to apply the intended styles. This demonstrates why correct server configuration is essential for proper web page functionality.

Content negotiation allows servers to serve different content based on client capabilities. Browsers send an `Accept` header indicating what MIME types they can handle. For example, a browser might send:

```
Accept: text/html, application/xhtml+xml, application/xml;q=0.9, */*;q=0.8
```

This means "I prefer HTML or XHTML, can handle XML with slightly lower priority (q=0.9), and will accept anything else at lower priority (q=0.8)." The `q` values are quality factors that express preference weighting, with 1.0 being the highest (and the default when not specified).

The server can use this information to choose which version of a resource to send. For instance, some servers serve WebP images to browsers that include `image/webp` in their Accept header, while serving JPEG to browsers that do not support WebP. This optimization delivers smaller file sizes to capable browsers without breaking compatibility for others.

The HTTP response includes a `Content-Type` header that specifies the MIME type and, for text types, often includes a charset parameter: `Content-Type: text/html; charset=UTF-8`. Browsers rely on this header to interpret the content correctly. If the header is missing, some browsers might attempt to sniff the content to determine its type. Internet Explorer's content-sniffing algorithms were particularly aggressive, sometimes leading to security issues. For example, interpreting an image as HTML if the image file happened to contain HTML-like patterns. Modern browsers follow stricter policies and trust the Content-Type header, which is why sending the correct MIME type from the server is crucial.

4.4.2　Plug-ins and Helper Applications

Even though browsers natively handle many types (HTML, images, common audio and video formats, etc.), there are types that historically required external help. Plug-ins are programs that integrate with the browser to handle content the browser cannot natively process, displaying the content within the browser window. Helper applications are external programs that the browser launches to open content in a separate window.

The distinction between plug-ins and helper applications can be subtle. A plug-in runs inside the browser window. For example, Adobe Flash Player would render Small Web Format (SWF) files embedded in a pagex, and PDF viewer plug-ins would display documents within a browser tab. A helper application, by contrast, is a separate program launched by the browser. If you click a link to an Excel spreadsheet and the browser does not have an in-tab viewer, it might launch Microsoft Excel to open the file. Similarly, clicking a `mailto:` link launches your default email client as a helper application.

Historically, common plug-ins included Adobe Flash Player (for `application/x-shockwave-flash` content), Adobe Reader for viewing PDFs within the browser, and Apple QuickTime or Windows Media Player for certain audio and video codecs. The browser would maintain a registry of plug-ins and the MIME types each could handle. When a server responded with a particular Content-Type, the browser would check if a plug-in was registered for that type and, if so, delegate rendering to that plug-in.

Modern browsers have largely moved away from plug-ins due to security concerns. Flash has been deprecated and is now disabled by default in all major browsers. NPAPI (Netscape Plugin Application Programming Interface) plug-ins are no longer supported in Chrome and most other browsers. Instead, browsers now rely on built-in capabilities as HTML5 provides native video and audio playback, and most browsers include built-in PDF viewers. This shift improves security because plug-ins often introduced vulnerabilities and had access to system resources that could be exploited.

The concept remains important for understanding web architecture: when a browser receives content with a MIME type it cannot handle natively, it must either use a plug-in (if available), launch a helper application, or prompt the user to download the file. If the server sends content with the proper MIME type, the appropriate handler should process it correctly; if the server sends the wrong type, the browser might attempt to render content incorrectly or simply offer it as a download.

4.4.3   MIME Types in HTML Markup

Web developers need to be aware of MIME types not just for server configuration, but also in the HTML markup itself. Several HTML elements accept type attributes that specify MIME types.

The `<link>` element for stylesheets can include a type attribute: `<link rel="stylesheet" type="text/css" href="style.css">`. Here `type="text/css"` explicitly specifies the MIME type. HTML5 allows you to omit this attribute for CSS stylesheets since `text/css` is the default for style links, but including it makes the intent explicit and maintains compatibility with older HTML versions.

Similarly, the `<script>` element historically required a type attribute: `<script type="text/javascript" src="app.js"></script>`. HTML5 changed this so that JavaScript is the default if no type is specified, and modern practice often omits the attribute entirely. However, the MIME type delivered by the server in the Content-Type header should still be `application/javascript` or `text/javascript`. The type attribute becomes important when using JavaScript modules (`type="module"`) or when embedding non-JavaScript content.

The `<embed>` and `<object>` elements use the type attribute to declare the MIME type of embedded content. For example, `<object data="file.swf" type="application/x-shockwave-flash">` would embed a Flash file (though this is now obsolete). The `<img>` tag typically does not require a type attribute because browsers determine the image format from the content itself.

The `enctype` attribute on forms is particularly important for controlling how form data is encoded when submitted. By default, form submissions use `application/x-www-form-urlencoded`, which corresponds to the simple `key=value&key2=value2` format in the URL or request body. When uploading files, you must change this to `multipart/form-data`:

```html
<form action = "/upload" method = "POST" enctype = "multipart/form-data">
    <input type = "file" name = "document">
    <input type = "submit" value = "Upload">
</form>
```

This tells the browser to send the form data as a MIME multipart message, where each field becomes a separate part with its own headers. The file field gets its own part with an appropriate Content-Type header based on the file being uploaded. Without the correct enctype, file uploads will not work properly since the browser would try to URL-encode the binary file data, corrupting it.

For multimedia elements, the type attribute helps browsers select appropriate sources. In a `<video>` element with multiple `<source>` children, each source can specify its type:

```html
<video controls>
    <source src = "movie.mp4" type = "video/mp4">
    <source src = "movie.webm" type = "video/webm">
</video>
```

This allows the browser to skip formats it does not support without downloading them first. For example, if a browser does not support WebM, it can immediately move to the MP4 source rather than attempting to load the WebM file only to discover it cannot play it.

4.4.4   MIME Types in Server Configuration

Web servers must be configured to send the correct MIME types for different file extensions. Apache uses directives like `AddType` in `httpd.conf` or `.htaccess` files:

```
AddType text/html .html
AddType text/css .css
AddType application/javascript .js
AddType image/jpeg .jpg .jpeg
AddType image/png .png
AddType image/svg+xml .svg
```

Alternatively, Apache can reference a `mime.types` file that contains a comprehensive list of extension-to-MIME mappings.

In Tomcat (a Java application server), MIME mappings are configured in `web.xml`:

```
1  <mime-mapping>
2      <extension>html</extension>
3      <mime-type>text/html</mime-type>
4  </mime-mapping>
```

This configuration tells the server what Content-Type header to send when serving files with each extension. If you introduce a new file type (say, a `.xyz` extension for proprietary data), you must configure the server to send an appropriate MIME type. You might use `application/x-xyz` (the `x-` prefix conventionally indicates an unofficial or experimental type) or register a standard type with Internet Assigned Numbers Authority (IANA) if the format becomes widely used.

Incorrect server configuration can cause significant problems. Consider a scenario where a developer sets up a site on Internet Information Services (IIS) but forgets to configure a MIME type for `.svg` files. The server might refuse to serve SVG files or send them as `application/octet-stream`, prompting browsers to download them rather than display them inline. The fix is to configure `.svg` to `image/svg+xml` so browsers recognize and render the graphics correctly.

Another common issue involves JSON files. If not configured, servers might serve `.json` files as `text/plain`, which may work for simple use cases but can cause problems when applications expect `application/json`. Proper configuration ensures consistent behavior across different client applications.

One technique for controlling browser behavior is deliberately sending an unexpected MIME type. If you want users to download an HTML file rather than view it, you can configure the server to send it as `application/octet-stream` (generic binary), which prompts browsers to show a save dialog. More commonly, servers use the `Content-Disposition: attachment` header alongside the correct MIME type to force a download while still indicating what type of file it is.

If you encounter situations where the browser shows raw source code instead of rendering a page, or offers to download a file that should be displayed, the cause is usually incorrect MIME type configuration on the server. Similarly, if a browser tries to display binary content as text (showing gibberish), the server probably sent a binary file with a text MIME type.

4.4.5 MIME Types and XHTML

The relationship between MIME types and XHTML illustrates how content types affect browser parsing behavior. If you send XHTML with `Content-Type: application/xhtml+xml`, browsers that support this type (which includes all modern browsers) will process it as strict XML. This means any well-formedness error will cause the browser to display an error message rather than attempting to recover and render the page. If you send the same content as `text/html`, browsers will use their HTML parser, which is more forgiving of errors.

For example, if you have a MathML equation embedded in an XHTML page served as `application/xhtml+xml`, Firefox and other supporting browsers will render the mathematics correctly because they're processing the document as XML and can handle the MathML namespace. Firefox includes `application/xhtml+xml` in its Accept header, indicating it can handle this content type.

This MIME type distinction historically caused compatibility issues with Internet Explorer, which did not support `application/xhtml+xml` and would prompt users to download pages served with this type. Some sites implemented content negotiation to address this: they would check the client's Accept header and send `application/xhtml+xml` to browsers that supported it (like Firefox) while sending `text/html` to browsers that did not (like IE). With Internet Explorer's replacement by Edge (which uses the Chromium engine and does support `application/xhtml+xml`), this is less of a concern today, but it illustrates the importance of MIME types in determining how content is processed.

Modern web development predominantly uses HTML5 with `text/html`, but MIME types remain important for other XML-based content. SVG graphics, for example, should be served with `image/svg+xml` when delivered as standalone files. If you erroneously serve an SVG as `text/html`, a browser may attempt to treat it as an HTML document, which will not work correctly. Some older server configurations did not include SVG mappings, causing SVG files to fail until administrators added the correct MIME type.

4.4.6 Content Negotiation in Practice

Content negotiation allows servers to serve different versions of a resource based on client capabilities or preferences. The server examines request headers like `Accept`, `Accept-Language`, and `Accept-Encoding` to determine which variant to send.

For MIME type negotiation, the server might check whether a client accepts `application/xhtml+xml`:

```php
if (stristr($_SERVER["HTTP_ACCEPT"], "application/xhtml+xml"))
{
    $mime = "application/xhtml+xml";
}
else
{
    $mime = "text/html";
}
header("Content-Type: $mime; charset=UTF-8");
header("Vary: Accept");
```

This code checks whether the Accept header contains "application/xhtml+xml" and sets the response MIME type accordingly. The `Vary: Accept` header is important for HTTP caching as it tells caches that this response varies depending on the Accept header, so they should store separate versions for different Accept values. Without this header, a cache might serve the wrong version to some clients.

Language negotiation works similarly. If a user's browser sends `Accept-Language: fr-CA,fr;q=0.8, en;q=0.5`, indicating a preference for Canadian French, then standard French, then English, the server could serve a French version of the page if available.

Image format negotiation has become increasingly common. Servers might deliver WebP images to browsers that include `image/webp` in their Accept header while serving JPEG to browsers that do not support WebP. This optimization reduces bandwidth for capable browsers without breaking compatibility. The server would include `Vary: Accept` so that caches store both versions appropriately.

The quality factor syntax (`q=0.9`) allows clients to express preferences beyond simple presence or absence. `Accept: */*;q=0.5` means "I accept any type at quality 0.5", which is a way to say the client prefers the explicitly listed types but will accept others at lower preference if necessary.

4.4.7 Email, MIME, and Base64 Encoding

MIME originated in email, predating its widespread use on the web. Understanding its email roots helps explain some aspects of web MIME usage, particularly around encoding binary content.

Email was originally designed for plain ASCII text. The core email transport protocol (SMTP) reliably handles only 7-bit characters, and certain byte values could be interpreted as control characters by mail servers. MIME solved the problem of sending rich content and attachments through this constrained channel.

An email uses `Content-Type` headers similar to HTTP. A plain text email might specify `Content-Type: text/plain; charset="UTF-8"`, while an HTML email would use `Content-Type: text/html; charset ="UTF-8"`.

For emails with attachments, MIME defines multipart structures. A `multipart/mixed` message contains multiple parts, each with its own headers. An email with a text message and a JPEG attachment would have one part of type `text/plain` containing the message body and another part of type `image/jpeg` containing the image data, all wrapped in a multipart container with boundary markers separating the parts.

The `multipart/alternative` type is used when sending the same content in different formats. For example, both plain text and HTML versions of the same message. The email client can choose which version to display based on its capabilities and user preferences.

When email parts contain binary data, the `Content-Transfer-Encoding` header specifies how that data is represented. The `base64` encoding is commonly used:

```
Content-Type: image/jpeg; name="photo.jpg"
Content-Transfer-Encoding: base64
```

Base64 encoding converts binary data into ASCII text that can safely traverse email systems. It takes 3 bytes of binary data and represents them as 4 ASCII characters using a 64-character alphabet consisting of A-Z, a-z, 0-9, plus sign (+), and forward slash (/), with equals sign (=) used for padding.

For example, the text "Man" consists of bytes 77, 97, and 110 (the ASCII values of M, a, and n). In binary, these are
01001101, 01100001, and 01101110. Base64 groups these 24 bits into four 6-bit chunks: 010011 (19), 010110 (22), 000101 (5), and 101110 (46). Looking up each value in the base64 alphabet yields T, W, F, and u, so "Man" encodes to "TWFu" in base64.

This encoding expands the data by approximately 33% (4 output characters for every 3 input bytes), but it ensures that only safe ASCII characters are transmitted. The receiving email client sees the Content-Transfer-Encoding header, knows to decode the base64 data, and recovers the original binary content.

While email usage of MIME and base64 might seem tangential to web development, these concepts appear in several web contexts. HTML forms can trigger email submissions (though usually through server-side scripts). Understanding MIME helps when debugging file uploads, which use similar multipart encoding. The same base64 encoding appears in data URLs, which allow embedding small resources directly in HTML or CSS:

```
1  <img src = "data:image/png;base64,iVBORw0KGgoAAAANSUhEUgAAAUA..." alt = "Tiny image">
```

4.4.8   Summary of MIME Types

MIME types form a fundamental part of web communication, determining how browsers interpret and handle content. Every resource on the web including HTML pages, stylesheets, scripts, images, videos, and downloadable files is associated with a MIME type that tells the browser what to do with it.

The correct MIME type ensures proper rendering: HTML pages display as web pages, images appear as graphics, and stylesheets apply to documents. Incorrect MIME types cause failures. For example, a CSS file served as `text/html` will not be applied as styles, and an HTML page served as `text/plain` displays as source code rather than a rendered page.

Form submissions use specific MIME types that developers must understand. Regular form submissions use `application/x-www-form-urlencoded` by default, encoding field names and values into a URL-compatible format. File uploads require `multipart/form-data`, which packages each field (including binary file content) as a separate part with its own headers and boundaries. Using the wrong encoding type will cause file uploads to fail.

Server configuration is essential for correct MIME type delivery. Web servers map file extensions to MIME types through configuration files, and administrators must ensure these mappings are complete and correct. Missing or incorrect mappings can break functionality or create security vulnerabilities. For example, user-uploaded content served with an executable MIME type could enable cross-site scripting attacks.

Content negotiation allows servers to serve different versions of resources based on client capabilities, improving efficiency by delivering optimized formats to capable browsers while maintaining compatibility with others. The `Vary` header ensures that caches store appropriate versions for different client types.

When developing and deploying web applications, always verify that your server sends correct MIME types. Test that HTML pages render correctly (`text/html`), that stylesheets apply (`text/css`), that JavaScript executes (`application/javascript`), that images display (`image/jpeg`, `image/png`, `image/svg+xml`), and that downloads work as expected (often `application/octet-stream` with `Content-Disposition: attachment`).

4.5   HTML5 Features

HTML5, finalized as a W3C Recommendation in 2014, represents a major evolution in web standards. Rather than pursuing the strict XML approach that characterized XHTML, the HTML5 working group took a pragmatic path that prioritized backward compatibility while introducing powerful new capabilities. The result is a specification that modernized web development by adding semantic elements that better describe page structure, native multimedia support that eliminated the need for plug-ins like Flash, enhanced form controls that reduce the need for JavaScript validation, and numerous APIs that extend what browsers can do. This section explores these HTML5 enhancements and how they improve web development.

4.5.1   The HTML5 Philosophy

HTML5's development was guided by several core principles that shaped its design philosophy. Understanding these principles helps explain why HTML5 looks and behaves the way it does.

Perhaps most importantly, backward compatibility ensured that existing web content would continue to function correctly even as new features were added. The web contains billions of pages created over decades, and breaking that content was not an option. This pragmatic stance recognized that theoretical purity must sometimes yield to practical reality. HTML5 would not require websites to be rewritten since old pages would continue to work, and new pages could gradually adopt new features.

The specification also emphasized clear error handling by explicitly defining how browsers should process malformed markup. Previous HTML versions left error handling undefined, leading each browser to develop its own recovery algorithms. When browsers encountered invalid HTML, they would guess at the author's intent, but different browsers guessed differently. HTML5 addressed this inconsistency by documenting exactly how browsers should handle common errors. This does not mean errors are encouraged, but it does mean that browsers behave consistently when they encounter them.

The principle of practical over theoretical meant the specification was written to support what web developers actually do rather than imposing idealistic constraints that would be ignored in practice. The working group studied real-world HTML, including common errors and unconventional patterns, and designed HTML5 to handle these cases gracefully. For example, HTML5 allows certain tags to be omitted, allows unquoted attribute values in specific circumstances, and does not require self-closing syntax for void elements. These are all reflecting patterns that developers commonly use.

Native capabilities aimed to reduce dependence on plug-ins like Flash, which had become essential for features like video playback but introduced security vulnerabilities and were not available on all platforms (notably, Apple's iOS devices never supported Flash). HTML5 introduced native `<video>` and `<audio>` elements, canvas for graphics, and numerous JavaScript APIs that provide functionality previously requiring plug-ins.

Finally, semantic markup emphasized that elements should describe content meaning, not just visual appearance. Rather than using generic `<div>` elements for all structural purposes, HTML5 introduced elements like `<header>`, `<nav>`, `<main>`, `<article>`, and `<footer>` that convey the purpose of content sections. This improves accessibility for screen readers, helps search engines understand page structure, and makes code more maintainable.

This philosophy produced a specification that is paradoxically both more permissive and more capable than its predecessors. HTML5 tolerates uppercase tags and certain syntax variations (for backward compatibility) while also providing sophisticated features like native video, client-side storage, and geolocation (for modern applications).

4.5.2 Semantic HTML5 Elements

HTML5 introduced numerous elements that describe the purpose of content rather than merely its visual presentation. Before HTML5, developers used generic `<div>` elements with class names like `class="header"` or `class="navigation"` to structure pages. These conventions worked but conveyed no meaning to browsers, search engines, or assistive technologies. HTML5's semantic elements provide standardized vocabulary for common page structures.

The benefits of semantic markup extend across several dimensions. For accessibility, screen readers can navigate pages more effectively when they understand the structure, and users can jump directly to the main content or navigate between articles rather than tabbing through every element sequentially. For search engine optimization (SEO), search engines can identify which content is primary (in `<main>`) versus supplementary (in `<aside>`), and can recognize article boundaries for featured snippets. For maintainability, semantic elements make code self-documenting, allowing a developer reading <nav> to immediately understand its purpose, while <div class="nav"> requires checking the CSS or JavaScript to understand what the element does. For styling, CSS can target semantic roles directly (article { margin-bottom: 2em; }) rather than relying on class names that might change.

Consider how a typical page structure looks with HTML5 semantic elements:

```html
<!DOCTYPE html>
<html lang = "en">
<head>
    <meta charset = "UTF-8">
    <title>Semantic HTML5 Example</title>
</head>
<body>
    <header>
        <h1>My Website</h1>
        <nav>
            <ul>
                <li><a href = "#home">Home</a></li>
                <li><a href = "#about">About</a></li>
                <li><a href = "#contact">Contact</a></li>
            </ul>
        </nav>
    </header>

    <main>
        <article>
            <header>
                <h2>Article Title</h2>
                <time datetime = "2025-06-14">June 14, 2025</time>
            </header>
            <section>
                <h3>Introduction</h3>
                <p>Article content here...</p>
            </section>
            <aside>
                <h4>Related Links</h4>
                <ul>
                    <li><a href = "#">Related Article 1</a></li>
                </ul>
            </aside>
        </article>
    </main>
```

```html
37
38      <footer>
39          <p>&copy; 2025 My Website. All rights reserved.</p>
40      </footer>
41  </body>
42  </html>
```

The <header> element represents introductory content or navigational aids. It can be used for the page header (as shown at the top of the example) or within sections and articles to contain their headings and metadata. Notice that the <article> element in the example contains its own <header> with the article title and publication date.

The <nav> element identifies a section containing navigation links. Using <nav> makes it clear which links constitute primary navigation versus incidental links within content. Screen readers can offer users the option to skip navigation and jump to main content, which is especially helpful for users who visit a site repeatedly and do not hear the navigation menu on every page.

The <main> element contains the dominant content of the document. There should be only one <main> element per page (excluding content repeated across pages like headers, footers, and navigation). This element directly answers the question "what is this page about?" and helps assistive technologies locate the primary content quickly.

The <article> element represents self-contained content that could be distributed independently and still make sense. Blog posts, news articles, forum posts, and user comments are typical uses. An article should be identifiable by its heading and could theoretically be syndicated or shared on its own.

The <section> element represents a thematic grouping of content, typically with its own heading. Unlike <article>, a <section> does not need to stand alone rather it is a way to organize content within a page or article.

The <aside> element contains content tangentially related to its surrounding content. Within an article, this might be pull quotes, related links, or supplementary information. At the page level, it might be a sidebar with links to other articles or advertisements. The key characteristic is that removing the aside would not diminish the main content's meaning.

The <footer> element represents a footer for its nearest sectioning ancestor or for the document. A page footer typically contains copyright information, contact details, or links to terms of service. Articles and sections can also have footers containing author information, related links, or publication details.

The <time> element represents a machine-readable date or time. The `datetime` attribute provides the standardized format (ISO 8601), while the element's content can be human-friendly. This allows browsers and search engines to understand the date even when it is displayed in various formats like "June 14, 2025" or "Yesterday."

Beyond structural elements, HTML5 introduced several other semantic elements. The <figure> element, paired with <figcaption>, wraps illustrations, diagrams, photos, code listings, or other content that is referenced from the main text but could be moved to an appendix without affecting the flow:

```
1  <figure>
2      <img src = "chart.png" alt = "Sales Chart">
3      <figcaption>Q1 2025 Sales Performance</figcaption>
4  </figure>
```

The `<mark>` element indicates text highlighted for reference purposes, like search results or key terms. The `<details>` and `<summary>` elements create expandable/collapsible content without JavaScript. The `<progress>` element shows completion status, while `<meter>` represents a scalar measurement within a known range.

When using semantic elements, choose the element that best matches your content's meaning. Do not use `<section>` for everything just because it is available. If content is truly self-contained and could be syndicated, use `<article>`; if it is tangential, use `<aside>`; if it is navigation, use `<nav>`. For generic containers that have no semantic meaning (purely for styling or scripting), `<div>` remains appropriate.

4.5.3 HTML5 Multimedia

Before HTML5, playing audio or video on web pages required plug-ins like Adobe Flash, Microsoft Silverlight, or Apple QuickTime. These plug-ins were often not installed by default, required users to click through security warnings, created accessibility challenges, drained battery life on mobile devices, and introduced security vulnerabilities. Apple's decision not to support Flash on iOS devices, announced by Steve Jobs in 2010, accelerated the push for native browser multimedia support.

HTML5 introduced the `<video>` and `<audio>` elements, making multimedia a first-class citizen on the web. Browsers now include built-in video and audio players, eliminating plug-in dependencies and providing consistent interfaces across platforms.

The `<video>` element embeds video content with optional playback controls:

```
1  <video width = "640" height = "360" controls poster = "thumbnail.jpg">
2      <source src = "movie.mp4" type = "video/mp4">
3      <source src = "movie.webm" type = "video/webm">
4      <source src = "movie.ogv" type = "video/ogg">
5      <!-- Fallback for browsers that do not support video -->
6      <p>Your browser doesn't support HTML5 video.
7          <a href = "movie.mp4">Download the video</a>.</p>
8  </video>
```

This structure demonstrates several important patterns. The `<video>` element itself sets display dimensions and behavior attributes. Multiple `<source>` elements provide the same video in different formats, allowing browsers to choose a format they support. Content between the opening `<video>` tag and the closing `</video>` tag (after the source elements) serves as fallback content for browsers that do not support HTML5 video at all, though such browsers are now rare.

The `controls` attribute tells the browser to display its built-in playback controls, including play/pause, progress bar, volume, and fullscreen toggle. Without this attribute, the video would have no visible interface, which is sometimes desirable when you want to provide custom controls via JavaScript.

The `poster` attribute specifies an image to display before playback begins. This serves as a preview and prevents the browser from showing a blank rectangle or an arbitrary frame from the video.

The `autoplay` attribute starts playback automatically when the page loads. However, modern browsers significantly restrict autoplay to prevent annoying user experiences. Most browsers only allow autoplay if the video is muted, the user has previously interacted with the site, or the site has been added to the user's allowlist. The `muted` attribute, which starts the video with sound turned off, is often combined with `autoplay` to enable automatic playback.

The `loop` attribute causes the video to restart automatically when it finishes, useful for background videos or short loops. The `preload` attribute provides hints about buffering behavior: `none` tells the browser not to preload any data (saving bandwidth if the user might not watch), `metadata` preloads only metadata like duration and dimensions, and `auto` (the default) allows the browser to preload as much as it deems appropriate.

The `<audio>` element works similarly but for audio content:

```html
<audio controls>
    <source src = "song.mp3" type = "audio/mpeg">
    <source src = "song.ogg" type = "audio/ogg">
    <p>Your browser doesn't support HTML5 audio.</p>
</audio>
```

One persistent challenge with HTML5 multimedia is format compatibility. Different browsers have historically supported different codecs due to patent licensing concerns. MP4 with H.264 video has the widest support and works in virtually all modern browsers, but H.264 is patent-encumbered, meaning companies using it in their products may owe royalty payments. WebM with VP8 or VP9 video is an open format backed by Google; it offers good compression and quality, and all modern browsers now support it. Ogg with Theora video is another open format but with more limited browser support and generally inferior compression.

For audio, MP3 (MPEG-1 Audio Layer 3) has universal browser support but is patent-encumbered (though many patents have now expired). Ogg Vorbis and Opus are open formats with good browser support.

Best practice is to provide multiple formats, listing them in order of preference. The browser will use the first format it supports. The `type` attribute helps browsers skip formats they can not play without attempting to download them.

JavaScript can control media elements programmatically:

```javascript
const video = document.querySelector('video');
video.play();           // Start playback
video.pause();          // Pause playback
video.currentTime = 30; // Jump to 30 seconds
video.volume = 0.5;     // Set volume to 50%
```

```
6 video.playbackRate = 2; // Double speed
```

The HTMLMediaElement interface (shared by video and audio elements) provides properties for current playback position, duration, buffered ranges, network state, and more. Events like play, pause, ended, timeupdate, and error allow JavaScript to respond to playback changes. This enables custom video players, analytics, synchronized content, and other interactive features.

4.5.4   HTML5 Graphics: Canvas and SVG

HTML5 provides two distinct approaches to graphics: Canvas for bitmap (raster) graphics drawn programmatically, and SVG for vector graphics defined declaratively. Each has strengths that make it suitable for different use cases.

The <canvas> element provides a rectangular drawing surface controlled entirely by JavaScript. The element itself defines only the size of the drawing area. All actual graphics are drawn using the Canvas API:

```
1  <canvas id = "myCanvas" width = "300" height = "200"></canvas>
2  <script>
3      const canvas = document.getElementById('myCanvas');
4      const ctx = canvas.getContext('2d');
5
6      // Draw a red rectangle
7      ctx.fillStyle = 'red';
8      ctx.fillRect(50, 50, 100, 75);
9
10     // Draw a blue circle
11     ctx.beginPath();
12     ctx.arc(150, 100, 50, 0, 2 * Math.PI);
13     ctx.fillStyle = 'blue';
14     ctx.fill();
15
16     // Draw text
17     ctx.font = '20px Arial';
18     ctx.fillStyle = 'black';
19     ctx.fillText('Hello Canvas!', 50, 180);
20  </script>
```

The getContext('2d') method returns a 2D rendering context, the object through which all drawing commands are issued. The 2D context provides methods for drawing rectangles, paths, text, and images; applying colors, gradients, and patterns; transforming the coordinate system; and compositing graphics.

Canvas works by manipulating pixels directly. When you draw something on canvas, it becomes part of the bitmap but the browser does not maintain a record of individual shapes. If you want to move a shape, you must clear the canvas (or the relevant portion) and redraw everything. This makes canvas well-suited for scenarios where you are drawing many objects that change frequently, like animations or games.

Canvas excels at games with many moving objects, where redrawing everything on each frame is necessary anyway. It is excellent for image manipulation, as you can access and modify individual pixels. Complex data visualizations with thousands of data points render efficiently on canvas. And when you need pixel-level control such as precise positioning, anti-aliasing control, or direct pixel manipulation canvas provides it.

SVG (Scalable Vector Graphics) takes a fundamentally different approach. SVG graphics are defined using XML-like markup, where each shape is a distinct element in the document:

```
<svg width = "300" height = "200">
    <rect x = "50" y = "50" width = "100" height = "75" fill = "red"/>
    <circle cx = "150" cy = "100" r = "50" fill = "blue"/>
    <text x = "50" y = "180" font-size = "20">Hello SVG!</text>
</svg>
```

This SVG creates the same visual result as the canvas example, but through markup rather than JavaScript. Each shape – the rectangle, circle, and text – is a separate element in the DOM.

Because SVG shapes exist as DOM elements, they can be styled with CSS, respond to events like `click` and `mouseover`, and be manipulated with JavaScript DOM methods. You can add a CSS rule like `circle:hover { fill: lightblue; }` to change the circle's color on hover, something that would require significant JavaScript with canvas.

SVG graphics scale infinitely without pixelation because they're defined mathematically rather than as pixels. This makes SVG ideal for icons and logos that must display crisply at any size, from tiny favicons to large hero images. Diagrams and charts benefit from SVG's scalability and interactivity. Users can hover over chart elements for details, and the chart remains sharp when zoomed. Graphics that need CSS styling or CSS animations work naturally with SVG. And because text in SVG remains selectable and searchable (unlike text drawn on canvas), SVG is more accessible.

The choice between canvas and SVG depends on what you are creating. Use canvas when you have many objects that change frequently, need pixel-level control, or are creating image effects. Use SVG when you need scalability, interactivity with individual shapes, CSS styling, or accessible text.

4.5.5 HTML5 APIs and JavaScript Features

HTML5 introduced numerous JavaScript APIs that extend browser capabilities far beyond document display. These APIs enable functionality that previously required plug-ins, native applications, or server-side processing.

The Geolocation API allows web applications to request the user's geographic location:

```
if (navigator.geolocation) {
    navigator.geolocation.getCurrentPosition(position => {
        console.log('Latitude: ' + position.coords.latitude);
        console.log('Longitude: ' + position.coords.longitude);
```

```javascript
5      }, error => {
6          console.error('Geolocation error: ' + error.message);
7      });
8  }
```

The browser prompts the user for permission before sharing location data, protecting privacy. The position object includes latitude, longitude, accuracy, and optionally altitude, heading, and speed. This enables location-aware features like local search, mapping, and location-based services.

The Web Storage API provides client-side data persistence with simpler syntax and larger capacity than cookies. Local Storage persists data indefinitely until explicitly cleared:

```javascript
1  // Store data
2  localStorage.setItem('username', 'Alice');
3  localStorage.setItem('preferences', JSON.stringify({theme: 'dark'}));
4
5  // Retrieve data
6  const username = localStorage.getItem('username');
7  const prefs = JSON.parse(localStorage.getItem('preferences'));
8
9  // Remove data
10 localStorage.removeItem('username');
11 localStorage.clear(); // Remove all data
```

Session Storage works identically but data persists only until the browser tab closes. Both provide approximately 5-10 MB of storage per origin (the exact limit varies by browser), far more than cookies' 4 KB limit. Data is stored as strings, so complex objects must be serialized with `JSON.stringify()` and parsed with `JSON.parse()`.

Web Workers enable JavaScript to run in background threads, preventing long computations from freezing the user interface:

```javascript
1  // main.js - runs in the main thread
2  const worker = new Worker('worker.js');
3  worker.postMessage({cmd: 'start', data: [1, 2, 3, 4, 5]});
4  worker.onmessage = (e) => {
5      console.log('Result from worker:', e.data);
6  };
7
8  // worker.js - runs in a separate thread
9  self.onmessage = (e) => {
10     if (e.data.cmd === 'start') {
```

```
11        const sum = e.data.data.reduce((a, b) => a + b, 0);
12        self.postMessage(sum);
13    }
14 };
```

Workers can not access the DOM directly (they have no `document` or `window` object), but they can perform calculations, make network requests, and process data without blocking the main thread. Communication happens through message passing with `postMessage()` and `onmessage`.

The File API allows web applications to access files selected by the user, enabling features like image preview before upload or client-side file processing. The Drag and Drop API provides native support for dragging elements within a page or dragging files from the desktop onto a web page. Combined with the File API, this enables intuitive file upload interfaces where users can drop files onto a designated area.

The History API allows JavaScript to manipulate the browser's history and URL without triggering a page reload. This enables single-page applications (SPAs) where JavaScript handles navigation, updates content, and maintains proper URL/history behavior so that back/forward buttons work correctly.

WebSockets provide full-duplex communication channels over a single TCP connection, enabling real-time communication between browser and server. Unlike HTTP, which is request-response, WebSockets allow either side to send messages at any time. This is essential for real-time applications like chat, live sports scores, collaborative editing, and multiplayer games.

IndexedDB provides a client-side database for storing significant amounts of structured data, including files and blobs. Unlike localStorage's simple key-value string storage, IndexedDB supports indexes, transactions, and can store JavaScript objects directly.

These APIs collectively transform browsers into application platforms capable of sophisticated functionality that once required native applications or browser plug-ins.

4.5.6 HTML5 Form Enhancements

While we covered form basics earlier in this chapter, HTML5 introduced specific improvements that reduce the need for JavaScript validation and improve user experience. These enhancements demonstrate HTML5's philosophy of making common tasks easier.

HTML5 added numerous new input types beyond the traditional text, password, checkbox, and radio. The `email` type provides a text field with built-in validation that checks for a valid email format. The `url` type validates URL format. The `tel` type indicates a telephone number (though validation rules vary by locale and are not enforced). The `search` type provides a text field styled appropriately for search queries (some browsers add a clear button).

Numeric inputs include `number`, which provides spinner controls and validates that input is numeric, and `range`, which displays a slider control. Both accept `min`, `max`, and `step` attributes to constrain values.

Date and time inputs address the longstanding challenge of date entry. The `date` type provides a date picker, `time` provides a time picker, `datetime-local` combines both, and `month` and `week` select entire months or weeks. These inputs display native controls appropriate to the device (calendar widgets on desktop, native date pickers on mobile). The `color` type displays a color picker, returning the selected color as a hex code.

HTML5 also introduced new attributes that enhance form usability. The `placeholder` attribute displays hint text inside an input field until the user begins typing. Unlike `value`, placeholder text is not submitted with the form and disappears as soon as the field has content.

The `required` attribute indicates that a field must be filled before the form can be submitted. Browsers display an error message and prevent submission if required fields are empty. The `pattern` attribute specifies a regular expression that the input must match. For example, `pattern="[A-Z]{3}"` requires exactly three uppercase letters.

The `autofocus` attribute places the cursor in a field when the page loads, saving users a click. Only one element per page should have this attribute. The `autocomplete` attribute controls browser autofill behavior; setting `autocomplete="off"` prevents browsers from suggesting previously entered values, which is appropriate for one-time codes or sensitive fields that should not be cached.

HTML5 also provides a Form Validation API for JavaScript, allowing custom validation logic while leveraging the built-in validation UI:

```javascript
const form = document.querySelector('form');
const email = document.querySelector('input[type="email"]');

email.addEventListener('input', () => {
    if (email.validity.typeMismatch) {
        email.setCustomValidity('Please enter a valid email address');
    } else {
        email.setCustomValidity(''); // Clear custom error
    }
});
form.addEventListener('submit', (e) => {
    if (!form.checkValidity()) {
        e.preventDefault();
        // Form is invalid; browser will show error messages
    }
});
```

The `validity` property provides details about why a field is invalid (typeMismatch, patternMismatch, valueMissing, tooLong, tooShort, rangeUnderflow, rangeOverflow, etc.). The `setCustomValidity()` method allows setting custom error messages that integrate with the browser's validation UI.

These form enhancements reduce the JavaScript code needed for common validation scenarios and provide consistent, accessible user experiences across browsers.

4.5.7 Microdata and Structured Data

HTML5 introduced microdata as a way to embed machine-readable information within HTML content. While humans can understand that a web page describes a person, product, or event, machines need structured hints to extract this information reliably.

```
1  <div itemscope itemtype = "http://schema.org/Person">
2      <h1 itemprop = "name">John Doe</h1>
3      <p>Job: <span itemprop = "jobTitle">Web Developer</span></p>
4      <p>Email: <a href = "mailto:john@example.com"
5                  itemprop = "email">john@example.com</a></p>
6  </div>
```

The `itemscope` attribute indicates that the element contains information about an item. The `itemtype` attribute specifies the vocabulary being used – in this case, Schema.org's Person type. The `itemprop` attribute on child elements identifies which property of the item each piece of content represents.

Search engines like Google, Bing, and Yahoo use structured data to enhance search results with rich snippets, additional information displayed alongside the standard title and description. A page about a recipe might show star ratings, cooking time, and calorie count directly in search results. A page about an event might display date, time, and venue information.

Schema.org, a collaboration between major search engines, provides vocabularies for describing common entities: people, organizations, products, events, reviews, recipes, and many more. Using Schema.org vocabularies increases the likelihood that search engines will understand and display your structured data.

While microdata is one approach to structured data, JSON-LD (JavaScript Object Notation for Linked Data) has become the preferred format for many applications. JSON-LD embeds structured data in a `<script>` tag rather than inline with content, separating structured data from presentation and making it easier to maintain.

4.5.8 HTML5 Best Practices

Effective use of HTML5 requires understanding not just what features are available, but when and how to apply them appropriately.

Use semantic elements for their intended purpose. The availability of `<section>`, `<article>`, `<aside>`, and other semantic elements does not mean everything should use them. Generic content that does not fit a semantic category should use `<div>`. Use `<article>` only for self-contained content that makes sense independently. Use `<section>` for thematic groupings that would appear in a document outline. Overusing semantic elements can be as problematic as not using them at all.

Provide fallbacks for multimedia content. While HTML5 video and audio are widely supported, include alternative content for edge cases. Provide multiple source formats for maximum compatibility. Include download links so users can access content even if playback fails. Consider transcripts for audio content and captions for video.

Test form inputs across browsers. Browser support for newer input types varies. The date picker, for example, provides an excellent native experience on some browsers but falls back to a plain text input on others. Consider whether the fallback experience is acceptable or whether you need JavaScript enhancements.

Consider accessibility throughout development. Semantic HTML helps accessibility but does not guarantee it. Use ARIA (Accessible Rich Internet Applications) attributes when HTML semantics are insufficient, such as when building custom widgets. Ensure keyboard navigation works for all interactive elements. Provide alternative text for images and captions for media. Test with screen readers and other assistive technologies.

Validate regularly. HTML5's permissive parsing does not mean validation is unnecessary. The W3C validator catches genuine errors that might cause rendering issues or indicate logical problems in your markup. Validation also helps ensure your code works consistently across browsers.

Practice progressive enhancement. Build core functionality with basic HTML that works everywhere, then enhance with CSS and JavaScript for capable browsers. This ensures content remains accessible even when advanced features fail or are unavailable.

4.5.9   The Future Beyond HTML5

While HTML5 was the last numbered version of HTML, the language continues to evolve as a "living standard" maintained by WHATWG (Web Hypertext Application Technology Working Group). Rather than periodic major releases, features are added continuously as they're developed and implemented by browsers.

Web Components allow developers to create custom, reusable HTML elements with encapsulated functionality. Custom elements let you define new tags like `<user-card>` or `<data-table>`. Shadow DOM provides encapsulation, preventing styles and scripts from leaking between components. HTML templates define reusable markup that is not rendered until activated.

WebAssembly enables running code written in languages like C, C++, Rust, and others in browsers at near-native speed. This opens web development to existing codebases and enables performance-intensive applications like games, image/video editing, and scientific simulations.

Ongoing improvements enhance security through features like Content Security Policy refinements, stricter cookie handling, and improved credential management. Performance APIs provide better metrics and control over resource loading. Accessibility features continue to expand with improved ARIA support and new semantic elements.

The HTML5 philosophy, including backward compatibility, practical standards based on real-world usage, and continuous improvement remains the guiding principle. The web platform has become stable enough that revolutionary changes are unnecessary; evolution happens through incremental additions that browsers can adopt gradually while maintaining compatibility with existing content.

For web developers, this means staying current with new features while building on a stable foundation. The core skills of HTML5 remain relevant even as new capabilities are added. Understanding semantic markup, multimedia, forms, and browser APIs provides a base from which to explore new features as they emerge.

4.6   Chapter Review

Problem 4.1 What is the difference between using the GET method and the POST method when submitting an HTML form? Explain how each method sends the form data to the server and in what situations you would use GET vs. POST.

Problem 4.2 In an HTML form, how do radio buttons and checkboxes differ in behavior and data submission? Contrast how a radio button group allows one selection versus a checkbox group allowing multiple selections, and describe how their values are sent in the request.

Problem 4.3 What steps must you take to allow users to upload a file via an HTML form? List the form attribute and method needed, and any server-side considerations (such as the form's encoding type) required for file uploads.

Problem 4.4 Name three new input types introduced in HTML5 and explain their purpose. For example, you might mention input types like `email`, `date`, `number`, `range`, or `color` and describe how they improve user input or validation.

Problem 4.5 What are semantic HTML5 elements and why are they useful? Give two examples. Define semantic elements (like `<header>`, `<article>`, `<nav>`, etc.) and provide examples (e.g., using `<nav>` for a menu or `<article>` for a blog post) including their benefits for structure and accessibility.

Problem 4.6 How do the HTML5 `<audio>` and `<video>` elements benefit web development compared to older plugin-based methods of embedding media? Discuss how these elements allow native media playback (controls, formats) without requiring Flash or other plugins, and mention the need for multiple source formats for broad browser support.

Problem 4.7 What is the difference between the `<canvas>` element and using SVG for graphics on the web? Compare the canvas (pixel-based, script-drawn, good for games and real-time drawing) with SVG (vector-based, XML markup for shapes, good for scalable graphics and diagrams), including how each is manipulated and typical use cases.

Problem 4.8 List two key syntactical differences between XHTML and HTML. For instance, mention requirements like lowercase tags, self-closing empty elements with `>`, mandatory closing of all tags, quoting all attribute values, etc., that XHTML imposes.

Problem 4.9 Why is including a DOCTYPE declaration important in an HTML document? Explain what the DOCTYPE does in terms of browser rendering mode (standards vs. quirks mode) and validation, and give the simple HTML5 doctype as an example.

Problem 4.10 How can you specify the character encoding of an HTML page and why is it important to do so? Describe the use of the `<meta charset="UTF-8">` tag (or equivalent HTTP header) and explain how declaring the encoding prevents text from appearing garbled by ensuring the browser decodes bytes correctly (especially for non-ASCII characters).

Problem 4.11 What is the purpose of HTML validation and what is a common error that a validator might catch? Define validation (checking against HTML standards) and give an example of a common error like an unclosed tag or improperly nested element that validation would highlight.

Problem 4.12 Why do we use character entity references like `<` or `&` in HTML, and when might you need to use them? Explain that `<` and `&` have special meaning in HTML, so they must be escaped to `<` and `&` when meant as literal characters. Also mention usage for non-keyboard symbols or non-breaking spaces (` `).

Problem 4.13 What is a MIME type and how does a web server use MIME types when serving files? Define MIME type (e.g., `text/html`, `image/png`) and describe how servers include `Content-Type` headers so the browser knows how to handle the file (display as webpage, image, download, etc.).

Problem 4.14 Give an example of how a browser plugin or helper application might be used based on MIME type. For instance: If a server sends `Content-Type: application/pdf`, how does the browser decide whether to display it with a PDF plugin/viewer or to download it or open with an external application?

Problem 4.15 Why do email attachments use Base64 encoding, and what does `Content-Transfer-Encoding: base64` indicate in an email header? Explain that email was historically text-only, so binary attachments are converted to Base64 text to safely transmit. The header indicates that the email body part is base64 and needs decoding to get the original file bytes.

5. Cascading Style Sheets

We have briefly touched on the HTML style element, style rules and properties used to fine-tune the appearance of text and elements on a web page. In this chapter we consider these issues in greater detail. So far we have restricted ourselves to the straightforward use of the style element; more generally such style specifications can be factored out of a page and maintained in separate style sheets (hence the terminology style sheets). A solid understanding of Cascading Style Sheets (CSS) is essential to developing modern web applications. While HTML provides the structure and content of web pages, CSS controls their visual presentation, enabling developers to create visually appealing, maintainable, and accessible websites. CSS was first proposed by Håkon Wium Lie in 1994, with CSS Level 1 becoming a W3C recommendation in 1996. The language has evolved through CSS2 (1998) and CSS3 (introduced in 1999 and continuously developed) into a powerful and comprehensive styling system. In this chapter, we explore CSS from its fundamental syntax through advanced features, including animations and responsive design.

Learning Objectives

By the end of this chapter, you should be able to:
- Write CSS rules using correct syntax and apply them to HTML documents using three different methods (inline, internal, and external stylesheets)
- Use CSS selectors effectively to target specific elements, from basic element selectors to advanced pseudo-classes and combinators
- Understand the cascade and specificity to predict which styles will apply when rules conflict
- Apply fundamental CSS properties for typography, colors, spacing, and layout using the box model
- Create responsive designs using media queries and flexible layouts that work across different devices
- Implement dynamic effects with CSS transitions and animations
- Leverage CSS frameworks like Bootstrap to accelerate development
- Follow CSS best practices for maintainability, performance, and accessibility

5.1 CSS History and Purpose

5.1.1 The Origins of CSS

Before CSS, web developers faced significant challenges in creating visually appealing websites. Early HTML mixed structure with presentation through attributes like `<font>` tags and `bgcolor` attributes, making websites difficult to maintain and update. Norwegian web pioneer Håkon Wium Lie recognized this problem and proposed Cascading Style Sheets as a solution. Working with Tim Berners-Lee and Robert Cailliau, Lie helped create a universal standardized style sheet system that would become an established web standard, significantly influencing the look and accessibility of the World Wide Web.

The evolution of CSS has progressed through three major versions. The first, CSS1 in 1996, introduced basic styling capabilities, allowing developers to select font styles and sizes, change text and background colors, and

DOI: 10.1201/9781003727651-5

control spacing. This first version established the fundamental concept of separating presentation from content. The second, CSS2 in 1998, expanded capabilities to include sophisticated page layout features, positioning, and media types. This version introduced the ability to create complex layouts without using HTML tables for non-tabular content. The third, CSS3 in 1999 through the present, rather than being a single monolithic specification, it is divided into modules that are developed independently. This modular approach has enabled features like animations, transformations, flexible box layout, grid layout, custom fonts, and advanced selectors. CSS3 continues to evolve with new modules being added regularly.

5.1.2   Benefits of Using CSS

CSS provides numerous advantages that have made it indispensable for modern web development. It offers improved control over formatting. It also provides fine-grained control over every aspect of presentation. Unlike HTML's limited styling attributes, CSS provides hundreds of properties for typography, colors, spacing, positioning, and visual effects. For example, while HTML might offer basic text alignment, CSS enables precise control over line height, letter spacing, text shadows, and even animated text effects.

CSS improves site maintainability. By separating presentation from content, it dramatically improves maintainability. A single CSS file can control the appearance of an entire website. Need to change your company's brand colors? Update a few lines in your CSS file rather than editing hundreds of HTML pages. This separation also makes it easier for teams to work together. Designers can focus on CSS while content creators work with HTML. CSS enhances accessibility by enabling accessibility by enabling semantic HTML markup. Screen readers and other assistive technologies can better understand content when it is not cluttered with presentational markup. CSS also supports features like high contrast modes, scalable text, and responsive designs that adapt to different user needs.

External CSS files improve page download speed. They are CSS files are cached by browsers, meaning they are downloaded once and reused across multiple pages. This caching significantly reduces bandwidth usage and improves page load times. Additionally, CSS can replace image-based designs with code-based solutions, further reducing file sizes.

CSS media queries provide improved output flexibility. They enable queries enable different styles for different output devices. The same HTML can be styled differently for screens, printers, mobile devices, or even speech synthesizers. This flexibility means you can create printer-friendly pages without duplicating content or provide optimized mobile experiences without separate mobile sites.

5.1.3   Important Considerations

It is important to note that different browsers have not always kept pace with W3C standards. While modern browsers have excellent CSS support, developers must still consider browser compatibility, especially when using newer CSS features. Tools like feature detection and fallback styles help ensure websites work across different browsers and versions.

5.2 CSS Syntax and Implementation Methods

5.2.1 Understanding CSS Rule Syntax

Every CSS rule follows a consistent structure consisting of two main parts: a selector that identifies which HTML elements to style, and a declaration block containing one or more property-value pairs. Let us examine this structure in detail.

A CSS rule starts with a selector, which identifies the element(s) in the HTML document that will be affected by the declarations in the rule. The selector is followed by a declaration block enclosed in curly braces. Each declaration consists of a property name, a colon, and a value, ending with a semicolon.

```
h1 {
    color: darkgreen;
    text-align: center;
    font-family: cursive;
}
```

In this example, `h1` is the selector, targeting all `<h1>` elements. The curly braces { } contain the declaration block. Inside the block, `color: darkgreen;` is a declaration setting the text color, `text-align: center;` centers the heading text, and `font-family: cursive;` sets the font to a cursive typeface. Note that the last semicolon before the closing brace is optional but recommended for consistency. The browser ignores whitespace (spaces, tabs, and line breaks) between CSS rules, allowing you to format your code for readability.

5.2.2 CSS Properties and Values

CSS3 defines over 100 different property names, each controlling a specific aspect of presentation. Below are the most commonly used properties organized by category.

Font and Text Properties:
- `font`, `font-family`, `font-size`, `font-style`, `font-weight`
- `@font-face` (for custom web fonts)
- `letter-spacing`, `line-height`, `text-align`, `text-decoration`, `text-indent`

When specifying font families, it is important to understand the main categories of typefaces. Serif fonts, such as Times New Roman and Georgia, have small decorative strokes (called serifs) at the ends of letters, which can improve readability in printed text. Sans-serif fonts, such as Arial and Helvetica, lack these decorative strokes (sans is French for without), giving them a cleaner, more modern appearance that is often preferred for screen display. Monospace fonts, such as Courier and Consolas, allocate the same horizontal space to every character regardless of its natural width, so a narrow letter like "i" occupies the same space as a wide letter like "W". This fixed-width property makes monospace fonts ideal for displaying code, where alignment is important.

CSS provides a shorthand `font` property that allows you to set multiple font-related properties in a single declaration. The general format is:

```css
selector {
    font: font-style font-weight font-size font-family;
}
```

The properties must be listed in the specified order. The `font-size` and `font-family` are required, while `font-style` and `font-weight` are optional. For example:

```css
p {
    font: italic bold 18pt 'Times New Roman', sans-serif;
}

/* Equivalent to: */
p {
    font-style: italic;
    font-weight: bold;
    font-size: 18pt;
    font-family: 'Times New Roman', sans-serif;
}
```

When using the shorthand, omitted optional properties are reset to their default values. Be careful with punctuation and spelling, as browsers will ignore incorrectly formatted font rules.

Color and Background Properties:

- `background`, `background-color`, `background-image`, `background-position`
- `background-repeat`, `box-shadow`, `color`, `opacity`

CSS supports multiple ways to specify colors. The simplest method uses color keywords. The W3C originally defined 16 standard color names: `aqua`, `black`, `blue`, `fuchsia`, `gray`, `green`, `lime`, `maroon`, `navy`, `olive`, `purple`, `red`, `silver`, `teal`, `white`, and `yellow`. Modern browsers support an extended set of 140 named colors. Note that `lime` represents full green (#00FF00), while `green` represents a darker shade (#008000). Colors can also be specified using hexadecimal notation (e.g., #FF5733), RGB values (e.g., `rgb(255, 87, 51)`), or RGBA for transparency (e.g., `rgba(255, 87, 51, 0.5)`).

CSS3 also introduced the HSL color model, which many designers find more intuitive than RGB. HSL stands for Hue, Saturation, and Lightness. Hue is a degree on the color wheel from 0 to 360, where 0 (and 360) is red, 120 is green, and 240 is blue. Saturation is a percentage from 0% (gray) to 100% (full color). Lightness is also a percentage from 0% (black) to 100% (white), with 50% being the normal color. For example, `hsl(0, 100%, 50%)` produces pure red, while `hsl(0, 100%, 25%)` produces a darker red. The HSLA variant adds an alpha channel for transparency, such as `hsla(120, 100%, 50%, 0.5)` for a semi-transparent green.

Historically, web developers were concerned with "web-safe colors," a palette of 216 colors that displayed consistently across early computer monitors. These monitors typically supported only 256 colors (8-bit color depth), and approximately 40 of those were reserved by operating systems. The web-safe palette consists of colors whose RGB components are multiples of 51 in decimal, or equivalently, combinations of the hexadecimal values 00, 33, 66, 99, CC, and FF. While this limitation is no longer relevant for modern displays, which support millions of colors, understanding this history helps explain why certain color values appear frequently in legacy code.

When selecting colors for web pages, accessibility is an important consideration. Statistically, 5 to 10 percent of males have a form of color blindness that makes it difficult for them to distinguish between red and green or between blue and yellow. This affects the choice of foreground (text) and background color combinations. For example, using red text on a green background creates readability problems for a significant percentage of viewers. Developers should ensure sufficient color contrast between text and backgrounds, and avoid relying on color alone to convey important information.

In addition to solid colors, CSS allows setting images as backgrounds using the background-image property. The syntax uses the url() function to specify the image path:

```css
.hero-section {
    background-image: url("images/banner.jpg");
    background-size: cover;       /* Scale image to cover entire element */
    background-position: center; /* Center the image */
    background-repeat: no-repeat; /* Do not tile the image */
}
```

The background-size property controls how the image is scaled: cover scales the image to completely cover the element (potentially cropping), while contain scales it to fit entirely within the element (potentially leaving empty space). The background-repeat property determines whether the image tiles horizontally, vertically, both, or not at all.

Border Properties:
- border, border-color, border-width, border-style
- border-top, border-right, border-bottom, border-left
- border-radius (for rounded corners)

Spacing Properties:
- padding, padding-top, padding-right, padding-bottom, padding-left
- margin, margin-top, margin-right, margin-bottom, margin-left

Sizing Properties:
- width, height, max-width, max-height, min-width, min-height

Layout Properties:
- display, position, top, right, bottom, left
- float, clear, overflow, z-index, visibility

List Properties:
- list-style, list-style-type, list-style-image

Effects and Animations:
- animation, filter, transform, transition, perspective

5.2.3   CSS Units of Measurement

Values in CSS often require units of measurement. CSS supports both relative units (based on other values) and absolute units (fixed measurements).

Common Units:

- `px` (pixels): The most common unit for precise control
- `em`: Relative to the parent element's font size
- `rem`: Relative to the root element's font size
- `%` (percentage): Relative to the parent element
- `vw/vh`: Viewport width/height units for responsive design

5.2.4   Three Methods of Implementing CSS

CSS can be added to HTML documents in three different ways, each with its own use cases and implications for maintainability.

1. Inline Styles

Inline styles are placed directly within an HTML element using the `style` attribute. This method is the most direct way to apply a style, but it mixes presentation with content, which is generally discouraged for large-scale projects.

```
1  <!-- Code that uses inline styling for h1, li and ul elements -->
2  <h1 style="color:blue; font-weight:bold; font-family:cursive">Countries To Visit</h1>
3
4  <ul>
5      <li style="color:green; font-size: 24pt">Ireland</li>
6      <ul style="font-style: italic">
7          <li>Dublin</li>
8          <li>Donegal</li>
9          <li>Dingle</li>
10     </ul>
11 </ul>
```

An inline style only affects the specific element it is defined on and overrides any other style definitions for the properties used. In the example above, the `<h1>` element has its text color set to blue, font-weight to bold, and font-family to cursive. The `<li>` element has its text color set to green, while the `<ul>` element has its font-style set to italic, which its children `<li>` elements inherit.

While handy for quick testing, inline styles have significant drawbacks. They cannot be reused across elements and they make HTML harder to read and maintain. They also have the highest specificity, making them difficult to override, and they increase file size and cannot be cached separately by the browser.

2. Internal/Embedded Stylesheets

Internal stylesheets (also called embedded stylesheets) place style rules within a `<style>` element inside the `<head>` section of an HTML document. This method keeps styles and content in the same file but separates them.

```html
<!doctype html>
<html>
<head>
    <meta charset="utf-8">
    <title>Embedded Styling Example</title>

    <!-- Code for embedded or internal style sheets -->
    <style>
        h1 {
            color: blue;
            font-weight: bold;
            font-family: cursive;
        }

        li {
            color: green;
            font-size: 24pt;
        }

        ul {
            font-style: italic;
        }
    </style>
</head>
<body>
    <h1>Countries To Visit</h1>
    <ul>
        <li>Ireland</li>
        <ul>
            <li>Dublin</li>
            <li>Donegal</li>
            <li>Dingle</li>
        </ul>
    </ul>
</body>
</html>
```

In the example above, the `<h1>` element has its text color set to blue, font-weight to bold, and font-family to cursive. The `<li>` element has its text color set to green, while the `<ul>` element has its font-style set to italic. Notice that all `<ul>` elements and all `<li>` elements are affected by the styling rules defined in the `<style>` block, not just specific instances as with inline styling. This demonstrates how embedded styles apply to all matching elements within the document. This method is useful for single-page websites or email templates.

3. External Stylesheets (Recommended)

External stylesheets are separate `.css` files containing only CSS rules. This is the recommended approach for production websites as it provides the best separation of concerns, reusability, and maintainability. The HTML document links to the external file using the `<link>` element in the `<head>`.

The HTML file (`countries.html`):

```html
<!doctype html>
<html>
<head>
    <meta charset="utf-8">
    <title>External Styling Example</title>

    <!-- Link to external style sheet for the page -->
    <link rel="stylesheet" href="countries.css" />
</head>
<body>
    <h1>Countries To Visit</h1>
    <ul>
        <li>Ireland</li>
        <ul>
            <li>Dublin</li>
            <li>Donegal</li>
            <li>Dingle</li>
        </ul>
    </ul>
</body>
</html>
```

The external CSS file (`countries.css`):

```css
/* External Style sheet For Countries to Visit */
h1 {
    color: blue;
    font-weight: bold;
```

```
5       font-family: cursive;
6  }
7
8  li {
9       color: green;
10      font-size: 24pt;
11 }
12
13 ul {
14      font-style: italic;
15 }
```

External stylesheets are the recommended approach for production websites because they offer numerous advantages over inline and embedded styles. They enable complete separation of content (HTML) and presentation (CSS) and offer reusability across multiple HTML pages, ensuring a consistent look. Also, browser caching improves performance; the `.css` file is downloaded once and reused. Furthermore, maintenance is made easier as changes to one `.css` file affect all linked pages. Finally, team collaboration is enabled as designers can work on CSS while developers focus on HTML.

5.2.5 Types of Stylesheets

Beyond the implementation methods, it is important to understand that browsers work with three different types of stylesheets:

- Author-created stylesheets: The styles you write as a web developer
- User stylesheets: Custom styles that users can define in their browsers (less common today)
- Browser stylesheets: Default styles that browsers apply to HTML elements

These three types interact through the cascade, which we will explore in detail later in this chapter. Note that the most effective approach to understanding and using CCS is through code examples, a strategy we employ extensively in the remaining sections of this chapter.

5.2.6 Style Inheritance

An important concept in CSS is inheritance, which determines whether a style applied to a parent element is automatically passed down to its descendant elements. Not all CSS properties are inherited. Properties related to text and fonts, such as `font-family`, `font-size`, `color`, and `line-height`, are inherited by default. This makes sense because you typically want all text within a container to share the same font characteristics unless explicitly overridden.

On the other hand, box model properties such as `border`, `margin`, `padding`, and `background` are not inherited. This is intentional: if borders were inherited, every element inside a bordered container would also have borders, cluttering the page with unintended visual effects. You can explicitly control inheritance using the `inherit` keyword (to force inheritance) or the `initial` keyword (to reset to the browser default).

5.3   CSS Selectors

Selectors are the foundation of CSS, allowing developers to target specific HTML elements for styling. Understanding selectors is crucial because they determine which elements your styles affect. CSS provides various selector types, from simple element selectors to complex combinators that target elements based on their relationships.

5.3.1   Basic Selectors

Element/Type Selectors

Element selectors (also called type selectors) target all instances of a specific HTML element. They use the element's tag name without angle brackets, as shown in the next code fragment which is followed by an HTML document demonstrating the use of element/type selectors.

```css
em {
    color: blue;
}

p {
    margin: 10px 0 5px 0;
    font-family: sans-serif, Times New Roman, Arial;
    font-size: 12pt;
    font-weight: bold;
}
```

```html
<!doctype html>
<html>
<head>
    <meta charset="utf-8">
    <title>Element/Type Selectors</title>
    <style>
        em {
            color: blue;
        }

        p {
            margin: 10px 0 5px 0;
            font-family: sans-serif, Times New Roman, Arial;
            font-size: 12pt;
            font-weight: bold;
        }
```

```
17        </style>
18   </head>
19   <body>
20      <p>
21          This page demonstrates the use of <em>Element/Type selectors</em>
22      </p>
23   </body>
24   </html>
```

The code above produces the following output:

This page demonstrates the use of *Element/Type selectors*

The em selector styles all `<em>` elements with blue text, while the p selector applies margins, font family, size, and weight to all paragraphs. Accordingly, the code above demonstrates how element selectors work. In this code two element/type selectors are styled: `<em>` and `<p>`. The `<em>` element's styling is accomplished on lines 7 through 9 of the code. It styles the text color to blue on line 8. The `<p>` element's styling is accomplished on lines 11 through 16. It styles the margins by creating space around the `<p>` element. Only the top margin and bottom margins are affected since they have the values of 10px and 5px (line 12). It also styles the font-family (line 13) using a web font stack. This stack, a list of font families, is used to ensure that the browser renders a desired font. The selector also styles the font-size to 12pt (line 13) and font-weight to bold (line 15).

Universal Selector

The universal selector ($*$) applies styles to all elements in the document. While powerful, it should be used sparingly due to performance considerations, as shown in the next code fragment which is followed by an HTML document demonstrating the use of universal selectors.

```
1  * {
2      color: blue;          /* color of all the elements is set to blue*/
3      font-weight: bold;    /* font weight for all the elements is set to bold*/
4      font-family: cursive; /*font family for all elements is set to cursive*/
5  }
```

```
1  <!doctype html>
2  <html>
3  <head>
4      <meta charset="utf-8">
5      <title>Universal Element Selector</title>
```

```
6      <style>
7        * {
8            color: blue;        /* color of all the elements is set to blue*/
9            font-weight: bold;  /* font weight for all the elements is set to bold*/
10           font-family: cursive; /*font family for all elements is set to cursive*/
11       }
12     </style>
13 </head>
14 <body>
15     <h1>The universal element selector</h1>
16     <p>This page demonstrates the use of * (universal element selector)</p>
17     <p>All the elements (h1, h2, p, ul, li) will have the same styling</p>
18     <h2>A simple list styled via the * selector</h2>
19     <ul>
20         <li>Item One</li>
21         <li>Item Two</li>
22         <li>Item Three</li>
23     </ul>
24 </body>
25 </html>
```

The code above demonstrates how universal selector ($*$) works. The universal selector applies the styling to all elements in the document. It is denoted by an $*$ (asterisk). Lines 7 through 11 accomplish the styling for all the elements in the document. The elements will have the following style: a text color of blue (line 8), a font-weight of bold (line 9), and a font-family of cursive (line 10).

Group Selectors

When multiple elements need identical styling, you can group their selectors using commas. This reduces code duplication and file size, as shown in the next code fragment which is followed by an HTML document demonstrating the use of group selectors.

```
1 h1, h2 {
2     color: blue;
3     font-weight: bold;
4     font-family: cursive;
5     text-align: center;
6 }
```

```
1  <!doctype html>
2  <html>
3  <head>
4      <meta charset="utf-8">
5      <title>Group Selectors</title>
6      <style>
7         h1, h2 {
8             color: blue;              /* color of all the elements is set to blue*/
9             font-weight: bold;        /* font weight for all the elements is set to bold*/
10            font-family: cursive;     /*font family for all elements is set to cursive*/
11            text-align: center;
12         }
13      </style>
14  </head>
15  <body>
16      <h1>Group Selectors</h1>
17      <p>This page demonstrates the use of group selectors</p>
18      <p>The styling for the elements h1 and h2 are grouped so they will have the same styling</p>
19      <h2>A simple list</h2>
20      <ul>
21          <li>Item One</li>
22          <li>Item Two</li>
23          <li>Item Three</li>
24      </ul>
25  </body>
26  </html>
```

The code above demonstrates how group selectors work. Group selectors reduce the size and complexity of your CSS files. Lines 7 through 12 style the `<h1>` and `<h2>` elements using a group selector. The group selector styles the text color to blue (line 8), the text font-weight to bold (line 9), the text font-family to cursive (line10), and the text alignment to center (line 11).

Class Selectors

Class selectors target elements with a specific `class` attribute value, regardless of element type. They are prefixed with a period (`.`) and are the workhorses of CSS, enabling reusable styles across different elements, as shown in the next code fragment which is followed by an HTML document demonstrating the use of class selectors.

```
1  .heading {
2      color: blue;
```

```css
3       font-weight: bold;
4       font-family: cursive;
5   }
6
7   .ireland {
8       color: green;
9   }
10
11  .spain {
12      color: goldenrod;
13  }
14
15  .italy {
16      color: red;
17  }
```

```html
1   <!doctype html>
2   <html>
3   <head>
4       <meta charset="UTF-8">
5       <title>Class Selectors</title>
6       <style>
7           .heading {
8               color: blue;
9               font-weight: bold;
10              font-family: cursive;
11          }
12
13          .ireland {
14              color: green;
15          }
16
17          .spain {
18              color: goldenrod;
19          }
20
21          .italy {
22              color: red;
23          }
24      </style>
25  </head>
26  <body>
```

```html
27    <!-- Create a heading styled to be blue, bold, and cursive -->
28    <h1 class="heading">Countries To Visit</h1>
29
30    <!-- Create an unordered list with class selectors -->
31    <ul>
32        <li class="ireland">Ireland</li>
33        <ul>
34            <li>Dublin</li>
35            <li>Donegal</li>
36            <li>Dingle</li>
37        </ul>
38        <li class="spain">Spain</li>
39        <ul>
40            <li>Valencia</li>
41            <li>Madrid</li>
42            <li>Barcelona</li>
43        </ul>
44        <li class="italy">Italy</li>
45        <ul>
46            <li>Rome</li>
47            <li>Florence</li>
48            <li>Venice</li>
49        </ul>
50    </ul>
51 </body>
52 </html>
```

Countries To Visit

- Ireland
    - ○ Dublin
    - ○ Donegal
    - ○ Dingle
- Spain
    - ○ Valencia
    - ○ Madrid
    - ○ Barcelona
- Italy
    - ○ Rome
    - ○ Florence
    - ○ Venice

Different classes apply different colors to list items. The `.ireland` class makes the text green, the `.spain` class makes the text goldenrod, and the `.italy` class makes the text red.

Class selectors simultaneously target different HTML elements regardless of their position in the document tree via the element's class attribute value. A class selector is created by placing a period (`.`) followed by the class name within the `<style>` element. Examining the code above we can see that lines 7 through 11 style the `<h1>` element found on line 28 which has a class attribute called "heading". It styles the element's text color to blue (line 8), font-weight to bold (line 9), and font-family to cursive (line10). Lines 13 through 15 style the `<li>` element found on line 32, which has a class attribute called "ireland". It styles this element's text color to green (line 14). Lines 17 through 19 style the `<li>` element on line 38, which has a class attribute called "spain". It styles this element's text color to goldenrod (line 18). Lines 21 through 23 style the `<li>` element on line 44, which has a class attribute called "italy". It styles this element's text color to red (line 22).

ID Selectors

ID selectors target a specific element by its `id` attribute. Since IDs must be unique within a page, ID selectors affect only one element. They are prefixed with a hash (#) symbol as shown in the next code fragment which is followed by an HTML document demonstrating the use of ID selectors.

```
1  #irelandlist {
2      font-family: Arial;
3      font-style: italic;
4      color: green;
```

```css
5  }
6
7  #spainlist {
8      font-family: Arial;
9      font-style: italic;
10     color: goldenrod;
11 }
12
13 #italylist {
14     font-family: Arial;
15     font-style: italic;
16     color: red;
17 }
```

```html
1  <!doctype html>
2  <html>
3  <head>
4      <meta charset="UTF-8">
5      <title>ID Selectors</title>
6      <style>
7          div {
8              width: 150px;
9              height: 100px;
10         }
11
12         .heading {
13             color: blue;
14             font-weight: bold;
15             font-family: cursive;
16         }
17
18         .ireland { color: green; }
19         .spain { color: goldenrod; }
20         .italy { color: red; }
21
22         #irelandlist {
23             font-family: Arial;
24             font-style: italic;
25             color: green;
26         }
27
28         #spainlist {
```

```
29            font-family: Arial;
30            font-style: italic;
31            color: goldenrod;
32        }
33
34        #italylist {
35            font-family: Arial;
36            font-style: italic;
37            color: red;
38        }
39      </style>
40  </head>
41  <body>
42      <h1 class="heading">Countries To Visit</h1>
43      <ul>
44          <div>
45              <li class="ireland">Ireland</li>
46              <ul id="irelandlist">
47                  <li>Dublin</li>
48                  <li>Donegal</li>
49                  <li>Dingle</li>
50              </ul>
51              <li class="spain">Spain</li>
52              <ul id="spainlist">
53                  <li>Valencia</li>
54                  <li>Madrid</li>
55                  <li>Barcelona</li>
56              </ul>
57              <li class="italy">Italy</li>
58              <ul id="italylist">
59                  <li>Rome</li>
60                  <li>Florence</li>
61                  <li>Venice</li>
62              </ul>
63          </div>
64      </ul>
65  </body>
66  </html>
```

Id selectors allow for targeting a specific element by its `id` attribute, regardless of its type or position. When an HTML element has been labeled with an id attribute you can target it for styling by using an id selector. This selector takes the form of pound/hash (#) followed by the id name. In the code above we have added id selectors to the code previously used to demonstrate class selectors. Lines 22 through 26 style the `<ul>` element found on line 46, which has an id attribute called `id="irelandlist"`, and its `<li>` elements via inheritance on lines 47 through 49. It styles the elements' font-family to Arial (line 23), font-style to italic (line 24), and color to green (line 25). Lines 28 through 32 style the `<ul>` element found on line 52, which has an id attribute called `"spainlist"`, and its `<li>` elements via inheritance on lines 53 through 55. It styles the elements' font-family to Arial (line 29), font-style to italic (line 30), and color to goldenrod (line 31). Lines 34 through 38 style the `<ul>` element found on line 58, which has an id attribute called "italylist", and its `<li>` elements through inheritance on lines 59 through 61. It styles the elements' font-family to Arial (line 35), font-style to italic (line 36), and color to red (line 37).

5.3.2 Advanced Selectors

Attribute Selectors

Attribute selectors target elements based on their attributes or attribute values. They use square brackets and offer powerful pattern matching capabilities as shown in the next code fragment which is followed by an HTML document demonstrating the use of attribute selectors.

```
1  [title~="Ireland"] {
2      border: 5px solid green;
3  }
4
5  [title~="Spain"] {
6      border: 5px solid goldenrod;
7  }
8
9  [title~="Italy"] {
10     border: 5px solid red;
11 }
```

```
1  <!doctype html>
2  <html>
3  <head>
4      <meta charset="UTF-8">
5      <title>Attribute Selectors</title>
6      <!-- Attribute Selectors for the various page elements -->
7      <style>
8          /* Previous styles omitted for brevity */
9          div { width: 150px; height: 100px; }
10         .heading { color:blue; font-weight:bold; font-family:cursive; }
11         .ireland { color: green; }
```

```html
12        .spain { color: goldenrod; }
13        .italy { color: red; }
14        #irelandlist { font-family:Arial; font-style:italic; color:green; }
15        #spainlist { font-family:Arial; font-style:italic; color:goldenrod; }
16        #italylist { font-family:Arial; font-style:italic; color:red; }
17
18        [title~="Ireland"] {
19            border: 5px solid green;
20        }
21
22        [title~="Spain"] {
23            border: 5px solid goldenrod;
24        }
25
26        [title~="Italy"] {
27            border: 5px solid red;
28        }
29    </style>
30 </head>
31 <body>
32    <h1 class="heading">Countries To Visit</h1>
33    <ul>
34        <div>
35            <li class="ireland">Ireland</li>
36            <ul id="irelandlist" title="Ireland">
37                <li>Dublin</li>
38                <li>Donegal</li>
39                <li>Dingle</li>
40            </ul>
41            <li class="spain">Spain</li>
42            <ul id="spainlist" title="Spain">
43                <li>Valencia</li>
44                <li>Madrid</li>
45                <li>Barcelona</li>
46            </ul>
47            <li class="italy">Italy</li>
48            <ul id="italylist" title="Italy">
49                <li>Rome</li>
50                <li>Florence</li>
51                <li>Venice</li>
52            </ul>
53        </div>
54    </ul>
```

```
55 </body>
56 </html>
```

Attribute selectors select elements either by the presence of an element attribute or by the value of an attribute. These selectors are not supported by all browsers. The code above adds attribute selectors to the code previously used to demonstrate class and id selectors. Lines 18 through 20 style the `<ul>` element found on line 36, which has a `title` attribute called "Ireland". The styling places a solid 5-pixel green border around the `<li>` elements on lines 37 through 39. Lines 22 through 24 style the `<ul>` element found on line 42, which has a `title` attribute called "Spain". The styling places a solid 5-pixel golden border around the `<li>` elements on lines 43 through 45. Lines 26 through 28 style the `<ul>` element found on line 48, which has a `title` attribute called "Italy". The styling places a solid 5-pixel green border around the `<li>` elements on lines 49 through 51. Table 5.1 lists common attribute selectors, their descriptions, and an example for each.

Table 5.1: Common attribute selectors.

Selector	Description	Example
`[attr]`	Matches elements with the specified attribute	`[title]` - any element with a title
`[attr="value"]`	Matches exact attribute value	`[type="email"]` - email inputs
`[attr~="value"]`	Matches if value is in space-delimited list	`[class~="warning"]`
`[attr^="value"]`	Matches if attribute starts with value	`[href^="https"]` - secure links
`[attr*="value"]`	Matches if attribute contains substring	`[src*="thumbnail"]`
`[attr$="value"]`	Matches if attribute ends with value	`[href$=".pdf"]` - PDF links

Pseudo-Element Selectors

Pseudo-element selectors style specific parts of elements or generate content that does not exist in the HTML. They allow selection of elements that do not exist explicitly in the DOM, such as the first line of a paragraph or content inserted before or after an element as shown in the next code fragment which is followed by an HTML document demonstrating the use of pseudo-element selectors.

```
1 h1::first-letter {
2     color: blueviolet;
3     font-weight: bold;
4     font-family: 'Snell Roundhand', cursive;
5     font-size: 2em;
6 }
7
```

```css
8  h1::after {
9      content: url("Flags.png");
10 }
11
12 p::first-line {
13     color: mediumorchid;
14     font-family: 'American Typewriter', serif;
15     font-weight: bold;
16 }
17
18 p::before {
19     content: "Please read carefully: ";
20     color: darkorange;
21 }
22
23 input::placeholder {
24     color: mediumvioletred;
25     font-style: italic;
26 }
27
28 li::marker {
29     color: crimson;
30     font-size: 1.5em;
31 }
32
33 ::selection {
34     color: darkorange;
35     background-color: yellow;
36 }
37
38 /* Other styles from previous examples omitted for brevity */
39 .heading { color: cornflowerblue; font-weight: bold; font-family: cursive; }
40 .ireland { color: green; }
41 .spain { color: goldenrod; }
42 .italy { color: red; }
```

```html
1 <!doctype html>
2 <html>
3 <head>
4     <meta charset="UTF-8">
5     <title>Pseudo-element Selectors</title>
6     <!-- Pseudo element Selectors for the various page elements -->
```

```
 7    <style>
 8          h1::first-letter {
 9              color: blueviolet;
10              font-weight: bold;
11              font-family: 'Snell Roundhand', cursive;
12              font-size: 2em;
13          }
14
15          h1::after {
16              content: url("Flags.png");
17          }
18
19          p::first-line {
20              color: mediumorchid;
21              font-family: 'American Typewriter', serif;
22              font-weight: bold;
23          }
24
25          p::before {
26              content: "Please read carefully: ";
27              color: darkorange;
28          }
29
30          input::placeholder {
31              color: mediumvioletred;
32              font-style: italic;
33          }
34
35          li::marker {
36              color: crimson;
37              font-size: 1.5em;
38          }
39
40          ::selection {
41              color: darkorange;
42              background-color: yellow;
43          }
44
45          /* Other styles from previous examples omitted for brevity */
46          .heading { color: cornflowerblue; font-weight: bold; font-family: cursive; }
47          .ireland { color: green; }
48          .spain { color: goldenrod; }
49          .italy { color: red; }
```

```
50        </style>
51   </head>
52   <body>
53        <h1 class="heading">Countries To Visit</h1>
54        <p>Below is a list of different countries and cities to visit<br>
55        If you do not see a country you like, type in a country name below</p>
56
57        <input type="text" placeholder="Enter the name of a country">
58        <br>
59
60        <ul>
61            <div>
62                <li class="ireland">Ireland</li>
63                <ul id="irelandlist">
64                    <li>Dublin</li>
65                    <li>Donegal</li>
66                    <li>Dingle</li>
67                </ul>
68                <li class="spain">Spain</li>
69                <ul id="spainlist">
70                    <li>Valencia</li>
71                    <li>Madrid</li>
72                    <li>Barcelona</li>
73                </ul>
74                <li class="italy">Italy</li>
75                <ul id="italylist">
76                    <li>Rome</li>
77                    <li>Florence</li>
78                    <li>Venice</li>
79                </ul>
80            </div>
81        </ul>
82   </body>
83   </html>
```

Pseudo-element selectors are used to style specified parts of an element such as the first line or first letter of an HTML element, or to insert content before or after the element's content. The code above uses several pseudo-element selectors. The `h1::first-letter` selector found on lines 8 through 13 targets the first letter of `<h1>` elements. The code has only one `<h1>` element, which is on line 53. The selector styles the letter "C" in countries, with a new text color of blueviolet (line 9), a font-weight of bold (line 10), a font-family of Snell Roundhand or cursive, if Snell Round is not available, (line 11), and a font-size of 2em (line 12). The `h1::after` selector found on lines 15 through 17 also targets `<h1>` elements. This selector places content after `<h1>` elements. In this code, it places a picture of three flags after the `<h1>` element on line 53. The `p::first-line` selector found on lines 19 through 23 styles the first line of `<p>` elements. Our code has only one `<p>` element, found on lines 54 through 55. It styles the element's text color to mediumorchid (line 20), the font-family to American Typewriter or serif, if American Typewriter is not available, (line 21), and the font-weight to bold (line 22). The `p::before` selector on lines 25 through 28 places content before `<p>` elements. In our code, it places the text "Please read carefully" before the `<p>`, element found on line 54. The `input::placeholder` selector on lines 30 through 33 styles the placeholder attribute of the `<input>` element, found on line 57. This selector changes the text color of the placeholder attribute of the `<input>` element to mediumvioletred (line31) and its font-style to italic (line 32). The `li::marker` selector on lines 35 through 38 styles the markers (bullets in this case) of the `<li>` elements on lines 62, 68 and 74. The markers will have their color styled as crimson (line 36) and their font-size as 1.5 em (line 37). The `::selection` selector on lines 40 through 43 styles any part of the page that is highlighted/selected by the user. When the user selects an item on the page, its color will be styled to dark orange (line 41) with a background color of yellow (line 42). Table 5.2 lists pseudo-element selectors and their descriptions.

Table 5.2: CSS pseudo-element selectors.

Selector	Description
`::first-letter`	Styles the first letter of an element
`::first-line`	Styles the first line of an element
`::before`	Inserts content before an element's content
`::after`	Inserts content after an element's content
`::marker`	Styles list item markers
`::selection`	Styles selected/highlighted text
`::placeholder`	Styles input placeholder text

Pseudo-Class Selectors

Pseudo-class selectors target elements based on their state or position in the DOM. They are essential for creating interactive styles and responding to user actions as shown in the next code fragment which is followed by an HTML document demonstrating the use of pseudo-class selectors. The order of pseudo-class selectors matters. For links, always use the LVHA order: `:link`, `:visited`, `:hover`, `:active`.

```
1  a:link {
2      color: green;
3      text-decoration: underline overline dotted red;
4  }
```

```css
 5
 6  a:visited {
 7      color: magenta;
 8      text-decoration-color: green;
 9  }
10
11  a:hover {
12      text-decoration: none;
13      color: cyan;
14      font-weight: bold;
15  }
16
17  a:active {
18      background-color: yellow;
19  }
20
21  li:first-child {
22      background-color: green;
23  }
24
25  li:last-child {
26      background-color: red;
27  }
28
29  .image img:only-child {
30      border: 4px solid goldenrod;
31      padding: 10px;
32  }
33
34  input:focus {
35      border: 2px solid blue;
36      background-color: blueviolet;
37      color: white;
38  }
39
40  input[type="radio"]:checked {
41      box-shadow: 0 0 7px 5px blueviolet;
42  }
43  div {
44      width: 150px;
45      height: 100px;
46  }
```

```html
1  <!doctype html>
2  <html>
3  <head>
4      <meta charset="UTF-8">
5      <title>Pseudo-class Selectors</title>
6      <!-- Pseudo-class Selectors -->
7      <style>
8          a:link {
9              color: green;
10             text-decoration: underline overline dotted red;
11         }
12
13         a:visited {
14             color: magenta;
15             text-decoration-color: green;
16         }
17
18         a:hover {
19             text-decoration: none;
20             color: cyan;
21             font-weight: bold;
22         }
23
24         a:active {
25             background-color: yellow;
26         }
27
28         li:first-child {
29             background-color: green;
30         }
31
32         li:last-child {
33             background-color: red;
34         }
35
36         .image img:only-child {
37             border: 4px solid goldenrod;
38             padding: 10px;
39         }
40
41         input:focus {
42             border: 2px solid blue;
```

```
43            background-color: blueviolet;
44            color: white;
45        }
46
47        input[type="radio"]:checked {
48            box-shadow: 0 0 7px 5px blueviolet;
49        }
50
51        div {
52            width: 150px;
53            height: 100px;
54        }
55    </style>
56 </head>
57 <body>
58    <p>Travel to the country of your dreams! To learn more visit
59    <a href="https://www.ourSite.com">OUR SITE</a> and start your adventure!</p>
60
61    <div class="image">
62        <img src="Flags.png" alt="Flags">
63    </div>
64
65    <div>
66        <nav>
67            <ul>
68                <li><a href="#">Ireland</a></li>
69                <li><a href="#">Spain</a></li>
70                <li><a href="#">Italy</a></li>
71            </ul>
72        </nav>
73    </div>
74    <p>If you did not find a country listed above then perhaps choose one from below</p>
75    England <input type="radio" name="destination">
76    France <input type="radio" name="destination">
77    Greece <input type="radio" name="destination">
78    Germany <input type="radio" name="destination">
79    <p>Otherwise type the name of the country you would like to visit below</p>
80    <input type="text" placeholder="Enter country name">
81 </body>
82 </html>
```

The pseudo-class selectors target an element based on its state or position. In the code above, the :linked selector found on lines 8 through 11 styles the text "OUR SITE" on line 59 when the link has not been visited. The :linked selector colors the text green (line 9) and places a dotted red line above and below the text (line 10). The `:visited` selector found on lines 13 through 16 styles the text "OUR SITE" on line 59 if the link has been visited. The `:visited` selector colors the text magenta (line 14) and places a dotted green line above and below the text (line 15). The `:hover` selector is found on lines 18 through 22. This selector styles the text "OUR SITE" on line 59 when the user mouses over the link. The `:hover` selector removes the line above and below the text (line 19), colors the text cyan (line 20), and bolds the text (line 21). The `:active` selector found on lines 24 through 26 styles the background-color of the text "OUR SITE" on line 59 to yellow (line 25) when the link is clicked by the user. The `:first-child` selector is found on lines 28 through 30. This selector styles the background color of the first child of a given element. In this case, it is the `<li>` element on line 68 and its background color is styled to green (line 29). The `:last-child` selector is found on lines 32 through 34. This selector styles the background color of the last child of a given element to red (line 33). In this case it targets the `<li>` element found on line 70. The `:only-child` selector found on lines 36 through 39 styles an element that is an only child of its parent element. This selector targets the `<img>` element on line 62 (a png file containing three flags), which is the only child of the `div.image`. It will surround the image with a 4-pixel border of goldenrod (line 37) that has a padding of 10-pixels (line 38). The `:focus` selector found on lines 41 through 45 styles an input element when it has focus (i.e., the user has clicked on it, in this case an `<input>` element. It styles the element by placing a solid 2-pixel blue border (line 42) around the input field, changes the background color to blueviolet (line 43), and the text color to white (line 44). The `:checked` selector found on lines 47 through 49 styles a radio button that has been selected. It adds a blueviolet shadow box to the selected radio button (line 48). Table 5.3 lists pseudo-class selectors and their descriptions.

Table 5.3: CSS pseudo-class selectors.

Selector	Description
`:link`	Unvisited links (default: blue underlined)
`:visited`	Previously visited links (default: purple underlined)
`:hover`	Elements being hovered over
`:active`	Elements being clicked (default: red underlined)
`:focus`	Elements that have received focus
`:checked`	Checked checkboxes or radio buttons
`:first-child`	First child of parent element
`:last-child`	Last child of parent element
`:only-child`	Only child of parent element

5.3.3   Contextual Selectors (Combinators)

Contextual selectors, also known as combinators, select elements based on their relationships in the document tree. They enable styling based on element context, adding specificity to your selectors as shown in the next code fragment which is followed by an HTML document demonstrating the use of contextual selectors.

```
1  div p {
2      color: blueviolet;
3      font-weight: bold;
4  }
5
6  nav > ul {
7      color: dodgerblue;
8  }
9
10 li > a {
11     color: orangered;
12     font-family: cursive;
13 }
14
15 div + h2 {
16     color: green;
17     font-family: cursive;
18 }
19
20 p ~ input {
21     background-color: cornflowerblue;
22 }
```

```
1  <!doctype html>
2  <html>
3  <head>
4      <meta charset="UTF-8">
5      <title>Contextual Selectors</title>
6      <!-- Contextual Selectors -->
7      <style>
8          div p {
9              color: blueviolet;
10             font-weight: bold;
11         }
12
```

```
13          nav > ul {
14              color: dodgerblue;
15          }
16
17          li > a {
18              color: orangered;
19              font-family: cursive;
20          }
21
22          div + h2 {
23              color: green;
24              font-family: cursive;
25          }
26
27          p ~ input {
28              background-color: cornflowerblue;
29          }
30      </style>
31 </head>
32 <body>
33      <div>
34          <p>Travel to the country of your dreams! To learn more visit
35          <a href="https://www.ourSite.com">OUR SITE</a> and start your adventure!</p>
36      </div>
37
38      <div class="image">
39          <img src="Flags.png" alt="Flags">
40      </div>
41
42      <div>
43          <nav>
44              <ul>
45                  <li><a href="#">Ireland</a></li>
46                  <li><a href="#">Spain</a></li>
47                  <li><a href="#">Italy</a></li>
48              </ul>
49          </nav>
50      </div>
51
52      <h2>If you did not find a country listed above then perhaps choose one from below</h2>
53
54      England <input type="radio" name="destination">
55      France <input type="radio" name="destination">
```

```
56      Greece <input type="radio" name="destination">
57      Germany <input type="radio" name="destination">
58
59      <p>Otherwise type the name of the country you would like to visit below</p>
60      <input type="text" placeholder="Enter country name">
61 </body>
62 </html>
```

Contextual selectors style elements based on their context or relationship in the document tree. The `div p` selector, a descendant combinator, is found on lines 8 through 11. It styles all the `<p>` elements that are descendants (meaning within) of `<div>` elements. The `<p>` element styled by this selector is found on line 34. The element's text color is styled to blueviolet (line 9) and its font-weight is bold (line 10). The nav > ul selector, a child combinator, is found on lines 13 through 15. It styles `<ul>` elements that are direct children of `<nav>` elements. The `<li>` elements within the `<ul>` element (line 44) affected by this selector are found on lines 45 through 47. The markers for the `<li>` elements are styled to the color dodgerblue (line 14). The li > a selector, found on lines 17 through 20, is also a child combinator that affects the `<a>` elements that are direct children of `<li>` elements. The `<li>` elements affected by this selector are found on lines 45 through 47. The style applied to the links of those elements is the text color orangered (line 18) and the font-family cursive (line 19). The `div + h2` selector, an adjacent sibling combinator, is found on lines 22 through 25. It styles the `<h2>` element on line 52 as it comes immediately after a `<div>` element (line 50). The `<h2>` element has its text color styled to green (line 23) and its font-family styled to cursive (line 24). The p   input selector is a general sibling combinator and is found on lines 27 through 29. It styles all the `<input>` elements that are next siblings (at the same level and come after) of `<p>` elements. The `<input>` element affected is found on line 60 as it is a sibling of the `<p>` element on line 59. It styles the element's background color to cornflowerblue (line 28). Table 5.4 lists contextual selectors, their names, descriptions, and an example for each.

Table 5.4: CSS contextual selectors (combinators).

Selector	Name	Description	Example
A B	Descendant	Selects all B elements inside A	div p
A > B	Child	Selects direct children only	li > a
A + B	Adjacent Sibling	Selects B immediately after A	div + h2
A ~ B	General Sibling	Selects all B siblings after A	p ~ input

5.4   The Cascade and Specificity

The "Cascading" in CSS refers to the algorithm browsers use to determine which styles apply when multiple rules target the same element and conflict with each other. Understanding the cascade is perhaps the most crucial skill for debugging CSS and writing predictable, maintainable stylesheets.

After you have used selectors, as described above, to target an element, the browser must decide which rule "wins" if multiple selectors target the same property.

5.4.1   How the Cascade Works

When multiple CSS rules conflict, the browser considers four factors, listed below, in a specific order to resolve any styling conflict. The first factor that resolves the conflict stops the process. These factors are: importance (`!important` declarations), origin (where the styles come from: author, user, or browser), specificity (how specific the selector is), and source order (which rule is defined last in the code).

Let us explore each factor in detail.

5.4.2   Importance: The !important Declaration

The `!important` flag is a special declaration you can add to a property-value pair. It immediately wins almost every conflict, overriding all other factors.

```css
/* In external stylesheet */
.warning-text {
    color: orange;
    font-size: 16px;
}

/* Later in the same file */
p {
    color: black !important;   /* This wins due to !important */
    font-size: 14px;
}
```

When applied to HTML:

```html
<p class="warning-text">
    This text will be BLACK (not orange) but 16px (not 14px).
</p>
```

The text color is black because `!important` overrides the more specific class selector. However, the font-size remains 16px because the class selector (`.warning-text`) is more specific than the `p` selector and no `!important` was used on `font-size`. `!important` should be used very sparingly, as it makes code difficult to debug. It is often reserved for utility classes that must always apply (e.g., `.d-none { display: none !important; }`).

5.4.3   Origin: Where Styles Come From

CSS can originate from three sources, listed here in order of increasing priority: user agent styles (the browser's default styles, e.g., `h1` is large and bold), user styles (custom styles a user defines in their browser, rare today), and author styles (your CSS - the `.css` files you write as the developer).

This means your stylesheets (author styles) will always override the browser's default styles, which is what you want.

5.4.4   Specificity: The Key to Understanding Conflicts

This is the most common and important factor. When multiple rules from the same origin (e.g., all from your own CSS) conflict, the browser uses a scoring system called specificity to determine which selector is more "specific." Specificity is calculated by counting four types of selectors. You can think of it as a four-part score (`Inline, IDs, Classes, Elements`):

- Inline styles (e.g., `style="\ldots{}"`) - Wins 1 in the first column (1,0,0,0).
- IDs (e.g., `#special`) - Wins 1 in the second column (0,1,0,0).
- Classes, attributes, and pseudo-classes (e.g., `.highlight`, `[type="text"]`, `:hover`) - Wins 1 in the third column (0,0,1,0).
- Elements and pseudo-elements (e.g., `p`, `::first-line`) - Wins 1 in the fourth column (0,0,0,1).

The following examples demonstrate specificity values ordered from lowest to highest:

```css
/* Specificity: 0,0,0,1 (one element) */
p {
    color: black;
}

/* Specificity: 0,0,1,0 (one class) */
.highlight {
    color: yellow;
}

/* Specificity: 0,0,1,1 (one class + one element) */
p.highlight {
    color: orange;
}

/* Specificity: 0,0,2,1 (two classes + one element) */
p.highlight.featured {
    color: purple;
}

/* Specificity: 0,1,0,0 (one ID) */
#special {
```

```
23      color: red;
24  }
25
26  /* Specificity: 0,1,1,1 (one ID + one class + one element) */
27  p#special.highlight {
28      color: green;
29  }
30
31  /* An inline style (1,0,0,0) would beat all of these. */
```

When these rules are applied to the same paragraph, the one with the highest score "wins":

```
1  <p id="special" class="highlight featured">
2      This text will be green.
3  </p>
```

The green from `p#special.highlight` (0,1,1,1) wins because its score is higher than the purple from `p.highlight.featured` (0,0,2,1). The second column (IDs) is more important than the third (Classes).

5.4.5 Source Order: The Tiebreaker

If two selectors have the exact same importance, origin, and specificity score, the simple tiebreaker rule is that the last rule defined wins:

```
1  /* Two rules with identical specificity (0,0,1,0) */
2  .button {
3      background-color: blue;
4      color: white;
5      padding: 10px;
6  }
7
8  /* This rule comes later in the file */
9  .button {
10      background-color: red;     /* This wins for background-color */
11      border: 2px solid black;   /* This is added */
12  }
```

The button will have a red background, white text, 10px padding, and a 2px black border. The `background-color: red` wins simply because it came last.

The same principle applies when styles come from different sources. Consider an external stylesheet that defines:

```
1  /* In external file: styles.css */
2  .highlight { color: red; background: yellow; }
```

And an internal stylesheet in the HTML document that defines:

```
1  /* In the HTML <style> element */
2  .highlight { color: cyan; }
```

When applied to `<p class="highlight">Hello</p>`, the paragraph will have a yellow background (from the external stylesheet, since no conflict exists for this property) and cyan text (from the internal stylesheet, which comes later in source order and overrides the external rule). This demonstrates that the cascade resolves conflicts on a property-by-property basis, not at the rule level.

5.5   The CSS Box Model

The CSS Box Model is fundamental to understanding how elements are sized and spaced on web pages. Every element in HTML is treated as a rectangular box, and the box model describes the different parts of that box and how they relate to each other.

5.5.1   Understanding the Box Model Components

Every element's box consists of four distinct areas, working from inside to outside: content (the actual content such as text, images, etc.), padding (space between the content and border), border (a line around the padding and content), and margin (space outside the border).

Let us visualize this with a practical example:

```
1   .box-model-demo {
2       /* Content dimensions */
3       width: 300px;
4       height: 150px;
5
6       /* Padding - inside the border */
7       padding: 20px;
8
9       /* Border - surrounds padding and content */
10      border: 5px solid #333;
11
12      /* Margin - outside the border */
13      margin: 30px;
14
```

```
15    /* Visual styling */
16    background-color: #e3f2fd;  /* Light blue - shows content + padding area */
17 }
```

5.5.2   Calculating Total Element Size

In the standard box model, the total space an element occupies is calculated as:

Total Width = margin-left + border-left + padding-left + width + padding-right + border-right + margin-right

Total Height = margin-top + border-top + padding-top + height + padding-bottom + border-bottom + margin-bottom

For our example:

- Total width = 30 + 5 + 20 + 300 + 20 + 5 + 30 = 410px
- Total height = 30 + 5 + 20 + 150 + 20 + 5 + 30 = 260px

5.5.3   The box-sizing Property

The traditional box model can be counterintuitive because setting `width: 300px` does not mean the element is 300px wide. Instead, it means the content is 300px wide. The `box-sizing` property changes this behavior:

```
1  /* Default box model */
2  .content-box {
3     box-sizing: content-box;  /* Default value */
4     width: 300px;
5     padding: 20px;
6     border: 5px solid black;
7     /* Actual width: 300 + (20 * 2) + (5 * 2) = 350px */
8  }
9
10 /* Border-box model (more intuitive) */
11 .border-box {
12    box-sizing: border-box;
13    width: 300px;
14    padding: 20px;
15    border: 5px solid black;
16    /* Actual width: 300px (padding and border included) */
17    /* Content width: 300 - (20 * 2) - (5 * 2) = 250px */
18 }
19
20 /* Common reset - apply border-box to everything */
21 *, *::before, *::after {
22    box-sizing: border-box;
23 }
```

The `box-sizing` property was introduced to address a historical inconsistency. In the early days of the web, browsers interpreted the box model differently depending on whether an HTML document included a proper DOCTYPE declaration. When a DOCTYPE is present, browsers render pages in "standards mode," where `width` and `height` refer only to the content area (the `content-box` behavior). However, when the DOCTYPE is missing or malformed, browsers enter "quirks mode" to maintain compatibility with older web pages. In quirks mode, some browsers (notably older versions of Internet Explorer) interpreted `width` and `height` to include padding and border (similar to `border-box` behavior). This inconsistency caused significant layout problems for developers. Today, always including a proper DOCTYPE (such as `<!DOCTYPE html>`) ensures standards mode, and explicitly setting `box-sizing: border-box` provides consistent, predictable behavior across all browsers.

5.5.4   Margin and Padding

Understanding the difference between margin and padding is crucial for controlling element spacing. Padding creates space inside the element, between the content and the border. The element's background color or image extends into the padding area. Padding values cannot be negative, and the padded area contributes to the element's clickable area, which is important for interactive elements like buttons and links. Margin creates space outside the element, between the border and surrounding elements. Margins are transparent, meaning the parent element's background shows through. Unlike padding, margin values can be negative, which allows elements to overlap. Additionally, vertical margins can collapse with adjacent margins, a behavior we will examine in the next section. Next is an example of controlling the spacing and layout of elements within a box model.

```css
/* Padding examples */
.card {
    padding: 20px;                 /* All sides */
    padding: 10px 20px;            /* Vertical | Horizontal */
    padding: 10px 20px 30px;       /* Top | Horizontal | Bottom */
    padding: 10px 20px 30px 40px; /* Top | Right | Bottom | Left */
}

/* Individual padding properties */
.specific-padding {
    padding-top: 10px;
    padding-right: 20px;
    padding-bottom: 30px;
    padding-left: 40px;
}

/* Margin examples - same syntax as padding */
.spaced {
    margin: 20px auto;  /* Vertical margins, horizontal centering */
```

```css
20 }
21
22 /* Negative margins for overlapping */
23 .overlap {
24     margin-top: -20px;   /* Pulls element up */
25 }
```

5.5.5 Margin Collapse

Adjacent vertical margins collapse into a single margin equal to the largest value:

```css
1 .paragraph {
2     margin: 20px 0;
3 }
4 /* Two adjacent paragraphs will have 20px between them, not 40px */
5
6 /* Preventing margin collapse */
7 .no-collapse {
8     /* Any of these prevent collapse: */
9     padding: 1px 0;
10    border: 1px solid transparent;
11    overflow: hidden;
12    display: flow-root;   /* Modern solution */
13 }
```

Understanding the box model is fundamental to CSS mastery. It affects every element on your page and influences how you approach layout, spacing, and sizing. With this knowledge, you can create precise, predictable layouts and debug spacing issues effectively.

5.6 Flexbox Layout

After mastering the CSS Box Model in Section 5.5, which controls the sizing and spacing of individual elements, the next logical step is to arrange those elements into a coherent page layout. Flexbox (the Flexible Box Layout module) is a one-dimensional layout model. It excels at distributing space and aligning items in a single direction, either as a row or as a column. It is a powerful tool for building responsive web designs that adapt to various screen sizes. To use Flexbox, you define a flex container by setting `display: flex` on a parent element. Its direct children automatically become flex items.

5.6.1 Core Concepts: The Main and Cross Axis

The most important concept to understand in Flexbox is that it works along two perpendicular axes that determine how items are distributed and aligned. The main axis is the principal axis along which the flex items are distributed, defined by the `flex-direction` property (which defaults to `row`, meaning left-to-right). As the figure below shows, the cross axis runs perpendicular to the main axis; if the main axis is a row, the cross axis is a column, and vice versa. Figure 5.1 shows flexbox layout, which operates along two axes: the main axis (determined by `flex-direction`) and the cross axis (perpendicular to the main axis). Items are distributed along the main axis and aligned along the cross axis.

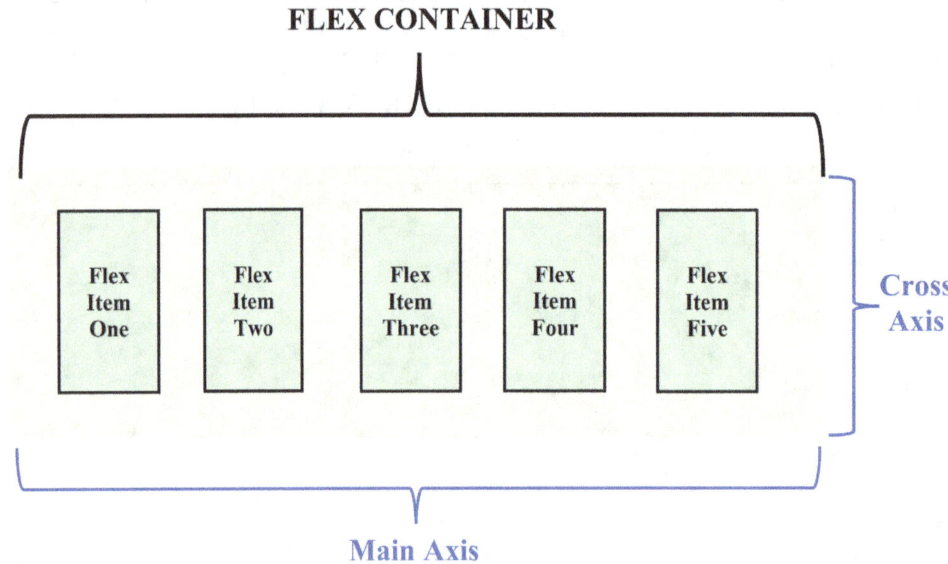

Figure 5.1: Flexbox layout.

5.6.2   Flex Container Properties

You control the overall layout by setting properties on the parent flex container.

display: flex

This is the property that enables Flexbox. Setting `display: flex` on an element turns it into a flex container, and its direct children become flex items.

flex-direction

This property indicates the direction that flex items will flow within the container. It establishes the main axis.
- `row` (default): Flows the flex items horizontally from left to right. The possible values are:
- `column`: Flows the flex items vertically from top to bottom.
- `row-reverse`: Flows the flex items horizontally in reverse order, from right to left.
- `column-reverse`: Flows the flex items vertically in reverse order, from bottom to top.

flex-wrap

By default, flex items will try to fit onto one line. This property controls whether flex items are allowed to wrap onto new lines if they do not fit. The possible values are:
- `nowrap` (default): The flex items do not wrap and may overflow the container.
- `wrap`: The flex items will wrap to a new line as needed.
- `wrap-reverse`: The flex items will wrap in reverse order (new lines are added above the previous line).

flex-flow

This is a shorthand property for setting both `flex-direction` and `flex-wrap` at the same time:

```css
.flex-container {
    flex-flow: row wrap; /* Sets direction to row and allows wrapping */
}
```

justify-content

This property justifies the flex items within the flex container along the main axis. It defines how unused space is distributed. The possible values are:
- `flex-start` (default): The flex items are placed at the start of the main axis (justified to the left for a `row`).
- `flex-end`: The flex items are placed at the end of the main axis (justified to the right for a `row`).
- `center`: The flex items are placed in the center of the main axis.
- `space-around`: Spacing is placed around the flex items. The space before the first item and after the last item is half the size of the space between items.
- `space-between`: Spacing is placed between the flex items. The first item is at the start edge and the last item is at the end edge.
- `space-evenly`: Spacing is placed evenly around all flex items, including before the first item and after the last item.

Figure 5.2 shows the `justify-content` property, which controls how flex items are distributed along the main axis. Common values include `flex-start`, `center`, `space-between`, and `space-evenly`.

Figure 5.2: The `justify-content` property.

align-items

This property determines the default alignment for flex items along the cross axis. The possible values are:
- `stretch` (default): The flex items are stretched to fill the container (from the start to the end of the cross axis).
- `flex-start`: The flex items are placed at the start of the cross axis (justified to the top for a `row`).
- `flex-end`: The flex items are placed at the end of the cross axis (justified to the bottom for a `row`).
- `center`: The flex items are placed in the middle of the cross axis.
- `baseline`: The flex items are placed at the baseline of the flex container (aligned by their text baseline).

align-content

This property aligns the flex lines within the container when there is extra space on the cross axis. Note: This property only has an effect when `flex-wrap: wrap` is set and there are multiple lines of items. The possible values are:
- `stretch` (default): The flex lines are stretched to fill the container.
- `flex-start`: The flex lines are positioned towards the start of the flex container.
- `flex-end`: The flex lines are placed at the end of the flex container.
- `center`: The flex lines are positioned towards the center of the container.
- `space-between`: Spacing between flex lines is distributed equally. The first line is at the start edge, the last is at the end edge.
- `space-around`: Spacing between flex lines is distributed equally, with half-space at the ends.
- `space-evenly`: Spacing of the flex lines is evenly distributed within the flex container.

5.6.3   Flex Item Properties

You can also set properties on individual flex items (the children) to control their behavior.

flex-basis

This property stipulates the initial size of a flex item before any growing or shrinking occurs. It can be a length unit (like 350px) or auto (the default, which uses the item's content size):

```css
.flex-container > div {
    flex-basis: 350px;
}
.flex-container div:nth-of-type(2) {
    flex-basis: 500px; /* This item will be wider */
}
```

flex-grow

This property stipulates how much a flex item can grow relative to other items if there is extra space in the container. It accepts a unitless number. A value of 0 (the default) means the item will not grow:

```css
.flex-container div:nth-of-type(2) {
    flex-grow: 3; /* This item will grow 3x as much as item 3 */
}
.flex-container div:nth-of-type(3) {
    flex-grow: 2; /* This item will grow 2x as much as item 1 */
}
/* Item 1 is flex-grow: 0 (the default) and will not grow */
```

flex-shrink

This property stipulates how much a flex item can shrink relative to other items if there is not enough space in the container. The default value is 1:

```css
.flex-container div:nth-of-type(2) {
    flex-shrink: 2; /* This item will shrink 2x as much as item 3 */
}
.flex-container div:nth-of-type(3) {
    flex-shrink: 1; /* This item will shrink */
}
/* If item 1 has flex-shrink: 0, it will not shrink at all */
```

flex

This is the shorthand property that sets `flex-grow`, `flex-shrink`, and `flex-basis` in one declaration. It is
the most common way to set these values:

```css
/* grow | shrink | basis  */
.item {
    flex: 0 1 auto; /* This is the default */
    flex: 1 1 300px; /* Grows and shrinks, starting from 300px */
    flex: 1;         /* Short for "flex: 1 1 0%" */
    flex: auto;      /* Short for "flex: 1 1 auto" */
}
```

align-self

This property allows you to override the container's `align-items` property for a single, specific flex item:

```css
.flex-container {
    align-items: baseline; /* All items align to baseline\ldots{} */
}

#spain-image {
    align-self: center; /* \ldots{}except this one, which is centered */
}

#spain-text {
    align-self: flex-start; /* \ldots{}and this one, which is at the top */
}
```

5.7   CSS Grid Layout

While Flexbox (Section 5.6) is a powerful tool for one-dimensional layout, CSS Grid (the Grid Layout Module)
is a two-dimensional layout system. It is designed to arrange content in both rows and columns simultaneously,
giving developers greater control and flexibility over large-scale page layouts than older methods like floats or
positioning. To use Grid, you define a grid container by setting `display: grid` on a parent element. Its direct
children automatically become grid items.

5.7.1   Core Concepts: Tracks, Cells, and Areas

The CSS Grid is formed by a series of horizontal and vertical lines that create a structure for your content, as
shown in the figure below.

- Grid Container: The parent element with `display: grid`.
- Grid Items: The direct children of the grid container.
- Grid Lines: The vertical and horizontal lines that form the grid structure.
- Grid Track: The space between two adjacent grid lines (a single column or row).
- Grid Cell: The smallest space in the grid, formed by the intersection of a row track and a column track.
- Grid Area: A rectangular space formed by one or more grid cells.

Figure 5.3 shows the CSS grid terminology where the grid container holds grid items, which are positioned using grid lines. The space between lines forms tracks (rows and columns), and the intersection of tracks creates cells. Multiple cells can form a grid area.

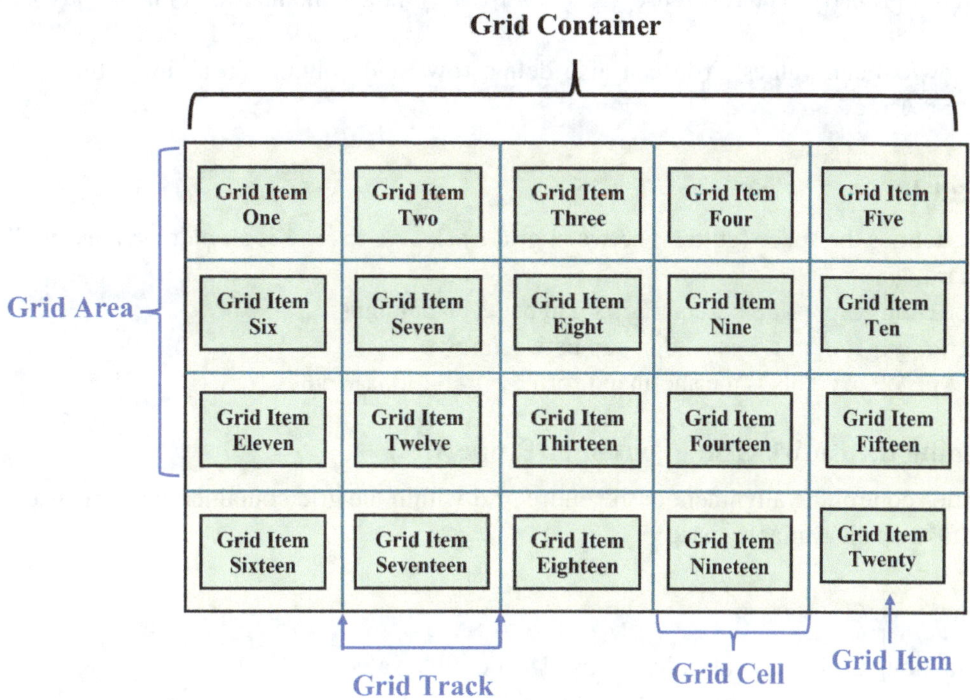

Figure 5.3: CSS grid terminology.

5.7.2 Defining the Grid (Container Properties)

The most important properties are set on the grid container to define the structure of the grid itself.

grid-template-columns

This property determines the width and number of columns in the grid container. You can use standard units (like `px`), flexible units (`fr`, or "fractional unit"), or keywords.

- `auto min-content 500px`: Creates a three-column grid. The first column is sized automatically, the second is sized to fit its content (`min-content`), and the third is 500px wide.

grid-template-rows

This property determines the height and number of rows in the grid container.

- `325px 400px`: Creates a two-row grid. The first row is 325px tall, and the second is 400px tall.

grid-template (Shorthand)

This is a shorthand property that can set `grid-template-rows`, `grid-template-columns`, and `grid-template-areas`.

- Using `grid-area` names: This allows you to "draw" your layout. First, you name an item with the `grid-area` property. Then, you use `grid-template` on the container to define the layout using those names.
- Using row/column values: You can also define rows and columns in a single line. The syntax is `grid-template: <rows> / <columns>`.

gap (and grid-gap)

This property defines the space (gutters) between grid tracks. `grid-gap` is an older syntax, while `gap` is the modern standard.

- `grid-column-gap: 25px`: Sets a 25px gap between columns.
- `grid-row-gap: 30px`: Sets a 30px gap between rows.
- `gap: 30px 25px`: This is the shorthand for `row-gap` (30px) and `column-gap` (25px).

5.7.3   Aligning the Entire Grid (Container Properties)

These properties control the alignment of the entire grid within the grid container, which is useful if the grid tracks do not take up all available space.

justify-content

Aligns the grid along the horizontal (inline) axis. The possible values are:
- `center`: Places the grid in the center of the grid container.
- `start`: Places the grid at the start of the container (left).
- `end`: Places the grid at the end of the container (right).
- `space-around`: Places space around the grid tracks.
- `space-between`: Places space between the grid tracks.
- `space-evenly`: Places space evenly around and between the grid tracks.

align-content

Aligns the grid along the vertical (block) axis. The possible values are:
- `center`: Places the grid in the middle of the grid container.
- `start`: Places the grid at the start of the container (top).
- `end`: Places the grid at the end of the container (bottom).

- `space-around`: Places space around the grid tracks.
- `space-between`: Places space between the grid tracks.
- `space-evenly`: Places space evenly around and between the grid tracks.

5.7.4 Aligning Items (Container & Item Properties)

These properties control the alignment of items inside their individual grid cells.

justify-items (Container Property)

This property sets the default horizontal alignment for all items within their grid cells. The possible values are:
- `right`: Aligns items to the right side of their cell.
- `left`: Aligns items to the left side of their cell.
- `center`: Aligns items to the center of their cell.
- `start`: Aligns items to the start of their cell (left).
- `end`: Aligns items to the end of their cell (right).
- `stretch` (default): Stretches items to fill the cell horizontally.

align-items (Container Property)

This property sets the default vertical alignment for all items within their grid cells. The possible values are:
- `center`: Aligns items to the middle of their cell.
- `start`: Aligns items to the top of their cell.
- `end`: Aligns items to the bottom of their cell.
- `baseline`: Aligns items to their text baseline.
- `stretch` (default): Stretches items to fill the cell vertically.

justify-self (Item Property)

This property is set on an individual grid item to override the container's `justify-items` property for that item only. The possible values are:
- `center`: Centers a specific item horizontally.
- `right`: Right-aligns a specific item horizontally.
- `baseline`: Aligns a specific item to its baseline.
- `left`: Left-aligns a specific item.

align-self (Item Property)

This property is set on an individual grid item to override the container's `align-items` property for that item only. The possible values are:
- `end`: Aligns a specific item to the bottom of its cell.
- `baseline`: Aligns a specific item to its text baseline.
- `center`: Centers a specific item vertically.
- `start`: Aligns a specific item to the top of its cell.

place-content (Shorthand)

This is a shorthand property that sets both `align-content` and `justify-content` in one declaration.

- `place-content: start space-evenly`: Sets `align-content: start` and `justify-content: space-evenly`.

5.7.5   Advanced Grid Functions

repeat()

The `repeat()` function saves you from typing out the same value multiple times.

- `grid-template-columns: repeat(2, 500px 1fr)`: This creates a 4-column track list of `500px 1fr 500px 1fr`.

minmax()

The `minmax()` function defines a size range (a minimum and a maximum) for a grid track. This is extremely useful for responsive design.

- `grid-template-columns: minmax(min-content, 250px) minmax(350px, 450px) 450px`:
- Column 1 will be at least the size of its content, but no wider than 250px.
- Column 2 will be at least 350px, but no wider than 450px.
- Column 3 is fixed at 450px.

5.7.6   When to Use Flexbox vs. Grid

Now that we have explored both layout systems, a common question is when to use one over the other. Table 5.5 makes some recommendations as to when to use Flexbox vs. Grid and explains why. However, the answer is simple: use them together. They are not competitors; they are collaborators.

- Use CSS Grid for the overall page layout (the "macro" layout), including things like your header, footer, sidebar, and main content area.
- Use Flexbox for the components inside those areas (the "micro" layout), including things like aligning items in your navigation bar, centering text in a card, or spacing out buttons.

Table 5.5: When to use flexbox vs. grid.

Use Case	Recommended	Why?
Overall Page Layout	Grid	Grid is two-dimensional (rows and columns)
Navigation Bar	Flexbox	Perfect for a one-dimensional row of links
A Gallery of Cards	Grid	`repeat(auto-fit, minmax(...))` is ideal
Aligning items in a Card	Flexbox	Simple 1D alignment
Form Layout	Grid	Easily align labels and inputs in columns

5.8   JavaScript and CSS Interaction

While CSS handles the static presentation of a page, JavaScript allows us to create dynamic, interactive user interfaces by manipulating CSS in response to user events, data changes, or the passage of time. Understanding how these two technologies interact is crucial for modern web development.

5.8.1   Accessing and Modifying Styles with JavaScript

JavaScript provides several methods to read and change an element's CSS, each with distinct advantages.

1. Direct Style Manipulation (The style Property)

The most direct way to change an element's CSS is by using its `style` property. This property corresponds to the element's inline `style` attribute. For example:

```javascript
// Get an element
const element = document.getElementById('myElement');

// Set individual style properties
element.style.backgroundColor = '#3b82f6';
element.style.padding = '20px';
element.style.borderRadius = '8px';
```

Notice that CSS properties containing a hyphen (like `background-color`) are converted to camelCase (like `backgroundColor`) in JavaScript.

While the `style` property provides direct access to inline styles, it has several important limitations that developers should understand:

- High Specificity: This method adds inline styles, which have the highest specificity (1,0,0,0) and can be difficult to override with external stylesheets.
- Read-Only for Stylesheet Styles: You cannot use `element.style` to read styles defined in an external stylesheet. `element.style.backgroundColor` will be empty unless you have set it inline.
- Mixes Concerns: It mixes styling logic (presentation) with your JavaScript (behavior), which can make code harder to maintain.

This method is best used for dynamic values, like calculating an element's position during a drag-and-drop operation.

2. Working with CSS Classes (The classList Property)

A much cleaner and more maintainable approach is to toggle CSS classes. You define your styles in your CSS file, and use JavaScript only to add or remove the class names. This keeps presentation and behavior separate. For example:

```css
1  /* In your stylesheet */
2  .is-active {
3      background-color: #3b82f6;
4      color: white;
5      box-shadow: 0 4px 10px rgba(0,0,0,0.2);
6      transform: scale(1.05);
7  }
```

```javascript
1  // In your script file
2  const button = document.querySelector('.my-button');
3
4  // Add a class
5  button.classList.add('is-active');
6
7  // Remove a class
8  button.classList.remove('is-active');
9
10 // Toggle a class (add if absent, remove if present)
11 button.classList.toggle('is-active');
12
13 // Check if a class exists
14 if (button.classList.contains('is-active')) {
15     console.log('Button is active');
16 }
```

This is the recommended method for most UI changes, such as highlighting a selected item or showing/hiding a modal.

3. Accessing Computed Styles (getComputedStyle)

To read the actual styles applied to an element (including those from external stylesheets, browser defaults, etc.), you must use the `window.getComputedStyle()` method. This method returns a read-only object containing all the CSS properties for that element. For example:

```javascript
1  const element = document.querySelector('.my-element');
2
3  // Get the computed styles
4  const styles = window.getComputedStyle(element);
5
```

```javascript
6  // Now you can read any property
7  console.log(styles.backgroundColor);    // e.g., "rgb(255, 255, 255)"
8  console.log(styles.width);              // e.g., "300px"
9  console.log(styles.marginTop);          // e.g., "10px"
10 console.log(styles.fontFamily);         // e.g., "Arial, sans-serif"
11
12 // Note: Computed styles are read-only. This will NOT work:
13 // styles.color = 'red'; // Fails
```

4. The CSS Object Model (CSSOM)

For advanced use cases, JavaScript can interact with the stylesheets themselves using the CSS Object Model (CSSOM). This allows you to add or remove entire CSS rules dynamically. For example:

```javascript
1  // Access the first stylesheet on the page
2  const stylesheet = document.styleSheets[0];
3
4  // Add a new rule to the end of the stylesheet
5  if (stylesheet.insertRule) {
6      stylesheet.insertRule('.new-dynamic-class { color: red; }', stylesheet.cssRules.length);
7  }
```

This is powerful but rarely needed for typical application development.

5. CSS Custom Properties (CSS Variables)

CSS Custom Properties (Variables) provide a powerful, modern bridge between CSS and JavaScript. You can set and get variable values on any element, most commonly the root (:root). For example:

```css
1  /* In your stylesheet */
2  :root {
3      --primary-color: #3b82f6;
4      --text-color: #333;
5  }
6  body {
7      background-color: var(--bg-color, #fff);
8      color: var(--text-color);
9  }
```

```javascript
// Get the root element (document.documentElement corresponds to <html>)
const root = document.documentElement;

// --- SET a CSS variable ---
root.style.setProperty('--primary-color', '#ff6b6b');
root.style.setProperty('--bg-color', '#1a1a1a');
root.style.setProperty('--text-color', '#f0f0f0');

// --- GET a CSS variable ---
const primaryColor = getComputedStyle(root)
    .getPropertyValue('--primary-color');

console.log(primaryColor); // Outputs: #ff6b6b
```

This method is the standard for implementing features like a "light/dark mode" theme switcher, as it allows you to change one variable that affects dozens of CSS rules instantly.

5.8.2   Browser Compatibility: Feature Detection vs. Browser Sniffing

When working with advanced CSS and JavaScript, you must account for browser differences. The old, discouraged method was "browser sniffing," which checks the browser's name (e.g., "is this Chrome?"). This is unreliable. The modern, recommended method is "feature detection," which checks if the browser supports the specific feature you want to use. For example:

```javascript
// Bad: Browser Sniffing (Discouraged)
if (navigator.userAgent.includes('Chrome')) {
    // This is fragile and can be faked
}

// Good: Feature Detection (Recommended)
if (CSS.supports('display', 'grid')) {
    // The browser understands CSS Grid
    element.style.display = 'grid';
} else {
    // Fallback for older browsers (e.g., Internet Explorer 11)
    element.style.display = 'flex';
}

if ('IntersectionObserver' in window) {
    // The browser supports this modern JavaScript API
    const observer = new IntersectionObserver(...);
```

```
18  } else {
19      // Fallback to older 'scroll' event listeners
20      window.addEventListener('scroll', ...);
21  }
```

The reason browser sniffing is discouraged is that it is fundamentally unreliable. Users can modify or spoof their browser's User-Agent string, and different versions of the same browser may support different features. Furthermore, new browsers emerge that may support features differently than expected based on their name alone.

Feature detection, on the other hand, directly tests whether the browser supports a specific capability. A common technique is to use the `typeof` operator to check if an object or method exists before using it:

```
1   // Check if a method exists before calling it
2   if (typeof document.querySelector === 'function') {
3       // Safe to use querySelector
4       const element = document.querySelector('.my-class');
5   }
6
7   // Check if a property exists on an object
8   if ('localStorage' in window && typeof window.localStorage !== 'undefined') {
9       // Safe to use localStorage
10      localStorage.setItem('key', 'value');
11  }
```

This approach ensures your code gracefully handles browsers with varying capabilities, rather than making assumptions based on browser identity.

5.8.3   Performance Considerations

Manipulating CSS with JavaScript can be performance-intensive. A key principle is to avoid changes that trigger "layout" or "reflow" (forcing the browser to recalculate the position of all elements, as shown below).

- Fast (Performant): Animating `transform` and `opacity`. (More on this below)
- Slow (Avoid in loops): Changing `width`, `height`, `margin`, `left`, or `top`.

```
1   // Bad: Causes multiple reflows
2   function badAnimation(element) {
3       element.style.left = '10px';      // Reflow
4       element.style.top = '10px';       // Reflow
5       element.style.width = '200px';    // Reflow
6       element.style.height = '200px';   // Reflow
```

```javascript
 7 }
 8
 9 // Good: Batch changes using a class
10 function goodAnimation(element) {
11     // All changes are applied in one step
12     element.classList.add('moved-and-sized');
13 }
14
15 // Best: Use transforms, which don't cause reflow
16 function bestAnimation(element) {
17     element.style.transform = 'translate(10px, 10px) scale(2)';
18 }
```

5.9 Responsive Design

Responsive web design (RWD) is an approach that ensures websites look and function well on all devices, from small mobile phones to large desktop monitors. Rather than creating separate, distinct sites for different devices (e.g., `m.website.com`), RWD uses a single, flexible codebase that adapts its presentation to the user's screen size and capabilities.

5.9.1 The Philosophy of Responsive Design

Responsive design, popularized by Ethan Marcotte in 2010, rests on three core technical principles: fluid grids (using relative units like percentages or fractional units for layout dimensions rather than fixed units like pixels, which allows the layout to "flow" or "flex" to fill the available space), flexible media (ensuring that media, primarily images and videos, can scale within their containing elements, which prevents large images from "breaking" the layout on small screens), and media queries (the CSS feature that makes RWD possible, which allow you to conditionally apply CSS rules only when certain device characteristics, such as viewport width, height, or orientation, are met).

5.9.2 Media Queries: The Foundation of Responsive CSS

Media queries are the cornerstone of responsive design. They allow you to define "breakpoints" in your design, meaning specific widths at which the layout should change to better suit the screen.

Basic Media Query Syntax

The most common use of media queries is to check the viewport's width. The syntax uses an `@media` rule:

```css
1 /* Mobile-first: Default styles for small screens */
2 .container {
3     width: 100%;
4     padding: 10px;
```

```css
5        background-color: #f0f0f0; /* Gray background on mobile */
6    }
7
8    /* Tablet styles: min-width means "at 768px and wider" */
9    @media (min-width: 768px) {
10       .container {
11           max-width: 750px;
12           margin: 0 auto;
13           padding: 20px;
14           background-color: #e0e0ff; /* Blue background on tablet */
15       }
16   }
17
18   /* Desktop styles: "at 1024px and wider" */
19   @media (min-width: 1024px) {
20       .container {
21           max-width: 960px;
22           padding: 30px;
23           background-color: #e0ffe0; /* Green background on desktop */
24       }
25   }
```

This "mobile-first" approach is the modern standard. All default styles (outside of any media query) target the smallest screens. Then, `@media` rules are used to add or override styles as the screen gets progressively larger.

Advanced Media Query Features

Media queries can do more than just check width. You can combine features and check for other device characteristics:

```css
1    /* 1. Combining conditions (a specific range) */
2    @media (min-width: 768px) and (max-width: 1023px) {
3        /* Styles specifically for tablets */
4    }
5
6    /* 2. Checking orientation */
7    @media (orientation: landscape) {
8        /* Styles for when the device is wider than it is tall */
9    }
10
11   /* 3. Checking for high-resolution (Retina) displays */
```

```css
12  @media (min-resolution: 192dpi),
13          (-webkit-min-device-pixel-ratio: 2) {
14      /* Use high-resolution background images */
15      .logo {
16          background-image: url('logo@2x.png');
17      }
18  }
19
20  /* 4. Checking user preferences (Accessibility) */
21  @media (prefers-reduced-motion: reduce) {
22      /* Turn off or reduce animations for sensitive users */
23      * {
24          animation-duration: 0.01ms !important;
25          transition-duration: 0.01ms !important;
26      }
27  }
28
29  @media (prefers-color-scheme: dark) {
30      /* Apply a dark theme */
31      body {
32          background-color: #1a1a1a;
33          color: #ffffff;
34      }
35  }
```

5.9.3   Flexible Layouts

As detailed in Section 5.6, the core of modern responsive layout is Flexbox and CSS Grid. By combining these layout systems with media queries, we can create powerful responsive experiences.

Flexbox for Responsive Layouts

A common pattern is a navigation bar that stacks vertically on mobile but becomes a horizontal row on desktops:

```css
1  /* Mobile-first (stacked column) */
2  .nav {
3      display: flex;
4      flex-direction: column;
5  }
6  .nav-item {
7      text-align: center;
8      border-bottom: 1px solid #ccc;
```

```css
 9  }
10
11  /* 768px and up (horizontal row) */
12  @media (min-width: 768px) {
13      .nav {
14          flex-direction: row;
15          justify-content: space-around;
16      }
17      .nav-item {
18          border-bottom: none;
19      }
20  }
```

CSS Grid for Complex Layouts

Grid is excellent for changing the entire page structure. A common pattern is a 1-column layout on mobile, 2-column on tablet, and 3-column on desktop:

```css
 1  /* Mobile-first (1 column) */
 2  .grid-container {
 3      display: grid;
 4      grid-template-columns: 1fr; /* A single flexible column */
 5      gap: 20px;
 6  }
 7
 8  /* 768px and up (2 columns) */
 9  @media (min-width: 768px) {
10      .grid-container {
11          /* Two equal-width flexible columns */
12          grid-template-columns: 1fr 1fr;
13      }
14  }
15  /* 1024px and up (3 columns) */
16  @media (min-width: 1024px) {
17      .grid-container {
18          /* A powerful auto-responsive grid:
19             Create as many columns as fit, with a minimum
20             width of 300px, and stretch them to fill. */
21          grid-template-columns: repeat(auto-fit, minmax(300px, 1fr));
22      }
23  }
```

5.9.4   Responsive Images and Media

The second principle of RWD is flexible media. The simplest way to achieve this is with a single CSS rule:

```css
img, video, iframe {
    max-width: 100%;  /* Prevents media from overflowing its parent */
    height: auto;     /* Maintains the original aspect ratio */
    display: block;   /* Fixes potential extra space below images */
}
```

This rule ensures that if an image is in a container that becomes narrower than the image's original width, the image will scale down proportionally. For more advanced control, such as loading smaller images on mobile to save bandwidth, you can use the `<picture>` element in your HTML.

5.9.5   Mobile-First Approach

The "mobile-first" approach, as shown in the examples above, is the modern standard for RWD.
- How it works: You write your base CSS styles (those outside any media query) to target the smallest mobile screens. This base style is simple, stacked, and single-column.
- Progressive Enhancement: You then use `min-width` media queries to add complexity as the screen gets larger by rearranging elements into columns, increasing font sizes, and adding effects that only make sense on larger devices.
- Why it is better: It forces you to prioritize content and results in cleaner, more efficient CSS. It is much easier to add complexity than to "undo" or "remove" complex desktop styles for a mobile view.

5.10   CSS Frameworks Introduction

CSS frameworks provide pre-written CSS and JavaScript code that helps developers build websites faster and more consistently. They typically include a grid system, pre-styled components (like buttons, navbars, and cards), utility classes, and JavaScript plugins for interactive elements. While writing custom CSS gives you complete control, frameworks offer rapid development, tested cross-browser compatibility, and established design patterns.

5.10.1   Why Use a CSS Framework?

Understanding the benefits and trade-offs is key to deciding when a framework is the right tool for the job. Frameworks offer several compelling advantages for development teams:
- Speed: Pre-built components and utilities dramatically accelerate development time.
- Consistency: Provides a standardized visual language and component set, which is crucial for teams.
- Responsive by Default: Most frameworks are "mobile-first" and include a powerful grid system.
- Cross-browser Compatibility: Framework authors have already tested and solved most browser quirks.
- Community: Large frameworks have extensive documentation, tutorials, and third-party resources.
However, frameworks also come with trade-offs that developers should carefully consider:

- File Size: Frameworks include a lot of code you might not use, which can lead to "bloat."
- Learning Curve: Each framework has its own class names and conventions that must be learned.
- Generic Look: Without customization, sites built with the same framework can look very similar.
- Override Complexity: Customizing default styles can sometimes require "fighting" the framework's specificity.

5.10.2 Bootstrap: The Most Popular Framework

Bootstrap, originally created by Twitter, is the most popular CSS framework. It provides a comprehensive component library and a powerful responsive grid system. We will look at Bootstrap 5 as our primary example.

Setting Up Bootstrap

To use Bootstrap, you do not need to download any files. You can link to it directly from a CDN (Content Delivery Network) in your HTML's `<head>`:

```html
<!DOCTYPE html>
<html lang="en">
<head>
    <meta charset="UTF-8">
    <meta name="viewport" content="width=device-width, initial-scale=1.0">
    <title>Bootstrap Demo</title>

    <!-- Bootstrap CSS -->
    <link href="https://cdn.jsdelivr.net/npm/bootstrap@5.3.0/dist/css/bootstrap.min.css"
          rel="stylesheet">
</head>
<body>
    <!-- Content goes here -->

    <!-- Bootstrap JavaScript Bundle (for components like dropdowns) -->
    <script
    src="https://cdn.jsdelivr.net/npm/bootstrap@5.3.0/dist/js/bootstrap.bundle.min.js"></script>
</body>
</html>
```

The "Utility-First" Philosophy

Modern frameworks like Bootstrap and Tailwind operate on a "utility-first" or "functional CSS" philosophy. Instead of writing custom CSS, you apply pre-defined, single-purpose classes directly to your HTML. With traditional CSS, you would write:

```html
<button class="my-button">Click Me</button>
```

```css
.my-button {
  background-color: blue;
  color: white;
  padding: 10px 15px;
  border-radius: 5px;
}
```

With Bootstrap utility classes, you can achieve the same result directly in HTML:

```html
<!--
  "btn" is a component class
  "btn-primary" is a modifier class
  "p-2" and "rounded" are utility classes
-->
<button class="btn btn-primary p-2 rounded">Click Me</button>
```

You can see how this approach allows you to style elements without ever writing a new line of CSS.

Bootstrap Grid System

Bootstrap's core feature is its 12-column responsive grid, which is built using Flexbox. It allows you to define layouts in your HTML, as the code below shows.

- `.container`: A wrapper that centers and sets the max-width of your content.
- `.row`: A flex container that holds columns.
- `.col-*`: Columns. You can specify how many of the 12 units a column should span:

```html
<div class="container text-center">
  <div class="row">
    <!-- This column spans 12 (all) units on small screens,
         but 6 (half) units on medium (md) screens and up -->
    <div class="col-12 col-md-6">
      Column 1 (Half width on desktop)
    </div>
    <!-- This column also spans 12 units on small,
         and 6 on medium and up -->
    <div class="col-12 col-md-6">
```

```
11        Column 2 (Half width on desktop)
12      </div>
13    </div>
14    <div class="row">
15      <!-- Three equal columns -->
16      <div class="col-4">Column A</div>
17      <div class="col-4">Column B</div>
18      <div class="col-4">Column C</div>
19    </div>
20  </div>
```

In this example, the first two `<div>` elements will stack vertically on mobile phones (`col-12`) but sit side-by-side on tablets and desktops (`col-md-6`). This is responsive design in action, achieved with just a few classes.

Bootstrap Components

Components are pre-styled, reusable elements. You simply copy their HTML structure. A "Card" is a common example:

```
1  <!-- A simple Bootstrap Card component -->
2  <div class="card shadow-sm" style="width: 18rem;">
3    <div class="card-body">
4      <h5 class="card-title">Card Title</h5>
5      <p class="card-text">
6        Some quick example text to build on the card title
7        and make up the bulk of the card's content.
8      </p>
9      <a href="#" class="btn btn-primary">Learn More</a>
10    </div>
11  </div>
```

This single block of HTML, without any custom CSS, produces a fully styled card with a shadow (`shadow-sm`), padding, and a styled button. Other popular components include Navbars, Modals (pop-ups), Alerts, and Forms.

Bootstrap Utilities

Utilities are single-purpose helper classes. This is where frameworks provide the most speed.

```
1  <!-- Spacing (m = margin, p = padding, t = top, b = bottom, s = start, e = end) -->
2  <div class="mt-5">Margin-top of 5 units</div>
3  <div class="p-3">Padding of 3 units on all sides</div>
4
5  <!-- Text (alignment, weight, color) -->
6  <p class="text-center">Centered text.</p>
7  <p class="fw-bold">Bold text.</p>
8  <p class="text-danger">Red (danger) text.</p>
9
10 <!-- Display and Flexbox -->
11 <div class="d-flex justify-content-between">
12   <span>Left</span>
13   <span>Right</span>
14 </div>
15 <div class="d-none d-md-block">Hidden on mobile, visible on desktop.</div>
```

5.10.3   Customizing Bootstrap

While Bootstrap provides excellent defaults, customization is often necessary. The best way is to override
Bootstrap's default SASS (Syntactically Awesome Style Sheets) variables (an advanced topic) or by overriding
the CSS variables it provides:

```css
1  /* Customizing Bootstrap with CSS Variables */
2  :root {
3      --bs-primary: #7c3aed; /* Change the primary color to purple */
4      --bs-border-radius: 0.5rem; /* Make all components more rounded */
5  }
```

You can also write your own custom utility classes to extend the framework.

5.10.4   When to Use Frameworks

Choosing between a CSS framework and custom CSS depends on your project's specific requirements, timeline,
and design goals. A framework is typically the better choice when building prototypes or MVPs (Minimum
Viable Products—products with just enough features to satisfy early users and gather feedback) that need to
ship quickly, when working in a team that requires high consistency across components, when creating admin
dashboards or internal tools where unique design is not the priority, or when you need battle-tested responsive
design and cross-browser support immediately.

On the other hand, custom CSS (or a utility-first framework like Tailwind) is often preferable when building
a unique, custom-branded website, when performance and minimal file size are absolute top priorities, when you
need full granular control over every style, or when the project is small and simple enough that a full framework

would be overkill. CSS frameworks like Bootstrap provide a solid foundation for rapid web development. They offer tested patterns, comprehensive documentation, and active communities. While they may not be suitable for every project, understanding how to use them effectively is a valuable skill for modern web developers.

5.11 CSS Animation

CSS animations bring websites to life by creating smooth, performant motion without JavaScript. Modern CSS provides three main approaches to animation: transitions for simple state changes, transforms for modifying element geometry, and keyframe animations for complex sequences.

5.11.1 Transitions: Smooth State Changes

CSS transitions are the simplest form of animation. They do not run on their own; instead, they react to a state change, such as an element being hovered (`:hover`) or a class being added via JavaScript (`.active`). You define a CSS property (like `background-color`) and a duration, and the browser handles the gradual change (or "tweening") between the start and end states.

Basic Transition Syntax

The `transition` property is a shorthand that defines the property to animate, the duration, the timing function, and any delay:

```css
.button {
    background-color: #3b82f6; /* Start state */
    color: white;
    padding: 10px 20px;
    border-radius: 5px;

    /* Define the transition */
    transition: background-color 0.3s ease-out;
}

.button:hover {
    background-color: #2563eb; /* End state */
}
```

In this example, the `.button` class defines the initial state. The `:hover` pseudo-class defines the end state. The `transition` property tells the browser: "If the `background-color` ever changes, take 0.3 seconds to animate it, using an `ease-out` timing function." You can transition multiple properties by separating them with a comma:

```css
.card {
    /* \ldots{} other styles \ldots{} */
    transition: transform 0.3s ease, box-shadow 0.3s ease;
}
```

Timing Functions

Timing functions control the acceleration curve of an animation, making it feel more natural rather than mechanical. CSS provides several built-in timing functions:

- `linear`: A constant speed.
- `ease` (default): Starts slow, speeds up, then ends slow.
- `ease-in`: Starts slow, then speeds up.
- `ease-out`: Starts fast, then slows down.
- `ease-in-out`: Like `ease`, but more pronounced.
- `cubic-bezier(n,n,n,n)`: A custom function for full control.

5.11.2 Transforms: Geometric Modifications

CSS transforms allow you to rotate, scale, skew, and translate (move) elements in 2D and 3D space. Importantly, `transform` does not affect the "flow" of the document. Moving an element with `transform: translateX(50px)` will not cause other elements on the page to reflow, making it highly performant for animation.

2D Transforms

These operate on the X and Y axes:

```css
/* Translate (move) */
.el { transform: translateX(50px); }  /* Move 50px right */
.el { transform: translateY(-20px); } /* Move 20px up */

/* Scale (resize) */
.el { transform: scale(1.5); }  /* 150% size */
.el { transform: scaleX(2); }   /* 200% width */

/* Rotate */
.el { transform: rotate(45deg); } /* Rotate 45 degrees clockwise */

/* Skew (slant) */
.el { transform: skewX(20deg); } /* Slant 20 degrees along X-axis */

/* You can combine multiple transforms in one declaration */
```

```
16  .el {
17      transform: translate(50px, -20px) rotate(45deg) scale(1.2);
18  }
```

3D Transforms

These operate in 3D space, requiring a `perspective` on a parent element to create the illusion of depth. A common example is a "card flip" effect:

```
1  <div class="flip-card">
2    <div class="flip-card-inner">
3      <div class="flip-card-front">Front</div>
4      <div class="flip-card-back">Back</div>
5    </div>
6  </div>
```

```
1   .flip-card {
2       perspective: 1000px; /* Defines the 3D "depth" */
3   }
4   .flip-card-inner {
5       transition: transform 0.6s;
6       transform-style: preserve-3d; /* Allows children to be 3D */
7   }
8   .flip-card:hover .flip-card-inner {
9       transform: rotateY(180deg); /* The flip animation */
10  }
11  .flip-card-front, .flip-card-back {
12      position: absolute;
13      width: 100%;
14      height: 100%;
15      backface-visibility: hidden; /* Hides the back of the element */
16  }
17  .flip-card-back {
18      transform: rotateY(180deg); /* Positions the back on the\ldots{} back */
19  }
```

5.11.3 Keyframe Animations

While transitions handle simple start-to-end state changes, keyframes allow for complex, multi-step animations. You define the animation's "stops" using `@keyframes`, and then apply it to an element.

Defining Keyframes

You define a sequence using percentages, from 0\% (start) to 100\% (end). The keywords `from` and `to` are aliases for 0\% and 100\%:

```css
/* A simple fade-in and slide-up animation */
@keyframes slideInUp {
    from {
        transform: translateY(50px);
        opacity: 0;
    }
    to {
        transform: translateY(0);
        opacity: 1;
    }
}

/* A more complex, multi-step "bounce" animation */
@keyframes bounce {
    0%, 20%, 50%, 80%, 100% {
        transform: translateY(0);
    }
    40% {
        transform: translateY(-30px);
    }
    60% {
        transform: translateY(-15px);
    }
}
```

Applying Keyframe Animations

Once defined, you use the `animation` property to attach the keyframes to an element and configure its behavior:

```css
.animated-element {
    /* Long-form properties */
    animation-name: slideInUp;
    animation-duration: 1s;
    animation-timing-function: ease-out;
    animation-delay: 0.5s;
    animation-iteration-count: 1; /* or 'infinite' */
```

```
8      animation-direction: normal;   /* 'normal', 'reverse', 'alternate' */
9      animation-fill-mode: both;     /* Retains the 'to' state after finishing */
10 }
11
12 /* Shorthand property for the same animation */
13 .animated-element-shorthand {
14     animation: slideInUp 1s ease-out 0.5s 1 normal both;
15 }
```

A common practical example is a loading spinner:

```
1 @keyframes spin {
2     to { transform: rotate(360deg); }
3 }
4
5 .spinner {
6     width: 50px;
7     height: 50px;
8     border: 5px solid #f3f4f6;
9     border-top-color: #3b82f6;
10     border-radius: 50%;
11     animation: spin 1s linear infinite;
12 }
```

In this example, the `.spinner` element will rotate 360 degrees over 1 second, linearly, and repeat infinitely, creating a continuous spinning motion.

5.11.4   Performance Considerations

When creating CSS animations, performance is crucial for a smooth user experience. Not all CSS properties are "cheap" to animate.

- Best (Performant): Animate `transform` and `opacity`. These properties can be handled by the browser's GPU (Graphics Processing Unit), resulting in hardware-accelerated, buttery-smooth animations that do not block the main browser thread.
- Avoid (Slow): Animate properties that trigger "layout" or "paint," such as `width`, `height`, `margin`, `padding`, or `left`/`top`/`right`/`bottom`. Animating these forces the browser to recalculate the layout of the page on every frame, which is slow and can cause "jank" or stuttering.

The following examples illustrate the difference between poor and optimal animation approaches. The first example triggers layout recalculation on every frame because it animates the `left` property:

```css
1  /* Bad: triggers layout recalculation */
2  @keyframes slide-bad {
3      from { left: 0; }
4      to { left: 100px; }
5  }
```

The better approach uses `transform`, which is hardware-accelerated:

```css
1  /* Good: hardware-accelerated */
2  @keyframes slide-good {
3      from { transform: translateX(0); }
4      to { transform: translateX(100px); }
5  }
```

You can hint to the browser that an element will be animated by using the `will-change` property. Use this sparingly, as it reserves GPU memory:

```css
1  .hover-element {
2      transition: transform 0.3s;
3      will-change: transform; /* Tell the browser to optimize for this */
4  }
5  .hover-element:hover {
6      transform: scale(1.1);
7  }
```

5.11.5   Accessibility and Animations

Always consider users who are sensitive to motion. CSS provides a media query, `prefers-reduced-motion`, to respect this user preference. You should wrap your animations in this media query, or use it to disable them:

```css
1  /* 1. Standard animations */
2  .animated-element {
3      animation: slideInUp 1s ease-out;
4  }
5  .hover-card {
6      transition: transform 0.3s;
7  }
8
```

```
 9   /* 2. Disable or reduce animations for sensitive users */
10   @media (prefers-reduced-motion: reduce) {
11       .animated-element {
12           animation: none; /* Turn off keyframe animation */
13       }
14       .hover-card {
15           transition: none; /* Turn off transition */
16       }
17
18       /* You could also opt for a more subtle 'fade-in' instead
19          of a 'slide-in' for a reduced-motion experience */
20   }
```

5.12 Chapter Review

Problem 5.1 What are the three main ways to include CSS in an HTML document, and when is each method most appropriate to use?

Problem 5.2 Explain the structure of a CSS rule, including what a selector, property, and value are. Provide an example of a complete CSS rule and identify each component.

Problem 5.3 Compare and contrast class selectors and ID selectors, explaining when you should use each one and what their specificity values are.

Problem 5.4 What is the CSS cascade and how are conflicts between rules resolved? Describe the four factors that determine which style wins when multiple rules target the same element.

Problem 5.5 Explain the universal selector ($*$) and its uses, giving an example of when it might be helpful and when it might cause performance issues.

Problem 5.6 What is the difference between descendant selectors and child selectors? Provide examples showing when each would select different elements.

Problem 5.7 Distinguish between pseudo-classes and pseudo-elements, giving three examples of each and explaining the fundamental difference between them.

Problem 5.8 Why is the LVHA order important for link pseudo-classes, and what problems might occur if you do not follow this order?

Problem 5.9 How do attribute selectors work in CSS? Provide examples of selecting elements based on:
- Presence of an attribute
- Exact attribute value
- Attribute value starting with specific text
- Attribute value containing a substring

Problem 5.10 Explain the CSS Box Model in detail, including the four components and how they relate to each other. How does `box-sizing: border-box` change the default behavior?

Problem 5.11 What is the difference between padding and margin? Explain margin collapse and when it occurs.

Problem 5.12 Describe three different ways JavaScript can interact with CSS, and include examples of each method.

Problem 5.13 What is the difference between computed styles and inline styles in JavaScript, and how do you access each programmatically?

Problem 5.14 Explain browser feature detection versus browser sniffing, and why feature detection is preferred. Provide a code example.

Problem 5.15 What are CSS media queries and how do they enable responsive design? Write a media query that applies styles only on screens wider than 768px.

Problem 5.16 What does "mobile-first" mean in responsive design, and how does this approach affect the way you write media queries?

Problem 5.17 Discuss the benefits and drawbacks of using CSS frameworks like Bootstrap, and when you would choose to use a framework versus writing custom CSS.

Problem 5.18 Compare CSS transitions and CSS animations, explaining when you would use each approach. Provide examples.

Problem 5.19 Which CSS properties can be animated performantly, and which properties should generally be avoided in animations and why?

Problem 5.20 How do you make CSS animations accessible, and what CSS features help users who prefer reduced motion?

Problem 5.21 What are CSS custom properties (CSS variables), and how do they differ from preprocessor variables? Show an example of defining and using them.

Problem 5.22 Explain CSS specificity in detail. Given the following selectors, order them from lowest to highest specificity:

- `p`
- `.content p`
- `#main p`
- `p.highlight`
- `body div p`
- `p[title]`

Problem 5.23 What is the difference between `display: none` and `visibility: hidden`, and how does each affect the document layout and accessibility?

Problem 5.24 When would you use the `!important` declaration, and why should it generally be avoided?

Problem 5.25 Describe the different types of CSS combinators and provide an example use case for each:

- Descendant combinator
- Child combinator
- Adjacent sibling combinator
- General sibling combinator

Problem 5.26 Building a Styled Navigation Bar: Create a horizontal navigation bar using CSS. Start with an unordered list containing five navigation links (Home, About, Services, Portfolio, Contact). Style the navigation bar so that list items display horizontally, remove default list styling (bullets and padding), and add hover effects that change the background color. Use the `:hover` pseudo-class to create smooth transitions when users mouse over each link. Implement the navigation using an external stylesheet to practice the separation of concerns between HTML structure and CSS presentation.

Problem 5.27 Card Layout with Flexbox: Design a responsive card layout using Flexbox. Create a container with six product cards, each containing an image placeholder, a title, a description, and a price. Use `display: flex` on the container with `flex-wrap: wrap` to allow cards to flow onto multiple rows. Each card should have a fixed width of approximately 300 pixels with appropriate margins. Apply the `justify-content` property to control spacing between cards. Add hover effects that slightly elevate the card using `transform: translateY()` and `box-shadow`.

Problem 5.28 Page Layout with CSS Grid: Create a complete page layout using CSS Grid. The layout should include a header spanning the full width, a main content area, a sidebar, and a footer. Use `grid-template-areas` to define named regions and place elements accordingly. The layout should be responsive: on screens wider than 768 pixels, display the sidebar next to the main content; on narrower screens, stack all elements vertically. Practice using the `fr` unit for flexible track sizing and `gap` for consistent spacing between grid areas.

Problem 5.29 CSS Specificity Challenge: Create an HTML document with multiple paragraphs that have various combinations of classes, IDs, and attributes. Write CSS rules using different selector types that target the same elements with conflicting styles. For example, create rules using element selectors, class selectors, ID selectors, and attribute selectors that all try to set different colors on the same paragraph. Predict which styles will be applied based on specificity rules, then verify your predictions in the browser. Document your findings by calculating the specificity value for each selector.

Problem 5.30 Animated Button Component: Design an interactive button component using CSS transitions and transforms. The button should have a base state with a solid background color, rounded corners, and appropriate padding. On hover, the button should smoothly transition to a different background color, slightly increase in size using `transform: scale()`, and display a subtle shadow. On click (using the `:active` pseudo-class), the button should appear pressed by reducing the scale and shadow. Use the `transition` property to ensure all state changes animate smoothly over 0.3 seconds.

Problem 5.31 Responsive Image Gallery: Build a responsive image gallery that adapts to different screen sizes. Use CSS Grid with `repeat(auto-fit, minmax(250px, 1fr))` to create a flexible grid that automatically adjusts the number of columns based on available space. Each gallery item should contain an image that fills its container while maintaining aspect ratio using `object-fit: cover`. Add a caption overlay that appears on hover using CSS positioning and opacity transitions. Include a media query that adjusts the minimum card size for mobile devices.

6. JavaScript

6.1   Introduction

This chapter covers the essentials of the client-side scripting language JavaScript, a language specifically designed to operate within web browsers. In a typical three-tier web application architecture, JavaScript runs in the client (browser) tier, i.e., the presentation layer, enabling interactive features in the user interface, while server-side languages handle the application logic and database interactions on the back-end.

To better understand JavaScript's role within web applications, it helps to visualize the standard three-tier architecture. The diagram below shows clearly the separation of responsibilities among the client tier (browser), server tier (web application server), and database tier (data storage). JavaScript primarily runs in the client tier, providing dynamic interactions and communicating asynchronously with the server tier. The server handles requests, performs logic or data operations, and responds back to the client. Figure 6.1 illustrates the roles of client, server, and database tiers.

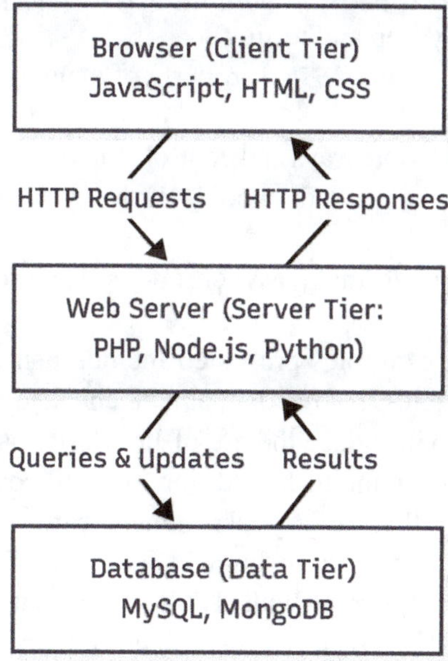

Figure 6.1: Three-tier web application architecture.

JavaScript code is interpreted by the browser and allows a web page user to interact dynamically with HTML elements and their content on the page. JavaScript code can be included directly in a web page (known as explicit embedding), or placed in a separate file that the page references and downloads (known as implicit embedding). For convenience, most examples here will use a `<script>` element embedded in the HTML

DOI: 10.1201/9781003727651-6

<head> to contain the code, or will show relevant code snippets in context. JavaScript functions can be written from scratch by the page designer (or reused from existing libraries) and are generally triggered or fired by events associated with the page, such as mouse clicks or when the page is loaded. We will introduce JavaScript syntax and concepts largely through illustrative examples, rather than a dry enumeration of syntax rules, as we believe this hands-on approach helps develop a practical understanding of the language and its uses.

Learning Objectives

By the end of this chapter, you should be able to:

- Data validation: How to use JavaScript to verify that data submitted by an HTML form satisfies various correctness criteria (e.g., non-empty, numeric format, etc.).
- Functions: How to define, implement, and invoke JavaScript functions.
- Event handling: What kinds of cursor or other browser events can trigger the execution of functions.
- DOM element access: How to use the HTML `id` attribute and the JavaScript `document.getElementById()` method in tandem to interact with specific HTML elements.
- Visual effects: How to implement simple dynamic effects like image rollovers.
- Language basics: Understanding general language characteristics of JavaScript, such as variable scope, control structures (loops, conditionals), operators, basic data types, etc.
- Development techniques: How to perform simple incremental program development in JavaScript (building up functionality step by step and testing).
- Dynamic content: How to use the `innerHTML` property of elements like `<div>` and `<span>` to insert or modify page content on the fly.
- Data structures: How to use JavaScript arrays and control structures like `for` loops and `switch` statements.
- Randomness: How to use and, if needed, modify JavaScript's built-in random number generation functions.
- AJAX: How AJAX allows a page to make asynchronous background HTTP requests to web servers without reloading the page.

Elaborating on the above list, the examples presented include using JavaScript to perform simple data validation for data entered into form fields, so that data can be checked on the client side for various criteria before being sent to the server. We also introduce the use of JavaScript patterns (regular expressions) to detect desirable or undesirable textual patterns in input. In addition, we will cover some of the browser events (such as mouse events and page load events) that can asynchronously trigger JavaScript functions, illustrating the use of the `document` and `window` objects, various built-in functions like `alert()`, and the key `document.getElementById()` method (used in conjunction with HTML `id` attributes) to read from or write to form fields. A simple rollover example will demonstrate visual effects achieved in response to cursor movements. The basic JavaScript language features including "variable scope (local vs. global variables and variable persistence), standard control statements like `if`, `if-else`, and `switch`, boolean conditions, and string manipulations " are addressed via examples. We also touch on the limited syntax diagnostic tools available in browsers (e.g., error consoles in Firefox and Chrome) to help debug scripts.

An example is presented that uses JavaScript with HTML image maps to create an interactive graphic. We will develop simple applications involving random numbers to explore how "random" JavaScript's random number generator really is, and along the way introduce additional language features while demonstrating incremental program development techniques. These examples illustrate the use of `for` loops, arrays, the built-in `Math.random()` function, and other features. The essential `innerHTML` property of HTML elements (which allows dynamic insertion or modification of page content) is also demonstrated. The chapter ends with a brief introduction to AJAX, a JavaScript technique that allows a page to make asynchronous background connections to a web server (and even to a back-end database via a server-side script), significantly enhancing the capabilities of web pages.

Caveat about Programming Style: In practice, the best approach is to use clear, descriptive names for HTML fields, variables, and functions so that code is easy to read and maintain. Because the numerous examples here are written for illustration purposes, the code may use very abbreviated, "telegraphic" names that would not be considered good style in a production setting. The reader should be aware that these code snippets are for educational purposes; when you write your own code (such as for assignments or professionally), you should follow normal best-practice naming conventions, even if this text does not always do so.

6.2 Development Tools for JavaScript

Just as with HTML, simple text editors like Notepad++ or TextPad provide syntax highlighting for JavaScript. In addition to basic text editors, several specialized tools can aid JavaScript development:

- Firefox Developer Tools: Modern browsers like Firefox and Chrome include developer consoles that provide useful diagnostic information on script errors. Firefox's old Error Console (and now the integrated Developer Tools) help identify JavaScript errors, and add-ons like Firebug (historically) or the built-in tools in Firefox/Chrome can assist in debugging and inspecting web applications (e.g., viewing HTTP requests, inspecting the DOM, etc.).
- jQuery: jQuery is a powerful JavaScript library that simplifies many common tasks and enables sophisticated visual effects that would be non-trivial to implement by hand. (We will discuss jQuery more later in the context of AJAX.) You can download it from the official site and include it in your pages. jQuery provides an accessible syntax for traversing the DOM and binding events to elements, among other capabilities.
- Komodo Edit: A free, open-source code editor that supports HTML, CSS, and JavaScript with features like syntax highlighting and code browsing.
- Aptana Studio: An open-source IDE for web development (HTML, CSS, JavaScript, etc.). Aptana provides JavaScript debugging, code completion, and a high-level HTML editor, which can improve productivity.
- JSLint: A code quality tool that checks whether JavaScript source code follows strict coding rules and best practices. It can be used to catch potential problems or deviations from conventions in your scripts.

6.3 JavaScript Output Methods

Before diving into complex examples, it is useful to understand how to produce output in JavaScript. There are several methods to display information or messages:

6.3.1 `alert()` Dialog

The `alert()` function displays a popup dialog with a message and an OK button. This is often used to show quick notifications or warnings. For example, the following page will show an alert as soon as it loads, by calling an `alert()` inside a function that is triggered on the page's load event:

```html
<!doctype html>
<html>
<head>
  <meta charset = "UTF-8">
  <title>alert() example</title>
</head>
<body onload = "displayWelcomeMessage()">
  <script>
    function displayWelcomeMessage() {
      alert("Welcome to Web Development");
    }
  </script>
</body>
</html>
```

In this example, when the page loads, the function `displayWelcomeMessage()` is automatically executed (via the `onload` attribute in the `<body>` tag). The function calls `alert("Welcome to Web Development")`, causing a dialog box to pop up with the welcome message.

6.3.2 `console.log()` Output

The `console.log()` method writes a message to the browser's JavaScript console. This does not show anything to the end user on the web page, but it is extremely useful for debugging and logging. Developers can open the console (in tools like Firefox Developer Tools or Chrome DevTools) to see these messages. The output will appear in the browser's console (press F12 or Cmd+Opt+I to open it, in most browsers). For example:

```html
<!doctype html>
<html>
<head>
  <meta charset = "UTF-8">
  <title>console.log() example</title>
</head>
<body>
  <h2>Displaying a message in the browser's console</h2>
  <script>
    let welcomeMessage = "Welcome to Web Development!";
```

```
11      console.log(welcomeMessage);
12    </script>
13  </body>
14  </html>
```

When this page is opened, it writes the text `"Welcome to Web Development!"` to the console. The `<h2>` in the body is just there to indicate what the script is doing. To see the output, one would open the browser's developer console. Using `console.log()` is a good way to check values or the flow of a program without interrupting the user with a dialog.

6.3.3 `document.write()` Output

The `document.write()` method writes content directly to the HTML document stream at the point where the script is executed. It can be used to print text or HTML into the page. This method is mainly useful for quick tests or simple pages; it is generally avoided in modern complex applications (where DOM manipulation or other methods are preferred) because if used after the page loads, it can overwrite the whole page.

In the example below, we call `document.write()` in two places: once in the head (as the page is loading, before the body content), and once in the body. Each call will output content at that location in the page:

```
1  <!doctype html>
2  <html>
3  <head>
4    <meta charset = "UTF-8">
5    <title>document.write() example</title>
6    <script>
7      document.write
8      ("<h2><font color='magenta'>This content is in the head element of the HTML
         document</font></h2>");
9      document.write("<br><br>");
10   </script>
11  </head>
12  <body>
13   <script>
14     document.write
15     ("<h2><font color = 'green'>This content is in the body element of the HTML
        document</font></h2>");
16     document.write("<br>");
17     document.write("<h1>Welcome to Web Development!</h1>");
18   </script>
19  </body>
20  </html>
```

When this page loads, the first `document.write` (in the head) will produce a magenta heading in the page before the body content appears. The second and third `document.write` calls occur when the body is loading, so their output (a green heading and a large welcome message) appears within the body. Essentially, `document.write()` writes whatever string is given to it into the HTML at the point the script runs. In this example, we inserted line breaks (`<br>`) to space things out. Keep in mind that using `document.write()` after the page has fully loaded (for example, in response to a user action) will overwrite the current page, so it is typically used only during initial page construction.

6.3.4   `prompt()` Dialog

The `prompt()` function displays a modal dialog that asks the user to input some text. It usually shows a message and provides a text field for the user, along with OK/Cancel buttons. The function returns the text that the user entered (or `null` if the user canceled). This method is useful for simple input but is not commonly used in modern interfaces except for quick tests or demos, because the appearance and flow are browser-native (and it can be intrusive).

For example, the following script will prompt the user for their name and then greet them with an alert using the name entered:

```html
<!doctype html>
<html>
<head>
  <meta charset = "UTF-8">
  <title>prompt() example</title>
</head>
<body>
  <script>
    let userName = prompt("Please enter your name:");
    if (userName !== null) {
      alert("Welcome to Web Development, " + userName + "!");
    }
  </script>
</body>
</html>
```

When this code runs, a dialog appears asking `"Please enter your name:"`. If the user enters a name and clicks OK, that value is stored in the variable `userName`. The script then checks if `userName` is not `null` (meaning the user did not cancel), and if so, it displays an alert welcoming the user by name. If the user had clicked Cancel at the prompt, `userName` would be `null` and the alert would be skipped.

Using `prompt()` and `alert()` together in this way allows a simple interaction without needing any HTML form elements on the page. However, for a better user experience, one would typically use proper form fields on the page. Still, these methods are good to know for quick experiments.

6.4 HTML Forms with Data Validation

Concepts: data validation, input patterns, regular expressions, string search, backreferences, testing, and test cases.

Syntax: HTML `<form>` onsubmit event, `alert()`, `isNaN()`, `document.getElementById()` method, `id` attribute, regex notation (anchors ^ $, repetition +, alternation |, character classes, and escapes)

Client-side JavaScript is often used to validate form data before it is submitted to a server. This allows immediate feedback to the user and can reduce unnecessary server requests when simple errors (like a missing field) can be caught in the browser. A prototype syntax for a form that validates its data might be:

```
1 <form action = "submit.php" onsubmit = "return validate()">
2   <input type = "text" id = "FirstName" name = "FirstName" />
3   <input type = "submit" value = "Send" />
4 </form>
```

In the example above, the form's `onsubmit` attribute calls a JavaScript function `validate()` when the user tries to submit the form. This function `validate()` will return `true` or `false` to indicate whether the form data is acceptable. If `validate()` returns `false`, the form submission is blocked (prevented from being sent to the server). If it returns `true`, the form will proceed to submit to the URL specified by its `action`.

The flowchart below illustrates the decision flow during client-side form submission with JavaScript validation. It shows how the `validate()` function intercepts the submission and either allows it to continue or blocks it based on the input data's validity. As Figure 6.2 shows, if the `validate()` check fails (returns `false`), an error alert is shown and the submission is halted; if the validation succeeds (returns `true`), the form data is sent to the server as intended.

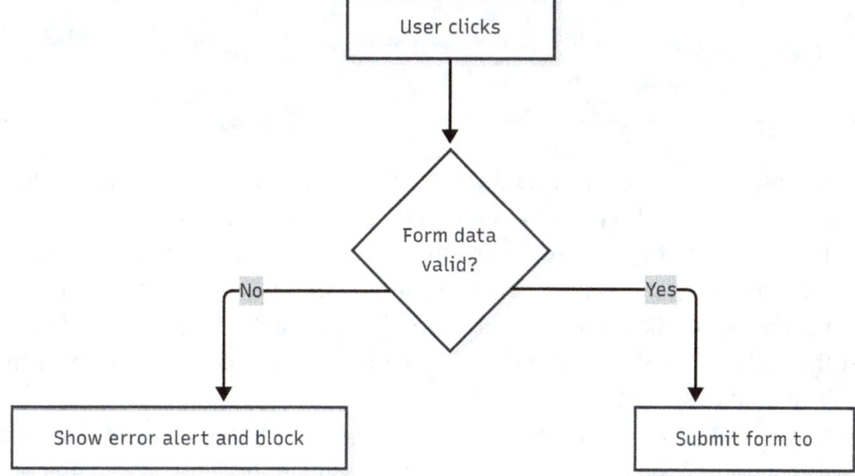

Figure 6.2: A flowchart depicting the client-side form submission process with validation.

When testing such a form, you can use a dummy URL or script (like a placeholder PHP file) for the `action` just to observe whether submission is blocked or allowed. If no `action` or an empty action is provided, it can be hard to tell if the form submission was attempted at all. It is good practice to provide an `action` (even a dummy one) so that when the form is submitted, you see a page navigation or some resulting behavior. That way, you can distinguish a prevented submission (nothing happens, no new page loaded) from a successful one.

To validate form inputs, the JavaScript function needs to access the values the user entered. Any form field can be given an `id` attribute, and using the `document.getElementById()` method we can retrieve a reference to the field and examine its `.value` property. For example, given an `<input type="text" id="FirstName" name="FirstName" />` as above, the following JavaScript expression yields its current text content:

```
document.getElementById("FirstName").value
```

Using this property, we can implement checks. Below is a trivial validation function `validate()` that checks if a field is empty, and alerts the user if so:

```
function validate()
{
  if (document.getElementById("FirstName").value == '')
  {
    alert('Please fill the empty field.');
    return false;
  }
  else
  {
    return true;
  }
}
```

This function works as follows: if the text field with `id="FirstName"` is empty (the value equals an empty string), it shows an alert message and returns `false` to block the form submission. If the field is not empty, it returns `true`, allowing submission to proceed. Notice that each `return` also terminates the function execution at that point. When `validate()` returns false, the form submission is aborted on the client side; if it returns true, the submission continues to the server (in our example, if the action were `"submit.php"`, the browser would then request that URL. If no such file exists, you would get a file not found error, which is one simple way to see that the form tried to submit).

We can extend this idea to perform more checks. Often, you will want to validate multiple fields and multiple conditions. For instance, you might check that a supposed number is actually numeric, or that an email field contains an "@" character. JavaScript provides tools like the `isNaN()` function (which checks if a value is "Not a Number") and regular expressions for pattern matching (more on those below).

Below, we illustrate a slightly more involved validation scenario: ensuring a form field contains a numeric value. Suppose we have a field for "Age" that should only contain digits. We can use `isNaN()` to detect non-numeric input:

```html
<input type = "text" id = "Age" name = "Age" />
```

```javascript
function validateAge() {
  let ageValue = document.getElementById("Age").value;
  if (ageValue == '') {
    alert('Age is required.');
    return false;
  }
  if (isNaN(ageValue)) {
    alert('Please enter a valid number for age.');
    return false;
  }
  // Additional checks (e.g., range) could go here
  return true;
}
```

In this `validateAge()` function, we first check if the field is empty and alert the user if so. Then we use `isNaN(ageValue)` to test if the entered value is not a number. If it is not numeric, we alert the user to enter a number and return false. If both checks pass, we return true (meaning the input is acceptable). We could call `validateAge()` as part of a larger `validate()` function or directly via an `onsubmit` attribute.

Rudimentary Data Validation

There is a vast range of validation tests one might perform on form data. Here are a few simple examples of questions we can ask about an input:

- Is the field non-empty?
- Is the value in a numeric range (e.g., 1—"100)?
- Does the input match a specific format (e.g., a date or email address format)?
- Do two fields (like "password" and "confirm password") match each other?

We saw above a basic approach to check for non-emptiness and numeric content. Each check is typically a simple `if` with a condition, possibly combined with logical operators (`&&`, `||`). For multiple fields, one might group related alerts or use a variable to track a final decision (e.g., set `let valid = true` and flip it to false for any failing test, then return that at the end).

Data Validation using Textual Patterns

JavaScript supports patterns through regular expressions, which are a powerful way to describe textual formats. A regular expression (regex) is essentially a pattern that a string can be tested against to see if it matches (or to find matches within the string). Regular expressions can get very complex, but even basic patterns can be useful for validation.

For example, consider an input for a US zip code. You might want to ensure it is exactly 5 digits. A regex for that could be `/^[0-9]{5}$/`, where `^` denotes the start of the string, and `$` the end (using both means the pattern must cover the entire string), and `[0-9]{5}` means exactly 5 characters, each a digit 0—"9.

If a string `"12345"` is tested against this pattern, it matches (valid zip); `"1234"` would fail (too short), `"123456"` fails (too long), `"1234a"` fails (not all digits).

JavaScript's `RegExp` or pattern literal can be used with string methods. For instance:

```javascript
let zipPattern = /^[0-9]{5}$/;
if (!zipPattern.test(userInput)) {
  alert("Please enter a 5-digit ZIP code.");
}
```

Here, `zipPattern.test(userInput)` returns true if the input matches the 5-digit pattern, false otherwise.

Regular expressions have their own mini-language with specific syntax for matching patterns. The most commonly used metacharacters and their meanings are:

- Character classes: `[A-Za-z]` means any letter, `[0-9]` any digit. You can also use `\d` for digit, `\w` for word character (letter/digit/underscore), `.` for any character.
- Repetition qualifiers: `{5}` means exactly 5 times, `+` means "one or more times", `*` means "zero or more times", `?` means "optional" (zero or one time). You can also specify ranges like `{2,4}` meaning 2 to 4 times.
- Anchors: `^` matches the start of the string, `$` matches the end. Use `^...$` to ensure the pattern covers the entire string.
- Alternation: `|` acts like OR. `(cat|dog)` matches either "cat" or "dog".
- Grouping and Backreferences: Parentheses group parts of patterns and also remember the matched text, which can be referenced as `\1`, `\2`, etc. later in the pattern or used in replacements.

In JavaScript, regex patterns are written between slashes (e.g., `/pattern/`). Functions like `String.match()`, `String.replace()`, or regex methods like `pattern.test(string)` can be used. For example:

```javascript
let pattern = /^[0-9]{3}-[0-9]{2}-[0-9]{4}$/;
let ssn = "123-45-6789";
if (pattern.test(ssn)) {
  console.log("Valid SSN format");
}
```

This regex checks a format of 3 digits, hyphen, 2 digits, hyphen, 4 digits (like a US Social Security Number). The `.test()` method returns true or false.

Regular expressions are powerful but can be complex. They should be used when appropriate and tested thoroughly with various inputs to ensure they match exactly what you intend.

6.4.1   Backreferences in Patterns

So far, we have seen patterns that enforce character rules in a single field. Regular expressions also support backreferences, which are a way to refer to earlier matched groups in the same pattern. This is useful, for example, to ensure that two parts of a string are identical.

Imagine a form that asks the user to enter a new password twice (to confirm it). You could use a regex with a backreference to check that both entries match. For example, the pattern `^([A-Za-z0-9]{6,})\1$` would enforce that the string consists of some sequence (letters or numbers, at least 6 long), immediately followed by the exact same sequence again. If the two inputs (entered consecutively in one string) are the same, this pattern matches. (This is a bit contrived for actual form handling, because usually you would get the two fields separately in JavaScript and compare them directly, but it illustrates backreferences.)

Backreferences are beyond basic usage, but they highlight how regex can not only check format but also relationships between parts of the text. In practice, for form validation, one would typically use simpler regex patterns for individual fields and use JavaScript logic to compare fields (like password confirmation) rather than one giant regex.

6.5   Functions and Events

JavaScript code on a web page typically runs in response to events (like a user action or a page loading). To organize code, we often write reusable functions (named blocks of code that perform specific tasks) and then set them to execute when certain events occur. In this section, we will look at how to define functions and handle events, and then how to use the browser's Document Object Model (DOM) to access and manipulate page elements.

6.5.1   Function Definitions

We usually place JavaScript function definitions inside a `<script>` tag. Often, this script is put in the HTML `<head>` section so that it loads before the body content (ensuring functions are ready to use when the body loads). However, scripts can also be placed at the end of the `<body>` for a more linear load (which can be beneficial for performance). Here is a simple example of defining and calling a function:

```
1  <head>
2    <script>
3      function showMessage() {
4        alert("Hello, world!");
5      }
6    </script>
7  </head>
8  <body>
9    <button onclick = "showMessage()">Click me</button>
10 </body>
```

In this snippet, we define a function `showMessage()` inside a script in the head. In the body, a button is set up so that when it is clicked (via the `onclick` attribute), it calls `showMessage()`. As a result, clicking the button triggers an alert dialog with "Hello, world!".

Any JavaScript code inside `<script>` tags will be executed as soon as that part of the HTML is processed, unless it is inside a function (in which case it only runs when the function is called later). In the above example, defining the function does not produce any immediate output by itself; the code inside runs only when invoked by clicking the button.

JavaScript functions can also take parameters (inputs). For example, `function greet(name) { alert('Hello ' + name); }` defines a function with one parameter. Calling `greet('Alice')` would pop up "Hello Alice." You do not need to specify data types for parameters or for the function's return value in JavaScript.

Parameter Passing: JavaScript uses pass-by-value for function arguments. This means the function gets copies of the values that are passed in. (For objects, this copy is actually a reference to the same object, so object properties can still be modified from inside the function.) Also, the number of arguments used to call a function does not have to match the number of parameters in its definition; extra arguments will be ignored, and missing ones will default to `undefined`.

Events

Defining a function is only part of the story. We typically want to invoke (run) that function when something happens, not immediately when the script loads. The simplest way to do this is to tie the function to a browser event via an HTML attribute (like the `onclick` we used above). Events can be things like mouse clicks, key presses, mouse movements, form submissions, page loads, and more, and they occur asynchronously (independent of the main page flow).

Consider a slightly different example: suppose we want to show a warning message if the user moves their mouse over a particular piece of text (maybe something sensitive). We could do:

```html
<p onmouseover = "alert('Please do not hover over this text')">
   Secret Information
</p>
```

Here we did not even use a named function; we directly put an `alert()` call in the `onmouseover` attribute of the `<p>` tag. When the mouse pointer hovers over that paragraph, the browser fires the mouseover event and triggers the alert. In practice, for anything complex, you would likely call a function instead (so you can reuse code or keep HTML cleaner). For example:

```html
<script>
  function warnUser() {
    alert("Please do not hover over this text");
  }
</script>
<p onmouseover = "warnUser()">Secret Information</p>
```

This does the same thing, but now the logic is defined inside the script as a function `warnUser()` rather than inline in the HTML. Either way, the code runs asynchronously in response to the user's action (in this case, moving the mouse over the paragraph).

Binding Events with JavaScript

The examples above illustrate the traditional approach of embedding event handlers directly in HTML attributes (e.g., `onclick="..."`). This mixes JavaScript with HTML, which can get messy in large projects. As an alternative, you can bind events to elements using JavaScript itself (after the elements exist in the DOM). For instance:

```html
<p id = "secretText">Secret Information</p>
<script>
  document.getElementById("secretText").onmouseover = warnUser;
</script>
```

In this snippet, we assume there is an element with `id="secretText"` (the `<p>` in the HTML). We then assign the `warnUser` function to its `onmouseover` property via a script, which effectively sets up the event handler without using an inline attribute. Many modern libraries (and the newer standard method `addEventListener`) provide cleaner ways to attach events, but the concept is the same.

The key point is that events (like a user hovering, clicking, typing, submitting a form, etc.) happen independently of the initial page load, and JavaScript functions can run in response, allowing interactive behavior on the page.

6.5.2   Event Handling Techniques and Examples

Typically, when an event is triggered (for example, a user clicking a button or pressing a key), a designated JavaScript function known as an event handler runs in response. There are many kinds of events in the browser. Some of the most commonly handled events include:

- load: Fired when a page or image has fully loaded (e.g., the window's `onload` event).
- DOMContentLoaded: Fired when the HTML document has been loaded and the DOM is ready (without waiting for images).
- click: A user clicks on an element (e.g., a button).
- dblclick: A user double-clicks an element.
- mouseover: The mouse pointer moves onto an element (hovers over it).
- mouseout: The mouse pointer leaves an element.
- focus: An element (like a text input or link) gains focus (e.g., user clicks or tabs into a form field).
- blur: An element loses focus (e.g., user clicks or tabs away from a form field).
- change: The value of an input or select element changes (e.g., a selection is made, or an input field is edited and then loses focus).
- submit: A form is submitted.
- keydown: A key on the keyboard is pressed down.

JavaScript can handle these events using three main techniques:

1. Inline HTML event handlers (DOM Level 0): Add event handler code directly in HTML attributes like `onclick="..."` or `onchange="..."`. This was the original way to handle events in early JavaScript; easy to set up, but it mixes JavaScript into HTML markup.

2. Event handler properties in script (DOM Level 0): Assign a handler function to a DOM element's property (e.g., `element.onclick = ...`) using JavaScript. This approach keeps the event logic in script instead of in HTML, but each event property can only have one handler (assigning a new one overwrites the old one).

3. Event listeners (DOM Level 2): Use the `addEventListener()` method to register one or more handlers for an event. This is the prevailing standard. It allows multiple handlers on the same event, and separates JavaScript from HTML. It also provides an event object with details and supports advanced features like event capturing and bubbling.

Each approach can be used to accomplish similar tasks. Below, we illustrate these techniques with examples for various event types, while keeping the general task the same for comparison (such as changing an element's style or showing a message when an event occurs).

Inline HTML Event Handlers

In the inline approach, you embed the JavaScript in the HTML tag via special `on...` attributes. When that event occurs, the specified code runs. This method is straightforward for simple actions but can become messy in large projects because the logic is mixed into the HTML structure.

For example, to run code when a page finishes loading, one could use an `onload` attribute in the `<body>` tag. In practice, this is often done by assigning to the global `window.onload` property in a script (which is equivalent to using `<body onload="...">`). Here is a simple example that prints messages when the page (or DOM) loads:

```
1  <script>
2    window.onload = function() {
3      console.log("The page has fully loaded.");
4    };
5    document.body.onload = function() {
6      console.log("The DOM is loaded.");
7    };
8  </script>
```

In the snippet above, the first handler tied to `window.onload` will run when the entire page (images, CSS, etc.) is loaded, and the second handler (using `document.body.onload`) will run when the HTML body's content is loaded. Both are set inline in the HTML (inside a `<script>` tag). Now, let us look at some user interaction events handled inline.

Inline click handler

Suppose we want to change the style of a heading when a button is clicked. We can use an `onclick` attribute on the button to call a function defined in a script. For instance:

```
<h1 id = "listHeading">My Favorite Foods Around the World</h1>

<button onclick = "changeHeadingStyle()">Change Heading Style</button>

<script>
  function changeHeadingStyle() {
    let heading = document.getElementById("listHeading");
    heading.style.color = "cornflowerblue";
    heading.style.fontFamily = "Times New Roman";
  }
</script>
```

Here, the `<button>` has an `onclick` attribute that calls `changeHeadingStyle()` when clicked. The function (defined in the script) finds the heading by its `id` and changes its text color and font. As a result, clicking the button immediately triggers the inline handler and updates the heading's style.

Inline change handler

We can similarly handle a change event on a dropdown `<select>` menu. The `onchange` attribute can call a function whenever the selection changes:

```
<label for = "myCountyChoice">Select a county:</label>
<select id = "myCountyChoice" onchange = "reportSelection()">
  <option value = "Kerry">County Kerry</option>
  <option value = "Donegal">County Donegal</option>
  <option value = "Dublin">County Dublin</option>
  <option value = "Cork">County Cork</option>
</select>

<script>
  function reportSelection() {
    let selected = document.getElementById("myCountyChoice").value;
    document.write("You selected: " + selected);
  }
</script>
```

In this example, when the user picks a different option in the dropdown, the `onchange` attribute triggers the `reportSelection()` function. That function grabs the selected value and writes out a message like "You selected: County Cork." Using `document.write()` in this way will replace the page content with the message. This is suitable for a simple demo, though in a real app you might update a specific part of the page instead.

Inline focus/blur handlers

Focus events occur when an element (typically a form field or link) gains focus, and blur events occur when it loses focus. Using inline handlers, we can, for example, highlight a text input when it is focused and then change it back when it blurs.

Focus example: When the text box is focused (e.g., clicked into), we will turn its background blue and preset its value:

```html
<input type = "text" id = "country" onfocus = "highlightField()" />

<script>
  function highlightField()
  {
    let field = document.getElementById('country');
    field.style.borderColor = "blueviolet";
    field.style.background = "cornflowerblue";
    field.value = "France";
  }
</script>
```

Blur example: When the same text box loses focus, we restore its style and change the value:

```html
<input type = "text" id = "country" onblur = "resetField()" />

<script>
  function resetField()
  {
    let field = document.getElementById('country');
    field.style.borderColor = "darkred";
    field.style.background = "red";
    field.value = "Lebanon";
  }
</script>
```

In practice, you would put both `onfocus` and `onblur` on the same input element (rather than have two separate inputs as above), but for illustration we show them separately. When the user clicks into the field, onfocus fires and highlightField() runs, turning the field violet/blue and pre-populating "France" as an example value. When the user clicks or tabs out, the onblur event fires and resetField() runs, changing the field to a red outline/background and setting its value to "Lebanon."

Inline mouseover/mouseout handlers

Mouse events can also be handled inline. Let us say we want to change a heading's style when the user hovers over it and revert when they move the mouse away. We can use onmouseover and onmouseout attributes:

```html
<h1 id = "listHeading"
    onmouseover = "makeHeadingFancy()"
    onmouseout = "makeHeadingPlain()">
  My Favorite Foods Around the World
</h1>

<script>
  function makeHeadingFancy()
  {
    let heading = document.getElementById("listHeading");
    heading.style.color = "cornflowerblue";
    heading.style.fontFamily = "Times New Roman";
  }
  function makeHeadingPlain()
  {
    let heading = document.getElementById("listHeading");
    heading.style.color = "blue";
    heading.style.fontFamily = "cursive";
  }
</script>
```

In this snippet, as the mouse pointer enters the <h1> element, the onmouseover triggers makeHeadingFancy(), which changes the heading text to a cornflower blue, serif-styled font. When the pointer leaves the area, onmouseout triggers makeHeadingPlain(), restoring the original blue cursive style. This happens instantly as the user moves the mouse in and out, creating a hover effect.

Inline handlers like the above examples are easy to understand: the HTML element literally "hooks" to a JavaScript function. However, as noted, mixing a lot of JavaScript into your HTML can make the code harder to maintain. Next, we will look at a cleaner way to attach events using JavaScript code.

Event Handler Properties (Dynamic Assignment in Script)

The event property approach still uses the old DOM Level 0 model, but keeps the JavaScript separate from HTML. Instead of putting on... attributes in the HTML, we wait until the element is available in the DOM, then use JavaScript to set the corresponding property (such as `.onclick`) to a handler function. This decouples the markup and logic (you could even do it from an external `.js` file) but one limitation remains: each event property can only have one handler at a time. Setting a second one will overwrite the first.

Using the same scenarios as before, we next discuss how we can attach events via script.

Click event via property

We include an HTML element with an `id`, then in a script, get a reference to that element and assign a function to its `onclick`. For example, to change our heading's style on button click using this method:

```html
<h1 id = "listHeading">My Favorite Foods Around the World</h1>
<button id = "changeBtn">Change Heading Style</button>

<script>
  const btn = document.getElementById("changeBtn");
  btn.onclick = function()
    {
      let heading = document.getElementById("listHeading");
      heading.style.color = "cornflowerblue";
      heading.style.fontFamily = "Times New Roman";
    };
</script>
```

Now, when the button with `id="changeBtn"` is clicked, the function we assigned to `btn.onclick` executes and updates the heading style. This approach moves the `onclick` logic out of the HTML attribute and into the script. If we wanted to reuse a named function, we could define `function changeHeadingStyle() { ... }` and then do `btn.onclick = changeHeadingStyle;`, although here we used an anonymous function directly.

Change event via property

Similarly, we can handle the dropdown selection change with JavaScript:

```html
<form>
  <label for = "myCountyChoice">Select a county:</label>
  <select id = "myCountyChoice">
    <option value = "Kerry">County Kerry</option>
    <option value = "Donegal">County Donegal</option>
    <option value = "Dublin">County Dublin</option>
    <option value = "Cork">County Cork</option>
  </select>
</form>
```

```
10
11 <script>
12   const choiceMenu = document.getElementById("myCountyChoice");
13   choiceMenu.onchange = function()
14   {
15     let selected = document.getElementById("myCountyChoice").value;
16     document.write("You selected: " + selected);
17   };
18 </script>
```

Here we grab the `<select>` element by ID and assign an `onchange` handler function to it. Whenever the user picks a different option, the function runs and writes out the selected county. This has the same effect as the inline example earlier, but the HTML `<select>` tag is now free of any `onchange` attribute; the relationship is set in script.

Focus and blur via property

We can attach multiple different event handlers to the same element (for different events) using this approach. For instance, to achieve the focus/blur behavior on the text field (highlight on focus, reset on blur) via script:

```
1 <input type = "text" id = "countryField" />
2
3 <script>
4   const field = document.getElementById("countryField");
5   field.onfocus = function()
6   {
7     field.style.borderColor = "blueviolet";
8     field.style.background = "cornflowerblue";
9     field.value = "France";
10   };
11   field.onblur = function()
12   {
13     field.style.borderColor = "darkred";
14     field.style.background = "red";
15     field.value = "Lebanon";
16   };
17 </script>
```

In the code above, we first get the text input element, then assign one function to `field.onfocus` and another to `field.onblur`. When the user focuses the field, the `onfocus` handler executes (coloring the field and setting a value), and when the user leaves the field, the `onblur` handler executes (changing the colors and value to something else). This is functionally equivalent to using inline `onfocus`/`onblur` attributes, but the logic is defined in the script. Note that if we were to set `field.onfocus` again later, it would replace the previous handler as only one function can be tied to the `onfocus` property at a time.

Mouseover/mouseout via property

Likewise, to handle the heading hover effect via script properties:

```html
<h1 id="listHeading">My Favorite Foods Around the World</h1>

<script>
  const heading = document.getElementById("listHeading");
  heading.onmouseover = function()
   {
    heading.style.color = "cornflowerblue";
    heading.style.fontFamily = "Times New Roman";
   };
  heading.onmouseout = function()
   {
    heading.style.color = "blue";
    heading.style.fontFamily = "cursive";
   };
</script>
```

We retrieve the heading element and then assign it two handlers: one for its `onmouseover` and one for `onmouseout`. As the user hovers, the first function runs to apply the "fancy" style, and as the mouse leaves, the second function restores the plain style. Again, this keeps our HTML clean (the `<h1>` tag has no inline event attributes), while our JavaScript sets up the desired interactive behavior.

The event property technique makes it easier to manage code (especially when placing scripts at the bottom of the page or in external files), but it still has the limitation of a single handler per event property. Modern JavaScript addresses this with event listeners, which allow multiple handlers and more flexibility.

Event Listeners (Modern Approach with `addEventListener`)

The Event Listener approach is the recommended modern way to handle events. All current browsers support the `addEventListener` method, which lets you register multiple event handlers on the same element and event type if needed. It also provides an Event object to the handler, which contains information about the event (such as the mouse position, key pressed, etc.). Event listeners are sometimes called DOM Level 2 events, and they participate in the DOM's event flow (capturing, target, and bubbling phases), though for most basic uses you do not need to worry about that detail.

The syntax is straightforward:

```
1  element.addEventListener(eventType, handlerFunction);
```

Here, `eventType` is a string like `"click"` or `"mouseover"`, and `handlerFunction` is the function to execute when that event fires on the given element. You can remove a listener later with `removeEventListener` if needed, and you can add multiple listeners of the same type without one canceling the other. (By default, listeners use the bubbling phase; a third boolean argument can specify the capture phase, but we will not delve into capturing here.)

Let us redo our examples using `addEventListener()`:

Page load events

Instead of using `window.onload`, we can listen for the load event on the window, or the DOMContentLoaded event on the document. For example:

```
1  <script>
2    window.addEventListener("load", function()
3      {
4        console.log("The page has been loaded");
5      });
6    document.addEventListener("DOMContentLoaded", function()
7      {
8        console.log("DOM content is ready");
9      });
10 </script>
```

In this snippet, we attach two listeners. The first logs a message when the entire page is loaded (equivalent to the earlier `window.onload`). The second logs a message when the HTML DOM is fully constructed, which is often slightly earlier (it does not wait for images and other external resources). We could also achieve the first by writing a separate named function and passing it, e.g., `window.addEventListener("load", pageLoaded);` `function pageLoaded() { ... }`, but here we used anonymous functions for brevity.

Click event with `addEventListener`

We can attach a click handler to our button in a similar way:

```
1  <h1 id = "listHeading">My Favorite Foods Around the World</h1>
2  <button id = "changeBtn">Change Heading Style</button>
3
4  <script>
```

```
5    function changeHeadingStyle()
6      {
7        let heading = document.getElementById("listHeading");
8        heading.style.color = "cornflowerblue";
9        heading.style.fontFamily = "Times New Roman";
10     }
11   document.getElementById("changeBtn").addEventListener("click", changeHeadingStyle);
12 </script>
```

Here we define the `changeHeadingStyle()` function and then register it as a listener for the `"click"` event on the button. Now, when the button is clicked, the function executes and updates the heading. This accomplishes the same as our earlier examples, but using `addEventListener`. We could register even more `"click"` listeners on the same `#changeBtn` if we wanted, each executing in the order added when the event fires.

Alternatively, we could have skipped defining a named function and passed an anonymous function directly: e.g., `addEventListener("click", function() { ... });`, which is common for simple one-off handlers.

Change event with `addEventListener`

For the dropdown selection:

```
1  <select id = "myCountyChoice">
2    <option value = "Kerry">County Kerry</option>
3    <option value = "Donegal">County Donegal</option>
4    <option value = "Dublin">County Dublin</option>
5    <option value = "Cork">County Cork</option>
6  </select>
7
8  <script>
9    function reportSelection()
10     {
11       let selected = document.getElementById("myCountyChoice").value;
12       document.write("You selected: " + selected);
13     }
14   document.getElementById("myCountyChoice").addEventListener("change", reportSelection);
15 </script>
```

We attach the `reportSelection` function as a listener to the `"change"` event of the select menu. Each time the user picks a new option, the listener fires and outputs the selection. Just as before, this will overwrite the page with the message via `document.write()` for demo purposes.

Focus/Blur with `addEventListener`

We can register listeners for focus and blur on the text field:

```html
<input type = "text" id = "countryField" />

<script>
  const countryField = document.getElementById("countryField");
  countryField.addEventListener("focus", function()
    {
      countryField.style.borderColor = "blueviolet";
      countryField.style.background = "cornflowerblue";
      countryField.value = "France";
    });
  countryField.addEventListener("blur", function()
    {
      countryField.style.borderColor = "darkred";
      countryField.style.background = "red";
      countryField.value = "Lebanon";
    });
</script>
```

This is very similar to the property assignment example, except we use `addEventListener` to attach the handlers. One immediate benefit is that we could, if desired, add more listeners to the same `"focus"` or `"blur"` events without overriding the first one. In this case, when the field gains focus, the first listener executes to style the field and set a value; when it loses focus, the second listener executes to revert the style and change the value. When these events fire, the browser creates an Event object and passes it into our anonymous functions. We have not needed to use it here, but we could access parameters like `event.target` or `event.type` inside those functions if we declared them to take an `e` or `event` parameter.

Mouseover/Mouseout with `addEventListener`

Again, for the heading hover effect:

```html
<h1 id = "listHeading">My Favorite Foods Around the World</h1>

<script>
  const headingEl = document.getElementById("listHeading");
  headingEl.addEventListener("mouseover", function()
    {
      headingEl.style.color = "cornflowerblue";
```

```
8      headingEl.style.fontFamily = "Times New Roman";
9    });
10   headingEl.addEventListener("mouseout", function()
11   {
12     headingEl.style.color = "blue";
13     headingEl.style.fontFamily = "cursive";
14   });
15 </script>
```

As the mouse enters the heading, the `"mouseover"` listener runs (applying the new style), and as it leaves, the `"mouseout"` listener runs (restoring the style). We could attach even more mouse event listeners (like `"mousemove"`, etc.) if needed in the same way.

Keydown event example

Event listeners make it easy to handle keyboard events as well. For instance, suppose we want to give immediate feedback when a user presses a key in a text box:

```
1 <input type = "text" id = "textInput"
2        value = "Press down on the text box"
3        style = "background-color:lightyellow;" />
4
5 <script>
6   document.getElementById("textInput").addEventListener("keydown", function(e)
7     {
8       let box = document.getElementById("textInput");
9       box.style.backgroundColor = "cornflowerblue";
10      box.value = "Key was pressed and keydown event triggered";
11    });
12 </script>
```

In this example, we have an input field with some placeholder text. We attach a `"keydown"` event listener to it. The moment any key is pressed while this field is focused, the listener executes: it changes the background color to cornflower blue and replaces the field's text with a message indicating that the keydown event was triggered. We capture the event object as `e` in the function signature here, though we did not explicitly use it, if we wanted, we could examine `e.key` to see which key was pressed, etc.

Submit event example

Finally, consider a form submission. We can use an event listener on a `<form>` to intercept the submit event:

```
1  <form id = "submitForm">
2    Enter your name: <input type = "text" id = "nameField">
3    <input type = "submit" value = "Submit">
4  </form>
5
6  <script>
7    document.getElementById("submitForm").addEventListener("submit",
8    function(e)
9      {
10       alert("The name entered is: " +
11             document.getElementById("nameField").value);
12       // e.preventDefault(); // uncomment to prevent actual form submission
13      });
14 </script>
```

Here we attach a listener to the form's `"submit"` event. When the user clicks the submit button, the listener function runs and pops up an alert showing the text that was entered. After our handler runs, by default the form will continue submitting (which usually reloads the page). If we wanted to stop the submission (perhaps to validate the input and prevent an undesired reload), we could call `e.preventDefault()` as shown in the comment. The ability to access the event object `e` (passed into our function) and call methods like `preventDefault()` or `stopPropagation()` is another advantage of using `addEventListener`. In this case, using the event object is not strictly necessary just to read the input value, but it gives us control over the event's default behavior (submission) if needed.

In summary, JavaScript's event handling can be achieved in multiple ways. The inline approach puts quick scripts right into your HTML via attributes, which is simple but intermixed with markup. The property assignment approach moves the code into your script, keeping HTML cleaner but still only allowing one handler per event. The event listener approach is the most flexible and clean method, letting you attach multiple handlers and giving you the event object for further control. In practice, you will often use `addEventListener` for modern web development, but understanding the older techniques is useful for reading legacy code and for context on how event handling in JavaScript has evolved.

6.5.3   HTML id, name, and value Attributes

Earlier, we saw how the HTML `id` attribute can be used to retrieve specific elements. Let us look more systematically at the relationship between HTML elements and JavaScript objects. When a web page loads, the browser creates a DOM, which is a tree of objects representing the structure of the page. Every HTML element becomes a DOM node that JavaScript can interact with.

When the browser loads an HTML document, it constructs a hierarchical structure, the DOM. Understanding this DOM structure helps in effectively selecting and manipulating elements using JavaScript. The following simplified diagram visually represents the DOM tree created from a small snippet of HTML containing an

<input> and a <button> element. Figure 6.3 illustrates how HTML elements become structured nodes accessible via JavaScript. Each element and text node is represented clearly in the hierarchy.

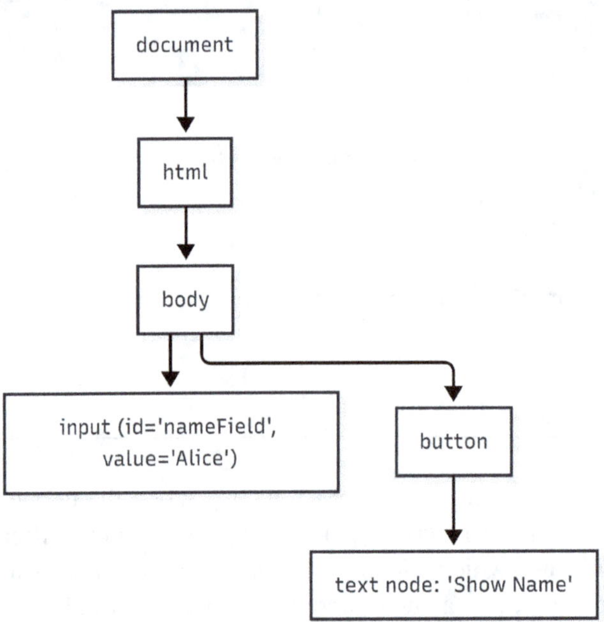

Figure 6.3: A simple DOM tree.

One of the most important connections is that the `id` attribute of an HTML element can be used to get a reference to that element in JavaScript. The `document.getElementById("...")` method quickly returns the one element whose `id` matches the string. For example:

```
1 <input type = "text" id = "nameField" value = "Alice">
2 <button onclick = "alert(document.getElementById('nameField').value)">
3 Show Name
4 </button>
```

Here the button's `onclick` handler uses `document.getElementById('nameField').value` to fetch the current text in the input field and then alerts it. This demonstrates how we can access and use the `.value` property of a form input element via its `id`. The `id` attribute should be unique on a page (no two elements share the same id) so that `getElementById` returns exactly one element. Once you have that element's object, you can read or write its properties (like `.value` for form fields, `.innerHTML` for container elements, `.src` for images, etc.), or even change its style or attach events to it.

In the example above, the <input> field has both an `id` and a `value` attribute. Many form elements also have a `name` attribute. The `name` attribute is not used by `getElementById` (which strictly matches only the `id`), but it can be useful in other contexts (for example, grouping form fields or when submitting form data to the server, the server references form fields by their name). In JavaScript, if you have a reference to an element, you can get its name or id as properties of that element object. Consider this snippet:

```html
<input type = "text" id = "employeeName" name = "employeeName" value = "John">
<script>
  const empInput = document.getElementById('employeeName');
  alert("ID is: " + empInput.id);        // shows "employeeName"
  alert("Name is: " + empInput.name);     // shows "employeeName"
  alert("Value is: " + empInput.value);   // shows "John"
</script>
```

In this example, document.getElementById('employeeName') returns the input element. We then alert its id property (which is "employeeName", the value of the id attribute), its name property ("employeeName", the value of the name attribute), and its value property ("John", the current text in the field). This shows that the DOM element's properties mirror the corresponding HTML attributes. The name attribute by itself does not do anything in our script, but it is used when the form is submitted (or could be used to retrieve the element via methods like document.getElementsByName() if needed).

6.5.4 Document and Window Objects

To summarize the interplay of objects: the document object represents the HTML document loaded in the browser, and allows access to its contents (forms, elements, etc.), while the window object represents the browser window (or tab) itself. The window is the global object in a browser environment, and it includes the document as window.document. Many functions like alert() and prompt() are actually methods of window (you could call window.alert() and it is the same as alert()), and global variables in scripts are, by default, properties of window. Similarly, when we use document, it is actually window.document.

Some useful properties and methods of these objects include:

- document.getElementById("id"): returns the element with a given id (as discussed above).
- document.forms: an array-like collection of all <form> elements on the page (each form can be accessed by index or name).
- document.getElementsByTagName("tag"): returns a collection of all elements with the given tag name.
- document.getElementsByClassName("class"): returns a collection of all elements with the given CSS class.
- window.location: can be used to read or change the current URL (for example, setting window.location will redirect the browser to a new page).
- window.setTimeout(func, milliseconds): calls the given function once after the specified time delay (used to schedule code to run later).
- window.setInterval(func, milliseconds): calls the given function repeatedly at the specified interval.

- `window.onload`: an event property where you can set a function to run when the page has fully loaded (useful for initialization code).

In our examples so far, we have not explicitly led with `window.` because it is implied. For instance, when we call `alert()`, it is implicitly `window.alert()`. Similarly, `document` is actually `window.document`. Understanding this hierarchy is useful when we consider the scope of variables and functions on a page.

6.5.5   Selecting DOM Elements

Beyond `getElementById`, the DOM provides several methods to select elements in the document using different criteria. Often you will want to get a list of elements (not just one) or select by tag name or class. Here are some common selection methods:

- `document.getElementsByTagName("tagName")`: Returns a collection of all elements with the given tag name. For example, `document.getElementsByTagName('li')` would find all `<li>` list items.
- `document.getElementsByClassName("className")`: Returns a collection of all elements that have the given CSS class. For instance, `document.getElementsByClassName('highlight')` would get all elements with `class="highlight"`.
- `document.getElementsByName("name")`: Returns a collection of elements with the given `name` attribute. This is often used for form fields (e.g., `document.getElementsByName('customerEmail')` to get all elements named "customerEmail").
- `document.querySelector("selector")`: Returns the first element that matches a given CSS selector string. This method is more flexible; the parameter is a CSS selector (like `"#content p.highlight"` for "a `<p>` with class highlight inside an element with id content"). If no element matches, it returns `null`.
- `document.querySelectorAll("selector")`: Returns all elements that match the CSS selector, as a static NodeList (which is similar to an array). For example, `document.querySelectorAll('div.note')` would retrieve every `<div class="note">` element on the page.

The older "getElementsBy..." methods return a live HTMLCollection (or NodeList) of elements, while the newer `querySelectorAll` returns a static NodeList. For most purposes, you can treat these collections like arrays (you can check their `length` property and access elements by index), although they are not true JavaScript Array objects.

Both approaches are fine to use; `querySelector`/`querySelectorAll` is very convenient with complex selectors, whereas the dedicated methods like `getElementsByTagName` or `getElementsByClassName` can be slightly faster and were the traditional way.

For example, suppose our HTML contains a list of foods:

```html
<div id = "foodList">
  <ul class="foodOfWorld">
    <li>Kibbeh</li>
    <li>Irish Soda Bread</li>
    <li>Lasagna</li>
    <li>Paella</li>
    <li>Pad Thai</li>
    <li>Tandoori</li>
```

```
9     </ul>
10   </div>
```

We can select various parts of this DOM structure with different methods:

```
1  <script>
2     // Using the classic DOM selection methods:
3     let foodDiv = document.getElementById("foodList");
4     let listItems = document.getElementsByTagName("li");
5     let listsByClass = document.getElementsByClassName("foodOfWorld");
6
7     // Using modern query selector methods:
8     let firstItem = document.querySelector("#foodList li");
9     let allItemsQuery = document.querySelectorAll("#foodList li");
10    let ulQuery = document.querySelector("#foodList ul");
11  </script>
```

In the above script, `foodDiv` will refer to the `<div id="foodList">` element. `listItems` will be a collection of all `<li>` elements on the page (in this case, 6 items). `listsByClass` will be a collection of all elements with class `"foodOfWorld"`, the single `<ul>` in our `foodList` div. Meanwhile, `firstItem` will capture the first `<li>` inside the element with id `"foodList"` (which would be "Kibbeh"), and `allItemsQuery` will be a list of all `<li>` elements inside `#foodList` (essentially the same 6 items as `listItems` in this example). We also grabbed `ulQuery` as the first `<ul>` inside `#foodList` (there was only one).

We can use these references just like we did with `getElementById` before. For example, `alert(ListItems.length)` would show 6 (the number of `<li>` items), and `alert(firstItem.textContent)` would show "Kibbeh". If we wanted to highlight the list dynamically, we could do something like `ulQuery.style.backgroundColor = "yellow"`, which would color the background of the `<ul>` element.

6.5.6   Traversing DOM Nodes

Each element node in the DOM is part of a hierarchy of nodes, and we can navigate this family tree using various properties. Starting from one node, you can move to its parent, its children, or its siblings. Some useful DOM node properties for traversal include:

- `parentNode`: The parent node of the current node (e.g., an element's parent element). For instance, a `<li>` element's `parentNode` might be the `<ul>` it is inside. If a node has no parent (for example, the document's root `<html>`), `parentNode` will be `null`.
- `childNodes`: A collection of a node's child nodes. This includes all types of child nodes (elements, text nodes, comment nodes, etc.). For example, a `<ul>` element's `childNodes` might include text nodes for whitespace in addition to `<li>` children. If a node has no children, `childNodes.length` will be 0.
- `firstChild` / `lastChild`: The first child node and last child node of a given node, respectively. These could be an element or a text node. If there are no children, these properties are `null`.

- previousSibling / nextSibling: The node immediately before or after the current node at the same level of the tree. These might be element nodes or text nodes (for example, whitespace between elements counts as a text node sibling). If there is no previous or next node (e.g., the node is the first or last child), the respective property is null.
- previousElementSibling / nextElementSibling: Similar to the above, but these give only sibling element nodes, skipping over text or comment nodes. These are handy if you want to move to the next HTML element and ignore any text nodes in between.
- children: An HTMLCollection of child elements (only the element nodes, ignoring text/comment children). For example, a <ul> element's children would only contain <li> elements.
- firstElementChild / lastElementChild: The first and last child that are element nodes (ignoring text nodes).
- textContent: A property that returns or sets the text content of a node and all its descendants. For example, a <p> element's textContent gives the full text inside that paragraph (without the HTML tags).
- nodeName: The name of the node. For element nodes, this is the tag name (usually in uppercase, e.g., "DIV" for a <div> element). For text nodes, it will always be #text.
- nodeType: A numeric code representing the type of node (1 for element nodes, 3 for text nodes, etc.). This is less commonly used in everyday scripting, but it exists if you need to distinguish node types.
- nodeValue: The value of the node. For text nodes, nodeValue contains the text itself. For element nodes, nodeValue is null (since the "value" of an element node is usually its children, not a direct text value).

Using these properties, we can navigate the DOM. For example, continuing with the food list above, suppose we have a reference to the <ul> element:

```
<script>
  let ul = document.querySelector("#foodList ul");
  alert(ul.parentNode.id);                          // "foodList" (the parent DIV's id)
  alert(ul.firstElementChild.textContent);          // "Kibbeh" (the first list item text)
  alert(ul.lastElementChild.textContent);           // "Tandoori" (the last list item text)
  alert(ul.firstElementChild.nextElementSibling.textContent); // "Irish Soda Bread"
</script>
```

Here, ul.parentNode is the <div id="foodList"> (whose id we alert). The firstElementChild of the <ul> is the first <li> ("Kibbeh"), and the lastElementChild is the last <li> ("Tandoori"). We then took the first <li> and accessed its nextElementSibling, which gave us the second <li> ("Irish Soda Bread"). If we used firstChild and nextSibling instead, we might get text nodes in between due to whitespace, which is why the ...ElementSibling versions are often more convenient for element traversal.

In addition to the tree navigation, remember that element nodes have their own useful properties as mentioned earlier (for example, .id, .className, .innerHTML, .style, etc., as well as things like .href for anchor <a> tags, .src and .alt for images, and .value for inputs). By combining element selection (from the previous section) with traversal properties, you can walk the DOM and manipulate any part of the page.

6.5.7   Creating and Removing Elements Dynamically

So far, we have been accessing existing elements, but the DOM also lets us create new elements on the fly, as well as remove or replace elements. This enables truly dynamic page updates with JavaScript. To create or remove nodes, you can use methods like:

- `document.createElement(tagName)`: Creates a new element node of the specified type. For example, `document.createElement('p')` makes a new `<p>` element (not yet attached to the page).
- `document.createTextNode(text)`: Creates a new text node containing the given text. (Often, instead of using this explicitly, you can just set `element.textContent`, but it is useful if you need to create text nodes manually.)
- `element.appendChild(node)`: Appends the given node as the last child of the specified element. This will add the node to the DOM (at the end inside that parent element).
- `element.insertBefore(newNode, referenceNode)`: Inserts `newNode` into the DOM as a child of `element`, positioned before `referenceNode` (which should already be a child of `element`).
- `element.removeChild(childNode)`: Removes the specified `childNode` from the DOM (`childNode` must be a child of that element). This returns the removed node, which you could reuse or simply discard.
- `element.replaceChild(newNode, oldNode)`: Replaces an existing child `oldNode` with a `newNode` within an element.
- `node.remove()`: Removes the specified node from the DOM (this is a convenient modern method that removes the node from its parent directly).

Using these, we can build or alter the page content dynamically. Let us say we want to add a new item to a list and then remove another item:

```html
<ul id = "desserts">
  <li>Ice Cream</li>
  <li>Pie</li>
</ul>
<script>
  // Create a new list item and add it to the list
  let list = document.getElementById("desserts");
  let newItem = document.createElement("li");
  newItem.textContent = "Cake";
  list.appendChild(newItem);   // adds <li>Cake</li> as the last child of the ul

  // Remove the first item from the list
  let firstItem = list.firstElementChild;
  list.removeChild(firstItem);
</script>
```

After this script runs, the `<ul id="desserts">` will have "Pie" and "Cake" as its two `<li>` items. We created a new `<li>` element, set its text content to "Cake", and appended it to the list. Then we removed the original first item ("Ice Cream") by calling `removeChild` on the list. (We could also have done `firstItem.remove()` to achieve the same removal more directly.)

You can use similar techniques to create entire new sections of a page, add paragraphs or images dynamically, or remove elements in response to user actions. For example, a script might create a new `<div>` with certain content and insert it into the document to show a popup message, then remove it after a timeout.

6.5.8   Image Rollover Visual Effects

A rollover effect is when moving the mouse on or off an element causes a visual change. We touched on a simple version of this using `onmouseover` and `onmouseout` events in the Secret Information example above. Let us do a more concrete example: changing an image when the mouse hovers over it, and changing it back when the mouse leaves (like a button that lights up when you hover over it).

HTML part

```
1  <img id = "myImage" src = "parrot.jpg" alt = "parrot"
2        onmouseover = "swapImage()" onmouseout = "swapImage()">
```

Here we have an image element. It starts by showing `parrot.jpg` (with alt text "parrot"). We have set both its `onmouseover` and `onmouseout` attributes to call the same function `swapImage()`. This means the function will run when the mouse enters the image area, and also when the mouse leaves.

JavaScript part

```
1  <script>
2    let showingParrot = true;
3    function swapImage()
4    {
5      if (showingParrot)
6      {
7        document.getElementById("myImage").src = "cardinal.jpg";
8        document.getElementById("myImage").alt = "cardinal";
9        showingParrot = false;
10     }
11     else
12     {
13       document.getElementById("myImage").src = "parrot.jpg";
14       document.getElementById("myImage").alt = "parrot";
15       showingParrot = true;
16     }}
17  </script>
```

Initially, the image is a parrot. We use a variable `showingParrot` to remember which image is currently shown. The `swapImage()` function checks this flag: if the parrot is currently showing (`showingParrot` is true), the function swaps the image to a cardinal (by changing the `src` property to `"cardinal.jpg"` and also updating the `alt` text to "cardinal"), and then sets `showingParrot` to false. If `showingParrot` was false (meaning the cardinal is showing), the function swaps the image back to the parrot and sets the flag back to true. We tied this one function to both the `onmouseover` and `onmouseout` events of the image. The net effect is that each time you hover over or off the image, the code toggles the image: when you move the mouse onto the picture it changes to the other image, and when you move it off, the function runs again and changes it back. In other words, the image flips each time you hover or un-hover, creating a simple rollover toggle. The state diagram below visualizes the image rollover toggle from the example above. It shows the two image states and how moving the mouse on or off the image triggers a swap between them. As Figure 6.4 illustrates, the image starts as a parrot; on a `mouseover` event it switches to the cardinal image, and on `mouseout` it reverts to the parrot, toggling back and forth with each hover.

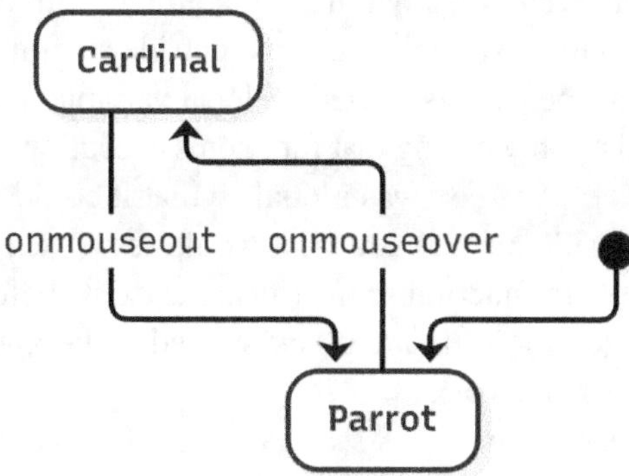

Figure 6.4: A state diagram of the two-image rollover effect.

In practice, if you wanted a classic rollover (where a specific image always appears on hover, and the original always returns on mouseout), you might use two different functions or an if/else that checks the event type. For simplicity, our example uses one function to toggle back and forth. One important detail: we should also swap the `alt` text, not just the image `src`. If we forgot to update the `alt`, the image would change but the alternative text (used by screen readers or shown if the image fails to load) would remain "parrot," which would be misleading when the cardinal is showing. Always keep such pairs (image src and its descriptive alt text) consistent when you script image changes.

Debugging Tip: If a dynamic effect is not working (say the image is not swapping when you expect it to), open your browser's developer console. A common error is a typo in a function name or in `getElementById`, or a missing quotation mark in your code. Modern browser consoles will usually show you an error message and even the line number where things went wrong. For example, forgetting the quotes around `"myImage"` in the `getElementById` call would cause an error that the console can pinpoint. Use the console for catching and fixing mistakes in your scripts.

6.6   Basic Language Concepts

This section reviews some fundamental JavaScript language concepts and features, illustrated through examples introduced above:

- Syntax: JavaScript is case-sensitive (uppercase vs. lowercase letters matter). Statements are generally terminated with a semicolon `;` (the interpreter will often insert them automatically, but it is best practice to include them for clarity). JavaScript largely ignores extra whitespace, so you can format code across multiple lines (typically breaking after operators or commas for readability). You can optionally enable a stricter mode by adding `'use strict';` at the top of a script or function, which enforces certain rules and helps catch common mistakes.

- Identifiers and naming: Names for variables, functions, etc., can only include letters, digits, underscores, and dollar signs, and cannot begin with a digit. They also cannot be any reserved keyword in JavaScript. Identifiers are case-sensitive (`myVar` vs. `myvar` are different). It is good practice to use descriptive names and follow a consistent naming convention (e.g., camelCase or snake_case) rather than single letters or unclear abbreviations, and avoid naming anything that conflicts with built-in global objects or functions.

- Variable scope and lifetime: A global variable (declared outside any function) is accessible to all scripts on the page and persists as long as the page is loaded. A local variable (declared with `var` inside a function, or with `let` inside a block) exists only during that function's execution (or within that block). For example, in the rollover example, `showingParrot` was global so that it could remember state between function calls. If it had been declared inside `swapImage()`, it would reset each time, defeating the purpose. Note that a `var` declaration is hoisted to function scope (its name exists before the declaration line, defaulting to `undefined`), whereas `let` (and `const`) are block-scoped and not accessible before their declaration (using them earlier would cause an error).

- Control structures: We have seen `if` and `if-else` statements for making decisions. The syntax is similar to C/C++/Java: `if (condition) { ... } else { ... }`. The braces `{}` group multiple statements into a single block that the if or else controls. If there is only a single statement, braces are optional, but it is safer to include them to avoid errors when adding statements later. We can also use `else if` to chain multiple conditions in sequence. JavaScript also provides a `switch` statement for multi-way branching based on a single value.

- Boolean conditions: Conditions in JavaScript `if`/`else` are expressions that evaluate to `true` or `false`. Common comparison operators are `==` (equality), `!=` (inequality), `>` (greater), `<` (less), `>=`, `<=`. Note that `==` compares value but not type (so `5 == "5"` is true), whereas `===` (strict equality) checks both value and type (so `5 === "5"` is false, because one is a number and the other is a string). Similarly, `!=` vs. `!==`. In our examples, we often used `==` for simplicity. Also, logical operators `&&` (and), `||` (or), and `!` (not) can combine or invert conditions. For example, you might see `if (x > 0 && x < 10) { ... }` which means "if x is between 1 and 9 (inclusive)".

- Loops: We use a `for` loop to repeat an action many times. A `for` loop in JavaScript has the form: `for (initialize; condition; update) { statements; }`. For instance, `for (var k = 0; k < N; k++) { ... }` will loop N times with k taking values from 0 up to N-1. There are also `while` and `do...while` loops for other looping needs. A `while` loop runs as long as its condition remains true, and a `do...while` loop is similar but guarantees at least one execution of the loop body (since the condition is checked at the end of each loop iteration). Additionally, JavaScript offers `for...in` and `for...of` loops (described below) for convenient iteration over object properties and array values, respectively.

- Operators: In addition to comparison and logical operators mentioned above, JavaScript has arithmetic operators `+`, `-`, `*`, `/`, `%` (modulus for remainder). It also has the auto-increment `++` and auto-decrement `--` operators. In our code, we used `count[k]++` to increment an array element. This is shorthand for `count[k] = count[k] + 1`. Similarly `k++` increments k by 1 (there is a prefix and postfix form, but in a standalone statement `k++` or `++k` have the same effect). It also includes a conditional (ternary) operator `?:` that can return one of two values based on a boolean condition (e.g., `result = (x > 0 ? "positive" : "non-positive")`).
- Strings: We have seen strings in use (e.g., `"Please don't do that!"`). Strings can be concatenated with the `+` operator. For example, in Select a Country above, we did: `document.write("You selected: " + selected);` This concatenated two strings into one. JavaScript will convert numbers to strings if needed when using `+` with a string (but be careful: `+` is also addition if both operands are numbers, so the context matters). You can also use the `+=` operator to append to an existing string (for example, `greeting += "!"` adds an exclamation mark to the end of the string in `greeting`).
- Comments: In JavaScript, `//` begins a single-line comment, and `/* ... */` is used for block comments spanning multiple lines. Comments are ignored by the interpreter and are there for human readers to annotate code.

The above basics were illustrated in various examples (form validation, rollover, etc.). Mastering these fundamentals of variables, control flow, and data types is crucial for writing effective JavaScript.

6.6.1 Control Structures and Operators

Let us take a closer look at the use of control structures in one of our examples, the image swap (rollover) toggling. We had:

```
if (showingParrot)
{
  document.getElementById("myImage").src = "cardinal.jpg";
  document.getElementById("myImage").alt = "cardinal";
  showingParrot = false;
}
else
{
  document.getElementById("myImage").src = "parrot.jpg";
  document.getElementById("myImage").alt = "parrot";
  showingParrot = true;
}
```

This is a straightforward if-else: if the condition (`showingParrot`) is true, execute the first block, otherwise execute the second block. In this case, because we set `showingParrot` inside each branch, it might look cleaner to some to use a different approach, but the logic is clear: one branch or the other will run depending on the state of `showingParrot`.

In fact, we could toggle the value of showingParrot and then use two separate if statements:

```javascript
showingParrot = !showingParrot;
if (showingParrot)
{
  document.getElementById("myImage").src = "parrot.jpg";
  document.getElementById("myImage").alt = "parrot";
}
if (!showingParrot)
{
  document.getElementById("myImage").src = "cardinal.jpg";
  document.getElementById("myImage").alt = "cardinal";
}
```

The logic above will work similarly (because once we flip showingParrot, exactly one of those conditions will be true and run). However, if we did not flip the variable first, using two separate if checks might cause both to run or one to never run, depending on how they are structured. In general, if two conditions are mutually exclusive (either one or the other), an if ... else is clearer and ensures only one branch executes. Our original approach was fine and arguably easier to read.

Another way to write a simple two-branch decision is the conditional operator (also called the ternary operator). This operator uses a condition ? valueIfTrue : valueIfFalse syntax, and produces a value. For example, instead of the if-else above, we could set the image source in one line using:

```javascript
document.getElementById('myImage').src = showingParrot ? 'cardinal.jpg' : 'parrot.jpg';
```

This will assign 'cardinal.jpg' if showingParrot is true, or 'parrot.jpg' if false. Similarly, you might use a ternary to choose a string or a number to assign to a variable based on some condition. The conditional operator is handy for short, simple choices, but for complex logic, regular if-else statements may be clearer.

Earlier, we also briefly touched on the switch statement. A switch is useful when you have to compare the same value against many possibilities. The syntax in JavaScript:

```javascript
switch(x)
{
  case 'Option1':
    // code for x == 'Option1'
    break;
  case 'Option2':
    // code for x == 'Option2'
```

```
8      break;
9    default:
10     // code if x doesn't match any above
11   }
```

Each `case` is checked, and if one matches, the code under it runs until a `break` is encountered, which exits the switch. If no case matches, the `default` section (if provided) runs.

As further illustration, consider the following simple examples of conditional statements and loops in isolation. Simple if example: The code below checks if a number (entered in a variable `monthEntered`) is between 6 and 8, and if so, displays an alert.

```
1 if (monthEntered >= 6 && monthEntered <= 8)
2 {
3   alert("WELCOME to Summer");
4 }
```

This represents a basic `if` statement; if the condition is true, the single statement (or block of statements) inside the braces executes. If the condition is false, nothing happens.

If-else example: In this variant, we handle two outcomes; one if the condition is true, and another if it is false.

```
1 if (monthEntered >= 6 && monthEntered <= 8)
2 {
3   alert("WELCOME to Summer");
4 }
5 else
6 {
7   alert("The month entered is not a Summer month");
8 }
```

Here, if `monthEntered` is between 6 and 8, the first alert runs; otherwise, the message in the `else` runs. This ensures exactly one of the two alerts will pop up.

If-else-if chain example: We can check multiple ranges or conditions by chaining `else if`. For example:

```
1 if (monthEntered >= 6 && monthEntered <= 8)
2 {
3   alert("WELCOME to Summer");
4 }
```

```
5  else if (monthEntered >= 9 && monthEntered <= 11)
6  {
7    alert("WELCOME to Fall");
8  }
9  else if (monthEntered >= 3 && monthEntered <= 5)
10  {
11    alert("WELCOME to Spring");
12  } else
13  {
14    alert("WELCOME to Winter");
15  }
```

This sequence of conditions will display a season-appropriate message depending on the numeric month (assuming 1-12 for Jan-Dec). The first `if` checks for summer months, the next `else if` for fall, then spring, and the final `else` catches all remaining cases (winter, which in this logic would be months 12, 1, 2). Only one branch will execute; the first one whose condition is true.

Switch example: The if-else-if above could also be written with a `switch` if we mapped months to seasons. For instance:

```
1  switch(season)
2  {
3    case "Summer":
4      alert("Summer time!");
5      break;
6    case "Fall":
7      alert("Leaves are falling!");
8      break;
9    default:
10      alert("It's neither summer nor fall.");
11  }
```

In this snippet, depending on the value of `season`, a different alert would run. A more concrete example: imagine `genre` holds the name of a movie genre. We could use a switch to display a related message:

```
1  switch(genre)
2  {
3    case "comedy":
4      console.log("You chose comedy. Get ready to laugh!");
5      break;
6    case "horror":
```

```
 7      console.log("You chose horror. Don't watch it alone!");
 8        break;
 9    case "drama":
10      console.log("You chose drama. Enjoy the story.");
11        break;
12    default:
13      console.log("Genre not recognized.");
14  }
```

If genre is "horror", for example, the console will log the horror message. If none of the cases match, the default runs.

For loop example: A for loop is used to repeat a block of code a known number of times. Consider a scenario where we want to print out a multiplication table for a given factor (say, 5). We can loop from 1 to 12 and multiply:

```
1  let factor = 5;
2  for (let counter = 1; counter <= 12; counter++)
3  {
4    let product = counter * factor;
5    document.write(counter + " multiplied by " + factor + " = " + product + "<br>");
6  }
```

This loop runs 12 times (counter from 1 through 12 inclusive). Each iteration calculates product and writes a line to the document like "3 multiplied by 5 = 15". We use document.write here for simplicity to demonstrate output, but in a real page you might accumulate this in a string or use DOM manipulation to display it.

While loop example: A while loop repeats as long as a condition remains true. The equivalent multiplication table example using while:

```
1  let factor = 5;
2  let counter = 1;
3  while (counter <= 12)
4  {
5    let product = counter * factor;
6    document.write(counter + " multiplied by " + factor + " = " + product + "<br>");
7    counter++;
8  }
```

This will perform the same output as the for-loop example. We manually increment counter at the end of the loop body. If we forget counter++, this would become an infinite loop (because counter would always be 1, always <=12, and never exit).

Do...while loop example: A `do...while` loop is similar to a while loop, but it guarantees the loop body runs at least once because the condition is checked after the first iteration:

```javascript
let factor = 5;
let counter = 1;
do
{
  let product = counter * factor;
  document.write(counter + " multiplied by " + factor + " = " + product + "<br>");
  counter++;
} while (counter <= 12);
```

This will also produce the same multiplication table. The structure is useful if the body of the loop should run at least one time regardless of the condition (for example, prompting a user at least once and then continuing to prompt while the input is invalid).

In summary, JavaScript's control structures (`if`, `if-else`, `switch`, loops) and operators (arithmetic, comparison, logical) behave in ways familiar to those who have used C-style languages, with a few quirks (like the `==` vs. `===` distinction and truthy/falsy values in conditions, where e.g., an empty string `""` or the number 0 is treated as false in an `if`). As you write more scripts, you will become comfortable with these constructs and when to use each.

6.6.2   Arrays

JavaScript arrays are list-like data structures used to store multiple values. Table 6.1 lists some useful methods and properties associated with arrays (including the `delete` operator for removing elements):

Table 6.1: Common JavaScript array methods and properties.

Method / Property / Operator	Description
`concat()`	Merges two (or more) arrays into a new array.
`delete`	Removes an element from an array (sets its value to `undefined` but does not change the array's length).
`find(fn)`	Returns the value of the first element in the array that satisfies the testing function `fn`, or `undefined` if none is found.
`findIndex(fn)`	Returns the index of the first element that satisfies the testing function, or `-1` if none satisfies it.
`indexOf(value[, start])`	Returns the index of the first occurrence of `value` in the array, searching from index `start` (default 0). Returns `-1` if not found.
`includes(value[, start])`	Returns `true` if the array contains `value` (searching from index `start`, default 0), otherwise `false`. (Also works on strings.)
`Array.isArray(obj)`	Returns `true` if `obj` is an array, otherwise `false`.
`lastIndexOf(value[, start])`	Returns the index of the last occurrence of `value` in the array, searching backwards from index `start` (default: end of array). Returns `-1` if not found.
`length`	Returns the number of elements in the array. (This is a property, not a function.)
`pop()`	Removes the last element of the array and returns that element. (The array's length decreases by 1.)
`push(element1, ..., elementN)`	Adds one or more elements to the end of the array and returns the new length of the array.
`sort()`	Sorts the elements of the array in place in ascending order. (By default, elements are compared as strings lexicographically.)

An array is written as a sequence of elements in square brackets. Arrays are zero-indexed (the first element is index 0). They are dynamic and can grow or shrink, and they can contain elements of any type (even mixing types in one array, though typically elements are related). For example:

```javascript
let pets = ["dog", "cat", "fish", "bird"];
console.log(pets[0]);       // "dog" (the first element)
console.log(pets.length);   // 4 (number of elements)
```

In the above, `pets[0]` accesses the first element, and `pets.length` gives the array's length. You can modify arrays by index (e.g., `pets[1] = "hamster";`) or use built-in methods. For instance, `pets.push("lizard")` would add a new element to the end (making the length 5), and `pets.pop()` would remove the last element.

Arrays can also be heterogeneous (contain different types) and even contain other arrays. For example, you could have `let randomStuff = ["Alice", 3.14, null, true]` mixing strings, numbers, etc. If an array element is another array, you effectively have a multi-dimensional array structure. For instance:

```
const matrix = [
  [1, 2, 3],
  [4, 5, 6]
];
console.log(matrix[1][2]); // 6
```

Here `matrix` is a 2×3 array (two sub-arrays). We access the element in the second row and third column with `matrix[1][2]` (indexes 1 and 2 because they start at 0). To iterate over arrays, you can use a standard `for` loop with an index or other constructs like `for...of` (covered next) to loop through values directly.

6.6.3 Objects and Constructors

JavaScript objects are collections of properties, which can be either data values or functions (methods). The most common way to create an object is using object literal notation, defining the object with its key-value pairs in braces. For example:

```
const movie =
{
  title: "Harry Potter",
  leadMaleCharacter: "Harry",
  leadFemaleCharacter: "Hermione"
};
```

This creates an object `movie` with three data properties. You can access properties with dot notation (e.g., `movie.title`) or with bracket notation using a string key (e.g., `movie["title"]`).

Another way to create an object is to first create an empty object and then add properties to it one by one:

```
const film = {};
film.title = "Harry Potter";
film.leadMaleCharacter = "Harry";
film.leadFemaleCharacter = "Hermione";
```

Often, when many objects of the same kind are needed, it is convenient to use a constructor function (or in modern ES6+, a class) to serve as a template for new objects. For example:

```javascript
function Movie(title, leadMale, leadFemale)
{
  this.title = title;
  this.leadMaleCharacter = leadMale;
  this.leadFemaleCharacter = leadFemale;
  // You can also define methods inside:
  this.getInfo = function()
  {
    return "Movie: " + this.title +
           ", Lead Male: " + this.leadMaleCharacter +
           ", Lead Female: " + this.leadFemaleCharacter;
  };
}
```

Calling `new Movie("Harry Potter", "Harry", "Hermione")` will create a new object with the given values. Using the `new` keyword with a constructor function involves several steps behind the scenes, as illustrated in Table 6.2:

Table 6.2: Steps when calling a constructor function with the `new` operator.

Step	What happens when `new Movie("Harry Potter", "Harry", "Hermione")` is called
1	A new empty object is created.
2	The constructor function `Movie` is invoked with `this` set to that new object.
3	The function body executes, adding properties (and methods) to `this`. This populates the new object with the provided data.
4	The new object is returned as the result of the `new` expression (and, in this example, gets assigned to the variable `movie1`).

In practice, object literal syntax is usually preferred for simplicity and performance when you need to create just one object. Constructor functions (or ES6 classes) are useful when you need to create multiple similar objects with the same structure.

Mastering these fundamentals of variables, control structures, data types (like strings and arrays), and objects is crucial for writing effective JavaScript.

6.6.4 Additional Loop Constructs: for...in and for...of

JavaScript provides two additional loop constructs that are handy in certain situations:

- `for...in`: loops over the property names of an object.
- `for...of`: loops over the values of an iterable (like an array or string).

For example, consider an object describing a pet:

```javascript
const pet =
{
  type: "dog",
  name: "Dante",
  owner: "Doug"
};
for (const key in pet)
{
  console.log(key + ": " + pet[key]);
}
// Output:
// type: dog
// name: Dante
// owner: Doug
```

The `for...in` loop above iterates over each property in the `pet` object (in no guaranteed order). Inside the loop, we used each `key` to access the corresponding value with `pet[key]`.

Likewise, you can use `for...of` to loop over array elements directly. Using the `pets` array from earlier:

```javascript
for (const animal of pets)
{
  console.log(animal);
}
// Output:
// dog
// cat
// fish
// bird
```

Here, each `animal` variable takes on the value of each element in the array in turn, and the loop logs each one. This is often more convenient and readable than using an index to access `pets[i]`. Technically, you could use `for...in` on an array as well, but that would iterate over the index keys (as strings) and is generally not recommended for arrays.

6.6.5   Switch Control Structure

We already covered the general idea of the `switch` statement. For completeness, let us connect it to the image map scenario: we could implement `Notify(p)` with a switch instead of the array:

```
1  function Notify(p)
2  {
3    let msg;
4    switch(p)
5     {
6       case 1: msg = "SUN"; break;
7       case 2: msg = "EARTH"; break;
8       default: msg = "Unknown";
9     }
10   document.getElementById("info").innerHTML = "<h2>" + msg + ": CLICK TO ENLARGE</h2>";
11  }
```

This does the same thing (with `default` catching any unexpected id). As you can see, as the number of cases grows, this can become unwieldy, which is why we opted for the array approach earlier. Still, switch is very useful in other situations, especially when you have distinct code to run for each case (not just setting a variable as in this simple mapping).

6.6.6   innerHTML Property

As we utilized above, `element.innerHTML` is one of the most useful properties for dynamic HTML manipulation. It allows you to get or set the HTML content of any element. For instance, you can empty an element by setting `innerHTML = ""` (empty string), or build up a chunk of HTML as a string (perhaps concatenating in a loop) and assign it to create a bunch of new content at once.

However, you should be cautious: setting `innerHTML` replaces the old content entirely. If you just want to append, you might do something like `element.innerHTML += "<p>more</p>";` (which reads the old HTML, adds your new string, and writes it back). For complex updates or performance-critical situations, manipulating the DOM via methods (like `createElement`, `appendChild`, etc.) is another approach. But `innerHTML` is often sufficient and simpler.

One should also avoid mixing `innerHTML` updates with maintaining references to DOM elements that were inside, as they might get recreated. In our simple usage, these concerns are minimal.

6.6.7   Interactive Mapped Images Example

Now, let us consider a more robust example using an interactive image map to apply some of the concepts we have just learned. Image maps are images with multiple clickable regions defined by `<area>` elements inside a `<map>`. We use JavaScript to provide dynamic feedback when the user hovers over specific regions of an image.

Imagine we have an image of the solar system with the Sun and Earth marked as regions[1]. The basic HTML might look like:

```html
<img src = "PIA06890_modest.jpg" alt = "Solar System" usemap = "#SolarSystemMap" />

<map name = "SolarSystemMap">
  <area shape = "rect" coords = "0,0,100,330" href = "sun_large.jpg" alt = "Sun" />
  <area shape = "circle" coords = "218,180,10" href = "earth_large.jpg" alt = "Earth" />
</map>
```

This sets up two regions: one rectangular area covering the Sun in the image (coordinates and size predetermined), linking to a larger image or page for the Sun; and one circular area around Earth, linking to an Earth image/page. Without JavaScript, if the user clicks these areas, they would go to the linked resource (e.g., a large image). But the user might not even realize the image is interactive. We want to provide a rollover tooltip/label effect: when the user hovers over a region, display a message like `"SUN: CLICK TO ENLARGE"` in a visible part of the page. When they move away or click, remove the message.

To implement this, we can use JavaScript event handlers on the `<area>` elements, and a dedicated `<div>` on the page to display the message. We will do the following:

- Give each `<area>` an `id` and add `onmouseover` and `onclick` handlers.

---

[1]NASA Photojournal Home Page Graphic. Wikimedia Commons. Jan 26, 2008. Accessed Jan 16, 2026. Creative Commons Attribution-Share Alike 4.0 International license.

- Use a `<div id="info">` as a container to show messages.
- Create two functions: `Notify(p)` to display the appropriate message for area with id `p` when hovered, and `Clear()` to clear the message (e.g., on mouseout or click).

First, modify the map HTML:

```html
<div id = "info"><h4>This image is segmented.</h4></div>

<map name = "SolarSystemMap">
  <area id = "1" shape = "rect" coords = "0,0,100,330"
        href = "sun_large.jpg" alt = "Sun"
        onmouseover = "Notify(1)" onclick = "Clear()" />
  <area id = "2" shape = "circle" coords = "218,180,10"
        href = "earth_large.jpg" alt = "Earth"
        onmouseover = "Notify(2)" onclick = "Clear()" />
</map>
```

We added `id="1"` and `id="2"` to the area tags (using numeric ids here for brevity; though note, IDs should ideally start with a letter. In a quick example it works in many browsers, but technically it is not valid in XHTML to start with a digit; HTML5 is more forgiving but it is best to use something like `id="area1"`). We also added `onmouseover="Notify(1)"` for the Sun area and `Notify(2)` for the Earth area. The `onclick` for each calls `Clear()`. We placed a `<div id="info">...</div>` above the map (it contains a default message `"This image is segmented."` initially).

Now the JavaScript part. We want `Notify(p)` to look up a message corresponding to area `p` and display it inside the `info` div. We could hardcode it with an if or switch: if `p == 1`, message = `"SUN"`; if `p == 2`, message = `"EARTH"`. But an easier way is to use an array of messages where the index corresponds to the id. For instance:

```javascript
var message = ["", "SUN", "EARTH"];
```

This creates an array where `message[1]` is `"SUN"` and `message[2]` is `"EARTH"`. (We leave `message[0]` as an empty string just to make the indexing align with our ids. Since we have no area 0, we will not use index 0.)

Now, `Notify(p)` can use this array:

```javascript
function Notify(p) {
  document.getElementById("info").innerHTML = "<h2>" + message[p] +
     ": CLICK TO ENLARGE</h2>";
}
```

This function takes the parameter `p` (which will be 1 or 2 as passed from onmouseover). It finds the `<div id="info">` element and sets its `innerHTML` content to an `<h2>` heading containing the message string and a prompt like `": CLICK TO ENLARGE"`. For example, if `p == 1`, `message[p]` is `"SUN"`, so it sets innerHTML to `<h2>SUN: CLICK TO ENLARGE</h2>`. That will replace whatever was previously inside the `info` div with this new content. The user will see the message appear (the text will replace the initial `"This image is segmented."` note, in a larger font since we wrapped it in `<h2>` for prominence).

The `Clear()` function just needs to restore the original note or clear the field. We could restore the original `<h4>This image is segmented.</h4>` or simply blank it out. Let us restore the original note:

```
1  function Clear() {
2    document.getElementById("info").innerHTML = "<h4>This image is segmented.</h4>";
3  }
```

Now, what will happen? When the page loads, the info div says `"This image is segmented."` When the user moves the mouse over the Sun area, `Notify(1)` runs and changes the div to say `"SUN: CLICK TO ENLARGE"`. When they move off or click (in our code we put `onclick="Clear()"` so the message will stay on screen when they move off, unless they click. We might also want to clear on `onmouseout` for completeness, but here we tied clear to click assuming once they click to go to the larger image, we remove the message. One could add `onmouseout="Clear()"` as well to each area if desired, to clear on hover-out without clicking).

If the user clicks on the area, two things happen: the link's default action navigates to `sun_large.jpg` (showing presumably a larger sun image or page) and the `onclick="Clear()"` triggers our JavaScript to clear the message. In practice, once they click and navigate away, clearing the message on the original page is not that important (since they will be looking at a new page). However, if the link opened in a new tab (sometimes image maps might target a new window), then the original page would remain and it is nice to clear the message after the click. It depends on how you implement the UX. For our demonstration, it is fine either way.

Using an array for messages made it easy to map area ID to a message. This approach scales: if we had many areas, we just fill the array with corresponding messages, and `Notify(p)` does not need to change. This is better than writing a long if/switch for each one. It also means adding a new area is as simple as giving it the next ID and adding an entry in the array.

We should mention that `innerHTML` is a very handy property: it represents the HTML content inside an element as a string. By setting it, we replaced the entire contents of the `div#info`. We included HTML tags (`<h2>` etc) in the string, which the browser parses and displays. This is an easy way to inject bits of HTML dynamically. The string could even include other elements, styles, etc. One just has to be careful not to break existing HTML structure (for example, do not put `<td>` tags via innerHTML in a context where there is no table, etc.). In our case, it is straightforward.

6.6.8   Random Numbers

Finally, recall our exploration of random numbers with `Math.random()`. We posed the question: "How uniformly random is `Math.random()`?" and outlined an approach to test it by generating many random samples and tallying them into intervals.

To summarize the outcome:

- `Math.random()` produces a pseudo-random number in the range [0, 1). That is, it can be 0 (inclusive) up to but not including 1. Each call gives a new double-precision floating-point number.
- If truly uniform, in the long run the distribution of values should be roughly even across the interval 0 to 1.
- We broke [0,1) into, say, 4 subintervals (quartiles: [0,0.25), [0.25,0.5), [0.5,0.75), [0.75,1)). We then generated N random numbers and counted how many fell into each quarter.
- Our code used an array `count[0..3]` to count hits in each interval, a loop `for(k=0; k<N; k++)` to generate numbers, and if/else statements to increment the appropriate counter (`count[0]++` if <0.25, etc.).
- After that, we converted counts to frequencies by dividing by N, and displayed the results in a `<div>` via `innerHTML`, perhaps with each frequency on a new line or as a list.

If we ran this experiment with a large N (say 10,000 or 100,000), we would likely observe the frequencies to be roughly 0.25 each (maybe not exact, but hovering around 25%). If one interval consistently got significantly more or fewer hits, then `Math.random()` might be suspect, but in practice it is usually quite uniform for general use.

6.7   JavaScript Prototypes

JavaScript is a prototype-based object system. This means it does not use traditional classes as in Java or C++; instead, it uses prototypes to enable objects to inherit properties and methods from other objects. In practice, every JavaScript function can act as a constructor, and has a special property called `prototype` (initially an empty object). When you create an object using the `new` keyword with a constructor function, the newly created object's internal `__proto__` links to the constructor's `prototype` object. All instances created from that constructor will share the properties and methods defined in its prototype. This allows JavaScript to mimic classical inheritance: objects can have shared behavior (via the prototype) while also maintaining their own state (via instance properties).

For example, consider a constructor function `PetInfo` that initializes some properties for a pet. We can add a method and a property to `PetInfo.prototype` so that all `PetInfo` objects share them. In the code below, we define `PetInfo`, then use its prototype to add a method `calculateBirthDate()` (to compute a pet's age) and a property `breed`. We then create two `PetInfo` instances to see how they inherit these prototype members:

```javascript
// Constructor function for PetInfo objects
function PetInfo(owner, petType, petName, petBirthYear)
{
  this.owner = owner;
  this.pettype = petType;
  this.petname = petName;
  this.petbirthdate = petBirthYear;
}

// Add a method to the PetInfo prototype to calculate the pet's age
PetInfo.prototype.calculateBirthDate = function()
```

```javascript
12  {
13    const todaysdate = new Date();
14    let currentYear = todaysdate.getFullYear();
15    console.log("The age of the pet is: " + (currentYear - this.petbirthdate));
16  };
17
18  // Add a prototype property (shared by all PetInfo instances)
19  PetInfo.prototype.breed = "Maltese";
20
21  // Create a PetInfo object (instance)
22  let petinfo1 = new PetInfo("Maria", "dog", "Murphy", 2020);
23  console.log(
24    "The Name of the Owner is " + petinfo1.owner +
25    ". The pet type is " + petinfo1.pettype +
26    " and the pet's name is " + petinfo1.petname +
27    " and the breed is " + petinfo1.breed + "."
28  );
29  petinfo1.calculateBirthDate();   // uses the prototype method, logs the age
30
31  // Modify the prototype's breed property
32  PetInfo.prototype.breed = "Jack Russell Terrier";
33
34  // Create a second PetInfo object after changing the prototype
35  let petinfo2 = new PetInfo("John", "dog", "Jackie", 2016);
36  console.log(
37    "The Name of the Owner is " + petinfo2.owner +
38    ". The pet type is " + petinfo2.pettype +
39    " and the pet's name is " + petinfo2.petname +
40    " and the breed is " + petinfo2.breed + "."
41  );
42  petinfo2.calculateBirthDate();   // logs the age for this pet
```

Let us break down how this works step by step:

1. Constructor Function: We define a function `PetInfo(owner, petType, petName, petBirthYear)` that sets up properties on the newly created object (`this.owner`, `this.pettype`, etc.). This function will serve as a constructor for pet info objects. By convention, constructor functions in JavaScript start with a capital letter.

2. Prototype Method: We add a function `calculateBirthDate` to `PetInfo.prototype`. This method calculates the pet's age by subtracting the birth year from the current year and prints the result to the console. Because it is on the prototype, we do not have to add this function to each object manually. Any object created by `new PetInfo()` will automatically inherit this method. For example, when we later call `petinfo1.calculateBirthDate()`, JavaScript finds `calculateBirthDate` on `PetInfo.prototype`

(since `petinfo1` itself does not have that property) and executes it with `this` referring to `petinfo1`.

3. Prototype Property: We also add a property `breed` to `PetInfo.prototype` and set its value to `"Maltese"`. This means all `PetInfo` instances will have a default `breed` property coming from the prototype. If an instance does not have its own `breed` property, accessing `instance.breed` will retrieve the value from the prototype. Initially, we set it to "Maltese".

4. Creating an Instance (petinfo1): We call `new PetInfo("Maria", "dog", "Murphy", 2020)` to create a new pet info object, `petinfo1`. The constructor function runs, assigning `owner="Maria"`, `pettype="dog"`, `petname="Murphy"`, and `petbirthdate=2020` on `petinfo1`. At this point, `petinfo1`'s own properties are set as above, but it does not have a `breed` property of its own. However, because `petinfo1` was created with `PetInfo`, its internal prototype is `PetInfo.prototype`, which does have a `breed`. Thus, `petinfo1.breed` will resolve to `"Maltese"` via the prototype chain.

5. Using the Prototype Members: We then log some info to the console using `console.log`. The first `console.log` for `petinfo1` outputs the owner, pet type, pet name, and breed. As explained, `petinfo1.breed` is found on the prototype, so it prints "Maltese". The next line calls `petinfo1.calculateBirthDate()`. Since `calculateBirthDate` was defined on the prototype, this call invokes that shared function. Inside the function, `this.petbirthdate` refers to `petinfo1.petbirthdate` (which is 2020), and `currentYear` is the current year (for example, 2025 if run this year). It then logs the pet's age. Expected output for `petinfo1`:

   - `"The Name of the Owner is Maria. The pet type is dog and the pet's name is Murphy and the breed is Maltese."`
   - `"The age of the pet is: 5"` (assuming currentYear is 2025, since 2025 - 2020 = 5)

   The first line comes from our explicit `console.log` and shows that `petinfo1` has inherited the breed "Maltese". The second line is from `calculateBirthDate()` and shows the calculated age.

6. Altering the Prototype: After creating `petinfo1`, we execute `PetInfo.prototype.breed = "Jack Russell Terrier";`. This changes the breed property on the prototype object for `PetInfo`. Now, any `PetInfo` instance that does not have its own `breed` field will reflect this new value. It is important to note that prototypes are live objects. Modifying a prototype affects all existing and future objects that rely on that prototype. In this case, even though we created `petinfo1` earlier, it does not have its own `breed` (it is using the prototype's value). Now that the prototype's `breed` is "Jack Russell Terrier", if we were to check `petinfo1.breed` again at this point, it would now yield `"Jack Russell Terrier"` instead of the old value. (No explicit log for this was shown, but this is how prototype inheritance works.)

7. Creating another Instance (petinfo2): Next, we create a second object `petinfo2` with `new PetInfo("John", "dog", "Jackie", 2016)`. The constructor runs again, setting `owner="John"`, `pettype="dog"`, `petname="Jackie"`, `petbirthdate=2016` on the new object. Like the first object, `petinfo2` does not have its own `breed` property, so it will also rely on `PetInfo.prototype.breed`. At this time, the prototype's breed has been changed to "Jack Russell Terrier", so `petinfo2.breed` will naturally be `"Jack Russell Terrier"`.

8. Using the Prototype Members on petinfo2: We then log the details of `petinfo2`. The `console.log` for `petinfo2` prints the owner, pet type, pet name, and breed. Because of the prototype change, this time the breed comes out as "Jack Russell Terrier". Calling `petinfo2.calculateBirthDate()` runs the same prototype method, but with `this` referring to `petinfo2`. It calculates `currentYear - 2016` and logs the age. Expected output for `petinfo2`:

- `"The Name of the Owner is John. The pet type is dog and the pet's name is Jackie and the breed is Jack Russell Terrier."`
- `"The age of the pet is: 9"` (if currentYear is 2025, since 2025 - 2016 = 9)

These lines confirm that `petinfo2` picked up the new prototype `breed` value and that the shared `calculateBirthDate` method correctly computes the age for the second pet.

The diagram below illustrates the prototype linkage in our `PetInfo` example. It shows the constructor function `PetInfo`, its prototype object, and the two instances (`petinfo1` and `petinfo2`) pointing to the shared prototype. This visual can help you see how both instances inherit the `calculateBirthDate` method and `breed` property from `PetInfo.prototype`. As Figure 6.5 illustrates, `PetInfo.prototype` (center) holds properties and methods shared by all `PetInfo` instances. Both `petinfo1` and `petinfo2` objects link to this prototype, allowing them to use the `calculateBirthDate()` function and `breed` value defined on it. The `PetInfo` constructor function has a `prototype` property that points to the same object. This diagram highlights how JavaScript objects created by a constructor share one prototype object (enabling inheritance of behavior).

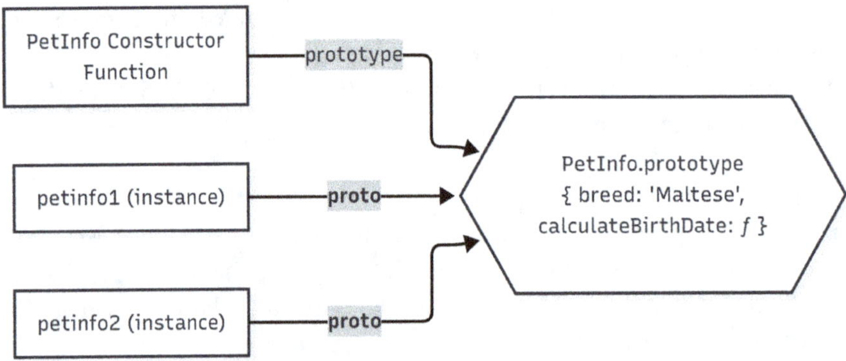

Figure 6.5: Prototype-based inheritance in JavaScript.

In summary, this example demonstrates JavaScript's prototype-based inheritance. We defined properties and a function on `PetInfo.prototype` and saw that all instances of `PetInfo` could use them. By using prototypes, you avoid duplicating methods for each object. The method is defined once on the prototype and referenced by every instance. Prototype inheritance also means that if we update a prototype property (like changing `PetInfo.prototype.breed`), that change is reflected in all existing objects that have not overridden that property. Conversely, if an instance defines its own property with the same name as something on the prototype, the instance's own property will mask (override) the prototype's value for that particular object. Overall, understanding prototypes is key to understanding how JavaScript implements inheritance and shared behavior among objects.

6.8   Regular Expressions

This topic was covered earlier in the context of form validation, where we introduced regular expressions as patterns for matching text. Below is a brief recap.

Regular expressions (regex) are sequences of characters that form a search pattern, often used for string matching and substitution. In JavaScript, regex is used for tasks like validating input formats (email addresses, phone numbers), searching within text, and find-and-replace operations.

We saw examples of regex in Data Validation using Textual Patterns. For instance, `/^[A-Za-z]+$/` is a regex that matches a string consisting entirely of one or more letters (no digits or symbols, and not empty). Let us recap some key regex elements (also mentioned earlier):

- Character classes: `[A-Za-z]` means any letter (uppercase or lowercase). `[0-9]` means any digit. You can combine ranges, e.g., `[A-Za-z0-9]` for alphanumeric. There are also predefined classes like `\d` (digit), `\w` (word character for letter/digit/underscore), and `\s` (whitespace).
- Repetition: `+` means "one or more", `*` means "zero or more", `?` means "zero or one" (optional). Curly braces can specify exact counts or ranges: `{3}` means exactly 3, `{3,6}` means between 3 and 6, and `{3,}` means 3 or more.
- Anchors: `^` matches the start of the string, `$` matches the end. For example, `^Hello$` would match exactly the string "Hello" and nothing else.
- Alternation: The `|` symbol works like OR inside a regex. For example, `^(yes|no)$` matches either "yes" or "no" exactly.
- Grouping: Parentheses `(...)` group parts of the pattern and also capture the text matched by that part. These captured groups can be referenced later in the pattern (with backreferences like `\1`) or used in a replacement string.

Table 6.3 shows common regex metacharacters and their meanings.

Table 6.3: Common regular expression metacharacters and their meanings.

Metacharacter	Meaning
.	Matches **any character** (except newline by default).
[ ]	Matches any **one character** from the set or range of characters inside the brackets.
\	Escape character – treats the next character literally. (For example, `\.` matches a literal dot instead of "any character".)
( )	**Groups** part of the pattern into a single unit (for applying quantifiers or alternation). Captures the matched substring for potential backreference (\1, \2, etc.).
^	**Anchor for start** of the string. (Inside a character class `[...]`, a leading `^` negates the set instead.)
$	**Anchor for end** of the string (matches the end of line/string).
|	**Alternation** – acts like a logical OR between subpatterns. (Example: `cat|dog` matches either "cat" or "dog".)
*	**Quantifier:** matches the preceding element **zero or more** times.
?	**Quantifier:** matches the preceding element **zero or one** time (makes it optional).
{ }	**Quantifier:** matches the preceding element a specified number of times. (For example, `{n}` = exactly n times; `{n,m}` = n to m times; `{n,}` = at least n times.)
+	**Quantifier:** matches the preceding element **one or more** times.

In JavaScript, regex patterns are commonly written as literals like `/pattern/flags`. For example,

`/^\d{5}$/` is a regex for a 5-digit string. We often use methods like `pattern.test(string)` (which returns a boolean) or `string.match(pattern)` (which returns the matched substring or an array of matches). For example:

```javascript
let pattern = /^[0-9]{3}-[0-9]{2}-[0-9]{4}$/;
let ssn = "123-45-6789";
if (pattern.test(ssn))
{
  console.log("Valid SSN format");
}
```

This uses `.test()` to check if the string `ssn` matches the pattern for a Social Security Number format. The `RegExp` object also provides other useful methods for pattern matching, as shown in Table 6.4.

Table 6.4: Common methods of the JavaScript `RegExp` object.

Method	Description
`exec()`	Executes the search on a string and returns the first match as an array (with captured groups) if found, or `null` if no match is found.
`test()`	Tests whether the pattern matches a given string. Returns `true` if a match is found, otherwise `false`.
`toString()`	Returns a string representing the regex (its source pattern and flags).

Remember that in JavaScript, strings can also use methods like `match`, `search`, and `replace` with regex. For instance:

```javascript
let text = "Hello World";
let result = text.replace(/World/, "JavaScript");
console.log(result); // "Hello JavaScript"
```

Regular expressions are very powerful for validating and manipulating strings, but they can be hard to read. It is often helpful to comment your regex or break it into parts if it is complicated, or use online tools to test them thoroughly with various inputs.

6.9   AJAX Programming Model

AJAX (Asynchronous JavaScript and XML) is a technique that enables web pages to request data from a server asynchronously, without reloading the entire page. Despite "XML" in the name, the data returned is often JSON or even plain text; the key concept is the asynchronous HTTP request in the background. AJAX allows for more dynamic and responsive web applications. For example, updating just a part of a page with new information (like live search suggestions or a stock ticker) without disrupting the user's interaction with the page.

In traditional web interactions (before AJAX became common), a user would fill a form or click a link, causing the browser to make an HTTP request and then load a new page from the server in response. AJAX allows the browser to behind the scenes call a server API (for example, a PHP script or a REST endpoint) and handle the response data in JavaScript, updating the existing page content.

Figure 6.6 compares the traditional page request cycle to the AJAX model. It demonstrates how a user action results in a full page reload in the traditional model, versus a background request and partial update in the AJAX model. In a traditional web request (top sequence), a user action sends an HTTP request and the server returns a full HTML page, causing the browser to reload the entire page. In the AJAX model (bottom sequence), the user's action triggers a background request (XHR or Fetch). The server returns data only (for example, JSON or XML), and the browser's JavaScript updates only the relevant part of the existing page. The result is a smoother experience as the page is partially updated without a full reload.

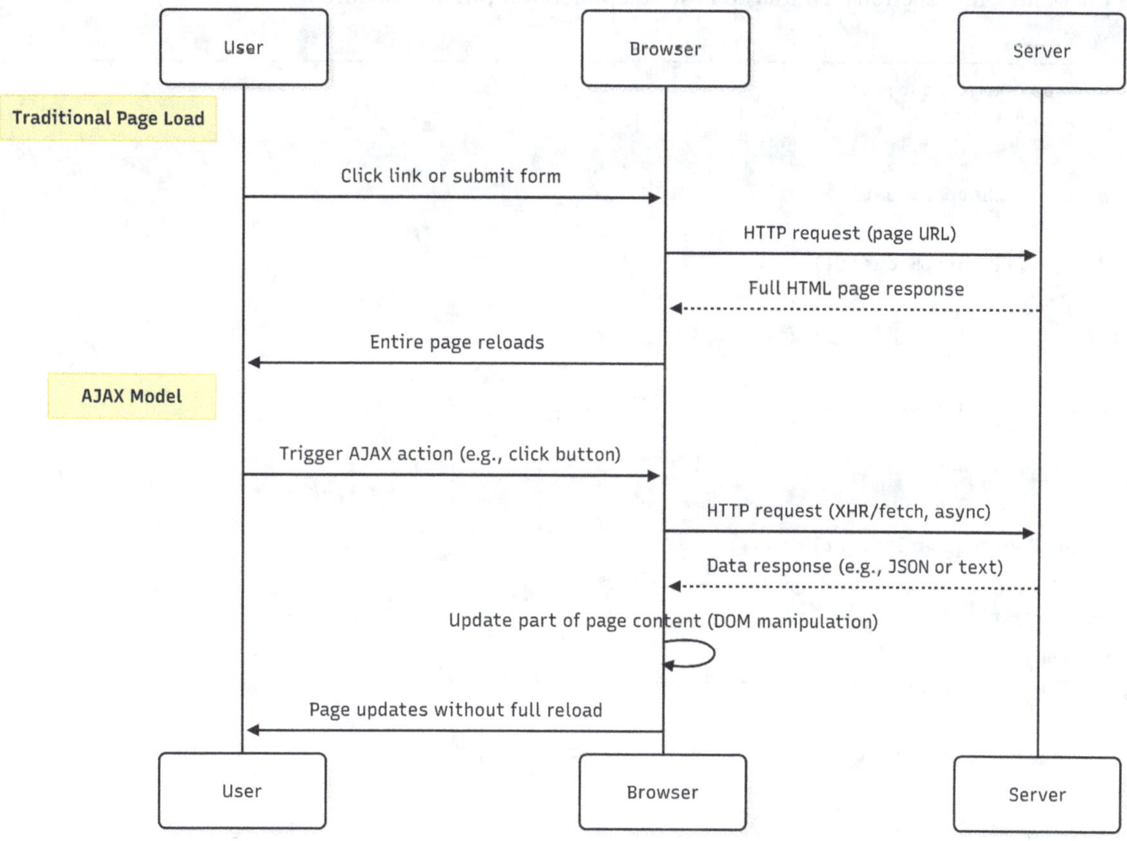

Figure 6.6: Traditional page load vs. AJAX workflow.

6.9.1   Illustrative Generic AJAX Functions

To use AJAX in JavaScript, one historically used the XMLHttpRequest (XHR) object. Newer APIs like fetch provide a simpler interface, but understanding XHR is useful for background and for certain custom scenarios. Below, we outline a basic AJAX workflow using XHR:

1. Create a request object. This is an instance of XMLHttpRequest in modern browsers. (Older IE used an ActiveXObject; modern code usually handles both for compatibility.)
2. Configure the request. Specify the HTTP method (GET or POST) and the URL/endpoint you want to hit.
3. Define a callback. Set up an event handler for when the server responds. With XHR, this is typically done by assigning a function to xhr.onreadystatechange or using xhr.addEventListener('load', ...). You check xhr.readyState and xhr.status to determine if the response is complete and successful, then get the response data (via xhr.responseText or similar).
4. Send the request. For GET requests, you usually send null or nothing; for POST, you send the request body (and set appropriate request headers like content type).

Let us illustrate with functions, similar to how an application might structure it:

```javascript
function createRequestObject()
{
  // Create an XMLHttpRequest object, with IE fallback
  if (window.XMLHttpRequest)
  {
    return new XMLHttpRequest();
  }
  else
  {
    return new ActiveXObject("Microsoft.XMLHTTP");  // for very old IE
  }
}

function sndReq(requestObj, url)
{
  // Configure the XMLHttpRequest
  requestObj.open("GET", url, true);  // true for asynchronous
  requestObj.onreadystatechange = function()
  {
    if (requestObj.readyState === 4)        // 4 = DONE
    {
      if (requestObj.status === 200)        // 200 = OK
      {
        responder(requestObj);
      }
      else
      {
```

```
28         console.error("AJAX error, status:", requestObj.status);
29       }
30     }
31   };
32   requestObj.send(null);
33 }
34
35 function responder(requestObj)
36 {
37   // Handle the response data
38   let responseText = requestObj.responseText;
39   // For example, update part of the page:
40   document.getElementById("result").innerHTML = responseText;
41 }
```

In this outline:

- `createRequestObject()` returns an XHR object (with a fallback for old IE).
- `sndReq(xhr, url)` sets up the request. We provide an anonymous function to handle state changes. This code checks for `readyState === 4` which means the operation is complete; then `status === 200` for a successful HTTP response. On success, it calls `responder()`.
- `responder(xhr)` is where we process the result. In this case, we simply took `xhr.responseText` (the server's response as text) and stuffed it into an element with id "result".

  (R) Modern practice might use `xhr.onload` for success and `xhr.onerror` for error, or use the Fetch API which returns a promise. But the above illustrates the moving parts of a classic AJAX call.

Also, when making repeated AJAX calls, one might want to prevent caching issues. Browsers might cache responses for identical GET requests. A common trick is to add a dummy query parameter like `?nocache=` (with a random number or timestamp) to the URL to ensure the request is seen as unique each time. e.g., `url = "/data?query=term&nocache=" + Math.random()` so that the browser fetches fresh data instead of a cached copy.

6.9.2 AJAX Example

Let us consider a concrete example: a simple page that has an input field and a button. The user enters a value, clicks the button, and the page will send that value to the server via AJAX and display the server's response without reloading.

Client HTML (ajaxExample.html):

```
1 <html>
2 <head><title>AJAX Example</title>
3 <script type = "text/javascript">
4 // Assume createRequestObject, sndReq, responder are defined as above.
```

```javascript
5  var http = createRequestObject();
6  function sendInput()
7  {
8    // Get value from input field with id="userInput"
9    var v = document.getElementById("userInput").value;
10   // Construct URL with query parameter
11   var url = "ajaxResponse.php?u=" + encodeURIComponent(v);
12   sndReq(http, url);
13 }
14 </script>
15 <style>
16   /* Just to make the output area visible */
17   #result { border: 2px solid black; background-color: #ffc; padding: 5px; }
18 </style>
19 </head>
20 <body>
21   <input type = "text" id = "userInput" value = "Enter something" />
22   <button id = "sendButton" onclick = "sendInput()">Send</button>
23   <div id = "result">Here I am.</div>
24 </body>
25 </html>
```

A few things are worth noting about this example. We included our script in the head, created one XHR object `http`, and a function `sendInput()` that uses it. We URL-encode the user input (`encodeURIComponent`) to safely include it in a URL query string. The result `<div id="result">` is initially populated with some placeholder text. When the button is clicked, `sendInput()` is called, which triggers the AJAX request; the response will be handled by the `responder` function (defined in our generic functions), which will replace the content of the `#result` `<div>` with the response text.

Server (ajaxResponse.php):

```php
1  <?php
2  $u = $_GET['u'];   // retrieve the 'u' query parameter
3  print "<b>Server Response:</b><br>";
4  for($k = 0; $k < 5; $k++)
5  {
6    print "Loop index k is: $k and u is $u <br>";
7  }
8  ?>
```

This PHP script simply takes the u parameter and prints a response: a bold header and then 5 lines showing the loop index and the value of u. For example, if the user entered "Test", the response might be:

```
Server Response:
Loop index k is: 0 and u is Test
Loop index k is: 1 and u is Test
... up to k is 4 ...
```

This text is sent back as the HTTP response. Once the client receives it, our responder function places it inside the #result div. The result on the page would be that the div now shows the lines from the server (formatted as HTML). Notably, the user did not navigate away from the page and the update was seamless. They could even continue typing new input and clicking the button to get new results, without full page reloads.

This is the essence of AJAX: background requests and partial page updates.

Often using low-level XHR as above is supplanted by easier methods:

- The Fetch API (window.fetch) returns a promise and uses a simpler syntax:

```
1  fetch("ajaxResponse.php?u=" + encodeURIComponent(v))
2    .then(response => response.text())
3    .then(text => { document.getElementById("result").innerHTML = text; })
4    .catch(err => console.error(err));
```

Fetch can also easily handle JSON via response.json(). This uses an arrow function (=>) for the callback, a shorthand for writing small functions in ES6.

- jQuery (a popular JS library) provides shorthand methods like $.ajax, $.get, $.post which further simplify sending AJAX requests and handling responses.

6.9.3   jQuery and AJAX

Using jQuery, the above example could be greatly simplified. jQuery normalizes the differences between browsers and provides a straightforward interface:

```
1  $("#sendButton").click(function()
2  {
3    $.get("ajaxResponse.php", { u: $("#userInput").val() })
4      .done(function(data)
5      {
6        $("#result").html(data);
7      })
8      .fail(function()
9      {
10       alert("Error fetching data");
11     });
12 });
```

Here, `$.get` performs a GET request. We passed it an object `{ u: value }` which jQuery converts to a query string. The `.done()` method attaches a success callback (which receives the response data and inserts it into the result div), and `.fail()` attaches an error handler. jQuery's AJAX methods (`$.get`, `$.post`, `$.ajax`, etc.) handle creating the XHR, listening for `readyState`, checking status, and so on for you. Similarly, `$.ajax` can be used with more options (it allows you to specify the `dataType` expected, like `"json"` so it will parse JSON automatically, custom headers, etc.).

A one-liner example with jQuery:

```
1  $.post("ajaxResponse.php", { u: "hello" }, function(response)
2  {
3    console.log("Server said: " + response);
4  });
```

This sends a POST request with data and logs the response.

 As of 2025, many developers might opt for the native Fetch API or other libraries for AJAX, but jQuery remains a simple way to handle it, especially if it is already included for other DOM manipulations.

6.10 JavaScript Frameworks Introduction

As web applications became more complex, developers turned to JavaScript frameworks to help organize code and build rich interfaces efficiently. Frameworks and libraries such as Angular and React (among others like Vue.js, etc.) provide abstractions and patterns for building modern web apps, often known as Single Page Applications (SPAs). In an SPA, after the initial page load, subsequent interactions fetch data (often via AJAX) and update the view without full page reloads. Frameworks help manage the state, rendering, and user interactions in these apps.

Below we give a very high-level introduction to Angular and React, two major players in this space, to illustrate the direction modern client-side development has taken. Both frameworks use JavaScript (or TypeScript, a superset of JS) but impose structure and provide powerful features beyond plain JS/DOM coding.

6.10.1 Angular Basics

Angular (sometimes called "Angular 2+" to distinguish it from the older AngularJS 1.x) is a full-featured framework maintained by Google. It uses TypeScript (a typed superset of JavaScript) and a component-based architecture. Angular's core concepts include Components, Templates, Data Binding, Services, and Dependency Injection.

- An Angular Component is a self-contained chunk of the interface, consisting of a template (HTML), a TypeScript class (which defines data and behavior), and metadata (decorators that tell Angular how to use this component). Components are organized in a hierarchy to build the app's UI.
- Templates in Angular are HTML with some additional syntax for data binding and logic. For example, you might see `{{ variableName }}` in an Angular template, which interpolates a component's variable

into the HTML. Angular templates can also include control structures using directives, like `<li *ngFor
="let item of items">{{ item }}</li>` which would repeat an `<li>` for each element in an array
(similar to a loop).

- Data Binding: Angular supports two-way data binding, particularly in forms. For example, `<input
  [(ngModel)]="username">` binds the input's value to the `username` property in the component, so that
  changes in the input update the property and vice versa.

- Services and Dependency Injection: Angular encourages separating business logic into services (usually
  classes annotated with `@Injectable`) that can be injected into components or other services. The
  framework's dependency injection system takes care of providing the right instances where needed. For
  instance, you might have a `UserService` that fetches user data via HTTP; Angular can inject this service
  into any component that needs it, rather than components manually creating service instances.

An extremely simplified example of an Angular component (using TypeScript):

```typescript
import { Component } from '@angular/core';

@Component({
  selector: 'hello-user',
  template: `<h1>Hello, {{name}}!</h1>`
})
export class HelloUserComponent
{
  name: string = 'Alice';
}
```

This defines a component `<hello-user>` that will render as `<h1>Hello, Alice!</h1>` (since `name` is "Alice"). If `name` were updated (perhaps via some user input bound to it), the template would automatically update
to reflect the new name.

Angular apps typically consist of many such components. Angular also includes powerful routing (for SPA
navigation without page reloads), form handling, built-in support for AJAX/HTTP via its HttpClient, and more.
It is a comprehensive framework, which means there is a steeper learning curve, but it provides structure for
large applications out of the box.

6.10.2 React Fundamentals

React, developed at Meta, takes a somewhat different approach. It is often described as a UI library rather than
a full framework, focusing mainly on the View aspect. React's key idea is building the UI using components
that describe what the interface should look like given certain data (called props and state in React). React
introduced the concept of a virtual DOM: rather than directly manipulating the browser DOM for every change,
React maintains a virtual representation of the DOM and efficiently updates the browser's DOM only where
changes are necessary. Some React basics:

- A React Component can be a JavaScript class or a function. Class components extend `React.Component` and implement a `render()` method. Function components (the modern preference) are simply functions that return what the UI should look like (in JSX form).
- JSX is an extension to JavaScript that allows you to write HTML-like syntax directly in your JS. It is not a string, and it gets compiled to JavaScript function calls. For example:

```
function HelloUser(props)
{
  return <h1>Hello, {props.name}!</h1>;
}
```

This is a React component (as a function) that takes `props` (properties) and returns a heading. `{props.name}` is how we insert a JS value into JSX (similar to Angular's `{{ }}` but here we are inside JS code so we use `{ }` to switch from HTML to an expression).

- Props and State: Props are inputs to components (like HTML attributes) that are passed from parent to child. State is internal to a component and can change over time (usually as a result of user actions or async data loading). When state or props change, React calls the component function (or `render` method) again to produce new JSX, and then it updates the DOM efficiently to match the new output.
- One-way data flow: Unlike Angular's two-way binding, React emphasizes one-way data flow. Parent components pass data to children via props; children notify parents of events via callbacks (which may cause the parent to update state and re-render children with new props). This unidirectional flow can make apps easier to understand as they grow.

React example using a class component:

```
class HelloUser extends React.Component
  {
  render() {
    return <h1>Hello, {this.props.name}!</h1>;
  }
}
// Usage:
ReactDOM.render(<HelloUser name="Bob" />, document.getElementById('root'));
```

Here we define a component that expects a prop `name`, and we render it into a DOM element with id 'root'. The output on the page would be `<h1>Hello, Bob!</h1>`.

React's ecosystem often includes other libraries for state management (like Redux or the built-in Context API) and for routing (React Router) because React itself is only concerned with rendering components.

One of the powerful aspects of React is that components can maintain internal state and re-render efficiently. For example, consider a simple counter component:

```
1  function Counter()
2  {
3    const [count, setCount] = React.useState(0);
4    return (
5      <div>
6        <p>You clicked {count} times</p>
7        <button onClick={() => setCount(count + 1)}>Click me</button>
8      </div>
9    );
10 }
```

Using React Hooks (`useState`), this functional component has a state variable `count`. Each time the button is clicked, `setCount` updates the state, and React re-renders the component, updating the displayed count. React handles the event (`onClick`) and re-render logic such that only the parts of the DOM that changed (the text in the `<p>`) are updated.

Angular vs. React: Angular is a complete framework with a prescribed way of structuring your app and a rich feature set (forms, HTTP, routing, etc. built-in). React is more minimal, focusing on building UI components and leaving other concerns to additional libraries. Angular uses templates with special syntax separate from the code (though closely linked), while React blends HTML and JavaScript via JSX, treating UI as a function of state. Both approaches have their merits, and the choice often depends on project requirements and developer preference.

What is common is that both Angular and React (and others like Vue) encourage developers to think in terms of components, to manage application state explicitly, and to use declarative rendering (you describe what the UI should look like for a given state, and the framework/library handles the DOM manipulations). This is a significant shift from older approaches where a lot of imperative DOM manipulation (e.g., using jQuery to find elements and update them) was the norm. The component-driven model helps manage complexity as applications grow larger.

6.11   Chapter Review

Problem 6.1 What are the two ways to include JavaScript code in an HTML page, and how do they differ?

Problem 6.2 Name at least two methods to display output or messages to the user using JavaScript. When might you use each?

Problem 6.3 In JavaScript, what is an "event" and how can events be used to trigger code execution? Give an example of an event and a corresponding event handler.

Problem 6.4 How do you define a function in JavaScript, and how can you invoke (call) it from your code or in response to an event?

Problem 6.5 Explain how you can access a specific HTML element from JavaScript and change its content or style. What method would you use and what HTML attribute must the element have?

Problem 6.6 Write a simple example of a JavaScript conditional using an `if` statement. In what situations would you use an `if...else` structure?

Problem 6.7 What is a loop in JavaScript? How does a `for` loop differ from a `while` loop, and when might you use each type of loop?

Problem 6.8 Why is client-side form validation useful? How can you use JavaScript to validate a form input (for example, to check that a number field contains only numbers)?

Problem 6.9 What is the `innerHTML` property in JavaScript, and how is it used to update the content of a web page dynamically?

Problem 6.10 What is AJAX and what does it allow a web page to do? Why is it important for creating dynamic, modern web applications?

Problem 6.11 What is a Single Page Application (SPA)? How do frameworks like Angular or React relate to the concept of an SPA?

Problem 6.12 Angular is described as a "full-featured framework." Who maintains Angular, and what language is it built with? Name one core concept of Angular.

Problem 6.13 React is often called a JavaScript library rather than a full framework. Who created React, and what is one key feature that makes React unique (for example, how it updates the DOM)?

Problem 6.14 If your JavaScript code is not working as expected in the browser, what tools or techniques can you use to debug the issue and find errors?

Problem 6.15 Which JavaScript function can generate a random number, and what range of values does this function return? How might you use it to simulate a dice roll or random selection?

Problem 6.16 Validating a Credit Card Form: Create a simple HTML form with a text input for a credit card number and a submit button. Use JavaScript to validate the format of the card number when the form is submitted. The credit card number should consist of 16 digits with a space after every 4 digits (e.g., `"1234 5678 9012 3456"`). Write a JavaScript function to check the input against this pattern using a regular expression (for example, use a regex like `/^([0-9]{4} ){3}[0-9]{4}$/`). If the input matches the pattern, display an alert message such as `"VALID CREDIT CARD ENTERED!"`. If the input does not match, display an alert message like `"INVALID CREDIT CARD ENTERED! RE-ENTER"` and prevent the form from submitting (for example, return `false` in the form's `onsubmit` event handler). Include appropriate attributes on the `<input>` field: set `type="text"`, give it an `id` (for example, `"card"`), a `name`, a `placeholder` (to show a hint like `"Enter Card Number"`), and a `title` that describes the required format.

Problem 6.17 Image Toggle on Click: Build a web page with an image that toggles between two pictures (for example, an image of a sunrise and an image of a full moon) each time the image is clicked. Place an `<img>` element in the HTML with the first image (e.g., the sunrise) as its `src`. Give the image an `id` and an appropriate `alt` attribute. Write a JavaScript function that switches the image's `src` between the sunrise image and the full moon image. Use an `if...else` statement to check which image is currently displayed. Trigger this function when the user clicks the image by adding an `onclick` attribute to the `<img>` tag or by using `addEventListener("click", ...)`. Make sure that after each click, the state is updated so that the next click toggles correctly.

Problem 6.18 Dynamic Text Style on Mouse Events: Make a piece of text on the page change its style when the mouse pointer enters or leaves it. Add a line of text in your HTML (for example, a `<p>` or `<span>`) and give it an `id` so you can select it in JavaScript. Use JavaScript to detect when the mouse enters or leaves this text element by setting up event handlers for the `"mouseover"` and `"mouseout"` events. When the mouse hovers over the text, change several of its style properties such as font size, font family, text color, and position. When the mouse leaves the text, revert the style changes. You can modify an element's style directly via JavaScript (for example, `element.style.color = "green"`), or define CSS classes for the hover state and non-hover state and toggle the element's `className`.

7. Web Application Security

In previous chapters, we have demonstrated how to build dynamic web applications using HTML, JavaScript, PHP, and SQL on a LAMP stack. Now, we turn our attention to securing these components and protecting our application and its users. Web application security is critical since web attacks are a leading cause of data breaches, as noted in the Black Duck Blog's analysis of the Equifax breach. An insecure form or query can expose sensitive user data or even compromise an entire server.

In this chapter, we will explore common web vulnerabilities and defensive techniques, focusing on authentication, authorization, secure password storage, session management, and data protection in PHP. We will learn how to defend against threats like SQL injection, Cross-Site Scripting (XSS), and Cross-Site Request Forgery (CSRF), and about using HTTPS to secure data in transit. In addition, we will address critical aspects of the security lifecycle, including managing third-party dependencies, implementing secure code review practices, and integrating security into our development workflow.

Furthermore, we include practical PHP examples and real-world case studies (like the Facebook Firesheep session hijacking and the Equifax breach) to illustrate failures and promote best practices. In addition, we explore how proper logging, monitoring, and secure deployment practices are essential components of a comprehensive security strategy.

Finally, you will be able to build web applications that not only function properly and correctly, but also withstand common attacks. This foundation in web application security will prepare you for the more advanced development topics covered in the next chapter.

Learning Objectives

By the end of this chapter, you should be able to:
- Explain the criticality of web application security and articulate the consequences of common security vulnerabilities.
- Identify and mitigate common misconceptions developers have regarding web security.
- Apply best practices in user authentication and secure password storage using PHP, including password hashing and verification techniques.
- Implement secure session management in PHP, including methods for protecting session identifiers.
- Defend your applications against common web attacks such as SQL injection, Cross-Site Scripting (XSS), and Cross-Site Request Forgery (CSRF).
- Validate and securely handle file uploads, ensuring the correct handling of MIME types and secure file storage.
- Configure HTTP security headers such as Content Security Policy (CSP), Strict Transport Security (HSTS), and others to enhance browser-side security.
- Implement comprehensive logging and monitoring practices to detect and respond to security incidents effectively.

DOI: 10.1201/9781003727651-7

- Manage third-party dependencies and keep components updated to prevent vulnerabilities from outdated software.
- Integrate security testing and code review practices into your development lifecycle.
- Outline secure deployment practices within Continuous Integration and Continuous Deployment (CI/CD) pipelines, including managing secrets securely.
- Summarize lessons learned from real-world security breaches and apply these insights to reinforce security in your applications.

7.1 Authentication and Secure Password Storage

Authentication is the process of verifying a user's identity (i.e., login), while authorization governs what an authenticated user is allowed to do (i.e., admin vs. regular user). Both are crucial for a secure application. If authentication is weak, attackers can impersonate users; if authorization is lax, users might access data or actions they should not. In a LAMP web app, PHP typically handles authentication by checking credentials against a MySQL database and then using sessions or cookies to remember the logged-in user. Let us examine how to implement these steps securely.

Secure Password Handling: Never store plaintext passwords in the database. Instead, store a one-way cryptographic hash of each password, as recommended in the OWASP Cryptographic Storage Cheat Sheet. PHP provides the `password_hash()` function to hash passwords using strong algorithms (like Bcrypt or Argon2) with automatic salting, as detailed in the OWASP Password Storage Cheat Sheet, and `password_verify()` to check a password against a stored hash. This way, even if the database is compromised, the actual passwords remain unknown (since hashes cannot feasibly be reversed). Many of the notorious breaches have been made worse because of plaintext or weakly-hashed passwords. Using weak hashing algorithms (like unsalted MD5 or SHA-1) is nearly as dangerous as using plaintext, since modern hardware can crack those hashes rapidly, according to the OWASP Password Storage Cheat Sheet. For example, in the 2009 RockYou breach, attackers exploited an SQL injection to retrieve 32 million user credentials, which were stored in cleartext, not hashed, as Reuters reported in their coverage of the incident. As a result, all those passwords became public, illustrating why hashing is vital.

Storing a Password Securely (PHP) Example:

```php
<?php
// Registration: hashing a new user's password before storing
$user = $_POST['username'];
$pass = $_POST['password'];

// Hash the password with a strong algorithm and salt (handled internally)
$hash = password_hash($pass, PASSWORD_DEFAULT);

// Store $user and $hash in the database (e.g., via PDO prepared statement)
$stmt = $pdo->prepare("INSERT INTO users(username, password_hash) VALUES (?, ?)");
$stmt->execute([$user, $hash]); ?>
```

In the above snippet, `PASSWORD_DEFAULT` uses a secure hashing algorithm (currently Bcrypt, and future PHP versions may use stronger algorithms by default). The hash contains a salt so that each user's password hashes to a unique value. To verify a login, we retrieve the stored hash and use `password_verify()`:

Verifying a Password at Login (PHP) Example:

```php
<?php
// Authentication: verifying login credentials
$user = $_POST['username'];
$pass = $_POST['password'];

// Look up the stored hash for this username
$stmt = $pdo->prepare("SELECT password_hash FROM users WHERE username = ?");
$stmt->execute([$user]);
$row = $stmt->fetch();

if ($row && password_verify($pass, $row['password_hash']))
{
    // Password is correct --- authentication successful
    session_start();
    session_regenerate_id(true); // prevent session fixation
    $_SESSION['username'] = $user;
    echo "Login successful!";
}
else
{
    // Authentication failed
    echo "Invalid username or password";
}
?>
```

Here we start a session for the user upon successful login (more on sessions in Section 7.3). The call to `session_regenerate_id(true)` ensures we issue a new session ID on login, thwarting session fixation attacks (discussed later). By using `password_verify()`, we avoid storing or comparing plaintext passwords.

Additional Authentication Best Practices:

- Account Lockout and Rate Limiting: Implement measures to thwart brute-force attacks. For example, if a user enters the wrong password five times, you might lock the account for a brief period or require a CAPTCHA. This prevents attackers from trying endless password guesses.
- Multi-Factor Authentication (MFA): Use MFA for extra security on accounts, especially those with sensitive access. MFA (e.g., one-time codes via SMS/email, authenticator apps, or hardware tokens) adds a second verification step beyond the password. Even if passwords are stolen, MFA can block unauthorized logins. Many large providers have shown that enabling MFA dramatically reduces account

compromises. While implementing MFA in a custom PHP app is complex (often involving generating and verifying time-based one-time passwords or integrating third-party services), it is a recommended practice for production systems handling sensitive data. For instance, after a 2016 breach, GitHub made SMS/email verification mandatory for some operations and later encouraged hardware security keys, reflecting an industry trend toward MFA to mitigate credential theft.

- Secure Transmission of Credentials: Always transmit login forms and credentials only over HTTPS (to prevent eavesdropping, as we will cover in Section 7.5). Never send passwords in plaintext over the network. Ensure your login page itself is served via HTTPS and that the cookies for the session (after login) have the Secure flag so they are never sent over an insecure connection. A thief on an open Wi-Fi should not be able to sniff credentials or session tokens in transit.

- Avoid Insecure Practices: Do not use or share passwords in insecure ways. For example, never email users their passwords (email is not secure), and discourage weak or common passwords. Do not reuse credentials in different contexts, such as the same password for your database admin user and an application user account. Use separate, strong credentials for backend systems. Also, do not store passwords in client-side code or in version control. There have been cases where API keys or passwords left in public code repositories led to major breaches (see the Uber case study below). Always assume that anything hard-coded or shared insecurely could become known to an attacker.

OAuth 2.0 and Third-Party Authentication: In modern web development, you can offload authentication to trusted providers like Google, Facebook, or GitHub using OAuth 2.0 and related protocols (such as OpenID Connect). OAuth 2.0 is an authorization framework that allows users to grant a third-party application access to their information on another service without sharing their password with the third party, as explained in the OWASP Authentication Cheat Sheet. For example, by implementing "Log in with Google," your application does not handle the user's password at all. Google authenticates the user and then provides your app with an access token or identity information. This can enhance security (you are not storing passwords, and you leverage the provider's robust authentication and MFA protections) and improve user convenience (fewer passwords to manage). If you integrate OAuth, use secure libraries and follow best practices. For example, use the Authorization Code grant flow (which keeps tokens off the URL), and verify tokens or authorization codes on the server side. Ensure you register redirect URLs exactly to prevent hijacking, and store client secrets safely. OAuth 2.0 relies on HTTPS for security and is widely adopted by APIs and websites for federated identity. It is important to note that OAuth by itself is about authorization (granting access to data), but with OpenID Connect on top, it can provide authentication (verifying identity). By using OAuth/OpenID Connect for login, you delegate the hard work of secure authentication to identity providers (like Google), but you must still implement proper authorization in your app for what an authenticated user can do.

JSON Web Tokens (JWT) for Session Management: Traditionally, after a user logs in, the server uses a session (stored server-side and identified by a cookie) to remember the user. An alternative approach popular in modern APIs and single-page applications is token-based authentication using JSON Web Tokens. A JWT is a compact, URL-safe token that consists of three parts (header, payload, signature) and can contain user identity information in its payload. After authentication, a server can issue a JWT, signed (digitally signed using a secret or private key) to prevent tampering, and the client (browser) stores it (often in a cookie or local storage) and sends it with each request. The server can then verify the token's signature and trust the data inside it without having to look up a session in memory or database as this makes JWTs useful for stateless auth, scaling across servers without sticky sessions. However, JWTs must be used carefully: treat them like passwords. If an attacker steals a JWT, they can impersonate the user until it expires. Therefore, it is wise to keep JWTs short-lived (add an `exp` expiration claim) and perhaps use refresh tokens for long sessions. Always use strong signing algorithms (e.g., HS256 with a strong secret, or RS256 with a private key). Never accept an unencrypted JWT over an insecure channel. Also, be aware of JWT implementation pitfall. For example, early on, some libraries mistakenly accepted tokens with `alg: "none"` (meaning no signature) as valid, as documented in the "Critical vulnerabilities in JSON Web Token libraries" report. This "alg=none" vulnerability meant an attacker could fabricate a token with any payload (e.g., marking themselves as an admin) and the library would accept it as authentic. Modern libraries have fixed this, but it underscores that you should always validate the token's signature and algorithm. If using JWTs in a browser context, prefer storing them in HttpOnly cookies (to mitigate XSS theft) with `Secure` (HTTPS only) and `SameSite` attributes set (to mitigate CSRF, as discussed later). JWTs are a powerful tool for decoupling session state from the server, but they require vigilant implementation of security best practices (signing, verification, short expiration, etc.). If your app is primarily server-rendered and running on a single server, standard PHP sessions are fine; JWTs shine when you have many microservices or need to authorize API requests directly without server session lookups.

Authorization and Access Control: Once authenticated, users should only perform authorized actions. Enforce permission checks on the server side for each request. For example, if your app has an "admin" role, verify `$_SESSION['role']` or similar before allowing admin-only operations. Do not rely on client-side checks (like hiding admin buttons via JavaScript) as attackers can easily bypass those. Implement logical access control to prevent users from accessing others' data (e.g., if user IDs are in URLs, ensure a user can only fetch their own `id` data, preventing Insecure Direct Object References). In PHP, this often means checking session user IDs against requested records in database queries (e.g., `SELECT * FROM orders WHERE id=? AND user_id = ?`).

Simple Authorization Check (PHP) Example:

```
# Only allow access if user is admin
session_start();
if ($_SESSION['role'] !== 'admin') {
    http_response_code(403);
    die("Forbidden: You do not have access to this resource.");
}
// ... proceed with admin-specific task ...
```

In practice, frameworks and libraries can help manage roles/permissions, but the core idea is to validate authorization on every protected action. A famous real-world failure of authorization was the 2012 GitHub incident, where an attacker discovered he could manipulate parameters to gain elevated privileges due to insufficient checks. GitHub had missed certain authorization validations, allowing the attacker to write to repositories he did not own. GitHub later confirmed this issue was due to a Ruby on Rails mass-assignment flaw that let the attacker add his public key to repositories and gain administrator access, as reported by The Hacker News. The lesson is that robust role-based access control and thorough permission checks are essential.

Case Study: Plaintext Passwords and SQL Injection (RockYou 2009). As mentioned earlier, RockYou.com suffered a major breach that exposed 30+ million user accounts, as Reuters reported. The attack started with an SQL injection vulnerability (discussed in detail later in this chapter) that allowed the attacker to dump the users table. Shockingly, all passwords were stored in plaintext. This meant the attacker immediately obtained millions of real passwords, which were later posted online. Many users had reused these passwords on other sites, causing a cascade of security issues beyond RockYou itself. This incident underscores two critical failures: lack of input validation (allowing SQL injection) and lack of password hashing. Modern PHP applications can easily avoid these mistakes by using prepared statements (to prevent injection) and `password_hash` (to secure passwords). RockYou paid fines and suffered reputational damage, but the broader web development community learned a hard lesson on the importance of basic security practices.

Case Study: Developer Credentials and OAuth Token Leak (Uber 2016). Proper authentication practices are not just for users; developers and deployment processes need protection too. In 2016, Uber experienced a major breach when attackers gained access to a private GitHub repository used by Uber engineers. Uber had not enabled MFA on their GitHub accounts, making it easier for attackers to compromise an account, according to The Register's reporting on the incident. Once inside the private repo, the intruders found AWS access credentials embedded in the code. Using those cloud server keys, they accessed Uber's AWS S3 storage and stole data on 57 million riders and drivers. Uber's engineers had essentially hard-coded a secret password in a place attackers eventually could get to, and insufficient access control on the code repository compounded the issue. The fallout was severe: Uber had to pay $148 million in fines for failing to notify users, and the incident remains a cautionary tale. Lessons: (1) Require MFA on developer code repositories and any other critical services. If Uber's GitHub had MFA, the attackers might have been foiled at the first step. (2) Never commit sensitive credentials to code; use secure vaults or environment variables for secrets. (3) Practice the principle of least privilege. The AWS keys Uber exposed had broad access; tighter permissions could have limited the damage. This case shows that "authentication" security is not only about user logins, but extends to how developers authenticate to services and how secrets are managed in code. Using OAuth tokens or keys in code is sometimes necessary, but they should be kept out of repositories (for example, use config files not checked into git, or services like AWS Secrets Manager) and rotated if exposed. And just as users should have MFA, developers should too, on all accounts that could lead to production access.

7.2   Session Management and User Sessions

Web applications use sessions to remember authenticated users and maintain state between page requests. In PHP, a session typically uses a session ID (often stored in a browser cookie named `PHPSESSID` by default) to associate a series of requests with a user's data on the server (e.g. login status, shopping cart contents). Secure session management is crucial. If an attacker hijacks a user's session, they can act as that user without knowing their password. In this section, we cover how to manage sessions safely and prevent common attacks like session hijacking and session fixation.

Starting Sessions Securely: Use `session_start()` to begin a session at the top of your PHP pages that require one. Always do this over HTTPS (so the cookie is not sent in plaintext) and ideally set session cookies with the Secure and HttpOnly flags. The Secure flag ensures the cookie is only sent over HTTPS, and HttpOnly makes it inaccessible to JavaScript (mitigating XSS-based theft of the cookie). You can configure these in PHP via `session_set_cookie_params()` or php.ini settings:

```php
1  // At the start of your script, before session_start():
2  // send cookie only over HTTPS
3  ini_set('session.cookie_secure', 1);
4  // prevent JavaScript access to session cookie
5  ini_set('session.cookie_httponly', 1);
6  // PHP will reject sessions supplied by user that don't exist (helps prevent fixation)
7  ini_set('session.use_strict_mode', 1);
8  session_start();
```

By enabling strict mode and regenerating the session ID at key points (like after login or privilege level change), you prevent session fixation. Session fixation is an attack where an adversary tricks a user into using a known session ID (for example, by sending them a link with `PHPSESSID=knownvalue`), then hijacks that session once the user logs in. Calling `session_regenerate_id(true)` after login ensures any pre-existing ID is not used going forward.

Session Timeout: Configure sessions to expire after an inactivity period. For example, you might invalidate a session if a user has been idle for 20 minutes, requiring them to log in again. This limits the window of opportunity for hijackers. PHP's `session.gc_maxlifetime` setting controls the lifetime of session files on the server. You can implement an inactivity timeout by storing a timestamp in `$_SESSION` (e.g., `$_SESSION['LAST _ACTIVITY']`) and checking it on each request.

Protecting Session Data: Only store necessary information in `$_SESSION`. Avoid storing sensitive personal data in session variables if possible and keep it in the database and fetch as needed. The session ID itself should be treated like a secret; do not expose it in URLs or logs. Use `session_destroy()` and unset session cookies on logout to invalidate the session immediately.

Session Hijacking and HTTPS: One common way to hijack sessions is by sniffing unsecured network traffic to steal session cookies. If a site is not fully on HTTPS, an attacker on the same network (e.g. public Wi-Fi) can intercept the session cookie and reuse it. A notorious example was the Firesheep tool in 2010, which demonstrated how easily one could take over accounts on sites like Facebook over open Wi-Fi. Firesheep listened for unencrypted session cookies on the network; when a victim logged into Facebook (which at the time would encrypt the password but then revert to HTTP for subsequent requests), Firesheep grabbed the user's session cookie. The attacker could then impersonate the victim's Facebook session without ever knowing their password. This session hijacking attack (also called sidejacking) prompted major websites to adopt always-on HTTPS for authenticated sessions. The lesson for developers is clear: always require HTTPS for any authenticated session so that cookies cannot be sniffed. (We will delve more into HTTPS in Section 7.5, but it is an integral part of session security.)

Case Study: Facebook Session Hijacking (Firesheep, 2010). In late 2010, a Firefox extension called Firesheep made headlines by allowing anyone to hijack web sessions over Wi-Fi, as documented on Wikipedia. With a single click, an eavesdropper could take over accounts on Facebook, Twitter, and other services that did not fully enforce HTTPS. Firesheep worked by sniffing packets for session cookies. When a logged-in user visited an insecure site, the cookie (like `Facebook_session=a1b2c3...`) was transmitted in plaintext. Firesheep captured that cookie and let the attacker act as the victim. This was possible because, at the time, Facebook protected the login page with SSL but did not require HTTPS for all subsequent traffic, a critical oversight. The immediate fix was for websites to use HTTPS everywhere and set the Secure flag on cookies. Indeed, Facebook and others soon did so, and browsers also started flagging non-HTTPS logins as insecure. Firesheep's impact was to dramatically raise awareness of session hijacking risks and usher in an era of ubiquitous web encryption. As a developer, remember that a user's session cookie is as powerful as their password. Protect it with the same zeal (via encryption in transit and HttpOnly flags to thwart XSS, etc.).

7.3 Input Validation and Output Escaping (Preventing SQL Injection and XSS)

One of the most dangerous assumptions in web development is trusting user input. All input is untrusted until proven otherwise. Attackers can craft malicious inputs to exploit your application. Two of the most prevalent exploits are SQL Injection (malicious SQL code in inputs) and Cross-Site Scripting (XSS) (malicious script injected into web pages). In a LAMP stack, these often arise from not properly handling data that flows from the browser to the database or to the page. In this section, we discuss how to rigorously validate inputs and safely output data, breaking down defenses for SQL injection and XSS.

7.3.1 SQL Injection: Dangers and Defenses

SQL Injection is a code injection technique where an attacker sends input that alters the intended SQL queries executed by the server. This occurs when an application builds SQL commands including externally influenced input without neutralizing special characters, allowing the input to modify the query's structure, as explained in CWE-89: SQL Injection. For example, if a PHP script builds a query by concatenating strings directly with user input, an attacker can input SQL syntax to prematurely end a string and add new commands. A classic example is a login form where the query is:

```
$query = "SELECT * FROM users WHERE username='$user' AND password='$pass'";
```

If an attacker sets `$user` to `anything' OR '1'='1` (and leaves `$pass` blank), the query becomes:

```
SELECT * FROM users WHERE username='anything' OR '1'='1' AND password='';
```

The condition `'1'='1'` is always true, so this would return all users, often bypassing authentication. In other cases, attackers can use `'; DROP TABLE users; --` to terminate the query and append a destructive command. The consequences are severe including data theft, data loss, or complete takeover of the database. According to security industry analyses, SQL injection is one of the most common web attack vectors, used to access information that was not intended to be displayed. Injection vulnerabilities have consistently been among the most critical web security issues, holding the #1 spot in the OWASP Top 10 for many years, and as of 2021 were still in the top three (OWASP Top 10 2021, category A03: Injection).

Use Prepared Statements (Parameterized Queries) for Prevention: The most effective way to prevent SQL injection in PHP is to use prepared statements with bound parameters (available with PDO or MySQLi extensions). In a prepared statement, the SQL command is defined with placeholders (`?` or named `:params`), and then variables are bound to those placeholders at execution. This separates the query structure from the data, so no matter what input is supplied, it cannot break out of the intended query format.

Using PDO Prepared Statements (PHP) Example:

```php
<?php
// Using PDO for a safe query
$user = $_POST['username'];
$pass = $_POST['password'];

$stmt = $pdo->prepare("SELECT * FROM users WHERE username = ? AND password = ?");
$stmt->execute([$user, $pass]);
$result = $stmt->fetch();
?>
```

In this example, even if `$user` contains quotes or SQL keywords, the database will not treat them as part of the SQL command; they will be treated only as data for the `username` parameter. Under the hood, the database receives the query structure and the data separately, eliminating the chance for injection. Note that we are still using a plaintext password in the query here for simplicity; in a real application, the password would be hashed. Even so, using a parameter for the password field prevents an attacker from injecting through the password input as well.

Additional SQL Injection Defenses: Use server-side input validation to reject or sanitize obviously malformed data (for instance, if you expect an integer, ensure the input is numeric). However, do not rely on blacklisting SQL keywords or special characters alone as attackers can often obfuscate inputs. Parameterized queries are a bulletproof approach because they do not attempt to sanitize but they simply avoid mixing data with code. Also, limit database user privileges: your web app's MySQL user should have the minimum rights needed (e.g., if the app never needs to drop tables, do not grant `DROP` privilege). This way, even if injection occurs, the damage is limited. Keeping database software updated is important too. A famous case of a missed update causing disaster was the Equifax breach (2017). While not SQL injection, it was an injection vulnerability (in Apache Struts, a web framework) that Equifax failed to patch. Attackers exploited it to run arbitrary code on the web server, stealing personal data of 147 million people, as reported by The Hacker News. The root cause was the same: unsanitized input reaching an interpreter (in this case, an expression language in the Struts framework). Equifax could have prevented the breach by applying the available patch or using a web application firewall rule to filter malicious input. The takeaway is that security flaws in the input processing chain, whether SQL, NoSQL, or other interpreters, must be promptly fixed and mitigated.

Case Study: Patch Your Software (Equifax Data Breach 2017). The Equifax breach is one of the largest in history, and it serves as a lesson about keeping web software up-to-date. Equifax's web application was built on Java using the Apache Struts framework. In March 2017, a critical Struts vulnerability (CVE-2017-5638) was disclosed and patched, allowing attackers to perform remote code execution via a malicious content-type header (an injection attack). Equifax, unfortunately, did not apply the patch on a key system. By May 2017, attackers exploited this flaw to penetrate Equifax's servers and exfiltrate data on nearly half of the US population, as The Hacker News reported. The breach was only disclosed in September 2017. Equifax confirmed that the attackers entered through the unpatched Struts vulnerability, according to the Black Duck Blog analysis. This case underscores that security is not only about your code, but also the frameworks and libraries you use. Regularly update your LAMP stack components (PHP, Apache, MySQL) and any libraries. A single outdated component with a known flaw can undermine all your other security measures. In summary: do not let a known injection flaw linger in your app, rather patch it or mitigate it before attackers find it.

Case Study: Cloud Misconfiguration and SSRF (Capital One 2019). Not all injection attacks target SQL or typical web forms; sometimes the injection is into an HTTP request or another service. In 2019, Capital One suffered a breach that exposed data of over 100 million customers. The attacker exploited a Server-Side Request Forgery (SSRF) vulnerability in Capital One's infrastructure. Capital One's web application firewall (WAF), based on an open-source module, was misconfigured. The attacker sent specially crafted requests that the WAF forwarded to an internal service (the AWS metadata service) that should not have been exposed, as detailed in Krebs on Security's analysis of the hack. Through the SSRF, the attacker obtained AWS credentials from the metadata endpoint, which had excessive permissions, including access to sensitive data stored in Amazon S3 buckets. In effect, an input (an HTTP header or parameter) that the WAF received was not properly validated and let the attacker "inject" a request to a protected internal URL. With the stolen credentials, the attacker downloaded massive amounts of personal data. The breach went undetected from March until July 2019, nearly four months, and was finally caught when an external security researcher tipped off Capital One. This incident shows that injection vulnerabilities can occur in many forms: here it was an HTTP request injection (SSRF), not a SQL or script injection, but the principle is similar. The defense is also similar: rigorous validation of inputs and internal communications. In cloud environments, one should block access to cloud metadata services by default or use mitigations like Instance Metadata Service v2 (which was introduced to prevent this exact attack). Also, limit the privileges of credentials available to any one component (Capital One's WAF role should not have been able to list and read all data from S3). This case is a lesson that security misconfiguration (an OWASP Top 10 issue) combined with an injection flaw can have catastrophic results. It is not just your application code but also your infrastructure that needs to be hardened.

7.3.2   Cross-Site Scripting (XSS): Dangers and Defenses

Cross-Site Scripting (XSS) is an attack where an application includes malicious client-side script (usually JavaScript) in a page, which then executes in other users' browsers. The root cause is usually an application taking user input and outputting it to a page without proper escaping or validation. In other words, whenever untrusted data is not neutralized before being placed in page output, arbitrary script can execute in the victim's browser, as explained in CWE-79: Cross-site Scripting. For example, a comment field on a blog that simply does `echo $_POST['comment']` could be misused: an attacker could submit a comment like `<script>evilCode()</script>` which the blog page would then render as active script. XSS allows attackers to hijack user sessions, deface websites, or redirect users. Effectively anything that JavaScript can do in the context of the affected site, including stealing cookies or sensitive data from forms. Unlike some attacks that target servers, XSS targets other users of the application by making the application itself an unwitting vehicle for attack.

There are three main types of XSS attacks:

- Reflected XSS: The malicious script is reflected off the server in the response, typically via a parameter in the URL or form submission. For instance, an error message page that prints back an invalid input without encoding could be exploitable. The attack is delivered when a victim is tricked into clicking a crafted link (with the script in the URL) and the server reflects that into the page.

- Stored XSS: The malicious script is stored on the server (e.g., in a database) and later displayed to users. Examples include malicious forum posts, product reviews, or profile fields. This can be particularly devastating as it can affect every user who views the compromised content (as happened in the classic MySpace Samy worm).
- DOM-based XSS: The vulnerability exists in client-side JavaScript that writes data to the DOM without proper handling, rather than involving the server generating the attack. (This type is less about server-side PHP, so we will not focus on it here, but front-end developers must be aware of it.)

Impact of XSS: Once an attacker can inject JavaScript into your site, they can perform actions as the victim or steal data. For example, an injected script can read cookies (unless marked HttpOnly) and send them to the attacker, leading to session hijacking. It could also display fake login forms (phishing), or propagate as a worm. A famous XSS incident was the Samy worm (2005) on MySpace, where a teenager injected a script into his profile that made anyone viewing it add him as a friend and copy the script to their own profile. Within 20 hours, over one million users had unwittingly run the worm's payload, making it one of the fastest-spreading web worms, according to the Wikipedia article on the Samy computer worm. Although Samy's payload was benign (it just displayed a message and self-propagated), it demonstrated the potent force of XSS. Modern web apps (including social networks) now strictly filter or escape user content to prevent such worms.

(XSS vs. CSRF) XSS attack example: In a reflected XSS scenario, an attacker lures a victim into clicking a URL that includes a malicious script. The website innocently loads the page and unknowingly sends the script back to the victim's browser, which executes it. The attacker's injected script ends up executing in the victim's browser, then sends private data back to the attacker.

Output Encoding and Input Sanitization for Defending Against XSS: The primary defense is to never inject raw user input into HTML output. Always escape or encode special characters in user-provided data before rendering. In PHP, the simplest method is using `htmlspecialchars()` or `htmlentities()`, which converts characters like <, >, " into their harmless HTML entity equivalents (<, >, ", etc.). For example:

```php
// Safe output example
$username = $_SESSION['username'];          // assume this came from user input originally
echo "Welcome, " . htmlspecialchars($username, ENT_QUOTES | ENT_HTML5, 'UTF-8');
```

This ensures that if `$username` contains something like `<script>alert('xss')</script>`, it will be output as literal `<script>...` tags on the page (visible text), rather than executing as a script. Any dynamic data that goes into HTML, JavaScript, or CSS context should be properly encoded for that context. Most XSS is prevented by this measure alone.

In cases where you want to allow some HTML (e.g., formatting tags in comments), you must sanitize the input by stripping dangerous tags/attributes. You can use tools or libraries (like HTML Purifier for PHP) to allow a safe subset of HTML and remove scripts. Simply blacklisting `<script>` tags is not enough, because attackers can use other vectors (onerror handlers, data URIs, etc.). A comprehensive sanitizer or a whitelist approach is required if you allow rich content.

Validate Inputs (but do not rely solely on validation): Many XSS payloads can be caught by input validation. For instance, if a field should only contain letters, reject anything with < or other symbols. However, some inputs (like messages or names) legitimately could include symbols, so output encoding is the stronger, more general solution. Validate inputs for length and type to reduce unexpected cases, but always encode on output regardless of validation.

Content Security Policy (CSP): As an advanced defense, web applications can employ CSP headers. A Content Security Policy instructs browsers to only execute scripts from permitted sources. For example, you can set a policy to disallow inline scripts (`script-src 'self'` to only allow scripts from your domain). CSP can significantly mitigate XSS impact by blocking the execution of injected scripts, though it requires careful configuration and testing to not break legitimate functionality. While CSP is a powerful tool, it complements but does not replace the need for proper output escaping in code.

Testing for XSS: During development, test pages by inputting harmless strings with `<script>alert('XSS')</script>` to see if an alert pops up; if it does, you have a vulnerability. Also test less obvious vectors (like `<imgsrc=xonerror=alert(1)>`). Developers should be familiar with XSS cheat sheets (like OWASP's) to know what patterns to defend against.

Case Study: Stored XSS (The MySpace Worm). The Samy worm mentioned above is a textbook example of stored XSS. Samy Kamkar found that MySpace did not properly sanitize the "About Me" field on profiles. He injected a script that would send him a friend request and copy itself to the viewer's profile, as documented in the Wikipedia article on the Samy computer worm. Because MySpace at the time allowed certain HTML but mistakenly allowed `<script>` via an attribute quirk, the payload executed on every profile view. In less than a day, over a million users had the string "samy is my hero" injected into their profiles, and Samy had amassed an enormous number of friend requests, according to the same source. The worm forced MySpace to temporarily shut down and fix their filters. For this prank, Samy faced legal consequences, but he also became an example in security circles of why output sanitization is critical. The lesson: even seemingly harmless user inputs (a profile bio) can be weaponized if not sanitized. As developers, we must assume that if there is a way to inject code, someone will, a reminder to always code defensively.

7.3.3   Cross-Site Request Forgery (CSRF): Protecting Actions from Silent Attack

While XSS exploits the browser's trust in content received from a site, Cross-Site Request Forgery (CSRF) exploits a website's trust in requests from a user's browser. In a CSRF attack, the victim is an authenticated user of a website, and the attacker tricks their browser into making a request on their behalf, without their knowledge. Since the request comes with the user's cookies/session, the website thinks it is legitimate and processes it. (In essence, the browser's automatic inclusion of credentials is being abused. The forged request includes the victim's session token, so the server cannot distinguish it from a real user action, as detailed in the OWASP CSRF Prevention Cheat Sheet.) For example, if a banking site's transfer form can be triggered by a simple POST request, an attacker could craft a hidden form on a malicious site that, when the victim visits it, auto-submits a fund transfer request from the victim's account to the attacker's account. The bank will see a valid session cookie and honors the request, unless extra precautions are in place.

CSRF attack flow: The victim is logged into their bank's website. The attacker crafts a malicious request, often by hosting a fake form or image on another site, that targets the bank. When the victim's browser unwittingly sends this request to the bank (for example, the victim visits a page that triggers the form submission), the bank sees the victim's valid session token and processes the request. Thus, the attacker's forged request is executed with the victim's privileges.

To guard against CSRF, web applications must ensure that every state-changing request is intentional and verifiable. Common defenses include:

- Anti-CSRF Tokens: The application generates a random token (unique per session or per request) and includes it in HTML forms (as a hidden input) or links. When a form is submitted, the server expects this token and verifies it against the user's session. An attacker's site cannot read this token (due to same-origin policy), so they cannot reproduce it in their forged requests. This is the most widely used protection. It requires adding token generation on the server side and verification logic on form submission endpoints.

- SameSite Cookie Attribute: Modern browsers support a cookie flag `SameSite` which, when set to `Strict` or `Lax`, will prevent cookies from being sent with cross-site requests (or at least not send them for cross-origin POSTs, depending on the mode). Setting `SameSite=Lax` on session cookies significantly reduces CSRF risk for most cases, and `SameSite=Strict` virtually eliminates it (but might interfere with legitimate cross-site usage like login flows). Many frameworks now enable SameSite by default on session cookies. This is a valuable defense in depth, though older browsers may not support it.

- Referer/Origin Header Validation: The server can check the `Origin` or `Referer` header of requests to ensure they came from the same site. For instance, if you receive a POST to `/transfer`, you expect the Origin to be your domain. If it is missing or different, you can reject the request. This is not foolproof (some clients might not always send Referer), but it is a useful check to log or block obvious cross-site attempts. Modern browsers do send an Origin header on most CSRF-prone requests (like POST, DELETE).

Implementing CSRF Tokens in PHP: Let us illustrate a simple anti-CSRF token mechanism. When rendering a form, generate a token and store it in the user's session:

```php
// Before generating form:
if (!isset($_SESSION)) session_start();
$token = bin2hex(random_bytes(32));        // create a random token
$_SESSION['csrf_token'] = $token;
```

Then include it as a hidden field in the HTML form:

```html
<form method="POST" action="/change_email.php">
    <input type="hidden" name="csrf_token" value="<?= htmlspecialchars($token)?>">
    New email: <input type="email" name="email">
    <button type="submit">Update Email</button>
</form>
```

When the form is submitted to `change_email.php`, verify the token:

```php
session_start();
if (!isset($_POST['csrf_token'], $_SESSION['csrf_token']) ||
    $_POST['csrf_token'] !== $_SESSION['csrf_token'])
{
    die("ERROR: Invalid CSRF token");
}
// Token is valid --- proceed with the requested action
$newEmail = $_POST['email'];
// ... update email in database ...
```

By tying the token to the user's session (or even to that specific form submission), we ensure that an external site cannot guess it. Even if an attacker places a hidden form on their own site pointing to /change_email.php, they will not know the user's token, so the server will reject the request. One must include such tokens in all state-changing forms or requests (login, settings update, posting a message, etc.).

For AJAX or API requests, the token can be included as a header or parameter that the server validates similarly. Some developers choose to rotate the CSRF token after each use for extra safety (to act like a one-time nonce).

 It is important that the token be unpredictable (secure random) and sufficiently long. random_bytes(32) provides 256-bit randomness which is plenty. Also, avoid using the session ID itself as a CSRF token. While it may seem convenient, if an attacker can steal a session (e.g., via XSS or other means), they would then also have the CSRF token. It is better to have a separate token.

Case Study: CSRF in the Wild (GitHub 2012). In February 2012, a security researcher discovered a CSRF vulnerability on GitHub that allowed adding a new SSH key to a user's account without their knowledge. By tricking a logged-in user into visiting a malicious page, a form on that page (targeting GitHub's URL) could auto-submit and add the attacker's SSH key to the victim's account. After that, the attacker could push code as that user. GitHub had inadvertently left out CSRF protection on that form. The researcher famously demonstrated the exploit and was briefly banned (until GitHub acknowledged the issue). This incident showed that even high-profile sites can miss a crucial CSRF check. The fix was straightforward: GitHub added CSRF tokens to that form and others, preventing unauthorized submissions. The lesson is to be thorough: Every state-changing endpoint needs protection. It is easy to overlook one, especially in a large application, which is why using frameworks or middleware that automate CSRF defenses is helpful.

In summary, to prevent CSRF: use tokens, enable SameSite cookies, verify origins, and ensure that sensitive operations require an extra step (for example, re-prompting for a password or OTP for very sensitive actions can mitigate CSRF since the attacker cannot simulate that second factor). Together, these layers will make CSRF nearly impossible to pull off.

7.3.4   Insecure Deserialization in PHP: Risks and Mitigations

What it is: Insecure deserialization occurs when an application deserializes data from an untrusted source without proper validation. PHP applications often use serialize() to package complex data (objects, arrays) for storage or transmission, and unserialize() to restore that data. The danger arises if an attacker can manipulate this serialized data. Deserialization flaws can lead to remote code execution (RCE). This is one of the most severe outcomes, as highlighted in the OWASP Top Ten 2017 "Insecure Deserialization" category. In practice, this means that if an application unserializes untrusted data, an attacker might craft malicious serialized objects that, when processed, execute arbitrary code on the server. For example, in PHP, using `unserialize()` on user input can be dangerous because an attacker could supply a serialized object that, upon being unserialized, triggers a magic method call to launch a payload. Always avoid unserializing data from untrusted sources. Use safer data formats (like JSON) or implement strict validation and allow-lists for any serialized objects. The key lesson is that any feature which processes attacker-controlled data (including serialization frameworks) must be treated with extreme caution, since a single deserialization vulnerability can compromise the entire application.

How it can be exploited: Suppose a PHP web forum uses `serialize()` to remember user session data on the client-side (instead of a secure server-side session). The serialized string might encode the user's ID, username, and role. An attacker intercepts their own session cookie and sees a serialized PHP object like: `a:3:{i:0;i:132; i:1;s:7:"Mallory"; i:2;s:4:"user";}` (in PHP's serialization format). By modifying the role value from `"user"` to `"admin"` and re-encoding the string, they obtain `...s:5:"admin";...` as part of the serialized data. If the application blindly calls `unserialize()` on this cookie, it will now treat the attacker as an administrator without any authentication check, as described in Veracode's security documentation on preventing insecure deserialization attacks. More dangerously, attackers can create a serialized object of a class that the application uses and populate it with data so that when it is unserialized, a magic method in that class runs malicious commands. PHP's flexibility means any class available to the autoloader can be instantiated via unserialization, so if that class's constructor or destructor does something unsafe (or can be made to do something unsafe by given properties), the attacker's data can exploit it, as explained in OWASP's Top Ten 2017 documentation on insecure deserialization. There are public exploit frameworks (for instance, gadget chains) that leverage PHP library classes to achieve RCE through this technique. For example, as shown in Figure 7.1 in an insecure deserialization attack, the attacker supplies a forged serialized object; when the server unserializes it, the object's magic methods execute malicious code.

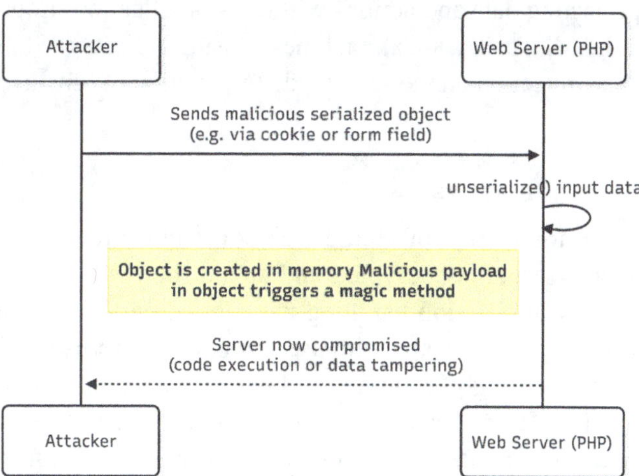

Figure 7.1: Sequence of a PHP insecure deserialization attack.

Prevention: The most effective defense is never deserialize data from an untrusted source. In practice, this means you should avoid using PHP's `unserialize()` on user-provided input altogether, as strongly recommended in both Veracode's security documentation and OWASP's guidance on preventing insecure deserialization attacks. If you need to maintain state or transmit data between requests, use safer formats like `JSON`. JSON only represents primitive types (numbers, strings, arrays) and not PHP objects, which greatly limits the risk because decoding JSON will not invoke unpredictable behaviors. Whenever possible, keep session or user data on the server side (e.g., in `$_SESSION` or a database) rather than trusting the client.

If you must use PHP serialization (for example, exchanging objects between trusted services), take extra precautions: use a cryptographic signature or MAC to ensure the serialized data has not been tampered with. For instance, you could `hash_hmac()` the serialized string with a secret key and verify the HMAC before unserializing, so that an attacker cannot supply an arbitrary object without detection. PHP 7+ provides an option to restrict allowed classes during unserialization: `unserialize($data, ["allowed_classes" => [...] ])`. Use this to whitelist classes or to forbid object deserialization entirely (`allowed_classes => false` will prevent any object from being instantiated, yielding an `__PHP_Incomplete_Class` instead, as explained in security researcher Vickie Li's detailed analysis of PHP's unserialize function). This way, even if an attacker injects a serialized object of an unexpected class, it will not be unserialized into a live object. Additionally, design your classes defensively: avoid dangerous operations in `__wakeup()` or `__destruct()` that could be abused. Finally, treat any deserialization operation as a potential code execution sink and place it in a low-privilege context (if possible) and log failures. If `unserialize` throws an error or you catch an inconsistent object state, consider it a possible attack and respond or alert accordingly, as recommended in OWASP's guidance on preventing insecure deserialization. In summary, prefer not to use PHP serialization for user data. Use JSON or other safe data formats and robustly validate any data before processing. By eliminating unsafe deserialization, you close a door that could lead straight to server takeover.

7.4   Secure Communication: HTTPS and Data Protection

So far, we have focused on protecting data and actions within the application. Equally important is protecting data in transit and at rest. In a LAMP stack context, that means using HTTPS (SSL/TLS) for all web traffic and following best practices for data protection on the server side (encryption of sensitive data, secure configuration, etc.).

7.4.1   HTTPS: Encrypting Data in Transit

HTTPS (HTTP over TLS) is the foundation of secure web communication. It ensures that data exchanged between the client (browser) and server is encrypted and cannot be read or modified by eavesdroppers or man-in-the-middle attackers. Any application handling passwords, personal information, financial data, or session cookies (which is virtually every web app with user accounts) must use HTTPS to be secure. Even for primarily public content, HTTPS is strongly recommended to protect the integrity of data and user privacy.

To implement HTTPS for a LAMP application, you will need an SSL/TLS certificate for your domain and configure your web server (Apache) to use it. Services like Let's Encrypt provide free certificates, making it easy to deploy HTTPS. In Apache, this involves enabling modules like `mod_ssl` and configuring a `<VirtualHost *:443>` with the certificate files. Once set up, you should redirect all HTTP traffic to HTTPS:

Example (.htaccess or Apache config redirect to HTTPS):

```
1  <If "%{HTTPS} == 'off'">
2    Redirect permanent "/" "https://YOURDOMAIN.com/"
3  </If>
```

Or in PHP, as a fallback, you could do:

```php
1  // Force HTTPS in PHP (early in execution)
2  if(empty($_SERVER['HTTPS']) || $_SERVER['HTTPS'] === "off")
3  {
4      $redirect = "https://" . $_SERVER['HTTP_HOST'] . $_SERVER['REQUEST_URI'];
5      header("Location: $redirect", true, 301);
6      exit();
7  }
```

This ensures users automatically switch to the secure URL.

When using HTTPS, mark cookies as Secure (as shown earlier) so they are not sent if a user accidentally goes to the HTTP version. Also consider using HTTP Strict Transport Security (HSTS) by sending an appropriate header:

```php
1  header("Strict-Transport-Security: max-age=31536000; includeSubDomains");
```

This tells browsers to remember to only use HTTPS for your site for the next year, preventing even manual `http://` attempts. Warning: Only enable HSTS when you are confident your site is fully on HTTPS, since it can lock out HTTP.

By deploying HTTPS, you defeat a host of network-based attacks: sniffing, tampering, and hijacking (like Firesheep). It is worth noting that since the Let's Encrypt initiative and others, virtually all major websites have transitioned to always-on HTTPS. Users have come to expect the padlock icon in their browser; not having it undermines user trust as well.

Beyond just "HTTPS or not," consider the quality of your TLS configuration: disable old, insecure protocols (SSLv3, TLS 1.0) and ciphers (like RC4, or known-weak ciphers) to prevent downgrade or cryptographic attacks. Tools like SSL Labs can test your site. Modern server configurations should use TLS 1.2+ and strong cipher suites, providing Perfect Forward Secrecy. This ensures that even if your server's key is compromised in the future, past traffic remains encrypted.

7.4.2 Data Encryption and Protection at Rest

On the server side, consider what happens if an attacker breaches your database or file system. We already covered password hashing for user passwords. For other sensitive data (social security numbers, medical information, credit card numbers), you should consider additional encryption at rest. For example, even if your database is stolen, you do not want raw credit card numbers to be readable. Common practices:

- Database encryption: Use encryption functions to encrypt sensitive fields before storing, and decrypt on access (with keys stored securely). For instance, MySQL offers `AES_ENCRYPT`/`AES_DECRYPT` functions. In PHP, you can use the OpenSSL library functions (e.g., `openssl_encrypt`). The key must be stored outside the database (and ideally not directly in the webroot code either, and sometimes a separate config or an environment variable is used). Encrypting at rest adds a layer of defense if backups or dumps are accessed. Note that database-level encryption can be complex; an alternative is full-disk encryption on the DB server, but that protects mainly against physical theft, not an attacker who has breached an active system.
- File system security: If your app allows file uploads, ensure that uploaded files (which might contain private data) are stored in non-public directories (outside the web root) and with proper access controls. Also sanitize file names and types to prevent malicious files (though that is more about protecting the server from a different kind of attack, like storing a PHP file that could be executed, discussed in Section 7.6). For any sensitive files generated by the app (reports, exports, etc.), apply least privilege: directories should have minimal access, and if possible, generate files with unique, unpredictable names or IDs (so they cannot be guessed).
- Backups and logs: Treat backups with the same security as the live data. Many breaches occur via old database backups left on a server. Logs can also contain sensitive info (like user IDs, or if you mistakenly logged passwords or other protected data which you should avoid). Secure or scrub logs as needed, and do not log sensitive personal data unnecessarily. If you must retain such logs (for compliance or debugging), protect them with access controls and encryption where feasible.
- Server and OS hardening: Since LAMP involves Linux and Apache, make sure the server OS is hardened. Use a firewall to limit access to only needed ports (80/443 for web, maybe 22 for SSH). Keep Linux packages updated (to fix vulnerabilities in Apache/PHP/MySQL). Use strong credentials for database access and never expose the database directly to the public internet if it can be avoided (it should listen on localhost or a private network). These system-level concerns are a bit beyond application code, but a secure app is only as secure as the environment it runs in. For example, no amount of PHP code security will save you if your Apache configuration allows directory traversal or your Linux user accounts have default passwords.
- Configuration secrets: Your PHP application might need to store protected data like database passwords, API keys, etc. Never commit these to public code or share them. Use configuration files with appropriate permissions (e.g., `chmod 600` so only the web server user can read them) or environment variables. You may also encrypt configuration values if they need to be stored in version control, but that requires a decryption step at runtime (which itself needs a key). The simpler approach: keep them in a file like `config.php` outside the web root (so it cannot be downloaded) and include it. Example:

```php
// in /var/www/html/index.php
include('/var/www/config/config.php'); // contains $db_password, etc.
```

If someone tries to request config.php via a browser, they cannot since it is not served by Apache from outside web root.
- Error Handling: Leaking detailed error messages can aid attackers. In development, you might display

MySQL or PHP errors, but in production, set `display_errors = Off` and log errors to a secure file instead. Attackers can trigger errors intentionally to glean information (stack traces, SQL fragments, file paths). Make sure your users see only generic error messages (e.g., "An error occurred, please try again later.") while you log the specifics for your debugging. This principle is called fail-safe: do not reveal internal workings on failure.

- Content and Protocol Security: Beyond HTTPS, ensure you are using secure protocols for any third-party integration. For example, if your PHP code calls an external API, use TLS to connect to it. If you have to store files (like user profile pictures), consider using cloud storage with proper access rules rather than serving them from an open directory.

Finally, always have a mindset of defense in depth. Each layer (the network, the server, the application, and the database) should have its own safeguards. Even if one layer is breached, the others provide additional protection. For instance, an attacker who somehow executes code via a PHP vulnerability might still be contained by file system permissions or SELinux rules; a stolen database dump might be useless if key data is encrypted; an XSS vulnerability might be mitigated by an active Content Security Policy.

7.5 Secure File Upload and MIME-Type Handling

Web applications often allow users to upload files, whether it is profile pictures, document attachments, or other media. File uploads introduce significant security risks if not handled properly. An unrestricted file upload vulnerability can lead to remote code execution, malware distribution, or attacks on other users. In this section, we cover how to securely handle file uploads, including validating file types (MIME types), storing files safely, and preventing common pitfalls.

The Dangers of Unrestricted File Uploads: If an attacker can upload an arbitrary file to your server, they may try to upload a web shell (a malicious script) and then execute it. For example, uploading a `.php` file with malicious code and somehow causing the server to interpret it could give full control to the attacker. Even if code execution is not possible, an attacker might upload huge files to fill disk space (denial of service), upload known viruses or malware (to infect other users who download them), or upload HTML/JS files that could perform XSS or phishing if served to others. In short, file uploads can serve as a trojan horse into your system if not strictly controlled.

File Type Validation: Always restrict which file types are allowed. Use a whitelist of acceptable file extensions (e.g., only `.jpg, .png, .gif` for images). But do not rely solely on the file extension, as it is trivial for an attacker to rename `evil.php` to `evil.jpg`. Instead, verify the file's content. You can check the MIME type reported by the browser (in the HTTP upload request) and more reliably, inspect the file's content on the server side. PHP's `finfo_file` or `mime_content_type` can help determine the file's real type by examining magic bytes. For images, you might try to create an image resource from the file (e.g., using GD library or ImageMagick); if it fails, the file is not a valid image. Reject any file that does not match the expected types. Also be cautious of files with multiple extensions (e.g., `shell.php.jpg`); some server configurations might only look at the last extension, others might not. It is best to strip or reject filenames containing multiple dots or unusual characters.

File Name Sanitation: Do not use the original filename supplied by the user when saving the file on the server. Attackers might include path traversal sequences (e.g., `../../etc/passwd`) in filenames to try to break out of the upload directory. Even if PHP's filesystem functions prevent traversal in upload handling, it is wise to

normalize names. A common approach is to ignore the user-provided filename and generate a random file name
or use a safe identifier (like the user's ID plus a timestamp). If you do keep original names (for user-friendliness),
sanitize them: remove any directory paths, remove dangerous characters (null bytes, quotes, backslashes, etc.),
and perhaps allow only alphanumeric and a dot. For example:

```php
$origName = $_FILES['upload']['name'];
$origName = basename($origName);                      // strip directory paths
$safeName = preg_replace("/[^A-Za-z0-9\.\-\_]/", "_", $origName); // replace unsafe chars
```

Even with this, consider storing with a unique prefix or in a location controlled by your application logic
(not directly accessible by user input as path).

Storage Location and Access Control: Store uploaded files in a directory that is not web-accessible or at
least not executable. The best practice is to put uploads in a folder outside the web root, so that no one can
access them by knowing a URL. If that is not feasible, configure the server such that this upload directory does
not execute scripts. For Apache, one might use an `.htaccess` or configuration to disable PHP execution in the
upload folder, for example:

```
# In the uploads directory .htaccess:
php_flag engine off
```

Or set the permissions such that the web server can read/write the files but will not run them as code. If the
uploads need to be accessible to users (like images), one approach is to store them outside web root and create a
PHP script to fetch and serve them (ensuring the user is authorized to get that file). This way, the PHP script can
control the output and set appropriate headers, and no direct URL can execute a file. Another approach is to use
a subdomain or separate static file server for user content, with strict MIME types.

MIME-Type Handling and Response Headers: When serving user-uploaded files, be cautious with the
content type. You do not want a user to upload an HTML file and have it served as HTML, because it could
contain malicious JS (XSS) executed in your domain context. Always set the `Content-Type` header based on
the actual file type. Additionally, for untrusted file types, consider forcing a download. For example, if you
allow `.pdf` or `.docx` uploads, you might serve them with a header `Content-Disposition: attachment` so
the browser does not try to render them inline (where they might run exploits in plugin viewers). Browsers
sometimes perform MIME sniffing. To avoid this send the header `X-Content-Type-Options: nosniff`
(covered in Section 7.7). This prevents the browser from interpreting a file as something else (for instance, an
attacker uploads a file with a `.jpg` extension but content of HTML; without `nosniff`, some browsers might
render it as HTML if opened directly).

Limit File Size and Scan Content: Enforce a maximum file size (both client-side and server-side). PHP has
`upload_max_filesize` and `post_max_size` settings; set them to reasonable values for your use case (and be
mindful of memory limits). This prevents attackers from uploading gigantic files to overwhelm storage. If your
application expects images of maybe up to 5 MB, there is no reason to accept a 500 MB upload. You can also

implement image dimension checks (if user claims it is an image but with 10000x10000 pixels, maybe reject or downscale). For file content, especially in enterprise contexts, consider integrating a virus/malware scan. There are open-source scanners (like ClamAV) that can be invoked on uploaded files to detect known malware. While this is more relevant if users will download each other's files (to prevent your service from spreading viruses), it can also detect if someone uploaded a known webshell script (signatures exist for common webshell code).

Secure File Upload Handling (PHP) Example:

```php
<?php
if(!empty($_FILES['upload']))
{
    $file = $_FILES['upload'];
    if($file['error'] !== UPLOAD_ERR_OK)
    {
        die("Upload failed with error code " . $file['error']);
    }
    // Validate file size (e.g., <= 2MB)
    if($file['size'] > 2*1024*1024)
    {
        die("File too large.");
    }
    // Validate MIME type
    $finfo = new finfo(FILEINFO_MIME_TYPE);
    $mime = $finfo->file($file['tmp_name']);
    $allowed = ['image/jpeg'=>'jpg', 'image/png'=>'png', 'image/gif'=>'gif'];
    if(!isset($allowed[$mime]))
    {
        die("Invalid file type.");
    }
    // Sanitize and generate target filename
    $ext = $allowed[$mime];
    $safeName = bin2hex(random_bytes(8)) . ".$ext";
    $destination = "/var/www/uploads/$safeName";
    // Move the file to the target directory
    if(!move_uploaded_file($file['tmp_name'], $destination))
    {
        die("Failed to save file.");
    }
    echo "File uploaded successfully.";
}
?>
```

In this example, we check for upload errors, enforce a size limit, verify the MIME type using `finfo_file` and allow only JPEG, PNG, or GIF. We then generate a random 16-character hex name (to avoid conflicts and guessing) with the appropriate extension, and move the file. The uploads directory `/var/www/uploads` should be configured as non-executable. If someone tries to upload `evil.php` renamed as `evil.jpg`, the MIME check will likely catch that it is not an actual image and reject it. Even if it slipped through, it would be saved as a random `.jpg` file in an uploads folder that does not execute PHP. And when serving it, one should send `Content-Type: image/jpeg` so a browser would not execute it as PHP; at worst it might just show broken image or text. This layered approach (validation, storage, serving) dramatically reduces risk.

Path Traversal and Other Tricks: Attackers might also try to use special characters in filenames to break your logic. Always use safe file APIs, for example avoiding directly concatenating untrusted input into file paths. In PHP, `basename()` helps remove directories, but be cautious of multibyte encodings or alternate directory separators. Ensure the final path is within your intended upload directory (one can double-check with `realpath` and ensuring it starts with your upload base path). By generating our own file name as above, we bypass most of these issues.

Case Study: Web Shell Upload in the Wild. A real example of file upload abuse occurred in a job recruitment site for Starbucks China (disclosed via a bug bounty). The site allowed applicants to upload their resumes, but it did not properly validate file type. An attacker uploaded an `.aspx` (ASP.NET) web shell script disguised as a resume. The server saved it in a web-accessible directory. The attacker then accessed the URL to that file, and since the server executed `.aspx` files, the web shell ran on the server, giving the attacker remote commands execution. They effectively owned the server via a simple file upload. This could have been prevented by disallowing `.aspx` uploads (or any non-PDF in that context), storing files outside the web root, and not executing user files. Many similar incidents have happened with PHP apps, including an outdated image upload plugin in WordPress,that allowed `.php` uploads, which were then executed, resulting in a compromised site. Lesson: Never assume users will only upload benign files. Validate and control everything about uploaded files including name, type, size, storage, and delivery.

In summary, to handle file uploads safely: accept only expected formats, validate the file content, sanitize names, store files in a non-executable location, set correct MIME types when serving, and limit size. And if file uploads are not needed, simply disable them to eliminate the risk entirely.

7.6   HTTP Security Headers

Besides implementing secure behaviors in your application code, you can also instruct browsers to enforce security by using HTTP security headers. These are special response headers that tell the browser to apply additional security policies when handling your web pages. Properly configured, they can prevent certain attacks or reduce their impact. Here are some important HTTP security headers and their uses:

- Strict-Transport-Security (HSTS): This header (as seen earlier) forces browsers to use HTTPS for all requests to your site. For example: `Strict-Transport-Security: max-age=31536000; includeSubDomains`. When a browser sees this, it will remember for one year to never use `http://` for your domain (including all subdomains). HSTS protects users from even accidentally making an HTTP request (which could be hijacked). It also thwarts SSL-stripping attacks (where an attacker downgrades a victim's connection to HTTP). Only enable HSTS after your site is fully HTTPS, and be careful with the preload directive (used to pre-load HSTS in browsers) that involves submitting your domain to a list and can be hard to undo. HSTS is a simple and very powerful header to reinforce always-on encryption.

- Content-Security-Policy (CSP): CSP is one of the most effective countermeasures against XSS and other injection attacks. It allows you to create a whitelist of content sources that the browser should accept. For example, a CSP header might be: `Content-Security-Policy: default-src 'self'; script-src 'self' https://apis.google.com; object-src 'none'; frame-ancestors 'none';`. This policy would allow content (by default) only from your own domain, scripts only from your domain and Google APIs, disallow all plugins/objects, and prevent your site from being framed. By limiting sources of scripts, styles, images, etc., CSP can prevent an injected malicious script from loading (because it is not from an allowed domain). You can also use CSP to disallow inline JavaScript (`'unsafe-inline'`) and eval-like functions (`'unsafe-eval'`). Implementing CSP can be complex on an existing site, as it may require changes to how you include resources. It often involves adding nonces or hashes for inline scripts you want to keep. Start with a report-only mode to see what would be blocked. While not trivial, a strict CSP can practically eliminate XSS (especially reflected and DOM XSS) by providing an external enforcement layer. Even in cases where XSS vulnerabilities exist, CSP can mitigate impact. However, CSP is not a set-and-forget; it must be maintained as your content changes.
- X-Frame-Options: This older header controls whether your pages can be loaded in an iframe on other sites (clickjacking protection). Its value can be `DENY` (disallow all framing), `SAMEORIGIN` (allow only if the parent page is from the same site), or `ALLOW-FROM <origin>` (allow a specific domain). For example: `X-Frame-Options: SAMEORIGIN`. This prevents attackers from embedding your site in a hidden frame and tricking users into clicking (e.g., a transparent overlay over a bank's site to capture clicks). Note: CSP's `frame-ancestors` directive supersedes this header in modern browsers, but X-Frame-Options is still widely used for simplicity.
- X-Content-Type-Options: Use `X-Content-Type-Options: nosniff`. This tells browsers not to MIME-sniff responses away from the declared Content-Type. In other words, if you send a file with `Content-Type: text/plain`, and it contains something that looks like HTML/JS, the browser should not try to execute it as such. This header prevents certain attacks where the browser guesses the content type and ends up executing untrusted content. It is especially important when serving user-uploaded content; combined with correct Content-Type headers, `nosniff` makes sure an image is treated as an image, a CSV as just text, etc.
- Referrer-Policy: This header controls what information is sent in the Referer header when navigating from your site elsewhere. It is about privacy and can indirectly have security benefits (e.g., not leaking sensitive URL params). For instance, `Referrer-Policy: no-referrer` means your pages will not send a Referer header at all. `strict-origin-when-cross-origin` (a common default) means full URL sent on same-site requests, but only origin on cross-site, and nothing if downgrading from HTTPS to HTTP. While not directly preventing attacks, a tight referrer policy can prevent leaking session IDs or query strings to third-party sites.
- Permissions-Policy (formerly Feature-Policy): This header lets you disable or enable certain browser features in the context of your site. For example, you can prevent your pages from using camera or microphone, or disable geolocation, payment request API, etc., if your site does not need them. A typical usage: `Permissions-Policy: camera=(), microphone=(), geolocation=(self)`. This does not address common web attacks, but it hardens the browser environment by limiting features that could be abused or that you simply do not need (reducing potential new vectors as browsers add capabilities).

- X-XSS-Protection: This header was used to control older browser XSS filters (e.g., in IE). One might set `X-XSS-Protection: 1; mode=block` or in some cases disable it with `0` if it conflicted with legitimate code. However, this header is now deprecated in modern browsers, as makers have moved toward CSP as a more comprehensive solution. Some security guidance actually suggests disabling it (setting `X-XSS-Protection: 0`) because in rare cases the old filter could introduce new problems. In summary, you generally do not need this header anymore, especially if you have a strong Content Security Policy. It is mentioned here for completeness.
- Cross-Origin Resource Sharing (CORS): CORS headers (such as `Access-Control-Allow-Origin` and related settings) specify which external origins are permitted to make requests to your server and read the responses. While CORS is primarily a browser mechanism for controlled resource sharing (and not a direct defense against attacks like XSS or SQL injection), a misconfigured CORS policy can become a serious vulnerability. For example, allowing all origins (`Access-Control-Allow-Origin:*`), especially in combination with allowing credentials, would let any website execute requests and read responses from your site as if it were the legitimate user. To prevent such abuse, configure CORS with the least permissive settings necessary. Only allow specific trusted origins to access your APIs, and avoid allowing credentials (cookies, auth headers) in cross-origin requests unless absolutely needed and restricted. In short, a careful CORS configuration ensures that malicious third-party sites cannot illicitly invoke privileged operations or steal sensitive data via a logged-in user's browser. (Remember, CORS is enforced by browsers but you should still implement proper server-side authorization for all requests, regardless of origin.)

7.6.1   Cross-Origin Resource Sharing (CORS): Safe Configuration

Modern web applications often provide APIs or resources that might be accessed from scripts on a different origin (domain). Cross-Origin Resource Sharing (CORS) is the mechanism that controls such access. By default, a web browser's same-origin policy prevents web pages from one origin from reading responses from a different origin. CORS works through special HTTP headers (e.g., `Access-Control-Allow-Origin`) that your server sends to tell browsers which origins are permitted to receive the response. While CORS is not an attack in itself, misconfiguring CORS can introduce serious vulnerabilities. A overly permissive CORS policy might allow untrusted websites to interact with your backend as if they were your own front-end. For instance, if your API sets `Access-Control-Allow-Origin: *` (allow any origin) on a sensitive endpoint, any malicious website can execute JavaScript in a victim's browser to call your API and read the results. This could expose user data or perform actions on behalf of an authenticated user, effectively a form of cross-site request hijacking.

How CORS works: When a browser makes a cross-origin request (using XHR/fetch or an HTML form), it includes an `Origin` header (the domain of the calling page). The server can respond with `Access-Control-Allow-Origin` to either echo back that origin or specify a list of allowed origins. The browser will only deliver the response to the calling script if the origin is allowed. Servers can also send additional headers like `Access-Control-Allow-Credentials: true` (to allow cookies/auth headers to be sent and received) and `Access-Control-Allow-Methods`/`Allow-Headers` (to whitelist which HTTP methods and request headers are permitted). CORS pre-flight requests (HTTP OPTIONS) are used for complex requests to check permissions. From a security standpoint, CORS is essentially a safety belt in the browser but it does not bypass authentication or other controls on the server; it only controls whether the calling frontend is allowed to receive the response.

If CORS is wide open, a malicious script can read the response of a cross-site request that it triggers. If CORS is correctly restricted, that script can still cause the request to be sent (the server will process it, possibly even perform a state-changing action if the user is logged in), but the browser will block the script from seeing the response. Thus, a lax CORS policy can turn what would have been a blind CSRF attack into an attack that exposes data to the attacker's site.

Security concerns: A common mistake is to set `Access-Control-Allow-Origin: *` indiscriminately. Using the wildcard `*` on protected resources is dangerous, as noted by security experts at Sucuri and SecureLayer7. It tells the browser to allow any site to make requests and read responses, effectively disabling the same-origin policy for those resources. An attacker can create a malicious web page, lure an authenticated user to visit it, and via JavaScript on that page call the vulnerable API endpoints. Because the user's browser includes their session cookie or token in the request, and because the API's CORS policy allows `*`, the browser will let the malicious script receive the response. The attacker's script can then steal the data (credit card info, personal details, etc.) and send it to the attacker. In one real-world scenario, attackers exploiting Magento shops set up malicious domains that exfiltrated customer data via wildcard CORS allowances. The store's own backend happily responded to the attacker's domain, as the CORS policy allowed all origins, enabling the theft of sensitive info. In short, CORS misconfiguration can lead to data leaks and abuse of user trust. It is categorized as a security misconfiguration issue in OWASP's Top 10 (part of "Security Misconfiguration") and is frequently reported in penetration tests of web APIs.

Best practices for CORS: Never set `Access-Control-Allow-Origin` to `*` for requests that require credentials or involve private data, as advised by security experts at SecureLayer7. Instead, explicitly specify the trusted origin(s) that need access. For example, if your web app is served from `https://myapp.example.com` and it needs to call an API at `api.example.com`, configure the API to allow only `https://myapp.example.com` as the origin. You can allow multiple specific origins by dynamically echoing back the `Origin` header if it is in your approved list (many server frameworks can do this). Always verify that the `Origin` header matches exactly an allowed domain and be cautious with partial matches or regex patterns. (A common mistake is using a permissive regex that unintentionally matches more domains than intended; e.g., the pattern `"^ https://mail.example.com$"` could be abused by an origin like `https://mailxexample.com` due to the way regex dot `.` can match characters, as pointed out in SecureLayer7's analysis of CORS vulnerabilities.) Allow credentials only when necessary: Setting `Access-Control-Allow-Credentials: true` allows cookies/token to be sent, but it also requires a specific origin (browsers will ignore `*` if credentials flag is true). If you need credentialed requests, double-check that `Access-Control-Allow-Origin` is not `*` in those responses. Furthermore, limit the HTTP methods and headers to only those needed: for instance, if your API should only be accessed with GET and POST, your CORS header should reflect that (`Access-Control-Allow-Methods: GET, POST`). Similarly, do not blindly allow all headers; specify only the ones your clients actually use (`Access-Control-Allow-Headers`). Tightening these reduces the abuse surface. For example, there is rarely a reason to allow PUT or DELETE from arbitrary origins unless your API explicitly needs those for cross-site use, as explained in Sucuri's guide on CORS.

On Apache, you can configure CORS in the server configuration or `.htaccess` using the `Header set Access-Control-Allow-Origin "https://myapp.example.com"` directive (and similarly for other CORS headers). In PHP, you can dynamically set CORS headers by detecting `$_SERVER['HTTP_ORIGIN']` and responding with the appropriate `Access-Control-Allow-*` headers via the `header()` function before output. However, be very careful: never reflect an Origin that you do not trust. A safe pattern is to maintain a list of allowed origins (domains) in a config, check if `$_SERVER['HTTP_ORIGIN']` is in that list, and if so, echo it; otherwise, do not set any CORS headers (or explicitly deny).

Ultimately, CORS should be as restrictive as possible. If your API is purely private (only called from your own front-end on the same domain), you might not need CORS at all. If it is used by known partners or services, limit it to those origins. There are tools like Mozilla Observatory and securityheaders.com that will flag overly permissive CORS settings in their scans, similar to how they check other HTTP headers. Always test your CORS configuration: ensure that a random site cannot fetch sensitive data from your application.

Figure 7.2 illustrates an attack due to permissive CORS. A malicious site's script uses the victim's credentials to call a vulnerable API. Because the API allowed `Access-Control-Allow-Origin: *`, the browser lets the evil script read the response, which is then sent to the attacker.

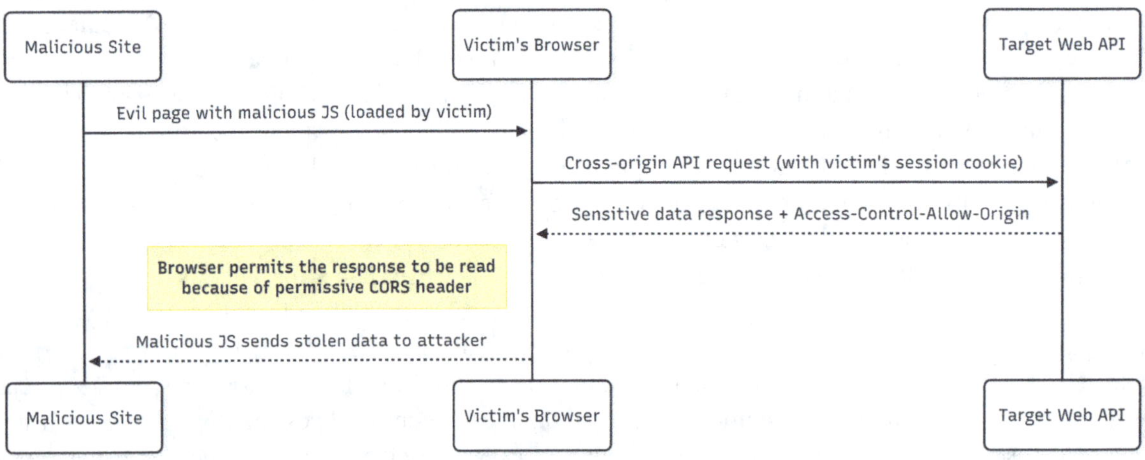

Figure 7.2: CORS misconfiguration scenario.

In summary, CORS is a powerful browser feature that must be configured with caution. To keep your PHP application safe, allow only specific origins that truly need access, avoid wildcards for anything sensitive, and regularly review CORS settings as your application evolves. By following the principle of least privilege for cross-origin access, you prevent unauthorized third-party sites from snooping on your APIs. CORS should work for you (enabling legitimate integrations) without opening doors to attackers.

Implementing Security Headers: In PHP, you send these headers via the `header()` function (before any output). For example:

```
header("Content-Security-Policy: default-src 'self'; frame-ancestors 'none';");
header("X-Frame-Options: DENY");
header("X-Content-Type-Options: nosniff");
header("Referrer-Policy: strict-origin-when-cross-origin");
```

You might also configure them at the web server level (Apache config or `.htaccess` using `Header set X-Frame-Options "DENY"`, etc.). Many frameworks and platforms provide easier ways or defaults for these. It is a good practice to review your site with tools like Mozilla Observatory or securityheaders.com to see if these headers are set and properly configured.

By using HTTP security headers, you add another layer of defense. They instruct the browser to behave more securely with your content. They cannot fix vulnerabilities in your code, but they can lessen the impact or likelihood of certain exploits. For instance, even if you had an XSS bug, a properly set CSP might block the malicious script; if you forget to enforce HTTPS, HSTS can cover you after first contact.

Combine headers for best effect: e.g., HSTS + Secure cookies + CSP + X-Frame-Options + Nosniff + Referrer-Policy. There is essentially no downside to most of these (except needing to ensure CSP does not break your site). Attackers will have a much harder time if the browser itself is helping police the boundaries.

7.7   Logging, Monitoring, and Incident Response

Up to now, we have focused on preventative measures, but detecting and responding to security incidents is just as critical. Even with all precautions, breaches or attacks may happen. Proper logging and monitoring can help you catch suspicious behavior early, and a solid incident response plan can mitigate damage. In this section, we outline how to log security-relevant events, monitor them, and what steps to take when an incident occurs.

Importance of Logging: At minimum, your application (and the web server, database, etc.) should log key events and errors. From a security perspective, things to log include: login attempts (especially failures), password reset requests, significant actions (account changes, data exports, admin actions), and any unexpected errors or input validation failures. These logs become invaluable for forensic analysis if something goes wrong. For example, if an account was compromised, the logs might show a brute-force login attempt or a login from an unusual IP. If data was accessed or altered, logs might pinpoint when and how. Be sure to include timestamps, user identifiers, source IPs, and event details. However, avoid logging sensitive data like passwords or full credit card numbers. If an attacker gets your logs, they should not find a treasure trove of plaintext secrets. Also be mindful of privacy; log what you need, but secure the logs.

Monitoring and Alerting: Logging is passive if no one looks at the logs. Implement monitoring: this could be as simple as setting up alerts for certain conditions, or as complex as a Security Information and Event Management (SIEM) system aggregating and analyzing logs. For a small app, you might at least send an email to admins on critical events (e.g., multiple failed logins for an account, indicating a brute force attempt, or an unexpected spike in 500 error responses indicating a possible attack). Many breaches go unnoticed for months because organizations were not effectively monitoring. In fact, studies have shown the average time to detect a breach is over 200 days, and often it is an external party (like law enforcement or a security researcher) that alerts the victim, not their own systems, as noted in OWASP's 2017 documentation on insufficient logging and monitoring. Do not let that be you; set up basic intrusion detection if possible. For web apps, consider using a Web Application Firewall (WAF) in logging mode or an IDS that watches traffic patterns. If using cloud services, take advantage of monitoring tools (AWS CloudWatch, etc.). At the very least, periodically review your authentication logs and error logs. Unusual patterns such as a spike in traffic at odd hours, repeated strange input patterns (could indicate someone probing for SQLi or XSS), or users logging in from new countries should be investigated.

Intrusion Detection Example: Suppose your PHP app writes to an `audit.log` file whenever an admin function is used. If you suddenly see in the logs that an admin password was changed or a new admin account was created and you (the real admin) did not do it, that is a big red flag that someone exploited something (like the GitHub CSRF or an XSS that stole admin session). By catching it soon (maybe your monitoring triggers an alert on "new admin account creation"), you can respond. For example, lock down the system, revert the change, force logouts, etc., before the attacker does more.

Incident Response Plan: Despite best efforts, assume a breach can occur and have a plan. Key steps in incident response include:

1. Identification: Determine if an incident occurred. This comes from monitoring/alerts or external notification. It might be a confirmed hack or just suspicious activity that needs checking.

2. Containment: If a breach is ongoing, you need to stop the bleeding. This could mean taking the site offline temporarily, disabling certain functionality, or applying quick patches. For example, if you discover an attacker's webshell on your server, immediately block access (change permissions or remove the file, and probably take the server off the network until cleaned). If user accounts are being stolen, maybe disable login or reset all sessions.

3. Eradication: Find the root cause and eliminate it. Patch the vulnerable code or update the software that was exploited. Remove any malware or backdoors the attacker may have left. This step often involves analysis such as checking logs to see what the attacker did, scanning for modified files or new accounts. Sometimes you may need to rebuild servers from scratch if you cannot fully trust the system integrity.

4. Recovery: Restore systems to normal operation, making sure the vulnerabilities are fixed. This might involve restoring from backups (if data was corrupted or wiped) or applying new configuration (e.g., stricter firewall rules). Monitor closely after recovery for any sign the attacker returns or the issue persists.

5. Notification: Depending on the incident, you may have legal obligations to notify users or authorities (especially if personal data was compromised). For instance, data breach laws often require notifying affected individuals within a certain timeframe. Even if not legally required, transparency with users (in a responsible way) is usually wise. Users can take their own measures (change passwords, etc.) if informed. In the 2016 Uber breach example, Uber chose to hide the incident for a year, which led to hefty fines and reputational damage when it eventually came out. Conversely, when GitHub had incidents, they were quick to write post-mortems explaining what happened and how it was fixed.

6. Lessons Learned: After the dust settles, do a retrospective. How did the attack happen? What can be improved to prevent it in future? This might lead to new coding guidelines, better testing (maybe add security tests or code review steps focusing on security), improved monitoring, or changes in policies (like enforcing MFA or stricter password rules if it was a credential issue).

Case in Point: The Capital One breach described earlier went undetected for months until an external tip. A robust monitoring system might have noticed unusual flows (why is a WAF server listing S3 buckets?). Furthermore, Capital One's incident response included cooperating with law enforcement; indeed, the FBI arrested the perpetrator (a former AWS employee) soon after discovery. In contrast, the Target 2013 breach triggered internal alerts (their security software actually caught the malware activity), but those alerts were ignored by the security team, leading to a full-blown compromise of 40 million credit cards. Target's lesson was to better train and staff their monitoring team to heed critical warnings.

Continuous Monitoring: Web security is not a "set it and forget it" thing. Keep an eye on your systems continuously. There are services that can monitor your site from outside (for defacement, uptime, or even attack surface changes). On the inside, ensure all logins, especially to admin accounts, are tracked. It is useful to log not just failures but successes for admin auth, so you know if an admin account logged in at an odd time. Automated anomaly detection (using AI or simpler threshold-based alerts) can pick up things humans might miss.

Protecting Logs: Note that logs themselves become a target for attackers once they are in. Many attackers will try to erase or tamper with logs to hide their tracks. Use append-only logging if possible, or send logs to a remote server or write-once media. That way an attacker cannot easily cover their trail. Also ensure proper access control: only authorized admins should be able to read sensitive logs, because logs could contain user data or clues about your system.

Data Backup and Recovery: Part of incident response is being able to recover if data is destroyed (whether by malicious act or accident). Regular backups, stored securely off-site, are essential. Test your backups occasionally to ensure you can restore when needed. Ransomware (malware that encrypts your data and demands ransom) is an increasing threat; good backups can turn a potential catastrophe into a simple restore operation (with some downtime as the main cost).

In summary, logging and monitoring are your eyes on the system. Make sure they are open and paying attention. Incident response is your fire drill that needs to be in place so that when something goes wrong, you know how to react calmly and effectively. The combination of proactive security measures we discussed and reactive measures in this section forms a complete security posture.

7.8   Secure Deployment and CI/CD Considerations

Writing secure code is vital, but how you deploy that code and manage your development pipeline also affects your application's security. Modern development often uses Continuous Integration and Continuous Deployment (CI/CD) pipelines, automated testing, and infrastructure as code. Missteps here can introduce vulnerabilities or expose your application to compromise before it is even live. In this section, we address securing the deployment process and CI/CD pipeline.

Separate Environments and Credentials: Maintain separate environments for development, testing, and production. Each should have its own database and credentials. Never use real customer data in dev/test; use anonymized or fake data. This way, if a non-production environment is compromised, it does not expose actual sensitive information. Also, development credentials (which might be shared more broadly or checked into code accidentally) should not grant access to production systems. For instance, your app might have a local dev config with `DB_USER=appuser_test` which only has privileges on a test DB, not the real one.

Protect Secrets in the Pipeline: A CI/CD pipeline often needs access to secrets (database passwords, API keys, etc.) to deploy or run tests. Use secure secret management such as most CI platforms(Jenkins, GitHub Actions, GitLab CI, etc.) allow you to store protected data securely and inject them as environment variables. Do not hardcode secrets in your pipeline scripts or config files in the repo. We saw in the Uber case that secrets in code can be disastrous. Many breaches (including some in 2021) occurred because developers accidentally committed API keys or credentials to public GitHub repositories, as reported by The Register in their coverage of the Uber breach. Use tools that scan commits for secrets (there are automated scanners that can catch AWS keys or other patterns in commits). If a secret does leak, assume it is compromised and rotate it (generate a new one) immediately.

Least Privilege for CI/CD: Your CI system (like Jenkins) itself should be secured. If an attacker can compromise your build server, they might inject malicious code into your app before it is deployed. So treat

CI servers as production-critical: lock them down, update them, and require strong auth (MFA if possible) to access them. Give the pipeline only the permissions it truly needs. For example, if it deploys code to a server via SSH, use a deploy key with limited scope rather than a general key with broad access. If the pipeline uses cloud credentials (like AWS keys to deploy infrastructure), ensure those keys have limited IAM roles (only allowed to perform the specific deployment actions).

Dependency Management and Build Security: CI can automatically run tests and also security checks. Integrate security scanning into your pipeline. Examples: run a static analysis tool or linter to catch things like use of `eval` or other risky functions. Use dependency checkers (like `npm audit` or `composer audit` for PHP dependencies) to fail the build if a known-vulnerable library is in use. Ensure you pin dependencies to specific versions (to avoid unexpected changes or malicious updates in third-party packages. There have been incidents where attackers compromised a widely-used library or its repository, and applications pulling the latest version automatically got backdoored code). In 2022, for example, an attacker inserted malware in a popular NPM package; applications that auto-updated it became infected. To mitigate, lock versions and review changelogs before updating.

Secure Build Artifacts: If your pipeline produces artifacts (like compiled code, Docker images, etc.), secure them. Sign artifacts or checksums so you know they have not been tampered with. If you build Docker images for your app, base them on official, minimal images (avoid unnecessary packages in the image, reducing attack surface) and scan them for vulnerabilities.

Continuous Integration Testing: Include security tests in CI. If you have a suite of unit/integration tests, add tests for security expectations. For example, a test to ensure that the "forgot password" flow requires the correct token, or that certain sensitive pages require authentication (you can write a test that tries to fetch an admin page without login and expects a 403/302 result). Consider using tools like OWASP ZAP in an automated way for dynamic analysis against a staging deployment as it can catch XSS, SQLi in a running app. While automated security testing will not find everything, it can catch low-hanging fruit early.

Deployment Pipeline Protections: Many orgs use infrastructure-as-code (like Terraform, CloudFormation, Ansible scripts, etc.) for deploying servers. Ensure those scripts are reviewed for security (for instance, check that security groups/firewall rules are not overly permissive, that S3 buckets created are private by default, etc.). If you deploy using containers or serverless, pay attention to their specific security (e.g., update base images, do not run containers as root, set resource limits). The pipeline should have checkpoints such as requiring manual approval for deploying to production, especially if the change touches authentication or other critical components, so someone can do a quick sanity check or ensure timing is right.

Access Control in CI/CD: Only trusted team members should be able to modify the CI configuration or deployment scripts. Because if someone (or an attacker who got their account) can modify the pipeline, they could introduce a subtle malicious step. For instance, adding a line to push code to another server or to send environment secrets to an external site. Use code reviews for changes to CI scripts and treat them with the same rigor as application code. Additionally, enforce code review for application changes too many source control systems allow branch protections (e.g., no push to main branch without review or without CI passing tests). This not only improves code quality but can catch security issues (if the reviewer spots something).

MFA and Secure Access for Developers: Ensure that developers use MFA for accessing critical services (code repository, CI dashboard, cloud consoles). Recall from Uber's case: lack of MFA on GitHub was a key weakness, according to *The Register's* report on the 2016 Uber breach. Many companies now require MFA for all Git providers and CI systems. Also, educate developers not to ignore security warnings from these platforms (like GitHub will warn if you commit an AWS key; take that seriously).

Supply Chain and Third-Party Services: If your deployment pulls code from third-party repositories or uses third-party actions/plugins in CI, verify their integrity. For example, if using a community GitHub Action in your workflow, ensure it is from a trusted source and pinned to a specific version or commit (to avoid the action updating to something malicious). Similarly, if your build downloads binaries or libraries from URLs, use checksums and secure URLs (HTTPS).

Continuous Delivery vs. Continuous Deployment: Continuous Delivery means each change passes through the pipeline and is ready to deploy, but might wait for manual release. Continuous Deployment means it deploys automatically. In either case, automation is high, which is great for consistency but also means a misconfiguration can propagate quickly. Use canary deployments or phased rollouts for critical changes including deployment to a small portion of users or to one server, monitor for issues (including security logs), then roll out further. This way if something goes wrong, impact is limited and you can rollback.

Rollback and Patching: The deployment process should include the ability to quickly rollback to a previous known-good version if a new deployment has problems (including security problems). Also, use the pipeline to push security patches quickly. For example, if a new vulnerability in a library is announced, having an automated test and deploy process means you can bump the library version and deploy to production faster, reducing the window of exposure. Time is critical for patching known issues (Equifax's breach was a failure to patch in time, something a well-oiled CI/CD could have potentially handled quickly).

Case Study: SolarWinds Build System Compromise (2020). Although not a web app scenario, a famous incident involved attackers inserting a backdoor into SolarWinds Orion software by compromising the company's build system. The attackers had access to build infrastructure and secretly modified the compiled code that was being delivered to customers (including many government agencies). This highlights that security of the build pipeline is as important as security of the code repository. If attackers get into your CI server or modify your build scripts, they can do tremendous damage. After this, many organizations started implementing techniques like build signing, multiple independent build verification, and stricter internal network segmentation for build servers.

In short, DevOps and DevSecOps go hand in hand: security must be woven into your development and deployment practices. As a LAMP developer, even if your team or project is small, following these CI/CD security guidelines will save headaches. Automate what you can (tests, scans), keep secrets out of the wrong places, enforce best practices (like MFA, code reviews), and treat your deployment pipeline as part of the attack surface to be defended. This ensures the code you worked hard to secure does not become insecure due to the way it is shipped or maintained.

7.9 Outdated Components and Dependencies: Managing Known Vulnerabilities

Thus far we have discussed securing the code you write, but equally important is the code you incorporate from others. Modern web apps rely heavily on frameworks (like Laravel, Symfony), libraries (for charts, PDF generation, etc.), and the underlying server stack (PHP itself, Apache/Nginx, OpenSSL, MySQL, etc.). Using outdated components or third-party libraries with known vulnerabilities can undermine all your other security measures. History has taught us this through painful examples: for instance, the massive Equifax data breach in 2017 was ultimately caused by an unpatched vulnerability in a third-party framework (Apache Struts) that

Equifax's system used. Attackers did not need to find a new bug in Equifax's code, they simply exploited the known Struts flaw (CVE-2017-5638) to execute commands on the server, as documented in the OWASP Top 10 2021 analysis of vulnerable components. In general, some of the largest breaches to date have resulted from attackers leveraging publicly documented vulnerabilities in out-of-date components that the target organization had not updated, according to OWASP's documentation on components with known vulnerabilities.

The risk: Third-party components often run with the same privileges as your application. If you include a vulnerable version of a library, an attacker may only need to send a specific request or input to trigger that library's weakness. Because these vulnerabilities are known (publicly disclosed in CVE databases and security advisories), attackers can easily scan the internet for applications using particular versions. There are even automated tools that try common exploits (for example, a scanner might attempt the Struts exploit on every web server it finds). If your app is using that vulnerable component, it could be compromised in seconds, regardless of how flawless your own code is. This issue is so prevalent that it consistently features in security top 10 lists (it was OWASP Top 10 2017 A9 "Using Components with Known Vulnerabilities" and remains in OWASP Top 10 2021 as "Vulnerable and Outdated Components"). The prevalence is partly due to development practices: teams may lose track of which libraries and versions they use, or postpone updates due to fear of breaking compatibility, as noted in OWASP's analysis. Meanwhile, exploit code for known flaws is often readily available or trivial to create, lowering the bar for attackers. An outdated component can be an easy backdoor into an otherwise secure system.

Best practices for dependency security: To mitigate this risk, you need a proactive strategy for managing updates and third-party code:

- Inventory and awareness: Maintain an up-to-date list of all components your application uses, including their version numbers. This includes server software (PHP version, database, etc.), backend libraries (composer packages), front-end libraries (JavaScript frameworks, CSS libraries), and even infrastructure components. You can use tools to automate this inventory, such as OWASP's Dependency-Check tool or built-in package manager audits. PHP's package manager Composer has `composer show --outdated` and security audit capabilities (`composer audit`) to list known vulnerable dependencies. Without knowing what you have, you cannot know what needs patching, as emphasized in both OWASP Top 10 2017 and 2021 documentation on vulnerable components.

- Subscribe to vulnerability feeds: Keep informed about security updates for the software you use. Most major projects have mailing lists or RSS feeds for security advisories. There are also aggregated feeds (like CVE and NVD databases) and tools that monitor these for you, as recommended in OWASP Top 10 2021. For instance, if you use a certain PHP framework, subscribe to its release announcements. When a new CVE is announced (e.g. "SQL injection in Library X version 1.2.3"), you should promptly check if you are using that version.

- Apply patches and updates promptly: Develop a routine process (a "patch management" policy) to update components in a timely manner, as advised in OWASP's guidance on managing components with known vulnerabilities. Delaying updates by months, or only updating on a infrequent schedule, leaves a window of exposure where attackers know your software is vulnerable. Aim to apply critical security patches as soon as possible; in days or weeks, not months. This might mean dedicating time each sprint to dependency upgrades or using automation to flag outdated components. When a critical zero-day issue emerges (e.g., the Log4j vulnerability in late 2021), treat it as an emergency: upgrade or apply workarounds immediately. Plan for compatibility by writing tests for your code. A good test suite will give you confidence that upgrading a library will not break functionality, making you more agile in applying updates.

- Use software composition analysis (SCA) tools: These tools can automatically scan your project's dependencies (and even nested transitive dependencies) for known vulnerabilities. Examples include OWASP Dependency-Check (open source), commercial services like Snyk, Dependabot (integrated with GitHub), or Composer's audit feature. Integrate these into your build process or CI pipeline. For instance, you can fail the build if a high-severity vulnerability is present in any dependency. This way, you catch vulnerable components early and can address them (by updating to a fixed version or applying a patch) before deploying. SCA tools reference databases of CVEs to identify if, say, the version of Twig or Guzzle you use has a known flaw.
- Version pinning and controlled upgrades: It is wise to pin your dependencies to specific versions (e.g., in Composer's `composer.lock`) rather than always pulling the "latest" on each deploy. Pinning ensures you have a predictable, tested set of components in production. However, pinning does not mean never upgrading but that you upgrade on your schedule, not unexpectedly. A good practice is to regularly review and update the pinned versions (e.g., update everything to latest patch releases every few weeks). This controlled approach prevents two extremes: on one hand, avoiding the situation of running years-outdated software; on the other, avoiding the chaos of an untested automatic update introducing breaking changes or malicious code. There have been incidents where attackers intentionally publish a fake "update" to a common library (or compromise an npm/PyPI package to insert malware); if your system blindly pulled the latest version, you could be running compromised code. Pinning plus review mitigates this. Always prefer official sources for updates (packagist.org for PHP libraries, etc.) and verify checksums or signatures when possible, as recommended in OWASP Top 10 2021.
- Remove or replace unsupported components: If a library or tool is no longer maintained by its author, strongly consider migrating to an alternative. Using an end-of-life component is risky as no one will issue fixes even if new vulnerabilities are found. For example, if you relied on an old image processing PHP library that has not been updated since 2015, an undiscovered vuln in it will stay unfixed. It might be better to replace it with a well-maintained library. Likewise, regularly prune dependencies you do not actually need (less code = less attack surface), as advised in OWASP's guidance on components with known vulnerabilities. Each extra plugin or package is another thing to monitor.

In summary, treat third-party code as an integral part of your attack surface. Your security is only as strong as the weakest link in your software stack. Keep your LAMP stack components (OS, PHP, web server, database) up to date with security patches. Do the same for application libraries: staying on top of updates can prevent opportunistic attacks. A well-maintained app that promptly patches its frameworks and libraries forces attackers to find new, harder ways in, whereas an outdated library is like an open invitation to be exploited. By using tools and good processes to manage dependencies, you significantly reduce the risk of a known bug in someone else's code becoming your problem. As OWASP advises, organizations should have an ongoing plan for monitoring and updating components over the entire lifecycle of the application. This continuous vigilance helps ensure that a brilliant defense in your own code is not defeated by a forgotten weakness in someone else's.

7.10　Secure Code Review and Automated Security Testing

Up to now, we have covered specific defenses and coding practices to secure your web application. In addition to writing secure code, a robust security program involves reviewing and testing that code for vulnerabilities on an ongoing basis. Humans make mistakes, and secure development is as much about catching and correcting those mistakes as it is about avoiding them in the first place. In this section, we focus on two critical processes: secure code reviews (usually manual inspections of code with security in mind) and automated security testing (using tools to find vulnerabilities). Incorporating these into your development lifecycle provides robust defense ensuring that weaknesses are identified and fixed before attackers can exploit them in production.

Secure code reviews: Code review is a common practice for improving quality; when done with a security mindset, it can uncover issues that automated tests might miss. This involves someone other than the author inspecting the code changes for potential security problems. For example, checking that input validation is in place, that queries use prepared statements, that passwords are handled properly, etc. Many vulnerabilities, such as missing access control or subtle logic flaws, can be spotted in a thorough review. It is best to integrate security review into your normal peer review process: use a checklist of common mistakes (for instance, the OWASP Top 10 or a company-specific secure coding checklist) and verify each code change against it. Some organizations require at least one security-focused approval on pull requests. The earlier you catch an issue, the cheaper it is to fix. Reviewing code during development (often called "shift-left" security) prevents vulnerabilities from ever making it to production. When reviewing, pay special attention to any use of dangerous functions or patterns (e.g., use of `eval`, direct SQL string concatenation, file system access, encryption logic, authentication flows). Security code review is a skill that improves with practice; developers can learn common anti-patterns and become adept at spotting things that "do not look right." It also helps spread security knowledge among the team. In a sense, every code review becomes a mini security audit. As mentioned earlier in the chapter, instituting requirements like "no code gets deployed without at least one peer review" and "no direct commits to main branch" can enforce that every change gets this scrutiny. Over time, this catches a lot of mistakes, from trivial (like a missing output escape on one line that could allow XSS) to complex (like an assumption in business logic that could be abused).

Static analysis (SAST): In addition to manual reviews, you can employ automated static code analyzers to scan source code for known vulnerability patterns. For PHP, examples include SonarQube with PHP rules, RIPS (now integrated into SonarCloud), Psalm or PHPStan with security plugins, and linters that flag risky functions. These tools look for things like SQL queries built from strings, usage of deprecated or insecure functions (e.g., `mysql_query` or `eval()`), cross-site scripting sinks (e.g., printing `$_POST` data without sanitization), and so forth. Static analysis can be integrated into your IDE (providing instant feedback to developers) and into your CI/CD pipeline. For instance, you might configure your GitHub Actions or Jenkins pipeline to run a SAST tool on each commit or pull request. If it finds a high-severity issue (say, user input being passed to `unserialize()`, which we know is dangerous), it can fail the build or at least report it for developers to fix. These tools are not perfect and can produce false positives, but they are extremely useful for catching the "low-hanging fruit" automatically. They act as a second pair of eyes. By using static analysis, you enforce a baseline of security hygiene, that ensures many obvious mistakes will be caught early, and developers will learn to avoid patterns that trigger the tool.

Dynamic testing (DAST) and vulnerability scanning: Static analysis examines code, but dynamic application security testing (DAST) examines a running application for vulnerabilities. Think of it like an automated penetration test. Tools like OWASP ZAP (Zed Attack Proxy) or Burp Suite can simulate malicious requests to your web app (running in a staging environment) and see if they can provoke a vulnerability. For example, ZAP can automatically crawl your application and attempt SQL injection in form fields, or try injecting script to detect XSS. It might flag responses that suggest a SQL error or check if content is reflected back unsanitized. You can integrate such a scanner into your test pipeline, including the deployment of the latest build to a test server and have ZAP run in automated mode against it, then produce a report. While DAST tools may not find logic flaws, they excel at discovering common configuration issues and injection flaws that static analysis might miss (because some issues only manifest with certain runtime conditions). They can also catch misconfigurations like overly verbose error messages or security headers missing (similar to what tools like Mozilla Observatory check). Keep in mind that DAST will generate a lot of traffic and possibly some false positives , essentially acting like an attacker, so you typically run it against non-production environments. Automated scanners can catch things like XSS, SQLi, missing HTTPOnly on cookies, default credentials, etc., giving you an opportunity to fix those before release.

Additionally, consider running dependency vulnerability scans (covered in the previous section) as part of testing ensure not only your code but also the packages you use are checked for known flaws. Some tools (like Nessus, OpenVAS) can scan deployed servers for known vulnerabilities in the stack (ensuring your PHP, Apache, OpenSSL versions are up-to-date), which straddles the line between app testing and infrastructure security.

Penetration testing and security audits: While automated tools are invaluable, they are not 100% comprehensive. Thus, it is recommended to periodically engage in manual penetration testing, either by an internal security team or external specialists. A skilled human tester can find logic bugs or complex issues that tools might overlook. They might perform threat modeling on your application, then attempt targeted attacks (for example, testing multi-step processes for logic gaps, trying privilege escalation not by code injection but by abusing a flawed access control check, etc.). Pen testers can also verify and triage the findings from automated scans to eliminate false positives and highlight the most critical real issues. Many organizations schedule pen-tests before major releases or on an annual (or more frequent) basis. The results of these tests then feed back into development: developers fix the discovered issues and learn not to repeat the same mistakes. Over time, this greatly improves the security posture of the application. Similarly, secure design reviews or architecture reviews at the planning stage can prevent whole classes of problems (though that is more about process than testing).

Continuous integration of security: The ideal state is to integrate these practices so that security checks happen continuously and automatically. This is often referred to as DevSecOps, essentially embedding security into DevOps pipelines. A possible workflow is: every code commit triggers automated tests, including unit tests, SAST, and dependency checks; when deploying to a staging environment, run DAST scans; for any critical code paths, require manual code review with a security checklist. Additionally, enforce things like formatting and linters (some insecure code patterns can also be caught by general lint rules). By making these steps part of normal development, you reduce the chance of pushing insecure code. Developers get rapid feedback if they introduce something risky, and it never becomes a production incident. It is much better to catch an unsafe use of `exec()` in a pull request than to deal with a breach months later.

Figure 7.3 shows a simplified diagram of how security activities can integrate into the development lifecycle. Code is reviewed and scanned before release, and even after deployment the application undergoes periodic security tests. This continuous feedback loop helps catch vulnerabilities early and often.

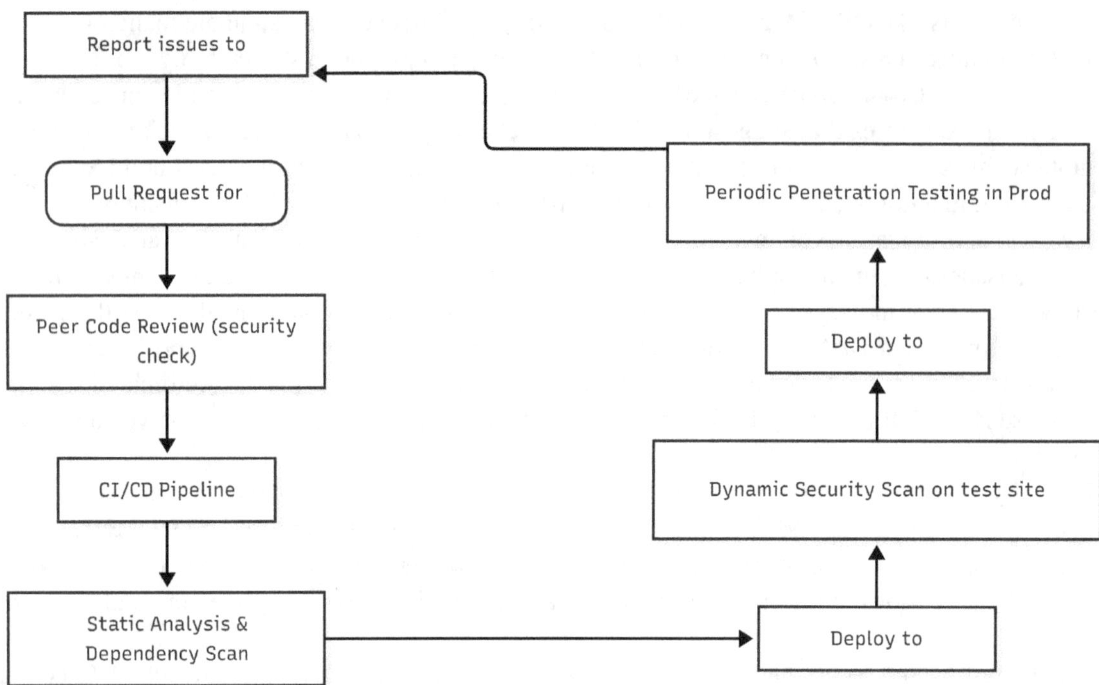

Figure 7.3: Integrating security into development.

A combined approach of automated vs. manual: Automated tools are great for consistency and speed, but humans are great at creativity and understanding context. For best results, use both. Let the tools handle the tedious work of checking every variable and request, and have skilled reviewers/pen-testers focus on the big picture and subtle issues. For example, a static analyzer might alert "possible SQL injection" in a snippet so the developer reviewing it can confirm and fix the code. A penetration tester might find that while your forms are secure, a certain undocumented admin URL has no CSRF protection, something a generic scanner might miss. Each method will catch things the other might not. Importantly, make sure to act on the findings. It is not enough to run scans; you need a process to review the results and remedy them. Incorporate the critical issues into your bug tracker and assign them priority just like functional bugs.

Cultivate a security mindset: Encourage developers to think like attackers when writing and reviewing code. Simple practices like threat modeling a new feature ("What could go wrong here? How might someone abuse this?") or using peer review as a learning opportunity ("I noticed you directly outputted this variable; could that enable XSS?") go a long way. Over time, your team will naturally produce more secure code, and the tools will have fewer issues to report.

In conclusion, secure code reviews and automated testing are essential companions to the secure coding techniques we have discussed. They provide assurance that the defenses are correctly implemented and help catch the one mistake you overlooked. By making these a routine part of development, you build security into the DNA of your project. Your web application should be not only well-designed and functional, but also continuously validated for security. This layered approach of prevent, detect, and fix is key to staying ahead of attackers and maintaining a robust security posture throughout your application's life cycle.

7.11 Real-World Lessons, Secure Coding Checklist, and Next Steps

Web application security is a vast field, and in this chapter we have focused on the core issues most relevant to LAMP stack developers: authenticating users securely, authorizing their actions properly, safeguarding their data (in the database, in transit, and in the browser), and coding defensively against common attacks. To put it in perspective, here is a summary of key best practices for a secure coding checklist:

- Never trust user input: validate it, sanitize it, or reject it. This stops many attacks at the gate.
- Use prepared statements for database queries: parameterized queries eliminate SQL injection risks.
- Escape output for HTML/JS: neutralize any injected scripts (XSS) by output encoding.
- Protect session cookies: use HttpOnly, Secure, and SameSite attributes, and always use HTTPS. Regenerate session IDs on privilege changes to thwart fixation.
- Implement anti-CSRF tokens: ensure state-changing requests are genuine by requiring an unguessable token (and/or use SameSite cookies and check Origin/Referer).
- Hash passwords and enforce strong auth: never store plaintext credentials, use one-way hashes (with salt and strong algorithms) and if possible enforce strong password policies (min length, complexity, avoid common passwords). Use MFA for critical accounts to add an extra layer.
- Enable HTTPS everywhere: transport-layer security is non-negotiable for modern web apps. Obtain a TLS certificate and redirect HTTP to HTTPS. Use HSTS to cement it.
- Validate and sanitize file uploads: if file uploads are needed, only accept allowed types, verify file content (MIME), use secure file names/locations, and never execute or serve unvalidated files as active content. Set appropriate content headers (`nosniff`, etc.).
- Use security headers: add HTTP response headers like Content-Security-Policy, X-Frame-Options, X-Content-Type-Options, Referrer-Policy, etc., to have the browser enforce important security constraints on your behalf.
- Keep software updated: many attacks (like Equifax's) exploit known holes that patches fix. Stay current on PHP, Apache, OpenSSL, and any libraries or frameworks you use. Apply security updates promptly.
- Plan for defense in depth: assume one layer (e.g., your code or the user's browser) might fail and have compensating controls. Example: even if an XSS slips in, a CSP header can mitigate it; if your app logic fails, a WAF might catch an injection attempt; if an attacker gets a foothold on the server, OS-level permissions might limit damage.
- Monitor and log actively: set up logging for logins, key actions, and errors. Monitor these logs for anomalies. Use alerts for repeated failed logins, odd admin activity, or other signs of attack. "Insufficient Logging and Monitoring" is itself a top security risk (OWASP Top 10 2017).
- Secure the development pipeline: use code reviews and automated tests to catch security issues early. Protect your source code repository (MFA, least privilege) and CI/CD pipeline (no plaintext secrets, run security scans, restrict who can deploy). A secure app can be undermined by an insecure deployment process (as seen in various supply-chain attacks).
- Learn from incidents: as we saw with RockYou, Firesheep, Samy worm, Equifax, Capital One, Uber, GitHub and others, each failure teaches what not to do. Stay informed of security news to learn about new threats and common pitfalls. Also, if you have minor incidents or near-misses in your own projects, analyze them and strengthen your defenses.

This secure coding checklist is a handy reference when building or reviewing application code and configuration. Checking off these items will help ensure you have not missed an obvious security measure. Web security is an ongoing process, not a one-time setup. It involves not just initial development but also constant maintenance: monitoring for suspicious activity, regular security testing (using tools or performing periodic penetration testing and code reviews with an eye for security), and improvement as new best practices emerge. Developers should familiarize themselves with resources like the OWASP Top 10 (the OWASP Top Ten is a regularly updated list of critical web security risks). Consider using security libraries or frameworks to handle tricky parts. For instance, using a framework like Laravel or Symfony in PHP can automatically provide protections (CSRF tokens, output escaping, ORM to prevent SQL injection, etc.), reducing the chances of making a mistake in those areas.

As we move to the next chapter, which covers more advanced topics in web development, remember that all those features must be built on the secure foundation we have established here. A web application can only be as strong as its weakest link. A single unchecked input or a misconfigured server can undermine an otherwise sound application. By applying the principles and practices from this chapter, you significantly raise the baseline security of your LAMP stack application. Keep security in mind at every stage of development, and you will be better equipped to build robust, trustworthy web applications.

7.12 Chapter Review

Problem 7.1 Why is it critical to adopt a proactive security mindset from the beginning of application development?

Problem 7.2 What is password hashing, and why is it essential for secure password storage?

Problem 7.3 Describe how the PHP functions `password_hash()` and `password_verify()` work together. Provide a brief code example.

Problem 7.4 What is session fixation, and how can it be prevented in PHP?

Problem 7.5 Explain the difference between authentication and authorization. Provide an example of each in the context of a PHP application.

Problem 7.6 How can prepared statements help prevent SQL injection? Give a PHP example using PDO.

Problem 7.7 What is Cross-Site Scripting (XSS), and how can output encoding mitigate it? Provide an example of using `htmlspecialchars()`.

Problem 7.8 Describe two effective methods for protecting against Cross-Site Request Forgery (CSRF).

Problem 7.9 What precautions should be taken when allowing users to upload files in a web application? Provide three specific recommendations.

Problem 7.10 What is MIME-type handling, and why is it important when serving user-uploaded files?

Problem 7.11 Explain the purpose of the HTTP security header Content Security Policy (CSP).

Problem 7.12 What does the Strict-Transport-Security (HSTS) header accomplish, and why is it valuable?

Problem 7.13 Describe at least three types of events or actions that should be logged for security purposes in a web application.

Problem 7.14 Why is monitoring important for web security, and what could happen if suspicious events are overlooked? Provide an example from the chapter.

Problem 7.15 Outline the key steps involved in an effective incident response plan.

Problem 7.16 Explain why credentials and API keys should never be committed directly into version control systems. Provide a brief real-world example of the consequences.

Problem 7.17 What security risks can arise from an insecure Continuous Integration/Continuous Deployment (CI/CD) pipeline?

Problem 7.18 How did the Equifax breach demonstrate the importance of timely software updates?

Problem 7.19 Provide two reasons why using Multi-Factor Authentication (MFA) is recommended for developer accounts and CI/CD systems.

Problem 7.20 Summarize three critical security practices from this chapter's secure coding checklist that every PHP developer should apply.

8. PHP

Server-side scripting allows web servers to generate dynamic content in response to client requests. Hypertext Preprocessor (PHP) is a widely-used open-source server-side scripting language that is especially suited for web development. PHP code is executed on the web server, producing HTML (or other output) that is sent to the client's browser. In a typical web application, the browser issues a request for a `.php` page; the web server's PHP engine processes the PHP code (possibly interacting with databases or files), and then sends back a response containing the resulting HTML. This differs from client-side scripts (like JavaScript) which run in the browser. PHP's syntax is C-like and it provides extensive capabilities for web application development, such as processing form data, interacting with databases, generating dynamic page content, handling file uploads, sending emails, and maintaining state with sessions and cookies. Figure 8.1 shows the PHP Request Processing Flow. When a browser requests a PHP page, the server executes the PHP code and returns the resulting HTML. The PHP source is not sent to the client; only the output produced by the PHP script is sent.

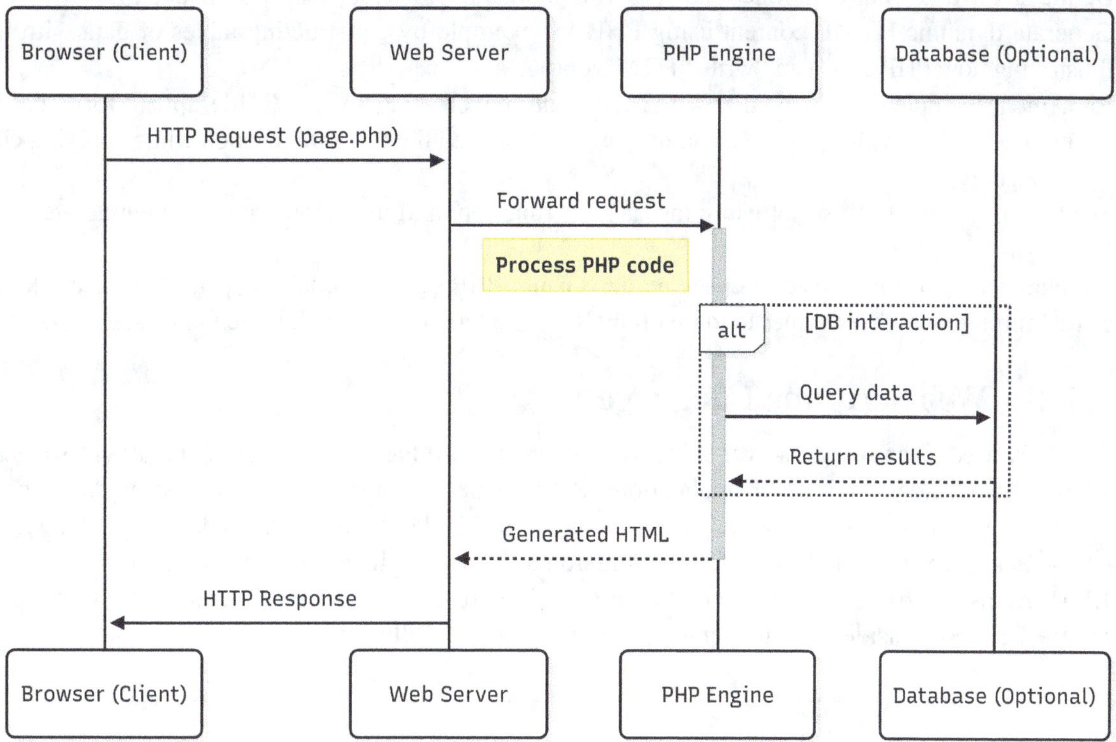

Figure 8.1: PHP request processing flow.

DOI: 10.1201/9781003727651-8

Learning Objectives

By the end of this chapter, you should be able to:

- Embed and execute PHP scripts within HTML pages, understanding the special `<?php ... ?>` delimiters and the importance of using the `.php` file extension for pages containing PHP code.
- Use development tools for PHP (or simple text editors) to write and debug PHP programs, and know how to view PHP error messages.
- Declare and use PHP variables (which are loosely typed) and understand PHP's basic data types and operators.
- Output data to the browser using PHP (e.g., with `echo` or `print`) and retrieve user input from HTML forms via the `$_GET` and `$_POST` superglobals.
- Apply control structures in PHP (conditional statements, loops, switch/case) and understand their syntax and behavior.
- Create and manipulate arrays and associative arrays in PHP, and understand how associative arrays (like `$_GET`, `$_POST`, `$_FILES`, and `$_SESSION`) use string keys.
- Utilize built-in PHP functions (for tasks like random number generation, string and type checking, date formatting, etc.) and understand the concept of a function.
- Define and invoke your own functions in PHP, and organize reusable code via include files.
- Generate dynamic HTML content using PHP, for example by constructing tables of data with loops, illustrating how PHP code can "write" HTML output.
- Implement file upload functionality with PHP, including creating an HTML file-upload form, handling the upload in PHP (with `$_FILES`), and moving the uploaded file to a safe location while applying checks on file size, type, etc.
- Send email from a PHP script using the `mail()` function, and understand how to include headers for HTML-formatted emails.
- Maintain state information across page requests using PHP sessions, enabling persistent data (like login status) throughout a user's interaction with the site, and handle cookies for client-side state persistence.

8.1   PHP – Web Scripting Language

PHP is a widely used, open source, server-side scripting language. It has a C-like syntax and provides extensive capabilities needed for developing web applications. PHP can perform functions like accessing data sent from HTML Forms, interacting with databases, processing using HTML Form and backend database data, wrapping data in dynamically created HTML tags for transmission to a browser, handling graphics, and so on.

PHP programs or scripts can be embedded in files that contain a mixture of HTML and PHP code by enclosing the PHP code inside special opening and closing tags as follows:

```
1  <?php
2     // PHP code goes here
3  ?>
```

The PHP filename must generally have the `.php` extension for the web server to recognize the contents as

PHP code to be interpreted rather than as HTML content to be passed through as-is to the browser (though the `.htaccess` file can be reconfigured to allow the PHP processor to recognize other file extensions). If a `.php` file contains both HTML and PHP code intermixed in an alternating fashion, the HTML segments are not enclosed within the `<?php ... ?>` delimiters. That would cause a syntax error since the HTML is not valid PHP and would be treated by the PHP processor as an error. The following illustrates the kind of alternation allowed:

```
1  <!-- Beginning HTML goes here, such as header contents. -->
2
3  <?php
4      // PHP code goes here.
5  ?>
6
7  <!-- More HTML here -->
8
9  <?php
10     // PHP code here.
11 ?>
12
13 <!-- Ending HTML here, such as footer contents. -->
```

Significantly, embedded HTML code can be placed under the control of PHP control structures (though kept outside the `<?php ?>` delimiters). For example, in the case of a PHP if statement, the corresponding conditionally executed HTML code would be transmitted to the browser only when the if (or other control) condition were satisfied. Often a PHP file may consist of just a single PHP segment. There are a variety of PHP coding styles as well as syntactical features such as the heredoc syntax to facilitate the intermixture of PHP and HTML code.

8.1.1 Embedding PHP in HTML

The most important fact about PHP is that it can be embedded within an HTML file. Below is a simple example of several ways PHP can be embedded in HTML code:

```
1  <!DOCTYPE html>
2  <html>
3  <head>
4  <meta charset = "UTF-8">
5  <title>Embedded PHP</title>
6  <!-- Style heading and paragraph colors -->
7  <style>
8  h3
```

```
 9  {
10      color:royalblue;
11  }
12  p
13  {
14      color:forestgreen;
15  }
16  </style>
17  </head>
18  <!-- PHP embedded in DOCTYPE -->
19  <?php
20  $courseName = "Web Applications"; //creates a variable called $courseName
21  ?>
22  <body>
23  <!-- PHP embedded in body of HTML code -->
24  <h3> Welcome to <?php echo $courseName; ?></h3> <!-- Prints out Welcome to Web Applications -->
25  <p>
26  <?php
27  echo "<strong>";
28  echo " Where we will learn HTML, CSS, JavaScript, PHP and SQL"; // Prints out the languages learned
29  echo"</strong>";
30  ?>
31  </p>
32  </body>
33  </html>
```

Notice in the example above that the PHP code can be placed before the DOCTYPE declaration and can be embedded within the various tag elements in the body of the HTML code.

What happens if you write `<? php` with a space before the php? Adding a space between the opening tag delimiter `<?` and `php` results in a syntax error. The PHP interpreter expects the exact sequence `<?php` with no spaces in between to recognize the beginning of a PHP code block.

8.1.2   PHP syntax errors

If you are using a PHP server environment installed on your own computer, then error messages can be accessed through the system error console. However, on a remote web server that provides PHP services when pages are requested by a client browser contacting it over the Internet, syntax error messages occurring during interpretation of a script are not sent to the browser, which makes it less convenient to debug scripts as they are developed.

In server environments, you can often access error messages by using a command prompt window if you have shell access. For example:

```
1 php filename.php
```

This command runs the script in the terminal (with output returned to the terminal, without browser rendering). You can also check the syntax without executing the file at the command line using:

```
1 php -l filename.php
```

using the option -l (lower case letter l for "lint").

The source code for a PHP program is executed on a web server. This source is not sent to the browser as the HTML tags are, though when developing the code it may sometimes be convenient to display it in the browser (being watchful of any passwords that would be disclosed). The following PHP built-in function displays the code for a file named in its argument:

```
1 show_source("example01.php");
```

The file argument used here is assumed to be in the same directory as the source PHP file (and of course may be the source file itself). Notably, the show_source function does not disclose the contents of any include file referred to in the source such as a file that contains database account information.

Comments in PHP are handled as in C with a pair of slashes (//) to introduce a single line comment and /* ... */ for multi-line comments.

Try the show_source instruction on a simple PHP example that also includes HTML content/tags. Then explain the source code of the returned file (as opposed to the rendered code), as displayed using View in the browser of the results. Observe that the source View contains many characters and lines that are not part of the original source file. Why is this? It is because the show_source command is aware of the syntax of PHP and HTML and special HTML characters like < and > that are intended to be displayed by the function, not interpreted or rendered by the browser as HTML tags. Thus all these special characters are converted to their correct entity representation.

The diagram in Figure 8.1 illustrates what happens when you request a PHP file. The file is retrieved, compiled, and the PHP statements in the file are executed. Output from PHP print and echo statements is sent to the browser, replacing the PHP code in the file that generated the output, whence no code is displayed, only its executed results, wrapped in any HTML tags they happened to be embedded in.

8.2   Development Tools for PHP

Much PHP professional development is done using tools as simple as NotePad++ that at least provide the key feature of language-dependent syntax-highlighting.

Komodo Edit: A free open source IDE that provides features like syntax autocompletion for PHP, Javascript, Ruby, Perl, etc. Komodo IDE is an upgraded commercial version of the basic free tool which provides more extensive capabilities.

Online Syntax Checking: Various online services provide basic PHP syntax checking and syntax error identification that can assist with simple applications.

CodeIgniter: At a more sophisticated level, there are open source development frameworks for PHP like CodeIgniter. CodeIgniter uses the Model-View-Controller programming paradigm with an emphasis on the Views and Controller aspect and an object-oriented approach to PHP.

Aptana: This is an open source IDE that supports Javascript, PHP and AJAX applications development.

For debugging, using `var_dump()` or `print_r()` to output variable values can help. More sophisticated debugging can be done with tools like Xdebug (which allows step-by-step execution, breakpoints, stack inspection, etc., in conjunction with an IDE). However, installing and configuring such tools can be complex, especially on hosted servers. In many educational settings or simpler projects, inserting temporary print statements or using error logs is sufficient for debugging purposes.

Another option is to use an online PHP shell or sandbox for quick tests. There are websites that offer an interactive PHP environment in the browser where you can run code and see output immediately.

8.3   Variables, Types and Operators

PHP is loosely typed: variables can be assigned values without being declared and the type of the variable is then dynamically determined by the PHP processor based on the data and context: string, integer, decimal or floating point, Boolean. The PHP variable names must begin with a `$_`. Forgetting this is a common syntax error. Names consist of the characters a–Z, 0–9, and the underscore _ and must begin with a letter or underscore (after the required `$`). Names are case-sensitive. These restrictions apply also to index variables in for-loops, for arrays and so on.

Variables act as stores of values, so two basic issues are: How to store values in the variables and how to see what is stored in a variable. We assign values to variables using the assignment statement (operator) as in:

```
1  $message = "This is a string.";
```

As previously indicated, the data does not have to be assigned a type since the PHP interpreter determines this from the data. To see (reveal, display) the contents of a variable (in a browser), we can send its value to the browser (naturally the one that requested the file containing the script) using the echo command (function) as in:

```
1  echo "This is from the PHP script.";
2
3  // Or using a variable:
4  $message = "This is from the PHP script.";
5  echo $message;
```

The string argument of echo can inter-mix text, PHP variables and HTML tags as in:

```
1 $value = 2;
2 echo "The value is: <b>$value</b>.<br>";
```

which is rendered by the receiving browser as:

```
The value is: 2.
```

The number 2 is displayed in bold (and followed by a period) because of the HTML bold tags and the content is followed by an HTML break tag which is interpreted as a newline character by the browser rather than displayed as text. Here the string argument of echo uses the PHP concatenation operator (denoted by the dot or period) to join the substrings transmitted (or sent to the browser) by echo. This operator behaves just like the concatenation operator in Javascript (denoted there by +). Notably, because PHP variables begin with a $ symbol the PHP compiler is able to recognize and therefore evaluate the variables even when they lie within a quoted string. The PHP naming restriction that variable names begin with a $ has an important benefit: the variable names are readily recognized as such by the PHP interpreter and so they can be (are) evaluated even within a string, though double quotes and single quotes are different in this so-called interpolation capability. The result may or may not be what is intended. For example, the above echo statement could be re-written as:

```
1 echo "The value is: <b>$value</b>.<br>";
```

which is far more succinct than the original version containing the concatenation dot operator (the remaining dot is a period which is part of the content, not an operator).

Watch out though because sometimes you may not get the intended effect. Thus if $value = 2, then:

```
1 echo "The value of $value is $value";
```

gives:

```
The value of 2 is 2
```

since both occurrences of $value in the string are interpreted as variables and so evaluated. In order to output where the $ was displayed in front of the x:

```
The value of $value is 2.
```

We could use the backslash escape character (\) before the special initial $ character we wish to display:

```php
echo "The value of \$value is $value.";
```

This handles the two $value occurrences differently: the first is displayed as literally $value, (since $ is displayed as a special character), while for the second the value of $value is output. An alternative is to use single quotes:

```php
$output = 'The value of $value is ' . "$value.";
```

Which has the effect that the first $value is not evaluated, contrary to what happens when double quotes are used. It yields:

```
The value of $value is 2.
```

8.3.1 PHP Basic Syntax Rules

PHP's basic syntax rules include the following: statements end with a semicolon, and extra whitespace in statements is ignored. PHP supports three styles of comments: single-line comments begin with a # (hashtag), end-of-line comments use //, and multiline comments begin with /* and encompass everything until a closing */.

Variables are used to store data. They are dynamically typed so their type does not have to be declared; the PHP engine makes a best guess as to the intended type based upon what is being assigned. Variables are also loosely typed, meaning they can be assigned different data types over time.

When declaring variables, you must preface the variable name with the dollar sign, followed by any combination of letters, numbers, or an underscore. Note that the combination must start with a letter or a single underscore. Variable names are case sensitive, so $final_cost and $final_Cost reference two different variables.

8.3.2 String Literals and Escape Sequences

In PHP string literals can be defined using either single or double quotes. Understanding the difference between the two is imperative! Single quotes define everything contained within them as is (literally), while double quotes interpret what is contained within them.

One example where we can see how this concept works is with string escape sequence characters used with string literals. Some of the most common of these string escape sequence characters are shown in Table 8.1.

Table 8.1: Common escape characters in PHP strings.

Escape Character	Description
\n	New line
\t	Horizontal tab
\\	Backslash
$	Dollar sign (Placing another $ after the first $ also works)
"	Double quote

Here is an example of how quotation marks work with string escape sequence characters:

```php
echo "See how double quotes in PHP interprets what is enclosed in double quotes.";
echo("<br>");
echo "Output a dollar sign: \$";
echo("<br>");
echo "Output double quotes \" Knowledge is power\" around a phrase";
echo ("<br><br>");
echo "See how single quotes in PHP do not interpret what is enclosed in single quotes.";
echo("<br>");
echo 'Output a dollar sign: \$';
echo("<br>");
echo 'Output double quotes \" Knowledge is power\" around a phrase';
```

OUTPUT:

Double Quotes

```
See how double quotes in PHP interprets what is enclosed in double quotes.
Output a dollar sign: $
Output double quotes " Knowledge is power" around a phrase
```

Single Quotes

```
See how single quotes in PHP do not interpret what is enclosed in single quotes.
Output a dollar sign: \$
Output double quotes \" Knowledge is power\" around a phrase
```

R Double quotes interpreted the escape sequences enclosed within them whereas single quotes defined everything exactly as is and therefore no escape sequences are expanded and thus are taken literally.

8.3.3 Operators

In addition to the concatenation operator for combining strings, other common PHP operators are the standard arithmetic operators (+, - *, /), the auto-increment operators familiar from languages like C (`variable++` and `variable--`), the modulus operator (`variable % number`) which gives the remainder of integer variable upon division by integer number, variations on the assignment operator (such as `variable += number` for `variable = variable + number`), and the logical and comparison operators, which are used to construct Boolean conditions. It is worth noting that some of these notations differ from those used in other languages. For example, in Java Server Pages (JSP) scripting language, the equality test for strings is implemented by a function that returns a Boolean value and requires the Java-like function call: `string1.equals(string2)` where `string1` and `string2` are strings. Table 8.2 lists logical and comparison operators in PHP along with their names and descriptions.

Table 8.2: Logical and comparison operators in PHP.

Logical Operator	Name	Description
and	AND	`$expressionA and $expressionB` – true if both expressions are true.
or	OR	`$expressionA or $expressionB` – true if either expression is true.
xor	Exclusive OR	`$expressionA xor $expressionB` – true if either expression is true but not both.
!	NOT	`!$expression` – true if `$expression` is not true.
&&	AND	`$expressionA && $expressionB` – true if both expressions are true (&& represents an AND).
||	OR	`$expressionA || $expressionB` – true if either expression is true (|| represents an OR).
==	Equal	`$expressionA == $expressionB` – true `$expressionA` equals `$expressionB`.
!=	Not Equal	`$expressionA != $expressionB` – true `$expressionA` is not equal to `$expressionB`.
>=	Greater than or equal	`$expressionA >= $expressionB` – true `$expressionA` is greater than or equal to `$expressionB`.
<=	Less than or equal to	`$expressionA <= $expressionB` – true `$expressionA` is less equal or equal to `$expressionB`.

8.4 Exchanging Data Between Browser and Script

A browser can transmit (send data) and receive data from a PHP script, and vice versa. The PHP `print` and `echo` commands send data to a browser. The PHP `var_dump` function sends the type and values of the objects listed in its parameters to the browser. A browser sends data to a PHP script via an HTML Form using either

HTTP GET or POST commands. A script acquires data sent by the browser to the web server using the global PHP arrays `$_GET` and `$_POST`.

We have already seen `echo`; the PHP print command works similarly. It can be used with or without parentheses:

```
1 print "Hello World";
2 print("Hello World");
```

Like echo, the output strings can inter-mix text, data, variables, and HTML (within quotes).

The PHP function var_dump displays the values of the variables listed in its parameter list. More generally it displays structured information about listed objects like arrays. Thus if `$valueA = 111` and `$valueB = 222` then `var_dump($valueA, $valueB);` displays the type and value of each listed parameter such as in:

Browser Output

```
int(111) int(222)
```

If the PHP array `$animals` has components: `$animals[1] = "cat"`, `$animals[2] = "dog"`, and the variable `$count = 111`, then `var_dump($animals, $count)` sends the following output to the browser:

Browser Output

```
array(2) { [1]=> string(3) "cat" [2]=> string(3) "dog" } int(111)
```

This gives us the detailed information that the array is of size 2, with components indexed by 1 and 2, the contents are strings with values "cat" and "dog", and the variable `$count` contains data of type int and has value 111.

8.4.1 GET and POST Methods

The GET and POST methods allow forms to interact with web servers.

Forms allow a user to input information and then usually via a button click the contents of the form are encoded and sent to a server. The server uses a program to decode the contents, perform some computation on the data and produces output that is sent back to the user.

The `<form>` element has a variety of attributes one of which is the method attribute. The method attribute determines how the data is sent to the handling page. The method attribute has two choices which refer to the HTTP request to be used:

GET is used when requesting specific information such as a particular DB record or the results of a search. It is less secure since the data is sent via URL parameters and thus are visible.

POST is used when some action is expected such as inserting data into a DB or updating a record. It is more secure since data is sent via the HTTP POST method and are not visible.

Data sent from an HTML Form can be accessed using globally available PHP associative arrays. Depending on whether the data is sent with an HTTP GET or POST command, a different global array is used. For an HTML Form that uses a GET command where the Form input field of interest has the element `name="userName"`, then the transmitted data is accessed by:

```php
$userName = $_GET["userName"];
```

where `$_GET` is the global array (associative array). The value of each named field on the Form is accessed in the same way. POST data is accessed analogously:

```php
$userName = $_POST["userName"];
```

The following code will work regardless of whether GET or POST is used on the Form. It uses the `(condition ? valueIfTrue : valueIfFalse)` notation from C which returns the value of `valueIfTrue` or `valueIfFalse`, depending on whether the condition is true or not:

```php
$userName = (!empty($_GET['userName'])) ? $_GET['userName'] : $_POST['userName'];
```

Recall that the notation `(condition ? valueIfTrue : valueIfFalse)` is the C-shortcut notation for an if-else statement:

```php
if (condition)
{
    statement = valueIfTrue;
}
else
{
    statement = valueIfFalse;
}
```

Filtering input data from a Form (validating data, etc) is critical to web applications. PHP provides built-in filter functions for validating and sanitizing input data.

8.4.2 Superglobal Arrays

A list of the various superglobal arrays is given in Table 8.3 along with their descriptions. The `$_GET` and `$_POST` allow the developer to access data sent by the client.

Table 8.3: Common PHP superglobal arrays.

Superglobal Array	Description
`$GLOBALS`	An array for storing data that needs superglobal scope.
`$_COOKIE`	An array of cookie data passed to the page via HTTP request.
`$_ENV`	An array of server environment data.
`$_FILES`	An array of file items uploaded to the server.
`$_GET`	An array of query string data passed to the server via the URL.
`$_POST`	An array of query string data passed to the server via the HTTP header.
`$_REQUEST`	An array containing the contents of `$_GET`, `$_POST` and `$_COOKIE`.
`$_SESSION`	An array that contains session data.
`$_SERVER`	An array that contains information about the request and the server.

8.5 Control Structures

The basic PHP control structures provide for conditional execution, loops, and case-based execution.

8.5.1 Conditional statements: if, if-else, elseif

The conditional statements in PHP are the if, if-else and the elseif statements. The if statement has the form:

```
if (condition)
{
    statements;
}
```

where the condition is a Boolean condition. If there is only a single statement afterwards, the braces { ... ; } can be omitted. That is, if the pair of braces contains just a single line of code, they can be omitted but the semicolon at the end of each line must be included in any case.

The standard if-else statement is:

```
if (condition)
{
    statements;
}
else
```

```
6  {
7      statements;
8  }
```

If multiple alternatives occur, one can use an elseif statement as in:

```
1  if (condition1)
2  {
3      statements;
4  }
5  elseif (condition2)
6  {
7      statements;
8  }
9  else
10 {
11     statements;
12 }
```

where the elseif part can be repeated as often as needed and the entire statement concludes with an else. Note that a semicolon is not included after the if-braces in the if-else or elseif statements. PHP also allows a colon alternative for braces in this context.

It is worth observing at this point that because of the shortcut way in which Boolean conditions are evaluated in PHP, the second part of a condition may be treated differently from the first. Thus, the second part of an $\&\&$ condition is not even evaluated if the first part of the condition already fails (because A $\&\&$ B is guaranteed to be false if A is false, regardless of the value of B). Similarly, the second part of an $||$ condition is not evaluated if the first part of the condition succeeds. For example, the outcome of the statement:

```
1  if (($fileType == "image/pjpeg") && ($fileSize < 20000))
2  {
3      echo "Allow.";
4  }
5  else
6  {
7      echo "Prevent.";
8  }
```

can be recognized as "Prevent" as soon as the image type test in the condition fails, regardless of the result of the size condition.

8.5.2 For-loop and foreach loop

The PHP for-loop statement has the standard use and form. It allows one to repeat a block of statements, as an index variable runs over a range of integers at a given increment, until a comparison condition on the index fails. For example, consider:

```php
for ($index = 0; $index < $limit; $index++)
{
    statements;
}
```

PHP also has a foreach loop that works as illustrated by the following example:

```php
$animals = array("dog", "cat", "bird"); //defines the array
foreach ($animals as $animal) //scans $animals array members
{
    echo "Value is: $animal <br>"; //prints current member value $animal
}
```

The array elements are successively scanned and their corresponding values are output. Here the successive values: dog, cat and bird.

We can exit a loop in several ways:

1. Complete the loop and exit normally with execution continuing with the next statement after the end of the loop.
2. If the loop is embedded in a function, we can exit the loop and return from the function using a return statement.
3. An exit function embedded in a loop will terminate the entire script and so automatically exit a loop.
4. The break statement will terminate the loop and continue with the next statement after the loop.

8.5.3 While loop

The while loop has the familiar C-format and works as follows. The while condition is tested when the loop is entered as well as at each subsequent repetition of the while body. When the condition fails, which can happen even before the body of the loop is entered for the first time, the loop stops iteration at that point and the script's execution continues at the next statement after the while loop. The general format of the while loop is as follows:

```php
// Initialization condition;
while (condition)
{
```

```
4       statements;
5 }
```

For example, the following while loop displays the numbers 1..10:

```
1 $counter = 1;
2 while ($counter <= 10)
3 {
4       echo $counter++;
5 }
```

Just as with a for-loop, a while loop can be exited at any point by executing a break statement in the body of the loop, as well as by the usual return and exit statements.

8.5.4   Case statement

The PHP switch statement is standard. It uses an expression to determine which one of a set of possible cases should be executed. A switch statement has the following components:

- switch expression
- case statement
- case statement label
- body of case statement
- break statement for case (optional but usual)
- default statement (optional)

The following example illustrates the general syntax:

```
1 switch ($fruitType)
2 {
3     case "apple":
4         echo "Apples are computers.";
5         break;
6     case "pineapple":
7         echo "Pineapples are tropical.";
8         break;
9     default:
10        echo "None of the above matches $fruitType.";
11 }
```

In this example, the switch expression is $fruitType. It can be either numeric or string valued and determines at which of the listed sequence of cases to start execution, based on the labels of the case statements

and the value of $fruitType. This example has three cases or possible outcomes. There are two cases
with explicit case labels "apple" and "pineapple" (with the format: case label :). The remaining default
statement is selected if $fruitType matches none of the labels. In this instance, each case but the last includes
a break statement which causes an exit from the switch at the end of the case, so only that case is executed if
$fruitType matches its label. In the example, only the second case is executed if the expression $fruitType
has the value "pineapple", while only the last (default) is executed if $fruitType = "orange". Thus: none
of the cases may occur or match if the default is omitted; multiple sequential cases may be executed if breaks
are omitted; non-matching cases may be handled using a default. If the expression value were numeric, then its
corresponding case label would be numeric rather than a string.

8.6   Arrays and Associative Arrays

Arrays and associative arrays are considered as the same type in PHP. Arrays are distinguished by having integer
indices and use the following kind of notation:

```
1  $mathConstants[1] = 3.14;
2  $mathConstants[2] = "PI";
```

Associative arrays (as well as arrays) map associative keys to values (keys => values) with the same kind of
indexing notation:

```
1  $constants["PI"] = 3.14;
2  $constants["1"] = "PI";
```

Thus they allow either strings or integers (like "1" or 1) on either side of the relation. Because access can
be done via strings, the associative array acts like a data structure that provides a rapid search table (also called a
dictionary or mapping). Accessing the value corresponding to the array index or key corresponds to a lookup. In
the mapping terminology, the key "PI" in the array above maps to the value 3.14. The array can also be thought
of as a so-called hash table that maps keys to values. Arrays can be created by using assignment statements as
above. There are also multi-dimensional arrays like:

```
1  $matrixValues[1][1] = 3.14;
2  $matrixValues[1][2] = "PI";
```

Arrays can also be defined using the following compact list notation:

```
1  $constants = array("PI" => 3.14, "1" => "PI");
```

We have previously noted how the `var_dump` command displays arrays and their structural information such as (assuming `$constants` as above and `$value = 111`):

```
echo var_dump($constants, $value);
```

Its output:

Browser Output

```
array(2) { ["PI"]=> float(3.14) [1]=> string(2) "PI" } int(111)
```

Here the array information is enclosed in braces.

We have already seen important built-in PHP associative arrays like `$_GET` and `$_POST` which are associatively indexed by the field names on HTML Forms as previously discussed. Later we consider the built-in PHP global two-dimensional array `$_FILES` whose pair of associative indices are Form field names and file properties like size and MIME type, respectively. We will introduce this global associative array when we consider file uploads using PHP.

8.6.1 Array Creation and Manipulation

PHP arrays are an ordered map which associates each value with a key. In most programming languages array keys are limited to integers that start at 0 and increment by 1, but in PHP array keys can be either integer (the default) or strings and need not be sequential.

Array values are not limited to integer or strings, rather they can be of any object type or primitive type supported in PHP.

Elements are accessed via subscripts. The subscript is enclosed in brackets [] and is called the key.

8.6.2 Different Types of Arrays

SIMPLE ARRAY WITH DEFAULT KEYS EXAMPLE (Indexed Array)

```
$pets = array("dog", "cat", "fish", "bird", "lizard", "hamster", "guinea pig");
```

Since the key values are not explicitly specified, the default values are used. The default for keys in PHP will start with 0 and will increment by 1 for each element in the array (0...n-1).

ARRAY WITH KEYS EXAMPLE (Associative Array)

Since the key values are given, the default values are not used and the keys associated with each array element are uniquely user-defined keys.

```
$petowner = array("dog"=>"Doug", "cat"=>"Cathy", "fish"=>"Finn", "bird"=>"Bianca", "lizard"=>"Liam",
"hamster"=>"Harper", "guinea pig"=>"Gil");
```

MULTI-DIMENSIONAL ARRAY EXAMPLES (Indexed Array)
Using default key values of 0...n-1:

```php
$childrenbook = array();
$childrenbook[] = array("Beatrix Potter", "The Tale of Peter Rabbit", 9780723247708);
$childrenbook[] = array("Eric Carle", "The Very Hungry Caterpillar", 9780399226908);
$childrenbook[] = array("Marcus Pfister", "The Rainbow Fish", 9783314015441);
```

MULTI-DIMENSIONAL ARRAY EXAMPLES (Associative Array)
Using keys:

```php
$childrenbook = array();
$childrenbook[] = array("author" => "Beatrix Potter", "booktitle" => "The Tale of Peter Rabbit",
 "ISBN" =>9780723247708);
$childrenbook[] = array("author" => "Eric Carle", "booktitle" => "The Very Hungry Caterpillar",
 "ISBN" =>9780399226908);
$childrenbook[] = array("author" => "Marcus Pfister", "booktitle" => "The Rainbow Fish", "ISBN" =>
 9783314015441);
```

8.6.3 Adding and Removing Array Elements

We know that arrays in PHP are dynamic and therefore elements can be added to and deleted from the array.

Adding to an array can be done by specifying an index or key and the array will add the new element at the given index/key and shift any elements that exist after it.

One dimensional array example with index specified:

```php
<?php
//Create a one dimensional array
$pets = array("dog", "cat", "fish", "bird", "lizard", "hamster", "guinea pig");

//Add a new element to the array by specifying the index
$pets[3] = "rabbit";
```

When you specify an index that already exists, PHP replaces the existing element with the new one.
One dimensional array example with no index specified:

```php
<?php
//Create a one dimensional array
```

```php
3  $pets = array("dog", "cat", "fish", "bird", "lizard", "hamster", "guinea pig");
4
5  //Add a new element to the array with no index specified
6  $pets[] = "rabbit";
```

When no index is specified, the element is added to the end of the array.

8.6.4   Removing Array Elements

The `unset` function removes an array element:

```php
1  <?php
2  //Create a one dimensional array
3  $pets = array("dog", "cat", "fish", "bird", "lizard", "hamster", "guinea pig");
4
5  //Use the unset() function to remove an array element
6  unset($pets[3]);
```

When you remove an element from an array, it creates gaps in the index sequence. To realign the indexes after elements are removed, use the `array_values()` function:

```php
1  // Array after unset leaves gaps: 0, 1, 2, 4, 5, 6
2  $pets = array_values($pets);
3  // Now the array has sequential indexes: 0, 1, 2, 3, 4, 5
```

8.6.5   Array Sorting Functions

PHP has four sorting functions as shown in Table 8.4:

Table 8.4: Common PHP array sorting functions.

Sort Function	Description
`sort()`	Sorts an array in ascending order.
`rsort()`	Sorts an array in descending order.
`asort()`	Sorts an associative array in ascending order (keeps the association between values and keys).
`ksort()`	Sorts an associative array in ascending order according to the key.

8.7 **Built-in Functions**

PHP has extensive libraries of built-in functions of which we mention here only a very few. We shall also indicate in the next subsection how PHP programmers can define their own user-defined functions and include files.

8.7.1 `rand()`

The PHP `rand()` function generates a random integer, unlike the analog in Javascript which generates a random decimal on [0, 1). The PHP function `rand(min, max)` generates a random integer on [min, max] where `min` and `max` are integers.

8.7.2 `exit($message)`

The function `exit($message)` – (alias `die`) – prints the string `$message` and terminates the current script.

8.7.3 `sleep(int seconds)`

The function `sleep(seconds)` delays program execution for `seconds` seconds. This is handy, for example, to enforce a small delay in a login script so a web traversing robot cannot repeatedly generate password attempts in any realistic time frame. The `sleep` function behaves differently than the in Javascript (which does not block subsequent code executions, unlike the sleep function). Other variations delay for microseconds or sleep until a specified time.

8.7.4 `is_numeric()`

There are many functions in PHP that determine whether an input is of a certain type or not. For example, recall that HTML Forms transmit strings, not integers, floating point numbers or Booleans. To verify that the input from such a Form is (say) numeric, one can use the variable handling function `is_numeric()` where `is_numeric($x)` returns true if the input `$x` is a number or numeric string, decimal, float, hexadecimal, etc.

8.7.5 `date(format string)`

The PHP `date` function has a complicated format string which is required as an argument. For example:

```
1 date("l dS \\of F Y h:i:s A")
```

This invocation gives detailed basic date information. The format controls are easily forgettable, like the first lowercase "L" (`l`) in the above which means that the day of the week is spelt out.

Other useful functions:
- `strlen($str)` gives the length of a string.
- `substr($str, $start, $len)` extracts a substring.
- `strpos($haystack, $needle)` finds the position of a substring.
- `str_replace($search, $replace, $string)` replaces occurrences of text.
- `count($array)` returns number of elements in an array.

- `array_keys($array)` and `array_values($array)` give the keys and values.
- `sort($array)` sorts an array (and `rsort`, `asort`, `ksort` for reverse, associative by value, associative by key sorting, respectively).
- `explode($delimiter, $string)` splits a string into an array.
- `implode($glue, $array)` joins an array into a string.

PHP's official documentation has a comprehensive function reference with examples for each function.

8.7.6 Predefined Arithmetic Functions

Some useful predefined arithmetic functions are shown in Table 8.5

Table 8.5: Common PHP arithmetic functions.

Arithmetic Function	Description
`abs($value)`	The absolute (positive) value of a number is returned.
`ceil($value)`	The number is rounded up to the nearest whole number and this value is returned.
`floor($value)`	The number is rounded down to the nearest whole number and its value returned.
`max($n1, $n2, ...)`	The highest value in an array or of several specified values is returned.
`min($n1, $n2, ...)`	The lowest value in an array or of several specified values is returned.
`pi()`	The value of PI ($\approx$ 3.141593) is returned.
`rand([$range1, $range2])`	A random integer number is generated based upon the range given as parameters.
`round($value [, $precision])`	The floating point number is rounded and returns the value from rounding to the number of decimal points specified.
`sqrt($value)`	The square root of the value is returned.
`srand([$seed])`	A random number generator that is seeded.

8.7.7 String Functions

Common PHP string functions that are used to manipulate the string literal are shown in Table 8.6.

Table 8.6: Common PHP string functions.

String Function	Description
chop()	Characters are removed from the right end of a string.
ltrim()	Characters are removed from the left side of a string.
rtrim()	Characters are removed from the right side of a string.
strcmp()	Comparison of two strings is performed. Returns 0 if the strings are equal; a negative value if the second string is greater; a positive value if the second string is less.
strlen()	Determines the length of a string and returns the value.
strpos()	Determines the position of the first occurrence of a string inside another string.
strtolower()	Converts the characters in a string to lowercase.
strtoupper()	Converts the characters in a string to uppercase.
substr()	Returns the substring of a string.
trim()	Removes characters from both sides of a string.

8.8   User-defined Functions

To define and apply user-defined functions, we need to know:
- How to define a function in PHP?
- How to include a PHP function definition in a script?
- How to invoke a user-defined function?
- How to define function parameters?
- How to return a function value?

We define a function in the usual way: by writing the code for the function prototype and its body:

```php
<?php
function functionName($parameter1, $parameter2, ...)
{
    // PHP code
    return $result; // optional
}
?>
```

The function can return values via a return statement such as using any of the following:

```php
return ($result); //returns value of $result
return (true);    //returns Boolean value true
return (false);   //returns Boolean value false
```

The function definition can be included directly in the PHP script (with the definition at the start of the PHP segment and the function invocation after that) or it can be enclosed (with its opening and closing PHP tags) in a separate file which is then cross-referenced by the script using an include statement. A typical file containing a user-defined function definition(s) or code segments might be named:

```
Functions.inc.php
```

The `.php` extension should be included to ensure the privacy of the function definition, while the rest of the name (`Functions.inc`) is user determined, with "inc" standing for "include". A script can then cross-reference this file using the PHP include statement:

```
1  include("Functions.inc.php");
```

Incidentally, the resulting included content does not show up if one uses a show_source call on the file containing the include. The included function is invoked in the conventional way by naming the function and listing its arguments:

```
1  functionName($parameterValue);
```

That is all the syntax we need to define and use PHP functions.

8.8.1   Function Definition Syntax

Having all your code in the main body of your script makes it harder to reuse, maintain and understand. Thus PHP allows for functions which are used to accomplish a single task. These functions can be made to behave differently based upon the values of their parameters.

Functions exist on their own and are called from code that needs to use them as long as they are in scope.

PHP has two types of functions: user defined functions, which are created by you the developer, and built-in functions, which come with the PHP environment that has a rich library of built-in functions.

When creating a user-defined function think about the function's purpose and its name. Functions can return values back to the function that called it or return no value, and they can have parameters or not have parameters.

The following piece of code shows the basic syntax of a function:

```
1  function name_of_function(list of parameters if needed)
2  {
3      // Code to execute
4  }
```

We can see a function definition:

- Requires the keyword `function`.
- The name of the function.
- Parentheses for whether it has parameters or not. If it has parameters they are separated by commas.
- The body of the function contained within curly brackets { }.

Example of a function that returns a value:

```php
<?php
//Function that calculates cost and returns the value of $cost
function totalCost()
{
    $cost = (100 + 50 + 50);
    return $cost += ($cost * .10);
}

//Print out the total cost after a call to the function totalCost which calculates the cost
echo ("The total cost is $" . totalCost());
?>
```

8.8.2 Return Type Declarations

PHP 7.0 added the ability to explicitly define a return type for a function, allowing the developer to force a function to return a certain type of value.

This is done via a Return Type Declaration that explicitly defines a function's return type. Accomplished by adding a colon and the return type after the parameter list when defining a function:

```php
<?php
//Must use this statement in order to use Return Type Declarations
declare(strict_types=1);

//Function that calculates cost based on what was spent and the tax rate
function totalCost(int $cost, float $taxRate) : int
{
    return $cost += $cost * $taxRate;
}

//Initialize variables which will become parameters for the function totalCost
$cost = 250;
$taxRate = 0.0675;
//Call the function totalCost and print out the value
echo "The final cost is $" . totalCost($cost, $taxRate);
?>
```

8.8.3   Parameters and Arguments

Parameters (or arguments) allow for values to be passed into functions. There are two types of parameters: formal parameters are those listed in parentheses after the function name in the function declaration, and they do not have a specific value but rather act as placeholders for the actual parameters when the function is called; actual parameters are those listed in parentheses after the function name when the function is called, and they contain the actual values passed into the function.

The actual parameters and formal parameters need to be in one-to-one correspondence in order and type. When using parameters in conjunction with a function, you must decide how many parameters will be passed in and what order they will be passed. Example of parameters and arguments:

```php
<?php
//Function to check if the number passed into a function is an integer or float value
function integerOrFloat($number)
{
    if (is_int($number))
    {
        echo ("The number " . $number . " is an integer");
        echo("<br><br>");
    }
    else
    {
        echo ("The number " . $number . " is a float");
    }
}

//Call/Execute the function
integerOrFloat(200);
integerOrFloat(25.75);
?>
```

8.8.4   Default Parameter Values

Defaults can be assigned to parameters in PHP. These values ensure that the specified parameter will have a value even when one is not passed into the function. It should be noted though once parameter default values are started all subsequent parameters must also have default values.

```php
<?php
//Function to check if the number passed into a function is an integer or float value
//Add a default value of 0
function integerOrFloat($number = 0)
{
```

```php
 6      if (is_int($number))
 7      {
 8          echo ("The number " . $number . " is an integer");
 9          echo ("<br><br>");
10      }
11      else
12      {
13          echo ("The number " . $number . " is a float");
14          echo ("<br><br>");
15      }
16 }
17
18 //Call/Execute the function
19 integerOrFloat(200);
20 integerOrFloat(25.75);
21 integerOrFloat();
22 ?>
```

8.8.5   Pass by Value vs. Pass by Reference

PHP allows parameters to be passed into functions in one of two different ways. When passed by value, a copy of the variable's value is passed into the function and thus it does not affect its memory location; any change made within the function is lost once the function finishes execution, and default values are passed by value. When passed by reference, the actual memory location of the variable is passed to the function and therefore any modifications that occur during the execution of the function remain once the function completes execution; an ampersand (&) is placed before any parameter's name in the function declaration when it is to be passed by reference. Example of pass by value:

```php
 1 <?php
 2 //Function that passes in a parameter by value
 3 function passByValue($number)
 4 {
 5     $number = ($number + 5) * 5 / 2 ;
 6 }
 7 //Initialize parameter value, print the value before function execution, call the function and print
 8   the value of the parameter after execution
 8 $num = 5;
 9 echo ("Value before function call: " . $num);
10 passByValue($num);
11 echo ("<br><br>");
12 echo ("Value after function call: " . $num);
13 ?>
```

Example of pass by reference:

```php
1  <?php
2  //Function that passes in a parameter by reference
3  function passByReference(&$number)
4  {
5      $number = ($number + 5) * 5 / 2 ;
6  }
7
8  //Initialize parameter value, print the value before function execution, call the function and print
   the value of the parameter after execution
9  $num = 5;
10 echo ("Value before function call: " . $num);
11 passByReference($num);
12 echo ("<br><br>");
13 echo ("Value after function call: " . $num);
14 ?>
```

8.8.6 Variable Scope

The scope of a variable determines whether a piece of code has access to it. A local variable is available and accessible only to the function it is defined in. A global variable is available and accessible outside of the function; to make the variable accessible inside the function, you need to use the keyword global before the variable name. Example of local scope:

```php
1  <?php
2  //Function demonstrating local scope
3  function localScope()
4  {
5      //Initialize message
6      $message = "Welcome to Web Development";
7      //Display the message
8      echo "Display the welcome message of: '" .$message . "' inside the function";
9  }
10
11 //Execute/Call function and then display message
12 localScope();
13 echo ("<br><br>");
14 echo "Display the welcome message of: '" .$message . "' outside the function";
15 echo ("<br><br>");
16 ?>
```

Example of global scope with keyword:

```php
1  <?php
2  //Initialize message
3  $message = "Welcome to Web Development";
4
5  //Function demonstrating global scope with keyword global
6  function globalKeywordScope()
7  {
8      //Initialize message so it is a global variable
9      global $message ;
10     echo "Display the welcome message of: '" .$message . "' inside the function";
11 }
12
13 //Execute/Call function and then display message
14 globalKeywordScope();
15 echo ("<br><br>");
16 echo "Display the welcome message of: '" .$message . "' outside the function";
17 ?>
```

> **R** From a programming design standpoint, the use of global variables should be minimized, and used only for objects that are truly global.

8.9 PHP Functions for Security

Web applications need to be secure by design. User input should never be trusted, and sensitive operations like authentication must be done carefully. PHP provides built-in functions and features to help with common security tasks such as input sanitization, password hashing, and encryption. While an exhaustive treatment of security is beyond the scope of this introduction, we will highlight a few crucial aspects.

8.9.1 Input Sanitization

Input sanitization is the process of cleaning up or validating data received from users (or any external source) before using it in our program (especially if that data will be used in a database query, displayed on a page, or included in an email, etc.). The goal is to prevent malicious data from causing harm. For example, preventing SQL injection by removing or escaping SQL syntax in a database query, or preventing XSS (Cross-Site Scripting) by escaping HTML characters in output.

PHP offers the `filter_var` function and related filter functions in the filter extension to validate and sanitize data easily. For example:

```php
$email = $_POST['email'];
if (filter_var($email, FILTER_VALIDATE_EMAIL))
{
    // $email is a valid email format
}
else
{
    // invalid email
}
```

This uses a built-in filter to check if the string is a valid email.

There are filters for validating integers, booleans, URLs, etc., and also for sanitizing (e.g., removing illegal characters from an email address, rather than validating format).

Another example, to sanitize a string to have only letters and numbers:

```php
$username = $_POST['username'];
$cleanUsername = preg_replace("/[^A-Za-z0-9]/", "", $username);
```

This uses a regular expression to remove any character that is not a letter or number.

It is important to choose the right approach depending on what you need:

- Validation (checking if input meets criteria) vs. Sanitization (modifying input to meet criteria or to be safe).
- For HTML output, use functions like `htmlspecialchars` or `htmlentities` to escape special characters ($<$, $>$, &, quotes) so they are not interpreted as HTML/JS.
- For database usage, use prepared statements with bound parameters or at least `mysqli_real_escape_string` for strings to avoid SQL injection.
- For file system usage (like filenames), remove/replace dangerous characters like `../` or null bytes which could lead to directory traversal or other issues.

In summary: Never directly trust `$_GET`, `$_POST`, `$_COOKIE`, etc. Always validate or sanitize as appropriate for the context.

8.9.2 Authentication Functions

Authentication typically involves verifying that a user is who they claim to be (usually by checking a username/email and password). PHP provides some built-in functions to help with password handling:

- `password_hash($password, PASSWORD_DEFAULT)` will hash a plaintext password using a strong algorithm (typically bcrypt) and a random salt. It returns a string (the hash) that you can store in a database.

- `password_verify($plaintext, $hash)` will verify a plaintext password against a hash (produced by `password_hash`) and return true if they match.
- `password_needs_rehash($hash, PASSWORD_DEFAULT)` can be used to check if an existing hash needs to be regenerated (e.g., if you update to a stronger algorithm).

These functions abstract away the details of salt generation and algorithm selection. You should always use them rather than using insecure approaches like MD5 or SHA1 without salt.

Example usage:

```php
// During registration:
$passwordHash = password_hash($_POST['password'], PASSWORD_DEFAULT);

// During login:
$hashFromDb = /* retrieve hash for the username */;
if (password_verify($_POST['password'], $hashFromDb))
{
    // Password is correct --- proceed with login (e.g., set session)
}
else
{
    // Incorrect password
}
```

Other security functions and features include `hash_hmac($algorithm, $data, $key)` for creating a message authentication code (MAC) to ensure data integrity using a secret key, and `openssl_encrypt` and `openssl_decrypt` for encryption using various algorithms (which requires understanding of cryptography to use correctly). PHP sessions and cookies (discussed later) can be used for managing logged-in state, with considerations for using secure flags (secure cookies, HTTPOnly, etc.). The function `ini_set('session.cookie_httponly', 1);` and similar configurations make cookies HTTPOnly (not accessible to JavaScript, mitigating XSS). Database libraries like PDO offer built-in protection against SQL injection via prepared statements.

Security is a vast topic. The key takeaway is to use established functions and best practices rather than writing custom security implementations.

8.9.3 Regular Expressions for Pattern Matching

Pattern matching in PHP can be accomplished via regular expressions. Regular expressions are a set of special characters that define a pattern, intended for matching and manipulation of text. They are commonly used to see if user input matches a predictable sequence of characters such as emails, and provide a concise way to eliminate conditional logic.

Regular expressions consist of two types of characters: literals, which are characters trying to match in the target, and metacharacters, which are special symbols that act as commands to the parser.

There are 11 metacharacters in PHP, as shown in Table 8.7. These PHP metacharacters are common with JavaScript.

Table 8.7: Regular expression metacharacters in PHP.

Metacharacter	Description
.	Matches any character in the pattern.
[ ]	Accepts any one of the characters within the square bracket or any character within the range.
\	Escape character that allows a metacharacter to be matched.
( )	Groups the part of the regular expressions enclosed within the ( ) together. Thus, allowing a quantifier to the entire group or restricts alternation (OR operator) to part of the REGEXP.
^	Anchor symbol that is used to force the pattern to match the entire comparison string from its beginning character until its last character. The ^ is the delimiter of the beginning character of the pattern. When it is inside brackets [ ] it means not.
$	Anchor symbol that is used to force the pattern to match the entire comparison string from its beginning character until its last character. The $ is the delimiter of the last character of the pattern.
|	Denotes the pattern for alternative patterns (OR operator).
*	Matches a pattern zero or more times.
?	Matches a pattern zero or one time.
{ }	Used to match exactly n instances of the preceding character or pattern.
+	Matches a pattern one or more times.

Additionally, a few common regular expressions and their descriptions are shown in Table8.8.

Table 8.8: Common regular expressions and their descriptions.

Common Regular Expression	Description
`^\s{0,8}$`	Matches 0 to 8 non-space characters.
`^\w{8,16}$`	Simple password expression indicating the password must be at least 8 characters in length, but no more than 16 characters long.
`^+\w*\d+\w*$`	Another password expression that requires at least one letter, followed by any number of characters, followed by at least one number, followed by any number of characters.
`^\d{5}(-\4{4})?$`	Matches a zip code.
`^((0[1-9]) | (1[0-2]))\ / (\d{4})$`	Matches a month and year in mm/yyyy format.
`^(.+)@([^\.]*)\.([a-z]{2,})$`	Matches a valid email address based on current standard naming rules.
`^((http | https)://)?([\w-]+\.)+[\w ]+(/[w-./?]*)?`	URL validation. Matches either http or https, matches word characters or hyphens, followed by a period followed either by a forward slash, word characters or a period.
`^4\d{3}[\s-]d{4}[\s-] d{4}[\s-]d{4}`	Matches a Visa credit card (four sets of four digits beginning with the number 4) separated by a space or a hyphen.
`^5[1-5]\d{2}[\s-]d{4}[\s-] d{4}[\s-]d{4}$`	Matches a Mastercard credit card (four sets of four digits beginning with the number 51-55) separated by a space or a hyphen.

8.10   Generating Dynamically Sized HTML Tables

One of the commonest Internet application problems is to retrieve data from a background database using a scripting language like PHP together with a query language like SQL to interact with the database, then structure the retrieved data with HTML markup tags for effective visual display in a browser. The data from the database is often displayed in a tabular layout, based on an HTML table sent to the browser and constructed dynamically by the PHP program.

In addition to its practical significance, it is conceptually interesting to understand how we can use one language (in this case PHP) to construct the code for another language (in this case the markup language HTML). Doing this requires not only an understanding of PHP and the environment it operates in, but also a thorough grasp of HTML constructs like tables and how to construct or manufacture the HTML code for the table using an algorithm written in PHP. The PHP program thus becomes a sort of software factory, which the PHP developer designs, that builds or constructs HTML code, based on parameters transmitted from an HTML Form. The constructed HTML code is thus dynamically generated rather than statically defined.

8.10.1   Pseudo-code Algorithm to Construct HTML Table

Consider how the logic of the following pseudo-code algorithm (for constructing a times table) correlates with the syntactical structure of an HTML table.

```
 1  Start table
 2  For I = 1 .. 12
 3  {
 4      Start row
 5      For K = 1 .. 12
 6      {
 7          Start cell
 8          Make Product I * K
 9          Stop cell
10      }
11      Stop row
12  }
13  Stop table
```

Figure 8.2 illustrates the logic needed to generate an HTML table showing the values of the 12 times multiplication table.

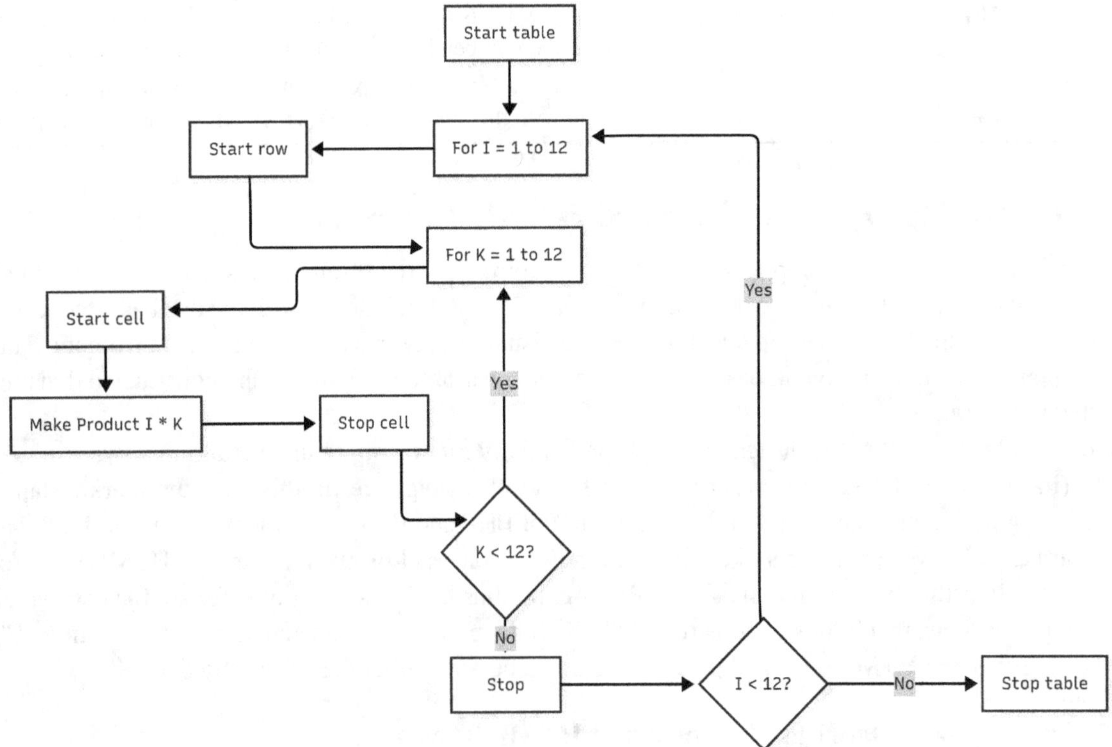

Figure 8.2: Flow chart for generating a multiplication table.

8.10.2   Sample Implementation

Implementation requires converting this pseudo-code into PHP. For example, the pseudo-code: Start table translates into the PHP code: print "<table>".

Refer to the skeletal HTML (times.html) and PHP (times.php) versions below. The PHP script `times.php` outputs a 12x12 multiplication table.

times.html:

```html
<form action = "times.php" >
    <input type = "text" name = "NAME" />YOUR NAME <br>
    <input type = "text" name = "M" />M (INTEGER) <br>
    <input type = "text" name = "N" />N (INTEGER) <br>
    <input type = "submit" value = "Make M by N times table." />
</form >
```

times.php:

```php
<?php
print "<table width=80% border=1 bordercolor=red>" ;
for ($row = 1; $row <= 12; $row++)
{
    print "<tr>" ;
    for ($column = 1; $column <= 12; $column++)
    {
        print "<td>" ;
        print "$row x $column = " . $row * $column ;
        print "</td>" ;
    }
    print "</tr>" ;
}
print "</table>" ;
?>
```

For illustrative purposes, we have included some simple HTML attributes in the PHP code. To finalize the solution, the PHP code needs to be enhanced to access the form values M and N in order to make the table size dynamic. This is done with the usual `$_GET` global array:

```php
$rows = $_GET["M"];
$columns = $_GET["N"];
$userName = $_GET["NAME"];
```

The form's NAME field is used for displaying the user name in a spanning cell at the top of the table so the code also needs the $userName$ variable.

We can obtain various style effects (dimensions for cell borders, font colors for cell text) using a style rule in the head element of the HTML header for the page, such as using the shorthand notation to designate a solid blue cell border:

```
1  <style>
2  td {font-color:blue; border:3px solid blue; }
3  </style>
```

The centered bold text in the first row (with default black text color) comes from including a th in a row with a colspan attribute that matches the (dynamic) table size. The code needs both $userName$ to show the form NAME and $columns$ to show the number of columns (since $columns$ controls the inner for-loop that generates the cell entries for each row). The slightly modified PHP code should now include:

```
1  print "<table width = 80% border = 1 bordercolor = red>";
2  print "<tr colspan = $columns><th>$userName</th></tr>";
```

The PHP variables $userName$ and $columns$ can be directly included in the print strings, positioned according to their HTML roles ($columns$ as the colspan attribute value and $userName$ as the first row's cell content).

Even as innocuous program as the multiplication table one is open to security risks. The above script does not check the input values for the size of the table, in violation of the usual (best practice) dictum to not trust user input. Always validate that the input values fall within an acceptable range to prevent potential resource exhaustion or other attacks.

 The variable `$_SERVER` is a PHP global array that contains server and execution environment information. For example, `$_SERVER['SERVER_PROTOCOL']` returns the protocol via which the page was requested. The argument `SERVER_NAME` returns the name of the host on which the script is running. The argument `HTTP_HOST` gives the contents of the host from the current request. `REMOTE_ADDR` gives the IP address from which the user is viewing the current page.

8.11   Uploading Files Using PHP

Seeing how to upload a file in a web environment using PHP is instructive because its implementation involves several important topics: system HTTP access privileges, as well as HTML and PHP capabilities. The following discussion introduces the relevant tools and ideas.

The administrative aspect entails the use of a server configuration to set what are called HTTP access privileges. The HTML capability involves an input element type that creates a widget that allows the user to browse their local file system in order to select a file for upload. The PHP script that handles the upload request relies on several PHP features, including a built-in associative array named `$_FILES` which provides detailed information about uploaded files. This information allows us to filter or selectively accept or reject requests for an upload. We will evolve the example incrementally starting with a primitive version by progressively adding filtering functionality, and exploring different control structures for implementing the example.

There are several concerns to be addressed when using PHP to upload a file to a web site:

1. The directory where the file is stored into must be given appropriate write permission on the server.
2. The HTML Form that requests the upload requires a special input field of type file that allows the user to browse their local file system for a file to be uploaded.
3. The PHP program must move the uploaded file from a temporary location and name provided by the web server to a target directory of the program's choice, and a name determined by the user (which may be the original filename).

We consider each of these issues in order.

8.11.1   Server Directory Permissions

The file uploaded by the browser is initially stored in a temporary directory on the file system, and under a temporary name assigned by the web server. The file must be moved by the PHP program that uploaded it from that temporary location to a directory in the user's file space. Otherwise, it will be automatically removed by the web server after the PHP program terminates. Figure 8.3 shows the transitions for uploading files.

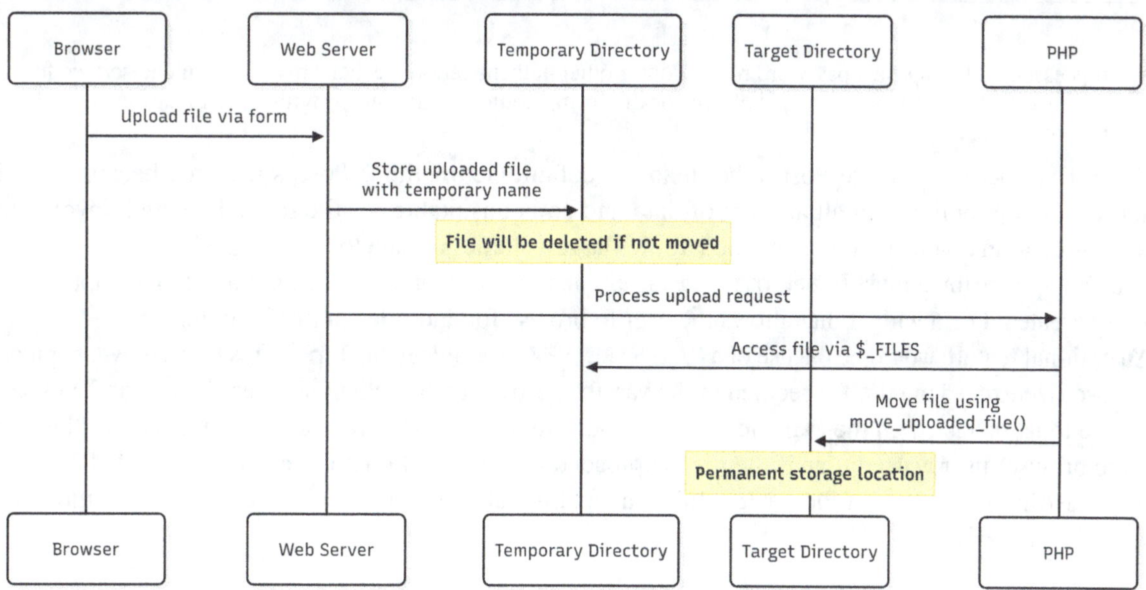

Figure 8.3: Transitions for uploaded file(s).

To enable the required move, the target directory for the move operation must be given appropriate write privileges on the server, otherwise any attempt by the PHP program to move the uploaded file into the directory will fail.

On Unix/Linux servers, this might involve using the chmod command to set appropriate permissions:

```
1  chmod 755 /path/to/upload/directory
```

For security reasons, it is generally advisable to place the upload directory outside of the web root if possible, or to use `.htaccess` files to prevent direct access to uploaded files if they could contain executable content.

8.11.2 HTML Form for File Input

The HTML syntax required for a Form to upload a file interoperates with the PHP program that handles the request and which may filter out requested files based on their type, size or other characteristics. The Form uses the Post method, a special encoding type, and an input element of type file. The basic syntax is as follows:

```
1  <form action = "upload.php" method = "POST" enctype = "multipart/form-data">
2      <input type = "file" name = "uploadedFile" />File to be uploaded<br>
3      <input type = "password" name = "accessCode" />Enter access code<br>
4      <input type = "submit" name = "submit" />
5  </form>
```

 It is essential to impose a password restriction or other authentication mechanism on any upload service for security reasons. The source code above for the form should be augmented with authentication controls before the service is deployed.

The HTTP method is set to Post rather than the default Get method. Post is required because the GET method is suitable only for small amount of data and so is unsuitable for file uploads, which involve large amounts of data; in contrast the Post method allows large volumes of data to be uploaded.

The enctype attribute must be set to `multipart/form-data` in order to transmit a file. The input type file is used to create a Form widget that allows the user to browse for and select a file for upload.

An optional feature would be the use of a `MAX_FILE_SIZE` variable in the form. This helps prevent uploading files whose size exceed the limits specified in the variable. However, this client-side restriction can be bypassed, so the size must be tested on the PHP side as well. Despite this, this HTML feature remains useful because it saves the browser user wasted time if the file is uploaded only to be ultimately rejected on the PHP side. The syntax to restrict the size is as follows. It requires an additional field that must be included before the type file element:

```
1  <input type = "hidden" name = "MAX_FILE_SIZE" value = "30000" />
```

8.11.3 Hidden Input Fields

Hidden input fields allow data to be sent to the PHP code that is not visible or modifiable by the user on the form:

```
1  <h1>A Hidden Input</h1>
2  <form action = "HiddenInput.php" method = "POST">
3      <label for = "Name">First name:</label>
4      <input type = "text" id = "Name" name = "Name"><br><br>
5      <input type = "hidden" id = "SSN" name = "SSN" value = "123-45-6789">
6      <input type = "submit" value = "Submit">
7  </form>
```

When using POST, the hidden data is sent via the HTTP POST request body and does not appear in the URL. When using GET, the query string (including hidden values) appears in the URL, making it visible to users.

8.11.4 Rudimentary Upload Program

We first illustrate a rudimentary upload service where the file is uploaded without restriction, which of course is not a good idea since it exposes your system to uploads of files of arbitrary size and type. This example is only for demonstration purposes. Later we will elaborate the example to allow filtering files according to a variety of restrictions as well as require password access for the upload service.

The web server uploads the file identified by a browser to a temporary location (with a temporary filename) from which it must be moved to a user directory before the PHP program terminates. The format of the PHP command to move an uploaded file from its original location to a user-specified target location is:

```
1  move_uploaded_file(string $filename, string $destination)
```

where string $filename is the temporary location of the uploaded file and $destination is the name and location where the file is to be moved.

PHP maintains the temporary location of the uploaded file in an associative array which is constructed when the file is uploaded. We will consider additional information provided by this array shortly, as well as the syntax for PHP associative arrays in general. For now we observe only that the reference:

```
1  $_FILES["uploadedFile"]["tmp_name"]
```

This returns the full path to the temporary uploaded file including its temporary name.

$_FILES is the reserved name for the associative array for an upload, "uploadedFile" is the name we gave to the file input field on the HTML Form, and "tmp_name" (not "temp_name") is a keyword used to access this temporary location and name.

The $destination path is only given relative to the current directory in which the PHP program file is located (which acts as the root of the relative addressing scheme). For simplicity, we will assume for now that we want to move the uploaded file to the same directory as the PHP program, under the name test.txt, regardless of its original file name or type, as in:

```php
1  <?php
2    move_uploaded_file($_FILES["uploadedFile"]["tmp_name"], "test.txt");
3  ?>
```

This is obviously only meaningful if the original file is of type txt, since if the type is other than txt then the uploaded file's extension would have to be changed even to open the file properly, but our point is that this illustrates the most primitive upload script.

A slight modification will move the temporary file to a subdirectory. Assume that the target directory is named upload and is a subdirectory of the current directory containing the upload script. We can change the move command to:

```php
1  move_uploaded_file($_FILES["uploadedFile"]["tmp_name"], "upload/test.txt");
```

Another slight modification to the code will preserve the name (and extension) of the original file as it was in the user's local file system. This is available from the $_FILES array as:

```php
1  $_FILES["uploadedFile"]["name"]
```

where the keyword name is used to access the $_FILES original name of the uploaded file (not a path to the file, just its name). Assuming the uploaded file is to be moved to the same directory as the PHP program, the move command becomes:

```php
1  move_uploaded_file($_FILES["uploadedFile"]["tmp_name"], $_FILES["uploadedFile"]["name"]);
```

Finally, if the file is to be moved to the upload subdirectory of the current directory, the corresponding command is:

```php
1  move_uploaded_file($_FILES["uploadedFile"]["tmp_name"], "upload/" . $_FILES["uploadedFile"]["name"]);
```

The second parameter concatenates the upload subdirectory with the original file name (and extension type) using the dot concatenation operator (.).

8.11.5 Associative Arrays and $_FILES Global Variable

PHP arrays are indexed tables that allow both integer and (associative) string indices whose values can be of any type. The following PHP code illustrates how to construct and display a user-defined (not a built-in or reserved) two-dimensional array $timesTable[][] with numeric indices:

```php
for ($row = 1; $row < 10; $row++)
{
  for ($column = 1; $column < 10; $column++)
  {
      $timesTable[$row][$column] = $row * $column;
      print(" " . $timesTable[$row][$column] . " ");
  }
   print("<br>");
}
```

In general, PHP array indices can be strings, so the array acts like an associative memory whose contents are accessed based on content references rather than (necessarily) via numbers as in:

```php
$animals["cat"]["feet"] = 4;
$animals["frog"]["feet"] = 4;
$animals["bird"]["eyes"] = 2;
print("cat " . $animals["cat"]["feet"] . "<br>");
print("frog " . $animals["frog"]["feet"] . "<br>");
print("bird " . $animals["bird"]["eyes"] . "<br>");
```

As previously observed $_FILES is a built-in PHP associative array created by a web server when a file is uploaded via HTTP to a web server. It contains information about the upload which is accessible by a PHP program running on the server. The $_FILES array has two component indices. The first is the name of the HTML file element corresponding to the upload ("uploadedFile" in our example). The second index is one of a set of keywords that identify various properties of the upload file. We have already used two of these components:

- $_FILES["uploadedFile"]["name"]
- $_FILES["uploadedFile"]["tmp_name"]

Other components useful for monitoring uploads and filtering upload requests are:

- $_FILES["uploadedFile"]["size"]
- $_FILES["uploadedFile"]["type"]
- $_FILES["uploadedFile"]["error"]

The "error" component is a binary flag (0 or 1) that indicates if an error has occurred during upload (0 means no error). The "size" component gives the integer number of bytes in the uploaded file. The "type" component gives the MIME type of the file as a MIME type/subtype pair, such as `"text/plain"` for a text file, `"text/html"` for an HTML file, `"image/gif"` for a GIF image file, or `"image/pjpeg"` for a jpg file. (Beware however that this property is under client control.) For example, when a sample file was uploaded these last three components were:

Table 8.9: Example of PHP $_FILES array output.

Key	Operator	Value
`$_FILES["uploadedFile"]["size"]`	=>	494
`$_FILES["uploadedFile"]["type"]`	=>	`"text/html"`
`$_FILES["uploadedFile"]["error"]`	=>	0

The values of program variables including associative arrays like `$_FILES` can be retrieved with the var_dump function and output to the requesting browser with an echo statement. For example, if `$_FILES["uploadedFile"]` and `$value` are program variables the following sends the values of its (arbitrary) list of parameters to the browser:

```
echo var_dump($_FILES["uploadedFile"], $value);
```

8.11.6   Filtering Upload Requests

So far our simple upload example does no screening on the upload requests. We will now show how to filter the requests based on file properties, but even more fundamentally we will first screen the requests to verify that we allow this user to have upload privileges. There are a variety of levels at which we could do this, but we shall just use a simple hard-coded password test. This is the first viable use of a password test we have encountered. Passwords could not be legitimately applied, for example, in a Javascript environment since the password testing code would be visible to the client. Since the PHP script runs on the web server, its code and hence any passwords are not visible or disclosed to the user.

We begin by enhancing the HTML Form with a password field:

```
Enter password here: <input type = "password" name = "accessCode" />
```

Here we use the "password" type in the Form to mask the typed text of the password as it is entered. On the server-side we need a password test and a corresponding accept/reject action such as:

```
if ($_POST["accessCode"] != "securePassword") exit("Invalid password.");
```

The exit() function has the form:

```
exit(string message)
```

The message argument is sent to the client and the script terminates after the command is executed.

Next we turn to filtering requests based on file properties. For example, file size restrictions (or violations) can be handled as follows:

```
if ($_FILES["uploadedFile"]["size"] > 30000) { exit("File Too Big."); }
```

This blocks requests for files larger than 30,000 bytes. This formulation of the filtering logic looks for a violation of a filtering criterion and exits as soon as one is spotted. The physically subsequent code in the script does not even have to be looked at for a reader to understand what happens if the condition succeeds.

We can then add other filtering conditions by appending them. For example, the most obvious way to handle restrictions on file MIME types is as follows. Suppose the objective is to only allow uploads for GIF and JPG files. Then an appropriate screening condition is:

```
if (
    ($_FILES["uploadedFile"]["type"] != "image/pjpeg") &&
    ($_FILES["uploadedFile"]["type"] != "image/gif")
)
{
   exit("File type not allowed.");
}
```

The boolean condition with the AND (&&) operator succeeds only if the file is neither GIF nor JPG, in which case the upload is disallowed and the script is immediately terminated at this line.

The sequencing of such filters (the first for size, the second for type) means a file has to pass all the tests or filters; otherwise the script exits with some "No can do." message. The filters above test for negative, non-satisfying conditions that cause the upload request to be blocked or stopped in its tracks if any condition violation is spotted. If the statements had been formulated in a positive fashion (like checking whether files satisfied a size or type test, rather than failed one), then we would be obliged to use nested if-else statements which would ultimately be more unwieldy to deal with. For example, in pseudo-code such logic would look like:

```
if (size < some limit)
{
   if (type is GIF or JPG)
      {
```

```
 5          --- upload the file ---
 6      }
 7      else
 8      {
 9          exit with message: file type wrong
10      }
11  }
12  else
13  {
14      exit with message: file too big
15  }
```

This is perfectly acceptable logic, but the construction becomes more complicated looking and harder to read as successive barriers are integrated into the test in the nested fashion shown. The perceptual/cognitive problem is that the action associated with the failure of a condition may be textually remote in the code from the condition it is related to. Furthermore, the exit actions also occur textually in the reverse of the order in which they are recognized by the code. For example, the "too big" exit above occurs at the last line of code even though the associated condition regarding size occurs at the first line of the code. The or die construct commonly used in PHP simplifies the logic further and allows us to state the filtering conditions in a more natural positive form that is easier to understand, as we shall describe next.

8.11.7   Pseudo-Code for Upload and die function

The filters for password authorization, size and file type can be described with the following pseudo-code description.

```
1  If wrong password
2      Message and exit
3  If file too big
4      Message and exit
5  If file wrong type
6      Message and exit
7  Otherwise
8      Move file and send message.
```

This is essentially what we implemented above, but an even cleaner logic can be accomplished with the PHP or die construct described below.

The PHP die function (which is like the PHP exit function) is frequently used in the following way:

```
1  (condition) or die("string message");
```

Observe that this is just an expression. In particular, there is no if used before the Boolean condition, and furthermore the die in this case is executed only if the condition fails, not if it succeeds as would happen in the case of an if statement. This works as follows. Because of the shortcut evaluation manner in which the or operator is evaluated in PHP, if the Boolean condition in the first parentheses succeeds, then execution of the program continues with the sequentially next statement in the code, not with the die function. The shortcut evaluation works because in an or-expression, such as: A or B, if A is true, then the overall expression is true and there is no need for the PHP processor to evaluate B; while if A is false then the B must be evaluated to determine the value of the overall expression. On the other hand, if the condition before the or fails, then the die function after the or operator must be executed to complete the evaluation of the overall expression and as a result its message is posted to the browser and the program terminates (dies) at that point, without executing any of the subsequent statements in the program. This is the reverse of the situation for the earlier implementation via if-constructs, which acted like violation detectors rather than requirement recognizers. This makes the role of the conditions or filters more natural and easier to understand. Using this construct, the previous pseudo-code can be modified as shown in Table 8.10.

Table 8.10: File upload filters using or die construct.

Condition	Operator	Action
(password OK?)	or	die("Invalid password.");
(size OK?)	or	die("File too big.");
(type OK?)	or	die("Invalid type.");

Otherwise move file and send status message to browser.

The conditions thus act like a chain of hurdles that the upload request must successfully overcome, pass or satisfy in order to reach the move operation. Stumbling at any hurdle ends the race to the goal or upload. The PHP code implementation of the hurdles is:

```php
// Password OK?
($_POST["accessCode"] == "securePassword") or die("Invalid password.");

// Size OK?
($_FILES["uploadedFile"]["size"] < 30000) or die("File too big.");

// Type OK?
(
    ($_FILES["uploadedFile"]["type"] == "image/pjpeg") ||
    ($_FILES["uploadedFile"]["type"] == "image/gif")
) or die("Invalid type.");
```

A final stylistic comment. An or expression is usually perceived to be symmetric, that is: (A or B) has the same meaning as (B or A). That is true if the terms A and B have no side-effects. However, in the present context the second B component has a very decided side-effect: it is a die function so its execution terminates the program. Thus in this context, the or expression is (anomalously) not symmetric.

8.11.8   Existing Files

The last and most complex hurdle we consider for our upload service involves over-writing existing files, which depends both on whether there is a file to overwrite in the first place and whether the user has allowed overwrites via the HTML Form. The basic pseudo-code is:

```
1  (file does not exist or (file does exist and overwrite is allowed))
2  or die("Overwrite not allowed.");
```

Here we assume the HTML Form has been extended to enable (or disable) overwriting an existing uploaded copy of a file. The condition above succeeds (in the first place) if there is no file with a matching name in the target directory, or there is such a file but the browser user wants to allow overwriting it. To implement this condition in PHP, we need, in addition to extending the HTML Form to let the user accept/reject the overload option, to use the built-in PHP function:

```
1  file_exists(string $filename);
```

This function returns true or false depending on whether the file named in the argument exists or not. The argument is the path to the file or directory (relative to the current directory of the script). For example:

```
1  file_exists("upload/" . $_FILES["uploadedFile"]["name"]);
```

This returns true if a file with the same name as the uploaded file already exists in the directory upload (assumed to lie in the same directory as the PHP program). We can also extend the HTML Form as follows:

```
1  Enter Yes (No) to enable (disable) uploads:
2  <input type = "text" name = "allowOverwrite" />
```

We can also use a pair of radio-buttons with the default choice set to not allow uploads.

These constructions allow us to implement the script as follows. We first define some Boolean variables that encode the overload option and the `file_exists` result which let us code this hurdle more succinctly. The first two statements provide logical variables that allow for a succinct statement of the hurdle defined in the third statement below:

```php
$allowOverwrite = ($_POST["allowOverwrite"] == "Yes");
$fileExists = file_exists("upload/" . $_FILES["uploadedFile"]["name"]);
(!$fileExists || ($fileExists && $allowOverwrite)) or die("Overwrite not allowed");
move_uploaded_file($_FILES["uploadedFile"]["tmp_name"],
                   "upload/" . $_FILES["uploadedFile"]["name"]);
```

This assumes the usual upload directory for the target of the move.

8.11.9 User-defined Functions

Determining whether an uploaded file belongs to an allowed MIME type is best described as a problem of set membership: does a given MIME type t belong to a set of MIME types T? In mathematical set-theory notation this would be written as $t \in T$ or $t \in \{$image/gif, image/pjpeg, text/plain, ...$\}$ for some list of types that the set represents. PHP does not have a set type so if we wish to simulate this behavior we need to define a function that captures this kind of functionality like:

```php
allowed_mime_type(string $file)
```

Note that:
- the parameter $file is the MIME type of the uploaded file, and
- the function returns true if $file belongs to the set of recognized MIME types.

There are two points to consider when implementing such a function: the syntax for defining functions in PHP and the design of the allowed_mime_type function. The syntax for defining and using user-defined functions was introduced earlier. Thus the next objective is to appropriately define and use the allowed_mime_type(string $file) function specified above. The pseudo-code for allowed_mime_type might be:

1. Define a list of allowed MIME types.
2. Scan the list for given input type $fileType, returning true if $fileType is found in list.
3. Otherwise, return false.

The code below directly implements this pseudo-code for a limited set of allowed MIME types stored in a one-dimensional array $mimeTypes defined in the function and which is indexed numerically so it can be scanned with an integer indexed for-loop. The loop performs the desired scan, exiting with true as the return value if the parameter $fileType matches any of the array values (that is, belongs to the set of types listed in the array). That return both exits the loop and the function. If the loop completes without a match, then the return false is executed.

```php
<?php
function allowed_mime_type($fileType) {
    $mimeTypes[1] = "images/gif";
    $mimeTypes[2] = "images/pjpeg";
```

```php
5      $mimeTypes[3] = "text/plain";
6      $mimeTypes[4] = "text/html";
7      $mimeTypes[5] = "application/msword";
8
9      for ($index = 1; $index < 6; $index++) {
10         if ($fileType == $mimeTypes[$index]) return(true);
11     }
12     return(false);
13 }
14 ?>
```

The function definition can be used as the contents of a PHP include file which can be referenced as described earlier. The resulting include file requires the usual PHP starting and closing tags.

The resulting hurdle for limiting upload requests to a (this) specific set of MIME types is readily implemented as:

```php
1 (allowed_mime_type($_FILES["uploadedFile"]["type"])) or die("Invalid type.");
```

The condition succeeds only if the upload type belongs to the allowed set of types identified in the function.

8.11.10   Including File Functionality

PHP allows for the inclusion/insertion of content from one file into another. It provides a mechanism for reusing both markup and PHP code. Specifically, PHP has four different functions for including files, as listed and described in Table 8.11.

Table 8.11: PHP file inclusion statements and their descriptions.

Name	Description
`include(filename or path to filename)`	The specified file is inserted into the file where the statement is placed and runs the specified file. If the function fails to insert the file the script will run, and a warning will be issued. The parentheses are optional.
`include_once(filename or path to filename)`	Works just like the include statement except it makes sure that the file is included only once.
`require(filename or path to filename)`	The specified file is inserted to the file where the statement is placed and runs the specified file. If the function fails to insert the file the script will not run and a fatal error occurs. The parentheses are optional.
`require_once(filename or path to filename)`	Works just like the require statement except it makes sure that the file is required only once.

Some examples of the include and require functions are given below:

- include `"myfile.php"`;
- include_once `"myfile.php"`;
- require `"myfile.php"`;
- require_once `"myfile.php"`;

The difference between include and require lies within what happens when the file specified cannot be found:

- The include issues a warning but allows for execution to continue.
- The require issues an error and stops execution of the script.

The `include_once` and `require_once` work exactly as include and require, but with the caveat that if the requested file has already been included once it will not be included again. It is recommended to use either of these statements for PHP pages that include multiple files.

It is important to mention scope when dealing with these 4 statements as the included file's code inherits the variable scope of the line on which the include occurred. Therefore the variables available at that line in the calling file will be available within the called file.

8.12 PHP Mail Function

The PHP built-in mail function allows the program to send email directly from the script. The following is an example of its invocation.

```
mail($recipientEmail, $subject, $message, "From: $senderEmail") or (print "Could not send mail.");
```

This tries to send the mail and posts an error message if the attempt fails. The above assumes fields like the following have already been defined (such as by assignment statement preceding the mail function):

```
$recipientEmail = "james.smith@example.edu";
$subject = "Meeting Confirmation";
$message = "This is to confirm our meeting tomorrow at 2pm.";
$senderEmail = "notifications@example.edu";
```

As noted, these must be defined before the mail function is invoked. The last parameter can be any of a variety of email headers. The general form of the mail invocation is:

```
mail($recipientEmail, $subject, $message, $headers);
```

The `$headers` string parameter can include a string consisting of so-called HTTP headers.

For a reliable mail system, it is important to verify that your server's mail configuration is correctly set up. Some hosting providers may restrict mail functions or require specific configuration.

Exercise: Send the mail parameters to the PHP program from a Form, then execute the mail function using those values. The data in the email could also include data from a database. A configuration consisting of:

- A client web browser
- An intermediate PHP program on a web server that collects data from a browser for mailing, and
- A mail function that executes in the program

might be thought of as a kind of pseudo-3-Tier software architecture (or a "2-Tier architecture") in which the background database component is supplanted by the actual human recipient of the mail message.

You can also include HTML markup in the email message. This requires including appropriate HTTP headers. For example, for text email only, the header would be: Content-Type: text/plain, while for a message containing embedded HTML markup, the message header would be: Content-Type: text/html; charset="iso-8859-1" identifying the content as HTML, as in this snippet:

```php
$headers = 'Content-type: text/html; charset=iso-8859-1' . "\r\n";
```

8.13   Sessions in PHP

When a PHP script finishes executing in response to a single HTTP request, normally all its variables and state are lost. If the same browser makes another request (like navigating to another page, or submitting a form to the next step of a process), the server has no built-in way to know it is the same user, or to carry over information (like login status, or items in a shopping cart). Sessions provide a way to retain data across multiple requests.

A session works by storing some data on the server (e.g., in files) and associating it with a unique ID. The browser receives that session ID (usually via a cookie) and sends it with each request. The PHP engine uses the session ID to find the stored data. Figure 8.4 shows a PHP session flow where a session ID is created and stored. When requested, the stored session ID is retrieved, used by the web server, and then the response is given to the browser.

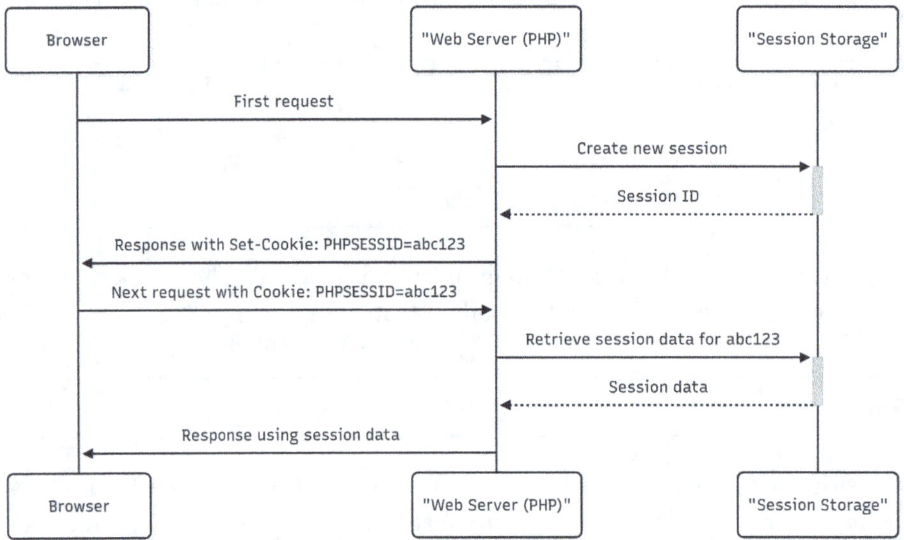

Figure 8.4: PHP session flow.

In PHP, using sessions is straightforward:

- At the top of any script where you want to use sessions, call `session_start()`. This will create a session (or resume the existing one if the user already has a session ID cookie).
- You can then read and write to the `$_SESSION` superglobal array. Data you store in this array will persist for that user between requests.

Example:

```
// page1.php
<?php
  session_start();
  $_SESSION['username'] = "Alice";
  echo "Session set.";
?>
```

```
// page2.php
<?php
  session_start();
  echo "Welcome, " . $_SESSION['username'];
?>
```

If the user visits `page1.php`, a session is started and `$_SESSION['username']` is set. The server sends a Set-Cookie header (e.g., `PHPSESSID=abcdef...; path=/; HttpOnly`). When the user then visits `page2.php`, the browser sends that cookie, `session_start()` finds the session, and `$_SESSION['username']` still holds "Alice".

How sessions work (conceptually):

- The session ID is a key (usually a random 32-character hex string).
- By default, PHP stores session data in files on the server (e.g., in a temp directory). The filename often is `sess_[session_id]`.
- When `session_start()` is called, PHP checks if the client sent a session cookie. If not, it creates a new session ID. If yes, it uses that ID (assuming the session has not expired).
- Data in `$_SESSION` is serialized and stored (e.g., in that file) at the end of the script.

Session configuration: PHP has settings in `php.ini` for session behavior (like cookie name, lifetime, storage path, etc.). The default cookie name is often `PHPSESSID`. Default storage is files. Default lifetime is until the browser is closed (session cookie) unless configured otherwise.

8.13.1 Life-cycle of a Session ID

Let us consider a simple scenario with two pages: an HTML form (P1) and a PHP processor (P2). The user goes to P1, which has a form. When they submit, it calls P2. Suppose P2 uses `session_start()` and maybe sets some session variables. Then P2 outputs some HTML, perhaps including a link or form that calls P2 again (or another page that also uses the session).

The life cycle of a session might be described in events:

1. Event 1: Browser (B) requests P1 (the initial HTML form page).
   Session status: No session exists yet (no session key).
2. Event 2: Server sends P1 to Browser.
   Session status: Still no session (just an HTML page, no session started).
3. Event 3: Browser submits the form (requests P2 with form data).
   Session status: Still none as the request does not include a session key yet because we have not started one.
4. Event 4: Server starts executing P2 (first time). Here `session_start()` is called.
   Session status: A session key (let us call it k) is created on the server. A new session file is made, identified by k.
5. Event 5: P2 completes execution and sends a response back to Browser. As part of this HTTP response, the server includes the session ID k in a Set-Cookie header to the browser.
   Session status: Session key k is transmitted to the browser.
6. Event 6: Browser receives the response. It sees the Set-Cookie for session ID k, and stores it (in memory or disk depending on cookie settings).
7. Event 7: Browser makes another request (say, the user clicks a link or auto-submits back to P2). This request includes the cookie with session ID k.
8. Event 8: Server receives request for P2 again. `session_start()` sees the incoming session ID cookie k. It locates the session file for k, and resumes that session (making the saved data available in `$_SESSION`).
9. Event 9: Script executes (maybe reading/modifying `$_SESSION` data), and sends response. No new cookie is sent (it is already set).
10. Event 10: Browser receives response, and the session persists as long as the cookie and server-side data are valid (cookie might expire when browser closes unless configured otherwise, and server data might expire after some inactivity timeout).

This cycle repeats for each subsequent request that needs the session.

8.13.2 Tracing the Session ID via HTTP Message Headers

We can actually observe the session ID being exchanged by looking at the HTTP headers. Using a browser's developer tools, you can see:

- When the server sends the Set-Cookie.
- That subsequent requests include the Cookie header.

For example:

- Response header from server after first `session_start()` might include:
  ```
  Set-Cookie: PHPSESSID=abc123def456...; path=/; HttpOnly
  ```
- Next request header from browser:
  ```
  Cookie: PHPSESSID=abc123def456...
  ```

This confirms the mechanism of session continuity.

8.13.3 PHP Syntax for Sessions

Now that we know how sessions work conceptually, lets look at the actual PHP syntax and usage:

Starting a session (at the top of a script, before any output is sent):

```php
session_start();
```

Storing data in the session:

```php
$_SESSION['key'] = $value;
```

Reading data:

```php
$value = $_SESSION['key'];
```

Removing a session variable:

```php
unset($_SESSION['key']);
```

Destroying a session completely:

```php
session_destroy();  // this clears the server-side data
setcookie(session_name(), "", time()-3600);  // this clears the cookie in the browser
```

Usually, to log out a user, you might unset session variables or destroy the session.

By default, session data persists until the user closes the browser (ending the session cookie) or until the server's session data is cleaned up (which might be 24 minutes of inactivity by default, depending on `session.gc_maxlifetime` setting, and the garbage collector probability settings).

8.13.4 Session Example: Simple Transaction Logging

To illustrate a more concrete use of sessions, consider a scenario: we want to log some "transactions" a user does, and then allow them to list all transactions they have done so far.

Page A: the user can perform an action (e.g., "add item to cart" or just a dummy action for our example). Page B: the user can view a log of all actions they have done. We will use a session to store the log:

```php
// perform.php (Page A)
<?php
session_start();
```

```php
4  $action = $_GET['action'];   // some action passed in URL, e.g., ?action=clicked_button
5  // Append action to session log
6  if (!isset($_SESSION['log']))
7  {
8     $_SESSION['log'] = array();
9  }
10 $_SESSION['log'][] = $action;
11 echo "Performed action: $action <br>";
12 echo "<a href = 'perform.php?action=test'>Do Test Action</a> | <a href = 'viewlog.php'>View Log</a>";
13 ?>
```

```php
1  // viewlog.php (Page B)
2  <?php
3   session_start();
4   if (!isset($_SESSION['log']))
5   {
6      echo "No actions in log.";
7   }
8   else
9   {
10     echo "Actions you performed:<ul>";
11     foreach ($_SESSION['log'] as $action)
12     {
13         echo "<li>" . htmlentities($action) . "</li>";
14     }
15     echo "</ul>";
16  }
17 echo "<a href='perform.php?action=test'>Do Test Action</a>";
18 ?>
```

In `perform.php`, we start a session, then we get an action from the query string. We ensure `$_SESSION['log']` exists and is an array, then append the new action. We output a link to itself (to perform another action) and to viewlog.php.

In `viewlog.php`, we start the session, then check if the log exists in session. If so, loop and print each action.

This log persists as the user does multiple actions because it is stored in the session. If the user closes the browser (session cookie lost), or we call `session_destroy()`, the log would reset.

8.13.5 Session Security

While sessions are powerful, they introduce security considerations. The session ID is essentially a "key" to impersonate a user's session. If an attacker gets hold of someone's session ID, they could hijack that user's session. Here are measures to mitigate common issues:

- Session ID exposure: By default, the session ID is kept in a cookie. Cookies are an HTTP-only mechanism, which is good (not directly accessible via JavaScript if `HttpOnly` flag is set). In the past, PHP had an option to propagate session IDs in URLs (called SID), which is risky if URLs are shared; it is largely disabled now. Ensure you do not expose session IDs in URLs or logs.
- Use HTTPS: If your site is over HTTPS, mark the session cookie as secure so it will not be sent over plain HTTP. This prevents network sniffing of the cookie.
- Regenerate session IDs: It is good practice to call `session_regenerate_id()` when a user logs in (and periodically) to avoid session fixation (where an attacker tricks a user into using a known session ID). Regenerating gives a new ID and invalidates the old one.
- Session timeout: Implement an inactivity timeout or an absolute timeout. For example, record `$_SESSION['LAST_ACTIVITY'] = time()` and check on each request if too much time has passed, then expire the session or require re-login.
- Destroy session on logout: Ensure `session_destroy()` is called and the cookie is cleared when the user logs out.
- Store minimal info in session: Do not store sensitive data in session if avoidable. Perhaps store a user ID, but not the password or extensive personal data. If you need to store very sensitive info, consider additional encryption on that data.
- Server-Side Security: The session files (e.g., in `/tmp` by default) are only as secure as your server. On a shared hosting, if not configured properly, other users might read them. Modern systems mitigate this, but just be aware.

By following these practices, sessions can be used securely to maintain state.

8.14 Cookies Management

Sessions use cookies behind the scenes, but you can also work with cookies directly in PHP. Cookies allow you to store small pieces of data on the client side, in the user's browser, and have the browser send that data back on each request to your site.

Typical uses of cookies:

- Remembering a user's preferences (like site theme or language).
- Keeping a user logged in ("Remember me" functionality).
- Tracking user behavior (though with modern privacy laws like GDPR, this is regulated).

Setting a cookie in PHP is done by sending a `Set-Cookie` header, which PHP provides via the `setcookie()` function.

8.14.1 Setting and Reading Cookies

Setting a Cookie: In PHP, you set a cookie by calling the `setcookie()` function. Its basic usage:

```
setcookie($name, $value, $expire, $path, $domain, $secure, $httponly);
```

- `$name` and `$value` are required. They will be URL-encoded by PHP.

- $expire is a timestamp for when the cookie should expire (if not set or 0, it is a session cookie that expires when browser closes).
- $path (optional) specifies the path on the server for which the cookie will be sent (default is "/", meaning the entire domain).
- $domain (optional) can make the cookie available to subdomains.
- $secure (optional, boolean) indicates the cookie should only be sent over HTTPS.
- $httponly (optional, boolean) indicates the cookie is HTTP only (not accessible via JavaScript).

Example:

```
1  setcookie("username", "Alice", time() + 3600);  // cookie "username" with value "Alice", expires in 1
   hour
```

This must be called before any output is sent (like headers).

When the browser receives this, it will store a cookie username=Alice that expires in one hour.

Reading a Cookie: PHP makes incoming cookies available in the $_COOKIE superglobal. For example, after the above cookie is set and the user makes another request:

```
1  echo $_COOKIE['username'];  // would output "Alice"
```

Cookie values are just strings. The browser will send them on each request to the same site until they expire or are deleted.

Updating a Cookie: Just call setcookie() again with the same name and a new value (and possibly a new expiration). It will overwrite the old one in the browser.

Deleting a Cookie: To remove a cookie, you set it with an expiration in the past:

```
1  setcookie("username", "", time() - 3600);
```

This tells the browser to delete the cookie (the value is set to empty and expiration is an hour ago). Note: to fully delete, the path and domain must match the original cookie set.

8.14.2   Security Considerations

Cookies can introduce security risks if not handled properly. Here is how to mitigate common issues:
- Sensitive data: Do not store highly sensitive information in cookies (like passwords, credit card numbers, etc.), because cookies reside on the client side and could be stolen or manipulated.
- Integrity: A user can edit cookies (there are browser extensions or just by using the developer console). So never trust the content of a cookie blindly. For example, do not just store isAdmin=true in a cookie and then trust it – a user could set that themselves. If you need to store something like that, use sessions or sign the cookie (e.g., include an HMAC).

- Secure flag: If your site is HTTPS, always set `secure=true` on cookies that contain any sort of important data (including session IDs).
- HttpOnly flag: Helps mitigate XSS by preventing JavaScript from reading the cookie's value (for session cookies or auth tokens, always use HttpOnly).
- Cookie theft (XSS): If an attacker can run JavaScript on your page (via XSS), they can potentially steal cookies (unless HttpOnly). So preventing XSS is crucial to cookie security.
- Cookie tampering (CSRF): Cookies are automatically sent by the browser. A malicious site could cause a user's browser to make a request to your site (e.g., by including an image or AJAX to your domain) and the browser will send cookies. This is Cross-Site Request Forgery. The malicious site cannot read the response (due to same-origin policy), but it can trigger actions. To mitigate, one uses anti-CSRF tokens to ensure requests are genuine.
- SameSite attribute: Modern cookies can be set with `SameSite` attribute to restrict cross-site sending of cookies (e.g., `SameSite=Lax` or `Strict`) to help against CSRF.

In summary, cookies are a useful tool for client-side state (and necessary for sessions to work by default), but should be used carefully.

8.14.3 Practical Example of Cookies

Imagine implementing a "Remember Me" checkbox at login:
- If user logs in and checks "Remember Me", after successful login, you set a cookie with a long expiration (e.g., 30 days) containing an auth token.
- On subsequent visits, if session is not active but cookie is present, you log the user in automatically by validating that token (checking against a database perhaps).
- The token in the cookie should be a secure random string, not something guessable. And if possible, tie it to the user account in the database, with an expiration and maybe IP or user-agent check.

Another example: site theme preference:
- User selects "dark mode".
- You set a cookie `theme=dark` that lasts a year.
- On each page load, you could have PHP or JavaScript check `$_COOKIE['theme']` and apply that theme.

8.14.4 Cookies vs. Sessions

- Use sessions when you want to store data securely on the server side and have a simple way to associate it with the user (via session ID cookie). Sessions are generally more secure for sensitive info because nothing sensitive is on the client, just an ID.
- Use cookies for lighter-weight things or when you explicitly want the client to have the data (or need the data even if the user has not interacted with the server in a while, e.g., remembering preferences even if the session expired).

Often they work together: you might store a user ID in a session (server side) after login, and also set a cookie for "remember me" to re-create the session if it expired.

8.14.5 Common Uses and Limitations of Cookies

Cookies are convenient for storing small amounts of data (a few kilobytes at most). They are sent on every request to the matching domain/path, which means overly large cookies can slow down web requests (since they bloat the headers).

Also, browsers limit the number of cookies per domain (often around 20) and total cookie size per domain.

From a privacy perspective, cookies have gotten a lot of attention because they can be used to track users across sites (especially third-party cookies). Modern browsers and regulations often require informing the user of cookies, and the `SameSite` attribute now defaults to Lax to prevent third-party use.

For our purposes (PHP apps), remember:

- Always consider the security flags (secure, HttpOnly, SameSite) when setting cookies that relate to authentication or sessions.
- Clean up cookies if they are no longer needed (set expiration in past).
- Validate cookie values (do not trust blindly).
- Understand that cookie data is visible to the end user (they can see it in their browser settings), so do not put anything there that might be problematic if seen.

By following these guidelines, you can safely harness cookies for better user experience (like persistent logins and personalization) without compromising the security of your application.

8.15 Chapter Review

Problem 8.1 What is PHP and how is it used in web applications?

Problem 8.2 Describe how PHP scripts are executed on the server and how the result is sent to the browser.

Problem 8.3 What special tags enclose PHP code in an HTML document?

Problem 8.4 Explain why PHP files must have the `.php` extension.

Problem 8.5 How do you declare and use variables in PHP? Provide an example.

Problem 8.6 What are the differences between indexed arrays and associative arrays in PHP?

Problem 8.7 Describe two ways data can be exchanged between the browser and PHP scripts.

Problem 8.8 What is the difference between using `$_GET` and `$_POST` in PHP?

Problem 8.9 Explain the difference between the equality (`==`) and identical (`===`) comparison operators in PHP.

Problem 8.10 What is a session in PHP and how does it maintain state across requests?

Problem 8.11 How do cookies differ from sessions, and when might you use cookies instead of sessions?

Problem 8.12 Give an example of how to securely handle file uploads using PHP.

Problem 8.13 What is the purpose of PHP's built-in function `filter_var()`?

Problem 8.14 Explain how PHP's `password_hash()` and `password_verify()` functions enhance security.

Problem 8.15 Write a short PHP script that dynamically generates an HTML table showing numbers from 1 to 10 and their squares.

9. SQL and MySQL

A basic understanding of the use and purpose of databases is essential to developing modern Internet applications. Most non-trivial web applications rely on a back-end database to store and manage data that the web application uses to provide services. MySQL is a popular open source relational database system widely used in the LAMP (Linux, Apache, MySQL, PHP) stack for Internet applications. MySQL provides a multi-user database server environment that allows concurrent access to a relational (table-based) database. In this chapter, we use MySQL as an example of a relational database in a typical three-tier web application architecture. The concepts and techniques covered (such as the SQL language) apply to other relational database systems as well.

Learning Objectives

By the end of this chapter, you should be able to:

- Describe the role of databases in web applications and identify what MySQL is in the context of the LAMP stack.
- Access a MySQL database (for example, via a tool like phpMyAdmin or the MySQL client) using appropriate credentials, and understand the basics of database accounts and permissions.
- Define and create relational database tables, choosing appropriate data types for each column, and understand how tables model real-world entities.
- Insert, retrieve, update, and delete data in a MySQL database using SQL commands (`INSERT`, `SELECT`, `UPDATE`, `DELETE`), including filtering query results with conditions (the `WHERE` clause).
- Apply basic relational design principles (normalization) to organize data into multiple related tables, using primary keys to uniquely identify records and foreign keys to link tables.
- Use SQL features for querying data such as selection of specific columns, pattern matching with `LIKE`, set membership with `IN`, range queries with `BETWEEN`, and aggregate functions like `COUNT` and `AVG`.
- Import and export data to and from MySQL tables using common formats (e.g., CSV) and understand how to backup/restore or migrate data.
- Recognize basic query optimization techniques, such as using indexes and limiting result sets, to improve database performance.
- Follow SQL security best practices, particularly to prevent SQL injection attacks by sanitizing inputs or using prepared statements, and understand the principle of least privilege for database access.

9.1 Accounts & Logon

To work with MySQL (or any database management system), you typically need to log on to a database server with a valid account. In a classroom or hosting environment, you might be provided with a database username, a password, and a database name. For example, many web hosting control panels and university systems offer phpMyAdmin, an open source web-based interface for MySQL. Using phpMyAdmin (or similar tools), you can enter your database username and password in a browser to access the MySQL server. In other cases, you

DOI: 10.1201/9781003727651-9

might use the MySQL command-line client or MySQL Workbench (a desktop GUI application) to connect to the database.

When working on a local development environment (such as a LAMP stack on your own PC), you may have a default MySQL user (commonly the `root` user with a password you set during installation). In hosted environments, your database credentials are often created for you. Once you have the credentials, you typically:

1. Navigate to the MySQL server interface for phpMyAdmin. This might be a URL like `http:// <your-server>/phpMyAdmin/` or a link in a control panel. For the MySQL CLI, you would run a command like `mysql -u <username> -p` and enter your password.

2. Enter your username and password to log in. MySQL will authenticate you and present the databases you have access to.

3. Select your database. In phpMyAdmin, your databases are listed on the left sidebar. Clicking on your database name will select it and show its tables. In SQL command-line, you might run `USE your_database;` to switch to it.

Once connected to the MySQL server and your database, you can create tables, execute SQL queries, and manage the data. In production systems, it is important to keep your database credentials secure and not share them. Database administrators often enforce privileges so that each application or user has only the necessary permissions (for example, a web app might only have rights to its own database, not to all databases on the server).

9.2   Database Tables: Definition, Creation, and Data Organization

A relational database like MySQL consists of a collection of one or more tables. A table is a structured collection of data organized into rows and columns. Each table represents a set of entities (things) of the same type, and each column of the table represents an attribute (a particular piece of information) that those entities have. Each row in the table corresponds to one individual record (or instance of the entity), with a value for each column.

For example, consider Table 9.1, which is a simple structure that stores information about persons, with columns for a person's name, age, and gender. Each row represents one person's record.

Table 9.1: A simple People table with three attributes: Name, Age, and Gender.

Name	Age	Gender
Bert	10	M
Sally	15	F
Harry	20	M
Betty	10	F

In this People table, the columns Name, Age, and Gender are the attributes describing each person. A table's schema is often summarized by listing its name and columns, e.g. People[Name, Age, Gender]. The table above lists four people. Each row's values fill in the attributes for one person (e.g. Bert is 10 years old and Male).

The columns (also called fields or attributes) define the type of data stored (Name is text, Age is a number, Gender is a short text or code). Each column in a MySQL table is assigned a specific data type when the table is created. For instance, a Name might be defined as a variable-length text string (VARCHAR), Age might be an integer (INT), and Gender could be defined as a CHAR(1) or an ENUM type (e.g., an ENUM that only allows values 'M' or 'F'). Choosing appropriate data types is important: for example, using a numeric type for Age allows numeric comparisons and calculations (like computing an average age), whereas storing ages as text would make such operations more difficult or inefficient. MySQL supports many data types (various integer sizes, floating-point numbers, dates and times, text types, etc.), and the choice depends on the nature of the data and how it will be used. For instance, if we plan to query or sort by age, a numeric type is appropriate; if we want to restrict Gender to a few possible values, an ENUM is convenient, as phpMyAdmin can even present those as radio buttons for data entry.

One concept central to relational databases is that each table should have a way to uniquely identify each row. In our initial People table above, none of the columns by itself is guaranteed unique as names might repeat (we could have two people named Harry, for example). A common practice is to add a special attribute that serves as a unique identifier for each record, often called a primary key. This could be something like an ID number. If we were dealing with students, perhaps a government-issued ID (like Social Security Number, in a U.S. context) could serve this purpose, or we could use an internal student ID. We might augment our People table by adding a unique ID column. For example, in Table 9.2, adding a column SSN (Social Security Number) for each person could make each row unique. Now even if two people share the same name (e.g., two entries for "Harry"), each can be distinguished by a unique SSN value.

Table 9.2: An augmented People table with a new SSN column as a unique identifier for each person.

Name	Age	Gender	SSN
Bert	10	M	110
Sally	15	F	112
Harry	20	M	770
Betty	10	F	771
Harry	30	M	772

In the augmented table above, SSN is intended to be unique for every person. Marking SSN as a primary key would enforce this uniqueness (the database will reject any attempt to insert a duplicate SSN). Primary keys are discussed more in Section 9.7, but note here that not all data types are eligible to be primary keys in MySQL. For example, very large text fields cannot be indexed as primary keys, whereas integer or short text/varchar fields are suitable.

Many real-world datasets are too complex to store in a single table. Instead, we organize data into multiple related tables to avoid duplication and to model relationships between entities. For example, if our People table refers to students, and we want to also keep track of which courses each student takes (and perhaps the grade each student earns in each course), it would be inefficient and non-normalized to add columns in People for every possible course. Instead, we would create a separate Courses (or enrollments) table to store this information. One simple design could include a People table with columns [SSN, Name, Age, Gender] containing each student's base information with SSN as primary key, and a Courses table with columns [SSN,

Course_ID, Course_Grade] where each row represents one student's grade in one course. The combination of `SSN` and `Course_ID` could serve as a composite primary key for this table, since one student can take a particular course only once (in our assumption here).

Using two tables like this avoids repeating course information in the People table for each student. If a student takes multiple courses, that student will have multiple rows in the Courses table (all sharing the same SSN to link back to the People table). If courses themselves have more attributes (like course name, credits, etc.), those could be in yet another table (e.g., a CourseCatalog table keyed by Course_ID). Organizing data into multiple tables with relationships is a process known as database normalization, which we will explore shortly.

Once you have defined tables in a database, you can interact with them in two general ways: manually or programmatically. Manually, you might use a graphical interface (like phpMyAdmin) or a command-line client to browse tables, insert or edit data, and run queries. Programmatically (from within a script or application), you would use the SQL language within your code (for example, PHP code) to query and update the database. In practice, most web applications interact with the database through code (the application issues SQL commands based on user input or application logic). Therefore, understanding the SQL commands to manipulate data is critical for developers, even if you often design and test queries manually, these commands will ultimately be executed by your programs. In the sections that follow, we will illustrate both the interactive use of MySQL (via phpMyAdmin) and the SQL commands themselves.

9.3   Database Normalization and Designing Relational Schemas

Storing all information in a single table can lead to a lot of redundancy and potential anomalies (problems when inserting, updating, or deleting data). Database normalization is the process of structuring the data into multiple related tables to minimize redundancy and dependency. The goal is to ensure that each table has a clear purpose (describes one type of entity or relationship) and that data is not unnecessarily duplicated across tables. Normalization typically involves several "normal forms" (1st, 2nd, 3rd normal form, etc.), but in essence, it means organizing the data so that each fact is stored in one place.

As an example, imagine we are designing a database for a collection of books. Suppose we tried to put everything about books into one big table: we might have columns for Title, Author(s), Author Bio, ISBN, Price, Subject(s), Publisher, Publisher Address, etc. A single book can have multiple authors and multiple subject categories. In one giant table, we might try to cram multiple authors into one row (e.g., Author1, Author2 columns) or multiple subjects into one field (like a comma-separated list). This approach would be problematic: it is hard to query, wastes space by repeating data (if a publisher publishes many books, the publisher address would be repeated in every row for each of those books), and makes updates error-prone (change an author name or publisher address, and you would have to update multiple records). These are signs of a design that is not normalized.

The normalized approach is to break this into separate tables, each representing one kind of entity. The Authors table (e.g., `Authors[Author_ID, Last_Name, First_Name, Bio]`) stores unique authors, one per row. The Subjects table (e.g., `Subjects[Subject_ID, Name]`) stores unique subjects or categories. The Publishers table (e.g., `Publishers[Publisher_ID, Name, Address, City, State, Zip]`) stores publishers with their address info. The Books table (e.g., `Books[ISBN, Title, Publisher_ID, Price, Pages, ...]`) stores books, with each row representing a book. Instead of storing publisher details here, we store a reference (Publisher_ID) to the Publishers table, and ISBN (or a similar book ID) could serve as the primary key for Books. Finally, the Books_Authors table handles the many-to-many relationship between books and authors (a book can have multiple authors, an author can write multiple books). We define `Books_Authors[ISBN, Author_ID]` where each row links one book to one author. The combination (ISBN, Author_ID) can be a composite primary key for this table, ensuring you do not list the same author twice for the same book. This table allows any number of authors per book without duplicating book or author information in one table.

By designing the database in this way, each piece of information is stored exactly once: an author's details are in the Authors table (and not repeated for every book they have written), a subject is listed once in Subjects, a publisher's address is stored once in Publishers, etc. The Books table references those by ID. This eliminates redundancy and prevents update anomalies, for example, if a publisher changes its address, we update one row in Publishers, instead of many book records.

Normalization has some requirements such as each table having a primary key, no repeating groups or arrays in a single row (1st normal form), and so on. For example, ensuring each table has a primary key is part of 1st normal form (1NF) and beyond. Primary keys uniquely identify rows within their own table, and when that key appears in another table (like Publisher_ID in the Books table), it is called a foreign key since it references a row in another table. In our example, Publisher_ID in Books is a foreign key referencing the Publishers table (Publisher_ID is a primary key in the Publishers table). Likewise, Author_ID in Books_Authors is a foreign key to Authors, and ISBN in Books_Authors is a foreign key to Books. We typically enforce these relationships by design and sometimes through database constraints; foreign key constraints ensure you cannot reference a non-existent author, for instance.

To summarize the normalization example: instead of one big table, we have several tables (Books, Authors, Publishers, etc.), each with a primary key. Many-to-many relationships (like books and authors) are handled via a JOIN table (Books_Authors). This structure avoids data duplication. It also means that to gather information across multiple tables, you will use JOIN operations in SQL or nested queries, which we will touch on later. But the benefits are consistency and scalability of the data. Designing a good schema often starts by identifying the entities (nouns) in the scenario (e.g., Students, Courses, Instructors, etc. in a school database; or Books, Authors, Publishers in a library database) and giving each its own table, then adding tables for relationships as needed.

Finally, normalization is sometimes balanced with practical considerations. Highly normalized schemas can require many JOINs to query, which can have performance impacts. In this course, we focus on 3rd Normal Form designs for clarity and simplicity. In real-world applications, sometimes a bit of denormalization is used for performance (storing certain derived or redundant data intentionally), but that should be done only with good reason. For starting out, it is best to fully normalize your schema and ensure you understand the relationships between tables. In the next section, we will see how to actually create tables in MySQL and then how to manipulate data with SQL.

9.4 Creating and Browsing Tables in MySQL (Using phpMyAdmin)

Now that we have a database design, let us see how to implement it in MySQL. You can create tables either by writing SQL `CREATE TABLE` statements or by using a graphical interface like phpMyAdmin. We will first illustrate using phpMyAdmin, as it provides a visual way to define tables, and then we will also look at the equivalent SQL commands.

After logging into phpMyAdmin and selecting your database, you can create a new table by using the Create Table form. phpMyAdmin will ask for a table name and the number of columns. For example, to create the People table, you would type "People" as the table name and, say, "4" as the number of columns (for Name, Age, Gender, SSN). Upon clicking Go, phpMyAdmin presents a form where you specify each column's details: the Name(the column name, e.g., `Name`, `Age`, `Gender`, `SSN`), the Type (the data type, e.g., `VARCHAR(50)` for Name, `INT` for Age, `CHAR(1)` or `ENUM` for Gender, `BIGINT` for SSN), the Length/Values (the size or allowed values, such as max length for `VARCHAR`, display width for `INT`, or allowed values like 'M','F' for `ENUM`), and other settings such as whether the column can be `NULL` or not, default values, and any index or primary key flags.

After filling in the details for each field, you click Save (or Create). MySQL will then create the table in the database. For instance, if we defined SSN as an integer type and marked it as the Primary Key, phpMyAdmin would execute an SQL statement under the hood to set that (more on primary keys later in this chapter). If all goes well, the new table appears in the database. The interface shown in Figure 9.1 includes each column's name, type, and attributes, and provides options to change the design (e.g., edit or drop columns, add indexes). In MySQL, after creating a table, you can always review its structure via this Structure tab.

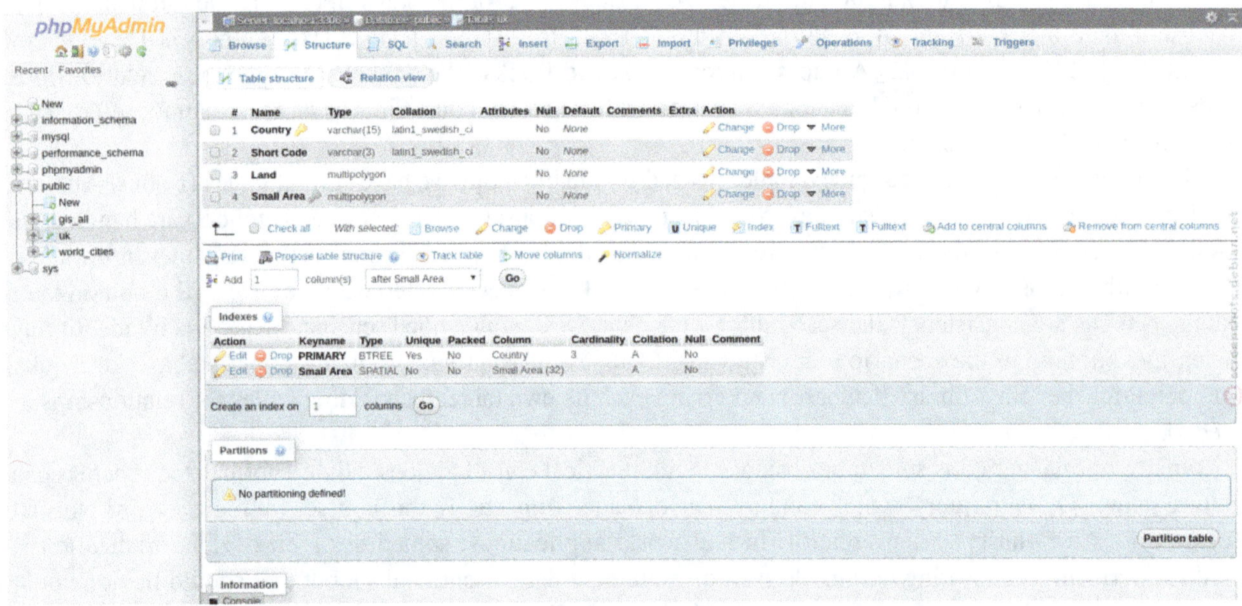

Figure 9.1: phpMyAdmin's structure view for a sample table (here, a table with columns Country, Short Code, Land, etc.).

PhpMyAdmin also provides an SQL tab where you can directly type SQL commands (queries or table creation statements) and execute them. In fact, everything done via the UI ultimately translates to SQL commands that MySQL executes. For example, after using the UI to create a table or insert data, phpMyAdmin often shows the exact SQL query it ran (e.g., it might display `INSERT INTO People (...) VALUES (...);`). This is a great way to learn the SQL syntax by example. While graphical tools are convenient for initial exploration and manual data entry, it is crucial to understand the SQL commands themselves. In an application, you will not have a person manually clicking Insert in phpMyAdmin; instead, your code will send an `INSERT` query to MySQL. In the remainder of this chapter, we focus on the core SQL commands for creating tables and manipulating data. We will use examples from our People table and others to illustrate each command. The interface shown in Figure 9.2 includes each row of data and, on the left, small icons to Edit or Delete individual records. The interface also allows filtering (searching within the table), and it shows the SQL query that was executed (here, `SELECT * FROM 'uk'` is displayed above the results).

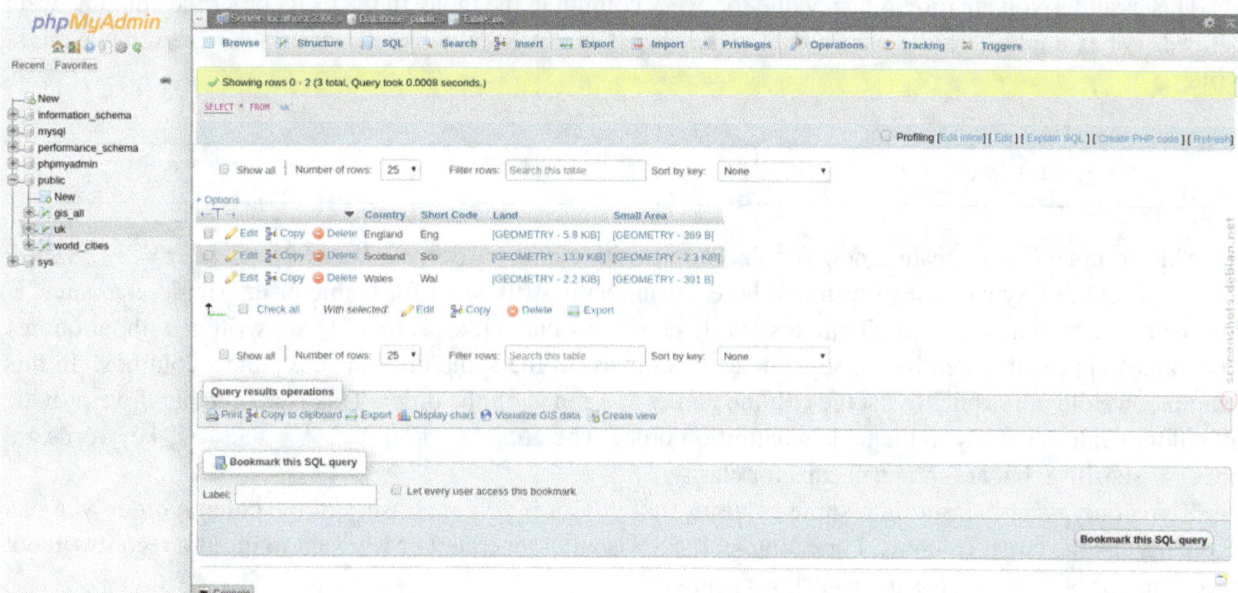

Figure 9.2: phpMyAdmin's browse view, showing sample data rows in a table (here, a table of geographic data).

9.5 SQL Commands: Creating and Modifying Data

The language used to interact with relational databases is SQL (Structured Query Language). SQL provides commands to create and alter the structure of tables (DDL – Data Definition Language) as well as to insert, update, delete, and query data (DML – Data Manipulation Language). SQL syntax is not case-sensitive (you can write `SELECT` or `select`), though keywords are often written in upper case by convention. The fundamental SQL commands covered in this section include CREATE TABLE for defining a new table, INSERT for adding new rows of data into a table, SELECT for retrieving data from one or more tables (covered later in the chapter), UPDATE for modifying existing rows in a table, DELETE for removing rows from a table, DROP TABLE for deleting an entire table and its data, and ALTER TABLE for changing the structure of an existing table (for example, adding or removing columns, or setting constraints like primary keys).

We will go through many of these, especially focusing on the ones used most frequently in application code (`INSERT`, `SELECT`, `UPDATE`, `DELETE`). As noted before, even if you use a GUI for development, your application will be executing these commands, so you need to know what they do.

9.5.1   Insert

The SQL INSERT command adds new records (rows) to a table. The basic syntax is:

```
INSERT INTO TableName VALUES (value1, value2, ..., valueN);
```

This assumes you are providing a value for every column in the table, in the exact order the columns were defined. For example, consider our People(Name, Age, Gender, SSN) table. To insert a new person, we might write:

```
INSERT INTO People VALUES ('Betty', 10, 'F', 771);
```

This command will create a new row in People with Name = 'Betty', Age = 10, Gender = 'F', SSN = 771. Notice a few syntax rules illustrated here. String values (like text for Name or the single-character 'F' for Gender) are enclosed in single quotes, while numeric values (like 10 or 771) are written without quotes. The values appear in parentheses, separated by commas, in the same order as the table's columns. In this example, we did not explicitly list the column names; we relied on the order. This is acceptable if we provide all column values exactly in the table's definition order. The INSERT INTO ... VALUES ... keywords are not case-sensitive, but are shown in caps for clarity.

If you only want to insert into some columns (not all), or if you are unsure of the column order, you can explicitly list the target columns. For example, if SSN is auto-generated or we want to insert a record without specifying SSN (maybe it has a default), we could do:

```
INSERT INTO People (Name, Age, Gender)
VALUES ('Julia', 22, 'F');
```

In this case, we list the columns we are providing. The unspecified column (SSN) must either have a default or be nullable (or auto-increment) for this to work.

You can also insert multiple rows in one SQL statement. For instance:

```
INSERT INTO People (Name, Age, Gender, SSN)
VALUES
  ('Bert', 10, 'M', 110),
  ('Sally', 15, 'F', 112);
```

This would insert two records at once. Each set of values in parentheses represents one row.

If the insert violates any constraints (for example, using a duplicate value in a primary key column, or a value of the wrong type), MySQL will reject it and return an error. We will see an example of a rejected insert when we discuss primary keys (later in this chapter).

9.5.2 Delete

The SQL DELETE command removes records from a table. You typically specify a condition to indicate which rows to delete (otherwise all rows would be removed, which is rarely intended). The general syntax is:

```
1  DELETE FROM TableName
2  WHERE <condition>;
```

For example, to delete the row for 'Betty' from the People table (assuming Name is unique in context or we specifically want to remove that one entry):

```
1  DELETE FROM People
2  WHERE Name = 'Betty';
```

This will remove any rows where the Name is 'Betty'. In our current data, that would delete the row we inserted for Betty. If there were multiple people named Betty, this command would delete all of them, because they all satisfy the condition. If no row matches the condition, the command still executes but deletes 0 rows but will not error out in that case.

The WHERE clause in a DELETE (and similarly in a SELECT or UPDATE) is a boolean condition that can use various operators to target specific rows. For instance, you can use comparisons (=, >, <, etc.), logical operators (AND, OR, NOT), and more. If we had two entries for 'Harry' and we wanted to delete both, we could do DELETE FROM People WHERE Name = 'Harry'; and both would be removed. If we try to delete something that is not there, like:

```
1  DELETE FROM People
2  WHERE Name = 'Marty';
```

As no one named Marty exists, MySQL will report that 0 rows were affected (essentially nothing happens, which is fine).

 Omitting the WHERE clause in a DELETE statement will delete all rows from the table. For example, DELETE FROM People; with no condition will wipe out every record in People. Use this with extreme caution. In cases where you truly want to remove all data but keep the table structure, a special command TRUNCATE TABLE People; can also be used, which typically is faster and resets any auto-increment counters, etc. phpMyAdmin's Empty operation uses TRUNCATE under the hood. Both TRUNCATE and an unconditional DELETE should be used carefully (and usually not at all in production, unless archiving or resetting data deliberately).

9.5.3 Empty (Truncate)

In phpMyAdmin, the Empty action (visible in the Operations tab or next to tables) will delete all the contents of
a table without deleting the table itself. This action uses the SQL TRUNCATE command. For example:

```
1 TRUNCATE TABLE People;
```

This quickly removes all rows from People, essentially resetting the table to empty state. Truncate is DDL-
like (Data Definition Language) in that it cannot be rolled back in the same way a delete can (in transactional
terms), but it is very efficient for bulk deletion. The end result of TRUNCATE TABLE People; is the same as
DELETE FROM People; (without a WHERE clause), with all data gone, but TRUNCATE is optimized for that
scenario.

Most of the time, you will use DELETE with specific conditions to remove individual records, but it is
useful to know about TRUNCATE for situations where you need to quickly clear a table (like resetting test
data).

9.5.4 Create Table

The CREATE TABLE command in SQL defines a new table schema. When using a GUI like phpMyAdmin, as
we did, the GUI ultimately runs a CREATE TABLE statement for you. Knowing the SQL lets you read or write
these definitions directly. The general syntax is:

```
1 CREATE TABLE TableName (
2     column_name1 data_type [constraints],
3     column_name2 data_type [constraints],
4     ...
5 );
```

You list all the columns and their types, and you can also include constraints like PRIMARY KEY or NOT
NULL, etc., as part of the definition.

For example, to create our People table via SQL (matching what we did in the GUI), one might write:

```
1 CREATE TABLE People (
2     Name    TEXT,
3     Age     INT,
4     Gender  TEXT,
5     SSN     BIGINT,
6     PRIMARY KEY (SSN)
7 );
```

This would create a table People with four columns, and declare SSN as the primary key, assuming we know SSN values will be unique for each person. In MySQL, `INT` by default is a 32-bit integer; `BIGINT` is a 64-bit integer, which we used for SSN in case we treat SSNs as numeric. We could also use `VARCHAR(9)` if treating SSN as a fixed-length string of digits. `TEXT` is a type for large text; a more appropriate type for Name might be `VARCHAR(100)` (to limit to, say, 100 characters). Here we keep it simple. The key point is the syntax: column name, then type, and multiple columns separated by commas, all enclosed in parentheses after the table name.

If we did not include the `PRIMARY KEY (SSN)` part initially, we can always add a primary key later. MySQL's variant of SQL also supports an `IF NOT EXISTS` clause (`CREATE TABLE IF NOT EXISTS People (...)`) to only create the table if it is not already present, which is useful in scripts where you do not want an error if the table exists.

Another example, if we wanted to make a table of inventory items:

```
1  CREATE TABLE Inventory (
2      ItemCode INT,
3      Description TEXT,
4      Amount INT,
5      PRIMARY KEY (ItemCode)
6  );
```

This defines an Inventory table with an item code, a description, and an amount (perhaps quantity in stock), and sets ItemCode as the primary key. We will use a variation of this in the UPDATE example later.

9.5.5   Drop Table

To remove a table, both its structure and all its data, from the database entirely, you use DROP TABLE. For example:

```
1  DROP TABLE People;
```

This will permanently delete the table named People from the database, including all data in it. This command should be used with caution as there is no easy "undo" for a drop (except restoring from backup). In phpMyAdmin, the Drop button corresponds to this command.

Sometimes, web applications might create and drop temporary tables on the fly, but generally dropping tables is something you do during development or schema migrations, not as a routine part of application logic.

With these basics covered (creating tables, inserting data, deleting data, etc.), we can now move on to some important nuances: setting primary keys, modifying table structures, and then the all-important task of retrieving data with SELECT queries.

9.6   Primary Keys and Handling Duplicate Keys

A primary key is a column (or combination of columns) that uniquely identifies each row in a table. Defining a primary key on a table is important for several reasons: it enforces data integrity (no two rows can have the same primary key value), it allows faster lookup of records (primary keys are indexed by default), and it establishes a way to reference rows from other tables (via foreign keys).

You can declare a primary key when creating the table (as we saw with `PRIMARY KEY (SSN)` in the CREATE TABLE example). If you did not do it at creation, you can add one later. MySQL offers an `ALTER TABLE` command to modify table structure. For example, to add a primary key on SSN after the fact:

```
ALTER TABLE People
ADD PRIMARY KEY (SSN);
```

Conversely, if you needed to remove a primary key, you could `ALTER TABLE People DROP PRIMARY KEY;`. MySQL allows only one primary key constraint per table, though it can cover multiple columns if it is a composite key.

In phpMyAdmin's Structure view, you can typically set a primary key by selecting the checkbox next to a column and clicking the key icon. In our People table example, if we had not already made SSN a primary key, we could check SSN and click the key icon. phpMyAdmin would run the appropriate ALTER TABLE command. It is worth noting that phpMyAdmin will only enable that key icon for columns of types that can be indexed. In our earlier text, we mentioned that in MySQL, pure TEXT columns cannot be a primary key because MySQL requires keys to be on a fixed-length or indexable column type. A `VARCHAR` (up to a certain length) can be a primary key, as can numeric types. In phpMyAdmin, if you see the key icon grayed out for a column, it likely means that column's type is not indexable or not suitable as a primary key. For instance, a `TEXT` or a very long `VARCHAR` might not allow indexing without a prefix.

When SSN is successfully made the primary key, MySQL will automatically ensure no two rows can have the same SSN. If you try to insert a new row with an SSN that already exists in the table, the database will reject it and issue an error. For example, suppose our People table currently has a row with SSN = 771 for Betty. If we inadvertently tried to insert Betty again (or another person) with SSN 771:

```
INSERT INTO People VALUES ('Betty', 10, 'F', 771);
```

MySQL would produce an error like:

```
ERROR 1062 (23000): Duplicate entry '771' for key 'PRIMARY'
```

In phpMyAdmin, this might be shown in a red error message stating the duplicate entry for key 1 (in older MySQL, the primary key is often referenced as key 1). The insertion would be blocked, and the data would remain unchanged, which is exactly what we want for data integrity.

In summary, always choose a primary key for your tables. If no natural unique identifier exists, it is common to use an auto-increment integer ID. In our example we could have had a `PersonID INT AUTO_INCREMENT PRIMARY KEY` as an arbitrary unique ID for People, instead of using SSN. In a production environment, using something like a student ID or employee ID is often better than using sensitive information like SSN as a key. But for our illustration we treated SSN as a unique key.

Primary keys can consist of multiple columns (this is called a composite key). For instance, in the Courses table example earlier, the combination of (SSN, Course_ID) could be the primary key, meaning a student can appear multiple times (in different courses), and a course can appear multiple times (for different students), but the same student-course pair is unique. You would define that with `PRIMARY KEY (SSN, Course_ID)` when creating the table (or via an ALTER TABLE add primary key).

If you ever need to change which column is the primary key, you would drop the existing primary key and add a new one (or do it in one ALTER statement by dropping and adding).

9.7 Importing and Exporting Data

MySQL provides ways to import data from external files and export data to files, which is very useful for populating a database from an existing dataset or for backing up/sharing data. PhpMyAdmin offers convenient tools for both actions.

- Importing Data: In phpMyAdmin, when you select a database or a specific table, you will see an Import tab. This allows you to upload a file containing data (or SQL commands) to be executed against the database. For example, if you have a CSV file of data that you want to load into a table, you can use Import to accomplish this. You would choose the file from your computer, select the format (CSV, SQL, etc.), and phpMyAdmin will handle the rest. If importing CSV into an existing table, you may need to ensure the columns match up or use the Columns option in phpMyAdmin to align CSV fields to table columns.

  Simple example: suppose we have a text file `words.txt` with a list of words (one per line) and we have a table `Words(word VARCHAR(100))`. In phpMyAdmin, we could go to the `Words` table and click Import, choose `words.txt`, select format CSV (since one line per entry, essentially CSV with no commas), and import. phpMyAdmin even lets you specify that each line is a new row and what the field separator is (in this case newline, and no explicit separator needed). After clicking Go, the file's contents would be inserted as rows in the table.

  When importing, be mindful of file size limits and timeouts. For very large data imports, it might be better to use the MySQL command-line tool (`LOAD DATA INFILE` command) or other bulk loading methods. In our environment or student accounts, you might be limited. For example, not being allowed to load extremely large files for performance reasons. Always check that the imported data looks correct by browsing the table afterwards.

- Exporting Data: phpMyAdmin's Export tab allows you to download the contents of a table or a whole database in various formats. Commonly, you might export as SQL (which gives you a `.sql` file with `CREATE TABLE` statements and `INSERT` statements to recreate the data) or as CSV (for use in Excel or other applications). For example, if you want to save the People table data, you could select the table, click Export, choose "Quick, display only the minimal options" and "SQL" format, and click Go. This would download a `.sql` file containing the SQL commands to reconstruct that table and its data. If you choose CSV, you can set options like what field delimiter to use, whether to put quotes around text, etc. Make sure to check "Save as file" so that the output is downloaded as a file instead of just displayed in the browser.

One handy use of exporting is to migrate data or to simply inspect the SQL. For instance, exporting as SQL can show you the exact `CREATE TABLE` statement for an existing table (including all indexes, which is useful documentation).

When importing/exporting, also consider data encoding (character set). phpMyAdmin usually defaults to UTF-8 which covers most text. If you have special characters, ensure the encoding is handled correctly.

In summary, Import is used to bulk load data into MySQL from files (CSV, SQL dumps, etc.), and Export is used to extract data (or entire schema) from MySQL to files. These features are vital for database backups and for populating tables with initial data. Just be cautious with large files and always verify a small sample of data after import.

9.8   Data Retrieval: The SELECT Query

Thus far, we have focused on defining tables and modifying data. The most common operation in database usage, however, is querying the data that is usually accomplished with the SQL SELECT command. The SELECT command allows you to retrieve rows from one or more tables, with various filtering and formatting options.

A basic SELECT query to get all data from a table looks like:

```
1  SELECT *
2  FROM TableName;
```

The * wildcard means "all columns." For example:

```
1  SELECT * FROM People;
```

This will retrieve all columns of all rows in the People table. In phpMyAdmin, this is exactly what the Browse tab does by default: executes SELECT * FROM People LIMIT 25; (with a limit for pagination) and shows the results. If you have a large amount of data, you might not want to select everything.

You can choose specific columns:

```
1  SELECT Name, Age
2  FROM People;
```

This would retrieve only the Name and Age columns for all rows.

Typically, you also want to filter the rows to those of interest. This is done with a WHERE clause, similar to in DELETE or UPDATE. For example, to get information on people named 'Harry':

```
1  SELECT *
2  FROM People
3  WHERE Name = 'Harry';
```

This will return all columns for any rows where Name is exactly 'Harry'. In our augmented data, we have two Harrys (with different ages and SSNs), and both would be returned.

You can use other operators in the WHERE clause. Suppose you want people within a certain age range:

```
1  SELECT Name, Age
2  FROM People
3  WHERE Age > 10 AND Age < 30;
```

This finds rows where Age is greater than 10 and less than 30. In our data, that would retrieve Sally (Age 15) and Harry (Age 20). We could also use the BETWEEN operator for a range check:

```
1  SELECT *
2  FROM People
3  WHERE Age BETWEEN 11 AND 14;
```

This would get rows with Age in the closed interval [11, 14]. (In MySQL, `BETWEEN 11 AND 14` means $\geq$ 11 and $\leq$ 14.) If our data had someone age 12, 13 or 14, those would appear; in our case, Age 15 is just outside that range, so we might get none from our small dataset.

Another useful operator is IN, which checks if a value matches any value in a list (or subquery). For example:

```
1  SELECT *
2  FROM People
3  WHERE Age IN (10, 20);
```

This finds rows where Age is either 10 or 20. With our data, Age 10 corresponds to Bert and Betty, and Age 20 corresponds to one of the Harry entries, so those rows would come back. The `IN` operator can make certain queries simpler than using multiple OR conditions. For instance, `Age IN (10, 20)` is equivalent to `(Age = 10 OR Age = 20)`.

We can also exclude a set using `NOT IN`. For example, `WHERE State NOT IN ('NJ','NY')` would find rows whose State is not 'NJ' or 'NY'. This is handy for filtering out certain categories.

9.8.1   Combining Conditions and Patterns

You can combine conditions with AND and OR. We saw AND in the Age example. Using OR: `WHERE Gender = 'M' OR Gender = 'F'` would give everyone (since each person is one or the other in our data). Typically OR is used for conditions like matching multiple possible values (though IN is often cleaner for that purpose).

Pattern Matching with LIKE

Sometimes you do not know an exact value, but you want to match a pattern. SQL provides the LIKE operator for pattern matching with wildcard characters. In SQL patterns (for MySQL and most databases), % represents any sequence of characters (including empty sequence), and _ (underscore) represents any single character.

For example, suppose we want to find all people whose name starts with "Har". We can query:

```sql
SELECT *
FROM People
WHERE Name LIKE 'Har%';
```

The pattern `'Har%'` means "starts with 'Har' followed by anything." This would match "Harry" as well as "Harold", "Harriet", etc. In our data, it matches "Harry". If we used `%Har%`, that would match any name containing "Har" anywhere (beginning, middle, or end). And `'%y'` would match any name ending in "y". The % wildcard can be used in combinations: e.g., `'H%y'` means "starts with H and ends with y" (would match "Harry", "Henry", etc.).

There is also the single-character wildcard _. For instance, `_ar%` would match "Harry" (because _ could be 'H', then "ar", then anything) as well as "Marvin" (_ = 'M', then "ar", then anything). Typically, % is used more often because it is more flexible.

One thing to note: different SQL dialects have different wildcard conventions for LIKE. In MySQL (and standard SQL), % and _ are used. In some other systems (notably Microsoft Access), * and ? are used instead. For example, an Access pattern "B*" is like MySQL "B%". Just be aware of this difference if you ever switch environments. In MySQL, always use % and _ with LIKE.

The LIKE operator is case-insensitive or case-sensitive depending on the collation of the column. By default, MySQL with a case-insensitive collation (like utf8_general_ci) will make LIKE `'Har%'` match "Harry" or "harry" or "HAROLD" (case-insensitive). There is also a ILIKE in some databases (not in MySQL, but MySQL has COLLATE clauses or you use LOWER() for case-insensitive matching explicitly). For our purposes, assume case-insensitive matching on text.

Using SELECT with Multiple Tables (JOINs)

A powerful feature of SELECT is the ability to draw data from multiple tables in one query, using JOINs. While a full treatment of JOIN is often a chapter of its own, we will introduce the basic idea here since our normalized designs often require combining tables to get a complete picture. For example, if we have a People table and a Courses (enrollment) table as described earlier, and we want to list, say, each student's name alongside the courses they take, we would need to JOIN People and Courses on the common field (SSN). A JOIN condition might look like:

```sql
SELECT People.Name, Courses.Course_ID, Courses.Course_Grade
FROM People
JOIN Courses ON People.SSN = Courses.SSN;
```

This query would produce a result combining data from both tables where the SSNs match (i.e., it pairs each person with their course records).

If tables are not joined correctly, you can get a Cartesian product (every combination of rows, which is usually not what you want). For instance, if you do:

```sql
SELECT *
FROM People, Courses;
```

With no WHERE or JOIN condition, MySQL will pair every person with every course entry in a massive result set (this is called an implicit JOIN without condition). That obviously mixes unrelated data and the results do not make sense (e.g., it might show a student with someone else's course). Always ensure that when selecting from multiple tables, you include appropriate JOIN conditions (e.g., matching foreign key to primary key relationships).

We will explore multi-table queries more in the next section (and in the PHP integration chapter), but keep this in mind: to get meaningful results from multiple tables, you must link them on the correct columns. Not doing so is a common error (you get too many results, often the product of the table sizes).

9.8.2 Ordering and Limiting Results

By default, SQL results come in whatever order the database finds it easiest (usually the order data is stored). Often, you will want to sort the results. You can add an ORDER BY clause to a SELECT query:

```sql
SELECT Name, Age
FROM People
WHERE Age > 10
ORDER BY Age ASC;
```

This would list the names and ages of people older than 10, sorted by Age in ascending order (youngest to oldest). You could use DESC for descending order. You can also sort by multiple columns (e.g., ORDER BY Age DESC, Name ASC to sort primarily by age (highest first) and tie-break by name alphabetically).

Another useful clause is LIMIT (specific to MySQL and some others, while SQL standard uses FETCH FIRST N ROWS, etc.). LIMIT 10 means "at most 10 results". If you combine it with an ORDER BY, you can get things like "top 10 oldest people" or "first 5 alphabetical names," depending on ordering. For example:

```sql
SELECT *
FROM People
WHERE Name LIKE 'H%'
ORDER BY Age DESC
LIMIT 10;
```

This would give at most 10 people whose names start with H, sorted by age (oldest first). If there are fewer than 10 such people, you just get however many there are; if there are more, you only get the first 10 in that sorted order.

MySQL also allows a shorthand to limit by percentage of results using LIMIT <percent> PERCENT in some environments, but the standard way shown in our doc uses the TOP clause (which is T-SQL or MS Access style). For example, MS Access might let you do SELECT TOP 50 PERCENT ... to get the top half of the results. MySQL does not use TOP; instead, you would calculate the number of rows and apply LIMIT. This is more advanced, but just know different SQL dialects handle it differently. In practice, LIMIT 10 (or LIMIT 0,10 with offset) is how MySQL does it.

Our focus will be mostly on retrieving the data we need via SELECT with appropriate conditions. The following section will discuss some more advanced aspects like nested queries, but even without those, you can answer a lot of questions with SELECT by filtering (WHERE), projecting specific columns, joining tables, sorting (ORDER BY), and limiting results.

9.8.3   Nested Select (Subqueries)

SQL allows you to nest one query inside another. These subqueries (also called nested selects) can be used in various ways, often in the WHERE clause to provide a list or condition. We saw a simple use of subquery in the context of the IN operator: WHERE Age IN (SELECT Age FROM ...) as an example.

Imagine a scenario: We want to find all male people who have an age that also occurs for some female person. One way to do this is with a subquery. We could first find "the set of ages of all female people", and then find all males whose age is in that set:

```
1  SELECT Name, Age, Gender
2  FROM People
3  WHERE Gender = 'M'
4    AND Age IN (
5        SELECT Age
6        FROM People
7        WHERE Gender = 'F'
8      );
```

Here the subquery SELECT Age FROM People WHERE Gender = 'F' produces a list of ages from the records in the People table where value for gender is female. The outer query then selects from People the records of those whose value for gender is Male and whose Age is also found in the subquery list. This is a somewhat contrived example (we could also do it with a self-JOIN), but it shows the principle. Another common use of subqueries is to filter based on results from another table, for example: "Find students (from People table) who are enrolled in course 'IT202' (which you would know by checking an enrollment table)". You could do:

```sql
1  SELECT Name
2  FROM People
3  WHERE SSN IN (
4        SELECT SSN
5        FROM Courses
6        WHERE Course_ID = 'IT202'
7  );
```

This inner query gets all SSNs of students taking IT202 from the Courses (enrollment) table, and the outer query finds the names of those students from People. This could also be achieved with a JOIN, but subqueries can be more readable in some cases.

One should ensure that the subquery returns data compatible with the outer query's expectation. In the above, the subquery returns a list of SSN values, which matches the type of People.SSN being compared. If you write a subquery, think: does the inner query return a scalar (single value), a column of values, or a full table? Depending on context, SQL expects certain types (IN expects a list, a straight = in a WHERE expects a single value. You could also use a subquery that returns one value, i.e., MAX).

Subqueries can also appear in the SELECT clause or FROM clause (derived tables), but that is beyond our current scope. A final note: sometimes a nested query can be rewritten as a simpler direct query or a JOIN. Database engines often optimize simple subqueries automatically. If a subquery is in the WHERE for each row of an outer query, it might be less efficient than a JOIN, but for learning purposes, subqueries are fine and often easier to conceptualize. We will see more meaningful uses of subqueries when dealing with multiple tables in queries (for example, ensuring some condition holds in a related set of rows).

9.9 The TOP Clause and LIMIT (Limiting Query Results)

As mentioned briefly, limiting the number of results returned is useful when you only need a sample or the first few results of a query. Different SQL implementations provide different ways to do this. In MySQL (and PostgreSQL, and SQLite), you use LIMIT. In Microsoft SQL Server or MS Access, you might use the TOP keyword at the beginning of the select (e.g., SELECT TOP 10 ...). In Oracle, there used to be a ROWNUM trick, and more modern standards use FETCH FIRST N ROWS ONLY.

In MySQL, if we want just the first 10 results of a query (perhaps we do not need the entire dataset), we can append LIMIT 10. If we wanted to start from a certain offset (say skip the first 5 and then take 10), we can do LIMIT 5, 10 (meaning offset 5, take 10).

The original course material referenced the TOP clause from MS Access. For completeness, an equivalent of:

```sql
1  SELECT TOP 10 *
2  FROM People
3  WHERE Name LIKE 'Har%';
```

in MySQL would be:

```
1  SELECT *
2  FROM People
3  WHERE Name LIKE 'Har%'
4  LIMIT 10;
```

Both intend to return at most 10 rows that match the condition. If there are fewer than 10 matches, you will just get however many exist. There is also mention of `TOP 50 PERCENT` which in MS Access would return half of the matching rows. MySQL does not have a direct percent, but one could calculate it or fetch all and then client-side take half. In practice, fixed limits are more commonly used.

For our purposes, understanding `LIMIT` (in MySQL) is enough. This is particularly useful in web applications for pagination (show 20 results per page, etc.), or to just prevent a runaway query from dumping thousands of rows when you only need a few.

9.10   Data Modification: Update Command

Thus far, we have inserted new data and deleted data. The UPDATE command allows us to modify existing data in one or more records. An update can change the values of one or multiple columns for those records that meet a given condition.

The general form is:

```
1  UPDATE TableName
2  SET column1 = value1,
3      column2 = value2,
4      ...
5  WHERE <condition>;
```

If you omit the WHERE clause, the update will apply to all rows in the table (so be careful!).

Let us use a simple example. Recall our Inventory table example from section 9.6 (ItemCode and Amount). Suppose we have:

```
1  INSERT INTO Inventory (ItemCode, Amount) VALUES (1010, 100), (2222, 300);
```

Now, ItemCode 1010 has an Amount of 100 (maybe representing stock quantity). If one item is sold or removed, we want to decrement the amount by 1. We can do:

```
1  UPDATE Inventory
2  SET Amount = Amount - 1
3  WHERE ItemCode = 1010;
```

This finds the inventory record with ItemCode 1010 and reduces its Amount by 1 (so it becomes 99). The SET clause can use the current value of the column (`Amount`) in the expression on the right side. This is very common (e.g., incrementing counters, deducting stock, adding balances, etc.).

If the WHERE clause matches multiple rows, all of them will be updated. For instance, if we had `UPDATE People SET Age = Age + 1 WHERE Gender = 'F';`, it would add 1 to the age of every female in the People table. That is probably not a realistic operation, but it illustrates multiple rows being updated. If the WHERE clause matches none, then zero rows are affected (and MySQL would report "Rows matched: 0 Changed: 0").

Here is another example: maybe we realized we entered someone's name incorrectly. Say we want to update Betty's age from 10 to 11. We could do:

```
1  UPDATE People
2  SET Age = 11
3  WHERE Name = 'Betty' AND Age = 10;
```

This will target the row(s) where Name is Betty and Age is 10, and set Age to 11 for those. If Betty was 10, now she becomes 11. If you had multiple Bettys of age 10 (unlikely if SSN is unique, but just as a scenario), all of them would get updated.

It is often safest to use the primary key in the WHERE clause for updates, to ensure you are updating exactly one specific row. For instance, `WHERE SSN = 771` to update Betty's record, rather than relying on Name which could duplicate.

You can also update multiple columns at once. For example:

```
1  UPDATE People
2  SET Age = 16, Gender = 'F'
3  WHERE Name = 'Sally';
```

This would set Sally's age to 16 and gender to F (the gender part is redundant if she is already F, but just to show multiple assignments). Each assignment is separated by a comma in the SET clause.

One must be mindful of constraints: if you update a primary key value to something that conflicts with another row, you will get a duplicate key error. If you update a value such that it violates a data type constraint (e.g., setting Age = 'abc'), you will get a type error.

A Note on Safe Updates and Transactions

While not a focus of this chapter, in practice you typically execute updates within transactions and check that you are not accidentally doing something unintended (like updating too many rows). Many database tools have a "safe updates" mode where they will not execute an update or delete without a WHERE clause unless you override it.

Our earlier example of decrementing inventory brings to mind a common application pattern: check-then-update. Usually, you might first check that ItemCode 1010 exists and maybe that Amount > 0 (if you are trying not to go below zero), then do the update. In SQL alone, you might incorporate that check into the query:

```
1 UPDATE Inventory
2 SET Amount = Amount - 1
3 WHERE ItemCode = 1010 AND Amount > 0;
```

Then you could check if any row was actually updated (MySQL provides an affected rows count). If 0 rows updated, perhaps the item was out of stock or not found. This is the kind of logic that an application would have to handle (maybe by giving a warning "item out of stock").

One more thing: as with insertion, SQL injection is a concern with updates if user input is directly used in constructing the query string. For example, if you had a web form to update a profile and you naively did `"... WHERE username = '$user'"` and $user came from input, an attacker could attempt to manipulate that. We will address SQL injection soon in the security section, but just remember that any SQL command (SELECT, INSERT, UPDATE, DELETE) can be vulnerable if not handled properly.

9.11   SQL Query Optimization

For small tables and simple queries, performance is not a big issue. As your data grows and your queries become more complex, it is important to consider how to optimize queries and design the database for efficiency.

Indexes are essential for performance. Ensure that columns used in `WHERE` clauses or JOINs are indexed (especially primary keys and foreign keys). Indexes are like lookup tables that the database uses to find rows faster. For example, if SSN is the primary key in People, MySQL automatically indexes it. If you often query People by Name, you might consider adding an index on Name as well, so that `WHERE Name = 'Harry'` runs faster. The trade-off is that indexes make writes slightly slower and use extra space, so you add them judiciously.

Selecting only needed columns can reduce the amount of data the database has to read and send. For instance, if you only need Name and Age, do not do `SELECT *` which reads Gender and SSN unnecessarily. This is especially true if some columns contain large text or BLOB data that you definitely do not need for that query.

Limiting the result set is also beneficial. Use `LIMIT` when you only need a subset of the results. This not only helps your application (less data to handle) but also can allow MySQL to optimize how it reads the data. For instance, if you have an index and you do `SELECT ... ORDER BY indexed_col LIMIT 10`, MySQL can stop after finding the first 10 in order, rather than processing the entire table.

When considering JOINs versus subqueries, note that in some cases a JOIN is more efficient than a subquery (and vice versa, depending on the scenario). With proper indexes (SSN indexed in People and SSN indexed in

Courses), both can be fine. But as a rule of thumb, try to write queries in a way that the database can use set operations and JOINs effectively, instead of repetitive nested lookups. Modern SQL optimizers are quite good, but giving them the simplest task (like a direct JOIN on keys) usually yields good performance.

Filtering early is another important technique. If you are joining multiple tables, use conditions to filter each table as much as possible before or during the JOIN. For example, if you only want students of a certain age in a JOIN between Students and Enrollments, putting `WHERE Students.Age > 20` will let the database consider only those students when joining with Enrollments, rather than joining everything and then filtering.

Avoiding unnecessary complexity is also important. Sometimes beginners will do things like select all rows in client code and then filter in the application, which is far less efficient than using a `WHERE` clause in the SQL to let the database filter (databases are optimized in C to do this stuff quickly). Always try to push the work to the database (it is optimized for set-based operations), but do not ask it to do arbitrary things that you could easily do in code if that is more straightforward (balance is key).

For analyzing queries, MySQL has an `EXPLAIN` feature where you can put `EXPLAIN` before a `SELECT` to see how it plans to execute it. It will show which indexes it uses, etc. If a query is slow, using EXPLAIN can help you identify if it is scanning a huge table (where an index might help) or if the JOIN order is suboptimal, etc. In a course setting, you might not need this, but it is good to know it exists.

Finally, regarding denormalization, very high-traffic systems sometimes denormalize certain data, for example storing a count in a table to avoid doing a `COUNT(*)` across many rows on the fly, or duplicating a frequently needed piece of info to avoid a JOIN. This can improve read performance but at the cost of more complex writes (you have to update in multiple places). For our purposes, we stick to normalized designs and trust the database engine, but be aware that there are exceptions where redundancy is deliberately introduced for speed (often in data warehousing or optimization after profiling the system).

In summary, for efficient queries: use indexes, select only what you need, filter and limit as appropriate, and design your schema intelligently (normalized but with indexes on relationships). Most of these will not even be felt with small-scale class project data, but as soon as you scale up (thousands or millions of rows), they become critical. It is a good habit to write clean, efficient SQL from the start.

9.12   SQL Security Best Practices

Security is paramount when interacting with databases, especially when those interactions involve user input (like form submissions that get turned into SQL queries). One of the most notorious vulnerabilities in web applications is SQL injection, which occurs when an attacker manipulates a query by inserting malicious input. We touched on this in the PHP chapter, but it is worth reiterating here in the context of SQL.

SQL Injection: This happens if you construct SQL commands as strings that include raw user input. For example, imagine you had a login form that sends a username and you naively create a query:

```
$query = "SELECT * FROM Users WHERE username = '$userInput';";
```

If `$userInput` is `alice` this becomes fine: `SELECT * FROM Users WHERE username = 'alice';`. But an attacker could input something like: `alice' OR '1'='1`. The query string would then become: `SELECT * FROM Users WHERE username = 'alice' OR '1'='1';`. The `OR '1'='1'` part will always be true, so this query would return all users instead of just alice, potentially bypassing login checks. In a worst-case scenario, they could try to terminate the quote and append additional SQL, e.g. `alice'; DROP TABLE Users; --`. If the application concatenated that, the query string would have an extra command to drop the table! This is obviously catastrophic if executed.

Preventing SQL Injection: Always treat user input as untrusted and incorporate it safely. The gold standard is to use prepared statements with bound parameters: instead of embedding the input directly, you use placeholders in your SQL (like `SELECT * FROM Users WHERE username = ?`) and then bind the actual value. The database driver then takes care of escaping it properly or sending it separately such that it cannot alter the query structure. In PHP, this can be done with PDO or MySQLi prepared statements. This way, even if the input contains quote characters or SQL keywords, they are not interpreted as part of the command.

If prepared statements are not available (or for legacy code), you should at least escape and sanitize inputs using escaping functions (like PHP's `mysqli_real_escape_string`) to neutralize characters like quotes in the input by turning them into harmless escaped versions. Sanitize by removing or rejecting inputs that contain suspicious patterns if they are not expected. For instance, if a numeric input contains letters or symbols, reject it.

Another important practice is to use a least privilege database user: connect to the database with a user account that has the minimum permissions necessary. For example, your web app's MySQL user typically should not have permission to DROP tables or DROP the database. It might only have SELECT/INSERT/UP-DATE/DELETE on the specific app database. That way, even if an injection attack sneaks in, the damage is limited (they cannot drop all tables if the user has no drop privilege, for instance).

You should also hide error details: when an SQL error occurs (maybe attacker is probing with malformed input), do not show the raw MySQL error message to the user. Those messages can reveal information about your database (table names, etc.). It is better to log the error on the server and show a generic message to the user. In PHP, for instance, you might turn off display_errors in production. This is more of general security hygiene but helps in SQL injection too (less feedback to attacker).

Finally, validate input formats: ensure that inputs conform to expected formats before using them in queries. For example, if an input is supposed to be an integer (like an ID), you can check that with code and reject anything that is not purely digits. If it is a username, maybe disallow characters that would not normally be in a username (like quotes, semicolons, etc.). While this alone will not stop a determined attacker (they can craft input that passes validation but is still malicious in context), it reduces the attack surface and can catch accidental issues.

On the MySQL side, there are also some best practices: use proper escaping of identifiers if you ever include those dynamically (less common, but e.g. dynamic table names should be backtick-escaped), keep the database software up to date as security patches often close off potential exploits, and if using newer MySQL you can use features like SQL modes to enforce stricter handling of bad input (though that is not directly about injection, more about not accepting bad dates or truncated data, etc.).

In summary, the primary concern is: never blindly concatenate untrusted input into SQL strings. Always parameterize or escape it. From the perspective of this chapter, when you write SQL queries by hand for practice, you do not worry about injection. But when these queries are generated by a web application, you must handle user input carefully.

Beyond SQL injection, other database security considerations include regular backups (in case something does happen, malicious or not, having backups of your data is crucial), encryption (store sensitive data like passwords in hashed form, e.g., use `SHA2()` or better, hash in application with salts and store the hash), access controls (use database permissions to restrict who can see or manipulate data, perhaps using views or stored procedures to limit direct access in advanced scenarios), and audit logging (log the queries or actions especially if they involve critical data, so you can trace what happened if something goes wrong).

For our context of Internet Applications, the biggest takeaway is to guard against SQL injection in any dynamic queries. The PHP code should use prepared statements or at least escape functions for any data that comes from the outside. By doing so, you ensure that the SQL commands executed are exactly what you intended, and not tweaked by a malicious actor.

9.13 SQL Examples for Creating Normalizing Tables

In this section, we bring together the SQL concepts discussed so far and apply them in practical scenarios. We will design a simple database, step through the normalization process, and demonstrate common SQL commands (for creating tables, inserting data, querying data, updating records, etc.) using illustrative case studies. The examples will use a LAMP stack context (Linux, Apache, MySQL, PHP), showing how SQL fits into an internet application.

9.13.1 Designing a Database for Children's Classics Books

Imagine we are tasked with creating a database to manage information about classic children's books and their authors. We need to decide what data to store and how to organize it into tables. When designing a database, several key steps guide the process.

First, identify the required data by listing all the information we need to store. For a book database, this might include book titles, authors, publication years, ISBNs, and so on. Consider looking at any existing systems, interviewing potential users, or researching similar applications to gather requirements. Next, eliminate unnecessary data by reviewing the list and removing anything that is not needed, focusing on the data elements that are essential.

With the data identified, group related data into tables by determining how to split the information into one or more tables. Each table should represent a single subject or entity (e.g., a table for Books, a table for Authors). Then break data into atomic fields: for each table, ensure that each field (column) holds the smallest useful unit of data. If an attribute can be subdivided, consider separating it. For example, an Author name could be split into `FirstName` and `LastName` instead of storing the full name in one field. Storing names in separate fields allows flexibility in sorting or formatting, and we can always concatenate them later in queries if we need the full name.

Determine primary keys by deciding on a primary key for each table, which is a column (or combination of columns) that uniquely identifies each record. A primary key should be unique and unchanging. For instance, an ISBN can serve as a unique identifier (primary key) for books, since no two books share the same ISBN. Additionally, consider table relationships by identifying how tables relate to one another. Will it be a one-to-one, one-to-many, or many-to-many relationship? Use primary keys and foreign keys to link tables. For example, if we have separate Books and Authors tables, one author can write many books, which is a one-to-many relationship. We would store a reference (foreign key) to the author in the books table.

Normalize the design by applying normalization rules to reduce data redundancy and avoid anomalies. This means eliminating repeating groups, removing partial dependencies, and removing transitive dependencies (discussed more below). Proper normalization typically results in each fact being stored only once, which makes the database more efficient and easier to maintain. Finally, plan indexes by identifying which columns to index for faster search and retrieval. Primary keys are automatically indexed in MySQL, and foreign keys or other frequently searched fields are good candidates for indexing to improve performance.

Following these steps, we can sketch an initial design. We will start with a single table for books and then refine it:

Suppose we create a table called `ChildrensClassics` to hold book information. It might have columns for the ISBN (as primary key), the book title, the author's name, and the year published. In a simple notation, we can represent it as: ChildrensClassics (Table) with PK ISBN, BookTitle, Author, YearPublished. Here, `ISBN` is the primary key (denoted by PK). For example, a couple of records might look like those shown in Table 9.3.

Table 9.3: Excerpt from an initial `ChildrensClassics` table, with the author's full name stored in each record.

ISBN	BookTitle	YearPublished	Author
978-0-72-324770-8	The Tale of Peter Rabbit	1902	Beatrix Potter
978-0-72-324773-9	The Tale of Benjamin Bunny	1904	Beatrix Potter
978-0-30-922690-8	The Very Hungry Caterpillar	1969	Eric Carle
...	...	...	...

While this single-table approach captures the data, it is not optimal. In the example above, the author "Beatrix Potter" appears in multiple rows (for each of her books), as do other authors. Storing the author's full name in every related book record is redundant and can lead to inconsistencies (e.g., if an author's name is misspelled in one record or if the author's name changes, it would need to be updated in many places).

To eliminate this redundancy, we split the data into two tables: one for books and one for authors. The `ChildrensClassics` table will hold book-specific details, and an `Authors` table will hold author details. Instead of storing the author's name in `ChildrensClassics`, we store an `AuthorID` (a code or number identifying the author). That `AuthorID` will serve as a foreign key linking to the `Authors` table where the actual name is stored. This design achieves a one-to-many relationship: one author (in the Authors table) can be linked to many books (in the ChildrensClassics table). After redesign, our tables look like this. The ChildrensClassics table has PK ISBN, BookTitle, YearPublished, and FK AuthorID. Each record is a book, where ISBN uniquely identifies a book and AuthorID indicates which author wrote the book, corresponding to an entry in the Authors table. The ChildrensAuthors table has PK AuthorID, AuthorFirstName, and AuthorLastName. Each record is an author, where AuthorID is a unique identifier for an author, and we store the author's name split into first and last name fields.

The newly created ChildrensAuthors table below reduces redundancy by placing the table in 1NF, adding a primary key called AuthorID.

ChildrensAuthors (Authors Table):

AuthorID	AuthorFirstName	AuthorLastName
20	Beatrix	Potter
40	Eric	Carle
60	Marcus	Pfister
80	A. A.	Milne
100	Maurice	Sendak

ChildrensClassics (Books Table):

ISBN	BookTitle	YearPublished	AuthorID
978-0-72-324770-8	The Tale of Peter Rabbit	1902	20
978-0-72-324773-9	The Tale of Benjamin Bunny	1904	20
978-0-30-922690-8	The Very Hungry Caterpillar	1969	40
978-0-24-113590-7	The Very Busy Spider	1984	40
978-3-31-401544-1	The Rainbow Fish	1999	60
978-0-73-584118-5	Dazzle the Dinosaur	1994	60
978-0-52-544443-5	Winnie-the-Pooh	1926	80
978-0-14-036122-3	The House at Pooh Corner	1928	80
978-0-06-443178-1	Where the Wild Things Are	1963	100
978-0-06-443253-5	Chicken Soup with Rice	1962	100

After normalization, the `ChildrensAuthors` table stores each author once, and the `ChildrensClassics` table references authors by ID. For instance, AuthorID 20 (Beatrix Potter) is linked to two books. In this improved design, an author's name is stored in only one place (the ChildrensAuthors table). If "Beatrix Potter" needed to be corrected or changed, we would update that name in the authors table, and it would apply to all her books. The books table references authors by ID, avoiding repeated names. This design adheres to normalization principles and reduces redundancy.

In our example, we have a one-to-many relationship between authors and books (one author, many books). It is useful to understand the general types of table relationships. A one-to-one relationship exists when two tables are related in such a way that each record in Table A corresponds to exactly one record in Table B, and vice versa. This is less common; an example might be a table of users and a table of user profile details, linked by the same user ID as primary keys in both tables. A one-to-many relationship exists when a record in Table A corresponds to multiple records in Table B. This is implemented by having a primary key in Table A that is referenced by a foreign key in Table B. Our authors-to-books relationship is one-to-many: each author (Table

A) can have many books (Table B). The AuthorID in the books table is a foreign key pointing to the primary key of the authors table. A many-to-many relationship exists when records in Table A relate to many records in Table B and vice versa. This is handled by introducing an intermediate table (often called a JOIN table or link table) that contains references (foreign keys) to both Table A and Table B. The intermediate table typically has a composite primary key made up of those two foreign keys. For example, if one wanted to track which authors collaborated on which books (assuming a book could have multiple authors and an author could collaborate on multiple books), a separate table (e.g., BookAuthors) would list pairs of BookID and AuthorID to represent the many-to-many relationships.

By designing our schema with proper table relationships and keys, we set the stage for efficient data management. Next, we will ensure our design is normalized, structured according to standard normal forms for relational databases, and look at some examples of normalization in practice.

Normalization Examples

Database normalization is the process of organizing data to minimize redundancy and prevent common update problems. The goal is to ensure each table stores a well-defined set of related data, with no unnecessary duplication. The normalization process is typically broken down into normal forms (1st normal form, 2nd normal form, 3rd normal form, etc.). Here we illustrate the first three normal forms with simple case studies:

First Normal Form (1NF)

A table is in 1st Normal Form if every column contains only atomic (indivisible) values, and there are no repeating groups or arrays in a single record. In other words, each field should contain a single value, not a list or a set of values. Let us take 1NF Violation as an example. Consider a `ToolTable` intended to list tools and their prices, as shown in Table 9.4.

Table 9.4: An example ToolTable that is not in 1NF.

ToolID	Tool	ToolPrice
1000	nut, bolt	5.50
2000	hammer	12.50
3000	nail	2.50
4000	hammer, nail	20.00
5000	drill	50.00
6000	bolt	2.75

Some records have multiple items listed in the `Tool` field, such as "nut, bolt" and "hammer, nail". This design violates 1NF because the `Tool` column in some rows contains more than one value (e.g., the entry "nut, bolt" for ToolID 1000 represents two tools in one field). This makes it hard to reliably query or update individual tool values.

Bringing the table to 1NF: To fix this, we need to eliminate multi-valued fields. One way is to break the data into two tables. We can create a Tools table that lists each tool separately (each ToolID may appear multiple times here, once per tool name if a single ToolID was originally used to group multiple tools), and a ToolPrices table that lists each ToolID with its price (each ToolID appears only once here, with the price). To remove the violations, the data in Table 9.4 could be reorganized.

Tools (ToolID $\rightarrow$ ToolName):

ToolID	ToolName
1000	nut
1000	bolt
2000	hammer
3000	nail
4000	hammer
4000	nail
5000	drill
6000	bolt

ToolPrices (ToolID $\rightarrow$ ToolPrice):

ToolID	ToolPrice
1000	5.50
2000	12.50
3000	2.50
4000	20.00
5000	50.00
6000	2.75

Now each field holds a single value: the Tools table has one tool per row, and the prices are stored separately. The `ToolID` serves as a link between the two tables (it is a primary key in ToolPrices, and a foreign key in Tools). This structure is in 1NF; no field contains a list of items. We have also achieved some degree of normalization by separating what might be considered two different entities: "Tool Item" and "Tool Pricing".

Second Normal Form (2NF)

A table is in 2nd Normal Form if it is already in 1NF and every non-key column is fully dependent on the table's primary key. This mainly applies to tables that have a composite primary key (a primary key made of more than one column). In a table with a composite key, each non-key attribute must depend on the whole key, not just part of it. If a non-key attribute depends on only one part of a composite key, that is called a partial dependency, and it violates 2NF. Let us take 2NF Violation as an example. Suppose we have a Table `AirlineCustomer` with the following structure and sample data, as shown in Table 9.5.

Table 9.5: An `AirlineCustomer` table not in 2NF.

TicketID	AirlineID	AirportLocation
120	50	Newark
140	100	Dublin
160	50	Newark
180	150	Paris
200	100	Dublin

Assume the primary key of this table is a combination of TicketID and AirlineID (meaning a ticket is uniquely identified by the combination of a ticket number and an airline code, with `AirportLocation` as a non-key column). Here, `AirportLocation` might represent the airport from which the customer departs. By examining the data, we notice a problem: the `AirportLocation` seems to depend only on `AirlineID` and not on the full composite key.

For instance, Airline 50 corresponds to "Newark" in every case (Ticket 120 and 160 both have AirlineID 50 and both list Newark), Airline 100 always corresponds to "Dublin" (for Ticket 140 and 200), and Airline 150 corresponds to "Paris" (Ticket 180). This indicates that AirportLocation is functionally dependent on AirlineID alone. In other words, given an AirlineID we know the AirportLocation, irrespective of the TicketID. This is a partial dependency (AirlineID → AirportLocation), because AirlineID is only part of the primary key.

Since `AirportLocation` does not depend on the entire primary key (TicketID + AirlineID), the table is not in 2NF. Bringing the table to 2NF, we should separate the data into two tables to remove the partial dependency:

1. An Airlines table that uses `AirlineID` as its primary key and stores attributes that depend on the airline (in this case, `AirportLocation`, presumably the hub or primary airport for that airline).
2. A Tickets table that uses the composite key or a single unique TicketID as primary key and includes `AirlineID` as a foreign key (and any other ticket-specific details).

Now, we apply this to the example in Table 9.5.

Airlines (AirlineID → AirportLocation):

AirlineID	AirportLocation
50	Newark
100	Dublin
150	Paris

Tickets (TicketID → AirlineID):

TicketID	AirlineID
120	50
140	100
160	50
180	150
200	100

Now, each non-key attribute is fully dependent on the primary key of its table. In the Airlines table, `AirportLocation` depends on the whole key (AirlineID, which is the sole primary key for that table). In the Tickets table, the only non-key attribute is AirlineID, and if we consider TicketID as the primary key (assuming each ticket has a unique ID), AirlineID is fully dependent on that TicketID. We have eliminated the partial dependency by isolating the `AirportLocation` in the Airlines table. The design is now in 2NF. This separation also saves storage and avoids inconsistencies: for example, if an airline's hub changes, we update it in one place (the Airlines table) rather than in multiple ticket records.

Second normal form helps remove redundant data and makes maintenance easier. It reduces the chance of inconsistent data by not storing the same fact (like an airline's location) in multiple rows.

Third Normal Form (3NF)

A table is in 3rd Normal Form if it is in 2NF and also has no transitive dependencies. A transitive dependency means a non-key column depends on another non-key column, which in turn depends on the primary key. In simpler terms, no non-primary-key attribute should depend on another non-primary-key attribute.

Let us extend the airline ticket scenario to a 3NF Violation by adding one more attribute to the `Tickets` table: the name of the airline (call it `AirlineName`). Now consider Table 9.6, our combined Tickets table (not fully normalized), where `TicketID` is the primary key; `AirlineName` and `AirportLocation` are both dependent on `AirlineID`, and `AirlineID` is in turn dependent on `TicketID` in this context.

Table 9.6: A `Tickets` table not in 3NF, as it contains a transitive dependency.

TicketID	AirlineID	AirlineName	AirportLocation
120	50	United	Newark
140	100	Aer Lingus	Dublin
160	50	United	Newark
180	150	Air France	Paris
200	100	Aer Lingus	Dublin

Here, we can assume that TicketID is the primary key (each ticket number is unique). We already know from earlier that `AirportLocation` depends on `AirlineID`. We have now added `AirlineName`, which also clearly depends on `AirlineID` (every time AirlineID 50 appears, the AirlineName is "United"; for 100 it is "Aer Lingus"; for 150 it is "Air France"). We have a situation where `TicketID` → `AirlineID` → `AirlineName`. In other words, `TicketID` determines `AirlineID` (because each ticket is associated with an airline), and `AirlineID` determines `AirlineName`. So, `TicketID` indirectly determines `AirlineName` via `AirlineID`. This is a transitive dependency: `TicketID` (the primary key) influences `AirlineName`, but not directly, the influence is through another non-key field (`AirlineID`).

Transitive dependencies violate 3NF. The presence of `AirlineName` in the Tickets table is redundant because that information really belongs with the Airline itself. To achieve 3NF, we remove the transitive dependency by splitting the table further:

- Keep the Tickets table with only the attributes that depend directly on the primary key. In this case, that could be `TicketID`, `AirlineID`, and perhaps `AirportLocation` if we consider that each ticket has a departure or destination airport. (Alternatively, as done in 2NF, `AirportLocation` might already reside in the Airlines table. We can decide to keep or remove it here, but let us focus on removing the new transitive dependency.)
- Create a separate Airlines table (if not already created in the 2NF step) that stores `AirlineID` and `AirlineName` (and it can also include the `AirportLocation` if that is a property of the airline rather than of the specific ticket).

Now, we apply this to the example in Table 9.6.

Airlines (AirlineID → AirlineName [and possibly AirportLocation]):

AirlineID	AirlineName
50	United
100	Aer Lingus
150	Air France

Tickets (TicketID → AirlineID [→ AirportLocation]):

TicketID	AirlineID	AirportLocation
120	50	Newark
140	100	Dublin
160	50	Newark
180	150	Paris
200	100	Dublin

Now, `AirlineName` is stored in the Airlines table and is linked to tickets via the `AirlineID`. In the Tickets table, every non-key column (here, `AirlineID` and possibly `AirportLocation`) depends directly on `TicketID`. And in the Airlines table, `AirlineName` depends on `AirlineID`. There are no transitive dependencies: `TicketID` does not determine `AirlineName` on its own, it only determines an `AirlineID`; then the

`AirlineName` is determined by that `AirlineID` in a different table. We have separated the concern of "airline information" from "ticket information." The design is in 3NF.

This final design for the airline scenario mirrors what we did for the books database: separate the entities (tickets and airlines, or books and authors) into different tables, and connect them with keys. The result is a set of tables that are easier to maintain and less prone to anomalies.

Benefits: With the database in 3NF, we avoid problems like update anomalies (e.g., changing an airline's name in one record but not another) or insertion anomalies (e.g., having to insert placeholder values for `AirlineName` if we add a ticket for a new airline without known details). Each fact (like an airline's name or base location) is stored in exactly one place.

9.13.2 Implementing the Database and SQL Command Examples

Now that we have a solid database design, we can implement it and manipulate the data using SQL. In this section, we will walk through common SQL commands (Data Definition Language commands for creating or altering tables, and Data Manipulation Language commands for querying and modifying data) using our Children's Classics database as the context.

Creating Tables (DDL)

To create a new database in MySQL, you would use the `CREATE DATABASE` statement. For example:

```
1  CREATE DATABASE ClassicsDB;
```

For our case study, let us assume we have a database ready, and we need to create the tables. We will start by creating an `Author` table (which we will later use for storing authors of children's books):

```
1  CREATE TABLE Author (
2      FirstName VARCHAR(50),
3      LastName  VARCHAR(50)
4  );
```

This SQL statement creates a table named Author with two columns: `FirstName` and `LastName` (each capable of holding up to 50 characters). At this stage, we have not added an `AuthorID` column or any primary key yet; we are just defining the basic structure.

 In practice, we would typically include a primary key in the create statement. For instance, we might add `AuthorID INT PRIMARY KEY AUTO_INCREMENT` to serve as a unique identifier for each author. However, for simplicity, we start with just the name fields and will demonstrate adding the ID using an ALTER statement.

Next, suppose we want to create the table for books (`ChildrensClassics`). A simple version of that table can be created with a statement like:

```sql
1  CREATE TABLE ChildrensClassics (
2      ISBN            VARCHAR(20),
3      BookTitle       VARCHAR(100),
4      YearPublished   YEAR,
5      AuthorID        INT
6  );
```

Here, ChildrensClassics is created with columns for ISBN, title, publication year, and AuthorID. We chose a VARCHAR(20) for ISBN to accommodate the ISBN strings (which can include hyphens) and a YEAR type for the publication year. AuthorID will be used to link each book to an author in the Author table. Again, in a full implementation we would likely set ISBN as the PRIMARY KEY for this table, and perhaps also declare AuthorID as a FOREIGN KEY referencing the Author table. Those details can be added via ALTER TABLE as we refine the design.

Altering Tables

As development progresses, we often need to modify table structures. For example, to add new columns, change data types, or rename the table. The SQL ALTER TABLE statement is used for such changes. Below are some common uses of ALTER TABLE, continuing with our example:

- Renaming a Table: After some thought, we decide to rename our Author table to ChildrensAuthors (to reflect that it contains authors of children's books). We can do this with:

```sql
1  ALTER TABLE Author
2  RENAME TO ChildrensAuthors;
```

This statement changes the table name from Author to ChildrensAuthors. All the data and columns remain intact, but any future references should use the new name.

- Adding a New Column: We realize that we need a unique identifier for each author. We choose to add an integer AuthorID column to the ChildrensAuthors table. An ALTER statement can add a column:

```sql
1  ALTER TABLE ChildrensAuthors
2  ADD AuthorID INT(4);
```

This adds a new column called AuthorID of type integer (with a maximum of 4 digits) to the end of the ChildrensAuthors table. By default, new columns are appended as the last column. If we immediately looked at the table structure after this operation, we would see columns: FirstName, LastName, AuthorID. (At this point, AuthorID is just a regular column; we might later designate it as a primary key or add an AUTO_INCREMENT attribute to generate IDs automatically.)

- Adding a Column at a Specific Position: SQL also allows specifying where to add the new column using the AFTER clause. For example, if we wanted to insert a middle initial column right after FirstName, we could do:

```
1  ALTER TABLE ChildrensAuthors
2  ADD COLUMN MiddleNameInitial VARCHAR(1) AFTER FirstName;
```

This inserts a column named MiddleNameInitial (a 1-character string) immediately after the FirstName column in the table. Now the column order would be: FirstName, MiddleNameInitial, LastName, AuthorID. We could use this if the natural logical position of a new column is not at the very end of the table.

- Modifying an Existing Column: Suppose we later realize that the AuthorID might need to allow more than 4 digits (perhaps our author IDs will grow beyond 9999). We can alter the column's definition with:

```
1  ALTER TABLE ChildrensAuthors
2  MODIFY AuthorID INT(6);
```

This changes the AuthorID column to an integer with up to 6 digits. The MODIFY clause lets us alter the data type or size of an existing column. After this, AuthorID can accommodate values up to 6 digits long. (If AuthorID was intended to be unique and used as a key, we would also add a PRIMARY KEY constraint on it, which could be done in the same or a separate statement.)

- Dropping a Column: If we decide we do not need the MiddleNameInitial after all, we can remove that column:

```
1  ALTER TABLE ChildrensAuthors
2  DROP MiddleNameInitial;
```

This will delete the column MiddleNameInitial (and all its data) from the ChildrensAuthors table. After executing this, the table goes back to having just FirstName, LastName, and AuthorID.

Each of these ALTER operations is executed on the structure of the table. When renaming or adding/dropping columns, MySQL will preserve existing data in other columns. (Renaming a table does not affect the data; dropping a column will obviously discard that column's data.) It is important to plan such schema changes carefully in a real-world setting, especially if the tables already contain data.

Inserting Data (DML)

Once tables are created, we can add data (records) to them using the INSERT statement. There are a couple of syntactic variations for INSERT in MySQL:

- Standard INSERT syntax: Specify the table name, list the columns, and then list the values to insert:

```
1  INSERT INTO ChildrensClassics (AuthorID, ISBN, BookTitle, YearPublished)
2  VALUES (120, "978-0-67-006336-9", "Corduroy", 1969);
```

This command adds a new record to the ChildrensClassics table. It will populate the AuthorID with 120, the ISBN with "978-0-67-006336-9", the BookTitle with "Corduroy", and the YearPublished with

1969. Each value corresponds to the respective column listed. (We are assuming here that AuthorID 120 refers to a new author, e.g., if Don Freeman, the author of Corduroy, was not already in our ChildrensAuthors table, we would add him with AuthorID 120. In practice, we should insert the author into ChildrensAuthors first and then use that ID in the books table.)

- MySQL-specific INSERT syntax (SET clause): MySQL offers an alternative syntax where you use SET to assign column values:

```
1  INSERT INTO ChildrensClassics
2  SET AuthorID = 120,
3      ISBN = "978-0-67-006336-9",
4      BookTitle = "Corduroy",
5      YearPublished = 1969;
```

This accomplishes the same thing as the previous statement, specifically inserting a record with those column values. Instead of a VALUES list, it explicitly sets each column. This format can be handy for clarity or when constructing queries programmatically, but it is specific to MySQL (not part of the standard SQL specification).

After executing an INSERT, the new row is added to the table. For instance, before the above insert, if we queried the table we might not see the book Corduroy. After insertion, a query would show that Corduroy (Year 1969, AuthorID 120) is now present.

(In our running example, AuthorID 120 would correspond to a new author we added to ChildrensAuthors – we would make sure to insert "Don Freeman" into the ChildrensAuthors table with AuthorID 120. Then the Corduroy book record links to that author.)

Querying Data with SELECT

The SELECT statement is the most frequently used SQL command. It retrieves data from one or more tables and returns a result set of rows that meet specified criteria. Let us demonstrate various ways to use SELECT on our book database:

- Select All Columns: To retrieve all columns for all books in the ChildrensClassics table, we use the wildcard * which means "all columns":

```
1  SELECT *
2  FROM ChildrensClassics;
```

This query will return every column (ISBN, BookTitle, YearPublished, AuthorID) for every record in the table. For example, part of the result might look like:

ISBN	BookTitle	YearPublished	AuthorID
978-0-72-324770-8	The Tale of Peter Rabbit	1902	20
978-0-72-324773-9	The Tale of Benjamin Bunny	1904	20
...	...	...	...

Using SELECT * is convenient when you want all the data, but if you have a lot of columns or only need specific ones, it is more efficient to list the needed columns explicitly.

- Select Specific Columns: You can choose which columns to retrieve. For example, if we only care about book titles and publication years (and not the ISBN or author ID), we can query:

```
1 SELECT BookTitle, YearPublished
2 FROM ChildrensClassics;
```

This will return a result set with just two columns, BookTitle and YearPublished, for every row in the table. For example:

BookTitle	YearPublished
The Tale of Peter Rabbit	1902
The Tale of Benjamin Bunny	1904
The Very Hungry Caterpillar	1969
. . .	. . .

In the SELECT clause, we listed the specific columns we wanted. The order of columns in the result will match the order we list them. Here, BookTitle comes first, then YearPublished.

- Filtering Rows with WHERE: Often we do not want all the data, but only those records that meet certain conditions. The WHERE clause allows us to filter the rows. For example, to find a book by title:

```
1 SELECT BookTitle, YearPublished
2 FROM ChildrensClassics
3 WHERE BookTitle = "The Tale of Peter Rabbit";
```

This query will search the ChildrensClassics table for rows where the BookTitle exactly matches "*The Tale of Peter Rabbit*". It will return only those rows (in this case, just the one record for *The Tale of Peter Rabbit*), showing the title and year:

BookTitle	YearPublished
The Tale of Peter Rabbit	1902

The WHERE clause can use various operators (like =, <, >, <=, >=, <> for not equal, etc.) and can match against numbers, strings, dates, etc. String comparisons by default are case-insensitive in MySQL (unless the collation says otherwise), but it is usually best to use the exact capitalization as stored.

- Complex Conditions (AND/OR): We can combine multiple conditions. For instance, suppose we want to find books published before 1970 and written by a certain range of authors (say, author IDs 20 or higher):

```
1  SELECT BookTitle, YearPublished, AuthorID
2  FROM ChildrensClassics
3  WHERE YearPublished < 1970
4    AND AuthorID >= 20;
```

This query uses AND to require both conditions to be true for a row to be returned. It will retrieve all books published before 1970 that also have an AuthorID of 20 or greater. Based on our sample data, this might return books like "The Very Hungry Caterpillar" (1969, AuthorID 40) and "Where the Wild Things Are" (1963, AuthorID 100), etc., while skipping books published after 1969 or books by an author with ID less than 20.

If we wanted to allow multiple alternative conditions, we could use OR. For example, WHERE YearPublished < 1970 OR AuthorID >= 20 would return any book either published before 1970 or with an authorID 20 and above (which in our data set would actually be almost everything, since most AuthorIDs are >= 20, but this is just to illustrate OR logic).

- Sorting Results (ORDER BY): By default, SQL does not guarantee any specific order of the result rows unless you request it. To sort the output, we use ORDER BY. For example, to get the list of books sorted by year:

```
1  SELECT BookTitle, YearPublished
2  FROM ChildrensClassics
3  ORDER BY YearPublished;
```

This will sort the results by the YearPublished column in ascending order (oldest to newest by year). If two books have the same year, their relative order is undefined (unless we add a secondary sort criteria). We can sort in descending order by adding the keyword DESC (descending) after the column name:

```
1  SELECT BookTitle, YearPublished
2  FROM ChildrensClassics
3  ORDER BY YearPublished DESC;
```

Now the latest year will appear first. We can also sort by multiple columns. Suppose we want to sort primarily by book title (alphabetically), but for books with the same title, we want the newest edition first. We could do:

```
1 SELECT BookTitle, YearPublished
2 FROM ChildrensClassics
3 ORDER BY BookTitle ASC, YearPublished DESC;
```

This sorts results by BookTitle in ascending (A–Z) order, and if there are ties (identical titles), it sorts those tie rows by YearPublished in descending order. For example, if there were multiple entries of a title in different years, they would appear grouped by title, with the most recent year first within each title group. (In our dataset, each title is unique, so the second ordering key would not really come into play.)

- Aggregate Functions and GROUP BY: SQL provides aggregate functions like COUNT(), SUM(), AVG(), MAX(), MIN() to perform calculations on sets of rows. When using these, we often group results by some column using GROUP BY. For instance, to find out how many books each author has in our database, we could use COUNT and GROUP BY on AuthorID:

```
1 SELECT AuthorID, COUNT(BookTitle) AS NumberOfBooks
2 FROM ChildrensClassics
3 GROUP BY AuthorID;
```

This query will group the rows in the ChildrensClassics table by AuthorID and count how many rows (books) are in each group. We use COUNT(BookTitle) to count the number of BookTitle entries (we could also use COUNT(*) which counts rows). We also use AS NumberOfBooks to give a descriptive name to the count result in the output.

The result might look like:

AuthorID	NumberOfBooks
20	2
40	2
60	2
80	2
100	2

Each AuthorID appears once, alongside the number of books associated with that author. In our sample data, each of the five authors had 2 books, hence the count of 2 for each author ID. If an author had no books in the table, they simply would not appear in this result (unless we did an outer JOIN with the Authors table, which is beyond our current scope).

We can combine GROUP BY with WHERE to filter which rows are counted. For example, if we only want to count books published after 1960 for each author:

```sql
1  SELECT AuthorID, COUNT(BookTitle) AS NumberOfBooks
2  FROM ChildrensClassics
3  WHERE YearPublished > 1960
4  GROUP BY AuthorID;
```

This will only consider books with `YearPublished > 1960` in the counting. The resulting counts per author might be different (some early 1900s books would be excluded, and authors who only wrote before 1960 would show 0 or be absent from the list).

When using `GROUP BY`, remember that any column in the `SELECT` that is not inside an aggregate function must be listed in the `GROUP BY` clause. In the above query, AuthorID is in the SELECT and not an aggregate, so we group by AuthorID. BookTitle is inside `COUNT()` (an aggregate), so it is fine. If we mistakenly tried to select BookTitle and AuthorID without grouping by BookTitle (which would not make sense in this context), SQL would throw an error.

Updating and Deleting Data (DML)

In addition to inserting new data, a database application often needs to update existing records or remove records. We use the `UPDATE` statement to change data in place, and the `DELETE` statement to remove data.

- UPDATE Example: Let us say we discover that the publication year for Corduroy was entered incorrectly as 1969, and we want to update it to 1968 (the actual publication year). Assuming we know Corduroy's AuthorID is 120 (from our earlier insert), we can correct the year with:

```sql
1  UPDATE ChildrensClassics
2  SET YearPublished = 1968
3  WHERE AuthorID = 120
4    AND BookTitle = "Corduroy";
```

This statement looks for records in ChildrensClassics that match the `WHERE` condition (AuthorID = 120 and BookTitle = "Corduroy") and sets the `YearPublished` for those records to 1968. In our case, that should target the single Corduroy record. After running this, Corduroy's YearPublished will be 1968. A breakdown of the syntax:

  - The `UPDATE ... SET ...` part specifies which table to update and what changes to make. We set `YearPublished = 1968`.
  - The `WHERE` clause identifies which row(s) to update. Without a WHERE clause, all rows in the table would be updated (which is rarely what we want). Here we narrowly target the specific book by a unique combination of author ID and title.
  - You can update multiple columns at once by listing them in the SET clause, e.g., `SET YearPublished = 1968, BookTitle = "Corduroy (Updated Title)" WHERE ....`

- DELETE Example: Now, suppose we want to remove the book Corduroy from the database entirely (perhaps it no longer falls under "classics"). We can delete that record with:

```
1  DELETE FROM ChildrensClassics
2  WHERE AuthorID = 120
3    AND BookTitle = "Corduroy";
```

This will delete any row that matches the condition (*Corduroy* by author 120). In our scenario, that should delete the *Corduroy* book we inserted. After executing the delete, a SELECT query on the table would no longer show that record.

As with UPDATE, the WHERE clause is crucial. DELETE FROM ChildrensClassics; with no WHERE would remove all records in the table (leaving an empty table). If you intend to delete all records, a more efficient way is to use TRUNCATE (discussed next). But if you intend to delete specific records, always use an appropriate WHERE filter.

- TRUNCATE (Deleting All Records Quickly): If we ever need to remove all rows from a table but keep the table itself, the TRUNCATE TABLE command is a convenient option. It is DDL (like a quick table reset) and typically faster than deleting rows one by one. For example:

```
1  TRUNCATE TABLE ChildrensAuthors;
```

This will instantly delete all data in the ChildrensAuthors table, but the table structure (columns, indexes, etc.) remains. After truncation, the ChildrensAuthors table is empty (0 rows). Truncate is often used during development or to clear staging tables because it is efficient; however, be cautious, as it cannot be rolled back in most settings and will free up storage space immediately.

(Our earlier example noted that before truncation the ChildrensAuthors table had 5 records. After TRUNCATE, it has 0 but the table still exists. Also, truncating resets any auto-increment counters back to the start in MySQL.)

- DROP (Deleting the Table): If we decide a table is no longer needed at all, we can remove the entire table (schema and data) using DROP. For instance:

```
1  DROP TABLE ChildrensAuthors;
```

This would completely delete the ChildrensAuthors table from the database, along with all its data. After a DROP, the table no longer exists; you would have to re-create it if you need it again. Use this with care, as dropping tables (or databases) is irreversible through SQL (unless you have backups).

In summary, INSERT, UPDATE, and DELETE allow us to add, modify, and remove data respectively, and they form the core of SQL's Data Manipulation Language (DML). Combined with SELECT (for retrieval), these commands enable full control over the data in our database.

Using SQL in an Application (Case: PHP Integration)

In a LAMP stack (Linux, Apache, MySQL, PHP) application, SQL commands are often executed from within a programming language like PHP to interact with the database dynamically. Let us look at a quick example of how a PHP script might incorporate a SQL query using our Children's Classics database.

Imagine we want to retrieve information about a particular book based on a user's input or some variable in our code. In PHP, it might look like this:

```php
<?php
    // Assume a connection to MySQL has been established and stored in $con
    include("connect.php");  // This file would set up the $con mysqli connection

    // Set a PHP variable for the book title we're searching for:
    $bookTitle = "The Very Hungry Caterpillar";

    // Construct an SQL query using the variable
    $query = "SELECT * FROM ChildrensClassics WHERE BookTitle = '$bookTitle'";

    // Execute the query against the database
    $result = mysqli_query($con, $query);

    // Fetch and display results (this is just conceptual, not full code)
    while($row = mysqli_fetch_assoc($result)) {
        echo $row['BookTitle'] . " - " . $row['YearPublished'];
    }
?>
```

In this PHP snippet:
- We include a `connect.php` file that sets up the connection (`$con`) to the MySQL database.
- We define `$bookTitle` as a PHP variable containing the title we want to search for.
- We then build the SQL query string, embedding the PHP variable inside the SQL string. Notice that the variable is enclosed in quotes within the SQL string: `... WHERE BookTitle = '$bookTitle'`. This results in a SQL command of: `SELECT * FROM ChildrensClassics WHERE BookTitle = 'The Very Hungry Caterpillar'`.
- We execute the query with `mysqli_query` and then hypothetically loop through results with `mysqli_fetch_assoc` to use them (e.g., printing the book title and year).

It is important to quote string variables inside the SQL query as shown, otherwise the database will interpret the words as column names or keywords rather than a string literal. In the above example, if we omitted quotes around `$bookTitle`, it would produce `... WHERE BookTitle = The Very Hungry Caterpillar`, which would cause an SQL error because the database would not recognize the unquoted text as a string value.

This example illustrates how an application can dynamically query the database. In a real-world scenario, we would also be careful to sanitize inputs or use prepared statements to prevent SQL injection, but those topics are beyond the scope of this section.

Using Aliases and Functions in Queries

SQL allows the use of aliases to temporarily rename columns or tables for the duration of a query. Aliases can make query results more readable or simplify writing complex queries (especially with self-JOINs or subqueries). They are created using the AS keyword (which is optional as you can just write the alias after the column name or table name).

For example, suppose we want to generate a single column that combines an author's first name and last name. In our ChildrensAuthors table, we have first and last names in separate columns. We can use the MySQL string concatenation function CONCAT() to JOIN them, and give that result an alias like "FullName":

```
1 SELECT CONCAT(FirstName, ' ', LastName) AS FullName
2 FROM ChildrensAuthors;
```

In this query:
- CONCAT(FirstName, ' ', LastName) will take the FirstName and LastName values for each record and combine them with a space in between. For instance, for a row where FirstName = "Beatrix" and LastName = "Potter", CONCAT will produce "Beatrix Potter".
- AS FullName assigns an alias name "FullName" to that resulting concatenated column.

The result of the SELECT query using the alias "FullName" to display combined names would be a single-column output showing each author's full name as follows:

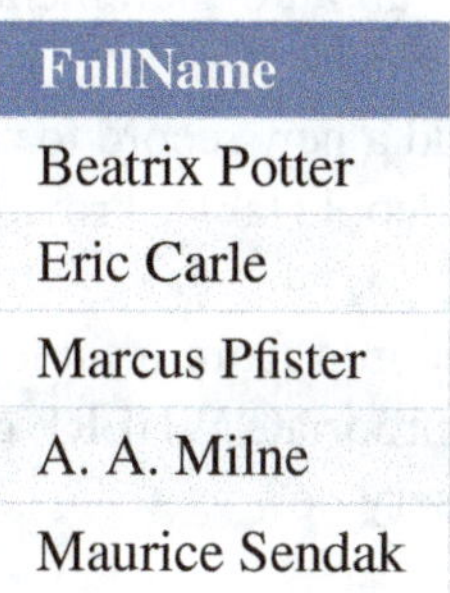

FullName
Beatrix Potter
Eric Carle
Marcus Pfister
A. A. Milne
Maurice Sendak

The underlying ChildrensAuthors table still has separate FirstName and LastName columns; the alias exists only for the duration of this query's result. We could just as well select other columns alongside the alias. For example, SELECT AuthorID, CONCAT(FirstName, ' ', LastName) AS FullName FROM ChildrensAuthors; would output two columns, the author ID and the full name, for each author.

Aliases are also useful for renaming table references (e.g., FROM ChildrensClassics AS C) especially in JOINs, but in this section we focus on column aliases as in the above example.

In summary, the AS clause improves the readability of results or queries. We used the CONCAT function here to demonstrate combining fields, but aliases apply broadly. Any time you want to label the result of an expression or give a more user-friendly name to a column in output, you can use an alias.

By working through this case study and the accompanying examples, we have seen how a well-designed database schema (with proper normalization and relationships) is implemented and manipulated using SQL.

We started with a real-world scenario (children's books and authors), designed tables, normalized the structure, and then used SQL commands to create tables, insert sample data, and query that data in various ways. We also demonstrated updating and deleting data, as well as using programmatic variables within SQL via a PHP example.

These examples illustrate the power of SQL in managing data for internet applications. A solid understanding of these fundamentals enables developers to build dynamic, data-driven websites and applications as part of the LAMP stack. The next chapters will build on this foundation, exploring more advanced database topics and how to interface MySQL with front-end components of web applications.

9.14   Chapter Review

Problem 9.1 Why are databases (and SQL) important in web applications? Explain the role of a database in a three-tier architecture and why most web apps use a database like MySQL on the back-end.

Problem 9.2 What is MySQL and how does it fit into the LAMP stack? Define MySQL and describe its general purpose in a Linux/Apache/MySQL/PHP environment.

Problem 9.3 What is the difference between an HTML table and a database table? Contrast the use of tables for layout in HTML vs. tables for data storage in a relational database.

Problem 9.4 In MySQL, how do you create a new database table via a web interface like phpMyAdmin? Outline the steps to create a table (such as providing table name, defining columns, setting data types, choosing a primary key) using phpMyAdmin.

Problem 9.5 Give an example of a good primary key for a table of people and explain why. For instance, compare using a Social Security Number vs. an auto-increment ID vs. a name as a primary key. Which is suitable and why (uniqueness, immutability, etc.)?

Problem 9.6 What is the SQL command to add a new record to a table? Write a sample command inserting a person Alice, age 30, female, SSN 999 into a People table. Provide an `INSERT` statement and be sure to get the syntax correct with quotes and parentheses.

Problem 9.7 How would you retrieve all records from a table named `Orders` where the `status` column "Shipped"? Write a `SELECT` query with an appropriate WHERE clause.

Problem 9.8 What does the following SQL query do?

```
1  DELETE FROM Students WHERE graduation_year < 2020;
```

Explain in plain words which records are affected and what happens to them. Also, note what would happen if the WHERE clause were omitted.

Problem 9.9 Explain the purpose of the `WHERE` clause in an SQL query. Give two examples of queries using ne with a simple condition, one with a compound condition). Ensure one example demonstrates a compound condition like using AND/OR.

Problem 9.10 What SQL clause or keyword would you use to sort query results? Write a query to select all columns `Employees` sorted by `LastName` alphabetically. The answer should mention `ORDER BY` and show usage in a SELECT.

Problem 9.11 How do you combine conditions in SQL? For example, how would you retrieve all rows from

`Products` where `category` is "Electronics" and `price` is below 100? (Expect a query with AND in the WHERE clause.)

Problem 9.12 What is the SQL `LIKE` operator used for? Provide an example query. Explain wildcard matching with %. For instance, selecting all users with email ending in "@gmail.com" using `LIKE '%%@gmail.com'`. (Ensure the use of % is correct, maybe like `'%%@gmail.com'` to allow any prefix.)

Problem 9.13 What are SQL aggregate functions? Name three and describe what they do. Expect mentions of COUNT (count rows), SUM (sum values), AVG (average values), MIN, MAX, etc., along with short descriptions.

Problem 9.14 Write an SQL query to find the average age of female employees in a table `Employees`. Something like `SELECT AVG(age) FROM Employees WHERE gender='F';`

Problem 9.15 What is a subquery (nested query) and when might you use one? Define a subquery and give a scenario, e.g., "finding customers who have placed an order in the Orders table by using a subquery in the WHERE of Customers query".

Problem 9.16 Describe the concept of database normalization in simple terms. Why might you split data into tables? Looking for an explanation of avoiding redundancy and ensuring each table has one theme (e.g., students vs. courses vs. enrollments) with relationships between them.

Problem 9.17 What is a SQL JOIN and why is it necessary in a relational database? Explain that a JOIN combines rows from multiple tables based on a related column (foreign key to primary key) to gather information that is spread across tables due to normalization.

Problem 9.18 Consider two tables: `Students(StudentID, Name, Age, Gender)` and `Enrollments(StudentID, CourseID, Grade)`. Write a query to list the names of all male students (Gender = 'M') who lled in course 'IT202'. This requires a JOIN or subquery. An answer could use a JOIN: `SELECT s.Name FROM Students s JOIN Enrollments e ON s.StudentID = e.StudentID WHERE s.Gender='M' AND e.CourseID="IT202";`

Problem 9.19 How can you limit the number of results returned by a query in MySQL? Give an example. Describe the `LIMIT` clause. Example: `SELECT * FROM Orders ORDER BY OrderDate DESC LIMIT 5;` (to get the 5 most recent orders, for instance).

Problem 9.20 What is SQL injection and one way to prevent it in application code? Define SQL injection (malicious input altering query intent) and mention using prepared statements or input sanitization/escaping as a prevention strategy.

Below is a set of problems that assume some hypothetical tables (like the earlier People table) where you can infer the general idea behind the problem while focus on the SQL constructs needed:

Problem 9.21 Using DISTINCT:

- List the different classes or majors that students are enrolled in. (For example, if a student table has a Major field, `SELECT DISTINCT Major FROM Students;` would give unique majors. Or if a courses table has course codes, distinct course prefixes might be obtained via pattern or substring if needed.)

Problem 9.22 Using IN and NOT IN:

- Which students are from either New York or New Jersey? (Assuming a student table with a State field, use `WHERE State IN ('NY','NJ')`.)
- Which students have grades that are not 2 or 3? (If grades are numeric like 1,2,3,4 or perhaps year levels, you could do `WHERE Grade NOT IN (2,3)` to filter those out.)

Problem 9.23 Using the LIKE operator:

- What are all the course sections that start with "IT102"? (If course sections are labeled like IT102-001, IT102-002, etc., use `WHERE Section LIKE 'IT102%'`.)
- Find all section IDs that end in "001". (`WHERE Section LIKE '%001'` will match "CS101-001", "IT202-001", etc.)
- List all students whose name begins with "B". (`WHERE Name LIKE 'B%'`.)

Problem 9.24 Complex queries with multiple conditions:

- Which male students are taking IT202? (This requires both a gender filter and a course filter across two tables: likely `SELECT s.Name FROM Students s JOIN Enrollments e ON s.SSN = e.SSN WHERE s.Gender='M' AND e.Course_ID='IT202';`.)
- Which courses have at least one female student? (One approach: JOIN students and enrollments, filter Gender='F', group by course, or use a subquery: e.g., `SELECT Course_ID FROM Enrollments WHERE SSN IN (SELECT SSN FROM Students WHERE Gender='F')`; this gives courses with a female enrolled.)
- Which courses have only male students? (This is trickier: one way is to find courses that do not have any female students. You could find courses that have female students as above, then do `NOT IN` that list. For example: `SELECT Course_ID FROM CoursesTable WHERE Course_ID NOT IN (SELECT Course_ID FROM Enrollments WHERE SSN IN (SELECT SSN FROM Students WHERE Gender ='F'));`. Alternatively, use grouping and a HAVING clause: group enrollments by course and put `HAVING SUM(Gender='F') = 0` by joining in the student gender, a more advanced SQL technique.)

10. PHP and MySQL Integration

Dynamic web applications almost always rely on a database to store and retrieve information. In this chapter, we focus on how PHP (the server-side script) integrates with MySQL (the database) to create fully functional data-driven websites. We will see how the pieces of the LAMP stack come together: PHP code running on the server can accept user input from the browser, interact with a MySQL database to store or fetch data, and then send the results back to the client in an HTML format. Proper PHP-MySQL integration enables features like user registrations, form submissions that save to a database, dynamic content display, authentication systems, and more. We will start from basic database operations in PHP and build up to more advanced techniques, including ensuring security and using prevailing best practices.

Learning Objectives

By the end of this chapter, you should be able to:

- Connect PHP to a MySQL database and perform fundamental SQL operations (INSERT, SELECT, UPDATE, DELETE) through PHP.
- Handle form data in PHP, and use it to insert new records into a database and query existing data.
- Retrieve data from MySQL and display it in web pages, formatting results into HTML (e.g., generating tables of query results).
- Implement basic authentication and session management using PHP with database-stored credentials, including securing passwords with hashing.
- Prevent SQL injection attacks by sanitizing inputs or (preferably) using prepared statements and bound parameters in database queries.
- Integrate AJAX to fetch database data asynchronously, creating dynamic features like autocomplete suggestions without full page reloads.
- Use modern PHP database extensions (MySQLi and PDO) instead of deprecated `mysql_*` functions, and understand the advantages of these improved interfaces.

10.1 PHP and MySQL

Server-side scripts act as the glue that ties together the three components of the three-tier architecture underlying most web applications. To visualize how the client, server, and database work together, Figure 10.1 shows the three-tier architecture flow in a typical PHP/MySQL web application, illustrating how the client tier (browser) communicates with the server tier (PHP script) which in turn interacts with the database tier (MySQL). In this model, a web browser (client tier) sends an HTTP request to the PHP application on the server (application tier), which then interacts with the MySQL database (database tier) and returns the results back to the client as an HTML response.

DOI: 10.1201/9781003727651-10

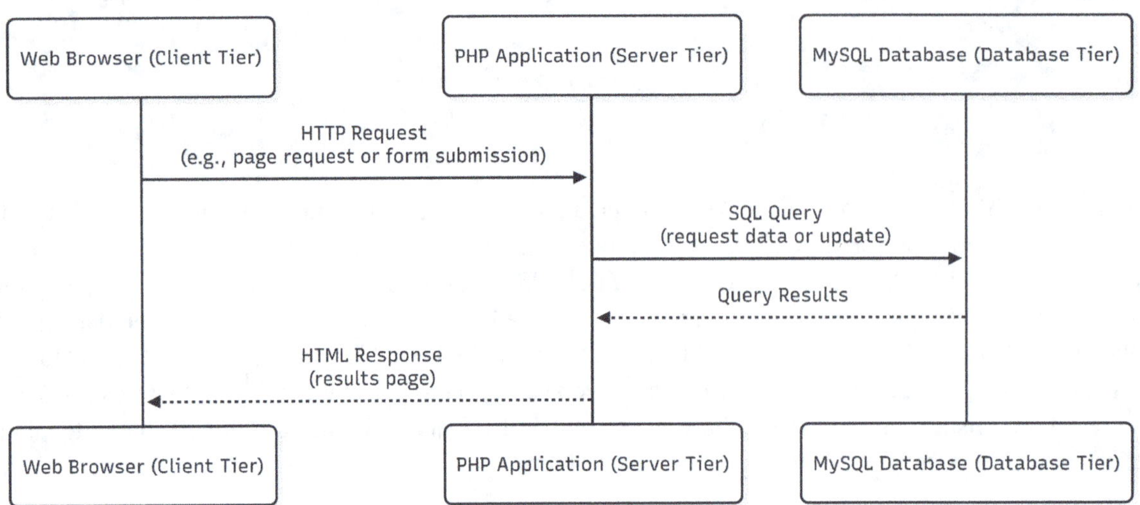

Figure 10.1: Three-tier architecture flow of a PHP web application.

Our focus here is on the PHP coding involved in database integration. We have already seen how PHP programs can interact with a browser, but these programs also serve as the intermediary between client-side views and back-end databases. PHP programs need many capabilities: they must connect to databases, send SQL commands for execution, accept and handle the results of those commands, process client-side inputs as well as database outputs, and wrap (or embed) these results in HTML tags for presentation by browsers (for example, in HTML tables). This chapter overviews these capabilities.

To do this, we will begin with a simple example that illustrates an HTML form accepting data and sending it to a PHP program for insertion into a database. Then we will consider the more elaborate process of retrieving data from a database and embedding it in HTML for the browser. We will briefly examine password-restricted access to PHP scripts, including keeping authentication information in a database and using encryption. We will also introduce the idea of sessions for enabling persistent interactions between browsers and server-side scripts. Finally, we conclude with an integrative AJAX-supported application that relies on database retrieval and employs all the various tools we have learned.

 To see the PHP version that your server is running, you can use the statement: `echo "<br>The PHP version here is: " . PHP_VERSION;` inside a PHP script. Including the statement `phpinfo();` in a script will output detailed information about the current PHP configuration. However, for security reasons, it is not advisable to leave such a script publicly accessible because of the sensitive configuration information it discloses. (See the `http://cwe.mitre.org/top25/#CWE-770` warning about information disclosure.)

10.2   Database Connection and Data Insertion via Form

This section demonstrates how to connect to a MySQL database from a PHP program and insert data from an HTML form into the database. We first present a simple example, beginning with a basic HTML form, and then elaborate on each aspect of the example.

10.2.1   HTML Form

The HTML form (with skeletal code only) is shown below:

```html
1 <form action="database.php" method="GET">
2     <label for="FullName"> Enter Your Full Name: </label>
3     <input type="text" name="FullName" />
4     <br>
5     <input type="submit" value="Submit" />
6 </form>
```

Sample Output

Enter Your Full Name: [   ]
[Submit]

The form's `action` attribute identifies the PHP program intended to service the form request (in this case, `database.php`). We have used the default HTTP GET method here (specified by `method="GET"` or by omission, since GET is default). When the user fills the text field and clicks Submit, the form data is sent to the web server. The server will start the requested PHP program (assumed to reside in the same directory as the form in this example) and make the transmitted form values available to that program. The `<input type="text" name="FullName" />` element creates a single-line text field and assigns the name FullName to the data entered, so that the PHP script can refer to this value by that name. The `<input type="submit">` creates the submission button that, when pressed, sends the form's content to the server for processing. The PHP program must know the name of the form field (in this case "FullName") in order to retrieve the value. Figure 10.2 illustrates the end-to-end process of an HTML form submission resulting in a new record in the database. The user fills out a form in the browser and submits it, the PHP script on the server receives the form data (via an HTTP POST request), connects to the MySQL database to execute an INSERT query, and then sends a confirmation back to the client.

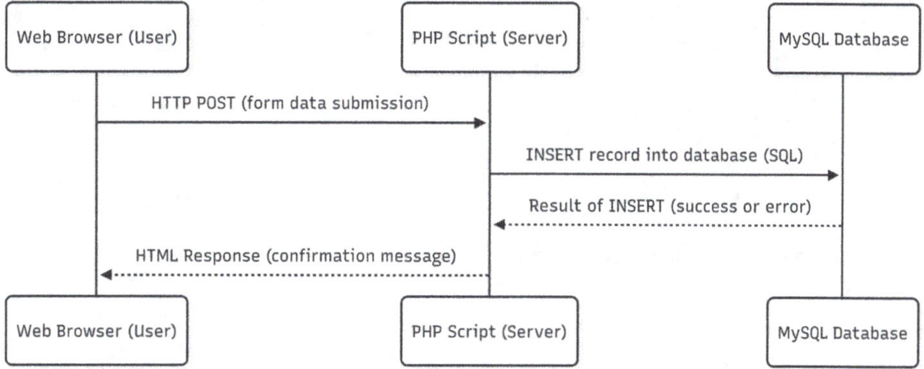

Figure 10.2: Form submission to database insertion flow.

Why GET vs. POST? We used the GET method above for simplicity, but for inserting data it is strongly recommended to use POST. If a GET request is used for an insertion and the user refreshes the results page, the browser may inadvertently resend the same form data, causing a duplicate insertion. (Unless the database schema prevents duplicates with a unique key, you could end up with the same record inserted twice.) In contrast, if the form uses POST and you refresh the results page, the browser will typically warn and require confirmation before resubmitting, preventing an accidental duplicate insert. Another practical difference is that POST can transmit a larger amount of data than GET and can include a broader range of characters. For these reasons, use POST for form submissions that cause database inserts or updates, and GET for idempotent requests (like data retrieval) which have no side effects on repeated execution.

10.2.2   PHP Program to Insert Data

Now let us look at the PHP code that will process the form and insert data into the MySQL database. In our initial example, we will insert a hard-coded value into the database (ignoring the form input for the moment) just to demonstrate the mechanics of database connectivity and insertion. Then we will discuss how to use the actual form input. Assume we have a MySQL table, called Table1, with three columns (for example: name, age, department) where the first and third columns are text and the second is an integer. Here is a simple PHP script that connects to the database and inserts a new row:

```php
<?php
// (Normally, you would include an external file with these credentials)
$hostname = "yourMySQL";        // MySQL server domain
$username = "youUserName";      // MySQL username
$password = "yourPassword";     // MySQL password
$dbname   = "yourDatabaseName"; // Database name

// 1. Connect to MySQL server and select the Database
$connect = mysqli_connect($hostname, $username, $password, $dbname);
if (!$connect) {
  die("Connection failed: " . mysqli_connect_error());
}
echo "Connected to the MySQL server and Database selected";

// 2. Define an SQL INSERT query (using hard-coded values for now)
$query = "INSERT INTO Table1 VALUES ('Howie', 11, 'IT')";

// 3. Execute the INSERT query
$insertrecord = mysqli_query($connect, $query);
if (!$insertrecord){
    print "<br>";
    die("Insert Failed: " . mysqli_error($connect));
}
```

```
25  // 4. Confirmation output
26  echo "<br>Record inserted into Table1.";
27  ?>
```

Sample Output if connection fails

```
Connection failed: Access denied for user 'yourusername'@'domain' (using password:
    YES)
```

Sample Output if connection successful and insertion fails due to invalid data

```
Connected to the MySQL server and Database selected Insert failed: Table
    'yourdatabase.Table1' doesn't exist
```

Sample Output if connection successful and insertion successful

```
Connected to the MySQL server and Database selected
Record inserted into Table1.
```

How it works: When the Apache web server receives a request to run this PHP script, it executes the code and returns the output (the HTML text generated by `print`/`echo` statements) to the browser. In the code above, step 1 uses `mysqli_connect()` to establish a connection to the MySQL server using the given hostname, username, password and database. If the connection fails (e.g., due to wrong credentials or server issues), the if statement executes the `die(...)` part and prints an error message and terminates the program. If the connection succeeds, the script prints a confirmation message "Connected to the MySQL server and Database selected" and an object representing the MySQL connection is stored in the variable `$connect`.

In step 2, we define our SQL query string `$query`. Here it is an INSERT statement that adds a new row to Table1 with the values `'Howie'` for the first column, `11` for the second, and `'IT'` for the third.

 In a PHP string that contains an SQL command, do not terminate the SQL with a semicolon `;` as the semicolon is used in the MySQL console or in phpMyAdmin to separate multiple statements, but when sending a single query via a API call like `mysqli_query()`, the semicolon should be omitted. The PHP statement itself does end with a semicolon as usual, but inside the quoted SQL string we do not include it.

Step 3 executes the query with `mysqli_query(connect, $query)`. This function has two parameter the connection object and the query string. The function sends the SQL string to the MySQL server for execution. If the query fails (for example, due to a syntax error in SQL, invalid data or a table that does not exist), `mysqli_query` returns false and the `die(mysqli_error($connect))` will output the error message from MySQL and halt execution. If it succeeds, for an INSERT query MySQL simply reports the number of rows inserted (which should be 1). The script does not explicitly print anything on success at this point, so without step 4 the page would just show "Connected to the MySQL server and Database selected". In step 4, we added a confirmation printout that a record was inserted. This is optional, but it provides feedback to the user or developer that the operation completed.

At this stage, our PHP program inserts a fixed data row every time it runs. To actually use the form input value (field FullName from our HTML form), we need to modify the script slightly. Instead of the hard-coded `'Howie'` in the INSERT statement, we should plug in the value that came from the form.

10.2.3 Syntax Recap

Before we adjust our code to use dynamic input, let us recap a few PHP syntax points illustrated so far.

In PHP, all variable names start with a dollar sign. For example, `$hostname`, `$username`, `$query` are variables. Variable names are case-sensitive and must start with a letter or underscore, followed by any number of letters, numbers, or underscores. PHP provides superglobal associative arrays like `$_GET` and `$_POST` to access form values sent via HTTP GET or POST. For instance, `$_GET["FullName"]` will retrieve the value of the form field named "FullName" sent via the query string. In our example, if the user typed "Howie" in the text field named FullName, then `$_GET["FullName"]` will evaluate to `"Howie"` in the PHP script.

Every PHP statement ends with a semicolon `;` as the statement terminator. This is required in PHP (unlike JavaScript, where it is sometimes optional). Forgetting a semicolon will cause a parse error. PHP's control structures (if, while, for, etc.) use syntax similar to C/Java/JavaScript. One key difference is that loop index variables or any variables in the condition must start with `$` as they are PHP variables, for example: `for($i = 0; $i < 10; $i++) { ... }`.

For browser output, the `print` (or `echo`) statement sends output to the browser. This can include HTML tags and variable values. When you include a PHP variable inside a double-quoted string, PHP will replace it with the variable's value in the output. For example, `print "Hello $name";` will output Hello Alice (if `$name` contains "Alice"). You can also concatenate strings and variables with the `.` operator, as we saw with the query string construction.

Now, as an experiment, try the above example on your own database (adjusting the connection credentials to your setup). Create a table in your database with the expected structure (for example, Table1 with columns for name, age, department). Upload the HTML form and PHP script to your web server. Use your browser to load the HTML form page from your site, enter some test data, and submit the form to run the PHP program.

At first, our provided PHP code inserts a fixed value `("Howie", 11, "IT")`, ignoring what you typed in the form. After verifying that works (and seeing the new row in the database via phpMyAdmin or the MySQL console), modify your PHP code so it actually inserts the value sent from the form, instead of the hard-coded "Howie". You can do this by building the INSERT query using `$_GET["FullName"]` for the first value. For example, if you stored `$_GET["FullName"]` in a variable `$name`, you could do:

```php
$name = $_GET["FullName"];
$query = "INSERT INTO Table1 VALUES ('$name', 11, 'IT')";
```

After uploading the modified PHP code, submit the form again with a new input value. Then check your database table to see if a row with the value you entered was added. (You may need to refresh the table view in phpMyAdmin to see the new entry. Also be aware there might be a slight delay before the change appears.)

The example above demonstrates the basics of sending data from a form to a database via PHP. Next, we will discuss some important details and variations: how the PHP script works in general, how to handle special characters to prevent security issues, and how to perform other SQL operations like DELETE and SELECT.

10.3   PHP Script

In the previous section, we introduced a specific example of inserting form data into a database. Now we will take a closer look at the general PHP script elements involved in database operations. This includes establishing the database connection, executing SQL commands (INSERT, DELETE, SELECT), and guarding against common security pitfalls like SQL injection. We continue to use the MySQL database in our examples.

10.3.1   Connecting to MySQL from PHP

Connecting to a MySQL database in PHP involves specifying the server, username, password, and database name; then, calling a function to initiate the connection. In our example, we used the old `mysql_connect()` function. PHP also provides the improved MySQLi extension and the general-purpose PDO (PHP Data Objects) for database connections, which we will explore those later. Here, we explain the basic connection logic.

The typical call to connect (using the older MySQL extension) is:

```php
mysql_connect($hostname, $username, $password) or die("Unable to connect to MySQL");
```

This one line attempts to connect to the MySQL server and, if it fails, outputs the error message and stops execution. The `or die(...)` part takes advantage of PHP's short-circuit evaluation: if `mysql_connect()` returns false (failure), the `die()` is executed; if `mysql_connect()` returns a truthy resource (success), the `die()` is skipped. We usually follow a successful connection by selecting the database:

```php
mysql_select_db($databaseName) or die(mysql_error());
```

If selecting the database fails (e.g., the database does not exist or the user has no access), `mysql_error()` will return a message describing the error, which then gets printed by `die()`. After a successful `mysql_select_db`, the connection is ready for queries.

Example:

```php
$hostname = "sql1.njit.edu";
$username = "yourUCID";
$password = "yourPassword";
$project  = "yourUCID";
mysql_connect($hostname, $username, $password) or die("Unable to connect to MySQL");
print "Connected to MySQL<br>";
mysql_select_db($project) or die(mysql_error());
```

When this snippet runs, if all credentials are correct, the browser would display "Connected to MySQL". If something is wrong (say, the password is incorrect), the script would die with "Unable to connect to MySQL" or a MySQL error message. The `mysql_error()` function, when called after a failed database call, returns the last error message from the MySQL server.

 In modern PHP, the old `mysql_*` functions are deprecated. You should use MySQLi or PDO for database connections. For example, using MySQLi (procedural style) the connection code would be:

```php
$connect = mysqli_connect($hostname, $username, $password, $project);
if (!$connect) {
    die("Connection failed: " . mysqli_connect_error());
}
```

We will discuss MySQLi and PDO in the Modern Database Approaches section, but it is good to be aware that `mysql_connect` is deprecated and replaced by these alternatives.

10.3.2   Insert Command

After connecting, one of the first tasks is often to insert new data. In PHP, you send an SQL INSERT command to the database using a function like `mysql_query()` (or `mysqli_query()` in MySQLi). For example, consider this line from our earlier script:

```php
$s = "INSERT INTO Table1 VALUES (`Howie`, 11, 'IT')";
mysql_query($s);
```

Here, `$s` is a string containing a valid SQL statement. The `mysql_query($s)` call delivers that SQL command to MySQL for execution. Recall that an SQL INSERT syntax is:

```sql
INSERT INTO table_name VALUES (value1, value2, ..., valueN)
```

All values must be listed in the order of the table's columns. In our example, Table1 has three columns, so we provide three values. The first and third are text types, which we wrap in quotes, and the second is numeric (no quotes).

In practice, you would rarely hard-code values as we did with 'Howie' and 11. Instead, you would use variables (perhaps obtained from a form). For instance, if `$x` held a name from the form, you might do:

```php
$x = $_GET["A"];                     // get name from form
$s = "INSERT INTO Table1 VALUES ('$x', 11, 'IT')";
mysql_query($s);
```

This would insert whatever name was provided (plus the fixed age 11 and department "IT"). Important: If the string comes from user input, you must be careful to sanitize it before using it in SQL. We will address this shortly.

We usually also want to handle errors for insert operations. A common idiom is:

```
mysql_query($s) or print(mysql_error());
```

This way, if the INSERT fails for some reason, the script prints the MySQL error but continues running (since we used `print` instead of `die`). You could also use `or die(mysql_error())` to halt execution on error. Even if you omit the error checking, a failed `mysql_query` will not stop the PHP script by itself; it will just return `false`. But it is good practice to check for errors so you are aware if something went wrong (for example, a typo in the SQL or a violation of a database constraint).

10.3.3 Security issue: Preventing SQL Injection with mysql_real_escape_string()

Whenever you include external input (like form data) in an SQL query, you risk SQL injection attacks. SQL injection is a technique where malicious users input special characters or SQL fragments that alter the intended meaning of your query. To mitigate this, you should sanitize inputs before using them in SQL statements.

One way to do this in PHP (when using the old MySQL extension) is `mysql_real_escape_string()`. This function takes a string and escapes special characters such as quotes, ensuring they are treated as plain characters in SQL, not as syntax. This function must be called after a successful `mysql_connect` (it needs a live database connection to determine the proper escaping).

For example, if `$x` is a string from a form that we plan to use in an INSERT:

```
$x = $_GET["A"];
$x = mysql_real_escape_string($x);
$s = "INSERT INTO Table1 VALUES ('$x', 11, 'IT')";
mysql_query($s);
```

By escaping `$x` first , any single quotes in the input become `\'` in the SQL string, and other special characters are similarly neutralized. This prevents a user from injecting something like `'); DROP TABLE Table1; --` or other harmful input. If we did not escape `$x`, a cleverly crafted input could break out of the value quotes and inject additional SQL commands. (We will see a concrete example of SQL injection in the Password Restricted Access section and how escaping thwarts it.)

 Always sanitize and validate form inputs. The `mysql_real_escape_string()` function (or its MySQLi/PDO equivalents) is one approach , but the most robust solution is to use prepared statements with parameter binding (which we'll touch on later in modern approaches), so that special characters do not need to be escaped at all as they are sent separately from the query. Also, never display raw database error messages to end users in a production environment, as they can leak information.

10.3.4   Delete command

In addition to inserting data, your PHP scripts may need to delete data. The process is similar: you build an SQL DELETE statement and execute it with a query function.

Under the same assumptions as before (say, Table1 has a text column "name"), the following PHP code uses a value from a form (in a variable $u) to delete all rows where the name matches that value:

```php
$u = $_GET["name"];                          // assume a form field named "name"
$u = mysql_real_escape_string($u);           // escape the value for safety
$s = "DELETE FROM Table1 WHERE name = '$u'";
mysql_query($s);
```

This will delete all records whose name equals the provided $u. If no records match, then nothing is deleted (the query simply affects 0 rows). Often, you might want to know how many rows were deleted. PHP's mysql_affected_rows() function returns the number of rows affected by the last DELETE, INSERT, or UPDATE query in the current connection. For example:

```php
mysql_query($s);
if (mysql_affected_rows() > 0) {
    print "<br>Successfully deleted some rows.<br>";
} else {
    print "<br>No rows deleted.<br>";
}
```

This will print "No rows deleted." if the DELETE matched nothing. You could also use the terse syntax:

```php
(mysql_affected_rows() > 0) or print "<br>No rows deleted.<br>";
```

which will print the message only if mysql_affected_rows() is 0.

 Be cautious with DELETE queries. If you leave out the WHERE clause, DELETE FROM Table1 (with no condition) will remove all rows from the table! Always ensure the intended condition is present.

10.4   Date and Temporal Data in MySQL and PHP

Having covered inserting and deleting data, we can now move on to handling data retrieval and displaying database query results in a web page. Many applications require working with dates and times (temporal data). For example, you might want to timestamp when a record was inserted or last updated. MySQL provides several data types and functions for dates and times, and PHP also has functions to obtain and format date/time values. Here we discuss a few common approaches to associating temporal information with database entries.

When creating a MySQL table, you can define a column with a date/time-related type such as TIMESTAMP, DATETIME, or DATE. These types store temporal values in different formats and ranges. One useful feature is that a column of type TIMESTAMP can automatically be set to the current date and time when a new row is inserted.

For example, suppose Table1 has a single column of type TIMESTAMP. You could insert the current date/time into that column by using the SQL function CURRENT_TIMESTAMP in your INSERT statement:

```
INSERT INTO Table1 VALUES (CURRENT_TIMESTAMP)
```

When MySQL executes this, it will insert a value like 2010-01-04 13:59:13 (this format is YYYY-MM-DD hh:mm:ss in 24-hour time). The exact value will be the date and time at the moment the INSERT happens. This is an easy way to record when a row was added.

MySQL also has a function NOW() which returns the current date and time in the same format as a DATETIME or TIMESTAMP. You could use it similarly in an INSERT or UPDATE statement. For example:

```
$s = "INSERT INTO Table1 VALUES ( NOW() )";
```

This would insert the current timestamp into Table1.

On the PHP side, you have the powerful date() function which can generate formatted date/time strings. The date() function takes a format string and an optional timestamp (in seconds since Jan 1, 1970 UTC, a.k.a. the Unix epoch). If you omit the timestamp argument, it uses the current server time. For example:

```
$d = date("l dS \\of F Y h:i:s A");
```

This will produce a string like "Saturday 19th of September 2009 03:33:34 PM". The format string "l dS \of F Y h:i:s A" uses various format codes, where l (lowercase L) produces the full name of the day of week ("Saturday"), d gives the two-digit day of month (19), and S provides the English ordinal suffix for day ("th"). The \of sequence literally outputs "of" (the backslash escapes the o so it is not treated as a format code). For the date portion, F gives the full month name ("September") and Y provides the four-digit year (2009). The time portion uses h for hour in 01-12 format, i for minutes, s for seconds, and A for the uppercase AM/PM indicator.

The result stored in $d could be printed or inserted into a database as a text field (enclosed in quotes for SQL). Many other format codes are available for date().

Another useful MySQL function is UNIX_TIMESTAMP(), which converts a MySQL date/time value to an integer (the number of seconds since Jan 1, 1970). This is essentially the inverse of PHP's date formatting. You could retrieve a timestamp from MySQL and then use date() in PHP to format it however you like. For example, if you had a MySQL DATETIME column, you could do:

```php
// $result is a MySQL result resource from a SELECT query that got a datetime column
$row = mysql_fetch_assoc($result);
$ts = strtotime($row['datetime_col']);   // convert datetime string to Unix timestamp
echo date("m/d/Y g:i A", $ts);
```

This would output the datetime in a format like `01/04/2010 1:59 PM`, if `datetime_col` was `2010-01-04 13:59:13`. (Here we used PHP's `strtotime` to parse the MySQL datetime string into a timestamp, then formatted it.)

In summary, MySQL offers server-side functions like `NOW()` and `CURRENT_TIMESTAMP` to capture the current time in queries, and PHP offers client-side functions like `date()` to format dates and times in a variety of ways. You can choose where to generate the timestamp depending on your needs. Often, using MySQL's automatic timestamp (via TIMESTAMP column default or `NOW()`) is convenient for logging when records are created. PHP's date functions are useful for displaying dates in user-friendly formats or when you need more control over time zones and formatting.

10.5   Retrieving Data and Embedding Results in HTML

So far we have focused on sending data to the database (inserts and deletes). Equally important is pulling data from the database and presenting it on a web page. In this section, we will walk through a PHP script that queries a MySQL database and then displays the results in an HTML format. We will use an example where a user can enter a name, and the PHP script will fetch records matching that name from a table and display the details.

10.5.1   Program code

Consider the following PHP script (we will call it database.php for this example). It expects a form to send a value via GET with the field name "A" (like our earlier HTML form). The script connects to the database, runs a SELECT query using the provided value, and then displays the results:

```php
<?php
// include file with $hostname, $username, $password, $project variables
include('account.php');

// Establish database connection
$dbh = mysql_connect($hostname, $username, $password)
     or die("Unable to connect to MySQL database");
print "Connected to MySQL<br>";
mysql_select_db($project) or die(mysql_error());

// Obtain HTML form data from server
$u = $_GET["A"];
```

```php
13
14  // Define SQL query based on the input
15  $s = "SELECT * FROM Table1 WHERE name = '$u'";
16  print("<br>Query is: $s<br><br>");
17
18  // Execute the select query
19  $data = mysql_query($s) or die(mysql_error());
20
21  // Process query results
22  while ($info = mysql_fetch_array($data)) {
23      print("<b>Name: </b>" . $info['name'] . "<br>");
24      print("<b>Age: </b>"  . $info['age']  . "<br><br>");
25  }
26  ?>
```

Sample Output (assume the user entered "Alice" in the form and there are two matching records in the table):

Sample Output

```
Connected to MySQL
Query is: SELECT * FROM Table1 WHERE name = 'Alice'

Name: Alice
Age: 22

Name: Alice
Age: 25
```

Let us break down how this script works, section by section.

10.5.2 Acquiring Form input

The PHP script accesses the form data (which the server has stored by the time the script runs) via the superglobal array $_GET (since we used method GET) or $_POST (if method POST was used). Consider the code snippet below:

```php
1  $u = $_GET["A"];
```

It retrieves the value of the form field named "A" and stores it in the PHP variable $u. We now have the user's input in $u for use in our script. If the form method were POST, we would use similarly $_POST["A"].

One nuance: when inserting a PHP variable into an SQL string, if the variable represents text, it needs to be enclosed in quotes in the SQL. In our code, we wrote:

```php
$s = "SELECT * FROM Table1 WHERE name = '$u'";
```

By including `'$u'` inside the double quotes, we ensure that the resulting SQL query has quotes around the value of $u. This is an easier alternative to doing:

```php
$u = "'" . $u . "'";
$s = "SELECT * FROM Table1 WHERE name = $u";
```

which concatenates quotes around the value. The method used in the code leverages the fact that PHP will replace $u with its value within a double-quoted string, so you can nest it inside single quotes for SQL. This leaves the actual $u variable unchanged (unquoted in PHP), which is fine.

Important: Just as with INSERT, if $u comes from user input, we should sanitize it. In a real script, you would likely see:

```php
$u = mysql_real_escape_string($_GET["A"]);
$s = "SELECT * FROM Table1 WHERE name = '$u'";
```

To prevent SQL injection. For brevity, the example above did not include that, but it should be understood as necessary in practice (or better yet, use a prepared statement as shown later).

10.5.3 Defining SQL statement

After getting the input, the script defines the SQL query string in the variable $s. In our case:

```php
$s = "SELECT * FROM Table1 WHERE name = '$u'";
```

This query will select all columns (*) from Table1 for rows where the "name" column matches the value in $u. If $u is "Alice", the query becomes `SELECT * FROM Table1 WHERE name = 'Alice'`. The script even prints out the query for debugging purposes:

```php
print("<br>Query is: $s<br><br>");
```

This is helpful during development to verify the query looks correct. (You might remove such debug prints in production.)

10.5.4 Executing SQL select

To execute the SELECT query, we use:

```
1  $data = mysql_query($s) or die(mysql_error());
```

Here, $data will hold the result of the query. Specifically, it returns a result set resource (sometimes called a result pointer) that references all rows returned by the query. If the query fails (say, there is a syntax error or the table does not exist), mysql_query returns false and die(mysql_error()) will output the error and exit. Assuming success, $data now contains zero or more rows of results.

10.5.5 Processing SQL results

After executing the query, the results reside on the MySQL server and can be fetched row by row by the PHP script. The code uses a while loop:

```
1  while ($info = mysql_fetch_array($data))
2  {
3      ...
4  }
```

mysql_fetch_array($data) fetches the next row from the result set $data as an array (and moves the internal pointer to the following row). On each iteration, $info is assigned to the array of the current row's data. When there are no more rows, mysql_fetch_array returns false and the loop ends. In our example, for each row fetched, the loop prints the name and age.

We have chosen mysql_fetch_array here, which by default can return both numeric indices and associative indices for the columns. Commonly, you might use mysql_fetch_assoc($data) instead, which returns only an associative array indexed by column names. In our usage, we only use associative indices ($info['name']), so mysql_fetch_assoc would be sufficient. Using the associative keys makes the code clearer than using numeric indices (like $info[0], $info[1] for name and age, respectively). We pass no second argument to mysql_fetch_array, so it returns a dual array; we could also call mysql_fetch_array ($data, MYSQL_ASSOC) to get the same effect as mysql_fetch_assoc.

10.5.6 Accessing retrieved data

Inside the loop, we access the retrieved row's columns via the $info array. For example:

```
1  $info['name']
```

gives us the value of the "name" column of the current row, and $info['age'] gives the "age" column value. These indices correspond to the column names in the SELECT query. (Column names are case-sensitive in PHP array indices exactly as they are defined in the database.) If our SELECT had specified aliases or specific columns, we would use those names/aliases as keys.

This associative array approach means we do not have to remember that, say, index 0 is name and index 1 is age; we can just use the actual names, which is less error-prone. Under the hood, each call to `mysql_fetch_array` (or `_assoc`) returns a fresh array for the row, and the previous row's array is overwritten or lost if not stored elsewhere. Typically, you process each row inside the loop and then discard it (or build a larger structure from parts of it if needed).

To illustrate, if Table1 had columns (name, age, dept) and a row (`'Alice'`, `22`, `'HR'`), after `mysql_fetch_array`, `$info["name"]` would be "Alice", `$info["age"]` would be "22", and `$info["dept"]` would be "HR". If the next row was (`'Alice'`, `25`, `'IT'`), the loop's next iteration would overwrite `$info` with that row's data.

How the loop works: Each time the `while` condition is evaluated, `mysql_fetch_array($data)` is called to get the next row. If a row is returned, it is truthy and assigned to `$info`, and the loop body executes. If no row is returned (end of results), the condition is falsy and the loop ends. This loop pattern is common for processing all rows in a result set.

10.5.7   Sending retrieved data to browser

Within the loop, we use `print()` to send output to the browser. In our example:

```
1  print("<b>Name: </b>" . $info['name'] . "<br>");
2  print("<b>Age: </b>"   . $info['age']  . "<br><br>");
```

This will output each record's name and age on the page. We included some HTML tags in the strings: `<b>...</b>` to make the labels "Name:" and "Age:" bold, and `<br>` to insert line breaks after each piece of information and an extra break between records.

Remember that when the browser receives this output, it will render those HTML tags appropriately (bold text and line breaks). If we had multiple records, as in the sample output, each record's information is separated by a blank line (`<br><br>` gives a blank line).

Also note, as a subtlety: in our code we wrote `print(... . $info['age']. "<br>")` without quotes around `age` inside `$info['age']`. That is correct because 'age' is a key in the array and not a variable. If we mistakenly wrote `$info[age]` without quotes, PHP would interpret `age` as a constant (which is not defined, leading to a notice). Always use quotes around array indices that are strings.

If the query returns no results (e.g., no name matches the input), the `while` loop will not execute at all, and the user would only see the "Query is: SELECT ... " line and nothing after. In a user-facing script, you might want to detect that case and print something like "No records found." if `$data` has zero rows. You can check this by `mysql_num_rows($data)` which gives the number of rows in the result. For example:

```
1  if (mysql_num_rows($data) == 0)
2  {
3      print("No records found for $u.");}
```

10.5.8 Wrapping (embedding) data in an HTML table

Our current output is functional but not very polished because the data is just listed with line breaks. For a more organized display, we can embed the results into an HTML table. This way, each row from the database can be a row in the table, and each column can be a cell, with headers at the top.

PHP allows us to print the necessary table tags before, during, and after the loop. For example:

```php
print("<table border='1'>");
print("<tr><th>Name</th><th>Age</th></tr>");  // header row

while ($info = mysql_fetch_array($data))
{
    print("<tr>");
    print("<td>" . $info['name'] . "</td>");
    print("<td>" . $info['age']  . "</td>");
    print("</tr>");
}

print("</table>");
```

In this snippet, we open an HTML table with a border, add a header row with two column headings ("Name" and "Age") using `<th>` cells, then for each data row we create a `<tr>` with two `<td>` cells. After the loop, we close the `</table>`. We must place the `<table>` start tag before the loop and the `</table>` after the loop so that they are output only once. The table header row is also printed once, before entering the loop. The loop then prints one table row per database record.

Each iteration outputs a `<tr> ... </tr>` row, with `<td>` cells containing the name and age. By the end, the browser will render a nice table with all the results. For example, if the query returned three people: The above is how the output would look (with a simple border for clarity). We used `border='1'` for the table to give it a visible border; you could style it with CSS for a better look. We also chose to duplicate the name "Alice" twice in the table, since there were two records for Alice, and each record appears as its own row.

In our code example, we used `print` with string concatenation to embed variables into the HTML tags. Another approach is to break out of PHP mode to directly write HTML, but in generated output like this, concatenating strings is fine. Just remember that when outputting HTML from PHP, you need to be careful with quotes. In our example, we used single quotes around the border attribute to avoid conflict with the double quotes delimiting the PHP string.

By wrapping data in a table, we make it more readable for the end user. Each column is aligned under a header, and each row is distinct. The principle is the same for more columns: you would add more `<td>` and corresponding `<th>` for each column of interest.

To summarize this example: The PHP script connects to the database, retrieves data based on user input, and demonstrates two ways of displaying it in two ways: simple line-by-line and as an HTML table. Now, the user who requested the data can see it neatly formatted on the webpage.

10.6   Password Restricted Access

In some cases, you will want to restrict access to a PHP script's functionality unless a user provides a valid password (or other credentials). There are a variety of ways to implement this. At the most basic level, you might "hard-code" a password in the script and check if the input matches it. However, hard-coding secrets in a script is not good practice for anything beyond trivial use, and it raises maintenance and security issues.

A better approach is to maintain authorized usernames and passwords in a database table, and have the PHP script check the provided credentials against the database. The benefits are that you can easily manage multiple users, assign different privileges, and update passwords without editing the script. Also, by leveraging the database, you can implement stronger protections (like hashed passwords, discussed shortly).

Let us consider a simple scenario: we want an "admin" password to protect certain actions (for example, to access a page that deletes entries or displays sensitive information). We will store this password in a database table and have the PHP script verify it.

10.6.1   Maintaining password information in database

Suppose we have a table Password with a single column `password` (text type) that contains the valid admin passwords (perhaps just one password for the whole application, or multiple if there are multiple admins). A very basic password-checking snippet in PHP could be:

```php
$p = $_GET["password"];  // get the password from a form field named "password"
$s = "SELECT * FROM Password WHERE password = '$p'";
mysql_query($s);
if (mysql_affected_rows() > 0)
{
    // password match found
    // (proceed with protected action)
}
else
{
    die("Invalid Administrative Password");
}
```

In this code, we take the user-provided password from the form, run a SELECT query to see if it exists in the Password table, and then use `mysql_affected_rows()` to check if the query matched any rows. If at least one row matched, `mysql_affected_rows()` returns a positive number (in this case it would equal the number of matching rows, likely 1), and we allow the script to continue. If none matched, we call `die()` to stop execution and output an "Invalid Administrative Password" message.

 A more appropriate function here would be `mysql_num_rows()` since we are dealing with a SELECT result. `mysql_affected_rows()` is typically for checking DML (INSERT/UPDATE/DELETE) results. In this context, `mysql_query($s)` without storing the result may not allow `mysql_num_rows()` to work directly. A clearer implementation would be:

```php
1  $result = mysql_query($s);
2  if (mysql_num_rows($result) > 0)
3  {
4      // password exists
5  }
6  else
7  {
8      die("Invalid password");
9  }
```

Nonetheless, the logic is that if the query finds a match, the password is correct; if not, it is incorrect.

Figure 10.3 shows a basic password-based authentication process using a database lookup. In this scenario, a user enters a username and password into a login form. The PHP script (server) queries the database to check for a matching username and password. Depending on the query result, the server either grants access (on a valid match) or denies access with an error message.

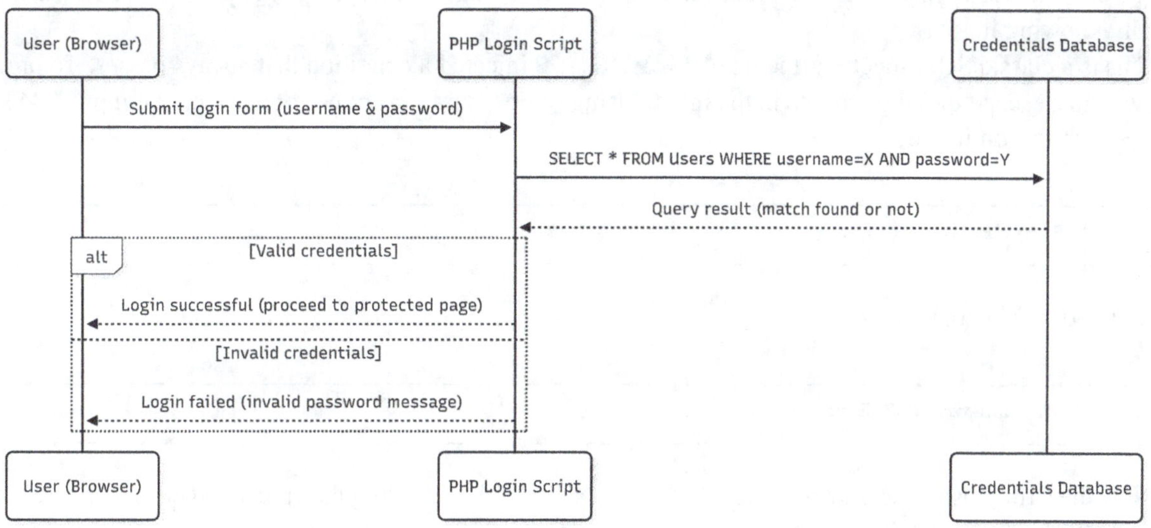

Figure 10.3: Password authentication flow using a plaintext credential check.

In this rudimentary approach, the PHP code is relying on the database to store the password and check it. The advantage is that the actual password value is not exposed in the PHP code sent to the client (PHP code never is, only output). However, simply matching plaintext passwords has security limitations. If someone gains read access to the database, they can see the password. This brings us to the next topic: encryption.

10.6.2   SQL Injection attack and mysql_real_escape_string function

Before encryption, we must emphasize the security issue we touched on earlier: SQL injection. The password-checking example above is vulnerable to injection if we do not escape the input. Consider if an attacker submits the string:

```
CAT' or 'B'='B
```

as the password. The query string becomes:

```
SELECT * FROM Password WHERE password = 'CAT' or 'B'='B'
```

Why is this bad? Because `'B'='B'` is a tautology (always true). The WHERE clause effectively becomes `(password = 'CAT') OR (TRUE)`. This will return all rows from the Password table (or at least one row regardless of what 'CAT' is), causing `mysql_num_rows` or `mysql_affected_rows` to report a match even though the password "CAT" was incorrect. In other words, the attacker bypasses the password check without actually knowing it.

This is a classic SQL injection: the input `' or 'B'='B` injected a condition that always passes. To prevent this, we must escape the single quote in the input. Using `mysql_real_escape_string` on the input "CAT' or 'B'='B" would turn it into:

```
CAT\' or \'B\'=\'B
```

So the query becomes:

```
SELECT * FROM Password WHERE password = 'CAT\' or \'B\'=\'B'
```

Now the string inside the quotes is literally `CAT' or 'B'='B` (including the embedded quotes as characters, thanks to the backslashes). The database will look for a password that literally equals `CAT' or 'B'='B` (which presumably none will). The `or 'B'='B` part is no longer a separate part of the SQL logic; it is just part of the search string. Thus, the tautology is eliminated. The query will properly return 0 rows for an incorrect password like that, and our check will fail (which is what we want for an invalid password input).

This example highlights why input sanitization is critical. By escaping special characters (especially quotes), `mysql_real_escape_string()` prevents malicious input from breaking out of the intended query structure. Always apply it (or a similar mechanism) to any data that will be used in SQL statements, unless you are using parameterized queries/prepared statements which handle this for you.

 `mysql_real_escape_string` is for the old MySQL extension. With MySQLi, you would use `mysqli_real_escape_string($connection, $string)`, and with PDO you would use prepared statements or `PDO::quote` as alternatives.

10.6.3   Password encryption

Even with injection prevented, storing plaintext passwords in a database is risky. If someone gains read access to the database or if the database is compromised, all passwords would be exposed. A further level of protection is to store only an encrypted (hashed) version of the password in the database, rather than the plaintext. Then, when a user submits a password, the script encrypts the submission and compares it to the stored encrypted value. Because cryptographic hash functions are one-way (computationally infeasible to reverse), an attacker who sees the hashed passwords cannot easily derive the original passwords.

One way to do this in PHP is by using the built-in `crypt()` function. The `crypt()` function takes a plaintext string (and optionally a "salt") and returns an encrypted hash string. The exact algorithm and format depend on the system and provided salt, but a useful property of `crypt()` is:

If y = `crypt($x)`, then `crypt($x, $y)` will return y.

In other words, if you encrypt a password and get some result y, using that result as the salt to encrypt the same original password will reproduce y. This is handy for verification: you can store y and later check a password by seeing if `crypt(password_attempt, stored_hash) == stored_hash`.

Modern PHP offers even better functions (`password_hash()` and `password_verify()`) which handle salting and hashing (using algorithms like Bcrypt or Argon2) automatically. But to illustrate the concept, we will use `crypt()` in this example.

The process involves two phases: registration (or setup) and login (verification).

Registration (Storing a Password): Suppose we have a table registeredUsers with columns `username` and `password` (both text). When a new user registers or when we set the admin password, we will insert not the raw password, but an encrypted version of it.

```php
$username = $_GET["username"];
$password = $_GET["password"];
// Encrypt the password using a one-way hash
$encrypted = crypt($password);
$s = "INSERT INTO registeredUsers VALUES ('$username', '$encrypted')";
mysql_query($s);
```

Here, `$encrypted` is the hashed password. We use `crypt($password)` without specifying a salt; PHP will generate a salt and produce a hash (often in Unix DES or MD5-based format by default, or stronger depending on system settings). We then store the username and this hash in the database. Important: We do not store the original `$password` anywhere because once hashed, the original password is not needed for storage. (In a real system, you would also want to ensure usernames are unique, etc., but we will focus on the password aspect.)

Login (Verifying a Password): When a user needs to authenticate (login), they will provide their username and password. Our script should check these against the database.

```php
$username = $_GET["username"];
$password = $_GET["password"];

// 1. Retrieve the stored encrypted password for this username
$s = "SELECT * FROM registeredUsers WHERE username = '$username'";
$results = mysql_query($s);
if (mysql_num_rows($results) == 0)
{
    die("Wrong username.");
}
$row = mysql_fetch_assoc($results);
$storedHash = $row["password"];   // the encrypted password from DB

// 2. Verify the password by encrypting the input using the stored hash as salt
if (crypt($password, $storedHash) == $storedHash)
{
    // Password is correct
    echo "Access granted!";
}
else
{
    die("Wrong password.");
}
```

In step 1, we query the database for the given username. If no such user exists, we terminate with "Wrong username.". If the user exists, we fetch the stored encrypted password $storedHash. In step 2, we call crypt($password, $storedHash). This uses the stored hash as the "salt" for the crypt function. Thanks to how crypt is designed, if $password is exactly the original correct password, this will reproduce the same hash as $storedHash. We then compare it with the stored hash. If they are equal, the password is correct. If not, it is wrong. This way, we verify the password without ever needing to see the original stored password (we only compare hashes).

The PHP program continues only if the username/password pair is valid. Otherwise, it dies with an error. Notice that even if someone looked at our database, they would see only the hashed passwords, not the plain text. And because cryptographic hashes are one-way, knowing the hash does not directly reveal the password. An attacker would have to perform a brute-force or dictionary attack to guess the password from the hash (which is computationally difficult if the password is strong).

Figure 10.4 illustrates an improved authentication flow where passwords are stored as hashes in the database. In this flow, the PHP script first retrieves the stored password hash for the given username from the database, then hashes the password provided by the user (using the same algorithm and salt) and compares the two hashes. Only if the computed hash matches the stored hash does the server consider the password correct and grant access. Otherwise, access is denied, and all of this happens without exposing the actual plaintext password.

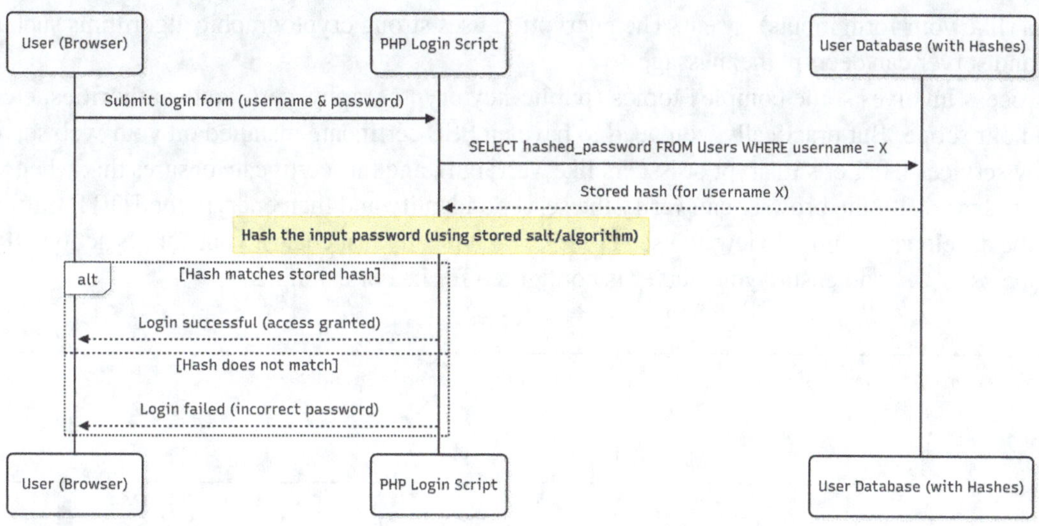

Figure 10.4: Password hashing verification flow.

Why use a salt? The salt (which is embedded in the stored hash when using crypt) ensures that the same password will result in different hashes each time, thwarting attackers from using precomputed tables (rainbow tables) to crack passwords, and also means two users with the same password will not have identical hashes in the database. In our code above, when we call `crypt($password)` for the first time without a second argument, PHP generates a random salt. That salt is part of the returned hash string (for example, the returned string might start with `$1$abc123...` where `abc123` is the salt in an MD5-based hash). When we later do `crypt($password_attempt, $storedHash)`, PHP extracts the salt from `$storedHash` and uses it to hash the attempt, ensuring consistency in comparison.

 The PHP 5.5+ `password_hash()` function simplifies all this. You would do `$hash = password_hash($password, PASSWORD_DEFAULT);` to store, and later `password_verify($password, $hash)` to check. These handle salt generation and a stronger algorithm (usually Bcrypt) internally.

10.6.4   HTTPS - Secure transmission of information

So far, we have focused on how data is handled on the server side and stored in the database. However, another critical aspect of security is how data is transmitted between the client (browser) and server. If you send sensitive information (like passwords) over an unencrypted connection, it could be intercepted by eavesdroppers on the network. This is where HTTPS comes in.

HTTPS stands for HTTP Secure (HTTP over SSL/TLS). When a form is submitted over HTTPS, the data is encrypted in transit, meaning that even if someone intercepts the packets, they cannot read the contents easily. Additionally, HTTPS ensures that the client is talking to the genuine server and not an imposter, through the use of certificates and trusted authorities.

For our context, if you deploy a login form or any password transmission, you should do it over `https://` instead of `http://`. Most production websites have an SSL certificate that enables HTTPS. When using an HTTPS URL, the browser and server perform a "SSL handshake" to establish an encrypted channel before any

HTTP data (like your form inputs) is sent. The encryption uses strong cryptographic algorithms such that only the client and server can decrypt the messages.

The process involves some complex topics (public-key cryptography, certificate authorities, etc.) which are beyond our scope. But practically, you need to have an SSL certificate installed on your web server (often provided by services like Let's Encrypt or issuers like VeriSign), and this certificate ensures that when you go to `https://yourdomain`, the browser can verify the server's identity and then encrypt the HTTP traffic.

From the developer's point of view, to use HTTPS, you typically just change your form's action URL or site URL to `https://...` and ensure your server is configured for it. For example:

```
1  <form action="https://yourdomain.com/secure/submit.php" method="post">
2      ...
3  </form>
```

If `submit.php` processes a password, using HTTPS will protect that password in transit. In contrast, if it were `http://yourdomain.com/secure/submit.php`, the password would go over the network in plain text (which could be read by any intermediate node or malicious listener).

Most modern websites redirect all HTTP traffic to HTTPS to enforce secure transmission. You might have noticed that when you visit `http://gmail.com`, it redirects to `https://mail.google.com/...` automatically. This is critical for security.

In summary, protecting data in web applications involves multiple layers: at the database layer, use secure practices like hashing passwords and guarding against SQL injection; at the application layer, enforce authentication checks; and at the transport layer, use HTTPS to encrypt data in transit.

10.7   AJAX and Database Supported Drop-down Menus

At this point, we have covered using PHP for database operations and integrating with HTML forms. Now we will explore an advanced integrative example that involves AJAX (Asynchronous JavaScript and XML) to create a dynamic, database-driven user interface component: an autocomplete drop-down menu (similar to Google's search suggestions).

Scenario: On the Google search homepage, when you start typing a query, a drop-down appears with suggested completions of what you might be searching for. This is an example of an autocompletion feature. As you type each character, a request is sent (behind the scenes, via AJAX) to a server that returns possible completions from a database, and the browser displays them in a list below the input field. Each suggestion can be clicked to automatically fill the input field and trigger the search. This provides a dynamic, user-friendly experience.

We will implement a simplified version of this: imagine we have a dictionary of words in our database. As the user types letters into a text box, we want to show a drop-down of up to 10 words from that dictionary that start with the letters typed so far. This requires coordination between HTML/JavaScript (on the client side) and PHP/SQL (on the server side), using AJAX to communicate.

This example ties together many pieces: HTML for the form, JavaScript for capturing events and making AJAX calls, PHP for querying the database, and the database (MySQL) for storing the word list. By now, we have the knowledge to understand each part, and AJAX is the glue that connects the client and server interactively.

10.7.1 Flow of Control

First, let us outline the sequence of events and interactions in this autocomplete feature, from the moment the user starts typing to the moment a suggestion is chosen:

1. User types a character in the text input field on the webpage (e.g., types "g"). This triggers a JavaScript onkeyup event (key released) on that input field.

2. The onkeyup event handler calls a JavaScript function (let us call it `sendReq`) that is our AJAX function. This function reads the current contents of the text field and sends an HTTP request to a specific PHP script on the server (via the `XMLHttpRequest` object). The request includes the current text (e.g., "g") as a parameter (likely via query string if using GET).

3. The PHP script (let us call it `autocomplete.php`) receives the request (with the partial string "g"), connects to the database, and performs an SQL SELECT query to fetch words that begin with "g". For example, `SELECT * FROM dictionary WHERE word LIKE 'g%' LIMIT 10`. The database returns the matching results (say, 10 words starting with "g").

4. The PHP script then takes those results and wraps them in HTML elements (such as `<div>` tags or `<tr>` table rows) with appropriate event attributes (onmouseover, onclick, etc.) so that they can behave like a dropdown menu on the client side. Essentially, the PHP script is constructing a small HTML snippet that contains the suggestions. It then prints this HTML snippet as the response to the AJAX call.

5. Back in the browser, the AJAX `sendReq` function has set up a callback (often called `onreadystatechange` or a promise) to handle the server's response. When the response arrives, the AJAX callback function (lets call it `handleResponse`) is triggered. This function takes the HTML snippet returned by PHP (which is just a text string from JavaScript's perspective) and inserts it into the webpage, specifically into a designated area just below the text input field. Typically, we have a placeholder element like an empty `<div id="suggestions"></div>` in the page, and `handleResponse` might do `document.getElementById("suggestions").innerHTML = responseText` to populate it.

6. Now the user sees a list of suggestions (each likely in its own clickable element) appear as a drop-down below the input field, while they are still on the same page (no full page reload). This all happened asynchronously via AJAX.

7. The suggestions are made interactive via the HTML that PHP generated. For example, each suggestion `<div>` might have an `onmouseover` event to highlight it (change background color when the user hovers), an `onmouseout` to un-highlight, and an `onclick` event to handle selection. The highlighting gives a visual cue as the user moves their mouse or arrow keys over suggestions.

8. If the user hovers over a suggestion, a JavaScript function (perhaps `highlightOn()`) is called to change its style (e.g., background color). When they move off, another function (`highlightOff()`) is called to remove the highlight.

9. If the user clicks one of the suggestions, an `onclick` event triggers another JavaScript function (let us call it `chooseSuggestion`). This function will take the content of that suggestion (the text of the word) and put it into the original text input field (completing the user's query). It likely also hides or clears the suggestions dropdown.

10. After filling the input with the chosen suggestion, the `chooseSuggestion` function can then programmatically submit the form to perform the actual search (in this case, perhaps submitting to Google or whatever the form's action is). This is done by calling something like `document.getElementById` `("searchForm").submit()` from JavaScript. In our outline, originally we intended to perhaps submit to Google's search URL, but in general it could submit to any action.

11. The form submission navigates the browser to the search results page (or whatever action was intended, possibly to another PHP that uses the final input value).

The key point is that steps 1-9 happen without a full page reload; only step 10 (the final submission) loads a new page. Steps 2-5 constitute the AJAX request-response cycle, which is asynchronous and does not interfere with the user's ability to keep typing.

To summarize the flow in simpler terms: Keyup event → AJAX call → PHP query → PHP responds with HTML → AJAX callback inserts HTML → user interacts with suggestions (mouseover, click) → click triggers filling input and form submission.

Figure 10.5 depicts the asynchronous flow of an AJAX-powered autocomplete feature that integrates PHP and MySQL. As the user types into a text field, client-side JavaScript captures the input (on each key-up event) and sends an AJAX request to the server with the partial query. The PHP script on the server receives the request, queries the MySQL database for matching entries (e.g., words beginning with the input letters), and returns an HTML snippet containing suggestion items. The browser then dynamically displays these suggestions below the input field without reloading the page. When the user clicks on one of the suggestions, that choice is inserted into the input field and can trigger the form's submission to perform the final action (such as executing a search or filling a form value).

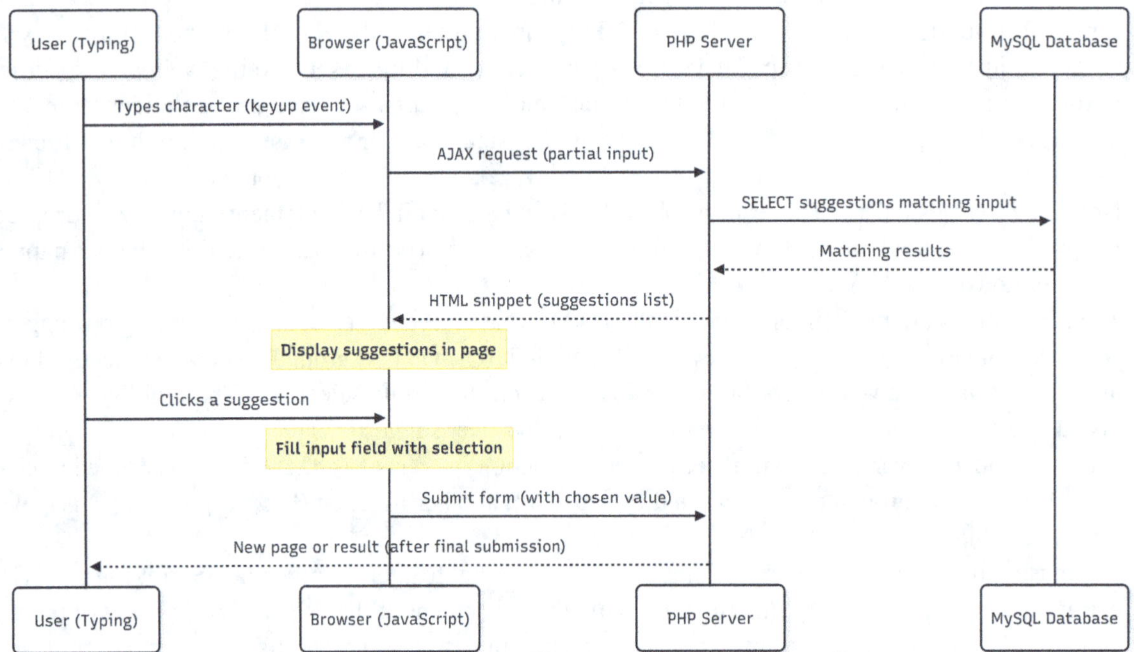

Figure 10.5: AJAX autocomplete flow.

10.7.2 Static div elements

Before diving into all the dynamic parts, it is helpful to construct a static prototype of what we want the drop-down suggestions to look like and how they behave. We can simulate two suggestion items in HTML to understand the necessary structure and JavaScript.

Here is a static example of two suggestion <div> elements in HTML, with events and IDs. Now consider the following code snippet:

```html
<div id="1" onmouseover="ON(1)" onmouseout="OUT(1)" onclick="MOVE(1)">
    <b>Wikipedia</b>
</div>
<div id="2" onmouseover="ON(2)" onmouseout="OUT(2)" onclick="MOVE(2)">
    <b>Google</b>
</div>
<input type="text" id="100" />
```

This snippet shows two `div` elements, each with a unique `id` (1 and 2) and three event attributes. The onmouseover="ON(1)" attribute calls JavaScript function `ON(1)` when the mouse enters the first div. The onmouseout="OUT(1)" attribute calls `OUT(1)` when the mouse leaves. The onclick="MOVE(1)" attribute calls `MOVE(1)` when clicked.

The content of the first div is `<b>Wikipedia</b>`, which will appear as "Wikipedia" in bold. The second div (id 2) contains `<b>Google</b>` (as an example second suggestion).

There is also an `<input type="text" id="100" />` which could represent our main text field (in static testing, we just put it there for the MOVE function to target).

Now, we define the JavaScript functions ON, OUT, and MOVE to handle these events:

```javascript
function ON(p)
{
    document.getElementById(p).style.background = '#8080ff';
}
function OUT(p)
{
    document.getElementById(p).style.background = '#ffffff';
}
function MOVE(p)
{
    document.getElementById(100).value = document.getElementById(p).innerHTML;
}
```

The `ON(p)` function highlights a suggestion by changing its background color to a light blue (hex `#8080ff`) when the mouse is over it. The parameter `p` is the numeric id of the div, and `document.getElementById(p)` finds the div element with that id (e.g., "1") and sets its background style. The `OUT(p)` function reverses this, setting the background back to white when the mouse moves away. The `MOVE(p)` function handles clicking a suggestion by moving the content of the clicked suggestion into the main input field. In this example, `document.getElementById(p).innerHTML` gets the HTML content of the suggestion div (which is the suggestion text in bold tags). Assigning it to `document.getElementById(100).value` places that text into the input field with id "100". (In practice, we might strip HTML tags if needed; here innerHTML of `<b>Wikipedia</b>` would include `<b>` tags. We might prefer to only use plain text in the suggestions to avoid that, or use a different property like `.innerText` if available.)

At this static stage, if you open an HTML file containing the above snippet and include those JS functions, you will see two boxes with "Wikipedia" and "Google". Hovering over them turns them blue (highlight), and clicking one will put its text into the text field below.

Two further aspects to consider in a full solution:

1. Styling the suggestions: We might want each suggestion div to have a border and a fixed width, etc., to look like a menu. We can do this with CSS. We will get to that in the "Style rule for div elements" section, but for instance, we might want each suggestion to have a thin border and be of a certain width so they stack neatly.

2. Submitting the form after selection: In our `MOVE` function above, we have not triggered the form submission. If our goal is that choosing a suggestion automatically performs a search (like Google does), we need to submit the form programmatically. Assuming the form itself has an id (say id="200"), we could enhance MOVE to submit it:

```
1  function MOVE(p)
2  {
3      document.getElementById(100).value = document.getElementById(p).innerHTML;
4      document.getElementById(200).submit();
5  }
```

This presumes the form has `id="200"` (we will ensure that in the HTML form). This way, once the suggestion is moved into the input, we immediately call the form's `submit()` method to send the final query. For now, keep in mind that final step; we will incorporate it when we tie everything together.

The static exercise above helps determine that each suggestion needs a unique identifier and that our JavaScript can manipulate those suggestions by id. In a dynamic scenario, our PHP script will generate multiple such divs with ids 1,2,3,... and corresponding event handlers pointing to the same ON, OUT, MOVE functions (just with different parameters).

Now, having verified how one or two static items behave, we proceed to build the actual dynamic components.

10.7.3   Javascript control of form submission

As noted, one part of this feature is that when a user chooses a suggestion, we want to submit the form automatically. This requires giving an id to the form and using JavaScript to call its `submit()` method.

Assume our search form in HTML is something like:

```html
<form action="http://www.google.com/search" id="200" method="get">
    <input type="text" name="q" id="100" />
    <input type="hidden" name="hl" value="en" />
    <!-- no submit button, because we'll submit via JS -->
</form>
```

Here we gave the form `id="200"` (we use 200 just as a number consistent with earlier usage; it could be any string, but we'll use numeric IDs for consistency in this example). The form is set to GET Google's search (with `name="q"` for query and `hl` for language, as Google expects). We intentionally omit a submit button because we want the user to trigger submission by selecting a suggestion or by pressing Enter normally (which would also submit the form if a default submit button were present or by capturing the Enter key event).

Now our `MOVE(p)` function from earlier can be expanded:

```javascript
function MOVE(p) {
    document.getElementById(100).value =
        document.getElementById(p).innerText || document.getElementById(p).textContent;
    document.getElementById(200).submit();
}
```

We use `.innerText` or `.textContent` to get just the text content of the suggestion (to avoid copying any HTML tags). Then we call `submit()` on the form with id 200. This will send the form to `http://www.google.com/search?q=<query>&hl=en` which performs a Google search for the selected query.

By controlling form submission via JavaScript, we ensure the flow is: User clicks suggestion $\rightarrow$ suggestion text goes to input $\rightarrow$ form auto-submits $\rightarrow$ user sees search results.

It is important to have given the form an id in the HTML so that our JS can reference it. Without an id, we could get the form via other means (e.g., `document.forms[0]`) but an id is straightforward.

So, the takeaway: JavaScript can submit forms programmatically using `formElement.submit()`. We use this technique to complete the search when a suggestion is chosen, eliminating the need for the user to press "Enter" or click a submit button after choosing.

10.7.4 Javascript onkeyup event in text input field

Next, we need to trigger the AJAX call whenever the user types into the search field. We do this by listening for the onkeyup event on the text input.

In our HTML form (or script that sets up events), we can add:

```html
<input type="text" name="q" id="100" onkeyup="sendReq()" />
```

Now, every time the user releases a key in that field, the `sendReq()` JavaScript function will be called. The `sendReq()` function is what will handle making the AJAX request to fetch suggestions.

One caveat: The text in the field can change not only by typing but also by our `MOVE()` function when a suggestion is clicked (it populates the field). That also fires onkeyup for the keystroke that was pressed to trigger the suggestion (like Enter or a mouse key). In our design, once a suggestion is clicked, we actually submit the form immediately, so we might not need to worry about additional key events at that point.

However, consider a user typing quickly letter by letter: each keyup triggers an AJAX call. We need to ensure `sendReq()` captures the current state of the input field each time. This is easy: inside `sendReq()`, we can read `document.getElementById(100).value` to get whatever is currently typed.

Also, we might want to introduce a small delay or check to avoid flooding the server with too many requests (some implementations introduce a short timeout so it does not fire on every single keystroke if they are in quick succession, but for simplicity we may ignore that).

In summary, the onkeyup event on the input field is the hook for our AJAX. Each character typed results in an AJAX query for matching words. If the user quickly types "goo", that will trigger sendReq three times (for "g", "go", "goo"). If implemented efficiently, the server responses will come and update the suggestions. Possibly earlier suggestions get overwritten by later ones (which is fine).

One more detail: We should consider the case when the input becomes empty (user deletes characters). In that case, we might want to clear the suggestions. We can handle that by having sendReq detect if the input string is empty and if so, maybe clear the suggestions div. Or our PHP could return nothing which our handleResponse can handle by clearing the container. For now, we assume the user will type at least one character for suggestions.

Now, let us proceed to implementing `sendReq()` and the rest of the AJAX interface.

10.7.5   AJAX interface

Now we tie in the AJAX components, including the JavaScript function that makes the asynchronous request (`sendReq`), and the PHP script that processes it. We will outline the JavaScript first, then the PHP.

JavaScript `sendReq() function example:`

```javascript
1  var http = new XMLHttpRequest();   // global XHR object
2
3  function sendReq()
4  {
5      var v = document.getElementById(100).value;        // get current input
6      var url = "autocomplete.php?u=" + encodeURIComponent(v);
7      url += "&sid=" + Math.random();   // add a random seed to avoid caching
8      http.open("GET", url, true);
9      http.onreadystatechange = handleResponse;
10     http.send(null);
11  }
```

Let us explain this step by step. We create an `XMLHttpRequest` object (here stored in a global variable `http` for simplicity). Modern browsers support this; older IE used `ActiveXObject` but we assume standard XHR here. In `sendReq()`, we first get the value of the input field (id 100). We construct a URL `url = "autocomplete.php?u=" + encodeURIComponent(v)` to request, which means we are calling autocomplete.php on the same server, passing the user input as a GET parameter u. We use `encodeURIComponent` to safely encode the value in case it has spaces or special characters.

We then append `&sid=` with a random number (`Math.random()`). This trick ensures that each request URL is unique so that the browser does not cache the response for a given query and reuse it. This is often done in AJAX calls because some browsers aggressively cache GET requests. By adding a dummy query parameter that is different each time, we force the request to actually go to the server. Next, we call `http.open("GET", url, true)`, which initializes the request as a GET to the specified URL, with `true` indicating asynchronous mode. We set `http.onreadystatechange = handleResponse;`, meaning whenever the readyState changes (particularly when the response is ready), our `handleResponse` function will be called to process it. Finally, we call `http.send(null);` to send the request (GET requests do not have a body, hence null).

So `sendReq()` prepares and sends off the asynchronous request to server `autocomplete.php`, passing the current partial query.

JavaScript `handleResponse() function:`

```javascript
function handleResponse()
{
    if (http.readyState == 4)
    {
        var response = http.responseText;
        document.getElementById("suggestions").innerHTML = response;
    }
}
```

This function is the callback that processes the server's answer. We check if `readyState == 4` which means the response is fully received. Then we grab `http.responseText`, which contains the textual data returned by the server (in our case, the HTML snippet of suggestions that the PHP will output). We find the element with id "suggestions" (which we need to have in our HTML, perhaps a `<div id="suggestions">``</div>` positioned beneath the input field) and set its innerHTML to the response text. This will render the suggestion `<div>`s that PHP sent, effectively displaying the drop-down.

Now, we need to ensure that in our HTML page we have an element with id "suggestions". We might create a placeholder div in the HTML form, for example:

```html
<div id="suggestions" class="style1"></div>
```

Maybe we give it a class (style1) that defines some base styling (like position or border). Actually, we might not give the container the class; instead, the dynamic divs inside will have class style1. The code above in handleResponse simply dumps whatever HTML the PHP gave into that container.

Now the PHP script `autocomplete.php`:

This script needs to read the input parameter (let us call it $u) from the URL (sent by AJAX), connect to the database (if not already a persistent connection), perform a SELECT query on the dictionary table to get matches that start with that input string, and generate HTML (divs or table rows) with those results, including the event attributes and unique ids, and output them.

For example:

```php
<?php
// get DB credentials ($hostname, $username, $password, $project)
include('account.php');

mysql_connect($hostname, $username, $password) or die(mysql_error());
mysql_select_db($project) or die(mysql_error());

$u = $_GET['u'];   // the partial string from AJAX
$u = mysql_real_escape_string($u);   // sanitize input for safety
$query = "SELECT word FROM dictionary WHERE word LIKE '$u%'";
$query .= " LIMIT 10";
$t = mysql_query($query) or die(mysql_error());

// Output results as divs
$k = 1;
while ($r = mysql_fetch_assoc($t))
{
    $word = htmlspecialchars($r['word']);   // escape any special HTML characters
    echo "<div class=\"style1\" id=\"$k\" ";
    echo "onmouseover=\"ON($k)\" onmouseout=\"OUT($k)\" onclick=\"MOVE($k)\">";
    echo "$word</div>";
    $k++;
}
?>
```

A breakdown of this: We connect to the database (using an include for credentials for brevity) and select the DB. We get the u parameter from the request and escape it to prevent any chance of SQL injection or harmful characters. We craft a SELECT query to get up to 10 words starting with u from a table `dictionary` (which we assume has a column `word`), using `LIMIT 10` to restrict to 10 results.

We execute the query. Then for each result row, we output a `<div>`. We use $k as an index starting at 1 for the first suggestion. We give each div the class "style1" (for styling), an `id` equal to the index $k, and the event handlers `onmouseover`, `onmouseout`, `onclick` calling ON, OUT, MOVE with the index. We put the actual word inside the div, using `htmlspecialchars` to escape any characters like < or & that might be in the word just to be safe (so that our output does not break HTML if the word contains, say, an ampersand). We increment $k for the next suggestion.

So, if the user typed "g" and the first few words in our dictionary are "Game", "Gamma", "Giraffe", "Google", ... the PHP might output:

```html
<div class="style1" id="1" onmouseover="ON(1)" onmouseout="OUT(1)" onclick="MOVE(1)">
    Game
</div>
<div class="style1" id="2" onmouseover="ON(2)" onmouseout="OUT(2)" onclick="MOVE(2)">
    Gamma
</div>
<div class="style1" id="3" onmouseover="ON(3)" onmouseout="OUT(3)" onclick="MOVE(3)">
    Giraffe
</div>
...
```

This is exactly the format our earlier static example and JS functions expect. These lines are sent back as the AJAX response.

The `handleResponse` JavaScript will insert these into the `<div id="suggestions">` container on the page. Because each inserted div has the class "style1", and we likely have CSS defined for `.style1`, they will appear styled accordingly.

We should also consider what happens if no results are found. Our PHP script will output nothing inside the while loop. That means `handleResponse` will set `suggestions.innerHTML = ""` (empty), effectively clearing any previous suggestions. This is the desired behavior: (if the user typed something that yields no matches, the dropdown disappears or shows nothing). We might choose to output a small message like "(No suggestions)" if `$k` stays 1 (meaning no loop iterations), but it is optional.

10.7.6 Style rule for div elements

Now let us address the styling. We want the suggestion divs to look like a dropdown menu: typically a white box, black text, maybe a border around each item or the whole group, and a consistent width so they align under the text field. We can define a CSS class (as mentioned, `.style1`) to style these suggestion divs. For example:

```css
<style>
  .style1
  {
     border: 2px solid black;
     width: 400px;
     height: 30px;
     background-color: white;
     cursor: pointer;
  }
</style>
```

This style gives each suggestion a thin black border (2px), fixes the width to 400px and height to 30px for each suggestion box, sets the background color to white by default, and sets `cursor: pointer;` so the mouse cursor shows as a hand when hovering (indicating clickable).

We could also style the container (`#suggestions` div) if needed (e.g., give it a border or position it). But since each item has a border, one could also just rely on that.

The class is applied in the PHP output (`<div class="style1">`). When inserted into the page, each suggestion div will be styled by this rule.

The width should be matched to the text input's width if we want them aligned. If our text input is ~400px, we set that accordingly. The height 30px is arbitrary; it should be enough to accommodate one line of text (with some padding possibly). We might refine it with `line-height` or padding for better vertical centering of text, but we will keep it simple.

We should also note that when we highlight a div on hover, we change its background to `#8080ff` (light blue) in the `ON()` function. This will override the white background set by the class. When we `(OUT)`, we set back to white. So our style and script work together for the hover effect.

 The `.style1` class name is arbitrary; it is named as in the content we have. In practice, you might call it `.suggestion` or something more descriptive.

This CSS can be placed in the `<head>` of the HTML page or an external stylesheet. As long as the page that will contain the suggestions (which is the main page with the input) has this style loaded, it will apply to the inserted suggestion divs.

To summarize, our CSS ensures each suggestion appears as a separate bordered box of equal size, stacked on top of one another (block-level divs will naturally stack vertically). The background is white until hovered, at which point our JS changes it (we could also use CSS `:hover` on `.style1`, but since we want to trigger via JS for compatibility, we did that).

10.7.7   SQL for retrieval based on partial string

We already touched on the SQL query used in the PHP script, but let us explicitly note the technique:

To retrieve entries that begin with a given string in SQL, we use the `LIKE` operator with a wildcard. For example:

```
SELECT *
FROM dictionary
WHERE word LIKE 'goo%';
```

This would retrieve all rows where the `word` column starts with "goo". The `%` is a wildcard that matches any sequence of characters. If we wanted to match the string anywhere, we would use `%goo%`. For ending with, `%goo`. But for starting with, `goo%` is correct.

We also might want to limit the number of results, because a common word fragment (like "a") could have thousands of matches. We used `LIMIT 10` to just get the top 10 results. In MySQL, if we wanted the first 10 alphabetically, we could add `ORDER BY word ASC LIMIT 10`. If not, MySQL will return in whatever order it finds (likely alphabetical if the table naturally is, but not guaranteed without `ORDER BY`).

Some SQL implementations (SQL Server, MS Access) use `SELECT TOP 10 ...` instead of `LIMIT`. MySQL uses `LIMIT`. Since our environment is MySQL, we use `LIMIT 10`.

In some of our PHP code, we did:

```
$query = "SELECT word FROM dictionary WHERE word LIKE '$u%'";
$query .= " LIMIT 10";
```

So that covers it: `LIKE '$u%'` is the crucial part for "begins with $u" retrieval.

One more thing to consider: if the database is large, these queries should ideally use an index (if the `word` column is indexed, a prefix search can use the index). For our demonstration, we will not delve into database indexing, but it is good to know for real performance you would index the `word` column.

10.7.8 Wrapping database content in HTML tags dynamically

We have essentially done this in our PHP code by echoing `<div>` tags around each database result. To reiterate the approach:

Our PHP script took each database row (a word) and wrapped it in the necessary HTML tags (div with events) before outputting. This is dynamic generation of HTML based on database content.

We started with a static model, then translated it to dynamic code. The keys were using a loop (while fetch) to handle an unknown number of results, using a counter $k to produce unique ids for each generated element, inserting the dynamic data (`$r['word']`) into the output while taking care to escape it properly (with `htmlspecialchars` in our code), and including necessary escaping for quotes within attributes. In our echo, notice we used double quotes around HTML attributes and echoed the numeric $k without quotes for onmouseover etc. That was fine because $k is numeric. If we had string parameters, we would need to quote them properly.

In our code, we concatenated strings with `echo` for readability:

```
echo "<div class=\"style1\" id=\"$k\" onmouseover=\"ON($k)\" ...>$word</div>";
```

We had to escape the double quotes around style1 by backslashes inside the PHP string, or we could have used single quotes around the whole string and not escape double quotes. Either way, the principle is building an HTML snippet with the data inserted.

This approach is relatively straightforward because the HTML needed for each piece is small. If it were more complex, sometimes one might use templating or an output buffer. But direct echo in a loop is common. The resulting HTML (as we saw) is then interpreted by the browser thanks to innerHTML injection.

One more detail from the original notes: the `this` notation is mentioned as an alternative, which we will cover next.

10.7.9 Modification using this notation

There is an alternative way to handle the events without assigning unique incremental IDs to each suggestion: using the JavaScript `this` keyword in the event handlers.

For example, instead of `onmouseover="ON(1)"`, we could have `onmouseover="ON(this)"`. In that case, the ON function could be defined to accept an object reference rather than an id. For example:

```
function ON(elem)
{
    elem.style.background = '#ff8080';
}
```

If we attach it as `onmouseover="ON(this)"` on a div, then inside ON, `elem` refers to the actual div element that triggered the event. So we can directly change its style. Similarly, `OUT(this)` would pass the element itself. For the MOVE function, if we do `onclick="MOVE(this)"`, then:

```
function MOVE(elem)
{
    document.getElementById(100).value = elem.textContent || elem.innerText;
    document.getElementById(200).submit();
}
```

Here, `elem` is the clicked div, so `elem.innerHTML` or `elem.textContent` gives its content. Then we submit the form as before. Using `this` simplifies the generation on the PHP side slightly because you no longer need to output a number or manage IDs for each event. You could output:

```
echo "<div class=\"style1\" onmouseover=\"ON(this)\" onmouseout=\"OUT(this)\" onclick=\"MOVE(this)\">
    {$word}
</div>";
```

No need for id attributes at all on those divs. And your JS functions use the element references directly. The original text suggests this as an incidental modification. It highlights that `this` in an event handler refers to the element on which the event occurred. The example given changes the ON function to the following code and ON is called as `onmouseover="ON(this)"`.

```
function ON(p)
{
    p.style.background = '#ff8080';
}
```

This demonstrates that `p.style.background = '#ff8080'` has the same effect as our earlier `document.getElementById(p).style...` when p was an id. It is just another way that some find cleaner, as it removes the need for global id variables and lookups.

The MOVE function was also adjusted to:

```
function MOVE(p)
{
    document.getElementById(100).value = p.innerHTML;
    document.getElementById(200).submit();
}
```

It is called as `onclick="MOVE(this)"`. (The snippet included the `submit()` call to show the whole cycle.)

Finally, an alternative approach is mentioned: using an HTML table instead of a series of divs for the suggestions. Indeed, one could create a small table with one column and multiple rows for suggestions. Each row `<tr>` could have an `onmouseover` etc., and the word in a `<td>`. It is a matter of taste; using a table might make alignment easier (one could also include multiple columns of info if needed). The original note just acknowledges that possibility but sticks with divs.

In summary, the `this` notation modification is a nice refinement that can simplify the code. It eliminates the need for numeric IDs for each suggestion element, thereby simplifying both the generated HTML and the JS functions (no need to manipulate strings to get elements by id, just use the element directly).

For completeness, we might keep our implementation as-is (with numeric IDs), or adopt the `this` approach. Both are valid. In a textbook scenario, showing both approaches is educational.

To avoid confusion, perhaps we will note the `this` approach as an aside (since we already have the numeric id approach working).

Now we have a fully integrated understanding: HTML/JS for dynamic behavior, PHP/SQL for data retrieval, and how they communicate via AJAX.

This AJAX example demonstrates how all three tiers (client UI, server logic, database) can work together to provide a seamless user experience.

10.8 Modern Database Approaches

Up to now, we have used the traditional MySQL PHP extension (via functions like `mysql_connect`, `mysql_query`, etc.) for database interactions. However, modern PHP development favors improved extensions and practices. The MySQLi (MySQL Improved) extension offers both procedural and object-oriented interfaces, support for prepared statements, and other enhancements. PDO (PHP Data Objects) is a database-neutral, object-oriented interface that supports many types of databases (MySQL, PostgreSQL, SQLite, etc.) with a single API, using prepared statements by default.

Using MySQLi or PDO is recommended because the old `mysql_*` functions are deprecated (they were removed as of PHP 7). Additionally, using prepared statements (with bound parameters) is a more secure way to handle user inputs, as it avoids the need for manual escaping and is less error-prone against SQL injection.

MySQLi vs. PDO: Table 10.1 compares a few core functions between MySQLi and PDO.

Table 10.1: Comparison of MySQLi and PDO functions.

MySQLi Function	PDO Equivalent	Description
`mysqli_connect()`	PDO constructor (`new PDO(...)`)	Connect to the MySQL database server.
`mysqli_query()`	`$pdo->query()` or `$pdo->exec()`	Execute an SQL query (query returns result set for SELECT, exec returns row count for INSERT/UPDATE/DELETE).
`mysqli_error()`	`$pdo->errorInfo()`	Retrieve the last error message (for PDO, `errorInfo()` is a method on the PDO or PDOStatement object).
`mysqli_close()`	Set PDO object to `NULL`	Close the database connection. (Destroying or setting the PDO object to null closes the connection.)

In addition to the above, the two tables below, Table 10.2 and Table 10.3, describe some other commonly used features in PDO and MySQLi. The ordering in each table allows you to compare the methods/functions one against the other.

Table 10.2: PDO methods and their usage.

PDO Method	Description	Syntax / Usage
PDO constructor	Selects a database (via DSN) when connecting (specify DB in DSN).	`new PDO($dsn, $user, $password)` e.g. `$dsn="mysql:host=host;dbname=name";`
Statement::rowCount	Returns the number of affected rows from a previous DML query (INSERT, UPDATE, DELETE).	`$stmt = $pdo->prepare($sql);` `$stmt->execute();` `$count = $stmt->rowCount();`
Statement::fetch	Fetches the next row from a result set. Mode can be specified to get associative or numeric array, etc.	`$stmt = $pdo->query($sql);` `$row = $stmt->fetch(PDO::FETCH_ASSOC);`
Statement::rowCount	(When used after a SELECT) Can return the number of rows fetched/available in the result set (for buffered queries or after `fetchAll`).	`$stmt = $pdo->query($sql);` `$rows = $stmt->rowCount();`

Table 10.3: MySQLi functions and their usage.

MySQLi Function	Description	Syntax / Usage
`mysqli_select_db`	Changes the default database for the current connection.	`mysqli_select_db($connection, $dbname)`
`mysqli_affected_rows`	Returns the number of rows affected by the last DML query (INSERT, UPDATE, DELETE).	`mysqli_affected_rows($connection)`
`mysqli_fetch_array`	Fetches a row from a result set as an array. By default, it returns both associative and numeric indices (can be limited with flags).	`$row = mysqli_fetch_array($result);`
`mysqli_num_rows`	Gets the number of rows in a result set (for SELECT queries).	`mysqli_num_rows($result)`

In this section, we will briefly introduce PDO for database access and show an example using it, and also discuss object-oriented approaches in PHP for organizing database code (for instance, using classes or the OOP style of MySQLi/PDO).

10.8.1 PDO for Database Access

What is PDO? PDO is a PHP extension that defines a consistent interface for accessing databases. Instead of having functions specific to MySQL or PostgreSQL, PDO provides a generic set of classes and methods. You use a "data source name" (DSN) to specify which database and server to connect to. Once connected, you can prepare SQL statements, bind parameters, execute, and fetch results in an object-oriented manner. PDO also supports transactions and error handling via exceptions, making robust database programming easier.

Basic PDO connection example:

```php
<?php
$dsn = "mysql:host=sql1.njit.edu;dbname=yourUCID";
$user = "yourUCID";
$pass = "yourPassword";

try
{
    $pdo = new PDO($dsn, $user, $pass);
    $pdo->setAttribute(PDO::ATTR_ERRMODE, PDO::ERRMODE_EXCEPTION);
    echo "Connected via PDO!<br>";
```

```php
11  }
12  catch (PDOException $e)
13  {
14      echo "Connection failed: " . $e->getMessage();
15      exit();
16  }
```

We set $dsn to "mysql:host=hostname;dbname=databaseName". For MySQL, the DSN starts with mysql:. You then specify host and dbname. (There are other options like charset that can be added, e.g. charset=utf8.) We specify $user and $pass for the database credentials. We then attempt to create a new PDO object with $pdo = new PDO($dsn, $user, $pass). This constructor connects to the database (and selects the database as specified in the DSN). We set an attribute on the PDO object: PDO::ATTR_ERRMODE to PDO::ERRMODE_EXCEPTION. This tells PDO to throw exceptions when a database error occurs, instead of just returning false. This is helpful for debugging and ensures errors are not silently ignored. We catch any PDOException that might be thrown if the connection fails, and handle it by printing an error message and exiting.

If successful, we have a $pdo object that represents the connection.

Executing queries with PDO: PDO offers two main ways to run queries: using the query() method for simple static queries, or using prepared statements with prepare() and execute() for queries that include parameters.

Direct query (no user input or already safe input):

```php
1  $sql = "SELECT name, age FROM Table1";
2  foreach ($pdo->query($sql) as $row)
3  {
4      echo $row['name'] . " - " . $row['age'] . "<br>";
5  }
```

Here, $pdo->query($sql) returns a PDOStatement object which is iterable (we can use foreach on it to get each row). Each $row is an associative array by default (or it could be an object if configured with a different fetch mode). We then output the name and age columns. This is a quick way to fetch results without explicitly preparing a statement when no external input is involved.

Prepared statements (for user input):

Prepared statements are the preferred way when building queries with external data. Instead of concatenating and escaping input values into SQL, you write the SQL with placeholders and then bind values to those placeholders.

Example of using named placeholders:

```php
1  // Imagine we have $name and $age from user input (e.g., from $_POST or $_GET)
2  $sql = "INSERT INTO Table1 (name, age) VALUES (:name, :age)";
```

```php
3  $stmt = $pdo->prepare($sql);
4  $stmt->bindParam(':name', $name, PDO::PARAM_STR);
5  $stmt->bindParam(':age', $age, PDO::PARAM_INT);
6  $stmt->execute();
```

We write the SQL with `:name` and `:age` as placeholders for the values. The method `$pdo->prepare($sql)` prepares the statement (sends it to the database for parsing, without executing it immediately). We bind PHP variables to those placeholders using `bindParam`, also specifying the type (string for name, int for age). Binding ensures the values are safely handled, and PDO will escape them or send them separately to avoid SQL injection. Finally, `$stmt->execute()` runs the statement with the bound values.

We could also combine binding and execution in one step by using `$stmt->execute([':name' => $name, ':age' => $age]);`, which passes an array of placeholder values. Or, alternatively, use question mark `?` placeholders and bind by position instead of name.

Example using positional placeholders (?):

Here, the values are provided in the code (not directly from user input), and question marks `?` are used as placeholders:

```php
1   // Assume $connect is our PDO connection (as created above)
2   try
3   {
4       $connect = new PDO(
5       "mysql:host=$servername;dbname=$dbname",
6       $username,
7       $password
8   );
9       $connect->setAttribute(PDO::ATTR_ERRMODE, PDO::ERRMODE_EXCEPTION);
10  }
11  catch (PDOException $e)
12  {
13      echo "Connection failed: " . $e->getMessage();
14      exit();
15  }
16  // Set values to insert
17  $Owner   = "Rose";
18  $PetType = "rabbit";
19  $PetName = "Remi";
20  // Create INSERT query with positional placeholders
21  $insertpet = "INSERT INTO Pets (Owner, PetType, PetName) VALUES (?, ?, ?)";
22  $query = $connect->prepare($insertpet);
23  $query->bindValue(1, $Owner);
24  $query->bindValue(2, $PetType);
```

```
25 $query->bindValue(3, $PetName);
26 $query->execute();
```

In the code above, we use `?` in the SQL and call `$query->bindValue(1, $Owner)`, etc., to bind values by their position (1-based index in this case). This inserts a new row into the Pets table with the given Owner, PetType, and PetName, avoiding any need to escape the values manually.

To visually illustrate the interaction process when using PDO prepared statements, Figure 10.6 demonstrates the sequence of operations involved. This sequence includes preparing the SQL statement with placeholders, securely binding the user-provided parameters to these placeholders, and finally executing the statement. Essentially, this figure shows the structured communication between the PHP PDO script and the MySQL database when using prepared statements. It highlights the critical separation of query preparation, parameter binding, and execution, offering clear security advantages over traditional query approaches (for example in mitigating SQL injection risks).

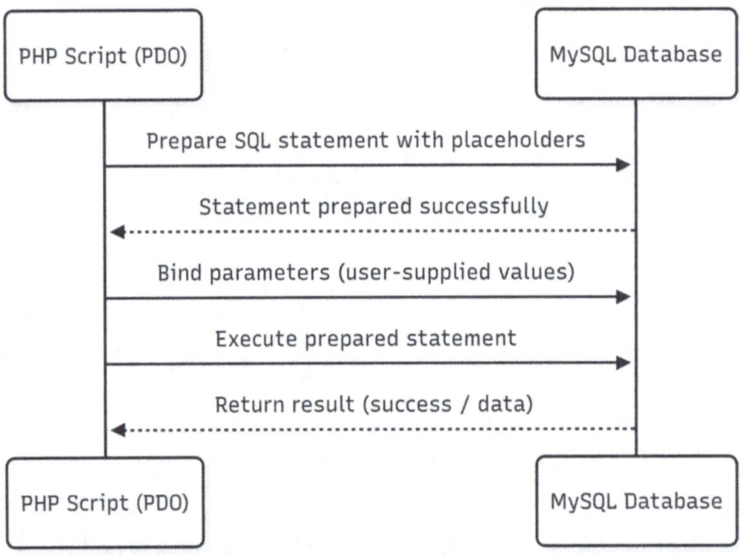

Figure 10.6: Prepared statement interaction flow.

For retrieving data with a condition using PDO, you would similarly use a placeholder in the WHERE clause:

```
1 $sql = "SELECT * FROM Table1 WHERE name = :name";
2 $stmt = $pdo->prepare($sql);
3 $stmt->execute([':name' => $nameInput]);
4 $results = $stmt->fetchAll(PDO::FETCH_ASSOC);
```

Here, `fetchAll(PDO::FETCH_ASSOC)` gets all result rows as an array of associative arrays. You could also do a loop with `while ($row = $stmt->fetch(PDO::FETCH_ASSOC)) { ... }` to iterate through the results one row at a time.

In a real application, your data often comes from an HTML form. You can still use prepared statements to handle such input. For example, imagine an HTML form that collects a pet owner's name, pet type, and pet name, and we want to insert that into the Pets table using PDO:

Example — inserting via an HTML form with PDO (prepared statement):

```php
1  <!DOCTYPE html>
2  <html lang="en">
3  <head>
4      <meta charset="UTF-8">
5      <title>Pet Insert Via a Form</title>
6  </head>
7  <body>
8  <?php
9  if ($_SERVER['REQUEST_METHOD'] == 'POST') {
10     // Variables to connect to MySQL server (replace with actual credentials)
11     $servername = "MySQL Servername";
12     $dbname     = "MySQL Database name";
13     $username   = "MySQL Username";
14     $password   = "MySQL Password";
15
16     // Try-catch block for connection
17     try {
18         // Connect to server and database
19         $connect = new PDO("mysql:host=$servername;dbname=$dbname", $username, $password);
20         $connect->setAttribute(PDO::ATTR_ERRMODE, PDO::ERRMODE_EXCEPTION);
21         echo "Connected successfully";
22     } catch (PDOException $e) {
23         echo "Connection failed: " . $e->getMessage();
24         exit();
25     }
26
27     // Prepare an INSERT query
28     $petinsert = "INSERT INTO Pets (Owner, PetType, PetName)
29                   VALUES (:Owner, :PetType, :PetName)";
30     $query = $connect->prepare($petinsert);
31     $query->bindValue(":Owner",   $_POST["Owner"]);
32     $query->bindValue(":PetType", $_POST["PetType"]);
33     $query->bindValue(":PetName", $_POST["PetName"]);
34     $query->execute();
```

```
35 }
36 ?>
37
38 <h1>Pet Table Insert</h1>
39 <form action="PDOInsert.php" method="POST">
40     <label for="Owner">Enter a Pet Owner's Name:</label>
41     <input type="text" id="Owner" name="Owner"><br>
42
43     <label for="PetType">Enter the Pet Type:</label>
44     <input type="text" id="PetType" name="PetType"><br>
45
46     <label for="PetName">Enter a Pet's Name:</label>
47     <input type="text" id="PetName" name="PetName"><br>
48
49     <input type="submit" value="Submit">
50 </form>
51 </body>
52 </html>
```

PDO Insert Form Interface

Pet Table Insert

Enter a Pet Owner's Name: [   ]
Enter the Pet Type: [   ]
Enter a Pet's Name: [   ]
[Submit]

In the above PDOInsert.php script, when the form is submitted via POST based on the input of user interface, we connect to the database, prepare an INSERT statement with named parameters :Owner, :PetType, :PetName, and then bind each of those to the data received from the form ($_POST array). Finally, we execute the statement to insert the new record. If the connection succeeds, the script echoes "Connected successfully". We do not, however, have to call any escape function on the form inputs. By using a prepared statement with bound values, PDO takes care of escaping special characters to prevent SQL injection. If the pet information has been inserted, the following output appears.

Sample Output:

```
Connected successfully Gil guinea pigGinger INSERT INTO Pets (Owner, PetType, PetName)
VALUES (:Owner, :PetType, :PetName)
```

For comparison, let us see how the same insertion could be done using MySQLi without prepared statements, using manual escaping of inputs.

Example of using `mysqli_real_escape_string()` (manual escaping):
The `mysqli_real_escape_string($connection, $string)` function can be used to escape special characters in a string before including it in an SQL query. Its syntax is:

```
mysqli_real_escape_string(connection, escapestring)
```

The parameter connection is the MySQL connection resource (or link) and escapestring is the string to be escaped.

This function will add backslashes before characters like NULL, newline, carriage return, the backslash itself, single-quote, double-quote, and Control-Z, so that they are treated as literal characters in SQL and not as part of SQL syntax.

Using manual escaping, our form-handling insert script might look like:

```php
<!DOCTYPE html>
<html lang="en">
<head>
    <meta charset="UTF-8">
    <title>Pet Insert Using MySQLi</title>
</head>
<body>
<?php
if ($_SERVER['REQUEST_METHOD'] == 'POST') {
    // Replace these with actual credentials
    $servername = "MySQL Servername";
    $dbname     = "MySQL Database name";
    $username   = "MySQL Username";
    $password   = "MySQL Password";

    // Connect using MySQLi
    $connect = mysqli_connect($servername, $username, $password, $dbname);

    if (mysqli_connect_errno()) {
        die("Failed to connect to MySQL: " . mysqli_connect_error());
    }

    echo "Connected successfully<br>";

    // Escape user input
    $Owner   = mysqli_real_escape_string($connect, $_POST["Owner"]);
```

```php
27    $PetType = mysqli_real_escape_string($connect, $_POST["PetType"]);
28    $PetName = mysqli_real_escape_string($connect, $_POST["PetName"]);
29
30    // Construct the INSERT query
31    $petinsertquery = "INSERT INTO Pets(Owner, PetType, PetName)
32                       VALUES ('$Owner', '$PetType', '$PetName')";
33
34    $petinsert = mysqli_query($connect, $petinsertquery);
35
36    if ($petinsert)
37    {
38       echo "One row inserted. " . mysqli_affected_rows($connect);
39    }
40    else
41    {
42       echo "Insert failed: " . mysqli_error($connect);
43    }
44    mysqli_close($connect);
45  }
46  ?>
47
48  <h1>Pet Table Insert</h1>
49  <form action="MySQLiInsert.php" method="POST">
50    <label for="Owner">Enter a Pet Owner's Name:</label>
51    <input type="text" id="Owner" name="Owner"><br>
52    <label for="PetType">Enter the Pet Type:</label>
53    <input type="text" id="PetType" name="PetType"><br>
54    <label for="PetName">Enter a Pet's Name:</label>
55    <input type="text" id="PetName" name="PetName"><br>
56    <input type="submit" value="Submit">
57  </form>
58  </body>
59  </html>
```

In this MySQLi example, we connect using `mysqli_connect`, then call `mysqli_real_escape_string` on each piece of user input to sanitize it. We construct an SQL string with the escaped values and execute it with `mysqli_query`. If the insert succeeds, we output a message indicating a row was inserted (and use `mysqli_affected_rows` to confirm how many rows were inserted, which should be 1). This procedural code achieves the same result (inserting a new row from form input) but requires manual handling of special characters. There is a risk of forgetting to escape a value or other mistakes when constructing the query. With PDO prepared statements (shown previously), these risks are minimized because the values are never directly concatenated into the SQL string.

Benefits of PDO: PDO is database agnostic. if tomorrow you switch from MySQL to PostgreSQL (or another database), you just change the DSN (and possibly a few SQL dialect differences), but much of the code can remain the same. Prepared statements make it easy to avoid SQL injection and handle data safely (no need for manual escaping like `mysql_real_escape_string` when using bound parameters). The OOP interface encourages a cleaner code structure, interacting with objects and exceptions, which can lead to more robust and organized error handling. As we set with `ERRMODE_EXCEPTION`, PDO can throw exceptions on errors (the option for exceptions), allowing you to catch and handle them, instead of having to check return values everywhere. PDO also offers flexibility in fetching: you can fetch results as associative arrays, numeric arrays, objects of a class, etc., by specifying the fetch mode. Finally, PDO makes it straightforward to use database transactions (e.g., `$pdo->beginTransaction()`, `$pdo->commit()`, `$pdo->rollBack()`).

Converting an earlier script to PDO (simplified):

Original (using old mysql_* functions):

```php
mysql_connect($host, $user, $pass);
mysql_select_db($db);
$res = mysql_query("SELECT * FROM Table1");
while ($row = mysql_fetch_assoc($res))
{
    echo $row['col1'];
}
```

PDO version:

```php
$pdo = new PDO("mysql:host=$host;dbname=$db", $user, $pass);
$stmt = $pdo->query("SELECT * FROM Table1");
while ($row = $stmt->fetch(PDO::FETCH_ASSOC))
{
    echo $row['col1'];
}
```

As you see, the overall logic is not too different. The PDO code is slightly more verbose in setting up (and we could similarly do this with MySQLi), but PDO offers more flexibility and features as needed.

In practice, once you learn PDO, you will rarely miss the old `mysql_*` functions. It might be slightly more typing at first (prepare, bind, execute) but the reliability and security gains are worth it.

10.8.2   PDO and MySQLi: Fetching Data

Both PDO and MySQLi provide multiple ways to fetch data from query result sets. This includes fetching rows as numeric arrays, associative arrays, or objects. Below we illustrate various fetch functions/modes in PDO and MySQLi and how they differ. For these examples, assume we have a Pets table and have executed a query like

`SELECT * FROM Pets`. We will print out some combination of the columns (e.g., Owner, PetType, PetName) from each row to demonstrate the result of each fetch mode.

PDO `fetch() (default mode)`: By default, `PDOStatement::fetch()` without a mode parameter returns the next row using the default fetch mode (which is `PDO::FETCH_BOTH`, meaning you can access columns by both name and number). For example:

```php
try
{
    $connect = new PDO("mysql:host=$servername;dbname=$dbname", $username, $password);
    $connect->setAttribute(PDO::ATTR_ERRMODE, PDO::ERRMODE_EXCEPTION);
}
catch (PDOException $e)
{
    echo "Connection failed: " . $e->getMessage();
    exit();
}
try
{
    $petquery = "SELECT * FROM Pets";
    $petresults = $connect->query($petquery);
    if ($petresults)
      {
        // Loop through result set using default fetch() (FETCH_BOTH)
        while ($row = $petresults->fetch())
          {
            echo "<h4>Owner    Pet Type</h4>";
            // Using numeric indices (default mode also allows assoc indices)
            echo $row[0] . "     " . $row[1];
            echo "<br>";
          }
      }
}
catch (PDOException $error)
{
    echo "Query failed: " . $error->getMessage();
}
$connect = null;
```

In the above code, `$petresults->fetch()` retrieves each row. By default, you can access the columns either by numeric index or column name. Here we used numeric indices `[0]` and `[1]` to print the first two columns (Owner and Pet Type). (We also output a small header in `<h4>` tags for clarity in the output.)

PDO `fetch(PDO::FETCH_NUM)`: This fetch mode returns the row as an enumerated array (numeric indices only, no associative keys).

```php
try
{
    $connect = new PDO ("mysql:host=$servername;dbname=$dbname", $username, $password);
    $connect->setAttribute(PDO::ATTR_ERRMODE, PDO::ERRMODE_EXCEPTION);
}
catch (PDOException $e)
{
    exit("Connection failed: " . $e->getMessage());
}
try
{
    $petquery = "SELECT * FROM Pets";
    $petresults = $connect->query($petquery);
    if ($petresults)
    {
        // Loop through result set using fetch(PDO::FETCH_NUM)
        while ($row = $petresults->fetch(PDO::FETCH_NUM))
        {
            echo "<h4>Owner    Pet Name</h4>";
            // Print the first and third columns using numeric indices
            echo $row[0] . "     " . $row[2];
            echo "<br>";
        }
    }
}
catch (PDOException $error)
{
    echo "Query failed: " . $error->getMessage();
}
$connect = null;
```

Here we explicitly pass `PDO::FETCH_NUM` to fetch. The code prints the Owner (index 0) and Pet Name (index 2) from each row. No associative keys are available in this mode.

PDO `fetch(PDO::FETCH_ASSOC)`: This mode returns each row as an associative array (column names as keys, no numeric indices).

```php
try
{
```

```php
 3      $connect = new PDO
 4          ("mysql:host=$servername;dbname=$dbname", $username, $password);
 5      $connect->setAttribute(PDO::ATTR_ERRMODE, PDO::ERRMODE_EXCEPTION);
 6  }
 7  catch (PDOException $e)
 8  {
 9      exit("Connection failed: " . $e->getMessage());
10  }
11  try
12  {
13      $petquery = "SELECT * FROM Pets";
14      $petresults = $connect->query($petquery);
15      if ($petresults)
16        {
17          // Loop through result set using fetch(PDO::FETCH_ASSOC)
18          while ($row = $petresults->fetch(PDO::FETCH_ASSOC)) {
19              echo "<h4>Owner    Pet Name</h4>";
20              // Access by column names
21              echo $row['Owner'] .
22                  "     " .
23                  $row['PetName'];
24              echo "<br>";
25          }
26        }
27  }
28  catch (PDOException $error)
29  {
30      echo "Query failed: " . $error->getMessage();
31  }
32  $connect = null;
```

Now each `$row` is an associative array, so we use `$row["Owner"]` and `$row["PetName"]` to access the data. This prints the Owner and Pet Name for each record.

PDO `fetch(PDO::FETCH_BOTH)`: This mode returns an array indexed by both column name and number (this is actually the default mode, as noted earlier). For completeness:

```php
 1  try
 2  {
 3      $connect = new PDO ("mysql:host=$servername;dbname=$dbname", $username, $password);
 4      $connect->setAttribute(PDO::ATTR_ERRMODE, PDO::ERRMODE_EXCEPTION);
 5  }
```

```php
6  catch (PDOException $e)
7  {
8      exit("Connection failed: " . $e->getMessage());
9  }
10 try
11 {
12     $petquery = "SELECT * FROM Pets";
13     $petresults = $connect->query($petquery);
14     if ($petresults)
15       {
16         // Loop through result set using fetch(PDO::FETCH_BOTH)
17         while ($row = $petresults->fetch(PDO::FETCH_BOTH))
18           {
19             echo "<h4>Owner    Pet Type</h4>";
20             // We can use both associative and numeric indices for the same row
21             echo $row['Owner'] . "     " . $row[1];
22             echo "<br>";
23           }
24       }
25 }
26 catch (PDOException $error)
27 {
28     echo "Query failed: " . $error->getMessage();
29 }
30 $connect = null;
```

In this example, we fetch with `PDO::FETCH_BOTH`. We demonstrate that `$row["Owner"]` and `$row[1]` can both be used (in this case, `$row[1]` corresponds to the PetType column, assuming the columns are ordered as Owner, PetType, PetName). This mode is handy for flexibility, but typically you will choose either numeric or assoc for clarity. By default, PDO uses `FETCH_BOTH` if not set otherwise.

Now let us look at MySQLi's fetch functions. We will perform similar tasks using MySQLi procedural functions:

`mysqli_fetch_array() (default)`: By default, `mysqli_fetch_array` returns the next row of a result set as an array with both associative and numeric indices (equivalent to `MYSQLI_BOTH` mode).

```php
1  $connect = mysqli_connect($servername, $username, $password, $dbname);
2  if (mysqli_connect_errno())
3  {
4      exit("Failed to connect to MySQL: " . mysqli_connect_error());
5  }
6  $query = "SELECT * FROM Pets";
```

```php
7  $petresults = mysqli_query($connect, $query);
8  if ($petresults)
9  {
10     // Loop through result set using mysqli_fetch_array (default both)
11     while ($row = mysqli_fetch_array($petresults))
12       {
13         echo "<h4>Owner    Pet Name</h4>";
14         // Using both associative and numeric indices
15         echo $row['Owner'] . "     " . $row[1];
16         echo "<br>";
17       }
18  }
19  else
20  {
21     echo "Query Failed: " . mysqli_error($connect);
22  }
23  mysqli_close($connect);
```

Here we used `mysqli_fetch_array` without specifying a second argument, so it returns both kinds of indexes. In the echo, `$row["Owner"]` and `$row[1]` refer to the same data (Owner column). We print Owner and Pet Name for each row.

`mysqli_fetch_array(MYSQLI_NUM)`: This returns the row as a numeric array (0-indexed, no associative keys).

```php
1  $connect = mysqli_connect($servername, $username, $password, $dbname);
2  if (mysqli_connect_errno())
3  {
4     exit("Failed to connect to MySQL: " . mysqli_connect_error());
5  }
6  $query = "SELECT * FROM Pets";
7  $petresults = mysqli_query($connect, $query);
8  if ($petresults)
9  {
10     // Loop through result set using mysqli_fetch_array(MYSQLI_NUM)
11     while ($row = mysqli_fetch_array($petresults, MYSQLI_NUM))
12       {
13         echo "<h4>Owner    Pet Name</h4>";
14         // Print the first and third columns by index
15         echo $row[0] . "     " . $row[2];
16         echo "<br>";
17       }
```

```php
18  }
19  else
20  {
21      echo "Query Failed: " . mysqli_error($connect);
22  }
23  mysqli_close($connect);
```

This prints Owner (index 0) and Pet Name (index 2) for each row, using purely numeric indexing.
`mysqli_fetch_array(MYSQLI_ASSOC)`: Returns the row as an associative array (column names as keys).

```php
1  $connect = mysqli_connect($servername, $username, $password, $dbname);
2  if (mysqli_connect_errno())
3  {
4      exit("Failed to connect to MySQL: " . mysqli_connect_error());
5  }
6  $query = "SELECT * FROM Pets";
7  $petresults = mysqli_query($connect, $query);
8  if ($petresults)
9  {
10     // Loop through result set using mysqli_fetch_array(MYSQLI_ASSOC)
11     while ($row = mysqli_fetch_array($petresults, MYSQLI_ASSOC))
12     {
13         echo "<h4>Owner    Pet Name</h4>";
14         // Access by column names
15         echo $row['Owner'] . "     " . $row['PetName'];
16         echo "<br>";
17     }
18  }
19  else
20  {
21      echo "Query Failed: " . mysqli_error($connect);
22  }
23  mysqli_close($connect);
```

This is similar to using `mysqli_fetch_assoc`. In fact, MySQLi provides a dedicated function for that:
`mysqli_fetch_assoc()`: This function fetches one row as an associative array (equivalent to `mysqli _fetch_array` with `MYSQLI_ASSOC`). It is essentially the same output as above, but we will show it for completeness:

```php
$connect = mysqli_connect($servername, $username, $password, $dbname);
if (mysqli_connect_errno())
{
    exit("Failed to connect to MySQL: " . mysqli_connect_error());
}
$query = "SELECT * FROM Pets";
$petresults = mysqli_query($connect, $query);
if ($petresults)
{
    // Loop through result set using mysqli_fetch_assoc
    while ($row = mysqli_fetch_assoc($petresults))
      {
         echo "<h4>Owner    Pet Name</h4>";
         echo $row['Owner'] . "     " . $row['PetName'];
         echo "<br>";
      }
}
else
{
    echo "Query Failed: " . mysqli_error($connect);
}
mysqli_close($connect);
```

As expected, this prints the Owner and Pet Name for each row, using only associative array access.

`mysqli_fetch_row()`: This function fetches one row as a numeric array (similar to `MYSQLI_NUM`, but returns only numeric indices and is slightly faster when you only need numeric index). For example::

```php
$connect = mysqli_connect($servername, $username, $password, $dbname);
if (mysqli_connect_errno())
{
    exit("Failed to connect to MySQL: " . mysqli_connect_error());
}
$query = "SELECT * FROM Pets";
$petresults = mysqli_query($connect, $query);
if ($petresults)
{
    // Loop through result set using mysqli_fetch_row
    while ($row = mysqli_fetch_row($petresults))
      {
         echo "<h4>Pet Type    Owner</h4>";
         // Print the second and first columns by index (just to show usage)
```

```
15        echo $row[1] . "     " . $row[0];
16        echo "<br>";
17      }
18  }
19  else
20  {
21    echo "Query Failed: " . mysqli_error($connect);
22  }
23  mysqli_close($connect);
```

Here $row is a pure numeric array. We chose to print Pet Type (index 1) followed by Owner (index 0) for each record.

In summary, MySQLi provides separate functions or flags for each fetch mode (`mysqli_fetch_assoc`, `mysqli_fetch_row`, or `mysqli_fetch_array` with flags), whereas PDO uses a single `fetch()` method with different mode constants. Both approaches allow you to retrieve data in the way you find most convenient.

Finally, if you want to simply count how many rows were returned by a SELECT query in MySQLi, you can use `mysqli_num_rows()`:

```
1   $connect = mysqli_connect($servername, $username, $password, $dbname);
2   $query = "SELECT * FROM Pets";
3   $petresults = mysqli_query($connect, $query);
4   if ($petresults)
5   {
6       $numRows = mysqli_num_rows($petresults);
7       echo "Number of rows in the table: " . $numRows;
8   }
9   else
10  {
11      echo "Query Failed: " . mysqli_error($connect);
12  }
13  mysqli_close($connect);
```

This will output the number of rows in the result set. (PDO does not have a direct equivalent function for unbuffered SELECT results; one common approach in PDO is to do `$stmt->rowCount()` after fetching all the results or to use `COUNT(*)` in SQL if you only need the count.)

10.8.3   Complete Examples: MySQLi and PDO in Action

To illustrate modern approaches with a concrete scenario, let us consider a simple Pets table in a MySQL database (with columns like Owner, PetType, PetName). We will demonstrate two PHP scripts, one using PDO and another using MySQLi, that perform a series of operations on this table: connecting to the database, selecting all records, inserting a new record, updating a record, deleting a record, and then closing the connection. The scripts print messages indicating whether each operation succeeded. In an alternate version, after each operation we also query and display the current contents of the table in an HTML format to verify the changes.

Complete CRUD (Create, Read, Update, Delete) Operations with PDO:

The following PHP script uses PDO to connect to MySQL and execute a sequence of SQL commands (SELECT, INSERT, UPDATE, DELETE), each wrapped in a try/catch for error handling. It echoes a success message for each query if it executes, or an error message if a query fails:

```php
<?php
// Variables to connect to MySQL server (replace with your actual credentials)
$servername = "MySQL Servername";
$dbname = "MySQL Database name";
$username = "MySQL Username";
$password = "MySQL Password";

try
{
    // Connect to MySQL server and select the database using PDO
    $connect = new PDO ("mysql:host=$servername;dbname=$dbname", $username, $password);
    $connect->setAttribute(PDO::ATTR_ERRMODE, PDO::ERRMODE_EXCEPTION);
    echo "Connected successfully to the MySQL server";
    echo "<br><br>";
}
catch(PDOException $error)
{
    echo "Connection failed: " . $error->getMessage();
    exit();
}

// SELECT all records from Pets
try
{
    $petquery = "SELECT * FROM Pets";
    $petresults = $connect->query($petquery);
    if ($petresults)
    {
        echo "SELECT QUERY EXECUTED SUCCESSFULLY";
    }
}
catch(PDOException $error)
{
    echo "SELECT failed: " . $error->getMessage();
```

```php
35  }
36
37  // INSERT a new record into Pets
38  try
39  {
40      $petinsert = $connect->exec("INSERT INTO Pets(Owner, PetType, PetName)
41          VALUES ('Rose','rabbit','Rem')");
42      if ($petinsert)
43      {
44          echo "<br><br>INSERT QUERY EXECUTED SUCCESSFULLY";
45      }
46  }
47  catch(PDOException $error)
48  {
49      echo "<br><br>INSERT failed: " . $error->getMessage();
50  }
51
52  // UPDATE a record in Pets
53  try
54  {
55      $petupdate =
56          $connect->exec("UPDATE Pets SET PetName='Remy' WHERE Owner='Rose'");
57      if ($petupdate)
58      {
59          echo "<br><br>UPDATE QUERY EXECUTED SUCCESSFULLY";
60      }
61  }
62  catch(PDOException $error)
63  {
64      echo "<br><br>UPDATE failed: " . $error->getMessage();
65  }
66
67  // DELETE the record from Pets
68  try
69  {
70      $petdelete = $connect->exec("DELETE FROM Pets WHERE Owner = 'Rose'");
71      if ($petdelete)
72      {
73          echo "<br><br>DELETE QUERY EXECUTED SUCCESSFULLY";
74      }
75  }
76  catch(PDOException $error)
77  {
```

```php
78      echo "<br><br>DELETE failed: " . $error->getMessage();
79  }
80
81  // Close the DB connection
82  $connect = null;
83  ?>
```

This PDO script performs the operations in sequence. We used `PDO::query()` for SELECT (since it returns a result set) and `PDO::exec()` for INSERT/UPDATE/DELETE (which return the number of affected rows). Each operation is wrapped in a try/catch to handle any exceptions. On success, a message is printed; on failure, the catch block prints the error. We then close the connection by setting `$connect = null`.

PDO Script with Table Output After Each Operation:

In the above script, we only printed confirmation messages. Alternatively, we can retrieve and display the table contents after each modification to verify the changes. The script below uses the PDO `exec` method for the INSERT/UPDATE/DELETE (since those return an integer count of affected rows) and performs a SELECT after each operation to output the current state of the Pets table in an HTML table format:

```php
1   <?php
2   // (Connection part is the same as above)
3   $servername = "MySQL Servername";
4   $dbname = "MySQL Database name";
5   $username = "MySQL Username";
6   $password = "MySQL Password";
7   try {
8       $connect = new PDO("mysql:host=$servername;dbname=$dbname", $username, $password);
9       $connect->setAttribute(PDO::ATTR_ERRMODE, PDO::ERRMODE_EXCEPTION);
10      echo "Connected successfully to the MySQL server";
11      echo "<br><br>";
12  } catch(PDOException $error) {
13      echo "Connection failed: " . $error->getMessage();
14      exit();
15  }
16
17  // Perform an initial SELECT and display the table
18  try {
19      displayPetsTable($connect, "Existing Table Using Select Statement");
20  } catch(PDOException $error) {
21      echo "SELECT failed: " . $error->getMessage();
22  }
23
24  // INSERT a record and then SELECT to display updated table
```

```php
25 try {
26     $petinsert = $connect->exec(
27         "INSERT INTO Pets(Owner, PetType, PetName)
28          VALUES ('Rose','rabbit','Rem')"
29     );
30     if ($petinsert) {
31         // Query and display table after insertion
32         displayPetsTable($connect, "Table After Insertion of Record");
33     }
34 } catch(PDOException $error) {
35     echo "<br>INSERT failed: " . $error->getMessage();
36 }
37
38 // UPDATE a record and display table after update
39 try {
40     $petupdate = $connect->exec(
41         "UPDATE Pets
42          SET PetName = 'Remy'
43          WHERE Owner = 'Rose'"
44     );
45     if ($petupdate) {
46         displayPetsTable($connect, "Table After Update of Record");
47     }
48 } catch(PDOException $error) {
49     echo "<br>UPDATE failed: " . $error->getMessage();
50 }
51
52 // DELETE the record and display table after deletion
53 try {
54     $petdelete = $connect->exec(
55         "DELETE FROM Pets
56          WHERE Owner = 'Rose'"
57     );
58     if ($petdelete) {
59         displayPetsTable($connect, "Table After Deletion of Record");
60     }
61 } catch(PDOException $error) {
62     echo "<br>DELETE failed: " . $error->getMessage();
63 }
64
65 // Close the DB connection
66 $connect = null;
67
```

```php
68  // Display pets table with a given title
69  function displayPetsTable($connection, $title) {
70      $petresults = $connection->query("SELECT * FROM Pets");
71      echo "<br>";
72      echo "<h3 align='center'>$title</h3>";
73      echo "<table align='center' border='2'
74              style='width: 600px; line-height: 30px;'>";
75      echo "<tr>
76              <th>Owner</th>
77              <th>Pet Type</th>
78              <th>Pet Name</th>
79          </tr>";
80      while ($row = $petresults->fetch(PDO::FETCH_ASSOC)) {
81          echo "<tr>";
82          echo "<td>" . htmlspecialchars($row['Owner']) . "</td>";
83          echo "<td>" . htmlspecialchars($row['PetType']) . "</td>";
84          echo "<td>" . htmlspecialchars($row['PetName']) . "</td>";
85          echo "</tr>";
86      }
87      echo "</table>";
88  }
89  ?>
```

In this version, each operation is followed by a fresh SELECT * query to print the contents of the table. The output is formatted as an HTML table (centered, with borders for clarity). This allows us to visually verify that the insert, update, and delete took effect: the inserted pet "Rose" appears in the table, then the name changes to "Remy", then the entry is gone after deletion. We used PDO::exec for the data-modifying statements, which returns the number of affected rows (we check this to confirm success). The PDO::query method returns a result set for the SELECT queries, which we then fetch and display.

Sample Output - Part 1-1

Existing Table Using Select Statement

Owner	Pet Type	Pet Name
Doug	dog	Dante
Cathy	cat	Calypso
Finn	fish	Flipper
Bianca	bird	Belle
Liam	lizard	Lizzie
Harper	hamster	Honey
Gil	guinea pig	Ginger
Gil	guinea pig	Ginger
Rose	rabbbit	Remy

Sample Output - Part 1-2

Table After Insertion of Record

Owner	Pet Type	Pet Name
Doug	dog	Dante
Cathy	cat	Calypso
Finn	fish	Flipper
Bianca	bird	Belle
Liam	lizard	Lizzie
Harper	hamster	Honey
Gil	guinea pig	Ginger
Gil	guinea pig	Ginger
Rose	rabbbit	Remy
Rose	rabbbit	Rem

Sample Output - Part 2-1

Table After Update of Record		
Owner	**Pet Type**	**Pet Name**
Doug	dog	Dante
Cathy	cat	Calypso
Finn	fish	Flipper
Bianca	bird	Belle
Liam	lizard	Lizzie
Harper	hamster	Honey
Gil	guinea pig	Ginger
Gil	guinea pig	Ginger
Rose	rabbbit	Remy
Rose	rabbbit	Remy

Sample Output - Part 2-2

Existing Table After Deletion of Record		
Owner	**Pet Type**	**Pet Name**
Doug	dog	Dante
Cathy	cat	Calypso
Finn	fish	Flipper
Bianca	bird	Belle
Liam	lizard	Lizzie
Harper	hamster	Honey
Gil	guinea pig	Ginger
Gil	guinea pig	Ginger

Complete CRUD Operations with MySQLi:

Now let us achieve the same tasks using MySQLi in procedural style. The following script connects using `mysqli_connect`, then performs the SELECT, INSERT, UPDATE, DELETE in sequence using `mysqli_query`, checking return values (and using `mysqli_error` for any failures). It prints similar success or failure messages for each step:

```php
<?php
// Variables for MySQL server connection
$servername = "MySQL Servername";
$dbname = "MySQL Database name";
$username = "MySQL Username";
$password = "MySQL Password";

// Connect to MySQL server and database using MySQLi
$connect = mysqli_connect($servername, $username, $password, $dbname);
if (!$connect)
{
    die("Failed to connect to MySQL and Database: " . mysqli_connect_error());
}
echo "Connected successfully to the MySQL server";

// SELECT all records from Pets
$petquery = "SELECT * FROM Pets";
$petresults = mysqli_query($connect, $petquery);
if ($petresults)
{
    echo "<br><br>SELECT QUERY EXECUTED SUCCESSFULLY";
}
else
{
    echo "<br><br>SELECT Query Failed: " . mysqli_error($connect);
}

// INSERT a new record into Pets
$petinsertquery = "INSERT INTO Pets(Owner, PetType, PetName) VALUES ('Rose','rabbit','Rem')";
$petinsert = mysqli_query($connect, $petinsertquery);
if ($petinsert)
{
    echo "<br><br>INSERT QUERY EXECUTED SUCCESSFULLY";
}
else
{
    echo "<br><br>INSERT Query Failed: " . mysqli_error($connect);
}

// UPDATE the pet's name in Pets
$petupdatequery = "UPDATE Pets SET PetName = 'Remy' WHERE Owner = 'Rose'";
$petupdate = mysqli_query($connect, $petupdatequery);
```

```php
43  if ($petupdate)
44  {
45      echo "<br><br>UPDATE QUERY EXECUTED SUCCESSFULLY";
46  }
47  else
48  {
49      echo "<br><br>UPDATE Query Failed: " . mysqli_error($connect);
50  }
51
52  // DELETE the record from Pets
53  $petdeletequery = "DELETE FROM Pets WHERE Owner = 'Rose'";
54  $petdelete = mysqli_query($connect, $petdeletequery);
55  if ($petdelete)
56  {
57      echo "<br><br>DELETE QUERY EXECUTED SUCCESSFULLY";
58  }
59  else
60  {
61      echo "<br><br>DELETE Query Failed: " . mysqli_error($connect);
62  }
63
64  // Close the database connection
65  mysqli_close($connect);
66  ?>
```

This MySQLi script is similar in structure to the PDO one. The main differences are the connection method and query functions. It uses `mysqli_connect` (with the database name provided as a parameter) and `mysqli_query` for all operations. On success, `mysqli_query` returns a result set object for SELECT or boolean `true` for successful INSERT/UPDATE/DELETE, which we check in the `if` conditions. We call `mysqli_close` at the end to close the connection.

MySQLi Script with Table Output After Each Operation:

Finally, here is the MySQLi version that, like the PDO alternate, prints the table after each operation to show the evolving data. We use `mysqli_fetch_array` to fetch results for displaying the table:

```php
1  <?php
2  $servername = "MySQL Servername";
3  $dbname = "MySQL Database name";
4  $username = "MySQL Username";
5  $password = "MySQL Password";
6  $connect = mysqli_connect($servername, $username, $password, $dbname);
7  if (!$connect) {
```

```php
 8      die("Failed to connect to MySQL and Database: " . mysqli_connect_error());
 9 }
10 echo "Connected successfully to the MySQL server<br><br>";
11 // Initial SELECT and display table
12 $petquery = "SELECT * FROM Pets";
13 $petresults = mysqli_query($connect, $petquery);
14 if ($petresults) {
15     displayPetsTable($connect, "Existing Table Using Select Statement");
16 } else {
17     echo "SELECT Query Failed: " . mysqli_error($connect);
18 }
19 // INSERT and display updated table
20 $petinsertquery = "INSERT INTO Pets(Owner, PetType, PetName)
21                    VALUES ('Rose','rabbit','Rem')";
22 $petinsert = mysqli_query($connect, $petinsertquery);
23 if ($petinsert) {
24     displayPetsTable($connect, "Table After Insertion of Record");
25 } else {
26     echo "<br>INSERT Query Failed: " . mysqli_error($connect);
27 }
28 // UPDATE and display updated table
29 $petupdatequery = "UPDATE Pets
30                    SET PetName = 'Remy'
31                    WHERE Owner = 'Rose'";
32 $petupdate = mysqli_query($connect, $petupdatequery);
33 if ($petupdate) {
34     displayPetsTable($connect, "Table After Update of Record");
35 } else {
36     echo "<br>UPDATE Query Failed: " . mysqli_error($connect);
37 }
38 // DELETE and display updated table
39 $petdeletequery = "DELETE FROM Pets
40                    WHERE Owner = 'Rose'";
41 $petdelete = mysqli_query($connect, $petdeletequery);
42 if ($petdelete) {
43     displayPetsTable($connect, "Table After Deletion of Record");
44 } else {
45     echo "<br>DELETE Query Failed: " . mysqli_error($connect);
46 }
47 // Close the database connection
48 mysqli_close($connect);
49
50 //Display pets table with a given title
```

```php
51  function displayPetsTable($connection, $title) {
52      $petquery = "SELECT * FROM Pets";
53      $petresults = mysqli_query($connection, $petquery);
54      echo "<br>";
55      echo "<h3 align='center'>$title</h3>";
56      echo "<table align='center' border='2'
57          style='width: 600px; line-height: 30px;'>";
58      echo "<tr>
59          <th>Owner</th>
60          <th>Pet Type</th>
61          <th>Pet Name</th>
62          </tr>";
63      while ($row = mysqli_fetch_array($petresults)) {
64          echo "<tr>";
65          echo "<td>" . htmlspecialchars($row['Owner']) . "</td>";
66          echo "<td>" . htmlspecialchars($row['PetType']) . "</td>";
67          echo "<td>" . htmlspecialchars($row['PetName']) . "</td>";
68          echo "</tr>";
69      }
70      echo "</table>";
71  }
72  ?>
```

This MySQLi script mirrors the PDO version with table outputs. It repeatedly queries the Pets table and prints it as an HTML table after each change. The HTML output and structure are the same as in the PDO example; here we use `mysqli_fetch_array` inside loops to fetch each row for display. By comparing these examples, you can see that both MySQLi and PDO can achieve the same goals. PDO offers more flexibility (supporting different databases and a richer set of options), whereas MySQLi is specific to MySQL. Importantly, both support prepared statements for better security (though we did not use prepared statements in these simple scripts). In practice, you would choose one approach and use it consistently, integrating techniques like prepared statements when handling user input to protect against SQL injection (as demonstrated earlier).

10.9   Chapter Review

To ensure you have understood the material in this chapter, answer the following review questions:

Problem 10.1 What PHP function is commonly used to select a MySQL database after connecting, and why is it necessary?

Problem 10.2 Why is using the POST method generally safer than GET for form submissions that modify database data (like inserts)?

Problem 10.3 In PHP, how do you fetch the next row from a query result using (a) the old mysql extension, and (b) MySQLi or PDO? Provide the function names for each.

Problem 10.4 Explain what SQL injection is and one technique we used to prevent it in this chapter.

Problem 10.5 The function `mysql_real_escape_string` was used to sanitize inputs. How do prepared statements (in MySQLi or PDO) improve on this approach?

Problem 10.6 Why should you not store plaintext passwords in your database? What PHP function can you use to securely hash passwords?

Problem 10.7 What does HTTPS encrypt, and why is it critical for transmitting login credentials?

Problem 10.8 In an AJAX request, what does the `onreadystatechange` (or analogous event) handler do in the JavaScript code?

Problem 10.9 In our autocomplete implementation, what is the benefit of using `onmouseover="ON(this)"` in the HTML, instead of `onmouseover="ON(1)"` with numeric IDs?

Problem 10.10 Name two advantages of using PDO for database access in PHP.

Problem 10.11 How can wrapping database logic into a PHP class (or using an ORM) benefit a larger application?

Problem 10.12 In the context of database operations, what is the advantage of using `PDO::ERRMODE_EXCEPTION`? What would happen if you do not handle an exception thrown by a PDO operation?

Problem 10.13 Create an HTML form that collects a person's name and age. Write a PHP script (`add_person.php`) that connects to a MySQL database and inserts the submitted name and age into a table `people(name, age)`. After inserting, the script should output a confirmation message. Test it by submitting the form and then verifying (via a SELECT query or phpMyAdmin) that the new record appears in the database.

Problem 10.14 Using the same `people` table, write a PHP script (`list_people.php`) that retrieves all entries and displays them in an HTML table. Each row in the HTML table should correspond to a row in the database, with columns for name and age. Style the table with some basic CSS (borders, header row, etc.).

Hint: Use a loop with `mysqli_fetch_assoc` (or PDO fetch) to get each row.

Problem 10.15 Create a table `admin(password TEXT)` and insert one row with a password (in plain text for this exercise, e.g., "secret"). Develop a PHP script (`admin_login.php`) that contains a simple HTML form with one password input field. When the form is submitted (to the same script or a separate handler), check whether the provided password matches the one in the database: if yes, display a "Login successful" message; if no, display `"Invalid password"`. Use the SQL approach shown in this chapter (SELECT query and check number of rows or use a fetch to see if a match exists). Then improve the script by hashing the stored password (using PHP's `password_hash`) and adjusting the login check to use `password_verify`. This will give you practice in storing and checking encrypted passwords.

Problem 10.16 Implement a simplified version of the AJAX autocomplete example. You can use a small dataset of words. For example, create a table `colors(name TEXT)` and populate it with some color names ("Red", "Green", "Blue", "Yellow", etc.). Then make an HTML page with a text input for searching colors. As the user types, use JavaScript to send the current input to a PHP script (like `search_color.php`) via AJAX (use `XMLHttpRequest` or the Fetch API). The PHP script queries `colors` for names starting with the input and returns matching names in an HTML list (e.g., `<li>` items or `<div>`s). Display the returned suggestions below the input field. Aim to get it working for basic typing and suggestions. You can skip implementing the highlight and click-to-select for this exercise if it is too complex; focus on the AJAX request/response flow.

Problem 10.17 Rewrite one of your earlier scripts (e.g., the insertion or the login check) to use PDO with prepared statements instead of `mysql_` or `mysqli` functions. For example, use `PDO::prepare` with `INSERT` in the add_person script, or use `prepare` with `SELECT` in the login script. Verify that your script still works as expected. This will help you compare the procedural vs. PDO approach.

11. Web Servers and Cloud DevOps

Modern web applications require more than just well-written code. They also need reliable infrastructure to serve content to users around the world. In this chapter, we explore how web servers operate within the LAMP stack, how to deploy applications to cloud platforms, and how DevOps practices help teams deliver software efficiently. We build upon the fundamental protocols discussed in Chapter 2 and examine the practical aspects of running web applications in production environments. Understanding these concepts is essential for anyone developing Internet applications, as the difference between a working application on your local machine and a successful production deployment often lies in proper server configuration, cloud architecture, and operational practices.

The rise of cloud computing has transformed how we think about web infrastructure. Rather than managing physical servers, developers now provision virtual resources on demand, scale applications automatically, and deploy updates continuously. This shift requires new skills beyond traditional programming, including understanding server configuration, automation tools, monitoring systems, and deployment pipelines. By mastering these concepts alongside your development skills, you become capable of not just building applications but ensuring they run reliably at scale.

Learning Objectives

By the end of this chapter, you should be able to:

- Configure and manage web servers like Apache and Nginx, understanding how they process requests and serve both static and dynamic content within the LAMP stack.
- Deploy web applications to cloud platforms, selecting appropriate services and understanding the trade-offs between different deployment models.
- Implement Infrastructure as Code principles using configuration management tools to automate server provisioning and maintain consistent environments.
- Monitor application performance and availability, setting up appropriate metrics, logs, and alerts to detect and resolve issues proactively.
- Design for scalability and high availability, understanding patterns like load balancing, caching, and content delivery networks.
- Apply DevOps practices to improve collaboration between development and operations, implementing continuous integration and deployment workflows.
- Troubleshoot common web server issues using appropriate tools and techniques, from analyzing logs to debugging configuration problems.
- Secure web server configurations, implementing best practices for access control, SSL/TLS certificates, and protecting against common attacks.

DOI: 10.1201/9781003727651-11

11.1   Introduction to Web Servers

11.1.1   What is a Web Server?

A web server is software that accepts HTTP requests from clients (typically web browsers) and responds with the requested content or an error message. To understand its role in web applications, think of a web server as a specialized waiter in a restaurant. Just as a waiter takes your order, communicates with the kitchen, and brings back your meal, a web server receives requests from browsers, coordinates with backend applications, and delivers the resulting web pages.

In the LAMP stack, Apache HTTP Server fills this critical role. Apache acts as the gateway between the outside world (users with web browsers) and your PHP applications. When someone types your website's URL into their browser, they are actually connecting to Apache, which then orchestrates the process of generating and delivering the appropriate response.

The fundamental responsibilities of a web server include several interconnected tasks. First, it must listen continuously on specific network ports for incoming connections. By default, web servers listen on port 80 for standard HTTP traffic and port 443 for secure HTTPS connections. When a connection arrives, the server must parse and understand the HTTP request to determine what the client wants. Based on this analysis, it either retrieves static content directly from the file system or invokes dynamic content generators like PHP scripts. Finally, it packages the result into a properly formatted HTTP response and sends it back to the client.

Consider the difference between serving static and dynamic content. When Apache receives a request for a static file like an image (`/images/logo.png`), it simply locates the file on disk and transmits it to the browser. This process is straightforward and fast. However, when the request is for a dynamic resource like `/products.php?category=electronics`, Apache recognizes that this requires PHP processing. It invokes the PHP interpreter, which executes the script, potentially queries the MySQL database, and generates HTML content on the fly. This dynamic generation allows websites to provide personalized, data-driven experiences rather than serving the same static content to everyone.

11.1.2   How Web Servers Process Requests

To truly understand web server operation, let us trace the complete journey of a typical request through the LAMP stack. This understanding proves invaluable when optimizing performance or debugging issues.

The process begins when a user clicks a link or enters a URL. Their browser first performs a DNS lookup to translate the domain name into an IP address, then establishes a TCP connection to the web server. Once connected, the browser sends an HTTP request that might look like this:

```
1  GET /products.php?category=books&sort=price HTTP/1.1
2  Host: www.example.com
3  User-Agent: Mozilla/5.0 (Windows NT 10.0; Win64; x64)
4  Accept: text/html,application/xhtml+xml
5  Accept-Language: en-US,en;q=0.9
6  Cookie: session_id=abc123def456
```

When Apache receives this request, it begins a multi-stage processing pipeline. First, it parses the request line to extract the HTTP method (GET), the requested resource (/products.php?category=books&sort=price), and the HTTP version. It then processes the headers, noting important information like the Host header (crucial for virtual hosting) and any cookies that might contain session information.

Apache's next task involves mapping the requested URL to a resource. This mapping process follows rules defined in Apache's configuration files. The server checks various configuration directives in the following order:

```
1 Request URL: /products.php?category=books&sort=price
2 $\downarrow$
3 DocumentRoot check: /var/www/html/products.php exists?
4 $\downarrow$
5 File type determination: .php extension $\rightarrow$ PHP handler
6 $\downarrow$
7 Access control: Does the client have permission?
8 $\downarrow$
9 Handler invocation: Execute through PHP interpreter
```

For our PHP example, Apache recognizes the .php extension and knows to invoke the PHP handler. The method of PHP invocation depends on the server configuration. With mod_php, PHP runs as an Apache module within the same process. With PHP-FPM (FastCGI Process Manager), Apache communicates with a separate PHP process pool through a socket or network connection.

The PHP interpreter then takes over, executing the script with access to the query parameters through the $_GET superglobal array. During execution, the PHP script might connect to databases, read files, call external APIs, or perform complex business logic. Here is a simplified example:

```php
1  // products.php - simplified example
2  $category = $_GET['category'] ?? 'all';
3  $sort = $_GET['sort'] ?? 'name';
4
5  // Connect to MySQL and fetch data
6  $db = new mysqli('localhost', 'user', 'pass', 'shop');
7  $stmt = $db->prepare("SELECT * FROM products WHERE category = ? ORDER BY ?");
8  $stmt->bind_param("ss", $category, $sort);
9  $stmt->execute();
10 $results = $stmt->get_result();
11
12 // Generate HTML output
13 echo "<html><head><title>Products</title></head><body>";
14 echo "<h1>Products in category: " . htmlspecialchars($category) . "</h1>";
15 while ($product = $results->fetch_assoc()) {
```

```
16      echo "<div class='product'>";
17      echo "<h2>" . htmlspecialchars($product['name']) . "</h2>";
18      echo "<p>Price: $" . number_format($product['price'], 2) . "</p>";
19      echo "</div>";
20 }
21 echo "</body></html>";
```

As PHP generates output, it typically buffers the content rather than sending it immediately. Once the script completes, PHP returns the generated HTML to Apache along with any headers set by the script (such as `Set-Cookie` headers for session management).

Apache then constructs the final HTTP response, adding its own headers:

```
1  HTTP/1.1 200 OK
2  Date: Thu, 15 Mar 2024 10:30:45 GMT
3  Server: Apache/2.4.41 (Ubuntu)
4  Content-Type: text/html; charset=UTF-8
5  Content-Length: 15234
6  Set-Cookie: session_id=abc123def456; Path=/; HttpOnly
7
8  <!DOCTYPE html>
9  <html><head><title>Products</title></head>
10 <body>
11 <!-- Generated HTML content here -->
12 </body></html>
```

This entire process, from request receipt to response transmission, typically occurs in milliseconds for well-optimized applications. However, each stage represents a potential bottleneck. Database queries might run slowly, PHP scripts could consume excessive memory, or Apache might struggle with too many concurrent connections. Understanding this flow enables developers to identify and address performance issues systematically. Figure 11.1 illustrates this complete request flow through the LAMP stack.

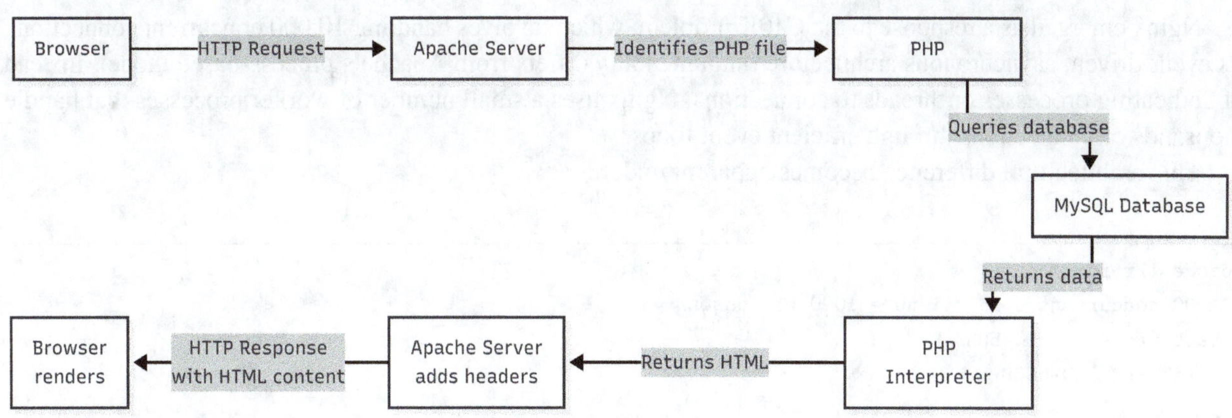

Figure 11.1: A complete request flow through the LAMP stack.

Understanding this architecture helps explain why certain optimizations work. For instance, caching database query results reduces the time spent in the MySQL stage. Implementing opcode caching for PHP eliminates the need to reparse PHP scripts on each request. Using a content delivery network (CDN) for static assets bypasses this entire flow for images, CSS, and JavaScript files.

11.1.3 Common Web Server Software

The web server landscape offers various options, each with distinct architectures and strengths. Understanding these differences helps architects choose the right tool for their specific needs.

Apache HTTP Server has dominated the web server market for decades, and for good reason. Its modular architecture allows administrators to load only the functionality they need, reducing memory footprint and attack surface. Apache's process-based model, particularly in its prefork MPM (Multi-Processing Module), creates separate processes to handle requests. This isolation provides excellent stability because if one request causes a crash, other requests remain unaffected.

Apache's configuration flexibility sets it apart. Through `.htaccess` files, developers can modify server behavior at the directory level without accessing main configuration files. This feature proves particularly valuable in shared hosting environments where users lack root access. Apache's extensive module ecosystem includes everything from URL rewriting (`mod_rewrite`) to security features (`mod_security`) to caching (`mod_cache`).

The server's request processing follows a series of phases, each allowing modules to intervene:

```
1  Connection Phase $\rightarrow$ Request Reading $\rightarrow$ URI Translation $\rightarrow$
2  Access Control $\rightarrow$ Authentication $\rightarrow$ Authorization $\rightarrow$
3  MIME Type Checking $\rightarrow$ Response Generation $\rightarrow$ Logging
```

This phase-based architecture enables sophisticated request handling but can impact performance under high load, as each phase adds processing overhead.

Nginx emerged as a response to the C10K problem, which involves handling 10,000 concurrent connections. Its event-driven, asynchronous architecture fundamentally differs from Apache's process-based model. Instead of dedicating processes or threads to connections, Nginx uses a small number of worker processes that handle thousands of connections through efficient event loops.

This architectural difference becomes apparent under load:

```
Apache (Prefork):
- 1000 concurrent connections = 1000 processes
- Each process: ~10-50MB RAM
- Total RAM: 10-50GB

Nginx:
- 1000 concurrent connections = handled by 4-8 workers
- Each worker: ~10-20MB RAM
- Total RAM: 40-160MB
```

However, Nginx's efficiency comes with trade-offs. It lacks Apache's extensive module system and `.htaccess` support. Dynamic module loading was not available until recently, and even now remains more limited than Apache's capabilities.

LiteSpeed offers an interesting middle ground, providing Apache compatibility (including `.htaccess` support) with performance approaching Nginx. Its event-driven architecture handles static content efficiently while maintaining compatibility with Apache modules and configurations. The commercial version includes built-in caching and advanced security features.

Caddy represents the new generation of web servers, focusing on simplicity and security. It automatically obtains and renews SSL certificates from Let's Encrypt, making HTTPS deployment trivial. Its configuration uses a simple, human-readable format:

```
example.com {
    root /var/www/html
    php_fastcgi localhost:9000
    encode gzip
}
```

For development environments, PHP's built-in server provides a zero-configuration option. Launched with `php -S localhost:8000`, it serves PHP applications without installing a full web server. However, it is strictly for development because it handles only one request at a time and lacks security features needed for production use.

When choosing a web server for LAMP deployments, consider several important factors. Compatibility is often paramount: Apache offers the best PHP integration and `.htaccess` support. In terms of performance, Nginx excels at serving static files and handling many connections. Apache provides greater flexibility through its extensive module system, offering solutions for complex requirements. For simplicity, Caddy or PHP's built-in server reduce configuration complexity. Finally, Apache's long history means extensive documentation and community knowledge, providing excellent support.

Many production deployments combine servers, using Nginx as a reverse proxy to handle static files and SSL termination while forwarding dynamic requests to Apache. This hybrid approach leverages each server's strengths while mitigating their weaknesses.

11.2 Web Server Configuration and Deployment

11.2.1 Apache Configuration Fundamentals

Before deploying web applications to a server, understanding Apache's configuration system is essential. When you rent a VPS (Virtual Private Server) or have access to a physical server, you typically start with a base Linux installation. The first step involves installing and configuring Apache to serve your PHP applications properly.

Apache's configuration resides in a hierarchical structure of files, typically located in `/etc/apache2/` on Debian-based systems (Ubuntu, Debian) or `/etc/httpd/` on Red Hat-based systems (CentOS, RHEL, Fedora). This structure allows for modular configuration management, making it easier to maintain complex setups.

The main configuration file (`apache2.conf` or `httpd.conf`) contains global settings that affect the entire server. Understanding each section helps you configure Apache appropriately for your application's needs:

```
# Server Root - defines the base directory for Apache's configuration
ServerRoot "/etc/apache2"

# Listen directive - tells Apache which port(s) to monitor
Listen 80
Listen 443

# User and Group - Apache drops privileges to these after starting
User www-data
Group www-data

# ServerAdmin - email address for error messages
ServerAdmin webmaster@example.com

# ServerName - helps Apache determine its own name
ServerName www.example.com
```

Each directive serves a specific purpose. The `Listen` directive tells Apache which network interfaces and ports to bind to. Running Apache as the `www-data` user (rather than root) follows the principle of least privilege, limiting damage if the server is compromised. The `ServerAdmin` email appears in default error pages, helping users report problems.

Module management represents another crucial aspect of Apache configuration. Modules extend Apache's functionality, and the LAMP stack requires several key modules:

```
# Essential modules for LAMP stack
LoadModule mpm_prefork_module modules/mod_mpm_prefork.so
LoadModule php_module modules/libphp7.4.so
LoadModule rewrite_module modules/mod_rewrite.so
LoadModule ssl_module modules/mod_ssl.so
LoadModule headers_module modules/mod_headers.so
```

On Debian-based systems, you enable modules using the a2enmod command:

```
# Enable required modules
sudo a2enmod php7.4
sudo a2enmod rewrite
sudo a2enmod ssl
sudo a2enmod headers

# Restart Apache to load modules
sudo systemctl restart apache2
```

The document root configuration determines where Apache looks for files to serve. The default configuration includes important security directives:

```
# Define the document root
DocumentRoot "/var/www/html"

# Configure permissions for the document root
<Directory "/var/www/html">
    # Options control what features are available
    Options Indexes FollowSymLinks

    # AllowOverride enables .htaccess files
    AllowOverride All

    # Access control in Apache 2.4+
    Require all granted
</Directory>
```

Understanding these options proves crucial for security and functionality. The `Options` directive controls server features: `Indexes` allows directory listings when no index file exists (often disabled in production), while `FollowSymLinks` permits Apache to follow symbolic links. The `AllowOverride All` setting enables `.htaccess` files, allowing per-directory configuration changes without modifying the main configuration file.

11.2.2 Deploying Applications on a Web Server

Deploying a LAMP application to a physical server or VPS involves several steps beyond basic Apache configuration. Let us walk through a complete deployment process for a typical PHP application.

First, prepare the server environment. After securing SSH access to your server, update the system and install the complete LAMP stack:

```
# Update system packages
sudo apt update && sudo apt upgrade -y

# Install Apache, MySQL, and PHP
sudo apt install apache2 mysql-server php libapache2-mod-php php-mysql -y

# Install additional PHP extensions commonly needed
sudo apt install php-curl php-gd php-mbstring php-xml php-zip -y

# Secure MySQL installation
sudo mysql_secure_installation
```

Next, create a dedicated directory structure for your application. Organizing files properly from the start prevents future complications:

```
# Create application directory
sudo mkdir -p /var/www/myapp/public_html
sudo mkdir -p /var/www/myapp/logs
sudo mkdir -p /var/www/myapp/ssl

# Set appropriate ownership
sudo chown -R $USER:www-data /var/www/myapp
sudo chmod -R 755 /var/www/myapp
```

The directory structure separates public files from logs and SSL certificates, improving security and organization. Setting proper ownership allows you to upload files while letting Apache read them.

Virtual hosts enable Apache to serve multiple websites from a single server. Create a new virtual host configuration for your application:

```apache
1  # /etc/apache2/sites-available/myapp.conf
2  <VirtualHost *:80>
3      ServerName myapp.com
4      ServerAlias www.myapp.com
5      ServerAdmin admin@myapp.com
6
7      DocumentRoot /var/www/myapp/public_html
8
9      # PHP configuration
10     <FilesMatch \.php$>
11         SetHandler application/x-httpd-php
12     </FilesMatch>
13
14     # Directory configuration
15     <Directory /var/www/myapp/public_html>
16         Options -Indexes +FollowSymLinks
17         AllowOverride All
18         Require all granted
19     </Directory>
20
21     # Logging
22     ErrorLog /var/www/myapp/logs/error.log
23     CustomLog /var/www/myapp/logs/access.log combined
24
25     # Security headers
26     Header always set X-Content-Type-Options "nosniff"
27     Header always set X-Frame-Options "DENY"
28     Header always set X-XSS-Protection "1; mode=block"
29  </VirtualHost>
```

This configuration establishes a complete environment for your application. The `ServerName` and `ServerAlias` directives tell Apache which domains this virtual host serves. Separate log files aid in troubleshooting and monitoring. Security headers protect against common web vulnerabilities.

Enabling the new site and disabling the default:

```bash
1  # Enable your site
2  sudo a2ensite myapp.conf
3
4  # Disable the default site
5  sudo a2dissite 000-default.conf
6
```

```
 7  # Test configuration
 8  sudo apache2ctl configtest
 9
10  # Reload Apache
11  sudo systemctl reload apache2
```

11.2.3   File Transfer and Deployment Methods

Transferring application files to the server represents a critical deployment step. Several methods exist, each with trade-offs between simplicity and sophistication.

The traditional approach uses SFTP (SSH File Transfer Protocol) for secure file transfer:

```
 1  # Connect via SFTP
 2  sftp user@your-server.com
 3
 4  # Navigate to the web root
 5  cd /var/www/myapp/public_html
 6
 7  # Upload all files from local directory
 8  put -r /local/path/to/app/* .
 9
10  # Set permissions after upload
11  chmod -R 755 .
12  chmod -R 777 storage/   # For writable directories
```

While simple, manual SFTP uploads are error-prone and make rollbacks difficult. A better approach uses version control with Git:

```
 1  # On the server, initialize a Git repository
 2  cd /var/www/myapp
 3  git init --bare repo.git
 4
 5  # Create a post-receive hook for automatic deployment
 6  cat > repo.git/hooks/post-receive << 'EOF'
 7  #!/bin/bash
 8  TARGET="/var/www/myapp/public_html"
 9  GIT_DIR="/var/www/myapp/repo.git"
10  BRANCH="main"
11
12  while read oldrev newrev ref
13  do
```

```
14      if [ "$ref" = "refs/heads/$BRANCH" ]; then
15          echo "Deploying $BRANCH branch to production..."
16          git --work-tree=$TARGET --git-dir=$GIT_DIR checkout -f $BRANCH
17
18          # Run post-deployment tasks
19          cd $TARGET
20          composer install --no-dev --optimize-autoloader
21          php artisan migrate --force
22          php artisan cache:clear
23
24          # Set permissions
25          chown -R www-data:www-data storage/
26          chmod -R 775 storage/
27
28          echo "Deployment complete."
29      fi
30  done
31  EOF
32
33  chmod +x repo.git/hooks/post-receive
```

This Git hook automatically deploys code when you push to the repository. From your local machine, run the following commands:

```
1  # Add the server as a remote
2  git remote add production user@your-server.com:/var/www/myapp/repo.git
3
4  # Deploy by pushing
5  git push production main
```

For PHP applications using Composer, deployment includes dependency management:

```
1  # Install Composer on the server
2  curl -sS https://getcomposer.org/installer | php
3  sudo mv composer.phar /usr/local/bin/composer
4
5  # During deployment, install dependencies
6  cd /var/www/myapp/public_html
7  composer install --no-dev --optimize-autoloader
8
```

```
 9  # Generate optimized autoload files
10  composer dump-autoload --optimize
```

11.2.4   Database Deployment and Migration

Deploying database changes requires careful coordination with application code. Start by creating the production database:

```
 1  -- Connect to MySQL as root
 2  mysql -u root -p
 3
 4  -- Create database and user
 5  CREATE DATABASE myapp_production CHARACTER SET utf8mb4 COLLATE utf8mb4_unicode_ci;
 6  CREATE USER 'myapp_user'@'localhost' IDENTIFIED BY 'strong_password_here';
 7  GRANT ALL PRIVILEGES ON myapp_production.* TO 'myapp_user'@'localhost';
 8  FLUSH PRIVILEGES;
```

Configure your application to use these credentials. Store sensitive configuration in environment files:

```
 1  // .env file (not committed to version control)
 2  APP_ENV=production
 3  APP_DEBUG=false
 4  APP_URL=https://myapp.com
 5
 6  DB_CONNECTION=mysql
 7  DB_HOST=localhost
 8  DB_DATABASE=myapp_production
 9  DB_USERNAME=myapp_user
10  DB_PASSWORD=strong_password_here
```

For initial database setup, import your schema:

```
 1  # Import database structure
 2  mysql -u myapp_user -p myapp_production < database/schema.sql
 3
 4  # Or use migrations if your framework supports them
 5  php artisan migrate --force
```

11.2.5   Performance Optimization for Production

Production servers require different configurations than development environments. Enable PHP opcode caching
for significant performance improvements:

```ini
; /etc/php/7.4/apache2/conf.d/10-opcache.ini
opcache.enable=1
opcache.memory_consumption=128
opcache.interned_strings_buffer=8
opcache.max_accelerated_files=4000
opcache.revalidate_freq=60
opcache.fast_shutdown=1
```

Configure Apache for production workloads. The default settings work for development but need adjustment
for production traffic:

```apache
# /etc/apache2/mods-available/mpm_prefork.conf
<IfModule mpm_prefork_module>
        StartServers              5
        MinSpareServers           5
        MaxSpareServers          10
        MaxRequestWorkers        150
        MaxConnectionsPerChild  3000
</IfModule>
```

These settings control how Apache handles concurrent requests. `StartServers` sets the initial number
of server processes. `MinSpareServers` and `MaxSpareServers` maintain a pool of idle processes ready
to handle requests. `MaxRequestWorkers` limits total concurrent connections, preventing server overload.
`MaxConnectionsPerChild` causes processes to restart after handling a certain number of requests, preventing
memory leaks.

Enabling compression to reduce bandwidth usage:

```apache
# Enable mod_deflate for compression
<IfModule mod_deflate.c>
    # Compress HTML, CSS, JavaScript, Text, XML
    AddOutputFilterByType DEFLATE application/javascript
    AddOutputFilterByType DEFLATE application/json
    AddOutputFilterByType DEFLATE application/xml
    AddOutputFilterByType DEFLATE text/css
    AddOutputFilterByType DEFLATE text/html
```

```
9     AddOutputFilterByType DEFLATE text/javascript
10    AddOutputFilterByType DEFLATE text/plain
11    AddOutputFilterByType DEFLATE text/xml
12
13    # Remove browser bugs
14    BrowserMatch ^Mozilla/4 gzip-only-text/html
15    BrowserMatch ^Mozilla/4\.0[678] no-gzip
16    BrowserMatch \bMSIE !no-gzip !gzip-only-text/html
17    Header append Vary User-Agent
18 </IfModule>
```

11.2.6   Security Hardening

Production servers face constant security threats. Implement these essential security measures.

Hiding sensitive information that could help attackers:

```
1 # Hide Apache version
2 ServerTokens Prod
3 ServerSignature Off
4
5 # Hide PHP version
6 # In php.ini:
7 expose_php = Off
```

Protecting sensitive files and directories:

```
1  # Deny access to version control directories
2  <DirectoryMatch "^/.*/\.(git|svn)/">
3      Require all denied
4  </DirectoryMatch>
5
6  # Protect sensitive files
7  <FilesMatch "(^\.htaccess|^\.htpasswd|\.ini$|\.log$|composer\.(json|lock))">
8      Require all denied
9  </FilesMatch>
10
11 # Prevent access to backup files
12 <FilesMatch "~$">
13     Require all denied
14 </FilesMatch>
```

Implement SSL/TLS for secure communications. First, obtain an SSL certificate. Let's Encrypt provides free certificates that can be easily installed using Certbot:

```
# Install Certbot
sudo apt install certbot python3-certbot-apache -y

# Obtain certificate
sudo certbot --apache -d myapp.com -d www.myapp.com
```

Configuring strong SSL settings:

```
# /etc/apache2/sites-available/myapp-ssl.conf
<VirtualHost *:443>
    ServerName myapp.com
    ServerAlias www.myapp.com
    DocumentRoot /var/www/myapp/public_html

    # SSL Configuration
    SSLEngine on
    SSLCertificateFile /etc/letsencrypt/live/myapp.com/fullchain.pem
    SSLCertificateKeyFile /etc/letsencrypt/live/myapp.com/privkey.pem

    # Modern SSL protocols only
    SSLProtocol -all +TLSv1.2 +TLSv1.3
    SSLCipherSuite ECDHE-ECDSA-AES128-GCM-SHA256:ECDHE-RSA-AES128-GCM-SHA256
    SSLHonorCipherOrder off

    # HSTS (HTTP Strict Transport Security)
    Header always set Strict-Transport-Security "max-age=31536000; includeSubDomains"

    # Other security headers
    Header always set X-Content-Type-Options "nosniff"
    Header always set X-Frame-Options "SAMEORIGIN"
    Header always set X-XSS-Protection "1; mode=block"
    Header always set Referrer-Policy "strict-origin-when-cross-origin"

    # ... rest of configuration ...
</VirtualHost>
```

11.2.7 Monitoring and Maintenance

After deployment, continuous monitoring ensures your application remains healthy.

Setting up basic monitoring using built-in tools:

```apache
# Monitor Apache status
sudo a2enmod status

# Configure status page (restricted access)
<Location /server-status>
    SetHandler server-status
    Require ip 127.0.0.1
    Require ip YOUR_ADMIN_IP
</Location>
```

Creating automated backup scripts for both files and databases:

```bash
#!/bin/bash
# /usr/local/bin/backup-myapp.sh

# Variables
BACKUP_DIR="/backup/myapp"
DATE=$(date +%Y%m%d_%H%M%S)
WEB_DIR="/var/www/myapp/public_html"
DB_NAME="myapp_production"
DB_USER="myapp_user"
DB_PASS="strong_password_here"

# Create backup directory
mkdir -p "$BACKUP_DIR"

# Backup database
mysqldump -u "$DB_USER" -p"$DB_PASS" "$DB_NAME" | gzip > "$BACKUP_DIR/db_$DATE.sql.gz"

# Backup files
tar -czf "$BACKUP_DIR/files_$DATE.tar.gz" -C "$WEB_DIR" .

# Keep only last 7 days of backups
find "$BACKUP_DIR" -name "*.gz" -mtime +7 -delete

# Log backup completion
echo "Backup completed at $(date)" >> /var/log/myapp-backup.log
```

Scheduling regular backups using cron:

```
1  # Add to crontab
2  0 2 * * * /usr/local/bin/backup-myapp.sh
```

This comprehensive approach to web server deployment ensures your LAMP applications run reliably on traditional server infrastructure. The next sections will explore how cloud platforms build upon these fundamentals while adding new capabilities for scaling and automation.

11.3   Cloud Computing Fundamentals

11.3.1   Introduction to Cloud Services

Cloud computing represents a fundamental shift in how organizations approach IT infrastructure. Rather than purchasing, housing, and maintaining physical servers, cloud computing allows you to rent computing resources on demand from massive data centers operated by providers like Amazon, Google, and Microsoft. This transformation affects every aspect of web application deployment, from initial development to global scaling.

To understand cloud computing's impact on LAMP deployments, consider the traditional approach. Previously, launching a web application meant purchasing server hardware, negotiating data center contracts, configuring network equipment, and maintaining all these components. This process required significant upfront investment and expertise in hardware management. Cloud computing eliminates these barriers by providing virtual resources that you can provision in minutes and pay for hourly or monthly.

The economic model shift proves particularly important for web applications. Traditional infrastructure requires estimating peak capacity and purchasing accordingly, leading to either wasted resources during quiet periods or insufficient capacity during traffic spikes. Cloud computing's pay-as-you-go model means you pay only for resources actually consumed. If your PHP application experiences a traffic surge, you can add servers within minutes and remove them when traffic subsides.

Cloud services organize into three primary service models, each offering different levels of abstraction and control. Understanding these models helps you choose the appropriate approach for your LAMP applications.

Infrastructure as a Service (IaaS) provides the fundamental building blocks of computing infrastructure. When you provision an IaaS resource, you receive a virtual server with specified CPU, memory, and storage characteristics. You maintain complete control over the operating system and all software installed on it. For LAMP deployments, IaaS resembles traditional server management most closely. You still install Linux, configure Apache, set up MySQL, and deploy PHP applications, but the underlying hardware becomes someone else's responsibility.

Consider Amazon EC2 (Elastic Compute Cloud) as a typical IaaS example. When you launch an EC2 instance, you select an Amazon Machine Image (AMI) that might contain a base Ubuntu installation. You then connect via SSH and proceed exactly as with a physical server: installing Apache, PHP, and MySQL, configuring virtual hosts, and deploying your application. The key difference lies in the infrastructure's virtual nature: you can resize the instance, snapshot it for backups, or terminate it when no longer needed.

Platform as a Service (PaaS) abstracts away infrastructure management, allowing developers to focus solely on application code. PaaS platforms handle operating system maintenance, security patches, load balancing, and scaling automatically. You provide application code and configuration; the platform manages everything else.

Heroku exemplifies the PaaS approach. Deploying a PHP application to Heroku involves pushing code via Git. Heroku automatically detects PHP applications, installs dependencies via Composer, configures the web server, and makes the application available at a public URL. While this simplicity accelerates development, it may limit configuration options important for complex LAMP applications.

Software as a Service (SaaS) delivers complete applications via web browsers. While you do not deploy your own applications as SaaS, understanding this model helps when integrating third-party services. Modern LAMP applications commonly incorporate SaaS offerings for functions like email delivery (SendGrid), payment processing (Stripe), error tracking (Sentry), or analytics (Google Analytics). These services provide sophisticated functionality without requiring you to build and maintain complex subsystems.

The boundaries between these models sometimes blur. AWS Elastic Beanstalk, for instance, provides PaaS-like simplicity while maintaining IaaS flexibility. You can deploy applications easily while retaining access to underlying EC2 instances for customization. This hybrid approach suits LAMP applications requiring both convenience and control.

11.3.2　Major Cloud Providers Overview

The cloud provider landscape features several major players, each with distinct characteristics affecting LAMP deployments. Understanding their differences helps select the most appropriate platform for your specific needs.

Amazon Web Services (AWS) pioneered public cloud computing and maintains the largest market share. AWS offers over 200 services covering every conceivable infrastructure need. For LAMP applications, the core services form a complete ecosystem. EC2 provides compute capacity with instances ranging from tiny t2.micro (1 vCPU, 1GB RAM) suitable for development to powerful m5.24xlarge (96 vCPUs, 384GB RAM) for demanding applications. RDS (Relational Database Service) offers managed MySQL with automated backups, updates, and failover. S3 (Simple Storage Service) handles file storage with effectively unlimited capacity and 99.999999999% durability.

AWS's comprehensiveness brings complexity. The service catalog can overwhelm newcomers, and the pricing model includes numerous variables. However, AWS provides unmatched flexibility and scale. If your LAMP application might grow from hundreds to millions of users, AWS offers the services to support that journey. The extensive documentation, large community, and mature ecosystem mean solutions exist for virtually any challenge.

Google Cloud Platform (GCP) leverages Google's internal infrastructure expertise. While offering fewer services than AWS, GCP excels in specific areas. Google's networking infrastructure provides exceptional global connectivity, beneficial for applications serving international audiences. BigQuery and machine learning services lead the industry, useful if your LAMP application requires advanced analytics.

For LAMP deployments, GCP's Compute Engine provides virtual machines with competitive pricing, including automatic sustained use discounts. Cloud SQL offers managed MySQL with interesting features like automatic storage increases and point-in-time recovery. GCP's Cloud Shell provides a browser-based terminal with pre-installed development tools, convenient for quick administration tasks.

Microsoft Azure historically focused on Windows workloads but now fully embraces Linux and open-source technologies. Azure's strength lies in hybrid cloud scenarios and enterprise integration. If your organization uses Active Directory, Office 365, or other Microsoft services, Azure provides seamless integration. Azure

DevOps offers comprehensive CI/CD pipelines well-suited for LAMP applications.

Azure's global presence rivals AWS, with data centers in more regions than any other provider. This geographic distribution helps meet data residency requirements and reduce latency. Azure Database for MySQL provides a managed service with built-in high availability and automatic backups. The Azure CLI and Cloud Shell offer consistent management experiences across platforms.

DigitalOcean takes a different approach, prioritizing simplicity and developer experience over comprehensive service offerings. Where AWS might require configuring multiple services for a basic LAMP deployment, DigitalOcean provides straightforward Droplets (virtual machines) that you can deploy in under a minute. The interface remains clean and intuitive, avoiding the complexity that can overwhelm developers new to cloud computing.

DigitalOcean's Managed Databases service handles MySQL administration tasks while maintaining the simplicity that defines their platform. Their documentation stands out for clarity and practical examples. While lacking advanced services like machine learning or big data analytics, DigitalOcean excels at core infrastructure needs. For straightforward LAMP applications without complex requirements, DigitalOcean's approach reduces operational overhead.

Other Notable Providers serve specific niches. Linode offers a DigitalOcean-like experience with competitive pricing. Vultr provides high-performance SSD instances with excellent global coverage. Hetzner, based in Germany, offers compelling prices for European deployments. These smaller providers often provide personalized support and simpler pricing models, though they may lack the advanced services and global scale of major providers.

11.3.3   Cloud Service Selection

Selecting appropriate cloud services requires evaluating multiple factors against your application's specific requirements. This decision impacts not only immediate deployment but also long-term scalability, costs, and operational complexity.

Understanding Cost Models proves essential for cloud deployments. Unlike traditional hosting with fixed monthly fees, cloud pricing involves multiple components. Compute costs form the foundation, where you pay for virtual machine time, typically hourly. A t3.small instance on AWS costs approximately \$0.0208 per hour (\$15 monthly if running continuously), while a similar Droplet on DigitalOcean costs \$12 monthly. However, compute represents only part of total costs.

Storage pricing includes multiple tiers. Block storage attached to instances costs around \$0.10 per GB monthly. Object storage for files costs less (around \$0.023 per GB on S3) but charges for requests and data transfer. Database services add another layer because RDS instances cost more than equivalent EC2 instances but include management, backups, and updates. Data transfer often surprises newcomers. While incoming traffic is typically free, outgoing traffic costs \$0.01-0.12 per GB depending on volume and destination.

Consider a typical LAMP application scenario. Your PHP application runs on a t3.small instance (\$15/month), uses 50GB of block storage (\$5/month), stores 100GB of user uploads in S3 (\$2.30/month), runs MySQL on a db.t3.small RDS instance (\$25/month), and transfers 100GB monthly (\$9/month). The total reaches approximately \$56 monthly, not including backups, monitoring, or traffic spikes. Understanding these components helps predict and optimize costs.

Performance Requirements shape instance selection and architecture decisions. CPU needs vary significantly between applications. A content management system might run adequately on 1-2 vCPUs, while a data processing application might require 8-16 vCPUs or more. Memory requirements often prove more critical for LAMP applications. PHP applications themselves might use modest memory, but MySQL benefits significantly from additional RAM for caching.

Storage performance affects application responsiveness more than many developers realize. Cloud providers offer various storage types. General-purpose SSD storage balances cost and performance for most LAMP applications. Provisioned Input/Output Operations Per Second (IOPS) storage guarantees specific performance levels for database workloads. Some providers offer local NVMe storage with exceptional performance but no persistence guarantees. Understanding these trade-offs helps optimize both performance and costs.

Geographic distribution impacts user experience significantly. Cloud providers operate data centers globally, allowing you to deploy applications near users. Latency between US East Coast and West Coast reaches 70-80ms, while transatlantic latency exceeds 100ms. For responsive web applications, deploying in multiple regions improves user experience but complicates architecture and increases costs.

Scalability Considerations influence initial architecture decisions. Vertical scaling (increasing instance size) provides the simplest growth path. Most cloud providers allow resizing instances with minimal downtime. However, vertical scaling faces limits, and even the largest instances may prove insufficient for popular applications. Horizontal scaling (adding instances) offers unlimited growth potential but requires architectural changes.

Preparing for horizontal scaling means designing stateless applications. Session data must move from local files to shared storage (like Redis). Uploaded files need centralized storage (like S3) rather than local directories. Database connections should support read replicas for distributing query load. These changes require effort but enable applications to scale beyond single-server limitations.

Auto-scaling capabilities vary between providers and service types. AWS Auto Scaling can automatically adjust Elastic Compute Cloud (EC2) instances based on metrics like CPU usage or request count. Google Cloud's autoscaling includes sophisticated predictive scaling. PaaS offerings like Elastic Beanstalk or App Engine handle scaling automatically. Understanding these options helps design systems that respond gracefully to traffic variations.

Security and Compliance requirements may dictate provider selection. Major cloud providers invest heavily in security, often exceeding what organizations could implement independently. However, the shared responsibility model means you remain responsible for application security, access management, and data protection.

Compliance certifications vary by provider and service. AWS, Azure, and Google Cloud Platform (GCP) maintain extensive certifications including Service Organization Control 2 (SOC 2), Payment Card Industry Data Security Standard (PCI DSS), Health Insurance Portability and Accountability Act (HIPAA), and ISO 27001. Smaller providers may offer fewer certifications but still maintain strong security practices. Understand which certifications your application requires and verify provider compliance.

Data residency laws affect global applications. General Data Protection Regulation (GDPR) requires keeping European users' data within the EU unless specific conditions are met. Some countries mandate local data storage for certain industries. Cloud providers' global infrastructure helps meet these requirements, but you must configure services appropriately. Understand where providers store data and whether you can control placement.

Making the Decision requires balancing these factors against your specific context. Start-ups with limited budgets might choose DigitalOcean for simplicity and predictable costs. Enterprises with complex requirements might select AWS for its comprehensive services. Organizations with existing Microsoft infrastructure might prefer Azure for integration.

Consider your team's expertise when selecting providers. AWS's complexity requires significant learning investment but provides unmatched flexibility. DigitalOcean's simplicity allows faster initial deployment but may require migration as needs grow. Factor in learning time and operational overhead when evaluating options.

Create decision matrices comparing providers across important criteria:

Criteria	Weight	AWS	GCP	Azure	DO
Cost	25%	3	4	3	5
Simplicity	20%	2	3	3	5
Services	20%	5	4	4	2
Performance	15%	5	5	4	4
Documentation	10%	4	4	3	5
Support	10%	3	3	4	4

This structured approach helps make objective decisions despite marketing claims and feature lists. Remember that migration between providers, while possible, requires effort. Choosing wisely initially saves future complications.

11.4　Deploying Web Applications to the Cloud

11.4.1　Setting Up Cloud Infrastructure for LAMP

Deploying a LAMP application to the cloud begins with provisioning the necessary infrastructure. Unlike traditional servers where you physically install hardware, cloud deployment starts with creating virtual resources through web consoles or command-line interfaces. Let us walk through a complete deployment process using AWS as our example, though the concepts apply to other cloud providers.

First, you need to create a virtual server instance. In AWS, this means launching an EC2 instance. Through the AWS Management Console, you select an Amazon Machine Image (AMI) as your starting point. For LAMP deployments, Ubuntu Server or Amazon Linux 2 are popular choices. The instance type determines your server's computing power. For example, a t3.small instance (2 vCPUs, 2GB RAM) suffices for small applications, while larger applications might require t3.large or bigger instances.

During instance creation, you configure several critical settings. The security group acts as a virtual firewall, controlling which traffic reaches your server. For a LAMP application, you typically need:

```
# Security group rules for LAMP application
Port 22 (SSH) - Source: Your IP address (for administration)
Port 80 (HTTP) - Source: 0.0.0.0/0 (anywhere)
Port 443 (HTTPS) - Source: 0.0.0.0/0 (anywhere)
Port 3306 (MySQL) - Source: Security group ID (only from app servers)
```

After launching the instance, you receive a public IP address or DNS name to access your server. Connect via SSH using the key pair you specified during creation:

```bash
# Connect to your EC2 instance
ssh -i your-key.pem ubuntu@ec2-xx-xx-xx-xx.compute-1.amazonaws.com

# Update the system
sudo apt update && sudo apt upgrade -y

# Install LAMP stack components
sudo apt install apache2 mysql-server php libapache2-mod-php php-mysql -y
sudo apt install php-curl php-gd php-mbstring php-xml php-zip php-bcmath -y
```

The cloud environment requires some configuration adjustments compared to traditional servers. For instance, EC2 instances have both public and private IP addresses. Your application should use the private IP for internal communications (like database connections) while Apache listens on all interfaces for public traffic.

11.4.2   Cloud-Native LAMP Deployment Architecture

Deploying to the cloud effectively means leveraging cloud services rather than simply replicating traditional server setups. A cloud-native LAMP architecture separates components across different services for better scalability and reliability.

Instead of installing MySQL on your EC2 instance, use Amazon RDS (Relational Database Service) for managed MySQL hosting. RDS handles backups, updates, and failover automatically.

Creating an RDS instance involves selecting MySQL as the engine, choosing an instance class (db.t3.micro for development, larger for production), and configuring networking to allow connections from your EC2 instances:

```php
# After creating RDS instance, configure your PHP application
# config/database.php
<?php
define('DB_HOST', 'myapp-db.cluster-xxxxx.us-east-1.rds.amazonaws.com');
define('DB_NAME', 'myapp_production');
define('DB_USER', 'admin');
define('DB_PASS', getenv('DB_PASSWORD')); // From environment variable
?>
```

File storage presents another consideration. On traditional servers, uploaded files reside in local directories. In cloud environments, especially with multiple servers, use object storage services like Amazon Simple Storage Service (S3). This approach ensures files remain accessible regardless of which server handles requests:

```php
// upload.php - Cloud-aware file upload handling
<?php
require 'vendor/autoload.php';
use Aws\S3\S3Client;

$s3 = new S3Client([
    'version' => 'latest',
    'region'  => 'us-east-1'
]);

if ($_FILES['upload']) {
    $file = $_FILES['upload'];
    $key = 'uploads/' . time() . '_' . $file['name'];

    try {
        // Upload to S3 instead of local directory
        $result = $s3->putObject([
            'Bucket' => 'myapp-uploads',
            'Key'    => $key,
            'Body'   => fopen($file['tmp_name'], 'r'),
            'ACL'    => 'public-read'
        ]);

        // Store S3 URL in database instead of local path
        $fileUrl = $result['ObjectURL'];
        $stmt = $pdo->prepare("INSERT INTO uploads (filename, url) VALUES (?, ?)");
        $stmt->execute([$file['name'], $fileUrl]);

    } catch (Exception $e) {
        error_log("Upload failed: " . $e->getMessage());
    }
}
?>
```

This architecture separates concerns: EC2 handles compute, RDS manages databases, and S3 stores files. Each service scales independently and provides features difficult to implement manually.

11.4.3   Automated Deployment Pipeline

Manual deployment to cloud servers shares the same problems as traditional deployment: human error, inconsistency, and downtime. Cloud platforms provide services to automate the entire deployment pipeline.

AWS CodeDeploy automates code deployment to EC2 instances. First, install the CodeDeploy agent on your instances:

```
1  # Install CodeDeploy agent on Ubuntu
2  sudo apt update
3  sudo apt install ruby wget -y
4  cd /home/ubuntu
5  wget https://aws-codedeploy-us-east-1.s3.us-east-1.amazonaws.com/latest/install
6  chmod +x ./install
7  sudo ./install auto
```

Next, create an `appspec.yml` file in your application root that tells CodeDeploy how to deploy your application:

```
1   # appspec.yml
2   version: 0.0
3   os: linux
4   files:
5     - source: /
6       destination: /var/www/html
7   hooks:
8     BeforeInstall:
9       - location: scripts/install_dependencies.sh
10        timeout: 300
11        runas: root
12    AfterInstall:
13      - location: scripts/change_permissions.sh
14        timeout: 300
15        runas: root
16    ApplicationStart:
17      - location: scripts/start_server.sh
18        timeout: 300
19        runas: root
20    ValidateService:
21      - location: scripts/validate_service.sh
22        timeout: 300
23        runas: root
```

In addition, the deployment scripts handle specific tasks at each stage, as demonstrated in the following script.

```bash
1  # scripts/install_dependencies.sh
2  #!/bin/bash
3  cd /var/www/html
4  composer install --no-dev --optimize-autoloader
5
6  # scripts/change_permissions.sh
7  #!/bin/bash
8  chown -R www-data:www-data /var/www/html
9  chmod -R 755 /var/www/html
10 chmod -R 777 /var/www/html/storage
11 chmod -R 777 /var/www/html/cache
12
13 # scripts/start_server.sh
14 #!/bin/bash
15 systemctl restart apache2
16 systemctl restart php7.4-fpm
17
18 # scripts/validate_service.sh
19 #!/bin/bash
20 curl -f http://localhost/health-check || exit 1
```

This automation ensures consistent deployments. Every deployment follows the same steps, reducing human error and enabling rollback if validation fails.

11.4.4   Container-Based Cloud Deployment

Containers provide consistency across environments and simplify dependency management. Docker containers package your LAMP application with all requirements, ensuring identical behavior across development, staging, and production.

Creating a `Dockerfile` for your LAMP application:

```dockerfile
1  # Dockerfile
2  FROM php:7.4-apache
3
4  # Install PHP extensions
5  RUN apt-get update && apt-get install -y \
6      libpng-dev \
7      libjpeg-dev \
8      libfreetype6-dev \
9      zip \
10     unzip \
```

```
11      && docker-php-ext-configure gd --with-freetype --with-jpeg \
12      && docker-php-ext-install gd pdo pdo_mysql mysqli
13
14  # Enable Apache modules
15  RUN a2enmod rewrite headers
16
17  # Install Composer
18  COPY --from=composer:latest /usr/bin/composer /usr/bin/composer
19
20  # Set working directory
21  WORKDIR /var/www/html
22
23  # Copy application files
24  COPY . /var/www/html/
25
26  # Install dependencies
27  RUN composer install --no-dev --optimize-autoloader
28
29  # Set permissions
30  RUN chown -R www-data:www-data /var/www/html \
31      && chmod -R 755 /var/www/html
32
33  # Configure Apache
34  COPY docker/apache.conf /etc/apache2/sites-available/000-default.conf
35
36  EXPOSE 80
37
38  CMD ["apache2-foreground"]
```

The Apache configuration for containerized deployment:

```
1   # docker/apache.conf
2   <VirtualHost *:80>
3       DocumentRoot /var/www/html/public
4
5       <Directory /var/www/html/public>
6           Options Indexes FollowSymLinks
7           AllowOverride All
8           Require all granted
9       </Directory>
10
11      ErrorLog ${APACHE_LOG_DIR}/error.log
```

```apache
12    CustomLog ${APACHE_LOG_DIR}/access.log combined
13 </VirtualHost>
```

Deploying containers to Amazon ECS (Elastic Container Service):

```json
1  // task-definition.json
2  {
3    "family": "myapp",
4    "networkMode": "awsvpc",
5    "requiresCompatibilities": ["FARGATE"],
6    "cpu": "512",
7    "memory": "1024",
8    "containerDefinitions": [
9      {
10       "name": "myapp",
11       "image": "123456789.dkr.ecr.us-east-1.amazonaws.com/myapp:latest",
12       "portMappings": [
13         {
14           "containerPort": 80,
15           "protocol": "tcp"
16         }
17       ],
18       "environment": [
19         {
20           "name": "DB_HOST",
21           "value": "myapp-db.cluster-xxxxx.us-east-1.rds.amazonaws.com"
22         },
23         {
24           "name": "APP_ENV",
25           "value": "production"
26         }
27       ],
28       "secrets": [
29         {
30           "name": "DB_PASSWORD",
31           "valueFrom": "arn:aws:secretsmanager:us-east-1:123456789:secret:db-password"
32         }
33       ],
34       "logConfiguration": {
35         "logDriver": "awslogs",
36         "options": {
37           "awslogs-group": "/ecs/myapp",
```

```
38              "awslogs-region": "us-east-1",
39              "awslogs-stream-prefix": "ecs"
40          }
41        }
42      }
43    ]
44 }
```

This container-based approach ensures consistency across environments and simplifies scaling. ECS manages container placement, health monitoring, and automatic recovery of failed containers.

11.5 Infrastructure as Code and Automation

11.5.1 Understanding the Paradigm Shift

You have now successfully deployed a web application by hand. While this is a crucial skill for understanding how servers work, it is not how modern applications are managed at scale. In this section, we will introduce you to the concept of 'Infrastructure as Code', a foundational principle of modern DevOps that automates this entire process. You are not expected to master these tools yet, but to understand the problem they solve and the new paradigm they represent.

From a web development perspective, this section plays a critical role. It is the conceptual bridge between traditional system administration and modern DevOps. The manual deployment processes you have learned, such as SSHing into servers, running apt-get commands, and editing configuration files, form the foundation of what we are about to automate. Understanding both approaches makes you a more effective developer and prepares you for the reality of modern web application deployment.

11.5.2 Configuration Management

Infrastructure as Code (IaC) fundamentally transforms how we manage servers and deploy applications. Instead of connecting to each server and manually running commands, we define our desired server state in text files. These files can be version controlled, reviewed, and executed repeatedly with consistent results.

Consider the problem: you have successfully configured one web server, but now you need ten more for scaling. Manually repeating the setup process on each server would take hours and inevitably lead to inconsistencies. Someone might forget a step, install a slightly different package version, or make a typo in a configuration file. These small differences accumulate into "configuration drift," making troubleshooting extremely difficult.

Configuration management tools solve this by treating infrastructure as software. Ansible, a popular choice for LAMP stacks, demonstrates this approach.

Here is a simple example that automates what you previously did manually:

```
1 # webserver.yml - Basic LAMP server configuration
2 ---
```

```yaml
 3  - name: Configure LAMP Server
 4    hosts: webservers
 5    become: yes
 6
 7    tasks:
 8      - name: Install Apache and PHP
 9        apt:
10          name:
11            - apache2
12            - php
13            - libapache2-mod-php
14            - php-mysql
15          state: present
16          update_cache: yes
17
18      - name: Start Apache service
19        service:
20          name: apache2
21          state: started
22          enabled: yes
23
24      - name: Deploy application code
25        git:
26          repo: https://github.com/company/myapp.git
27          dest: /var/www/html
28          version: main
29
30      - name: Set proper permissions
31        file:
32          path: /var/www/html
33          owner: www-data
34          group: www-data
35          recurse: yes
```

This playbook replaces dozens of manual commands with a declarative description of the desired state. Running `ansible-playbook webserver.yml` configures any number of servers identically. If you need to add Redis caching to all servers, you simply add a task and run the playbook again.

The real power emerges when managing multiple environments. Variables allow the same playbook to configure development, staging, and production differently:

```yaml
1  # group_vars/production.yml
2  app_debug: false
```

```
3  php_memory_limit: "256M"
4  domain: "myapp.com"
5
6  # group_vars/development.yml
7  app_debug: true
8  php_memory_limit: "128M"
9  domain: "dev.myapp.local"
```

11.5.3 Automated Provisioning

While configuration management handles software installation on existing servers, automated provisioning creates the servers themselves. This represents an even more dramatic shift from traditional approaches. Instead of ordering physical hardware or manually launching cloud instances, you describe your infrastructure in code. Terraform exemplifies this approach.

Here is a minimal example that creates the infrastructure for a LAMP application:

```
1  # main.tf - Basic LAMP infrastructure
2  provider "aws" {
3    region = "us-east-1"
4  }
5
6  # Create a web server
7  resource "aws_instance" "web" {
8    ami           = "ami-0c02fb55956c7d316"  # Ubuntu 20.04
9    instance_type = "t3.small"
10
11   tags = {
12     Name = "lamp-web-server"
13   }
14
15   user_data = <<-EOF
16     #!/bin/bash
17     apt-get update
18     apt-get install -y apache2 php libapache2-mod-php php-mysql
19     systemctl start apache2
20   EOF
21 }
22
23 # Create a database
24 resource "aws_db_instance" "mysql" {
25   identifier    = "lamp-database"
26   engine        = "mysql"
```

```
27   engine_version = "8.0"
28   instance_class = "db.t3.micro"
29   allocated_storage = 20
30
31   db_name  = "myapp"
32   username = "admin"
33   password = "changeme123!"   # Use secrets management in production
34
35   skip_final_snapshot = true
36 }
37
38 # Output connection information
39 output "web_server_ip" {
40   value = aws_instance.web.public_ip
41 }
42
43 output "database_endpoint" {
44   value = aws_db_instance.mysql.endpoint
45 }
```

Running `terraform apply` creates this entire infrastructure. Running `terraform destroy` removes it completely. This ability to create and destroy infrastructure on demand revolutionizes how we think about servers. They become ephemeral resources rather than long-lived pets we carefully maintain.

The implications are profound. Need a test environment for two hours? Create it, use it, destroy it. Want to ensure staging exactly matches production? Use the same Terraform code with different variables. Concerned about disaster recovery? Your entire infrastructure can be recreated from these text files.

11.5.4 Practical Integration

Understanding how these tools work together helps clarify their roles. A typical workflow proceeds in three stages. First, Terraform creates the infrastructure, including servers, databases, and load balancers. Second, Ansible configures the servers by installing software and deploying code. Third, Git manages both sets of files, treating infrastructure and configuration as code.

Here is a simplified example showing the integration:

```
1 # Step 1: Create infrastructure
2 cd terraform/
3 terraform init
4 terraform apply
5
6 # Step 2: Get the server IPs from Terraform
7 terraform output -json > ../ansible/inventory.json
```

```
 8
 9  # Step 3: Configure the servers
10  cd ../ansible/
11  ansible-playbook -i inventory.json site.yml
12
13  # Everything is version controlled
14  git add .
15  git commit -m "Add web server infrastructure and configuration"
16  git push
```

This automation does not eliminate the need for understanding the underlying processes. When Terraform fails to create a security group, you need to understand networking. When Ansible cannot connect, you need to understand SSH. The tools automate repetitive tasks but require solid foundational knowledge to use effectively.

11.5.5   The Learning Path Forward

As a web developer, you do not need to become a Terraform expert immediately. Start by understanding the problems these tools solve. Repeatability ensures you can deploy the same application identically every time. Version control allows you to track infrastructure changes like code changes. Collaboration improves because team members can review and understand infrastructure. Speed increases dramatically, allowing you to deploy complete environments in minutes instead of days. Finally, cost optimization becomes possible because you can create resources only when needed and destroy them when finished.

Begin with simple experiments. Use Ansible to automate one repetitive task. Create a single server with Terraform. Gradually expand as you become comfortable with the concepts.

Most importantly, recognize that Infrastructure as Code represents a fundamental shift in how we think about servers and deployment. Instead of artisanal, hand-crafted servers, we have reproducible, disposable infrastructure. This shift enables the rapid deployment and scaling that modern web applications require.

The next sections will explore how these automated approaches enable sophisticated deployment strategies and operational practices that would be impossibly complex with manual processes. The foundation you have built understanding manual deployment makes these advanced concepts accessible and practical.

11.6   Monitoring and Performance

11.6.1   Application Monitoring

Effective monitoring serves as the eyes and ears of your production environment, providing visibility into how your LAMP application performs under real-world conditions. Without proper monitoring, problems often go unnoticed until users complain, by which time significant damage to user experience or business operations may have already occurred. Modern monitoring encompasses multiple layers, from infrastructure metrics like CPU usage to application-specific measurements like page load times and business metrics like order completion rates.

The foundation of any monitoring strategy begins with understanding what to monitor. Infrastructure metrics tell you about the health of your servers and services. These include CPU utilization, memory usage, disk I/O, and network throughput. For a LAMP stack, you also need to monitor Apache's request handling, PHP's execution times, and MySQL's query performance. However, infrastructure metrics alone provide an incomplete picture. Application metrics reveal how your code performs in production, tracking response times, error rates, and throughput. Business metrics connect technical performance to business outcomes, measuring user registrations, order values, or any other key performance indicators relevant to your application.

Let us start with basic server monitoring using built-in Linux tools, then progress to comprehensive monitoring solutions. Every Linux system provides fundamental monitoring capabilities through command-line tools.

Understanding these tools helps diagnose problems even when sophisticated monitoring systems are unavailable:

```bash
#!/bin/bash
# basic-monitoring.sh - Server health check script

echo "=== Server Health Report - $(date) ==="

# CPU Usage
top -bn1 | grep "Cpu(s)" | awk '{print "CPU: User: " $2 "%, System: " $4 "%"}'

# Memory Usage
free -h | grep "Mem:" | awk '{print "Memory: " $3 " used of " $2}'

# Disk Usage
df -h / | grep -v Filesystem | awk '{print "Disk: " $5 " used"}'

# Service Status
for service in apache2 mysql php7.4-fpm; do
    systemctl is-active --quiet $service && echo "$service: Running" || echo "$service: DOWN"
done

# Recent Errors
echo "Recent Apache Errors:"
tail -n 5 /var/log/apache2/error.log
```

While command-line tools provide immediate insight, production environments require continuous monitoring with historical data and alerting capabilities. Prometheus has emerged as a leading open-source monitoring solution, particularly well-suited for cloud-native environments. Combined with Grafana for visualization, it provides a powerful monitoring stack for LAMP applications.

Setting up Prometheus begins with installing the server and configuring it to scrape metrics from your applications and infrastructure:

```yaml
# /etc/prometheus/prometheus.yml - Prometheus configuration
global:
  scrape_interval: 15s
  evaluation_interval: 15s

scrape_configs:
  # System metrics via Node Exporter
  - job_name: 'node'
    static_configs:
      - targets: ['localhost:9100']

  # Apache metrics
  - job_name: 'apache'
    static_configs:
      - targets: ['localhost:9117']

  # MySQL metrics
  - job_name: 'mysql'
    static_configs:
      - targets: ['localhost:9104']

  # PHP-FPM metrics
  - job_name: 'php-fpm'
    static_configs:
      - targets: ['localhost:9253']
```

Each exporter collects specific metrics. The Node Exporter provides system-level metrics, Apache Exporter monitors web server performance, MySQL Exporter tracks database metrics, and PHP-FPM Exporter monitors PHP process pools.

Installing these exporters on your servers enables comprehensive monitoring:

```bash
# Install Node Exporter
wget https://github.com/prometheus/node_exporter/releases/download/v1.3.1/node_exporter-1.3.1.linux-amd64.tar.gz
tar xvf node_exporter-1.3.1.linux-amd64.tar.gz
sudo cp node_exporter-1.3.1.linux-amd64/node_exporter /usr/local/bin/
sudo systemctl enable --now node_exporter
```

For Apache monitoring, enable the status module and configure the exporter:

```
1  # Enable Apache status module
2  <Location "/server-status">
3      SetHandler server-status
4      Require ip 127.0.0.1
5  </Location>
6  ExtendedStatus On
```

Grafana transforms raw metrics into actionable insights through visualization. Create comprehensive dashboards that display system health, application performance, and business metrics. A well-designed dashboard includes request rates showing traffic patterns, response time percentiles revealing user experience, error rates highlighting problems, system resource usage preventing capacity issues, and business metrics demonstrating value.

11.6.2 Performance Optimization

Performance optimization transforms monitoring insights into tangible improvements. The process begins with establishing baselines, identifying bottlenecks, implementing optimizations, and measuring results. Each layer of the LAMP stack offers optimization opportunities, from Apache configuration to PHP code efficiency to MySQL query tuning.

Apache optimization starts with selecting the appropriate Multi-Processing Module (MPM) for your workload. The prefork MPM creates separate processes for each request, providing excellent stability but consuming more memory. The worker MPM uses threads within processes, reducing memory usage but requiring thread-safe PHP extensions.

The event MPM, recommended for modern deployments, handles static content efficiently while delegating dynamic requests to PHP-FPM:

```
1  # /etc/apache2/mods-available/mpm_event.conf
2  <IfModule mpm_event_module>
3      StartServers              2
4      MinSpareThreads          25
5      MaxSpareThreads          75
6      ThreadsPerChild          25
7      MaxRequestWorkers        150
8      MaxConnectionsPerChild   1000
9  </IfModule>
```

These settings require careful tuning based on your server's resources and traffic patterns. Each worker consumes memory, so MaxRequestWorkers multiplied by average memory per request should not exceed available RAM. Monitor memory usage during peak traffic and adjust accordingly. Setting MaxConnectionsPerChild prevents memory leaks by periodically restarting worker processes.

Enabling compression to reduce bandwidth usage and improve page load times:

```apache
1  # Enable compression for text-based content
2  <IfModule mod_deflate.c>
3      AddOutputFilterByType DEFLATE text/html text/css text/javascript
4      AddOutputFilterByType DEFLATE application/javascript application/json
5      SetEnvIfNoCase Request_URI \.(?:gif|jpe?g|png|zip)$ no-gzip
6  </IfModule>
```

Browser caching reduces server load by instructing browsers to reuse static assets:

```apache
1  # Configure browser caching
2  <IfModule mod_expires.c>
3      ExpiresActive On
4      ExpiresByType text/html "access plus 0 seconds"
5      ExpiresByType text/css "access plus 1 month"
6      ExpiresByType application/javascript "access plus 1 month"
7      ExpiresByType image/jpeg "access plus 1 year"
8      ExpiresByType image/png "access plus 1 year"
9  </IfModule>
```

PHP optimization dramatically impacts application performance. OpCache, included with PHP 5.5+, caches compiled PHP bytecode, eliminating the need to parse and compile scripts on each request:

```ini
1  ; /etc/php/7.4/apache2/conf.d/10-opcache.ini
2  [opcache]
3  opcache.enable=1
4  opcache.memory_consumption=128
5  opcache.max_accelerated_files=4000
6  opcache.revalidate_freq=60
7  opcache.fast_shutdown=1
```

Monitoring OpCache effectiveness using built-in functions:

```php
1  <?php
2  // opcache-status.php - Simple OpCache monitor
3  $status = opcache_get_status();
4  $memory = $status['memory_usage'];
5  $stats = $status['opcache_statistics'];
6
```

```php
7  echo "Memory: " . round($memory['used_memory'] / 1024 / 1024, 2) . " MB used\n";
8  echo "Scripts: " . $stats['num_cached_scripts'] . " cached\n";
9  echo "Hit Rate: " . round($stats['hits'] / ($stats['hits'] + $stats['misses']) * 100, 2) . "%\n";
10 ?>
```

Database optimization often provides the greatest performance improvements. Start by analyzing slow queries:

```sql
1  -- Enable slow query log
2  SET GLOBAL slow_query_log = 'ON';
3  SET GLOBAL long_query_time = 2;
4
5  -- Analyze query performance
6  EXPLAIN SELECT u.*, COUNT(o.id) as order_count
7  FROM users u
8  LEFT JOIN orders o ON u.id = o.user_id
9  GROUP BY u.id;
10
11 -- Add appropriate indexes
12 CREATE INDEX idx_orders_user_id ON orders(user_id);
```

Application-level caching reduces database load by storing frequently accessed data:

```php
1  <?php
2  class CacheManager {
3      private $redis;
4      private $ttl = 3600;
5
6      public function __construct() {
7          $this->redis = new Redis();
8          $this->redis->connect('127.0.0.1', 6379);
9      }
10
11     public function remember($key, callable $callback) {
12         $cached = $this->redis->get($key);
13         if ($cached !== false) {
14             return unserialize($cached);
15         }
16
17         $data = $callback();
```

```php
18        $this->redis->setex($key, $this->ttl, serialize($data));
19        return $data;
20    }
21
22    public function forget($key) {
23        return $this->redis->del($key);
24    }
25 }
26
27 // Usage
28 $cache = new CacheManager();
29 $products = $cache->remember('featured_products', function() use ($db) {
30     return $db->query("SELECT * FROM products WHERE featured = 1 LIMIT 10")->fetchAll();
31 });
32 ?>
```

11.6.3   Alerting and Incident Response

Monitoring without alerting is like having smoke detectors without alarms. Effective alerting notifies the right people at the right time with actionable information, enabling rapid response to issues before they impact users.

Define alerts based on Service Level Objectives (SLOs) that reflect user experience rather than arbitrary thresholds. Instead of alerting when CPU usage exceeds 80%, alert when response times exceed acceptable limits or error rates spike:

```yaml
1 # /etc/prometheus/rules/alerts.yml
2 groups:
3   - name: lamp_application
4     rules:
5       - alert: HighErrorRate
6         expr: rate(app_errors_total[5m]) / rate(app_requests_total[5m]) > 0.05
7         for: 5m
8         annotations:
9           summary: "Error rate exceeds 5%"
10
11      - alert: SlowResponseTime
12        expr: histogram_quantile(0.95, app_request_duration_seconds_bucket) > 2
13        for: 10m
14        annotations:
15          summary: "95th percentile response time exceeds 2 seconds"
16
17      - alert: DatabaseDown
18        expr: mysql_up == 0
```

```
19        for: 1m
20        annotations:
21          summary: "MySQL database is unreachable"
```

Configuring Alertmanager to route alerts appropriately and prevent alert fatigue:

```
1  # /etc/alertmanager/alertmanager.yml
2  route:
3    receiver: 'team-backend'
4    routes:
5      - match:
6          severity: critical
7        receiver: 'pagerduty-critical'
8      - match:
9          team: database
10       receiver: 'team-database'
11
12 receivers:
13   - name: 'team-backend'
14     email_configs:
15       - to: 'backend-team@example.com'
16   - name: 'pagerduty-critical'
17     pagerduty_configs:
18       - service_key: 'your-service-key'
```

Document incident response procedures to ensure consistent and effective responses. Create comprehensive runbooks that guide engineers through common issues. A well-structured runbook should include severity levels, response processes, and specific solutions for common problems.

Start with defining severity levels that match your organization's needs. P1 Critical issues represent complete service outages or data loss risks requiring response within 15 minutes. Examples include database failures or site unreachability. P2 High severity covers major functionality impairments like payment processing failures requiring response within one hour. P3 Medium issues affect minor functionality with 4-hour response times, while P4 Low severity covers minimal impact issues addressed during business hours.

The response process should follow a consistent pattern. First, acknowledge the alert through your chosen system (whether Slack or PagerDuty) within the defined SLA. Create a dedicated incident channel using a naming convention like `incident-YYYY-MM-DD-description`. Perform initial assessment using quick health checks.

Communication remains critical throughout the incident. Update your status page immediately, notify stakeholders from a pre-defined list, and post updates every 30 minutes even if just to confirm ongoing investigation. During investigation and mitigation, follow specific runbooks for the issue type, consider immediate rollback if a recent deployment caused the problem, and implement temporary fixes when permanent solutions require more time.

For high response time issues, systematically check each layer. Start with the database by examining current processes and identifying long-running queries. Verify PHP-FPM status and restart if necessary. Check cache systems for corruption or connectivity issues.

Database connection errors require verifying basic connectivity first. Test the connection directly, check maximum connection settings, and monitor for connection leaks that might indicate application bugs. If connections are exhausted, increase the limit temporarily while investigating the root cause.

Memory issues require identifying the largest consumers. In emergencies, free memory carefully by clearing caches or restarting memory-heavy services. Always investigate the root cause after immediate mitigation to prevent recurrence.

Rollback procedures vary by deployment method. For containerized deployments, use orchestration tools to revert to previous versions. For traditional deployments, use version control to checkout previous commits and redeploy. Database rollbacks require extra care, using migration systems when possible or restoring from backups when necessary.

Maintain an updated contact list including on-call engineer rotation tracked in PagerDuty, team lead contacts, database administrator numbers, infrastructure team contacts, and management escalation paths. Store these securely but accessible to all team members who might respond to incidents.

This comprehensive monitoring and alerting system provides visibility into your LAMP application's health while enabling rapid response to issues. Regular review and refinement of alerts based on actual incidents ensures the system remains effective without causing alert fatigue.

11.7 Scalability and High Availability

11.7.1 Horizontal vs. Vertical Scaling

Scalability represents the ability of your LAMP application to handle increased load gracefully, whether from growing user bases, seasonal traffic spikes, or viral content. Understanding the two fundamental approaches to scaling helps make informed architectural decisions that balance performance, cost, and complexity.

Vertical scaling, also known as scaling up, involves adding more resources to existing servers. This might mean upgrading from a server with 4GB RAM to one with 16GB, or moving from 2 CPU cores to 8 cores. Vertical scaling offers the simplest path to improved performance because it requires no application changes. Your PHP code continues running on a single server, database queries work unchanged, and file uploads remain in local directories. This simplicity makes vertical scaling the natural first choice for growing applications.

Consider a typical progression for a LAMP application experiencing growth. Initially, your application runs comfortably on a modest server, perhaps a t3.small instance on AWS with 2 vCPUs and 2GB RAM. As traffic increases, you notice response times lengthening during peak hours. The immediate solution involves upgrading to a t3.medium (2 vCPUs, 4GB RAM) or t3.large (2 vCPUs, 8GB RAM). This upgrade process typically requires only a brief downtime for instance resizing:

```
# Stop the instance
aws ec2 stop-instances --instance-ids i-1234567890abcdef0
```

```
3
4  # Modify instance type
5  aws ec2 modify-instance-attribute \
6      --instance-id i-1234567890abcdef0 \
7      --instance-type "{\"Value\": \"t3.large\"}"
8
9  # Start the instance
10 aws ec2 start-instances --instance-ids i-1234567890abcdef0
```

However, vertical scaling faces inherent limitations. Even the largest available instances have finite resources. AWS's largest general-purpose instance, the m5.24xlarge, provides 96 vCPUs and 384GB RAM, but costs over $4,000 per month. More critically, vertical scaling creates a single point of failure. If your one large server fails, your entire application becomes unavailable. This risk becomes unacceptable for business-critical applications.

Horizontal scaling, or scaling out, addresses these limitations by distributing load across multiple servers. Instead of one large server, you run multiple smaller servers behind a load balancer. This approach offers virtually unlimited scaling potential since you can always add more servers. It also provides redundancy, as the failure of one server does not bring down the entire application. However, horizontal scaling requires significant application changes to handle distributed state and resources.

The transition from vertical to horizontal scaling represents a crucial architectural evolution. Applications designed for single servers often make assumptions that break in distributed environments. PHP sessions stored in local files will not be accessible when users hit different servers. File uploads saved to local directories disappear when accessed from another server. Database connections may overwhelm a single MySQL instance when multiple application servers connect simultaneously.

Preparing for horizontal scaling requires addressing each of these challenges systematically. Session management must move from local file storage to a centralized system. Redis provides an excellent solution for distributed session storage:

```
1  // config/session.php - Configure Redis session handling
2  ini_set('session.save_handler', 'redis');
3  ini_set('session.save_path', 'tcp://redis-server.example.com:6379?auth=password');
4
5  // Alternatively, use PHP configuration
6  session_save_path("tcp://redis-server.example.com:6379?auth=password");
7  session_save_handler("redis");
8
9  // For clustered Redis
10 ini_set('session.save_path',
11     'tcp://redis1:6379?auth=pass&weight=1&timeout=2.5,' .
12     'tcp://redis2:6379?auth=pass&weight=2&timeout=2.5'
13 );
```

File storage requires similar centralization. Instead of saving uploads to local directories, use object storage services:

```php
// upload-handler.php - Centralized file storage
use Aws\S3\S3Client;

class FileUploadHandler {
    private $s3;
    private $bucket;

    public function __construct() {
        $this->s3 = new S3Client([
            'version' => 'latest',
            'region'  => 'us-east-1'
        ]);
        $this->bucket = 'myapp-uploads';
    }

    public function handleUpload($file) {
        // Generate unique filename
        $filename = uniqid() . '_' . $file['name'];
        $key = 'uploads/' . date('Y/m/d') . '/' . $filename;

        try {
            // Upload to S3 instead of local filesystem
            $result = $this->s3->putObject([
                'Bucket' => $this->bucket,
                'Key'    => $key,
                'Body'   => fopen($file['tmp_name'], 'r'),
                'ACL'    => 'public-read',
                'ContentType' => $file['type']
            ]);

            return $result['ObjectURL'];
        } catch (Exception $e) {
            error_log("Upload failed: " . $e->getMessage());
            return false;
        }
    }

    public function serveFile($key) {
        // Generate presigned URL for private files
```

```php
40        $cmd = $this->s3->getCommand('GetObject', [
41            'Bucket' => $this->bucket,
42            'Key'    => $key
43        ]);
44
45        $request = $this->s3->createPresignedRequest($cmd, '+20 minutes');
46        return (string) $request->getUri();
47    }
48 }
```

Database scaling presents unique challenges since databases maintain state and require consistency. Read-heavy applications benefit from read replicas that distribute SELECT queries across multiple database instances while maintaining a single primary for writes:

```php
1  // database-manager.php - Read replica support
2  class DatabaseManager {
3      private $primary;
4      private $replicas = [];
5      private $currentReplica = 0;
6
7      public function __construct($primaryConfig, $replicaConfigs) {
8          // Connect to primary database
9          $this->primary = new PDO(
10             "mysql:host={$primaryConfig['host']};dbname={$primaryConfig['db']}",
11             $primaryConfig['user'],
12             $primaryConfig['pass']
13         );
14
15         // Connect to read replicas
16         foreach ($replicaConfigs as $config) {
17             $this->replicas[] = new PDO(
18                 "mysql:host={$config['host']};dbname={$config['db']}",
19                 $config['user'],
20                 $config['pass']
21             );
22         }
23     }
24
25     public function query($sql, $params = []) {
26         // Determine if query is read or write
27         $isWrite = preg_match('/^\s*(INSERT|UPDATE|DELETE|CREATE|ALTER|DROP)/i', $sql);
28
```

```php
29          if ($isWrite) {
30              // All writes go to primary
31              $stmt = $this->primary->prepare($sql);
32              $stmt->execute($params);
33              return $stmt;
34          } else {
35              // Distribute reads across replicas
36              $replica = $this->getNextReplica();
37              $stmt = $replica->prepare($sql);
38              $stmt->execute($params);
39              return $stmt;
40          }
41      }
42
43      private function getNextReplica() {
44          if (empty($this->replicas)) {
45              // Fall back to primary if no replicas
46              return $this->primary;
47          }
48
49          // Round-robin replica selection
50          $replica = $this->replicas[$this->currentReplica];
51          $this->currentReplica = ($this->currentReplica + 1) % count($this->replicas);
52
53          return $replica;
54      }
55
56      public function beginTransaction() {
57          // Transactions must use primary
58          return $this->primary->beginTransaction();
59      }
60 }
```

Load balancing distributes incoming requests across multiple application servers. Hardware load balancers provide excellent performance but cost significantly. Software load balancers like HAProxy or Nginx offer cost-effective alternatives. Cloud providers offer managed load balancing services that handle the complexity of health checks, SSL termination, and traffic distribution.

Implementing a basic Nginx load balancer demonstrates the concept:

```nginx
# /etc/nginx/sites-available/load-balancer.conf
upstream lamp_backend {
```

```nginx
 3      # Define backend servers
 4      server web1.internal:80 weight=3;
 5      server web2.internal:80 weight=2;
 6      server web3.internal:80 weight=1;
 7
 8      # Enable session persistence (sticky sessions)
 9      ip_hash;
10
11      # Mark servers as down after failures
12      server web1.internal:80 max_fails=3 fail_timeout=30s;
13      server web2.internal:80 max_fails=3 fail_timeout=30s;
14      server web3.internal:80 max_fails=3 fail_timeout=30s;
15  }
16  server {
17      listen 80;
18      server_name www.example.com;
19
20      # Forward all requests to backend
21      location / {
22          proxy_pass http://lamp_backend;
23          proxy_set_header Host $host;
24          proxy_set_header X-Real-IP $remote_addr;
25          proxy_set_header X-Forwarded-For $proxy_add_x_forwarded_for;
26          proxy_set_header X-Forwarded-Proto $scheme;
27
28          # Timeouts
29          proxy_connect_timeout 60s;
30          proxy_send_timeout 60s;
31          proxy_read_timeout 60s;
32
33          # Buffering
34          proxy_buffering on;
35          proxy_buffer_size 4k;
36          proxy_buffers 8 4k;
37      }
38      # Health check endpoint
39      location /health {
40          access_log off;
41          return 200 "healthy\n";
42          add_header Content-Type text/plain;
43      }
44  }
```

11.7.2 High Availability Patterns

High availability ensures your application remains accessible despite hardware failures, software bugs, or maintenance activities. The goal involves eliminating single points of failure and implementing automatic recovery mechanisms. Achieving high availability requires redundancy at every layer of your application stack.

The fundamental principle of high availability involves having at least two of everything. Two load balancers prevent the load balancer from becoming a single point of failure. Multiple web servers ensure the application remains available if one server fails. Database replication provides continuity if the primary database server crashes. Even seemingly minor components like DNS benefit from redundancy through multiple name servers.

Implementing high availability starts with load balancer redundancy. Active-passive configurations use virtual IP addresses that float between servers:

```
# keepalived.conf - High availability for load balancers
global_defs {
    router_id LB1
}
vrrp_script check_nginx {
    script "/usr/local/bin/check_nginx.sh"
    interval 2
    weight 2
}
vrrp_instance VI_1 {
    state MASTER
    interface eth0
    virtual_router_id 51
    priority 101
    advert_int 1

    authentication {
        auth_type PASS
        auth_pass secretpass
    }

    virtual_ipaddress {
        192.168.1.100/24
    }

    track_script {
        check_nginx
    }
}
```

The check script monitors Nginx health:

```bash
#!/bin/bash
# /usr/local/bin/check_nginx.sh
if ! pgrep -x "nginx" > /dev/null; then
    exit 1
fi

# Check if Nginx responds
if ! curl -f http://localhost/health > /dev/null 2>&1; then
    exit 1
fi

exit 0
```

Database high availability requires careful planning since databases maintain state. MySQL replication provides the foundation, but automatic failover requires additional orchestration.

Tools like MHA (Master High Availability) or Orchestrator manage failover processes:

```ini
# MHA configuration - /etc/mha/app1.cnf
[server default]
manager_workdir=/var/log/mha/app1
manager_log=/var/log/mha/app1/manager.log

ssh_user=mha
repl_user=replication
repl_password=replpass

master_binlog_dir=/var/lib/mysql
remote_workdir=/tmp

[server1]
hostname=db1.example.com
candidate_master=1
[server2]
hostname=db2.example.com
candidate_master=1
[server3]
hostname=db3.example.com
no_master=1
```

Application-level high availability involves designing for graceful degradation. When external services fail, applications should provide reduced functionality rather than complete failure:

```php
// resilient-service.php - Graceful degradation
class ResilientPaymentService {
    private $primary;
    private $fallback;
    private $cache;

    public function __construct($primaryGateway, $fallbackGateway, $cache) {
        $this->primary = $primaryGateway;
        $this->fallback = $fallbackGateway;
        $this->cache = $cache;
    }

    public function processPayment($order) {
        // Try primary payment gateway
        try {
            $result = $this->primary->charge($order);
            $this->logSuccess('primary', $order->id);
            return $result;
        } catch (Exception $e) {
            error_log("Primary gateway failed: " . $e->getMessage());
        }

        // Try fallback gateway
        try {
            $result = $this->fallback->charge($order);
            $this->logSuccess('fallback', $order->id);
            return $result;
        } catch (Exception $e) {
            error_log("Fallback gateway failed: " . $e->getMessage());
        }

        // Queue for later processing
        return $this->queueForLater($order);
    }

    private function queueForLater($order) {
        // Store in persistent queue
        $this->cache->rpush('payment_queue', json_encode($order));

```

```php
40          // Return pending status
41          return [
42              'status' => 'pending',
43              'message' => 'Payment will be processed shortly',
44              'reference' => $order->id
45          ];
46      }
47
48      public function processQueue() {
49          while ($orderJson = $this->cache->lpop('payment_queue')) {
50              $order = json_decode($orderJson);
51              $this->processPayment($order);
52          }
53      }
54  }
```

Health checks enable automatic detection and recovery from failures. Comprehensive health checks verify all critical components:

```php
1  // health-check.php - Comprehensive health monitoring
2  class HealthChecker {
3      private $checks = [];
4
5      public function addCheck($name, $callback) {
6          $this->checks[$name] = $callback;
7      }
8
9      public function runChecks() {
10         $results = [];
11         $healthy = true;
12
13         foreach ($this->checks as $name => $check) {
14             $start = microtime(true);
15
16             try {
17                 $result = $check();
18                 $results[$name] = [
19                     'status' => 'healthy',
20                     'duration' => microtime(true) - $start,
21                     'details' => $result
22                 ];
23             } catch (Exception $e) {
```

```php
                $healthy = false;
                $results[$name] = [
                    'status' => 'unhealthy',
                    'duration' => microtime(true) - $start,
                    'error' => $e->getMessage()
                ];
            }
        }

        return [
            'status' => $healthy ? 'healthy' : 'unhealthy',
            'timestamp' => time(),
            'checks' => $results
        ];
    }
}

// Configure health checks
$health = new HealthChecker();

$health->addCheck('database', function() {
    $pdo = new PDO('mysql:host=localhost;dbname=app', 'user', 'pass');
    $result = $pdo->query('SELECT 1')->fetchColumn();
    return ['connected' => true, 'response' => $result];
});

$health->addCheck('cache', function() {
    $redis = new Redis();
    $redis->connect('localhost', 6379);
    $redis->set('health_check', time());
    return ['connected' => true, 'latency' => $redis->ping()];
});

$health->addCheck('filesystem', function() {
    $testFile = '/tmp/health_check_' . uniqid();
    file_put_contents($testFile, 'test');
    $contents = file_get_contents($testFile);
    unlink($testFile);
    return ['writable' => true, 'content_match' => $contents === 'test'];
});

// Expose health endpoint
if ($_SERVER['REQUEST_URI'] === '/health') {
```

```php
67    header('Content-Type: application/json');
68    $results = $health->runChecks();
69    http_response_code($results['status'] === 'healthy' ? 200 : 503);
70    echo json_encode($results);
71    exit;
72 }
```

11.7.3   Content Delivery Networks

Content Delivery Networks (CDNs) represent a crucial component of scalable web architecture, distributing static content across global edge locations to reduce latency and server load. For LAMP applications, CDNs dramatically improve user experience by serving images, CSS, JavaScript, and other static assets from servers geographically close to users.

Understanding CDN operation helps optimize their use. When a user requests a static asset, the CDN checks if it has a cached copy at the nearest edge location. If found, the asset is served immediately with minimal latency. If not, the CDN fetches the asset from your origin server, caches it, and serves it to the user. Subsequent requests for the same asset from that geographic region are served from the cache until it expires.

Implementing CDN support requires modifying how your application generates asset URLs. Instead of relative paths, use absolute URLs pointing to the CDN:

```php
1 // cdn-helper.php - CDN URL generation
2 class CDNHelper {
3     private $cdnUrl;
4     private $version;
5     private $enabled;
6
7     public function __construct($config) {
8         $this->cdnUrl = $config['cdn_url'];
9         $this->version = $config['app_version'];
10        $this->enabled = $config['cdn_enabled'];
11    }
12
13    public function asset($path) {
14        // Strip leading slash
15        $path = ltrim($path, '/');
16
17        // In development, use local assets
18        if (!$this->enabled) {
19            return '/' . $path;
20        }
21
22        // Add version for cache busting
```

```php
        $separator = strpos($path, '?') === false ? '?' : '&';
        $versionedPath = $path . $separator . 'v=' . $this->version;

        // Return full CDN URL
        return $this->cdnUrl . '/' . $versionedPath;
    }

    public function image($path, $options = []) {
        $url = $this->asset($path);

        // Add image transformation parameters if CDN supports it
        if (!empty($options)) {
            $params = http_build_query($options);
            $separator = strpos($url, '?') === false ? '?' : '&';
            $url .= $separator . $params;
        }

        return $url;
    }
}

// Usage in templates
$cdn = new CDNHelper([
    'cdn_url' => 'https://cdn.example.com',
    'app_version' => '1.2.3',
    'cdn_enabled' => true
]);

// In your HTML
echo '<link rel="stylesheet" href="' . $cdn->asset('css/style.css') . '">';
echo '<script src="' . $cdn->asset('js/app.js') . '"></script>';
echo '<img src="' . $cdn->image('images/logo.png', ['w' => 200, 'h' => 100]) . '">';
```

Configuring your web server to set appropriate cache headers for CDN optimization:

```apache
# .htaccess - CDN-friendly headers
<IfModule mod_expires.c>
    ExpiresActive On

    # Images
    ExpiresByType image/jpeg "access plus 1 year"
    ExpiresByType image/png "access plus 1 year"
```

```apache
8      ExpiresByType image/gif "access plus 1 year"
9      ExpiresByType image/webp "access plus 1 year"
10     ExpiresByType image/svg+xml "access plus 1 year"
11
12     # CSS and JavaScript
13     ExpiresByType text/css "access plus 1 month"
14     ExpiresByType application/javascript "access plus 1 month"
15
16     # Fonts
17     ExpiresByType font/woff2 "access plus 1 year"
18     ExpiresByType font/woff "access plus 1 year"
19     ExpiresByType font/ttf "access plus 1 year"
20 </IfModule>
21
22 <IfModule mod_headers.c>
23     # CORS headers for CDN
24     Header set Access-Control-Allow-Origin "*"
25
26     # Cache-Control for CDN
27     <FilesMatch "\.(jpg|jpeg|png|gif|webp|css|js|woff|woff2|ttf)$">
28         Header set Cache-Control "public, max-age=31536000, immutable"
29     </FilesMatch>
30
31     # Vary header for proper caching
32     Header append Vary Accept-Encoding
33 </IfModule>
```

Implementing a CDN pull zone requires configuring the CDN to fetch content from your origin server. Most CDNs support custom cache keys and purging mechanisms:

```php
1  // cdn-purge.php - Purge CDN cache when content updates
2  class CDNPurger {
3      private $apiKey;
4      private $zoneId;
5      private $apiUrl;
6
7      public function __construct($apiKey, $zoneId) {
8          $this->apiKey = $apiKey;
9          $this->zoneId = $zoneId;
10         $this->apiUrl = 'https://api.cdn.com/v1';
11     }
12
```

```php
13    public function purgeUrl($url) {
14        $response = $this->makeRequest('POST', '/purge', [
15            'urls' => [$url]
16        ]);
17
18        return $response['success'];
19    }
20
21    public function purgeTag($tag) {
22        $response = $this->makeRequest('POST', '/purge', [
23            'tags' => [$tag]
24        ]);
25
26        return $response['success'];
27    }
28
29    public function purgeAll() {
30        $response = $this->makeRequest('POST', '/purge', [
31            'purge_all' => true
32        ]);
33
34        return $response['success'];
35    }
36
37    private function makeRequest($method, $endpoint, $data) {
38        $ch = curl_init($this->apiUrl . $endpoint);
39
40        curl_setopt_array($ch, [
41            CURLOPT_CUSTOMREQUEST => $method,
42            CURLOPT_POSTFIELDS => json_encode($data),
43            CURLOPT_RETURNTRANSFER => true,
44            CURLOPT_HTTPHEADER => [
45                'Authorization: Bearer ' . $this->apiKey,
46                'Content-Type: application/json'
47            ]
48        ]);
49
50        $response = curl_exec($ch);
51        $httpCode = curl_getinfo($ch, CURLINFO_HTTP_CODE);
52        curl_close($ch);
53
54        if ($httpCode !== 200) {
55            throw new Exception("CDN API error: HTTP $httpCode");
```

```php
56          }
57
58          return json_decode($response, true);
59      }
60 }
61
62 // Usage when updating content
63 $cdn = new CDNPurger('your-api-key', 'zone-123');
64
65 // Purge specific URL
66 $cdn->purgeUrl('https://cdn.example.com/images/header.jpg');
67
68 // Purge by tag
69 $cdn->purgeTag('homepage-assets');
70
71 // Purge everything (use sparingly)
72 $cdn->purgeAll();
```

Monitoring CDN performance ensures optimal configuration. Track cache hit ratios, bandwidth savings, and response times:

```php
1 // cdn-analytics.php - Monitor CDN performance
2 class CDNAnalytics {
3     private $apiClient;
4
5     public function getCacheHitRatio($startDate, $endDate) {
6         $stats = $this->apiClient->getStats([
7             'start' => $startDate,
8             'end' => $endDate,
9             'metrics' => ['requests', 'cache_hits']
10        ]);
11
12        $totalRequests = $stats['requests'];
13        $cacheHits = $stats['cache_hits'];
14
15        return $totalRequests > 0 ? ($cacheHits / $totalRequests) * 100 : 0;
16    }
17
18    public function getBandwidthSavings($startDate, $endDate) {
19        $stats = $this->apiClient->getStats([
20            'start' => $startDate,
21            'end' => $endDate,
```

```
22          'metrics' => ['bandwidth_cached', 'bandwidth_total']
23      ]);
24
25      return [
26          'saved_gb' => $stats['bandwidth_cached'] / 1024 / 1024 / 1024,
27          'total_gb' => $stats['bandwidth_total'] / 1024 / 1024 / 1024,
28          'savings_percent' => ($stats['bandwidth_cached'] / $stats['bandwidth_total']) * 100
29      ];
30  }
31
32  public function getPopularAssets($limit = 10) {
33      return $this->apiClient->getTopAssets([
34          'limit' => $limit,
35          'order_by' => 'requests',
36          'period' => '24h'
37      ]);
38  }
39 }
```

Advanced CDN features enhance performance further. Edge computing allows running code at CDN edge locations, reducing origin requests. Image optimization automatically resizes and compresses images based on device capabilities. HTTP/2 server push preemptively sends assets the browser will need.

Implementing these scalability and high availability patterns transforms LAMP applications from single-server deployments to globally distributed systems capable of handling millions of users. The journey requires careful planning and systematic implementation, but the result is a robust application that remains available and responsive regardless of load or failures.

11.8　Troubleshooting and Maintenance

11.8.1　Common Web Server Issues

Every web application encounters issues. Systematic troubleshooting resolves problems efficiently.

504 Gateway Timeout: Often indicates PHP scripts running too long:

```
# Check PHP-FPM status
systemctl status php7.4-fpm

# Review PHP-FPM logs
tail -f /var/log/php7.4-fpm.log

# Increase timeout settings
# In Apache
```

```
9  TimeOut 300
10 ProxyTimeout 300
11
12 # In PHP-FPM pool configuration
13 request_terminate_timeout = 300
14
15 # In PHP
16 max_execution_time = 300
```

403 Forbidden Errors: Usually permission or configuration issues:

```
1  # Check file permissions
2  ls -la /var/www/html/
3  # Fix ownership
4  chown -R www-data:www-data /var/www/html/
5
6  # Check Apache configuration
7  apache2ctl configtest
8
9  # Review .htaccess for deny rules
10 cat /var/www/html/.htaccess | grep -i deny
11
12 # Check SELinux (if enabled)
13 getenforce
14 semanage fcontext -a -t httpd_sys_content_t "/var/www/html(/.*)?"
15 restorecon -Rv /var/www/html/
```

Memory Exhaustion: PHP running out of memory:

```
1  // Temporary increase for specific script
2  ini_set('memory_limit', '512M');
3
4  // Better: Optimize the code
5  // Instead of loading all records:
6  $allUsers = $db->query("SELECT * FROM users")->fetchAll();
7
8  // Process in batches:
9  $offset = 0;
10 $limit = 1000;
11 while ($users = $db->query("SELECT * FROM users LIMIT $limit OFFSET $offset")->fetchAll()) {
```

```php
12    foreach ($users as $user) {
13        // Process user
14    }
15    $offset += $limit;
16
17    // Free memory
18    unset($users);
19 }
```

Slow Page Loads: Requires systematic investigation:

```bash
1  # 1. Check server resources
2  top
3  iostat -x 1
4
5  # 2. Monitor Apache requests
6  watch -n 1 'apache2ctl fullstatus | grep -E "requests|Scoreboard"'
7
8  # 3. Enable slow query log in MySQL
9  SET GLOBAL slow_query_log = 'ON';
10 SET GLOBAL long_query_time = 2;
11
12 # 4. Profile PHP execution
13 # Install XDebug or use built-in profiling
14 <?php
15 $start = microtime(true);
16 // Code to profile
17 $duration = microtime(true) - $start;
18 error_log("Operation took: $duration seconds");
```

11.8.2 Debugging Tools and Techniques

Effective debugging combines multiple tools and approaches.

Log Analysis: Centralize and analyze logs systematically:

```bash
1  # Combine logs for analysis
2  tail -f /var/log/apache2/error.log /var/log/php7.4-fpm.log /var/log/mysql/error.log
3
4  # Search for patterns
5  grep -i "fatal error" /var/log/apache2/error.log | tail -20
6
```

```
7  # Count errors by type
8  awk '{print $9}' /var/log/apache2/access.log | sort | uniq -c | sort -rn | head -20
9
10 # Monitor real-time with filtering
11 tail -f /var/log/apache2/access.log | grep -v "GET /health"
```

Browser Developer Tools: Modern browsers provide powerful debugging capabilities. The Network tab shows request timing and identifies slow resources. The Console reveals JavaScript errors that might affect functionality. Performance profiling identifies rendering bottlenecks.

Application Profiling: Use APM tools or add custom profiling:

```
1  class Profiler {
2      private $timers = [];
3
4      public function start($name) {
5          $this->timers[$name] = microtime(true);
6      }
7
8      public function end($name) {
9          if (!isset($this->timers[$name])) return;
10
11         $duration = microtime(true) - $this->timers[$name];
12         error_log(sprintf("Profile: %s took %.4f seconds", $name, $duration));
13
14         if ($duration > 1.0) {
15             error_log("WARNING: Slow operation detected: $name");
16         }
17     }
18 }
19
20 // Usage
21 $profiler = new Profiler();
22
23 $profiler->start('database_query');
24 $results = $db->query($complexQuery);
25 $profiler->end('database_query');
26
27 $profiler->start('api_call');
28 $response = file_get_contents('https://api.example.com/data');
29 $profiler->end('api_call');
```

Debugging Production Issues: Sometimes issues only occur in production. Safe debugging techniques include:

```php
// Conditional debug logging
if ($_GET['debug'] === 'secret_key') {
    ini_set('display_errors', 1);
    error_reporting(E_ALL);
}

// Detailed logging for specific users
if ($_SESSION['user_id'] === 12345) {
    error_log("Debug for user 12345: " . print_r($_POST, true));
}

// Feature flags for gradual rollout
if (FeatureFlag::isEnabled('new_checkout_flow', $user)) {
    // New code
} else {
    // Old code
}
```

11.8.3 Maintenance Best Practices

Regular maintenance prevents issues and ensures optimal performance.

Automated Backups:

```bash
#!/bin/bash
# backup.sh - Daily backup script
DATE=$(date +%Y%m%d)
BACKUP_DIR="/backups/$DATE"

# Create backup directory
mkdir -p $BACKUP_DIR

# Backup database
mysqldump -u root -p$MYSQL_PASSWORD \
    --all-databases \
    --single-transaction \
    --routines \
    --triggers \
    > $BACKUP_DIR/mysql_backup.sql
```

```bash
16
17 # Backup application files
18 tar -czf $BACKUP_DIR/www_backup.tar.gz /var/www/html/
19
20 # Backup Apache configuration
21 tar -czf $BACKUP_DIR/apache_config.tar.gz /etc/apache2/
22
23 # Upload to S3
24 aws s3 sync $BACKUP_DIR s3://my-backup-bucket/daily/$DATE/
25
26 # Clean old local backups (keep 7 days)
27 find /backups -type d -mtime +7 -exec rm -rf {} +
28
29 # Verify backup
30 if [ -f $BACKUP_DIR/mysql_backup.sql ]; then
31     echo "Backup successful for $DATE"
32 else
33     echo "Backup failed for $DATE" | mail -s "Backup Failure" admin@example.com
34 fi
```

Security Updates:

```bash
1  # Regular security patching
2  #!/bin/bash
3  # security-updates.sh
4
5  # Update package lists
6  apt-get update
7
8  # Check for security updates
9  UPDATES=$(apt-get -s upgrade | grep -i security | wc -l)
10
11 if [ $UPDATES -gt 0 ]; then
12     echo "Security updates available: $UPDATES"
13
14     # Apply security updates only
15     apt-get -y upgrade $(apt-get --just-print upgrade | \
16         grep -i security | \
17         awk '{print $2}')
18
19     # Restart services if needed
20     systemctl restart apache2
```

```bash
21    systemctl restart php7.4-fpm
22    systemctl restart mysql
23
24    # Log update
25    echo "$(date): Applied $UPDATES security updates" >> /var/log/maintenance.log
26 fi
```

Performance Monitoring:

```bash
1  # Create monthly performance report
2  #!/bin/bash
3  # performance-report.sh
4
5  REPORT_FILE="/tmp/performance_report_$(date +%Y%m).txt"
6  echo "Monthly Performance Report" > $REPORT_FILE
7  echo "==========================" >> $REPORT_FILE
8  echo "" >> $REPORT_FILE
9
10 # Apache statistics
11 echo "Apache Statistics:" >> $REPORT_FILE
12 apache2ctl status | grep -E "Total accesses|Total Traffic" >> $REPORT_FILE
13 echo "" >> $REPORT_FILE
14
15 # MySQL statistics
16 echo "MySQL Statistics:" >> $REPORT_FILE
17 mysql -e "SHOW GLOBAL STATUS LIKE 'Questions';
18         SHOW GLOBAL STATUS LIKE 'Slow_queries';
19         SHOW GLOBAL STATUS LIKE 'Connections';" >> $REPORT_FILE
20 echo "" >> $REPORT_FILE
21
22 # Disk usage trends
23 echo "Disk Usage:" >> $REPORT_FILE
24 df -h | grep -E "Filesystem|/dev/" >> $REPORT_FILE
25 echo "" >> $REPORT_FILE
26
27 # Top processes
28 echo "Top Processes by CPU:" >> $REPORT_FILE
29 ps aux --sort=-%cpu | head -10 >> $REPORT_FILE
30
31 # Send report
32 mail -s "Monthly Performance Report" admin@example.com < $REPORT_FILE
```

Documentation Maintenance: Keep documentation current:

```
# Production Runbook

## Server Information
- Web Servers: web1.example.com, web2.example.com
- Database: db1.example.com (primary), db2.example.com (replica)
- Load Balancer: lb.example.com
- Monitoring: monitor.example.com

## Common Procedures

### Rolling Restart
1. Remove server from load balancer
2. Perform maintenance
3. Verify service health
4. Return to load balancer
5. Wait 5 minutes before next server

### Database Failover
1. Verify replica is in sync
2. Stop replication on replica
3. Promote replica to primary
4. Update application configuration
5. Redirect traffic

## Emergency Contacts
- On-call Engineer: +1-555-0123
- Database Admin: +1-555-0124
- Network Team: +1-555-0125
```

11.9   DevOps Culture and Practices

11.9.1   DevOps Principles

DevOps represents a fundamental shift in how organizations approach software development and operations. Rather than maintaining separate development and operations teams with conflicting goals and limited communication, DevOps promotes collaboration throughout the entire application lifecycle. This cultural transformation proves particularly valuable for LAMP applications, where the traditional separation between developers writing PHP code and administrators managing Apache servers often creates inefficiencies and delays.

The core principle of DevOps involves breaking down silos between teams. In traditional organizations, developers focus on delivering new features quickly while operations teams prioritize stability and uptime.

These competing objectives create friction, with developers frustrated by slow deployment processes and operations teams overwhelmed by unstable releases. DevOps resolves this conflict by making both teams responsible for the entire application lifecycle, from initial development through production support.

Implementing DevOps begins with establishing shared ownership and accountability. When developers understand the operational implications of their code and operations teams participate in architecture decisions, better outcomes emerge. A developer who receives alerts when their code causes production issues writes more robust error handling. An operations engineer who participates in design reviews can suggest infrastructure optimizations early when changes remain inexpensive.

Continuous Integration and Continuous Deployment (CI/CD) embodies DevOps principles through automation. Rather than manual, error-prone deployment processes occurring weekly or monthly, CI/CD enables multiple daily deployments with confidence. Each code commit triggers automated tests, and successful builds deploy automatically to staging environments. This rapid feedback cycle catches issues early when fixes remain simple.

Implementing CI/CD for a LAMP application requires careful orchestration of multiple components. The pipeline must handle PHP code testing, database migrations, asset compilation, and deployment across multiple environments. Modern CI/CD tools like GitLab CI, Jenkins, or GitHub Actions provide the framework, but success requires thoughtful implementation specific to LAMP architecture.

11.9.2   Pipeline Configuration and Structure

A comprehensive GitLab CI pipeline for a LAMP application demonstrates these principles through systematic automation. The pipeline begins with fundamental configuration that establishes stages and shared variables:

```yaml
stages:
  - build
  - test
  - security
  - deploy

variables:
  PHP_VERSION: "7.4"
  MYSQL_DATABASE: test_db

cache:
  paths:
    - vendor/
```

This configuration establishes four sequential stages that organize the pipeline workflow. Variables centralize configuration values, making updates straightforward. Caching reduces execution time by preserving dependencies between pipeline runs.

11.9.3   Build Stage

The build stage prepares the application by installing dependencies:

```
1  build:dependencies:
2    stage: build
3    image: php:${PHP_VERSION}
4    script:
5      - apt-get update && apt-get install -y unzip
6      - curl -sS https://getcomposer.org/installer | php
7      - php composer.phar install --optimize-autoloader
8    artifacts:
9      paths:
10       - vendor/
```

This simplified build process focuses on essential tasks. The stage uses official PHP Docker images, installs Composer, and manages dependencies. Artifacts preserve the vendor directory for subsequent stages.

11.9.4   Testing Implementation

The test stage validates code through multiple approaches. Unit testing verifies individual components:

```
1  test:unit:
2    stage: test
3    image: php:${PHP_VERSION}
4    services:
5      - mysql:5.7
6    script:
7      - ./vendor/bin/phpunit tests/Unit
8    coverage: '/Lines:\s*(\d+\.\d+)%/'
```

Integration testing validates component interactions:

```
1  test:integration:
2    stage: test
3    image: php:${PHP_VERSION}
4    services:
5      - mysql:5.7
6    script:
7      - php artisan migrate --env=testing
8      - ./vendor/bin/phpunit tests/Integration
```

Code quality analysis maintains standards:

```
1  test:code_quality:
2    stage: test
3    script:
4      - ./vendor/bin/phpcs --standard=PSR12 app/
5      - ./vendor/bin/phpstan analyse app/
```

Each test job serves a specific purpose. Unit tests run quickly and catch basic errors. Integration tests verify database operations and API endpoints. Code quality tools enforce consistent standards across the team.

11.9.5 Security Scanning

Security scanning identifies vulnerabilities early in the development process:

```
1   security:dependencies:
2     stage: security
3     script:
4       - composer audit
5     allow_failure: true
6
7   security:code_patterns:
8     stage: security
9     script:
10      - grep -r "eval(" app/ && exit 1 || true
11      - grep -r "\$_GET\[" app/ | grep -v "filter_input" && exit 1 || true
```

Dependency scanning checks third-party libraries against vulnerability databases. Pattern matching identifies dangerous code constructs. The `allow_failure` flag prevents non-critical issues from blocking deployments while still alerting developers.

11.9.6 Deployment Automation

Deployment stages handle environment-specific requirements. Staging deployments provide final validation:

```
1  deploy:staging:
2    stage: deploy
3    script:
4      - rsync -av --exclude='.env' ./ $STAGING_SERVER:$DEPLOY_PATH/
5      - ssh $STAGING_SERVER "cd $DEPLOY_PATH && composer install --no-dev"
6      - ssh $STAGING_SERVER "cd $DEPLOY_PATH && php artisan migrate"
```

```yaml
7   environment:
8     name: staging
9   only:
10    - develop
```

Production deployments require manual approval:

```yaml
1  deploy:production:
2    stage: deploy
3    script:
4      - ./scripts/deploy-production.sh
5    environment:
6      name: production
7    when: manual
8    only:
9      - main
```

Staging deployments run automatically for `develop` branch commits, enabling rapid feedback. Production deployments require explicit approval, ensuring human oversight for critical changes.

This pipeline demonstrates several DevOps best practices. Automated testing catches bugs before deployment, with unit tests verifying individual components and integration tests ensuring proper system behavior. Security scanning identifies vulnerabilities in dependencies and code patterns that might create security issues. Code quality checks enforce consistent standards across the team. The deployment process itself uses Infrastructure as Code principles, with all deployment steps codified and version controlled.

11.9.7   Monitoring and Observability

Monitoring and observability represent another crucial DevOps principle. Traditional operations teams often discovered issues only when users complained. DevOps practices emphasize proactive monitoring and alerting, with developers receiving immediate feedback about their code's production behavior. This tight feedback loop encourages better coding practices and faster issue resolution.

Implementing comprehensive monitoring requires instrumenting applications to expose relevant metrics:

```php
1  namespace App\Services;
2
3  class MetricsService
4  {
5      private $requestCounter;
6      private $errorCounter;
7
```

```
 8      public function __construct()
 9      {
10          // Initialize Prometheus metrics
11          $this->requestCounter = $this->register('http_requests_total');
12          $this->errorCounter = $this->register('errors_total');
13      }
14
15      public function recordRequest($method, $status)
16      {
17          $this->requestCounter->inc([$method, $status]);
18      }
19
20      public function recordError($type)
21      {
22          $this->errorCounter->inc([$type]);
23      }
24  }
```

This simplified metrics service demonstrates the core concept of application instrumentation. The service tracks HTTP requests and errors, providing visibility into application behavior. Real implementations would expand this pattern to include response times, business metrics, and resource utilization.

Infrastructure as Code represents another fundamental DevOps practice. Rather than manually configuring servers through SSH sessions, infrastructure becomes reproducible and version controlled. This approach eliminates configuration drift and enables rapid provisioning of new environments.

11.10   Chapter Review

Problem 11.1 What is the difference between Apache's prefork MPM and event MPM? When would you choose one over the other for a LAMP application?

Problem 11.2 Explain the request flow when a user accesses a PHP page through Apache. What components are involved and in what order?

Problem 11.3 Compare IaaS, PaaS, and SaaS in the context of deploying a LAMP application. Give an example of each and discuss the trade-offs.

Problem 11.4 What is a blue-green deployment? How does it differ from a rolling deployment? What are the advantages and disadvantages of each approach?

Problem 11.5 How do environment variables help in managing different deployment environments? Write a PHP code example showing how to use environment-specific database credentials.

Problem 11.6 What is Infrastructure as Code? How does it improve upon traditional server management? Name two tools used for IaC and their primary differences.

Problem 11.7 Design a monitoring strategy for a LAMP application. What metrics would you track at each layer (infrastructure, web server, application, database)?

Problem 11.8 A user reports that your website is slow. Describe a systematic approach to diagnose the issue, including specific commands or tools you would use.

Problem 11.9 What are the key differences between vertical and horizontal scaling? What application changes are typically required to support horizontal scaling?

Problem 11.10 How does a CDN improve web application performance? What types of content are best served through a CDN, and what headers should be configured?

Problem 11.11 Explain the concept of "high availability." What does "five nines" (99.999%) uptime mean in practical terms? Design a high-availability architecture for a LAMP application.

Problem 11.12 What are some common security misconfigurations in Apache? List at least five security hardening steps you would take for a production web server.

Problem 11.13 How do you handle PHP sessions in a horizontally scaled environment? Describe at least two approaches with their pros and cons.

Problem 11.14 What is a "blameless post-mortem" and why is it important in DevOps culture? What key elements should be included in a post-mortem document?

Problem 11.15 Describe the stages of a typical CI/CD pipeline for a PHP application. What tests or checks would you include at each stage?

Problem 11.16 Set up Apache with two virtual hosts on your local machine, each serving a different PHP application. For example, create one virtual host for a simple blog application at `blog.local` and another for a contact form application at `contact.local`. Configure different PHP settings for each virtual host using `.htaccess` files, such as different memory limits or error reporting levels. Test that each virtual host correctly serves its respective application and that the PHP settings are properly isolated between the two sites. Document the configuration files you created and explain how Apache determines which virtual host should handle each request.

Problem 11.17 Create a simple deployment script that implements the blue-green deployment strategy. Your script should maintain two directory structures (blue and green) for your application code. When deploying a new version, the script should copy the new code to the inactive environment, run basic health checks to verify the application starts correctly, switch a symbolic link to activate the new version, and provide a rollback mechanism that can quickly revert to the previous version if problems are detected. Test your script by deploying several versions of a simple PHP application and practicing both successful deployments and rollbacks.

Problem 11.18 Using free tools like Prometheus and Grafana, build a monitoring dashboard for a LAMP application. Set up monitoring for Apache and MySQL by configuring appropriate exporters. Create a dashboard showing key metrics including request rates, response times, and error rates. Configure an alert that triggers when error rates exceed 5%. Document the installation process and explain how each component contributes to the monitoring solution. Test the alert by intentionally causing errors in your application.

Problem 11.19 Write an Ansible playbook that automates the complete setup of a LAMP server. The playbook should install Apache, MySQL, and PHP with appropriate configurations. It should configure a virtual host for your application and set up SSL certificates using Let's Encrypt for HTTPS support. The playbook should deploy a sample PHP application and configure basic security settings such as firewall rules and disabling unnecessary services. Test your playbook by running it against a fresh virtual machine and verify that the resulting server is fully functional and secure.

Problem 11.20 Set up a load-balanced environment that demonstrates horizontal scaling. Configure two or more Apache/PHP servers running identical copies of your application. Set up Nginx as a load balancer to distribute requests across the backend servers. Implement shared session storage using Redis so that users can be served by any backend server without losing their session data. Create a simple PHP application that displays the server name handling each request to demonstrate that load balancing is working correctly.

Problem 11.21 Using GitLab CI or GitHub Actions, create a continuous integration and deployment pipeline for a PHP application. The pipeline should run PHP linting and unit tests automatically when code is committed. Configure the pipeline to build a deployment artifact containing all necessary files. Set up automatic deployment to a staging environment when tests pass. Require manual approval before deploying to a production environment. Document the pipeline configuration and explain how each stage contributes to software quality and deployment reliability.

Problem 11.22 Take a sample PHP application and implement various performance optimizations. Enable and configure OPcache to cache compiled PHP code. Implement Redis caching for database queries to reduce database load. Add browser caching headers for static assets like CSS, JavaScript, and images. Use Apache Bench or a similar tool to measure performance before and after each optimization. Document the performance improvements achieved and explain why each optimization technique is effective.

Problem 11.23 Design and implement a disaster recovery solution for a LAMP application. Create automated MySQL backups that run on a schedule and store backup files to S3 or similar cloud storage. Write a restoration script that can recover the database from these backups. Create documentation for the recovery process that could be followed by any team member. Test the recovery process by simulating a failure scenario and restoring from backup. Measure the Recovery Time Objective (RTO) and document any improvements that could reduce recovery time.

12. Modern Web Development

The web development landscape has evolved dramatically since the early days of static HTML pages and simple server-side scripts. While the LAMP stack remains a robust foundation for web applications, modern development practices have introduced new paradigms, frameworks, and tools that fundamentally change how we build for the web. This chapter explores the current state of web development, examining both the evolution beyond traditional server-side rendering and the integration of sophisticated front-end frameworks with back-end services. Understanding these modern approaches equips you to build applications that meet contemporary user expectations for interactivity, performance, and user experience.

The shift toward more dynamic, responsive web applications has been driven by several factors: increased browser capabilities, faster internet connections, mobile device proliferation, and rising user expectations. Modern web applications often feel more like desktop software than traditional websites, offering real-time updates, offline functionality, and smooth interactions without page refreshes. This transformation requires developers to master new architectures, tools, and ways of thinking about web applications. By understanding both the traditional LAMP foundation and modern development practices, you can choose the right approach for each project and even combine techniques for optimal results.

Learning Objectives

By the end of this chapter, you should be able to:

- Compare and contrast traditional server-side rendering with modern client-side approaches, understanding the trade-offs and appropriate use cases for each.
- Understand the architecture of Single Page Applications (SPAs) and how they differ from traditional multi-page applications in terms of routing, state management, and server communication.
- Work with modern JavaScript frameworks and libraries like React, Vue, and Angular, understanding their core concepts and how they integrate with back-end services.
- Implement RESTful APIs and GraphQL services to provide data to front-end applications, following best practices for API design and documentation.
- Apply modern development workflows including version control with Git, automated testing, continuous integration, and deployment pipelines.
- Optimize web applications for performance using techniques like code splitting, lazy loading, caching strategies, and Content Delivery Networks (CDNs).
- Build Progressive Web Apps (PWAs) that work offline, install like native apps, and provide enhanced user experiences across devices.
- Understand microservices architecture and how it contrasts with monolithic applications, including when to consider this approach.

DOI: 10.1201/9781003727651-12

12.1 Evolution Beyond Server-Side Rendering

12.1.1 The Limitations of Traditional Approaches

To appreciate modern web development, we must first understand the limitations of traditional server-side rendering that dominated web development for decades. In the classic LAMP model we have studied, each user interaction typically triggers a full page reload. When a user clicks a link or submits a form, the browser sends a request to the server, PHP processes the request and queries MySQL if needed, generates a complete HTML page, and sends it back to the browser, which then renders the entire page fresh.

This approach, while simple and straightforward, creates several challenges:

Performance Overhead: Every interaction requires a full round-trip to the server and complete page regeneration. Even if only a small portion of the page changes (like updating a shopping cart count), the entire page must be transmitted and re-rendered. This creates noticeable delays, especially on slower connections or when servers are under load.

Consider a typical e-commerce product listing page. In a traditional LAMP application, applying a filter (such as selecting a price range) would require:

1. Submitting the filter criteria to the server
2. PHP re-querying the database with the new criteria
3. Regenerating the entire HTML page with the filtered results
4. Sending the complete page back to the browser
5. The browser re-rendering everything, including unchanged elements like headers and navigation

Limited Interactivity: Traditional server-side applications struggle to provide the rich, interactive experiences users have come to expect. Features like real-time search suggestions, drag-and-drop interfaces, or instant form validation require awkward workarounds or simply are not feasible within the request-response model.

State Management Challenges: Maintaining application state across page loads requires server-side sessions, cookies, or hidden form fields. This becomes cumbersome for complex applications where users expect their interface state (like expanded sections, sort preferences, or partially completed forms) to persist seamlessly.

Scalability Concerns: Since the server must generate every page dynamically, scaling requires proportionally more server resources. Caching helps but introduces complexity when dealing with personalized content or frequently changing data.

12.1.2 The Rise of Client-Side Rendering

Modern web development addresses these limitations by shifting more responsibility to the client (browser). Instead of generating complete HTML pages on the server, modern applications often send data (typically as JSON) and let JavaScript in the browser handle presentation and interaction. This paradigm shift introduces several key concepts, as discussed next.

First, Separation of Concerns: Modern architectures clearly separate the back-end API (data and business logic) from the front-end presentation layer. The server focuses on data management, authentication, and business rules, while the client handles user interface and interaction logic. This separation allows front-end and back-end teams to work more independently and enables the same API to serve multiple clients (web, mobile, desktop).

Second, Single Page Applications (SPAs): Instead of loading new pages for each interaction, SPAs load once and then dynamically update content as users interact with the application. Navigation happens client-side through JavaScript routing, creating smooth, app-like experiences. Popular examples include Gmail, Google Maps, and most modern web applications you interact with daily.

Third, API-First Development: Modern applications typically expose their functionality through well-defined APIs (Application Programming Interfaces) that front-end applications consume. This approach enables multiple front-end clients (web, mobile apps, third-party integrations), easier testing and documentation, better scalability through API caching and CDN distribution, and microservices architectures where different services handle specific functionality.

Fourth, Component-Based Architecture: Modern front-end frameworks organize code into reusable components, each encapsulating its own logic, styling, and markup. This modular approach improves code organization, enables better testing, and allows teams to build complex interfaces from simpler building blocks.

12.1.3   Modern JavaScript and ECMAScript Evolution

The transformation of web development closely tracks JavaScript's evolution from a simple scripting language to a robust platform for building complex applications. Understanding modern JavaScript is crucial for contemporary web development.

European Computer Manufacturers Association Script (ECMAScript): JavaScript follows the ECMAScript (ES) specification, with major updates bringing powerful new features. ES6/ES2015 introduced game-changing features including arrow functions for cleaner syntax (`const add = (a, b) => a + b`), classes for object-oriented programming, modules for organizing code (`import` and `export` statements), promises for handling asynchronous operations, template literals for string interpolation (`` `Hello ${name}` ``), and destructuring for extracting values (`const { name, age } = person`).

ES2017 added `async/await` for more intuitive asynchronous code:

```javascript
async function fetchUserData(userId) {
  try {
    const response = await fetch(`/api/users/${userId}`);
    const user = await response.json();
    return user;
  } catch (error) {
    console.error('Failed to fetch user:', error);
  }
}
```

Recent additions to ECMAScript include optional chaining (`user?.address?.street`), nullish coalescing (`value ?? defaultValue`), and private class fields.

Build Tools and Transpilation: Modern JavaScript development relies on build tools that transform and optimize code. Babel transpiles modern JavaScript to older versions for browser compatibility. Webpack bundles modules and assets, enabling code splitting and optimization. TypeScript adds static typing to JavaScript, catching errors during development. Development servers provide hot module replacement for instant updates during development.

These tools enable developers to use cutting-edge language features while maintaining compatibility with older browsers, a crucial consideration for public-facing applications.

12.1.4   The Role of AJAX in the Transition

AJAX (Asynchronous JavaScript and XML) served as the bridge between traditional server-side applications and modern client-side approaches. By enabling partial page updates without full reloads, AJAX demonstrated the potential for more dynamic web applications.

However, modern development has moved beyond basic AJAX to more sophisticated patterns. Fetch API, the modern replacement for XMLHttpRequest, provides a cleaner promise-based interface:

```javascript
// Old AJAX approach
var xhr = new XMLHttpRequest();
xhr.open('GET', '/api/products');
xhr.onload = function() {
  if (xhr.status === 200) {
    var products = JSON.parse(xhr.responseText);
    displayProducts(products);
  }
};
xhr.send();

// Modern Fetch approach
fetch('/api/products')
  .then(response => response.json())
  .then(products => displayProducts(products))
  .catch(error => console.error('Error:', error));
```

Real-time Communication: Modern applications often require real-time updates beyond what traditional AJAX polling can efficiently provide. WebSockets enable full-duplex communication channels between client and server. Server-Sent Events (SSE) allow servers to push updates to clients. Web Real-Time Communication (WebRTC) enables peer-to-peer communication for video chat and file sharing.

These technologies enable features like collaborative editing, live notifications, and real-time dashboards that would be impractical with traditional page-based approaches.

12.2   Single Page Applications and Modern Frameworks

12.2.1   Understanding Single Page Applications

Single Page Applications represent a fundamental shift in how web applications work. To understand this shift, we must first examine how traditional multi-page applications operate. In the conventional approach we have studied throughout this book, each user interaction triggers a complete page reload. When a user clicks a link or submits a form, the browser sends a request to the server, which processes it through PHP and MySQL, generates a complete HTML page, and sends it back. The browser then renders this entirely new page, causing the familiar flicker and loss of scroll position.

Single Page Applications eliminate this constant reloading by handling navigation and content updates within the browser itself. After the initial page load, which downloads the application's JavaScript code, CSS styles, and basic HTML structure, all subsequent interactions happen without full page refreshes. Instead of requesting complete HTML pages from the server, the application requests only the data it needs, typically in JSON format, and updates the relevant portions of the page dynamically.

This architectural difference creates significant implications for user experience. As shown in Figure 12.1, the contrast between traditional and SPA architectures is evident in how they handle page transitions. Consider navigating between sections of an e-commerce site. In a traditional application, clicking from the product list to a specific product causes the entire page to reload, losing any client-side state like filter selections or scroll position. In a SPA, only the main content area updates while maintaining the rest of the interface state, creating a seamless experience similar to desktop applications.

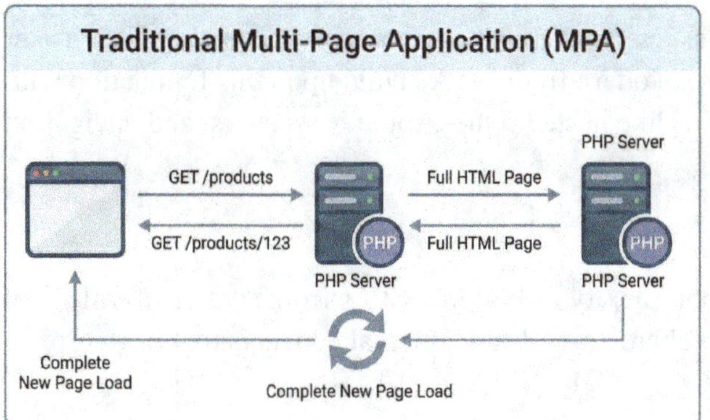

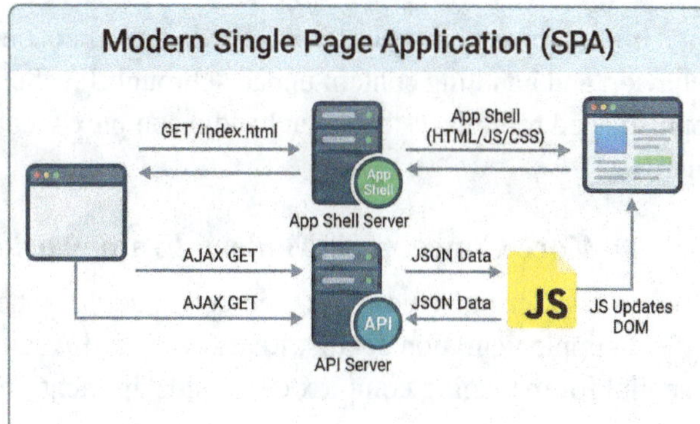

Figure 12.1: Traditional vs. SPA request flow.

The client-side routing mechanism that enables this behavior intercepts navigation events and updates the browser's URL without triggering a page reload:

```javascript
// Simple client-side routing concept
window.addEventListener('click', (e) => {
  // Intercept clicks on links
  if (e.target.tagName === 'A') {
    e.preventDefault();
    const path = e.target.getAttribute('href');

    // Update browser URL without reload
    window.history.pushState({}, '', path);

    // Load appropriate content based on path
```

```javascript
12      loadContent(path);
13    }
14 });
15
16 function loadContent(path) {
17   // Fetch data from API based on route
18   fetch('/api${path}')
19     .then(response => response.json())
20     .then(data => {
21       // Update page content with data
22       document.getElementById('content').innerHTML = renderContent(data);
23     });
24 }
```

This example demonstrates the fundamental concepts: intercepting navigation, preventing default browser behavior, and handling content updates through JavaScript. Modern frameworks build upon this foundation with sophisticated routing systems that handle complex scenarios like nested routes, route parameters, and navigation guards.

12.2.2   Core Concepts of Modern Frameworks

Modern JavaScript frameworks emerged to address the complexity of building SPAs from scratch. While they differ in implementation details, React, Vue, and Angular share several fundamental concepts that have proven essential for managing complex client-side applications.

Component-Based Architecture

Components form the building blocks of modern web applications. Each component encapsulates a piece of user interface along with its logic and styling, creating reusable units that can be composed into complex applications. This approach mirrors how we naturally think about user interfaces given that a page contains a header, which contains a navigation menu, which contains individual menu items:

```javascript
1 // Conceptual component structure
2 class ProductCard {
3   constructor(product) {
4     this.product = product;
5   }
6
7   render() {
8     return `
9       <div class="product-card">
10         <img src="${this.product.image}" alt="${this.product.name}">
```

```
11          <h3>${this.product.name}</h3>
12          <p class="price">$${this.product.price}</p>
13          <button onclick="addToCart(${this.product.id})">
14            Add to Cart
15          </button>
16        </div>
17      `;
18    }
19 }
20
21 // Using components to build interfaces
22 const products = fetchProducts();
23 const productCards = products.map(p => new ProductCard(p).render());
24 document.getElementById('product-list').innerHTML = productCards.join('');
```

The power of components becomes apparent when building complex interfaces. This `ProductCard` component can be reused throughout the application including in search results, featured products sections, or shopping cart previews. When you need to change how products appear, you modify one component rather than hunting through multiple templates.

Reactive Data Binding

Traditional web development requires manually updating the DOM when data changes. Modern frameworks introduce reactive systems where the UI automatically updates when underlying data changes. This declarative approach lets developers focus on the data and let the framework handle DOM updates:

```
1  // Traditional imperative approach
2  let count = 0;
3  function increment() {
4    count++;
5    // Manually update every place count is displayed
6    document.getElementById('counter').textContent = count;
7    document.getElementById('cart-badge').textContent = count;
8    // Must remember to update all locations
9  }
10
11 // Modern reactive approach (conceptual)
12 const state = reactive({
13   count: 0
14 });
15
16 // Define UI as function of state
```

```
17  function render() {
18    return '
19      <div>
20        <span id="counter">${state.count}</span>
21        <span id="cart-badge">${state.count}</span>
22        <button onclick="state.count++">Increment</button>
23      </div>
24    ';
25  }
26  // Framework automatically re-renders when state.count changes
```

This reactive approach fundamentally changes how developers think about user interfaces. Instead of imperatively manipulating the DOM, you declare relationships between data and UI, making applications more predictable and maintainable.

Virtual DOM and Efficient Updates

Direct DOM manipulation is computationally expensive, especially when making many small changes. The Virtual DOM concept addresses this by providing a lightweight JavaScript representation of the actual DOM.

```
1   1. State Change Triggered
2      state.items = [...state.items, newItem]
3
4   2. New Virtual DOM Tree Created
5      VirtualDOM =
6        {
7        tag: 'ul',
8        children:
9        [
10          {tag: 'li', text: 'Item 1'},
11          {tag: 'li', text: 'Item 2'},
12          {tag: 'li', text: 'NEW Item 3'} // New item
13        ]
14        }
15
16  3. Diff with Previous Virtual DOM
17     Difference found: One new <li> element
18
19  4. Apply Minimal Changes to Real DOM
20     document.querySelector('ul').appendChild(newListItem)
```

This process ensures optimal performance by batching updates and applying only necessary changes to the actual DOM, enabling smooth user interfaces even with frequent updates.

12.2.3 React: A Library for Building UIs

React, created by Facebook to address challenges in building their increasingly complex web interface, introduced several innovative concepts that have influenced modern web development. At its core, React treats UI as a function of application state; given the same state, a component will always render the same output.

React components are JavaScript functions that return JSX, a syntax extension that combines JavaScript with HTML-like markup:

```
// Simple React component
function Welcome(props) {
  return <h1>Hello, {props.name}!</h1>;
}

// Component with state using Hooks
function Counter() {
  const [count, setCount] = useState(0);

  return (
    <div>
      <p>You clicked {count} times</p>
      <button onClick={() => setCount(count + 1)}>
        Click me
      </button>
    </div>
  );
}

// Composing components
function App() {
  return (
    <div>
      <Welcome name="Maria" />
      <Counter />
    </div>
  );
}
```

React's introduction of Hooks revolutionized how developers write components. The useState Hook manages component state, while useEffect handles side effects like API calls:

```jsx
function ProductList() {
  const [products, setProducts] = useState([]);
  const [loading, setLoading] = useState(true);

  // Fetch products when component mounts
  useEffect(() => {
    fetch('/api/products')
      .then(res => res.json())
      .then(data => {
        setProducts(data);
        setLoading(false);
      });
  }, []); // Empty array means run once

  if (loading) return <div>Loading...</div>;

  return (
    <div className="product-grid">
      {products.map(product => (
        <ProductCard key={product.id} product={product} />
      ))}
    </div>
  );
}
```

React's unidirectional data flow ensures predictable application behavior. Data flows down through props, while events bubble up through callback functions. This pattern, combined with React's component model, makes it easier to understand how changes propagate through an application.

The React ecosystem provides solutions for every aspect of application development. React Router handles client-side navigation, Redux and Context API manage complex state, and Next.js adds server-side rendering capabilities. This rich ecosystem, combined with React's flexibility, has made it the most popular choice for building modern web applications.

12.2.4 Vue.js: The Progressive Framework

Vue.js takes a different approach, emphasizing approachability and incremental adoption. Created by Evan You after working with Angular at Google, Vue combines the best aspects of other frameworks while maintaining a gentler learning curve. Its template-based syntax feels familiar to developers with HTML experience:

```html
<template>
  <div class="counter">
```

```
3     <p>Count: {{ count }}</p>
4     <button @click="increment">Increment</button>
5     <button @click="decrement">Decrement</button>
6   </div>
7 </template>
8
9 <script>
10 export default {
11   data() {
12     return {
13       count: 0
14     };
15   },
16   methods: {
17     increment() {
18       this.count++;
19     },
20     decrement() {
21       this.count--;
22     }
23   }
24 };
25 </script>
26
27 <style scoped>
28 .counter {
29   text-align: center;
30   padding: 20px;
31 }
32 </style>
```

Vue's single-file components encapsulate template, logic, and styling in one file, providing excellent organization while keeping related code together. The framework's reactivity system automatically tracks dependencies and updates the DOM efficiently:

```
1 // Vue 3 Composition API
2 import { ref, computed, watch } from 'vue';
3
4 export default {
5   setup() {
6     // Reactive references
7     const firstName = ref('John');
```

```javascript
8      const lastName = ref('Doe');
9
10     // Computed property automatically updates
11     const fullName = computed(() => {
12       return `${firstName.value} ${lastName.value}`;
13     });
14
15     // Watch for changes
16     watch(fullName, (newValue, oldValue) => {
17       console.log(`Name changed from ${oldValue} to ${newValue}`);
18     });
19
20     return { firstName, lastName, fullName };
21   }
22 };
```

Vue's progressive nature means you can adopt it incrementally. You might start by adding Vue to enhance a single form on a traditional server-rendered page:

```html
1  <!-- Enhancing existing HTML with Vue -->
2  <div id="search-form">
3    <input v-model="searchQuery" @input="searchProducts">
4    <div v-if="searching">Searching...</div>
5    <ul>
6      <li v-for="product in results" :key="product.id">
7        {{ product.name }} - ${{ product.price }}
8      </li>
9    </ul>
10 </div>
11
12 <script>
13 new Vue({
14   el: '#search-form',
15   data: {
16     searchQuery: '',
17     results: [],
18     searching: false
19   },
20   methods: {
21     searchProducts() {
22       this.searching = true;
23       // Debounced API call
```

```
24      clearTimeout(this.searchTimeout);
25      this.searchTimeout = setTimeout(() => {
26        fetch(`/api/search?q=${this.searchQuery}`)
27          .then(res => res.json())
28          .then(data => {
29            this.results = data;
30            this.searching = false;
31          });
32      }, 300);
33    }
34  }
35 });
36 </script>
```

This incremental adoption path makes Vue particularly attractive for teams modernizing legacy applications or those wanting to experiment without committing to a complete rewrite.

12.2.5 Angular: The Full Framework

Angular represents a complete platform for building web applications. Unlike React or Vue, which focus primarily on the view layer, Angular provides everything needed for large-scale application development. This comprehensive approach includes a powerful Command Line Interface (CLI), built-in routing, forms handling, HTTP client, and testing utilities.

Angular embraces TypeScript as its primary language, providing strong typing throughout:

```
1 // Angular component with TypeScript
2 import { Component, OnInit } from '@angular/core';
3 import { ProductService } from './product.service';
4
5 @Component({
6   selector: 'app-product-list',
7   template: `
8     <div class="product-list">
9       <h2>Products</h2>
10      <div *ngIf="loading">Loading products...</div>
11      <div *ngFor="let product of products" class="product-card">
12        <h3>{{ product.name }}</h3>
13        <p>{{ product.price | currency }}</p>
14        <button (click)="addToCart(product)">Add to Cart</button>
15      </div>
16    </div>
17  `
```

```
18 })
19 export class ProductListComponent implements OnInit {
20   products: Product[] = [];
21   loading = true;
22
23   constructor(private productService: ProductService) {}
24
25   ngOnInit() {
26     this.productService.getProducts().subscribe(products => {
27       this.products = products;
28       this.loading = false;
29     });
30   }
31
32   addToCart(product: Product) {
33     this.productService.addToCart(product);
34   }
35 }
```

Angular's dependency injection system manages object creation and dependencies:

```
1  // Angular service
2  import { Injectable } from '@angular/core';
3  import { HttpClient } from '@angular/common/http';
4  import { Observable } from 'rxjs';
5
6  @Injectable({
7    providedIn: 'root'   // Singleton service
8  })
9  export class ProductService {
10   private apiUrl = '/api/products';
11   constructor(private http: HttpClient) {}
12
13   getProducts(): Observable<Product[]> {
14     return this.http.get<Product[]>(this.apiUrl);
15   }
16
17   addToCart(product: Product) {
18     // Cart logic
19   }
20 }
```

Angular's use of RxJS for reactive programming provides powerful tools for handling asynchronous operations and data streams. While this adds a learning curve, it excels at complex scenarios like typeahead searches, real-time updates, and cancellable requests.

12.2.6 Choosing the Right Framework

Selecting a framework requires balancing multiple considerations beyond technical capabilities. Each framework can build sophisticated applications, so the decision often depends on your specific context.

For project size and complexity, Vue often works best for smaller projects or when enhancing existing applications due to its incremental adoption path and gentle learning curve. React suits projects of all sizes but particularly shines for interactive user interfaces requiring fine-grained control. Angular makes most sense for large applications where its comprehensive structure and enterprise features justify the initial complexity.

Team experience plays a crucial role in framework success. Developers comfortable with HTML and CSS often find Vue's template syntax intuitive, as it extends familiar concepts. React appeals to JavaScript developers who appreciate functional programming and JavaScript XML (JSX)'s power despite its initial unfamiliarity. Angular resonates with developers from enterprise backgrounds familiar with dependency injection, strong typing, and structured architectures from languages like Java or C#.

Performance considerations rarely dictate framework choice, as all three can be optimized for excellent performance. Initial bundle sizes tend to favor Vue and React over Angular, but proper code splitting and lazy loading minimize these differences. Runtime performance depends more on implementation quality. Efficient component design, minimizing re-renders, and proper state management matter more than framework choice.

The ecosystem and community support surrounding each framework provide important long-term considerations. React's massive ecosystem offers solutions for every conceivable need but requires careful evaluation among many options. Vue provides a more curated ecosystem with official solutions for routing, state management, and build tools. Angular's batteries-included approach means less time evaluating options but also less flexibility in technology choices.

Consider also the hiring market and long-term maintenance. React's popularity makes finding experienced developers easier in most markets. Vue's growing adoption and excellent documentation help developers ramp up quickly. Angular's enterprise focus means developers often command higher salaries but bring experience with large-scale applications. All three frameworks have proven their longevity and continue to evolve with web standards, making any choice a safe long-term investment with proper architectural decisions.

12.3 Modern API Design and Integration

12.3.1 RESTful API Principles

The separation of front-end and back-end in modern web development relies on well-designed APIs that enable communication between client applications and servers. REST (Representational State Transfer) has emerged as the dominant architectural style for web APIs, not because it represents the perfect solution, but because it aligns naturally with the existing infrastructure and conventions of the web. Understanding REST principles enables developers to create APIs that feel intuitive to consumers while leveraging proven patterns that have scaled across millions of applications.

REST treats everything as a resource that can be accessed through a unique URL, representing a fundamental shift from older RPC (Remote Procedure Call) approaches that focused on actions and methods. Instead of endpoints like `/getProduct` or `/updateProduct`, REST uses the URL to identify the resource (`/products /123`) and HTTP methods to specify the intended action. This alignment with HTTP's design makes REST APIs feel natural to developers already familiar with web technologies while providing consistent patterns that reduce cognitive overhead when working with multiple APIs.

The standard HTTP methods map directly to common database operations, creating a consistent interface for manipulating resources across different domains and applications. GET retrieves resources without side effects, enabling safe caching and repeated execution. POST creates new resources, typically returning the created object with server-assigned identifiers. PUT replaces entire resources with new representations, providing idempotent updates. DELETE removes resources, also offering idempotent behavior that supports retry mechanisms:

```javascript
// Express.js RESTful API implementation
const express = require('express');
const app = express();

// GET - Retrieve resources
app.get('/api/products', async (req, res) => {
  const products = await Product.findAll();
  res.json(products);
});

app.get('/api/products/:id', async (req, res) => {
  const product = await Product.findById(req.params.id);
  if (!product) {
    return res.status(404).json({ error: 'Product not found' });
  }
  res.json(product);
});

// POST - Create new resource
app.post('/api/products', async (req, res) => {
  const product = await Product.create(req.body);
  res.status(201).json(product);
});

// PUT - Replace entire resource
app.put('/api/products/:id', async (req, res) => {
  const product = await Product.findByIdAndUpdate(req.params.id, req.body);
  res.json(product);
});

// DELETE - Remove resource
```

```
32  app.delete('/api/products/:id', async (req, res) => {
33    await Product.destroy({ where: { id: req.params.id } });
34    res.status(204).send();
35  });
```

This implementation demonstrates several REST principles in practice. The URL structure clearly identifies resources using consistent patterns that developers can predict and understand. HTTP methods indicate the intended action without ambiguity, eliminating the need for custom action names in URLs. Status codes communicate results using web standards that tools and developers recognize universally. The approach provides a foundation for building larger API surfaces that maintain consistency and predictability.

Statelessness represents another core REST principle that significantly impacts API design and scalability characteristics. Each request must contain all information necessary to understand and process it, without relying on server-stored session state that couples clients to specific server instances. This constraint might seem limiting compared to traditional session-based web applications, but it enables horizontal scaling and improved reliability by eliminating server affinity requirements:

```
1   // Stateless authentication using JWT tokens
2   app.get('/api/user/orders', async (req, res) => {
3     const token = req.headers.authorization?.split(' ')[1];
4     if (!token) {
5       return res.status(401).json({ error: 'Authentication required' });
6     }
7
8     const decoded = jwt.verify(token, process.env.JWT_SECRET);
9     const orders = await Order.findAll({ where: { userId: decoded.userId } });
10    res.json(orders);
11  });
```

By including authentication information in each request rather than relying on server sessions, the API can scale horizontally across multiple servers without complex session synchronization mechanisms. Any server can handle any request, improving reliability and performance while simplifying deployment architecture.

12.3.2 Designing Effective RESTful APIs

Creating APIs that developers appreciate using requires thoughtful design beyond simply following REST principles. Consistency, predictability, and comprehensive documentation distinguish APIs that accelerate development from those that create frustration and support burdens. Effective API design considers the entire developer experience, from initial discovery through long-term maintenance and evolution.

Resource naming deserves careful consideration as it forms the foundation of API usability and developer productivity. Resources should use plural nouns that clearly indicate their purpose and scope. Hierarchical relationships can be expressed through URL nesting, but excessive depth creates complexity that outweighs organizational benefits. Well-designed resource hierarchies feel natural to developers while avoiding overly complex nested structures that become difficult to understand and maintain:

```
// Good resource naming examples
GET /api/products                    // Product collection
GET /api/products/123                // Specific product
GET /api/products/123/reviews        // Reviews for a product
GET /api/categories/45/products      // Products in a category

// Avoid these patterns
GET /api/product                     // Singular form
GET /api/getProducts                 // Verb in URL
GET /api/products/123/reviews/456/comments/789   // Excessive nesting
```

Filtering, sorting, and pagination become essential as collections grow beyond trivial sizes. Rather than creating separate endpoints for different views of data, query parameters provide flexible collection modification while maintaining clean URL structures. This approach enables clients to request exactly the data they need without requiring numerous specialized endpoints that increase API surface area and maintenance overhead:

```
// Flexible collection endpoint with query parameters
app.get('/api/products', async (req, res) => {
  const {
    category,
    minPrice,
    maxPrice,
    sort = 'name',
    order = 'asc',
    page = 1,
    limit = 20
  } = req.query;

  // Build query dynamically based on parameters
  const where = {};
  if (category) where.category = category;
  if (minPrice || maxPrice) {
    where.price = {};
    if (minPrice) where.price[Op.gte] = minPrice;
    if (maxPrice) where.price[Op.lte] = maxPrice;
  }

  const offset = (page - 1) * limit;
```

```javascript
23    const { count, rows } = await Product.findAndCountAll({
24      where,
25      order: [[sort, order]],
26      limit: parseInt(limit),
27      offset
28    });
29
30    res.json({
31      data: rows,
32      pagination: {
33        page: parseInt(page),
34        limit: parseInt(limit),
35        total: count,
36        pages: Math.ceil(count / limit)
37      }
38    });
39 });
```

This implementation provides flexibility while maintaining clean URL structures. Clients can control pagination, filtering, and sorting through intuitive query parameters. The response includes pagination metadata that helps clients understand result sets and implement navigation controls. The approach scales well as data grows while providing the flexibility that modern applications require.

Error handling in APIs requires special attention because clients depend on consistent, informative error responses to handle problems gracefully. Well-designed error formats include sufficient information for debugging while maintaining security by avoiding exposure of internal implementation details. Consistent error structures across an API reduce client-side error handling complexity and improve the overall developer experience:

```javascript
1  // Consistent error response format
2  app.use((err, req, res, next) => {
3    const status = err.status || 500;
4    const message = status === 500 ? 'Internal server error' : err.message;
5
6    res.status(status).json({
7      error: {
8        message,
9        status,
10       timestamp: new Date().toISOString(),
11       path: req.path
12     }
13   });
```

```
14 });
15
16 // Usage in route handlers
17 app.post('/api/products', async (req, res, next) => {
18   try {
19     if (!req.body.name || !req.body.price) {
20       const error = new Error('Name and price are required');
21       error.status = 400;
22       throw error;
23     }
24
25     const product = await Product.create(req.body);
26     res.status(201).json(product);
27   } catch (error) {
28     next(error);
29   }
30 });
```

This error handling approach provides consistent response formats while protecting sensitive information. Client applications can rely on predictable error structures for implementing robust error handling logic. The approach balances debugging utility with security considerations by avoiding exposure of internal system details.

12.3.3   GraphQL: A Query Language for APIs

While REST has served web development effectively for many years, it presents limitations that become apparent in complex applications with diverse client needs. Over-fetching occurs when endpoints return more data than clients need, wasting bandwidth and processing resources. Under-fetching requires multiple requests to gather related data, increasing latency and complexity. GraphQL, developed by Facebook to address these specific challenges, allows clients to specify exactly what data they need in a single request, eliminating both over-fetching and under-fetching problems.

The fundamental difference between REST and GraphQL lies in their approach to data fetching and API surface design. REST provides multiple endpoints, each returning a fixed data structure defined by server developers. GraphQL provides a single endpoint where clients send queries describing their precise data requirements. This flexibility enables different clients to request exactly the data they need without requiring server-side changes for each use case.

GraphQL's type system forms the foundation of its flexibility and developer experience benefits. By defining a comprehensive schema that describes all available data and operations, GraphQL provides a contract between client and server that enables powerful tooling and automatic validation. The schema serves as living documentation that stays synchronized with implementation while enabling features like auto-completion, error checking, and automatic code generation:

```
1  # GraphQL Schema Definition
2  type Product {
3    id: ID!
4    name: String!
5    price: Float!
6    description: String
7    category: Category!
8    reviews(first: Int = 10): [Review!]!
9    inStock: Boolean!
10 }
11
12 type Category {
13   id: ID!
14   name: String!
15   products: [Product!]!
16 }
17
18 type Query {
19   product(id: ID!): Product
20   products(filter: ProductFilter, first: Int = 20): [Product!]!
21   categories: [Category!]!
22 }
23
24 type Mutation {
25   createProduct(input: CreateProductInput!): Product!
26   updateProduct(id: ID!, input: UpdateProductInput!): Product!
27 }
```

This schema definition illustrates several GraphQL concepts that enhance developer productivity. Required fields marked with exclamation points provide compile-time guarantees about data availability. Optional fields enable flexible data modeling without breaking existing clients. Arguments on fields like `reviews(first: Int = 10)` allow clients to control data volume while providing sensible defaults. The schema enables powerful development tools while serving as comprehensive API documentation.

The real power of GraphQL becomes apparent when clients can request exactly the data they need using the defined schema. Different applications can use the same GraphQL endpoint while receiving completely different data sets based on their specific requirements. This flexibility eliminates the need for multiple API versions or specialized endpoints for different client types:

```
1  # Minimal client query
2  query GetProductBasics($id: ID!) {
```

```graphql
 3    product(id: $id) {
 4      name
 5      price
 6    }
 7  }
 8
 9  # Comprehensive client query
10  query GetProductDetails($id: ID!) {
11    product(id: $id) {
12      name
13      price
14      description
15      category {
16        name
17      }
18      reviews(first: 5) {
19        rating
20        comment
21      }
22    }
23  }
```

Both queries use the same GraphQL endpoint but return different data sets based on client needs. The first query returns minimal product information suitable for a simple product listing. The second query includes detailed information including related category data and customer reviews, perfect for a comprehensive product page. This flexibility eliminates over-fetching while enabling rich client experiences.

Implementing GraphQL requires resolvers that fetch data for each field in the schema. This resolver-based architecture provides fine-grained control over data fetching while enabling sophisticated optimization strategies. Each field resolves independently, allowing GraphQL to fetch only requested data while enabling advanced patterns like data loader batching to prevent N+1 query problems:

```javascript
 1  const resolvers = {
 2    Query: {
 3      product: async (parent, { id }) => {
 4        return await Product.findById(id);
 5      },
 6
 7      products: async (parent, { filter, first = 20 }) => {
 8        const where = {};
 9        if (filter?.category) where.categoryId = filter.category;
10
```

```
11      return await Product.findAll({ where, limit: first });
12    }
13  },
14
15  Product: {
16    category: async (product) => {
17      return await Category.findById(product.categoryId);
18    },
19
20    reviews: async (product, { first = 10 }) => {
21      return await Review.findAll({
22        where: { productId: product.id },
23        limit: first,
24        order: [['helpful', 'DESC']]
25      });
26    }
27  }
28 };
```

This resolver implementation demonstrates how GraphQL enables precise data fetching while maintaining clean separation of concerns. Query resolvers handle top-level data fetching, while field resolvers manage related data. The lazy evaluation approach ensures that complex operations only execute when clients request the corresponding data, optimizing performance automatically based on usage patterns.

12.3.4 API Documentation and Developer Experience

Excellent API documentation can make the difference between widespread adoption and obscurity. Modern tools and standards have made creating comprehensive, interactive documentation easier than ever, transforming API documentation from static text into dynamic, explorable interfaces that developers can immediately test and understand.

Open Application Programming Interface (OpenAPI), formerly Swagger, has become the standard for describing RESTful APIs. By writing a specification in YAML Ain't Markup Language (YAML) or JSON, you can generate interactive documentation, client Software Development Kits (SDKs), and even server stubs:

```
1 openapi: 3.0.0
2 info:
3   title: E-commerce API
4   version: 1.0.0
5
6 paths:
7   /products:
8     get:
```

```yaml
 9        summary: List products
10        parameters:
11          - name: category
12            in: query
13            schema:
14              type: string
15        responses:
16          '200':
17            description: Product list
18            content:
19              application/json:
20                schema:
21                  type: array
22                  items:
23                    $ref: '#/components/schemas/Product'
24
25 components:
26   schemas:
27     Product:
28       type: object
29       properties:
30         id:
31           type: string
32         name:
33           type: string
34         price:
35           type: number
```

This specification enables automatic validation and code generation. Tools like Swagger UI transform this into interactive documentation where developers can explore endpoints and make test requests. The declarative approach ensures documentation stays synchronized with implementation while providing a single source of truth for API contracts.

For GraphQL APIs, the built-in introspection capabilities provide automatic documentation. Tools like GraphQL Playground or GraphiQL offer interactive exploration with autocompletion, allowing developers to discover available types and fields dynamically. The strongly typed nature of GraphQL schemas means documentation generates automatically from the schema definition, eliminating the documentation drift common with manually maintained API docs.

Beyond technical specifications, effective API documentation requires clear examples and practical use cases that help developers understand integration patterns:

```javascript
1  // Clear SDK example with error handling
2  import { ApiClient } from '@example/api-client';
3
4  const client = new ApiClient({
5    apiKey: process.env.API_KEY,
6    baseURL: 'https://api.example.com/v1'
7  });
8
9  async function searchProducts(query) {
10   try {
11     const response = await client.products.search({
12       q: query,
13       category: 'electronics',
14       sort: 'price_asc'
15     });
16
17     return response.data;
18   } catch (error) {
19     if (error.status === 429) {
20       console.error('Rate limit exceeded, please retry later');
21     } else {
22       console.error('Search failed:', error.message);
23     }
24     return [];
25   }
26 }
```

Practical code examples demonstrate real-world usage patterns while showing proper error handling techniques. These examples should cover common integration scenarios, authentication flows, and edge cases that developers frequently encounter. The investment in comprehensive examples reduces support burden while accelerating developer adoption.

Rate limiting and API versioning represent crucial considerations for public APIs that require clear communication to developers. Rate limiting policies should be documented transparently, including specific limits for different operations and guidance on handling rate limit responses:

```javascript
1  // Rate limiting communication through headers
2  app.use((req, res, next) => {
3    res.set({
4      'X-RateLimit-Limit': req.rateLimit?.limit,
5      'X-RateLimit-Remaining': req.rateLimit?.remaining,
```

```
6    'X-RateLimit-Reset': new Date(req.rateLimit?.resetTime).toISOString()
7  });
8  next();
9 });
```

API versioning strategies affect long-term maintainability and should be documented clearly. Whether using URL versioning, header versioning, or content negotiation, the approach should be consistent and well-communicated to API consumers. Documentation should explain migration paths between versions and provide adequate notice for deprecation timelines.

Modern API design extends beyond technical implementation to encompass the entire developer experience. Comprehensive documentation, consistent interfaces, helpful error messages, and practical examples create APIs that developers recommend to others. This investment in developer experience generates significant returns through increased adoption, reduced support requests, and the development of thriving ecosystems around successful APIs. The most successful APIs treat documentation not as an afterthought but as a core product feature that enables developer success.

12.4   Modern Development Practices

12.4.1   Version Control with Git and GitHub

The evolution of web development from simple HTML pages to complex applications has made version control indispensable. While early web developers might have managed files through careful naming conventions or manual backups, modern development requires sophisticated tools to track changes, collaborate with teams, and manage releases. Git has emerged as the dominant version control system, fundamentally changing how developers work individually and collectively.

Figure 12.2 contrasts the centralized vs. distributed version control. Understanding Git requires grasping its distributed nature. Unlike older centralized systems where a single server holds the authoritative version, Git gives every developer a complete copy of the repository history. This design provides resilience against server failures, enables offline work, and allows flexible workflows that adapt to different team structures and project needs.

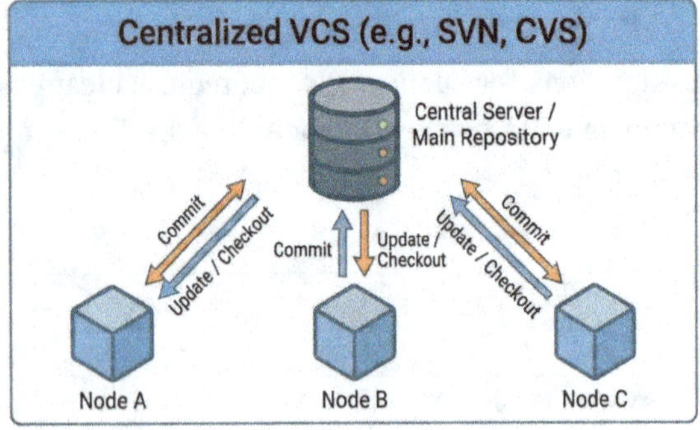

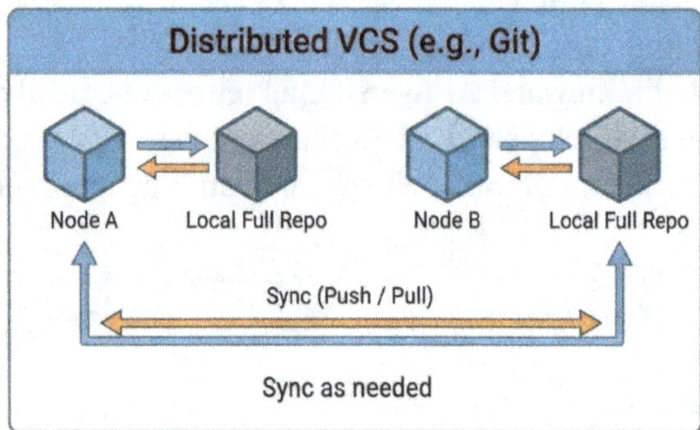

Figure 12.2: Centralized vs. distributed version control.

The basic Git workflow revolves around three states that files can exist in. The working directory contains your current files as they exist on disk. The staging area (also called the index) holds a snapshot of changes you intend to commit. The repository stores the permanent record of your project's history. Figure 12.3 describe three states of Git.

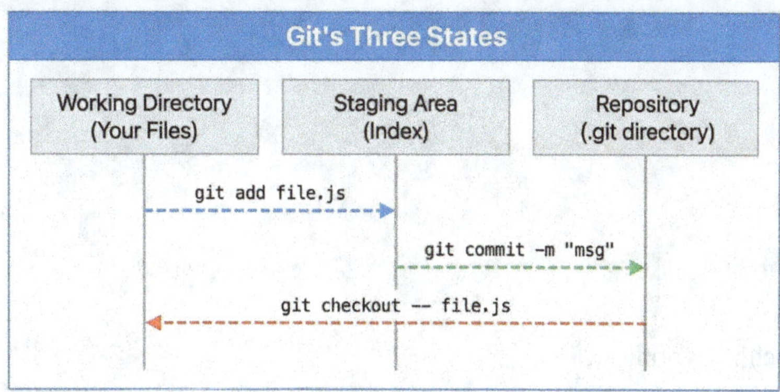

Figure 12.3: Git's three states.

This three-state architecture provides fine-grained control over exactly what changes you record. For example, you might modify several files while working on a feature but commit them separately to create a cleaner history:

```
# Check what files have changed
git status

# Stage only specific files for a focused commit
git add src/auth.js
git commit -m "Add user authentication module"

# Stage another related change
git add src/middleware/auth-check.js
git commit -m "Add authentication middleware for protected routes"
```

The power of Git becomes apparent when managing parallel development through branches. Rather than everyone working on the same code simultaneously, branches allow isolated development that can be merged when ready.

Figure 12.4 describes the Git branching workflow. This branching model enables several important workflows. Feature branches isolate new development from the stable main branch. Developers can experiment freely without affecting others' work. Code review happens before merging, ensuring quality. The main branch remains deployable at all times.

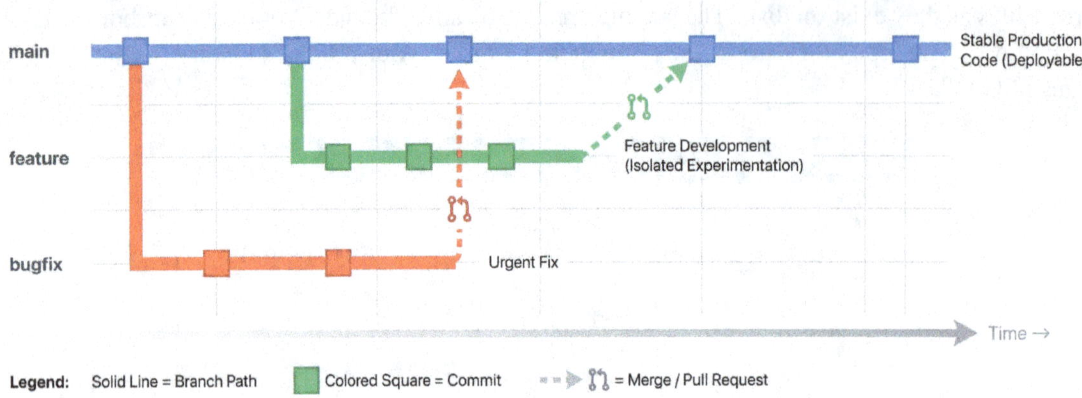

Figure 12.4: Git's branching workflow.

GitHub and similar platforms have transformed Git from a version control tool into a complete collaboration platform. The pull request workflow has become standard for team collaboration:

```
# 1. Create feature branch from updated main
git checkout main
git pull origin main
git checkout -b feature/shopping-cart

# 2. Make changes and commit
git add src/components/ShoppingCart.js
git commit -m "Implement shopping cart component with local storage persistence"

# 3. Push to GitHub
git push origin feature/shopping-cart

# 4. Create pull request via GitHub UI or CLI
gh pr create --title "Add shopping cart functionality" \
  --body "Implements persistent shopping cart using local storage"
```

Pull requests serve multiple purposes beyond code review. They document why changes were made, provide a forum for discussing implementation decisions, and create a permanent record of project evolution. Teams can require reviews before merging and maintain high code quality standards.

Effective commit messages contribute significantly to project maintainability. A well-crafted commit history tells the story of your project's development. The conventional commits specification provides a structured approach:

```
1  # Structure: <type>(<scope>): <subject>
2  # Types: feat, fix, docs, style, refactor, test, chore
3
4  git commit -m "feat(auth): add JWT token refresh mechanism"
5  git commit -m "fix(cart): prevent duplicate items when adding quickly"
6  git commit -m "docs(api): update authentication endpoint documentation"
```

This structure enables automated changelog generation and helps team members quickly understand the nature of changes.

12.4.2   Development Environments and Tooling

Modern web development involves numerous languages, frameworks, and build tools that must work together seamlessly. Creating consistent, productive development environments has become crucial for individual productivity and team collaboration.

Node.js fundamentally changed JavaScript development by providing a runtime environment outside the browser. The Node Package Manager (npm) has become the world's largest software registry. A typical modern project starts with a `package.json` file that defines all dependencies and scripts:

```json
1  {
2    "name": "modern-web-app",
3    "version": "1.0.0",
4    "scripts": {
5      "start": "webpack serve --mode development",
6      "build": "webpack --mode production",
7      "test": "jest",
8      "lint": "eslint src/**/*.js"
9    },
10   "dependencies": {
11     "react": "^18.2.0",
12     "axios": "^1.4.0"
13   },
14   "devDependencies": {
15     "webpack": "^5.88.0",
16     "jest": "^29.5.0",
17     "eslint": "^8.43.0"
18   }
19 }
```

This manifest file serves several critical purposes. It documents all project dependencies with specific versions, ensuring everyone uses compatible packages. Scripts provide consistent commands across different environments. The separation between dependencies (needed in production) and devDependencies (only for development) optimizes deployment size.

Build tools like Webpack have become essential for modern development. They handle numerous tasks that would be tedious or error-prone to manage manually. A basic Webpack configuration demonstrates the complexity it manages:

```js
// webpack.config.js
module.exports = {
  entry: './src/index.js',
  module: {
    rules: [
      {
        test: /\.jsx?$/,
        exclude: /node_modules/,
        use: 'babel-loader'  // Transpile modern JS for browsers
      },
      {
        test: /\.css$/,
        use: ['style-loader', 'css-loader']  // Process CSS
      }
    ]
  },
  devServer: {
    hot: true  // Enable hot module replacement
  }
};
```

This configuration enables several powerful features. Modern JavaScript syntax gets transpiled for browser compatibility. CSS files can be imported directly into JavaScript modules. The development server automatically refreshes when code changes, dramatically improving developer productivity.

Code quality tools have become integral to modern workflows. ECMAScript Lint (ESLint) catches potential errors and enforces coding standards:

```js
// .eslintrc.js
module.exports = {
  extends: ['eslint:recommended'],
  rules: {
    'no-unused-vars': 'warn',
    'no-console': ['warn', { allow: ['warn', 'error'] }]
  }
};
```


These tools catch common mistakes before code review. They enforce consistent style across team members. Integration with editors provides immediate feedback. Automation ensures standards are maintained.

Docker has revolutionized development environment consistency by containerizing applications:

```dockerfile
FROM node:18-alpine
WORKDIR /app
COPY package*.json ./
RUN npm ci
COPY . .
EXPOSE 3000
CMD ["npm", "start"]
```

This Dockerfile ensures identical environments across all developers and deployment targets. New team members can start contributing immediately without complex setup. Platform-specific configuration issues become obsolete.

12.4.3 Code Quality and Standards

Modern development practices emphasize maintaining high code quality through automated tools and established conventions. These practices prevent bugs, improve maintainability, and facilitate team collaboration while focusing specifically on the development-time aspects of application creation.

Static analysis tools examine code without executing it, identifying potential issues early in the development process. Beyond basic linting, tools like TypeScript add compile-time type checking to JavaScript, catching entire categories of runtime errors during development:

```typescript
// TypeScript catches type mismatches at compile time
interface User {
  id: number;
  email: string;
  preferences: UserPreferences;
}

function updateUser(user: User, updates: Partial<User>): User {
  return { ...user, ...updates };
}

// This would cause a TypeScript error:
// updateUser(user, { id: "invalid" }); // Error: Type 'string' is not assignable to type 'number'
```

Prettier handles automatic code formatting, eliminating debates about style preferences and ensuring consistent formatting across teams:

```
1  // .prettierrc
2  {
3    "semi": true,
4    "trailingComma": "es5",
5    "singleQuote": true,
6    "printWidth": 80,
7    "tabWidth": 2
8  }
```

Code reviews facilitate knowledge sharing and quality assurance. Modern platforms provide sophisticated review tools that integrate with version control workflows. Effective code reviews focus on logic correctness, architectural decisions, and adherence to team standards rather than formatting issues that automated tools handle.

Documentation practices have evolved beyond traditional comments to include automated documentation generation, inline type annotations, and comprehensive README files. Well-documented code reduces onboarding time and maintenance costs. Tools like JSDoc generate documentation from code annotations, ensuring documentation stays synchronized with implementation:

```
1  /**
2   * Calculates the total price including taxes and discounts
3   * @param {Object[]} items - Array of cart items
4   * @param {number} items[].price - Item price
5   * @param {number} items[].quantity - Item quantity
6   * @param {number} [items[].discount=0] - Discount percentage (0-1)
7   * @param {number} taxRate - Tax rate percentage (0-1)
8   * @returns {number} Total price including tax and discounts
9   */
10 function calculateTotal(items, taxRate) {
11   const subtotal = items.reduce((sum, item) => {
12     const itemTotal = item.price * item.quantity;
13     const discount = item.discount || 0;
14     return sum + (itemTotal * (1 - discount));
15   }, 0);
16
17   return subtotal * (1 + taxRate);
18 }
```

Modern development practices have transformed web development from individual craft to collaborative engineering discipline. Version control provides the foundation for team collaboration and project history. Sophisticated development environments boost productivity through automation and consistency. Code quality tools catch issues early and maintain standards. These practices require initial investment in learning and setup but pay substantial dividends through reduced bugs, easier maintenance, and more confident development cycles.

12.5 Mobile Considerations

12.5.1 The Mobile-First Imperative

The proliferation of smartphones and tablets has fundamentally altered how people access the web. Mobile devices now account for over half of global web traffic, with some regions seeing mobile usage exceed 70%. This shift demands more than simply making websites "work" on smaller screens; it requires rethinking how we design, develop, and optimize web applications from the ground up.

The mobile-first approach represents a philosophical shift in web development. Rather than designing for desktop and then adapting for mobile, developers now start with mobile constraints and progressively enhance for larger screens. This approach forces clarity and prioritization, as mobile's limited screen space demands focusing on essential features and content.

Consider the constraints that mobile devices impose on web applications. Screen sizes range from 320 pixels wide on older phones to over 400 pixels on modern devices, still far smaller than desktop monitors. Touch targets must be large enough for fingers rather than precise mouse pointers. Network connections vary wildly from fast WiFi to spotty cellular coverage. Battery life becomes a concern for JavaScript-heavy applications. Device capabilities differ significantly across the vast mobile ecosystem.

These constraints, rather than being limitations, drive better design decisions. When you must fit essential functionality into a 375-pixel wide screen, you eliminate clutter and focus on what truly matters. When you optimize for slow 3G connections, everyone benefits from faster load times. When you design for touch interaction, you create interfaces that are more intuitive and accessible for all users.

12.5.2 Responsive Web Design Principles

Responsive web design enables web applications to adapt gracefully to different screen sizes and devices. This approach relies on flexible grids, fluid images, and CSS media queries to create layouts that respond to their viewing environment.

The foundation of responsive design lies in the viewport meta tag, which tells mobile browsers how to scale and display content:

```
<meta name="viewport" content="width=device-width, initial-scale=1.0">
```

Without this tag, mobile browsers assume websites are designed for desktop viewing and zoom out to fit the entire page width, resulting in tiny, unreadable text that users must pinch to zoom. The viewport tag instructs browsers to match the device's width and display content at a readable scale.

Fluid Grids and Flexible Layouts

Traditional web design often used fixed pixel widths, creating rigid layouts that broke on different screen sizes. Responsive design embraces relative units and flexible containers:

```css
/* Traditional fixed layout */
.container {
  width: 960px;
  margin: 0 auto;
}

/* Responsive fluid layout */
.container {
  width: 100%;
  max-width: 1200px;
  margin: 0 auto;
  padding: 0 20px;
}

/* Flexible grid system */
.row {
  display: flex;
  flex-wrap: wrap;
  margin: 0 -15px;
}

.col {
  flex: 1;
  padding: 0 15px;
  min-width: 0; /* Prevent flex items from overflowing */
}

/* Responsive columns */
@media (max-width: 768px) {
  .col {
    flex: 0 0 100%; /* Full width on mobile */
  }
}
```

This flexible approach allows content to reflow naturally as screen sizes change. The container expands to fill available space while respecting a maximum width for readability on large screens. Padding provides breathing room on mobile devices where content might otherwise touch screen edges.

Media Queries and Breakpoints

Media queries enable different styles for different screen sizes, device capabilities, and viewing contexts. Rather than creating separate mobile and desktop sites, media queries allow one codebase to adapt intelligently:

```css
/* Base mobile-first styles */
.navigation {
  position: fixed;
  bottom: 0;
  width: 100%;
  display: flex;
  justify-content: space-around;
  background: white;
  box-shadow: 0 -2px 10px rgba(0,0,0,0.1);
}

.nav-item {
  flex: 1;
  text-align: center;
  padding: 10px;
}

/* Tablet styles */
@media (min-width: 768px) {
  .navigation {
    position: static;
    bottom: auto;
    box-shadow: none;
    border-bottom: 1px solid #eee;
  }

  .nav-item {
    flex: 0 0 auto;
    padding: 15px 20px;
  }
}

/* Desktop styles */
@media (min-width: 1024px) {
  .navigation {
    padding: 0 40px;
  }
}
```

```css
39    .nav-item:hover {
40      background: #f5f5f5;
41      transition: background 0.3s ease;
42    }
43  }
```

Figure 12.5 depicts the responsive layout transformation. This mobile-first approach starts with the simplest mobile layout, a fixed bottom navigation common in mobile apps. As screen size increases, the navigation moves to a traditional top position and gains hover effects that make sense only with mouse interaction.

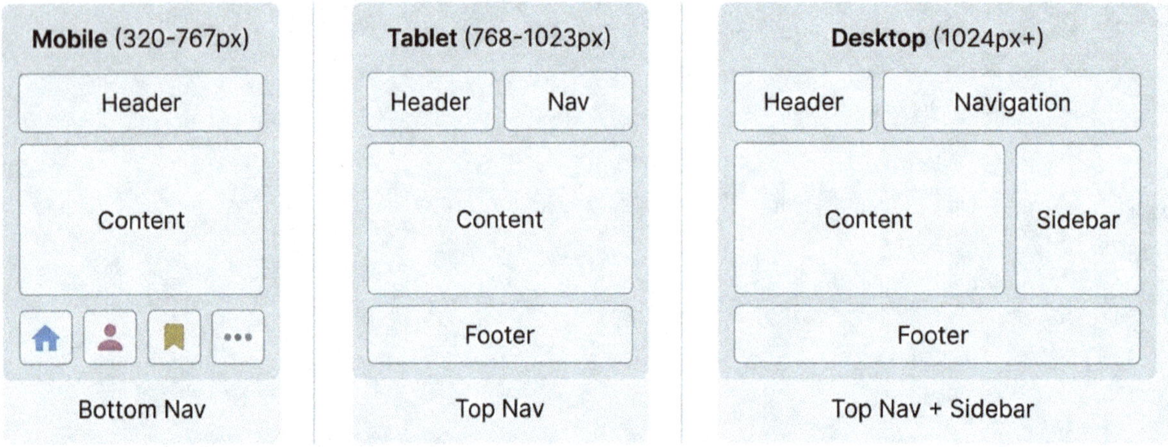

Figure 12.5: Responsive layout transformation.

Responsive Images and Media

Images present particular challenges in responsive design. A high-resolution image suitable for desktop viewing wastes bandwidth on mobile devices, while a small mobile image appears pixelated on high-resolution displays. Modern HTML provides several solutions:

```html
1  <!-- Responsive images with srcset -->
2  <img
3    src="product-400.jpg"
4    srcset="product-400.jpg 400w,
5            product-800.jpg 800w,
6            product-1200.jpg 1200w"
7    sizes="(max-width: 600px) 100vw,
8           (max-width: 1200px) 50vw,
9           33vw"
10   alt="Product photo"
```

```
11  >
12
13  <!-- Art direction with picture element -->
14  <picture>
15    <source
16      media="(max-width: 599px)"
17      srcset="product-mobile.jpg"
18    >
19    <source
20      media="(min-width: 600px)"
21      srcset="product-desktop.jpg"
22    >
23    <img src="product-desktop.jpg" alt="Product photo">
24  </picture>
```

The `srcset` attribute allows browsers to choose appropriately sized images based on device capabilities and network conditions. The `sizes` attribute tells browsers how large the image will be displayed at different viewport widths, enabling intelligent image selection before layout calculation. The `picture` element goes further, allowing different images for different contexts, such as a cropped square image for mobile and a wide banner for desktop.

Responsive Typography

Text readability on mobile devices requires careful attention to font sizes, line lengths, and spacing. Responsive typography scales smoothly across devices:

```
1   /* Base typography with fluid scaling */
2   html {
3     font-size: 16px;
4   }
5
6   body {
7     font-family: -apple-system, BlinkMacSystemFont, 'Segoe UI',
8                  Roboto, sans-serif;
9     line-height: 1.6;
10    color: #333;
11  }
12
13  /* Fluid typography using clamp() */
14  h1 {
15    font-size: clamp(1.75rem, 5vw, 3rem);
16    line-height: 1.2;
```

```css
17      margin-bottom: 0.5em;
18  }
19
20  p {
21      font-size: clamp(1rem, 2vw, 1.125rem);
22      max-width: 65ch; /* Optimal line length */
23  }
24
25  /* Responsive spacing */
26  .section {
27      padding: clamp(2rem, 5vw, 4rem) 0;
28  }
29
30  /* Adjust for reading distance on mobile */
31  @media (max-width: 600px) {
32      body {
33        font-size: 18px; /* Slightly larger for mobile reading */
34      }
35  }
```

The `clamp()` function creates truly fluid typography that scales smoothly between minimum and maximum values. This approach eliminates jarring jumps at breakpoints while ensuring text remains readable at all screen sizes. The `ch` unit for maximum paragraph width ensures optimal line length regardless of font size.

12.5.3   Touch Interactions and Mobile UX

Designing for touch requires fundamental changes in how we think about user interaction. Mouse pointers offer pixel-perfect precision, while fingers are relatively large and imprecise. This difference affects every interactive element in your application.

Touch targets must be large enough for comfortable interaction. Research shows that touch targets should be at least 44x44 pixels to ensure reliable interaction:

```css
1  /* Ensure adequate touch targets */
2  button,
3  .btn {
4      min-height: 44px;
5      min-width: 44px;
6      padding: 12px 24px;
7  }
8
9  /* Increase clickable area for small icons */
10  .icon-button {
```

```css
11    position: relative;
12    width: 24px;
13    height: 24px;
14  }
15
16  .icon-button::before {
17    content: '';
18    position: absolute;
19    top: -10px;
20    left: -10px;
21    right: -10px;
22    bottom: -10px;
23  }
```

Touch interactions differ from mouse interactions in several important ways. Touch devices support gestures like swipe and pinch that have no mouse equivalent. Hover states do not exist on touch devices, requiring alternative ways to reveal information.

Implementing touch-friendly interfaces requires handling these differences gracefully:

```javascript
1   // Touch-friendly carousel implementation
2   class TouchCarousel {
3     constructor(element) {
4       this.element = element;
5       this.startX = 0;
6       this.isDragging = false;
7
8       this.bindEvents();
9     }
10
11    bindEvents() {
12      this.element.addEventListener('touchstart', this.handleStart.bind(this));
13      this.element.addEventListener('touchmove', this.handleMove.bind(this));
14      this.element.addEventListener('touchend', this.handleEnd.bind(this));
15    }
16
17    handleStart(e) {
18      this.isDragging = true;
19      this.startX = e.touches[0].clientX;
20    }
21
22    handleMove(e) {
```

```
23     if (!this.isDragging) return;
24
25     e.preventDefault();
26     const currentX = e.touches[0].clientX;
27     const diff = currentX - this.startX;
28
29     this.element.style.transform = `translateX(${diff}px)`;
30   }
31
32   handleEnd() {
33     this.isDragging = false;
34     // Snap to nearest item based on swipe distance
35     this.snapToNearestItem();
36   }
37 }
```

This implementation handles touch events naturally while preventing default scrolling behavior during swipes. The simplified approach focuses on essential touch handling without overwhelming complexity.

12.5.4 Progressive Web Apps

Progressive Web Apps (PWA) represent the convergence of web and native mobile applications. They combine the reach of the web with capabilities traditionally reserved for native apps, including offline functionality, push notifications, and home screen installation.

The foundation of a PWA is the service worker, a JavaScript file that runs in the background and acts as a proxy between your application and the network:

```
1  // service-worker.js
2  const CACHE_NAME = 'app-v1';
3  const urlsToCache = [
4    '/',
5    '/styles/main.css',
6    '/scripts/app.js',
7    '/offline.html'
8  ];
9
10 // Install event - cache essential files
11 self.addEventListener('install', event => {
12   event.waitUntil(
13     caches.open(CACHE_NAME)
14       .then(cache => cache.addAll(urlsToCache))
15   );
```

```javascript
16 });
17
18 // Fetch event - serve from cache when offline
19 self.addEventListener('fetch', event => {
20   event.respondWith(
21     caches.match(event.request)
22       .then(response => {
23         return response || fetch(event.request);
24       })
25       .catch(() => {
26         return caches.match('/offline.html');
27       })
28   );
29 });
```

This service worker enables basic offline functionality by caching essential resources and providing fallbacks when network requests fail.

The Web App Manifest provides metadata that allows PWAs to be installed on devices:

```json
1 {
2   "name": "My Shopping App",
3   "short_name": "Shop",
4   "start_url": "/",
5   "display": "standalone",
6   "theme_color": "#2196F3",
7   "background_color": "#ffffff",
8   "icons": [
9     {
10       "src": "/icons/icon-192.png",
11       "sizes": "192x192",
12       "type": "image/png"
13     },
14     {
15       "src": "/icons/icon-512.png",
16       "sizes": "512x512",
17       "type": "image/png"
18     }
19   ]
20 }
```

This manifest enables home screen installation with proper app icons and full-screen display without browser chrome.

PWAs can also leverage advanced capabilities through modern web APIs:

```javascript
// Push notifications
async function subscribeToPushNotifications() {
  const registration = await navigator.serviceWorker.ready;

  const subscription = await registration.pushManager.subscribe({
    userVisibleOnly: true,
    applicationServerKey: publicVapidKey
  });

  // Send subscription to server
  await fetch('/api/push-subscribe', {
    method: 'POST',
    body: JSON.stringify(subscription),
    headers: { 'Content-Type': 'application/json' }
  });
}

// Background sync for offline actions
navigator.serviceWorker.ready.then(registration => {
  return registration.sync.register('sync-data');
});
```

These capabilities enable PWAs to provide native-like experiences while maintaining the advantages of web distribution. Users can install PWAs without app stores, receive push notifications, and work offline with synchronized data.

12.6   Performance Optimization

12.6.1   Understanding Web Performance

Web performance has become a critical factor in the success of modern applications. Studies consistently show that users abandon sites that take more than three seconds to load, with mobile users being even less patient. Performance affects not only user satisfaction but also business metrics, with faster sites demonstrating higher conversion rates, better search engine rankings, and increased user engagement. Understanding and optimizing performance requires a holistic approach that considers every aspect of how web applications load and run.

The journey of a web page from server to screen involves numerous steps, each presenting opportunities for optimization. When a user enters a URL or clicks a link, the browser must resolve the domain name through DNS, establish a TCP connection with the server, negotiate SSL/TLS encryption for HTTPS, send the HTTP request, wait for the server to process and respond, download the HTML response, parse the HTML and construct the DOM, discover and download additional resources like CSS and JavaScript, parse and execute

CSS and JavaScript, render the page layout, and finally paint pixels to the screen. Any delay in these steps compounds into perceived slowness.

Modern browsers provide sophisticated performance measurement APIs that help developers understand exactly where time is spent. The Navigation Timing API exposes detailed timing information about the page load process:

```javascript
// Measure key performance metrics
window.addEventListener('load', () => {
  const perfData = window.performance.timing;
  const pageLoadTime = perfData.loadEventEnd - perfData.navigationStart;
  const dnsTime = perfData.domainLookupEnd - perfData.domainLookupStart;
  const tcpTime = perfData.connectEnd - perfData.connectStart;
  const requestTime = perfData.responseEnd - perfData.requestStart;
  const domProcessing = perfData.domComplete - perfData.domLoading;

  console.log('Performance Metrics:', {
    'Total Page Load': `${pageLoadTime}ms`,
    'DNS Lookup': `${dnsTime}ms`,
    'TCP Connection': `${tcpTime}ms`,
    'Request/Response': `${requestTime}ms`,
    'DOM Processing': `${domProcessing}ms`
  });
});
```

Understanding these metrics helps identify bottlenecks. High DNS lookup times might indicate the need for DNS prefetching. Slow TCP connections could suggest exploring HTTP/2 or HTTP/3. Long request times might point to server-side performance issues. Extended DOM processing could indicate overly complex HTML or inefficient JavaScript.

12.6.2 Critical Rendering Path Optimization

The critical rendering path represents the sequence of steps browsers must complete before rendering content on screen. Understanding this process is fundamental to web performance optimization because it directly affects the time users wait before seeing meaningful content. The browser must parse HTML to construct the Document Object Model, process CSS to build the CSS Object Model, combine these to create the render tree, calculate layout geometry, and finally paint pixels to the screen. Each step in this sequence can introduce delays that compound into poor user experience.

The most significant bottleneck in this process is CSS, which blocks rendering by design. Browsers refuse to display content until they have processed all stylesheets because doing so would create a flash of unstyled content. While this behavior protects visual consistency, it can severely delay the initial render when CSS files are large or slow to load. The solution involves identifying critical CSS, which is the minimum styles needed for above-the-fold content, and delivering it immediately while deferring non-essential styles:

```html
<!DOCTYPE html>
<html>
<head>
  <meta charset="UTF-8">
  <meta name="viewport" content="width=device-width, initial-scale=1.0">
  <title>Optimized Page</title>

  <!-- Critical CSS inlined -->
  <style>
    body { margin: 0; font-family: sans-serif; }
    .header { background: #333; color: white; padding: 1rem; }
    .hero { padding: 2rem; text-align: center; }
  </style>

  <!-- Non-critical CSS loaded asynchronously -->
  <link rel="preload" href="/css/main.css" as="style"
        onload="this.onload=null;this.rel='stylesheet'">
  <noscript><link rel="stylesheet" href="/css/main.css"></noscript>
</head>
<body>
  <header class="header">
    <h1>My Fast Site</h1>
  </header>

  <section class="hero">
    <h1>Welcome</h1>
    <p>Critical content loads immediately</p>
  </section>

  <script async src="/js/app.js"></script>
</body>
</html>
```

This optimization strategy provides immediate visual feedback to users while maintaining a polished appearance. The inlined critical CSS ensures that users see properly styled content within milliseconds of the HTML arriving. The preload directive instructs the browser to fetch the complete stylesheet in the background while the async loading pattern prevents it from blocking the initial render. This approach typically reduces time to first contentful paint by several hundred milliseconds, creating a noticeably faster experience.

JavaScript presents additional challenges for critical rendering path optimization because scripts block HTML parsing by default. Modern applications require substantial JavaScript to function, but loading it all upfront creates unacceptable delays. Progressive enhancement addresses this challenge by delivering core functionality immediately while loading enhanced features on demand:

```javascript
// Progressive enhancement pattern
document.addEventListener('DOMContentLoaded', () => {
  // Core functionality available immediately
  initializeBasicFeatures();

  // Load enhanced features on demand
  const enhanceButton = document.querySelector('.enhance-button');
  enhanceButton?.addEventListener('click', () => {
    loadScript('/js/enhanced-features.js', () => {
      window.EnhancedFeatures.init();
    });
  }, { once: true });
});

function loadScript(src, callback) {
  const script = document.createElement('script');
  script.src = src;
  script.async = true;
  script.onload = callback;
  document.body.appendChild(script);
}
```

This progressive loading strategy ensures that users can interact with the application immediately while enhanced features load in the background. The pattern respects user agency by loading additional functionality only when requested, reducing bandwidth usage and improving performance for users who never access advanced features. The async attribute prevents these dynamically loaded scripts from blocking user interactions, maintaining responsiveness throughout the loading process.

12.6.3   Code Splitting and Lazy Loading

Traditional web applications ship all JavaScript code in a single bundle that users must download entirely before the application becomes functional. This approach works well for small applications but becomes problematic as codebases grow. Modern e-commerce sites, social media platforms, and productivity applications can easily exceed several megabytes of JavaScript, creating unacceptable load times even on fast connections. Code splitting addresses this challenge by breaking applications into smaller chunks that load on demand, dramatically reducing the time to interactive.

Figure 12.6 articulates the code splitting strategy. The benefits of code splitting extend beyond initial load performance. Route-based splitting ensures users download only the code needed for their current page, while feature-based splitting loads functionality as users access it. This approach respects user bandwidth and device capabilities while providing a smooth experience that scales with application complexity. Modern bundlers make code splitting straightforward through dynamic imports, which tell the bundler to create separate chunks automatically.

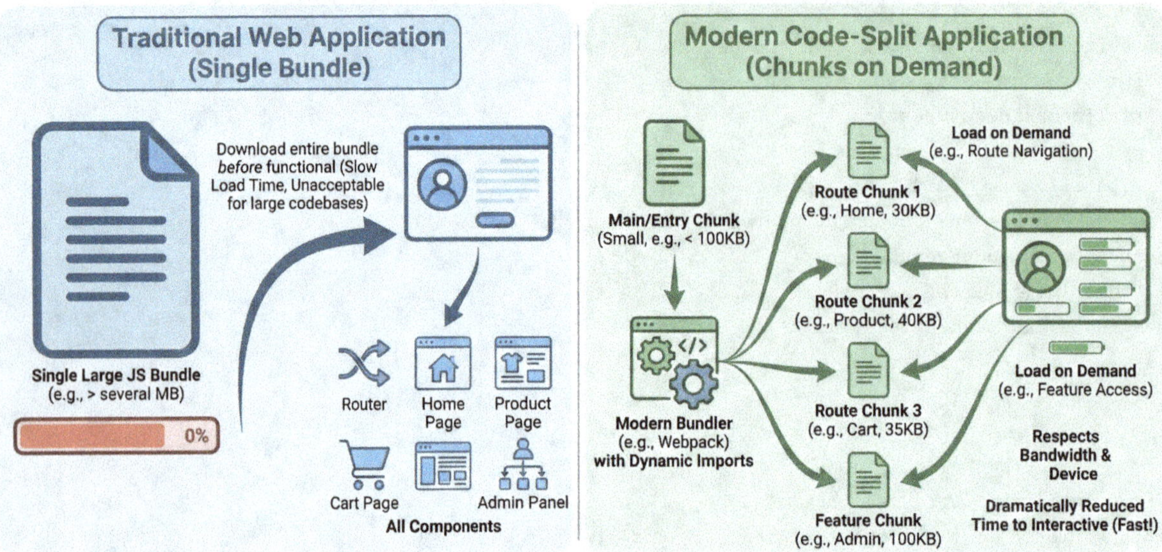

Figure 12.6: Code splitting strategy.

This transformation from a monolithic bundle to strategically split chunks represents a fundamental shift in how applications load. Instead of waiting for 500KB of JavaScript to download and parse, users can begin interacting with the application after downloading just 50KB. Additional functionality loads seamlessly as users navigate, creating the impression of instant page transitions while actually downloading code in the background:

```javascript
// Route-based code splitting with React
import React, { lazy, Suspense } from 'react';
import { BrowserRouter, Route, Switch } from 'react-router-dom';

// Lazy loaded route components
const Home = lazy(() => import('./pages/Home'));
const Products = lazy(() => import('./pages/Products'));
const Admin = lazy(() =>
  import(/* webpackChunkName: "admin" */ './pages/Admin')
);

function App() {
  return (
    <BrowserRouter>
      <Suspense fallback={<div>Loading...</div>}>
```

```
16        <Switch>
17          <Route exact path="/" component={Home} />
18          <Route path="/products" component={Products} />
19          <Route path="/admin" component={Admin} />
20        </Switch>
21      </Suspense>
22    </BrowserRouter>
23  );
24 }
```

React's lazy loading implementation demonstrates how modern frameworks have embraced code splitting as a core feature. The `lazy` function creates a component that loads only when needed, while Suspense provides a graceful fallback during loading. The webpack magic comment allows developers to name chunks for better debugging and cache optimization. This approach typically reduces initial bundle size by 60–80% while maintaining smooth user experience through intelligent preloading and caching.

Lazy loading extends beyond JavaScript to encompass all types of media and resources. Images represent the largest portion of most web pages by file size, making them prime candidates for lazy loading optimization. The goal is to load images just before users would see them, avoiding wasted bandwidth while maintaining the illusion of instant availability:

```
1  // Modern lazy loading implementation
2  class LazyImageLoader {
3    constructor() {
4      this.init();
5    }
6
7    init() {
8      if ('loading' in HTMLImageElement.prototype) {
9        this.useNativeLazyLoading();
10     } else {
11       this.useIntersectionObserver();
12     }
13   }
14
15   useNativeLazyLoading() {
16     const images = document.querySelectorAll('img[data-src]');
17     images.forEach(img => {
18       img.src = img.dataset.src;
19       img.loading = 'lazy';
20     });
21   }
```

```
22
23   useIntersectionObserver() {
24     const observer = new IntersectionObserver((entries) => {
25       entries.forEach(entry => {
26         if (entry.isIntersecting) {
27           const img = entry.target;
28           img.src = img.dataset.src;
29           img.classList.add('loaded');
30           observer.unobserve(img);
31         }
32       });
33     });
34
35     document.querySelectorAll('img[data-src]').forEach(img => {
36       observer.observe(img);
37     });
38   }
39 }
40
41 new LazyImageLoader();
```

This implementation demonstrates progressive enhancement at its finest. Modern browsers support native lazy loading through the `loading` attribute, providing optimal performance with minimal code. Older browsers fall back to the Intersection Observer API, which provides efficient scroll-based loading without the performance penalties of traditional scroll event listeners. The approach gracefully handles edge cases while providing excellent performance across all browser generations.

12.6.4   Client-Side Caching Strategies

Effective client-side caching represents one of the most impactful performance optimizations available to web developers. By storing previously fetched resources locally, applications can eliminate network requests entirely, providing instant responses to user actions. However, caching introduces complexity around cache invalidation, storage limits, and data freshness that requires careful strategy to manage effectively. Modern web applications employ multiple caching layers that work together to optimize both performance and reliability.

Service workers have revolutionized client-side caching by providing programmatic control over network requests. Unlike traditional browser caching, which relies entirely on HTTP headers, service workers enable sophisticated caching strategies that adapt to application needs. The cache-first strategy works excellently for static assets that rarely change, while network-first strategies ensure fresh data for dynamic content while providing offline fallbacks:

```
1  // Service worker with multiple caching strategies
2  const CACHE_VERSION = 'v2';
```

```javascript
3  const STATIC_CACHE = `static-${CACHE_VERSION}`;
4  const DYNAMIC_CACHE = `dynamic-${CACHE_VERSION}`;
5
6  // Cache-first strategy for static assets
7  async function cacheFirst(request) {
8    const cachedResponse = await caches.match(request);
9    if (cachedResponse) {
10     return cachedResponse;
11   }
12
13   const networkResponse = await fetch(request);
14   if (networkResponse.ok) {
15     const cache = await caches.open(STATIC_CACHE);
16     cache.put(request, networkResponse.clone());
17   }
18
19   return networkResponse;
20 }
21 // Network-first strategy for API calls
22 async function networkFirst(request) {
23   try {
24     const networkResponse = await fetch(request);
25
26     if (networkResponse.ok) {
27       const cache = await caches.open(DYNAMIC_CACHE);
28       cache.put(request, networkResponse.clone());
29     }
30
31     return networkResponse;
32   } catch (error) {
33     return await caches.match(request);
34   }
35 }
36 self.addEventListener('fetch', event => {
37   const { request } = event;
38
39   if (request.url.match(/\.(js|css|woff2?)$/)) {
40     event.respondWith(cacheFirst(request));
41   } else if (request.url.includes('/api/')) {
42     event.respondWith(networkFirst(request));
43   }
44 });
```

This service worker implementation demonstrates how different resources require different caching approaches. Static assets like JavaScript files, stylesheets, and fonts benefit from cache-first strategies because they rarely change and users expect them to load instantly. API responses require network-first strategies to ensure data freshness while providing offline capabilities when networks fail. The versioned cache names enable clean cache management during application updates, preventing stale content from interfering with new functionality.

In-memory caching provides additional performance benefits for computationally expensive operations that produce deterministic results. While service worker caching optimizes network requests, in-memory caching eliminates redundant calculations and data processing. This approach particularly benefits applications that perform complex mathematical calculations, image processing, or data transformations that might be repeated with the same inputs:

```javascript
// Simple LRU cache for expensive calculations
class LRUCache {
  constructor(maxSize = 50) {
    this.maxSize = maxSize;
    this.cache = new Map();
  }

  get(key) {
    if (this.cache.has(key)) {
      const value = this.cache.get(key);
      this.cache.delete(key);
      this.cache.set(key, value);
      return value;
    }
    return null;
  }

  set(key, value) {
    if (this.cache.size >= this.maxSize) {
      const firstKey = this.cache.keys().next().value;
      this.cache.delete(firstKey);
    }
    this.cache.set(key, value);
  }
}

const calculationCache = new LRUCache();

function expensiveCalculation(input) {
  const cacheKey = JSON.stringify(input);
  const cached = calculationCache.get(cacheKey);
```

```
32
33   if (cached !== null) {
34     return cached;
35   }
36
37   const result = performComplexCalculation(input);
38   calculationCache.set(cacheKey, result);
39   return result;
40 }
```

The Least Recently Used cache implementation provides automatic memory management while maintaining excellent hit rates for frequently accessed data. This pattern works particularly well for operations like search result processing, data aggregation, or format conversions that users might repeat within a single session. The cache automatically evicts old entries to prevent memory growth while preserving recently accessed results that users are likely to need again.

12.6.5 Measuring Client-Side Performance

Performance optimization without measurement is merely guesswork. Understanding how applications perform in real-world conditions across diverse devices, networks, and user patterns requires comprehensive monitoring that captures both technical metrics and user experience indicators. The Web Vitals initiative has standardized the most important performance metrics that correlate with user satisfaction, providing a foundation for performance measurement that aligns technical optimization with business outcomes.

Core Web Vitals represent the essential metrics that every web application should monitor. Largest Contentful Paint measures loading performance by tracking when the largest element becomes visible. First Input Delay captures interactivity by measuring the delay between user input and browser response. Cumulative Layout Shift quantifies visual stability by tracking unexpected layout changes that frustrate users. These metrics provide objective measures of subjective user experience:

```
1  // Measuring Core Web Vitals
2  import { getCLS, getFID, getLCP } from 'web-vitals';
3
4  function sendToAnalytics(metric) {
5    const body = JSON.stringify({
6      name: metric.name,
7      value: metric.value,
8      url: window.location.href,
9      timestamp: Date.now()
10   });
11
12   if (navigator.sendBeacon) {
13     navigator.sendBeacon('/api/metrics', body);
```

```
14    }
15 }
16
17 // Measure core metrics
18 getCLS(sendToAnalytics);      // Cumulative Layout Shift
19 getFID(sendToAnalytics);      // First Input Delay
20 getLCP(sendToAnalytics);      // Largest Contentful Paint
```

Web Vitals provide standardized metrics that enable comparison across applications and tracking improvement over time. However, applications often require custom metrics that reflect specific user journeys or business-critical operations. Custom performance monitoring captures application-specific timings that help identify bottlenecks in user workflows and track the performance impact of feature changes:

```
1  // Custom performance monitoring
2  class PerformanceMonitor {
3    start(name) {
4      performance.mark(`${name}-start`);
5    }
6
7    end(name) {
8      performance.mark(`${name}-end`);
9      performance.measure(name, `${name}-start`, `${name}-end`);
10
11     const measure = performance.getEntriesByName(name)[0];
12     const duration = measure.duration;
13
14     if (duration > 100) {
15       console.warn(`Slow operation: ${name} took ${duration.toFixed(2)}ms`);
16     }
17
18     sendToAnalytics({
19       name: `custom.${name}`,
20       value: duration
21     });
22   }
23 }
24
25 const perfMonitor = new PerformanceMonitor();
26
27 // Usage example
28 async function loadProductData(productId) {
```

```
29   perfMonitor.start('product-load');
30
31   try {
32     const data = await fetch(`/api/products/${productId}`);
33     const product = await data.json();
34     perfMonitor.end('product-load');
35     return product;
36   } catch (error) {
37     perfMonitor.end('product-load');
38     throw error;
39   }
40 }
```

This custom monitoring approach provides insights into application-specific performance characteristics that Web Vitals cannot capture. By measuring operations like product loading, search execution, or checkout completion, development teams can identify performance regressions before they impact user experience. The automated warning system helps catch performance problems during development, while the analytics integration enables long-term performance tracking across releases and user segments. The combination of standardized Web Vitals and custom application metrics provides comprehensive visibility into performance that guides optimization efforts and validates improvements.

12.7   API Design and Consumption

12.7.1   The Evolution of Web APIs

Web APIs have transformed from simple data endpoints into sophisticated interfaces that power the modern web ecosystem. The journey from early Extensible Markup Language Remote Procedure Call (XML-RPC) and Simple Object Access Protocol (SOAP) services to today's RESTful and GraphQL APIs reflects the web's evolution toward simplicity, flexibility, and developer experience. Understanding this evolution helps developers appreciate why certain patterns have emerged and how to design APIs that stand the test of time.

The early days of web services were dominated by SOAP, which brought enterprise-style service-oriented architecture to the web. SOAP required complex XML envelopes for every request and response, with strict contracts defined in WSDL (Web Services Description Language) files. While this approach provided strong type safety and comprehensive tooling, it proved cumbersome for web developers accustomed to the simplicity of HTTP. A simple request to fetch user data might require dozens of lines of XML, specialized libraries to parse responses, and careful namespace management.

REST emerged as a return to web fundamentals, embracing HTTP's design rather than abstracting it away. Roy Fielding's dissertation introduced REST not as a protocol but as an architectural style that leverages the web's existing infrastructure. This alignment with HTTP made REST APIs immediately familiar to web developers. Instead of complex XML envelopes, developers could make simple HTTP requests to URLs representing resources. The simplicity of using standard HTTP methods (GET, POST, PUT, DELETE) to manipulate resources revolutionized how developers thought about web services.

Today's API landscape continues to evolve with GraphQL offering query flexibility, gRPC Remote Procedure Call (gRPC) providing high-performance binary protocols, and WebSocket enabling real-time bidirectional communication. Each approach serves specific needs, but REST remains dominant due to its simplicity and broad support. Understanding when to use each technology requires evaluating your specific requirements for performance, flexibility, caching, and developer experience.

12.7.2   Designing RESTful APIs That Scale

Creating APIs that remain maintainable and performant as they grow requires thoughtful design from the beginning. Well-designed APIs become assets that accelerate development, while poorly designed ones become technical debt that hampers progress. The principles of REST provide a foundation, but successful APIs require additional considerations around versioning, security, and developer experience.

Resource modeling forms the core of RESTful design. Rather than thinking in terms of functions or procedures, REST encourages modeling your domain as resources that can be manipulated through standard operations. Consider how we might model a user resource:

```javascript
// RESTful routes for user resources
app.get('/api/users/:id', getUser);
app.patch('/api/users/:id', updateUser);
app.delete('/api/users/:id', deleteUser);
app.get('/api/users/:id/orders', getUserOrders);
```

This resource-oriented approach reveals several important principles. The URL structure clearly identifies what resource we are working with (/api/users/123 refers to the user with ID 123). The HTTP method indicates the intended operation without needing custom action names in the URL. Related resources are accessed through logical paths that mirror their relationships (/api/users/123/orders fetches orders belonging to user 123).

When implementing these endpoints, consistency in response formats helps clients handle data predictably:

```javascript
async function getUser(req, res, next) {
  try {
    const user = await User.findById(req.params.id);

    if (!user) {
      return res.status(404).json({
        error: {
          code: 'USER_NOT_FOUND',
          message: 'The requested user does not exist'
        }
      });
    }
```

```
13
14    res.json({
15      data: {
16        id: user.id,
17        email: user.email,
18        name: user.name,
19        createdAt: user.createdAt,
20        _links: {
21          self: `/api/users/${user.id}`,
22          orders: `/api/users/${user.id}/orders`
23        }
24      }
25    });
26  } catch (error) {
27    next(error);
28  }
29 }
```

This response structure demonstrates several best practices. The actual user data is wrapped in a `data` property, allowing room for metadata at the top level. Error responses follow a consistent format with machine-readable codes and human-readable messages. The `_links` object provides hypermedia links, enabling clients to discover related resources without hardcoding URLs.

API versioning represents one of the most challenging aspects of API design. Once clients depend on your API, any breaking change can cause widespread issues. URL versioning provides the clearest approach:

```
1  // Version 1 response format
2  app.get('/api/v1/products/:id', (req, res) => {
3    const product = await Product.findById(req.params.id);
4    res.json({
5      id: product.id,
6      title: product.name,    // V1 used 'title'
7      price: product.price
8    });
9  });
10
11 // Version 2 with improved structure
12 app.get('/api/v2/products/:id', (req, res) => {
13   const product = await Product.findById(req.params.id);
14   res.json({
15     data: {
16       id: product.id,
```

```
17      name: product.name,  // V2 uses 'name'
18      price: {
19        amount: product.price,
20        currency: product.currency
21      }
22    }
23  });
24 });
```

The versioning strategy shows how APIs evolved over time. Version 1 used a flat structure with field names that seemed reasonable initially. Version 2 improves the design by wrapping the response in a data object (allowing for future metadata), using more accurate field names, and providing richer data structures for complex fields like price. Supporting both versions simultaneously allows existing clients to continue functioning while new clients benefit from improvements.

Handling collections efficiently becomes crucial as data grows. Pagination, filtering, and sorting must be designed thoughtfully:

```
1  app.get('/api/products', async (req, res) => {
2    const page = parseInt(req.query.page) || 1;
3    const limit = parseInt(req.query.limit) || 20;
4    const skip = (page - 1) * limit;
5
6    const filter = {};
7    if (req.query.category) filter.category = req.query.category;
8    if (req.query.minPrice) filter.price = { $gte: parseFloat(req.query.minPrice) };
9
10   const [products, total] = await Promise.all([
11     Product.find(filter).skip(skip).limit(limit),
12     Product.countDocuments(filter)
13   ]);
14
15   res.json({
16     data: products,
17     pagination: {
18       page,
19       limit,
20       total,
21       pages: Math.ceil(total / limit)
22     },
23     links: {
24       next: page < Math.ceil(total / limit)
```

```
25          ? `/api/products?page=${page + 1}&limit=${limit}`
26          : null
27      }
28   });
29 });
```

This implementation demonstrates how query parameters enable flexible data retrieval. Clients can control pagination through `page` and `limit` parameters. Filters like `category` and `minPrice` allow targeted queries without creating separate endpoints. The response includes pagination metadata, helping clients understand the result set and navigate through pages. Including `next` and `prev` links in the response enables clients to paginate without constructing URLs manually.

12.7.3 GraphQL Implementation Patterns

GraphQL represents a paradigm shift in API design, moving from fixed endpoints to flexible queries. While REST organizes around resources accessed through URLs, GraphQL provides a single endpoint where clients specify exactly what data they need. This flexibility comes with its own patterns and best practices for successful implementation.

The schema-first approach to GraphQL development ensures that API contracts are well-defined before implementation begins. Consider this schema for a user type:

```
1 type User {
2   id: ID!
3   email: String!
4   name: String!
5   profile: UserProfile
6   orders(first: Int = 20, after: String): OrderConnection!
7   createdAt: DateTime!
8 }
9
10 type UserProfile {
11   bio: String
12   avatar: String
13   preferences: JSON
14 }
```

This schema definition illustrates several GraphQL concepts. The exclamation marks indicate required fields that will never be null. The `profile` field is optional (no exclamation mark), meaning it might be null if the user has not created a profile. The `orders` field accepts arguments for pagination, with default values provided. This allows clients to request a user's orders with control over how many to fetch.

The real power of GraphQL becomes apparent when clients can request exactly the data they need:

```graphql
# Client requests only specific fields
query GetUserBasics($id: ID!) {
  user(id: $id) {
    name
    email
  }
}

# Another client needs more data
query GetUserWithOrders($id: ID!) {
  user(id: $id) {
    name
    email
    profile {
      avatar
    }
    orders(first: 5) {
      edges {
        node {
          id
          total
          status
        }
      }
    }
  }
}
```

Both queries hit the same GraphQL endpoint, but return different data based on client needs. The first query returns minimal user information, perfect for displaying a simple greeting. The second query includes profile data and recent orders, suitable for a user dashboard. This flexibility eliminates over-fetching (getting data you do not need) and under-fetching (requiring multiple requests).

Implementing resolvers requires careful attention to performance. Each field in the schema needs a resolver function that knows how to fetch its data:

```javascript
const resolvers = {
  User: {
    // Simple field resolvers often aren't needed if names match

    // Async resolver for related data
    profile: async (user) => {
```

```
7      return await UserProfile.findOne({ userId: user.id });
8    },
9
10   // Resolver with arguments
11   orders: async (user, { first, after }) => {
12     const orders = await Order.find({ userId: user.id })
13       .limit(first)
14       .sort({ createdAt: -1 });
15
16     return {
17       edges: orders.map(order => ({ node: order })),
18       pageInfo: { hasNextPage: orders.length === first }
19     };
20   }
21  }
22 };
```

The resolver pattern provides fine-grained control over data fetching. Each field can be resolved independently, allowing GraphQL to fetch only requested data. The `profile` resolver only runs if the client requests the profile field. Similarly, the `orders` resolver receives pagination arguments directly from the query. This lazy evaluation prevents unnecessary database queries.

However, naive resolver implementation can lead to the N+1 query problem. If you fetch 10 users and request their profiles, you might execute 11 queries (1 for users, 10 for profiles). DataLoader solves this by batching and caching requests:

```
1  const DataLoader = require('dataloader');
2
3  // Create a batch loading function
4  async function batchLoadProfiles(userIds) {
5    const profiles = await UserProfile.find({
6      userId: { $in: userIds }
7    });
8
9    // Map results back to match input order
10   const profileMap = {};
11   profiles.forEach(profile => {
12     profileMap[profile.userId] = profile;
13   });
14
15   return userIds.map(id => profileMap[id] || null);
16 }
```

```javascript
17
18  // Use DataLoader in context
19  const context = {
20    loaders: {
21      profile: new DataLoader(batchLoadProfiles)
22    }
23  };
24
25  // Updated resolver using DataLoader
26  const resolvers = {
27    User: {
28      profile: (user, args, context) => {
29        return context.loaders.profile.load(user.id);
30      }
31    }
32  };
```

DataLoader transforms multiple individual requests into a single batch query. When resolving multiple users' profiles, DataLoader collects all the user IDs and makes one database query instead of many. It also caches results within a single request, preventing duplicate fetches. This optimization is crucial for maintaining performance as query complexity grows.

GraphQL subscriptions add real-time capabilities, completing the query-mutation-subscription triad:

```graphql
1  type Subscription {
2    orderStatusChanged(orderId: ID!): Order!
3  }
```

This subscription allows clients to receive real-time updates when an order's status changes. Clients establish a persistent connection and receive pushed updates, eliminating the need for polling. This pattern works well for notifications, live dashboards, and collaborative features.

12.7.4   API Security and Authentication

Security considerations permeate every aspect of API design. Beyond basic authentication and authorization, modern APIs must defend against sophisticated attacks while maintaining performance and usability. A defense-in-depth approach layers multiple security measures to protect both the API and its consumers.

Token-based authentication has become the standard for modern APIs due to its stateless nature. JSON Web Tokens (JWTs) provide a self-contained way to transmit user identity:

```javascript
const jwt = require('jsonwebtoken');
// Generate tokens with appropriate claims
function generateAccessToken(user) {
  return jwt.sign(
    {
      id: user.id,
      email: user.email,
      roles: user.roles
    },
    process.env.JWT_SECRET,
    {
      expiresIn: '15m',
      issuer: 'api.example.com'
    }
  );
}

// Verify tokens in middleware
async function authenticateToken(req, res, next) {
  const token = req.headers.authorization?.split(' ')[1];

  if (!token) {
    return res.status(401).json({
      error: { code: 'NO_TOKEN', message: 'Authentication required' }
    });
  }

  try {
    const payload = jwt.verify(token, process.env.JWT_SECRET);
    req.user = await User.findById(payload.id);
    next();
  } catch (error) {
    res.status(401).json({
      error: { code: 'INVALID_TOKEN', message: 'Invalid authentication' }
    });
  }
}
```

This authentication system demonstrates several security principles. Tokens have short expiration times (15 minutes) to limit exposure if compromised. The issuer claim helps prevent tokens from being used across different services. The middleware extracts and verifies tokens on each request, maintaining stateless authentication. By storing only the user ID in the token and fetching full user data on each request, the system ensures fresh authorization information.

Rate limiting protects APIs from abuse while ensuring fair usage. A sliding window approach provides smooth limiting:

```javascript
// Simple in-memory rate limiter
const rateLimitMap = new Map();

function rateLimit(maxRequests = 100, windowMs = 60000) {
  return (req, res, next) => {
    const key = req.user?.id || req.ip;
    const now = Date.now();

    // Get or create user's request history
    let requests = rateLimitMap.get(key) || [];

    // Filter out old requests outside the window
    requests = requests.filter(time => now - time < windowMs);

    if (requests.length >= maxRequests) {
      return res.status(429).json({
        error: {
          code: 'RATE_LIMIT',
          message: 'Too many requests',
          retryAfter: Math.ceil((requests[0] + windowMs - now) / 1000)
        }
      });
    }

    requests.push(now);
    rateLimitMap.set(key, requests);
    next();
  };
}
```

This rate limiter tracks request timestamps for each user or IP address. It uses a sliding window that counts requests within the past minute, providing smoother limiting than fixed windows. The implementation includes helpful error responses with retry timing. For production systems, this in-memory approach would be replaced with Redis or similar distributed storage to work across multiple servers.

Input validation prevents injection attacks and ensures data integrity. Using a validation library provides consistent, declarative validation:

```javascript
const { body, validationResult } = require('express-validator');

// Define validation rules
const validateProduct = [
  body('name')
    .trim()
    .notEmpty().withMessage('Name is required')
    .isLength({ max: 100 }).withMessage('Name too long'),

  body('price')
    .isFloat({ min: 0 }).withMessage('Price must be positive')
    .toFloat(),

  body('category')
    .isMongoId().withMessage('Invalid category ID')
];
// Handle validation results
function handleValidation(req, res, next) {
  const errors = validationResult(req);

  if (!errors.isEmpty()) {
    return res.status(400).json({
      error: {
        code: 'VALIDATION_ERROR',
        message: 'Invalid input',
        details: errors.array()
      }
    });
  }

  next();
}
// Apply to routes
app.post('/api/products',
  validateProduct,
  handleValidation,
  createProduct
);
```

This validation approach separates concerns cleanly. Validation rules are declarative and reusable. The middleware pattern allows easy application to routes. Detailed error messages help clients correct their requests. The validation runs before any business logic, failing fast on invalid input.

API security requires constant vigilance and evolution. Regular security audits, dependency updates, and monitoring for unusual patterns help maintain a robust security posture. The principle of least privilege should guide all authorization decisions, granting only the minimum access necessary for each operation. By treating security as a core feature rather than an afterthought, APIs can provide powerful functionality while protecting both the service and its users from evolving threats.

12.8   Microservices and Modern Architectures

12.8.1   From Monoliths to Microservices

The evolution from monolithic architectures to microservices represents one of the most significant shifts in how we design and deploy web applications. Traditional LAMP applications typically follow a monolithic pattern where all functionality resides in a single codebase, shares one database, and deploys as a unified application. While this approach offers simplicity for smaller applications, it presents challenges as systems grow in complexity and scale.

Monolithic architectures served the web well for decades. A typical LAMP monolith might contain user authentication, product management, order processing, and payment handling all within the same PHP codebase. This design offers several advantages including simple development with all code in one place, straightforward debugging with a single application to trace through, easy deployment with one artifact to manage, and consistent data management with a shared database. However, as applications grow, these same characteristics become limitations.

The challenges of monolithic architectures become apparent at scale. When a small change requires redeploying the entire application, deployment risk increases significantly. Different components often have conflicting scaling needs. For example, the product catalog might need horizontal scaling for read-heavy traffic while order processing requires different optimization strategies. Team coordination becomes difficult when dozens of developers work on the same codebase. Technology choices affect the entire application, preventing teams from selecting the best tool for each specific problem.

Microservices architecture addresses these challenges by decomposing applications into small, independent services that communicate over networks. Each service owns its data, deploys independently, and can be developed by a small team using the most appropriate technology stack. Consider how an e-commerce platform might be decomposed:

```
// User Service - Handles authentication
class UserService {
  async login(req, res) {
    const { email, password } = req.body;
    const user = await User.findOne({ email });

    if (!user || !await bcrypt.compare(password, user.password)) {
```

```
 8        return res.status(401).json({ error: 'Invalid credentials' });
 9      }
10
11      const token = generateToken(user);
12      res.json({ token, user: user.toPublicJSON() });
13    }
14  }
15
16  // Product Service - Manages catalog with caching
17  class ProductService {
18    async getProduct(req, res) {
19      const cached = await cache.get(`product:${req.params.id}`);
20      if (cached) return res.json(JSON.parse(cached));
21
22      const product = await Product.findById(req.params.id);
23      await cache.setex(`product:${req.params.id}`, 300, JSON.stringify(product));
24      res.json(product);
25    }
26  }
```

Each service encapsulates specific business capabilities. The User Service owns all authentication logic and user data. The Product Service manages the product catalog with its own caching strategy. Services communicate through well-defined APIs, allowing internal implementation changes without affecting other services. This separation enables teams to work independently, deploy on different schedules, and scale services based on their specific needs.

12.8.2 Service Communication Patterns

Microservices must communicate effectively to provide cohesive functionality. Unlike monolithic applications where function calls happen in-process, microservices require network communication with all its complexities including latency, potential failures, and data consistency challenges. Understanding communication patterns helps build reliable distributed systems.

Synchronous communication through HTTP APIs provides the most straightforward approach. When the Order Service needs user and product information, it makes direct requests:

```
 1  // Order Service coordinating with other services
 2  async createOrder(req, res) {
 3    const { userId, items } = req.body;
 4
 5    try {
 6      // Fetch user information
 7      const userResponse = await axios.get(
```

```
 8       `${USER_SERVICE_URL}/users/${userId}`,
 9       { headers: { Authorization: req.headers.authorization } }
10     );
11
12     // Validate products exist
13     const productIds = items.map(item => item.productId);
14     const productsResponse = await axios.post(
15       `${PRODUCT_SERVICE_URL}/products/validate`,
16       { ids: productIds }
17     );
18
19     // Create order with gathered information
20     const order = await Order.create({
21       userId,
22       userEmail: userResponse.data.email,
23       items,
24       total: calculateTotal(items, productsResponse.data)
25     });
26
27     res.status(201).json(order);
28   } catch (error) {
29     handleServiceError(error, res);
30   }
31 }
```

This synchronous approach offers simplicity and immediate consistency but introduces challenges. The order creation depends on the availability of both user and product services. Latency accumulates as requests chain through services. Error handling becomes complex when any service in the chain fails.

Circuit breaker patterns help manage failure scenarios by preventing cascading failures:

```
 1 class CircuitBreaker {
 2   constructor(request, options = {}) {
 3     this.request = request;
 4     this.failureThreshold = options.failureThreshold || 5;
 5     this.resetTimeout = options.resetTimeout || 60000;
 6     this.state = 'CLOSED';
 7     this.failures = 0;
 8   }
 9
10   async call(...args) {
11     if (this.state === 'OPEN') {
```

```
12      throw new Error('Circuit breaker is OPEN');
13    }
14
15    try {
16      const response = await this.request(...args);
17      this.onSuccess();
18      return response;
19    } catch (error) {
20      this.onFailure();
21      throw error;
22    }
23  }
24 }
```

The circuit breaker monitors service health and "opens" after several failures, immediately failing requests instead of waiting for timeouts. This protects both the failing service from overload and the calling service from long delays.

Asynchronous communication through message queues provides an alternative approach that decouples services temporally. Services publish events without waiting for processing:

```
1  // Event-driven order processing
2  async createOrder(req, res) {
3    const order = await Order.create({
4      userId: req.body.userId,
5      items: req.body.items,
6      status: 'pending'
7    });
8
9    // Publish event for other services
10   await messageQueue.publish('order.created', {
11     orderId: order.id,
12     userId: order.userId,
13     items: order.items
14   });
15
16   res.status(202).json({
17     order,
18     message: 'Order accepted for processing'
19   });
20 }
21
```

```
22  // Pricing Service processes orders asynchronously
23  messageQueue.subscribe('order.created', async (event) => {
24    const total = await calculateOrderTotal(event.items);
25
26    await messageQueue.publish('order.priced', {
27      orderId: event.orderId,
28      total
29    });
30  });
```

Event-driven architecture offers several advantages. Services remain loosely coupled, knowing only about events rather than other services' APIs. The system gains natural resilience as message queues buffer events during service outages. Services can be added or removed without changing existing services. Processing happens at each service's pace without blocking others.

12.8.3   Data Management in Microservices

One of the most challenging aspects of microservices architecture involves data management. The principle of service autonomy dictates that each service should own its data, preventing direct database access between services. This approach ensures loose coupling but introduces complexity in maintaining data consistency and performing cross-service queries.

The database-per-service pattern enforces service boundaries at the data layer. Each service maintains its own database and exposes data only through its API:

```
1   // User Service owns user data
2   class UserService {
3     async updateUser(id, updates) {
4       const user = await User.findByIdAndUpdate(id, updates, { new: true });
5
6       // Publish event for other services
7       await publishEvent('user.updated', {
8         userId: id,
9         changes: updates
10      });
11
12      return user;
13    }
14  }
15
16  // Order Service maintains necessary user data copy
17  class OrderService {
18    async handleUserUpdate(event) {
```

```
19      // Update local copy of user data
20      await UserCache.updateOne(
21        { userId: event.userId },
22        { $set: event.changes }
23      );
24    }
25 }
```

This pattern shows how services maintain autonomy while sharing necessary data. The User Service owns the authoritative user data and publishes events when changes occur. The Order Service maintains a cached copy of relevant user information, updating it based on events. This approach trades some data duplication for service independence and performance.

Implementing distributed transactions across services requires careful consideration. The Saga pattern (a sequence of local transactions) coordinates multi-service transactions without distributed locks. A saga breaks the transaction into steps, each with a compensating action:

```
1  class OrderSaga {
2    constructor() {
3      this.steps = [
4        {
5          name: 'reserve_inventory',
6          forward: this.reserveInventory,
7          compensate: this.releaseInventory
8        },
9        {
10         name: 'charge_payment',
11         forward: this.chargePayment,
12         compensate: this.refundPayment
13       }
14     ];
15   }
16
17   async execute(orderData) {
18     const executedSteps = [];
19
20     try {
21       for (const step of this.steps) {
22         const result = await step.forward(orderData);
23         executedSteps.push({ step, result });
24       }
25       return { success: true };
```

```
26      } catch (error) {
27        // Compensate in reverse order
28        await this.compensate(executedSteps);
29        return { success: false, error };
30      }
31    }
32  }
```

The Saga pattern maintains eventual consistency without locking resources across services. If any step fails, compensating actions undo previous steps, ensuring the system returns to a consistent state.

12.8.4 Container Orchestration and Deployment

Microservices architecture demands sophisticated deployment and orchestration strategies. With dozens or hundreds of services to manage, manual deployment becomes impossible. Container orchestration platforms like Kubernetes have become essential for running microservices at scale.

Containerizing services ensures consistent deployment across environments. A production-ready Dockerfile demonstrates best practices:

```
1  FROM node:18-alpine AS builder
2  WORKDIR /app
3  COPY package*.json ./
4  RUN npm ci --only=production
5
6  FROM node:18-alpine
7  WORKDIR /app
8  COPY --from=builder /app/node_modules ./node_modules
9  COPY . .
10 EXPOSE 3000
11 USER node
12 CMD ["node", "server.js"]
```

This multi-stage build keeps images small by separating dependency installation from the final image. Running as a non-root user improves security. The Alpine base minimizes size and attack surface.

Kubernetes manages how services run in production through declarative configurations:

```
1  apiVersion: apps/v1
2  kind: Deployment
3  metadata:
4    name: user-service
5  spec:
```

```
 6    replicas: 3
 7    template:
 8      spec:
 9        containers:
10        - name: user-service
11          image: myregistry/user-service:v1.2.3
12          resources:
13            requests:
14              memory: "256Mi"
15              cpu: "250m"
16          livenessProbe:
17            httpGet:
18              path: /health
19              port: 3000
```

This configuration ensures high availability through multiple replicas, prevents resource exhaustion through limits, and enables automatic recovery through health checks. Kubernetes monitors service health and replaces unhealthy instances automatically.

Service mesh technologies add advanced networking capabilities without changing application code. Traffic management, security policies, and observability features are configured declaratively:

```
 1  # Canary deployment with traffic splitting
 2  apiVersion: networking.istio.io/v1beta1
 3  kind: VirtualService
 4  spec:
 5    http:
 6    - route:
 7      - destination:
 8          host: user-service
 9          subset: v1
10        weight: 90
11      - destination:
12          host: user-service
13          subset: v2
14        weight: 10
```

This configuration implements canary deployment (a risk mitigation strategy for releasing new versions of software) by routing 10% of traffic to the new version, enabling safe testing in production.

12.8.5 Monitoring and Observability

The distributed nature of microservices makes monitoring and debugging significantly more complex than monolithic applications. Modern observability practices combine metrics, logging, and distributed tracing to provide visibility into distributed systems.

Structured logging provides consistent, searchable logs across services:

```javascript
class Logger {
  log(level, message, metadata = {}) {
    console.log(JSON.stringify({
      timestamp: new Date().toISOString(),
      level,
      service: this.serviceName,
      message,
      ...metadata,
      traceId: getTraceId()
    }));
  }
}

// Usage in request handlers
logger.info('User retrieved', {
  userId,
  duration: Date.now() - startTime,
  traceId: req.headers['x-trace-id']
});
```

JSON format enables powerful log analysis and correlation across services. Including trace IDs links logs from different services handling the same request.

Distributed tracing reveals the complete request journey:

```javascript
// Trace context propagation
async function callUserService(userId, traceContext) {
  const span = tracer.startSpan('call-user-service');

  try {
    const response = await axios.get(
      `${USER_SERVICE_URL}/users/${userId}`,
      { headers: { 'x-trace-id': traceContext.traceId } }
    );
    span.setStatus({ code: 'OK' });
```

```
11    return response.data;
12  } catch (error) {
13    span.setStatus({ code: 'ERROR' });
14    throw error;
15  } finally {
16    span.end();
17  }
18 }
```

Each service creates spans representing units of work. Trace context propagates through headers, linking spans across services to show timing, dependencies, and errors.

Metrics provide quantitative monitoring:

```
1  // Define application metrics
2  const httpDuration = new Histogram({
3    name: 'http_request_duration_seconds',
4    labelNames: ['method', 'route', 'status']
5  });
6
7  const ordersCreated = new Counter({
8    name: 'orders_created_total',
9    labelNames: ['status']
10 });
11
12 // Track metrics in application code
13 ordersCreated.labels('success').inc();
14 httpDuration.labels(req.method, req.path, res.statusCode).observe(duration);
```

Technical metrics track latency and error rates while business metrics monitor application-specific behavior. Prometheus format enables powerful querying and alerting.

The combination of logging, tracing, and metrics creates comprehensive observability. When issues arise, metrics show what is wrong, traces reveal where problems occur, and logs explain why failures happen. This observability proves essential for operating microservices reliably at scale.

Microservices architecture represents a significant evolution in web application design. While the added complexity requires new skills and tools, the benefits of independent deployment, technology flexibility, and scalability make microservices compelling for large-scale systems. Success requires careful service design, robust communication patterns, comprehensive monitoring, and strong operational practices. As the ecosystem continues to mature, microservices will likely become even more accessible to teams of all sizes.

12.9   Emerging Technologies and Future Trends

12.9.1   WebAssembly and Next-Generation Performance

WebAssembly represents one of the most significant advances in web platform capabilities since JavaScript itself, fundamentally expanding what applications can accomplish within browsers. This binary instruction format enables near-native performance for computationally intensive tasks that have traditionally been impossible or impractical on the web platform. Understanding WebAssembly's capabilities and limitations helps developers identify opportunities to enhance application performance while maintaining the web's universal accessibility and deployment advantages.

The fundamental challenge that WebAssembly addresses stems from JavaScript's design as a high-level, dynamically typed language optimized for flexibility rather than raw computational speed. While modern JavaScript engines achieve remarkable performance through sophisticated just-in-time compilation and optimization techniques, certain categories of applications push beyond JavaScript's comfortable performance boundaries. Scientific simulations requiring precise floating-point calculations, image and video processing operations manipulating millions of pixels per frame, cryptographic operations demanding constant-time execution, and real-time games maintaining consistent sixty-frames-per-second rendering all strain JavaScript's capabilities despite increasingly powerful hardware.

WebAssembly provides a compilation target for systems programming languages like C++, Rust, and Go, enabling developers to leverage decades of optimized native code within web applications. The performance improvements can be dramatic for appropriate workloads, with computational tasks often executing five to ten times faster than equivalent JavaScript implementations. However, WebAssembly's true power emerges not from replacing JavaScript entirely but from complementing it in hybrid architectures that leverage each technology's strengths:

```javascript
// JavaScript image processing (simplified example)
function processImageJS(imageData) {
  const pixels = imageData.data;
  const output = new Uint8ClampedArray(pixels.length);

  // Complex image processing operations
  for (let i = 0; i < pixels.length; i += 4) {
    output[i] = pixels[i] * 0.5;         // Red channel
    output[i + 1] = pixels[i + 1] * 0.5; // Green channel
    output[i + 2] = pixels[i + 2] * 0.5; // Blue channel
    output[i + 3] = pixels[i + 3];       // Alpha channel
  }

  return output;
}

// WebAssembly module usage
```

```
18  async function processImageWASM(imageData) {
19    const wasmModule = await WebAssembly.instantiateStreaming(
20      fetch('/image-processor.wasm')
21    );
22
23    const { memory, process } = wasmModule.instance.exports;
24
25    // Copy data to WASM memory and process
26    const ptr = wasmModule.instance.exports.allocate(imageData.data.length);
27    const wasmArray = new Uint8Array(memory.buffer, ptr, imageData.data.length);
28    wasmArray.set(imageData.data);
29
30    process(ptr, imageData.width, imageData.height);
31
32    return new Uint8ClampedArray(wasmArray);
33  }
```

This comparison illustrates the typical performance characteristics of WebAssembly versus JavaScript for computational workloads. The JavaScript implementation, while functionally correct, suffers from the overhead of dynamic typing, bounds checking, and garbage collection pressure from temporary object creation. The WebAssembly version, compiled from optimized C++ or Rust code, executes the same algorithm with predictable memory access patterns, explicit memory management, and processor-optimized instruction sequences. For a typical four-megapixel image, the performance difference might range from ten-fold to fifty-fold improvement, transforming an operation that requires several seconds into one that completes in milliseconds.

The architectural integration between JavaScript and WebAssembly creates powerful hybrid applications that exceed the capabilities of either technology alone. JavaScript maintains its role as the orchestration layer, handling user interface updates, event management, and application state coordination. WebAssembly handles computationally intensive operations that benefit from low-level optimization. This division of responsibilities enables applications to provide responsive user experiences while performing complex calculations that would otherwise require native application development:

```
1   // Hybrid application architecture
2   class ImageEditor {
3     constructor() {
4       this.wasmReady = this.initializeWASM();
5     }
6
7     async initializeWASM() {
8       const response = await fetch('/image-processing.wasm');
9       const bytes = await response.arrayBuffer();
10      const module = await WebAssembly.instantiate(bytes);
```

```
11    this.wasm = module.instance.exports;
12  }
13
14  async applyFilter(imageData, filterType) {
15    await this.wasmReady;
16
17    this.showProcessingIndicator();
18    const result = await this.processInWASM(imageData, filterType);
19    this.displayResult(result);
20  }
21 }
```

The ecosystem surrounding WebAssembly continues expanding rapidly, with tooling and frameworks that lower adoption barriers while expanding capabilities. Emscripten provides a mature compilation toolchain that transforms existing C++ codebases into WebAssembly modules, enabling the web deployment of sophisticated libraries developed over decades for native platforms. The Rust programming language has embraced WebAssembly as a first-class compilation target, offering memory safety guarantees alongside performance benefits. AssemblyScript provides a TypeScript-like syntax that compiles directly to WebAssembly, enabling web developers to access WebAssembly performance without learning systems programming languages.

Future developments in WebAssembly promise even greater capabilities and broader adoption. The WebAssembly System Interface specification aims to provide standardized access to system resources, enabling WebAssembly modules to run securely outside browsers in server environments, edge computing platforms, and embedded systems. Thread support will unlock parallel processing capabilities that leverage modern multi-core processors effectively. Garbage collection proposals will enable managed languages like Java, C#, and Python to target WebAssembly efficiently, expanding the ecosystem beyond systems programming languages. These developments position WebAssembly as a universal compilation target that could transform software distribution and deployment across all computing platforms.

12.9.2   Edge Computing and Distributed Applications

Edge computing represents a fundamental architectural shift that moves computational resources closer to users and data sources rather than centralizing processing in distant data centers. This distributed approach addresses the physical limitations of centralized architectures while enabling new categories of applications that require ultra-low latency, high bandwidth utilization, or localized data processing. Understanding edge computing principles and implementation patterns helps developers design applications that can leverage distributed infrastructure effectively while maintaining consistency and reliability across geographically distributed deployments.

The motivation for edge computing becomes apparent when examining the constraints imposed by physical distance and network topology on modern applications. A user in Tokyo accessing a server located in Virginia must contend with approximately one hundred fifty milliseconds of round-trip latency due to the fundamental speed of light limitations, regardless of network infrastructure quality. This delay, while imperceptible for traditional web browsing, becomes problematic for interactive applications that require immediate feedback.

Video conferencing applications suffer from noticeable communication delays that disrupt natural conversation flow. Real-time gaming becomes unplayable when user inputs require hundreds of milliseconds to register. Augmented reality applications fail to maintain the illusion of digital objects existing in physical space when tracking updates lag behind head movements.

Edge computing addresses these limitations by distributing computational resources geographically, placing servers within milliseconds of users rather than continents away. Content Delivery Networks pioneered this approach for static assets, demonstrating the performance benefits of proximity. Modern edge computing platforms extend this concept to dynamic computation, enabling sophisticated applications to execute close to users while maintaining global consistency and coordination:

```javascript
// Edge worker for personalized content delivery
addEventListener('fetch', event => {
  event.respondWith(handleRequest(event.request));
});

async function handleRequest(request) {
  const country = request.headers.get('CF-IPCountry');
  const cached = await cache.match(request);

  if (cached && !isStale(cached)) {
    return cached;
  }

  // Add location context to request
  const originRequest = new Request(request);
  originRequest.headers.set('X-User-Country', country);

  let response = await fetch(originRequest);

  // Transform response based on location
  if (response.headers.get('content-type')?.includes('text/html')) {
    response = await personalizeContent(response, country);
  }

  return response;
}
```

This edge worker implementation demonstrates several key capabilities that distinguish edge computing from traditional CDN caching. The worker can modify requests before they reach origin servers, adding geographic context that enables location-aware processing. Response transformation occurs at the edge without round-trips to centralized servers, reducing latency while enabling personalization. Intelligent caching considers user context to improve cache hit rates while reducing origin server load. The entire processing pipeline executes at the edge, milliseconds away from users, providing performance characteristics impossible with centralized architectures.

Edge computing enables fundamentally new architectural patterns for distributed applications that go beyond simple caching and content transformation. Rather than treating edge nodes as passive content distributors, developers can build truly distributed systems where computation occurs across multiple geographic locations with sophisticated coordination mechanisms:

```javascript
// Distributed rate limiting at the edge
class EdgeRateLimiter {
  async shouldAllow(userId, action) {
    const key = `rate:${userId}:${action}`;
    const limit = 100;
    const window = 60000; // 1 minute

    const current = await RATE_LIMIT_STORE.get(key, 'json') || {
      count: 0,
      resetAt: Date.now() + window
    };

    // Reset if window expired
    if (Date.now() > current.resetAt) {
      current.count = 0;
      current.resetAt = Date.now() + window;
    }

    if (current.count >= limit) {
      return { allowed: false, remaining: 0 };
    }

    current.count++;
    await RATE_LIMIT_STORE.put(key, JSON.stringify(current));

    return { allowed: true, remaining: limit - current.count };
  }
}
```

This distributed rate limiting example illustrates how edge computing enables sophisticated coordination across multiple locations without centralized bottlenecks. Each edge location maintains its own view of rate limits while synchronizing through eventually consistent storage mechanisms. This approach scales horizontally across thousands of edge locations while maintaining sub-millisecond response times, something impossible with centralized rate limiting systems.

The implications of edge computing extend far beyond performance optimization into areas of regulatory compliance, data sovereignty, and privacy protection. Many jurisdictions now require personal data processing to occur within specific geographic boundaries, making edge computing not just a performance optimization but a legal necessity. Privacy-sensitive applications can analyze user data locally without transmitting it to centralized servers, reducing exposure while maintaining functionality. Internet of Things deployments can process sensor data at edge locations, reducing bandwidth requirements while enabling real-time responses to local conditions.

Edge computing also enables new business models and application categories that were previously impractical. Augmented reality applications can perform object recognition and spatial tracking at edge locations, reducing latency below perception thresholds while maintaining acceptable battery life on mobile devices. Autonomous vehicle coordination can occur at edge nodes positioned along transportation corridors, enabling real-time traffic optimization without relying on distant cloud servers. Industrial automation systems can process sensor data and control equipment through edge computing infrastructure, ensuring consistent operation despite network disruptions.

12.9.3　The Future of Web Standards

Web standards continue evolving to meet the changing needs of developers and users, driven by the relentless advancement of hardware capabilities, shifting user expectations, and emerging use cases that push the boundaries of what web applications can accomplish. Understanding the trajectory of web standards development helps developers prepare for future capabilities while designing applications that can gracefully adopt new features as they become available across browser implementations. The standards development process, coordinated through organizations like the World Wide Web Consortium (W3C) and the Web Hypertext Application Technology Working Group (WHATWG), balances innovation with backward compatibility and accessibility requirements.

Web Components represent one of the most significant additions to web standards in recent years, providing native browser support for custom, reusable user interface elements that work across frameworks and development approaches. These standards solve the long-standing problem of component portability by enabling developers to create encapsulated, reusable elements that integrate seamlessly with any web application regardless of the underlying framework or library choices:

```javascript
// Custom element with modern features
class EnhancedButton extends HTMLElement {
  static observedAttributes = ['variant', 'loading'];

  constructor() {
    super();
    this.attachShadow({ mode: 'open' });
    this.render();
  }

  connectedCallback() {
```

```
12    this.addEventListener('click', this.handleClick);
13  }
14
15  handleClick = async (event) => {
16    if (this.hasAttribute('loading')) return;
17
18    this.setAttribute('loading', '');
19
20    this.dispatchEvent(new CustomEvent('enhance-click', {
21      detail: { timestamp: Date.now() },
22      bubbles: true
23    }));
24
25    this.removeAttribute('loading');
26  }
27
28  render() {
29    const variant = this.getAttribute('variant') || 'primary';
30    const loading = this.hasAttribute('loading');
31
32    this.shadowRoot.innerHTML = `
33      <style>
34        button {
35          padding: 0.5em 1em;
36          border: none;
37          border-radius: 4px;
38          background: #007bff;
39          color: white;
40        }
41      </style>
42      <button>
43        <slot></slot>
44        ${loading ? '<span> Loading </span>' : ''}
45      </button>
46    `;
47  }
48 }
49
50 customElements.define('enhanced-button', EnhancedButton);
```

Web Components provide true encapsulation through Shadow DOM, preventing style conflicts that have plagued web development for decades. Custom elements work seamlessly with any framework or vanilla

JavaScript, reducing vendor lock-in and enabling long-term code reuse. Lifecycle callbacks enable sophisticated component behavior that rivals framework-specific solutions while maintaining standards compliance. This standardization represents a significant step toward framework-agnostic component development that could reduce the fragmentation currently seen in the JavaScript ecosystem.

Cascading Style Sheets continue gaining powerful features that reduce JavaScript dependencies while enabling increasingly sophisticated visual effects and layout capabilities. These additions represent a philosophical shift toward moving presentation logic back into CSS, where it belongs architecturally, while providing the dynamic capabilities that modern applications require:

```css
/* Container queries enable component-based responsive design */
.card-container {
  container-type: inline-size;
}

@container (min-width: 400px) {
  .card {
    display: grid;
    grid-template-columns: 150px 1fr;
  }
}
/* CSS custom properties with @property enable typed variables */
@property --progress {
  syntax: '<percentage>';
  initial-value: 0%;
  inherits: false;
}

.progress-bar {
  background: linear-gradient(
    to right,
    #007bff 0%,
    #007bff var(--progress),
    #e0e0e0 var(--progress)
  );
  transition: --progress 0.3s ease;
}

/* :has() selector enables parent selection */
.form-group:has(input:invalid) {
  border-color: red;
}
```

These CSS advances solve long-standing problems in web development while improving performance by moving logic from JavaScript to the browser's optimized CSS engine. Container queries finally enable truly component-based responsive design, where components adapt to their container size rather than viewport dimensions. Custom properties with type definitions provide compile-time checking and animation capabilities previously impossible. The has selector enables parent selection patterns that required JavaScript workarounds for decades.

New JavaScript APIs continue expanding the web platform's capabilities, bringing features previously exclusive to native applications to web browsers. These APIs represent a careful balance between providing powerful capabilities and maintaining the web's security and privacy principles:

```javascript
// File System Access API
async function editLocalFile() {
  const [fileHandle] = await window.showOpenFilePicker({
    types: [{ accept: { 'text/plain': ['.txt'] } }]
  });

  const file = await fileHandle.getFile();
  const contents = await file.text();

  // Edit contents
  const updatedContents = contents.toUpperCase();

  // Write back to file
  const writable = await fileHandle.createWritable();
  await writable.write(updatedContents);
  await writable.close();
}

// Web Share API
async function shareContent(title, text, url) {
  if (navigator.share) {
    await navigator.share({ title, text, url });
  } else {
    showCustomShareDialog({ title, text, url });
  }
}
```

These emerging APIs demonstrate the web platform's evolution toward providing native application capabilities while maintaining web principles of security and user agency. File system access enables document editors and development tools that were previously impossible as web applications. Web Share integrates with platform sharing mechanisms, providing native user experiences while maintaining cross-platform compatibility.

Progressive enhancement ensures applications work everywhere while leveraging advanced features where available.

The future trajectory of web standards points toward even greater capabilities and closer parity with native applications. WebGPU will provide direct access to graphics processing units for high-performance computing and rendering applications. Project Fugu initiatives continue adding native capabilities like device hardware access, advanced networking, and system integration features. WebAssembly's continued evolution will enable more languages and use cases while maintaining security and performance benefits.

These developments collectively represent a transformation of the web from a document delivery platform to a comprehensive application development and deployment environment. The distinction between web and native applications continues blurring as web standards provide increasingly powerful capabilities while maintaining the web's fundamental advantages of universal accessibility, instant deployment, and cross-platform compatibility. Developers who understand these evolving standards and plan for their adoption will be positioned to create the next generation of web applications that fully leverage the platform's expanding capabilities.

12.10 Final Word

This chapter has explored the dramatic transformation of web development from traditional server-side rendering to modern, sophisticated architectures. We began by examining how Single Page Applications revolutionized user experience through client-side routing and reactive interfaces. The major JavaScript frameworks (React, Vue, and Angular) each offer unique approaches to building these applications, with React emphasizing component composition, Vue providing approachable template syntax, and Angular delivering a comprehensive enterprise solution.

Modern API design has evolved beyond simple data endpoints to become the backbone of distributed systems. RESTful principles provide a solid foundation for resource-oriented APIs, while GraphQL offers flexible query capabilities that eliminate over-fetching and under-fetching problems. The importance of comprehensive API documentation, versioning strategies, and security considerations cannot be overstated in creating APIs that developers enjoy using.

The shift toward microservices architecture represents a fundamental change in how we structure large applications. By decomposing monoliths into focused services, teams gain independence, scalability, and technology flexibility. However, this architecture introduces complexity in service communication, data management, and operational concerns that require sophisticated solutions like circuit breakers, event-driven patterns, and comprehensive observability.

DevOps practices and continuous delivery have transformed how we build, test, and deploy applications. Infrastructure as Code brings software engineering practices to infrastructure management. CI/CD pipelines automate the path from code commit to production deployment. Modern deployment strategies like blue-green deployments and feature flags enable frequent, safe releases that would have seemed impossibly risky just a decade ago.

Looking toward the future, emerging technologies promise even more dramatic changes. WebAssembly enables near-native performance for computationally intensive tasks. Edge computing brings processing closer to users for unprecedented responsiveness. AI integration creates more intelligent, helpful applications. Evolving web standards continue expanding platform capabilities, blurring the line between web and native applications.

The key insight throughout this evolution is that modern web development is not about choosing a single technology or approach, but rather understanding how to combine multiple tools and patterns to solve specific problems. The LAMP stack that formed the foundation of our learning remains relevant, but it now exists within a much richer ecosystem of possibilities. Success in modern web development requires not just technical knowledge but also the judgment to select appropriate tools for each situation and the flexibility to adapt as the landscape continues to evolve.

12.11   Chapter Review

Problem 12.1 Compare and contrast server-side rendering with Single Page Applications. What are the key advantages and disadvantages of each approach? In what scenarios would you choose one over the other?

Problem 12.2 Explain the concept of the Virtual DOM in React. How does it improve performance compared to direct DOM manipulation? Describe the reconciliation process that occurs when state changes.

Problem 12.3 What problems does GraphQL solve that REST APIs struggle with? Provide specific examples of over-fetching and under-fetching. How does GraphQL's type system benefit both API developers and consumers?

Problem 12.4 Describe the differences between authentication and authorization in API security. How do JSON Web Tokens (JWTs) work, and what security considerations must be addressed when using them?

Problem 12.5 What is the circuit breaker pattern in microservices architecture? Explain how it prevents cascading failures and describe the three states (closed, open, half-open) with examples.

Problem 12.6 Compare synchronous and asynchronous communication patterns in microservices. What are the trade-offs between them? Provide examples of when each pattern is most appropriate.

Problem 12.7 Explain the concept of Infrastructure as Code. How does it differ from traditional infrastructure management? What problems does it solve, and what new challenges does it introduce?

Problem 12.8 Describe the differences between blue-green deployment and canary deployment. What are the advantages and risks of each approach? How do feature flags complement these deployment strategies?

Problem 12.9 What is WebAssembly and how does it differ from JavaScript? Provide examples of use cases where WebAssembly offers significant advantages. How do JavaScript and WebAssembly work together in modern applications?

Problem 12.10 Explain edge computing in the context of web applications. How does it differ from traditional centralized cloud computing? What types of applications benefit most from edge computing?

Problem 12.11 How do container orchestration platforms like Kubernetes help manage microservices? Describe key concepts including pods, services, and deployments.

Problem 12.12 What is distributed tracing and why is it essential for microservices architectures? How does it differ from traditional application logging? Explain how trace context propagates across services.

Problem 12.13 Describe the testing pyramid and explain why it is shaped as a pyramid. What types of tests belong at each level? How do you balance test coverage with maintenance burden?

Problem 12.14 What are Web Components and how do they differ from framework-specific components? Explain Shadow DOM, Custom Elements, and HTML Templates. What problems do Web Components solve?

Problem 12.15 How does AI integration change web application capabilities? Provide examples of practical AI use cases in web applications. What ethical considerations should developers keep in mind when implementing AI features?

Problem 12.16 Create a product catalog Single Page Application using React that demonstrates modern development practices. Begin by setting up a new React application using `Create React App` or Vite. Implement client-side routing with React Router to navigate between a product list, individual product pages, and a shopping cart. Create reusable components for product cards, navigation, and cart management.

For the backend, build a RESTful API using Node.js and Express that serves product data from a JSON file or simple database. Implement proper CORS configuration to allow your React application to communicate with the API. Add pagination to the product list endpoint, accepting `page` and `limit` query parameters. Include error handling that returns appropriate status codes and error messages.

Connect your React frontend to the API using the Fetch API or Axios. Implement loading states while data fetches, error boundaries to catch component errors gracefully, and optimistic updates when adding items to the cart. Use React hooks effectively, including `useState` for component state, `useEffect` for data fetching, and custom hooks for shared logic.

Problem 12.17 Transform the REST API from Problem 12.16 into a GraphQL API that demonstrates the advantages of flexible querying. Start by defining a complete GraphQL schema including `Product`, `Category`, and `Review` types with appropriate relationships. Implement `Query` types for fetching single products and paginated lists. Add `Mutation` types for creating reviews and updating product information.

Build resolvers that efficiently fetch data, implementing the N+1 query solution using `DataLoader` for related data. Create a context object that passes through authentication information and database connections. Implement field-level resolvers that only fetch data when requested by the client.

Test your GraphQL API using GraphQL Playground or Apollo Studio. Write queries that demonstrate partial field selection, where clients request only needed data. Show nested resource fetching in a single query and implement pagination using cursor-based patterns. Compare the network efficiency with the REST approach from Problem 12.16.

Problem 12.18 Enhance the product catalog from Problem 12.16 into a full Progressive Web App. Begin by creating a web app manifest that includes app name, icons, display modes, and theme colors. Generate icons in multiple sizes for different devices and platforms. Configure the manifest for standalone display mode.

Implement a service worker that enables offline functionality. Start with a basic caching strategy for static assets, then implement runtime caching for API responses. Create an offline fallback page that displays when users have no connection. Implement background sync to queue actions taken offline and sync when connectivity returns.

Add advanced PWA features including push notification capability with user permission handling, app installation prompts at appropriate moments, and periodic background sync for fresh content. Test your PWA using Lighthouse to ensure it meets PWA criteria and achieves good performance scores.

Problem 12.19 Create a complete CI/CD pipeline for the applications built in previous exercises. Start with a Git repository structure that includes clear branch naming conventions and a pull request workflow. Configure pre-commit hooks using Husky that run linting and basic tests before allowing commits.

Set up a CI pipeline using GitHub Actions, GitLab CI, or CircleCI. Configure the pipeline to run on every push and pull request. Implement stages for dependency installation with caching, linting and code quality checks, unit test execution with coverage reporting, and building production artifacts.

For continuous deployment, configure automatic deployment to a staging environment for the `develop` branch. Implement manual approval gates for production deployment. Use environment variables for configuration management and implement health checks that verify deployment success. Add rollback capabilities in case of deployment failures.

Problem 12.20 Build a simplified e-commerce system using microservices architecture to understand service communication patterns. Create three separate services: User Service for authentication and user profiles, Product Service for catalog management, and Order Service for order processing. Each service should have its own database and expose a RESTful API.

Implement synchronous communication where the Order Service calls User and Product services to validate orders. Add proper error handling and timeout configuration. Implement a circuit breaker pattern that prevents cascading failures when services are unavailable.

Add asynchronous communication using a message queue (RabbitMQ or Redis Pub/Sub). Implement an event-driven pattern where the Order Service publishes "order.created" events that other services consume. Create event handlers in each service that react to relevant events. Demonstrate how this decoupling allows services to process at their own pace.

For bonus learning, implement distributed tracing using OpenTelemetry to visualize request flow across services. Add structured logging that includes trace IDs for correlating logs across services. Create a simple monitoring dashboard that shows service health and communication patterns.

Index

Index

For Product Safety Concerns and Information please contact our EU
representative GPSR@taylorandfrancis.com
Taylor & Francis Verlag GmbH, Kaufingerstraße 24, 80331 München, Germany